FORECASTING

Methods and Applications
Third Edition

Spyros Makridakis
European Institute of Business
Administration (INSEAD)

Steven C. Wheelwright
Harvard University, Graduate
School of Business Administration

Rob J. Hyndman
Monash University, Department of
Mathematics and Statistics

John Wiley & Sons, Inc.

Acquisitions Editor	Beth L Golub
Marketing Manager	Leslie Hines
Production Editor	Kelly Tavares
Senior Designer	Laura Boucher

This book was set in Computer Modern Roman by one of the authors and printed and bound by Malloy Lithographing. The cover was printed by Lehigh Press.

This book is printed on acid-free paper. ∞

This work is dedicated to Nikolas, Yiorgus, Petros and Ari
Margaret
Leanne, Naomi, Timothy, David and Abigail, whose patience
and support make such a project possible and worthwhile.

To order books or for customer service please, call 1(800)-CALL-WILEY (225-5945).

Makridakis, Spyros G.
Forecasting: methods and applications. —3rd ed. / Spyros Makridakis, Steven C. Wheelwright, Rob J. Hyndman.
p. cm.
Includes bibliographical references and index.
ISBN 0-471-53233-9 (cloth: alk. paper)
I. Forecasting—Statistical methods. I. Wheelwright, Steven C., 1943- . II. Hyndman, Rob J. III. Title.
HD30.27.M34 1998
338.5'442—dc21
97-44416
CIP

Printed in the United States of America

PREFACE

The field of organizational forecasting, born in the 1950s, is reaching maturity. Significant theoretical developments in estimation and prediction, powerful and inexpensive computers coupled with appropriate software, several large scale empirical studies investigating the accuracy of the major forecasting methods, and, most importantly, the considerable experience gained through the actual application of such methods (in business and non-profit organizations) have contributed toward achieving this maturity. Today, the field of (organizational) forecasting rests on solid theoretical foundations while also having a realistic, practical base that increases its relevance and usefulness to practicing managers.

The preparation of this third edition, like the previous two, is based on the authors' view that the book should: (1) cover the full range of major forecasting methods, (2) provide a complete description of their essential characteristics, (3) present the steps needed for their practical application, (4) avoid getting bogged down in the theoretical details that are not essential to understanding how the various methods work, (5) provide systematic comparison of the advantages and drawbacks of various methods so that the most appropriate method can be selected for each forecasting situation, and (6) cover a comprehensive set of forecasting horizons (from the immediate to the long-term) and approaches (time series, explanatory, mixed) to forecasting.

New in this edition

While meeting the above criteria, this third edition includes major revisions of all the chapters and the addition of several completely new chapters. Our purpose has not been to merely revise the second edition, but rewrite it to include the contributions of the latest theoretical developments, and practical concerns, while presenting the most recent empirical findings and thinking. We have tried to make this edition both complete and fully updated, as well as theoretically correct and relevant, for those who want to apply forecasting in practice.

Some of the new material covered includes

- the X-12-ARIMA and the STL methods of time series decomposition
- local regression smoothing, best subsets regression and regression with time series errors.
- the use of Akaike's Information Criterion (AIC) for model selection
- neural networks and non-linear forecasting
- state space modeling and vector autoregression
- a modern approach to forecasting the long-term based on mega trends, analogies and scenarios
- new ideas for combining statistical and judgmental forecasts.
- experience gained from forecasting competitions including the latest M3-IJF Competition.
- recent research on forecast accuracy.
- the features of the major forecasting packages
- forecasting resources on the internet.

Unique features

This book is distinctive for its attention to practical forecasting issues, its comprehensive coverage of both statistical models and how to implement them in practice within a modern business environment, and the inclusion of many recent developments in forecasting research. In particular:

- There are dozens of real data examples and a number of examples from the authors' consulting experience. All data sets in the book are available on the internet (see below).
- We emphasise graphical methods and using graphs to help understand the analyses.

- Our perspective is that forecasting is much more than fitting models to historical data. While explaining the past is important, it is not adequate for accurately predicting the future.
- Much of the modern research on forecasting accuracy, based on surveys of forecast users, is summarized.
- Many recent developments in forecasting methodology and implementation are included.

Chapter outline

The book is divided into twelve chapters and three appendices.

Chapter 1: The forecasting perspective. This chapter provides a conceptual framework for understanding existing methodologies of forecasting and the tasks for which they can be used. It also provides an overview of the forecasting task and gives a useful structure for studying various forecasting methods.

Chapter 2: Basic forecasting tools. Chapter 2 outlines the basic quantitative foundations for the remainder of the book. It gives an overview of the notations and computations required to apply quantitative methods. Furthermore, it summarizes the various measures commonly used in evaluating and comparing the forecasts of different methods.

Chapter 3: Time series decomposition. Chapter 3 looks at the smoothing and decomposition of time series. These are not strictly forecasting methods, but they are useful tools for understanding time series better, and therefore they assist in forecasting.

Chapter 4: Exponential smoothing methods. Chapters 4 to 8 focus on quantitative (time series and explanatory) forecasting methods. In Chapter 4 exponential smoothing methods are examined, particularly single exponential smoothing, Holt's method and Holt-Winters' method.

Chapter 5: Simple regression. The explanatory regression methods (simple regression, multiple regression and econometric models) are discussed in Chapters 5 and 6. Chapter 5 deals with the case where there is only one explanatory variable.

Chapter 6: Multiple regression. Regression methods involving more than one explanatory variable are discussed in Chapter 6.

Chapter 7: The Box-Jenkins methodology for ARIMA models. In Chapter 7, the modeling approach of Box and Jenkins is described and extended using more recent methods such as the AIC.

Chapter 8: Advanced forecasting models. A collection of more advanced time series methods is discussed in Chapter 8 including regression with ARIMA errors, dynamic regression (or transfer function) models, intervention analysis, state space models and neural networks.

Chapter 9: Forecasting the long-term. This chapter discusses the problems and challenges when making long-term forecasts. It also provides three approaches (mega trends, analogies and scenarios) for arriving at such forecasts.

Chapter 10: Judgmental forecasting and adjustments. Chapter 10 describes the various biases and limitations that affect our judgment, as they relate to forecasting, and proposes ways to avoid or minimize them.

Chapter 11: The use of forecasting methods in practice. This chapter presents information about the usage of the various forecasting methods in business organizations as well as empirical findings about the accuracy of such methods. In addition it discusses the value of combining forecasts and the ability to improve the accuracy of the resulting forecasts through such combining.

Chapter 12: Implementing forecasting: its uses, advantages and limitations. The final chapter is concerned with practical implementation issues while also dealing with the usages, advantages and limitations of forecasting.

Appendix I: Forecasting resources. Several resources available to assist in the pursuit of forecast are discussed in Appendix I. These include software, journals, associations and useful Internet sites.

Appendix II: Glossary of forecasting terms. Appendix II is a glossary of forecasting terms covering the techniques, concepts,

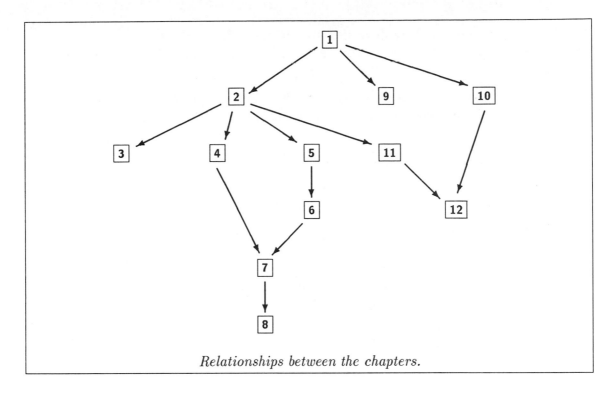

Relationships between the chapters.

and tools that are the essential components of forecasting. This glossary can serve as a dictionary and reference for terms that may be new or not clearly understood by readers

Appendix III: Statistical tables. Appendix III contains statistical tables for the various tests of significance used in evaluating quantitative forecasts and methods.

These chapters need not be covered in the order given. The diagram above shows the relationships between the chapters and the necessary prerequisites for studying the material in each chapter.

Supplementary resources

There is a web page for the book at

www.maths.monash.edu.au/~hyndman/forecasting/

This contains a number of resources including all the data sets used throughout the book. Over 500 other data sets may also be obtained from this site as well as the 3003 series used in the latest M3-IJF Competition.

An instructor's manual is also available from the publisher. This includes course outlines, teaching suggestions, solutions to all exercises, and some suggestions for case studies and projects.

Acknowledgments

We would like to thank a number of reviewers for carefully reading our manuscript and providing many helpful suggestions. Leonard E. Ross (California State Polytechnic University) and Elaine L. Tatham (University of Kansas) reviewed the entire book, Gary Grunwald (University of Colorado) and Mindi Nath (Monash University) reviewed Chapters 1 to 8, and Brian Monsell (U.S. Bureau of the Census) reviewed Chapter 3, particularly the X-12-ARIMA methodology. Gary Grunwald also provided some ideas for exercises at the ends of the chapters. Victoria Briscoe, Betsy Brink and Linda Mayer provided excellent administrative assistance for which we are also grateful.

Spyros Makridakis
Fontainebleau, France

Steven Wheelwright
Boston, Massachusetts

Rob Hyndman
Melbourne, Australia

CONTENTS

1

THE FORECASTING PERSPECTIVE

1/1 Why forecast?

Frequently there is a time lag between awareness of an impending
event or need and occurrence of that event. This lead time is the
main reason for planning and forecasting. If the lead time is zero
or very small, there is no need for planning. If the lead time is
long, and the outcome of the final event is conditional on identifiable
factors, planning can perform an important role. In such situations,
forecasting is needed to determine when an event will occur or a need
arise, so that appropriate actions can be taken.

In management and administrative situations the need for planning
is great because the lead time for decision making ranges from several
years (for the case of capital investments) to a few days or hours
(for transportation or production schedules) to a few seconds (for
telecommunication routing or electrical utility loading). Forecasting
is an important aid in effective and efficient planning.

Opinions on forecasting are probably as diverse as views on any
set of scientific methods used by decision makers. The layperson may
question the validity and efficacy of a discipline aimed at predicting an
uncertain future. However, it should be recognized that substantial
progress has been made in forecasting over the past several centuries.
There are a large number of phenomena whose outcomes can now
be predicted easily. The sunrise can be predicted, as can the speed
of a falling object, the trajectory of a satellite, rainy weather, and a
myriad of other events. However, that was not always the case.

The evolution of science has increased the understanding of various
aspects of the environment and consequently the predictability of
many events. For example when the Ptolemaic system of astronomy
was developed almost 1900 years ago, it could predict the movement
of any star with an accuracy unheard of before that time. Even then,
however, systematic errors were common. Then came the emergence
of Copernican astronomy, which was much more accurate than its
Ptolemaic predecessor and could predict the movement of the stars
to within hundredths of a second. Today, modern astronomy is far
more accurate than Copernican astronomy. The same increase in
accuracy is shown in the theory of motion, which Aristotle, Galileo,
Newton, and Einstein each improved.

The trend to be able to more accurately predict a wider variety of events, particularly those in the economic/business environment, will continue to provide a better base from which to plan. Formal forecasting methods are the means by which this improvement is occurring.

Regardless of these improvements, two important comments must be kept in view. The first is that successful forecasting is not always directly useful to managers and others. More than 100 years ago, Jules Verne correctly predicted such developments as submarines, nuclear energy, and travel to the moon. Similarly, in the mid-1800s, Charles Babbage not only predicted the need for computers, but also proposed the design and did the actual construction for one. In spite of the accuracy of these forecasts, they were of little value in helping organizations to profit from such forecasts or achieve greater success.

A second important point is the distinction between uncontrollable external events (originating with the national economy, governments, customers, and competitors) and controllable internal events (such as marketing or manufacturing decisions within the firm). The success of a company depends on both types of events, but forecasting applies directly to the former, while decision making applies directly to the latter. Planning is the link that integrates both.

decision making
planning

For the important areas of sales forecasting, planning, and decision making, these relationships are shown in Figure 1-1. Recognizing the role of forecasting in its organizational and managerial context is usually as important as selecting the forecasting method itself, and thus it will be addressed throughout this book.

A wide variety of forecasting methods are available to management (see, for example, Makridakis and Wheelwright, 1989). These range from the most naïve methods, such as use of the most recent observation as a forecast, to highly complex approaches such as neural nets and econometric systems of simultaneous equations. In addition, the widespread introduction of computers has led to readily available software for applying forecasting techniques. Complementing such software and hardware has been the availability of data describing the state of economic events (GNP, consumption, etc.) and natural phenomena (temperature, rainfall, etc.). These data in conjunction with organizational statistics (sales, prices, advertising, etc.) and technological know-how provide the base of past information needed for the various forecasting methods.

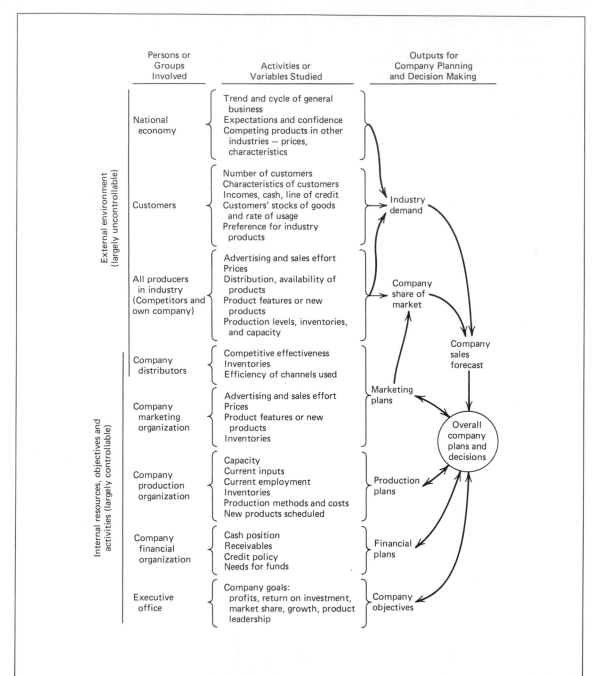

Figure 1-1: *Information flows in sales forecasting and business planning. (Adapted from Lippitt, 1969. Used by permission.)*

As suggested above, forecasting is an integral part of the decision making activities of management. An organization establishes goals and objectives, seeks to predict environmental factors, then selects actions that it hopes will result in attainment of these goals and objectives. The need for forecasting is increasing as management attempts to decrease its dependence on chance and becomes more scientific in dealing with its environment. Since each area of an organization is related to all others, a good or bad forecast can affect the entire organization. Some of the areas in which forecasting currently plays an important role are:

1. *Scheduling:* Efficient use of resources requires the scheduling of production, transportation, cash, personnel, and so on. Forecasts of the level of demand for product, material, labor, financing, or service are an essential input to such scheduling.

2. *Acquiring resources:* The lead time for acquiring raw materials, hiring personnel, or buying machinery and equipment can vary from a few days to several years. Forecasting is required to determine future resource requirements.

3. *Determining resource requirements:* all organizations must determine what resources they want to have in the long-term. Such decisions depend on market opportunities, environmental factors, and the internal development of financial, human, product, and technological resources. These determinations all require good forecasts and managers who can interpret the predictions and make appropriate decisions.

Although there are many different areas requiring forecasts, the preceding three categories are typical of the short-, medium-, and long-term forecasting requirements of today's organizations. This range of needs requires that a company develop multiple approaches to predicting uncertain events and build up a system for forecasting. This, in turn, requires that an organization possess knowledge and skills covering at least four areas: identification and definition of forecasting problems; application of a range of forecasting methods; procedures for selecting the appropriate methods for a specific situation; and organizational support for applying and using formalized forecasting methods.

A forecasting system must establish linkages among forecasts made by different management areas. There is a high degree of interdependence among the forecasts of various divisions or departments, which cannot be ignored if forecasting is to be successful. For example, errors in sales projections can trigger a series of reactions affecting budget forecasts, operating expenses, cash flows, inventory levels, pricing, and so on. Similarly, budgeting errors in projecting the amount of money available to each division will affect product development, modernization of equipment, hiring of personnel, and advertising expenditures. This, in turn, will influence, if not determine, the level of sales, operating costs, and cash flows. Clearly there is a strong interdependence among the different forecasting areas in an organization.

A major aim of this book is not only to examine the techniques available for meeting an organization's forecasting requirements, but also to consider the interdependence of needs in areas such as purchasing, production, marketing, finance, and general management.

1/2 An overview of forecasting techniques

Forecasting situations vary widely in their time horizons, factors determining actual outcomes, types of data patterns, and many other aspects. Figure 1-2 shows graphs of four variables for which forecasts might be required.

Figure 1-2a Monthly Australian electricity production from March 1956 to August 1995. (Source: Australian Bureau of Statistics.) Note the increasing trend, increasing variation each year, and the strong seasonal pattern that is slowly changing in shape. These strong historical patterns make this variable an easy one to forecast. Because of the changing seasonal patterns, some of the early data may not be useful in constructing a model. Forecasts are important for future planning of electricity production facilities and for ensuring existing facilities can meet peak demands.

Figure 1-2b U.S. Treasury Bill contracts on the Chicago market for 100 consecutive trading days in 1981. The downward trend is interesting, but it may only be a short downward movement

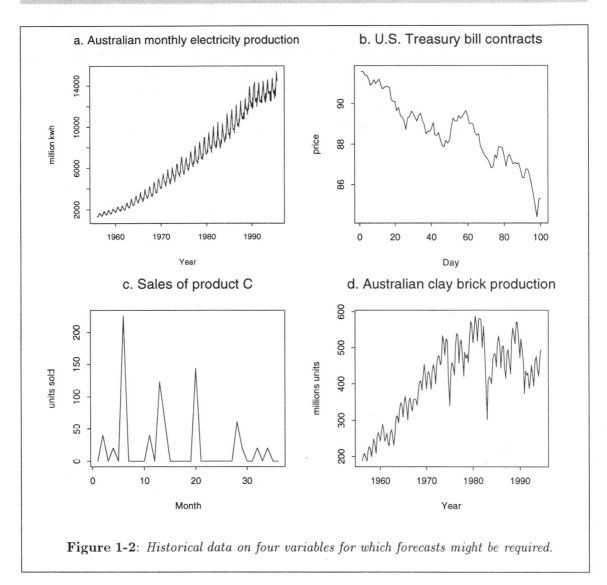

Figure 1-2: *Historical data on four variables for which forecasts might be required.*

in the middle of a highly variable series of observations. The critical question is whether this downward trend is likely to continue.

Figure 1-2c Sales of "product C" from a major oil company. This product was a lubricant sold only in units of large volume. To forecast a variable of this nature, it is necessary to investigate the nature of the product market, who is buying it, and what their future needs are likely to be.

Figure 1-2d Australian monthly clay brick production from March
    1956 to September 1994. (Source: Australian Bureau of
    Statistics.) Clearly, the market is seasonal and quite volatile.
    Accurate forecasts are very difficult unless the cause of the
    fluctuations can be identified.

To deal with such diverse applications, several techniques have
been developed. These fall into two major categories: quantitative
and qualitative methods. Table 1-1 summarizes this categorization
scheme and provides examples of situations that might be addressed
by forecasting methods in these categories.

QUANTITATIVE: *Sufficient quantitative information is available.*
- **Time series:** Predicting the continuation of historical patterns such as
  the growth in sales or gross national product.
- **Explanatory:** Understanding how explanatory variables such as prices
  and advertising affect sales.

QUALITATIVE: *Little or no quantitative information is available, but sufficient qualitative knowledge exists.*
- Predicting the speed of telecommunications around the year 2020.
- Forecasting how a large increase in oil prices will affect the consumption
  of oil.

UNPREDICTABLE: *Little or no information is available.*
- Predicting the effects of interplanetary travel.
- Predicting the discovery of a new, very cheap form of energy that
  produces no pollution.

Table 1-1: *Categories of forecasting methods and examples of their application.*

Quantitative forecasting can be applied when three conditions exist:

1. Information about the past is available.
2. This information can be quantified in the form of numerical data.
3. It can be assumed that some aspects of the past pattern will continue into the future.

This last condition is known as the *assumption of continuity*; it is an underlying premise of all quantitative and many qualitative forecasting methods, no matter how sophisticated they may be.

Quantitative forecasting techniques vary considerably, having been developed by diverse disciplines for different purposes. Each has its own properties, accuracies, and costs that must be considered in choosing a specific method. Quantitative forecasting procedures fall on a continuum between two extremes: intuitive or ad hoc methods, and formal quantitative methods based on statistical principles. The first type is based on empirical experience that varies widely from business to business, product to product, and forecaster to forecaster. Intuitive methods are simple and easy to use but not always as accurate as formal quantitative methods. Also, they usually give little or no information about the accuracy of the forecast. Because of these limitations, their use has declined as formal methods have gained in popularity. Many businesses still use these methods, either because they do not know about simple formal methods or because they prefer a judgmental approach to forecasting instead of more objective approaches.

Formal statistical methods can also involve extrapolation, but it is done in a standard way using a systematic approach that attempts to minimize the forecasting errors. There are several formal methods, often requiring limited historical data, that are inexpensive and easy to use and that can be applied in a mechanical manner (see Chapter 4). These methods are useful when forecasts are needed for a large number of items and when forecasting errors on a single item will not be extremely costly.

Persons unfamiliar with quantitative forecasting methods often think that the past cannot describe the future accurately because everything is constantly changing. After some familiarity with data and forecasting techniques, however, it becomes clear that although nothing remains exactly the same, some aspects of history do repeat themselves in a sense. Application of the right method can often identify the relationship between the variable to be forecasted and time itself (or several other variables), making improved forecasting possible.

1/2/1   Explanatory versus time series forecasting

An additional dimension for classifying quantitative forecasting methods is to consider the underlying model involved. There are two major types of forecasting models: time series and explanatory models.

explanatory models

Explanatory models assume that the variable to be forecasted exhibits an explanatory relationship with one or more independent variables. For example,

$$\text{GNP} \quad = \quad f(\text{monetary and fiscal policies, inflation,} \qquad (1.1)$$
$$\text{capital spending, imports, exports, error).}$$

Notice that the relationship is not exact. There will always be changes in GNP that can not be accounted for by the variables in the model, and thus some part of GNP changes will remain unpredictable. Therefore, we include the "error" term on the right which represents random effects, beyond the variables in the model, that affect the GNP figures.

Explanatory models can be applied to many systems—a national economy, a company's market, or a household. The purpose of the explanatory model is to discover the form of the relationship and use it to forecast future values of the forecast variable. According to explanatory forecasting, any change in inputs will affect the output of the system in a predictable way, assuming the explanatory relationship will not change (assumption of continuity).

The procedure for selecting an appropriate functional form of equation (1.1) and estimating its parameters will be discussed in detail later on. At this point it should be emphasized that according to (1.1), GNP depends upon, or is explained by, the factors on the right-hand side of the equation. As these factors change, GNP will vary in the manner specified by (1.1).

time series models

Unlike explanatory forecasting, time series forecasting treats the system as a black box and makes no attempt to discover the factors affecting its behavior. Therefore, prediction of the future is based on past values of a variable and/or past errors, but not on explanatory variables which may affect the system. The objective of such time series forecasting methods is to discover the pattern in the historical data series and extrapolate that pattern into the future.

There are two main reasons for wanting to treat a system as a black box. First, the system may not be understood, and even if it were understood it may be extremely difficult to measure the relationships assumed to govern its behavior. Second, the main concern may be only to predict what will happen and not to know why it happens. During the eighteenth, nineteenth, and first part of the twentieth centuries, for example, there were several people concerned with the magnitude of sunspots. There was little known at that time as to the reasons for the sunspots or the sources of energy of the sun. This lack of knowledge, however, did not hinder many investigators who collected and analyzed the frequency of sunspots. Schuster (1906) found that there was a regular pattern in the magnitude of sunspots, and he and several others were able to predict their continuation through time series analysis.

If the only purpose is to forecast future values of GNP without concern as to why a certain level of GNP will be realized, a time series approach would be appropriate. It is known that the magnitude of GNP does not change drastically from one month to another, or even from one year to another. Thus the GNP of next month will depend upon the GNP of the previous month and possibly that of the months before. Based on this observation, GNP might be expressed as follows:

$$\text{GNP}_{t+1} = f(\text{GNP}_t, \text{GNP}_{t-1}, \text{GNP}_{t-2}, \text{GNP}_{t-3}, \dots, \text{error}), \quad (1.2)$$

where t is the present month, $t+1$ is the next month, $t-1$ is the last month, $t-2$ is two months ago, and so on.

Equation (1.2) is similar to (1.1) except that the factors on the right-hand side are previous values of the left-hand side. This makes the job of forecasting easier once (1.2) is known, since it requires no special input values as (1.1) does. However, a requirement with both equations (1.1) and (1.2) is that the relationship between the left- and right-hand sides of the equations must be discovered and measured.

Both time series and explanatory models have advantages in certain situations. Time series models can often be used more easily to forecast, whereas explanatory models can be used with greater success for policy and decision making. Whenever the necessary data are available, a forecasting relationship can be hypothesized either as a function of time or as a function of explanatory variables, and tested. As demonstrated by the GNP example, quite often it is possible to forecast by using either explanatory or time series approaches. It is also possible to combine the two approaches. Models which involve both time series and explanatory features are discussed in Chapter 8.

1/2/2 Qualitative forecasting

qualitative
forecasting

Qualitative forecasting methods, on the other hand, do not require data in the same manner as quantitative forecasting methods. The inputs required depend on the specific method and are mainly the product of judgment and accumulated knowledge. (See Table 1-1.) Qualitative approaches often require inputs from a number of specially trained people.

As with their quantitative counterparts, qualitative techniques vary widely in cost, complexity, and value. They can be used separately but are more often used in combination with each other or in conjunction with quantitative methods.

It is more difficult to measure the usefulness of qualitative forecasts. They are used mainly to provide hints, to aid the planner, and to supplement quantitative forecasts, rather than to provide a specific numerical forecast. Because of their nature and cost, they are used almost exclusively for medium- and long-range situations such as formulating strategy, developing new products and technologies, and developing long-range plans. Although doubts are often expressed about the value of qualitative forecasting, it frequently provides useful information for managers. It is a premise of the authors that qualitative methods can be used successfully in conjunction with quantitative methods in such areas as product development, capital expenditures, goal and strategy formulation, and mergers, by even medium and small organizations. Whatever the shortcomings of qualitative methods, frequently the only alternative is no forecast at all.

The forecaster has a wide range of methods available that vary in accuracy, scope, time horizon, and cost. Key tasks are deciding which method to apply in each situation, how much reliance to place on the method itself, and how much modification is required to incorporate personal judgment before predictions are used as a basis for planning future actions. These issues will be addressed throughout this book.

1/3 The basic steps in a forecasting task

There are five basic steps in any forecasting task for which quantitative data are available.

Step 1: Problem definition

problem definition

The definition of the problem is sometimes the most difficult aspect of the forecaster's task. It involves developing a deep understanding of how the forecasts will be used, who requires the forecasts, and how the forecasting function fits within the organization. It is worth spending time talking to everyone who will be involved in collecting data, maintaining databases, and using the forecasts for future planning.

Consider the following statement by the manager of a paper products manufacturing company:

> We have a computerized inventory control system and we can get daily, weekly, and monthly reports at the drop of a hat. But our inventory situation is bad. We have far too much inventory at the factories, in the warehouses, and in the pipeline. Can we get better forecasts of future production and demand so we can reduce our inventory and save storage costs?

A forecaster has a great deal of work to do to properly define the forecasting problem, before any answers can be provided. For example, we need to know exactly what products are stored, who uses them, how long it takes to produce each item, what level of unsatisfied demand the company is prepared to bear, and so on.

Step 2: Gathering information

gathering information

There are always at least two kinds of information available: (a) statistical (usually numerical) data, and (b) the accumulated judgment and expertise of key personnel. Both kinds of information must be tapped.

It is necessary to collect historical data of the items of interest. We use the historical data to construct a model which can be used for forecasting. In the case of the paper products inventory, the data collected may consist of monthly demand and production for each item of interest over the previous three years. Other relevant data such as the timing and length of any significant production downtime due to equipment failure or industrial disputes may also need to be collected.

Step 3: Preliminary (exploratory) analysis

preliminary analysis

What do the data tell us? We start by graphing the data for visual inspection. Then we compute some simple descriptive statistics (e.g., mean, standard deviation, minimum, maximum, percentiles) associated with each set of data. Where more than one series of historical data is available and relevant, we can produce scatter plots of each pair of series and related descriptive statistics (e.g., correlations). These graphical and numerical summaries are discussed in Chapter 2. Another useful tool is decomposition analysis (Chapter 3) to check the relative strengths of trend, seasonality, cycles, and to identify unusual data points.

The purpose in all cases at this stage is to get a feel for the data. Are there consistent patterns? Is there a significant trend? Is seasonality important? Is there evidence of the presence of business cycles? Are there any outliers (extreme points) in the data that need to be explained by those with expert knowledge? How strong are the relationships among the variables available for analysis?

Such preliminary analyses will help suggest a class of quantitative models that might be useful in the forecasting assignment.

Step 4: Choosing and fitting models

forecasting models

This step involves choosing and fitting several quantitative forecasting models. In this book we will be discussing many types of quantitative forecasting models and will explain the technical details with completely worked-out examples. For now, we merely mention that the preliminary analysis (Step 3 above) serves to limit the search for an appropriate forecasting model and we would pursue one or two leading contenders for subsequent analysis.

Each model is itself an artificial construct. It is based on a set of assumptions (explicit and implicit) and usually involves one or more parameters which must be "fitted" using the known historical data. We will discuss exponential smoothing methods (Chapter 4), regression models (Chapters 5 and 6), Box-Jenkins ARIMA models (Chapter 7), and a variety of other topics including non-linear models, regression with ARIMA errors, intervention models, transfer function models, multivariate ARMA models, and state space models (Chapter 8).

When forecasting the long-term, a less formal approach is often better. This can involve identifying and extrapolating mega trends going back in time, using analogies, and constructing scenarios to consider future possibilities. These issues are discussed in Chapter 9.

Step 5: Using and evaluating a forecasting model

Once a model has been selected judiciously and its parameters estimated appropriately, the model is to be used to make forecasts, and the users of the forecasts will be evaluating the pros and cons of the model as time progresses. A forecasting assignment is not complete when the model has been fitted to the known data. The performance of the model can only be properly evaluated after the data for the forecast period have become available.

In this book, we have made a clear distinction between "fitting errors" and "forecasting errors." We will examine a variety of accuracy measures for both fitting and forecasting (in Chapter 2) and we will emphasize that, in practice, the model's forecasts are seldom used without modification. Expert judgment is invariably brought to bear on the use of the forecasts. The incorporation of expert judgment is addressed in Chapter 10.

It is important to be aware of how each forecasting method has performed in practice in other forecasting contexts. There has now been quite a lot of research on this issue looking at users' preferences and experiences with a range of forecasting methods. This research is summarized in Chapter 11.

In addition, the accuracy of future forecasts is not the only criterion for assessing the success of a forecasting assignment. A successful forecasting assignment will usually also be a stimulus to action within the organization. If the forecasts suggest a gloomy picture ahead, then management will do its best to try to change the scenario so that the gloomy forecast will not come true. If the forecasts suggest a positive future, then the management will work hard to make that come true. In general, forecasts act as new information and management must incorporate such information into its basic objective to enhance the likelihood of a favorable outcome. Implementing forecasting is often at least as important as the forecasts themselves. Chapter 12 addresses this important subject.

References and selected bibliography

ARMSTRONG, J.S. (1978) *Long-range forecasting: from crystal ball to computer*, New York: John Wiley & Sons.

ASHER, W. (1978) *Forecasting: an appraisal for policy makers and planners*, Baltimore: Johns Hopkins University.

BAILS, D.G. and L.C. PEPPER (1993) *Business fluctuations: forecasting techniques and applications*, 2nd ed., Englewood Cliffs, N.J.: Prentice-Hall.

BRIGHT, J.R. (1978) *Practical technological forecasting*, Austin, Texas: Industrial Management Center.

CHAMBERS, J.C., S.K. MULLICK, and D.D. SMITH (1971) How to choose the right forecasting technique, *Harvard Business Review*, July–August, 45–57.

——————————— (1974) *An executive's guide to forecasting*, New York: John Wiley & Sons.

CLARK, A.C. (1971) *Profiles of the future*, New York: Bantam Books.

CLEARY, J.P. and II. LEVENBACH (1982) *The professional forecaster: the forecasting process through data analysis*, Belmont, Cal.: Lifetime Learning Publications.

CLIFTON, P., H. NGUYEN, and S. NUTT (1991) *Market research using forecasting in business*, Stoneham, Mass.: Butterworth and Heinemann.

KWONG, K.K., C. LI, V. SIMUNEK, and C.L. JAIN (1995) *Bibliography on forecasting and planning*, Flushing, N.Y.: Graceway Publishing Company.

LIPPITT, V.G. (1969) *Statistical sales forecasting*, New York: Financial Executives Institute.

MAKRIDAKIS, S. and S.C. WHEELWRIGHT (1979) "Forecasting," *TIMS studies in forecasting*, Vol. 12, Amsterdam: North-Holland.

——————————— (1981) "Forecasting an organization's futures," in *Handbook of organizational design*, Vol. 1, eds. P.C. Nystrom and W.H. Starbuck, Oxford: Oxford University Press, 122–138.

——————————— (1989) *Forecasting methods for management*, 5th ed., New York: John Wiley & Sons.

SCHUSTER, R. (1906) On the periodicity of sunspots, *Philosophical Transactions*, Series A, **206**, 69–100.

STEINER, G.A. (1979) *Strategic planning*, New York: The Free Press.

THOMOPOULOS, N.T. (1980) *Applied forecasting methods*, Englewood Cliffs, N.J.: Prentice-Hall.

Exercises

1.1 Several approaches have been suggested by those attempting to predict stock market movements. Three of them are described briefly below. How does each relate to the different approaches to forecasting described in this chapter?

  (a) Dow Theory: There tend to be support levels (lower bounds) and resistance levels (upper bounds) for stock prices both for the overall market and for individual stocks. These levels can be found by plotting prices of the market or stock over time.

  (b) Random Walk Theory: There is no way to predict future movements in the stock market or individual stocks, since all available information is quickly assimilated by the investors and moves market prices in the appropriate direction.

  (c) The prices of individual stocks or of the market in general are largely determined by earnings.

1.2 You are asked to provide sales forecasts of several products for a large biscuit manufacturing company. Define the five steps of forecasting in the context of this project.

2

BASIC FORECASTING TOOLS

To develop an understanding of the field of quantitative forecasting requires some basic notation and terminology. This chapter presents such fundamentals. In Appendix 2-A the notation used throughout the book is presented, and in the body of this chapter the following topics are discussed: graphical methods for visualizing data to be used for forecasting (Section 2/2), the most important summary statistics (Section 2/3), and the various measures of forecasting accuracy that are used to help judge the appropriateness of a model (Section 2/4), calculation of prediction intervals (Section 2/5), the least squares procedure for estimating parameters of a model (Section 2/6), and the use of transformations to simplify data patterns (Section 2/7).

2/1 Time series and cross-sectional data

Throughout this chapter, we will use two data sets to illustrate ideas.

- Price ($US), mileage (mpg), and country of origin for 45 automobiles from *Consumer Reports*, April 1990, pp. 235 255.
- Monthly Australian beer production (megaliters, Ml) from January 1991–August 1995.

These data are given in Tables 2-1 and 2-2.

Often our historical data will consist of a sequence of observations over time. We call such a sequence a *time series*. For example, monthly sales figures, daily stock prices, weekly interest rates, yearly profits, daily maximum temperatures, annual crop production, and electrocardiograph measurements are all time series.

time series

In forecasting, we are trying to estimate how the sequence of observations will continue into the future. To make things simple, we will assume that the times of observation are equally spaced. This is not a great restriction because most business series are measured daily, monthly, quarterly, or yearly and so will be equally spaced.

Of the two examples above, the beer data form a time series as they are monthly figures over a period of time. However, the automobile data do not form a time series. They are *cross-sectional* data; all observations are from the same time.

cross-sectional data

Make	Country	Mileage (mpg)	Price ($)
Chevrolet Caprice V8	USA	18	14525
Chevrolet Lumina APV V6	USA	18	13995
Dodge Grand Caravan V6	USA	18	15395
Ford Aerostar V6	USA	18	12267
Ford Mustang V8	USA	19	12164
Mazda MPV V6	Japan	19	14944
Nissan Van 4	Japan	19	14799
Chevrolet Camaro V8	USA	20	11545
Acura Legend V6	Japan	20	24760
Ford LTD Crown Victoria V8	USA	20	17257
Mitsubishi Wagon 4	Japan	20	14929
Nissan Axxess 4	Japan	20	13949
Mitsubishi Sigma V6	Japan	21	17879
Nissan Stanza 4	Japan	21	11650
Buick Century 4	USA	21	13150
Mazda 929 V6	Japan	21	23300
Oldsmobile Cutlass Ciera 4	USA	21	13150
Oldsmobile Cutlass Supreme V6	USA	21	14495
Chrysler Le Baron Coupe	USA	22	12495
Chrysler New Yorker V6	USA	22	16342
Eagle Premier V6	USA	22	15350
Ford Taurus V6	USA	22	13195
Nissan Maxima V6	Japan	22	17899
Buick Skylark 4	USA	23	10565
Oldsmobile Calais 4	USA	23	9995
Ford Thunderbird V6	USA	23	14980
Toyota Cressida 6	Japan	23	21498
Buick Le Sabre V6	USA	23	16145
Nissan 240SX 4	Japan	24	13249
Ford Tempo 4	USA	24	9483
Subaru Loyale 4	Japan	25	9599
Chrysler Le Baron V6	USA	25	10945
Mitsubishi Galant 4	Japan	25	10989
Plymouth Laser	USA	26	10855
Chevrolet Beretta 4	USA	26	10320
Dodge Daytona	USA	27	9745
Honda Prelude Si 4WS 4	Japan	27	13945
Subaru XT 4	Japan	28	13071
Ford Probe	USA	30	11470
Mazda Protege 4	Japan	32	6599
Eagle Summit 4	USA	33	8895
Ford Escort 4	USA	33	7402
Honda Civic CRX Si 4	Japan	33	9410
Subaru Justy 3	Japan	34	5866
Toyota Tercel 4	Japan	35	6488

Table 2-1: *Price, mileage, and country of origin for 45 automobiles from* Consumer Reports, *April 1990, pp. 235–255.*

Month	1991	1992	1993	1994	1995
January	164	147	139	151	138
February	148	133	143	134	136
March	152	163	150	164	152
April	144	150	154	126	127
May	155	129	137	131	151
June	125	131	129	125	130
July	153	145	128	127	119
August	146	137	140	143	153
September	138	138	143	143	
October	190	168	151	160	
November	192	176	177	190	
December	192	188	184	182	

Table 2-2: *Monthly Australian beer production: January 1991–August 1995.*

2/2 Graphical summaries

The single most important thing to do when first exploring the data is to visualize the data through graphs. The basic features of the data including patterns and unusual observations are most easily seen through graphs. Sometimes graphs also suggest possible explanations for some of the variation in the data. data visualization

For example, industrial disputes will often affect time series of production; changes in government will affect economic time series; changes in definitions may result in identifiable changes in time series patterns. Graphs are the most effective way of identifying the effect of such events in the data. Where possible, these events should be adjusted for or included in the eventual model.

The type of data will determine which type of graph is most appropriate. Figures 2-1, 2-2, and 2-3 show three plots that provide useful information for forecasting. These graphical forms should be routinely used in forecasting projects and will be utilized throughout the rest of the book.

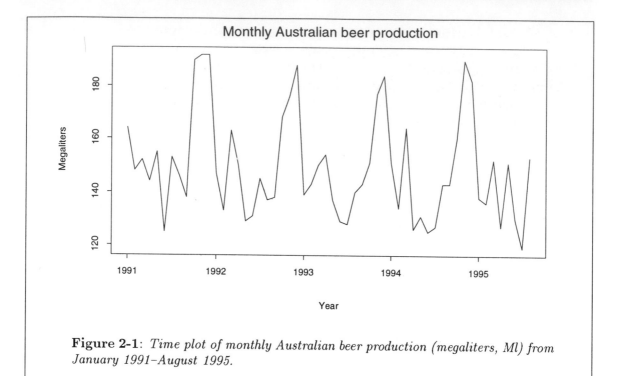

Figure 2-1: *Time plot of monthly Australian beer production (megaliters, Ml) from January 1991–August 1995.*

2/2/1 Time plots and time series patterns

time plot

For time series, the most obvious graphical form is a *time plot* in which the data are plotted over time. Figure 1-2 (p. 7) shows some examples. A time plot immediately reveals any trends over time, any regular seasonal behavior, and other systematic features of the data. These need to be identified so they can be incorporated into the statistical model.

Figure 2-1 shows a time plot of the beer data. This reveals the range of the data and the time at which peaks occur. It also shows the relative size of the peaks compared with the rest of the series and the randomness in the series since the data pattern is not perfect.

An important step in selecting an appropriate forecasting method is to consider the types of data patterns, so that the methods most appropriate to those patterns can be utilized. Four types of time se-

time series patterns

ries data patterns can be distinguished: horizontal, seasonal, cyclical, and trend.

1. A *horizontal* (H) pattern exists when the data values fluctuate   horizontal
   around a constant mean. (Such a series is called "stationary"
   in its mean.) A product whose sales do not increase or decrease   stationary
   over time would be of this type. Similarly, a quality control situation involving sampling from a continuous production process
   that theoretically does not change would also show a horizontal
   pattern.

2. A *seasonal* (S) pattern exists when a series is influenced by   seasonal
   seasonal factors (e.g., the quarter of the year, the month, or
   day of the week). Sales of products such as soft drinks, ice
   creams, and household electricity consumption all exhibit this
   type of pattern. The beer data show seasonality with a peak
   in production in November and December (in preparation for
   Christmas) each year. Seasonal series are sometimes also called
   "periodic" although they do not exactly repeat themselves over   periodic
   each period.

3. A *cyclical* (C) pattern exists when the data exhibit rises and   cyclical
   falls that are *not of a fixed period*. For economic series, these
   are usually due to economic fluctuations such as those associated with the business cycle. The sales of products such
   as automobiles, steel, and major appliances exhibit this type
   of pattern. The clay brick production shown in Figure 1-2d
   (p. 7) shows cycles of several years in addition to the quarterly
   seasonal pattern. The major distinction between a seasonal
   and a cyclical pattern is that the former is of a constant length
   and recurs on a regular periodic basis, while the latter varies
   in length. Moreover, the average length of a cycle is usually
   longer than that of seasonality and the magnitude of a cycle is
   usually more variable than that of seasonality.

4. A *trend* (T) pattern exists when there is a long-term increase or   trend
   decrease in the data. The sales of many companies, the gross
   national product (GNP), and many other business or economic
   indicators follow a trend pattern in their movement over time.
   The electricity production data shown in Figure 1-2a (p. 7)
   exhibit a strong trend in addition to the monthly seasonality.
   The beer data in Figure 2-1 show no trend.

Many data series include combinations of the preceding patterns.
For example, Figure 1-2d (p. 7) shows trend, seasonality, and cyclical

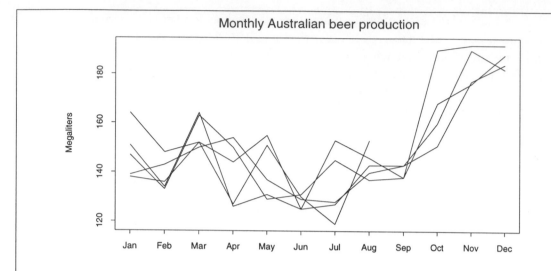

Figure 2-2: *A seasonal plot of the Australian beer production data. Note that production peaks in November and December in preparation for the southern hemisphere summer and is least in winter.*

behavior. One of the things that makes forecasting interesting and challenging is the huge variety of patterns that commonly occur in real time series data. Forecasting methods that are capable of distinguishing each of the patterns must be employed if a separation of the component patterns is needed. Similarly, alternative methods of forecasting can be used to identify the pattern and to best fit the data so that future values can be forecasted.

2/2/2 Seasonal plots

seasonal plot

For time series data that are seasonal, it is often useful to also produce a seasonal plot. Figure 2-2 shows a seasonal plot of the beer data. This graph consists of the data plotted against the individual "seasons" in which the data were observed. (In this case a "season" is a month.) This is something like a time plot except that the data from each season are overlapped. A seasonal plot enables the underlying seasonal pattern to be seen more clearly, and also allows any substantial departures from the seasonal pattern to be easily

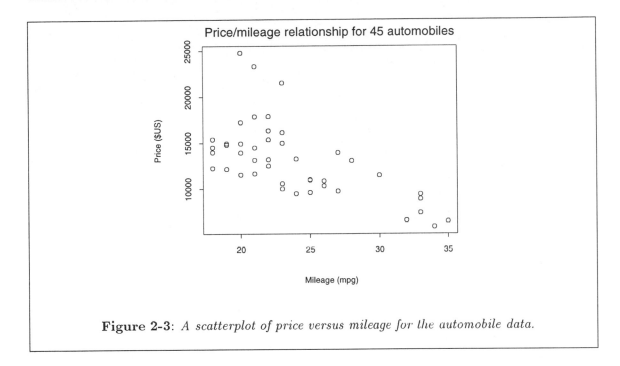

Figure 2-3: *A scatterplot of price versus mileage for the automobile data.*

identified. For example, there is one year (1991) in which the October beer production was higher than the pattern evident in the other years.

2/2/3 Scatterplots

The automobile data of Table 2-1 are not a time series making time or seasonal plots inappropriate for these data. However, these data are well suited to a scatterplot (see Figure 2-3) such as that of price against mileage. In Figure 2-3 we have plotted the variable we wish to forecast (price) against one of the explanatory variables (mileage). Each point on the graph represents one type of vehicle. The plot shows the relationship between price and mileage: vehicles with high mileage per gallon are generally cheaper than less fuel-efficient vehicles. (Both price and fuel-efficiency are related to the vehicle and engine size.) Vehicles with low mileage per gallon are generally priced over a range from around $12,000 to $18,000, with three vehicles much more expensive than other vehicles of comparable efficiency. The scatterplot helps us visualize the relationship and suggests that a forecasting model must include mileage as an explanatory variable.

scatterplot

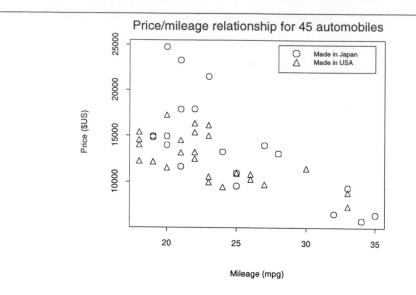

Figure 2-4: *A scatterplot showing price, mileage, and the country of origin for the automobile data.*

With the automobile data there is an additional explanatory variable, country of origin, which is a categorical (qualitative) variable rather than a numerical variable (its values are categories rather than numbers). Thus we cannot plot price against country in the same way. However, we can augment our scatterplot of price against mileage to also show the country of origin information. This is displayed in Figure 2-4. Here we have a scatterplot showing three variables. It shows that the two most efficient automobiles and the three expensive automobiles are all Japanese. It also shows that overall U.S.A. automobiles may be more efficient than the Japanese ones. A forecasting model might also include the country of origin as an explanatory variable, but that it is probably going to be less effective than mileage in giving accurate predictions.

2/3 Numerical summaries

statistic

In addition to graphics, it is also helpful to provide numerical summaries. A summary number for a data set is called a *statistic*.

For a single data set (univariate data) or a single time series, **univariate data** the most common descriptive statistics are the mean, the standard deviation, and the variance. Section 2/3/1 deals with these univariate statistics.

For a pair of random variables (bivariate data) it is of interest **bivariate data** to describe how the two data sets relate to each other. The most widely used summary numbers (statistics) for this purpose are the covariance and the correlation, and these will be defined in Section 2/3/2.

Then for a single time series, it is very useful to compare the observation at one time period with the observation at another time period. The two most common statistics here are the autocovariance and the autocorrelation, which are defined in Section 2/3/3. These measures will be used extensively in Chapter 7.

2/3/1 Univariate statistics

Consider the mileage of the 19 Japanese automobiles given in Table 2-1, reproduced in Table 2-3. The vehicles have been numbered from 1 to 19 for easy reference.

Using the letter M to denote mileage and a subscript i ($i = 1, 2, 3, \ldots, 19$) to denote the ith vehicle, the mean mileage can be **mean** written[1]

$$
\begin{aligned}
\bar{M} &= (M_1 + M_2 + M_3 + \cdots + M_{19})/19 \\
&= \frac{1}{19} \sum_{i=1}^{19} M_i \\
&= 469/19 = 24.68 \text{ mpg.}
\end{aligned}
$$

The mean should not be confused with the *median*, which is the **median** middle observation. So for the preceding 19 vehicles, the median is the mileage of the tenth vehicle when they are arranged in increasing order as shown in Table 2-3. That is, the median of the mileage data is 23. Both the mean and the median are designed to provide a numerical measure of the center of the data set.

---

[1]The summation notation, Σ, used here is explained in Appendix 2-A.

Make	Vehicle	Mileage (mpg)	
Mazda MPV V6	1	19	
Nissan Van 4	2	19	
Acura Legend V6	3	20	
Mitsubishi Wagon 4	4	20	
Nissan Axxess 4	5	20	
Mitsubishi Sigma V6	6	21	
Nissan Stanza 4	7	21	
Mazda 929 V6	8	21	
Nissan Maxima V6	9	22	
Toyota Cressida 6	10	23	← median
Nissan 240SX 4	11	24	
Subaru Loyale 4	12	25	
Mitsubishi Galant 4	13	25	
Honda Prelude Si 4WS 4	14	27	
Subaru XT 4	15	28	
Mazda Protege 4	16	32	
Honda Civic CRX Si 4	17	33	
Subaru Justy 3	18	34	
Toyota Tercel 4	19	35	

Table 2-3: *Mileage of Japanese automobiles listed in Table 2-1.*

As well as measuring the center of a data set, it is also valuable to measure the spread of the data. That is, we want a numerical measure indicating if the data are tightly bunched together or spread across a wide range.

To develop a measure of spread, we first need to calculate for each vehicle how far its mileage is from the mean mileage. The mean $\bar{M}$ is subtracted from each M_i to give the ith deviation from the mean, $(M_i - \bar{M})$.

deviation from mean

The sum of the deviations will always equal zero (as shown under column 3 of Table 2-4). Therefore, to develop a useful descriptive statistic from these deviations, they are either squared (as in column 5 of Table 2-4), or, occasionally, the absolute value is taken (as in column 4). The mean of the absolute deviations is denoted MAD,

mean absolute deviation

and for the mileage data

$$\text{MAD} = \frac{1}{19} \sum_{i=1}^{19} |M_i - \bar{M}| = 83.1/19 = 4.37 \text{ mpg}.$$

The mean of the squared deviations is designated MSD:

mean squared deviation

$$\text{MSD} = \frac{1}{19} \sum_{i=1}^{19} (M_i - \bar{M})^2 = 514.11/19 = 27.1.$$

Closely related to the mean squared deviation (MSD) is the *variance*, which is defined as the sum of squared deviations divided by one less than the total number of observations.[2] For the mileage data the variance of age is

variance

$$S^2 = \frac{1}{18} \sum_{i=1}^{19} (M_i - \bar{M})^2 = 514.11/18 = 28.6.$$

Note that since the variance formula uses 18 in the denominator and MSD formula uses 19, S^2 is larger than MSD. The variance S^2 is less intuitive than MSD but it has some desirable mathematical properties.[3]

The deviations $(M_i - \bar{M})$ are defined in units of miles per gallon. Therefore, the squared deviations are in units of squared mpg and so the mean squared deviation, MSD, and the variance, S^2, are also defined in units of squared mpg. By taking the square root of these two summary numbers, we get summary statistics in the same units as the data. In particular, we will define the *standard deviation* as

standard deviation

$$S = \sqrt{S^2} = \sqrt{28.6} = 5.34.$$

Both the MAD and the standard deviation S provide measures of spread. They (roughly) measure the average deviation of the

measures of spread

---

[2]The sum of squared deviations is divided by the "degrees of freedom" which can be defined as the number of data points minus the number of parameters estimated. When calculating a variance, we have to estimate the mean using the data, so the degrees of freedom is one less than the total number of observations.

[3]In statistics, a distinction is made between a biased estimator and an unbiased estimator. For sample data, the MSD is a biased estimator of population variance and the variance S^2 is an unbiased estimator of the population variance. See Rice (1995), p. 192, for a definition of unbiasedness.

observations from their mean. If the observations are spread out,
they will tend to be far from the mean, both above and below.
Some deviations will be large positive numbers, and some will be
large negative numbers. But the squared deviations (or the absolute
deviations) will be all positive. So both MAD and S will be large
when the data are spread out, and small when the data are close
together. Both MAD and S have the same units as the observations.

For many data sets the following useful rules of thumb hold:

- approximately two-thirds of the observations lie within 1 standard deviation of the mean; and

- approximately 95% of the observations lie within 2 standard deviations of the mean.

To summarize, suppose there are n observations and the individual
observations are denoted by Y_i for $i = 1, \ldots, n$. Then the univariate
statistics (summary numbers) that will be used in this text are defined
(generally) as follows:

mean
$$\bar{Y} = \frac{1}{n}\sum Y_i \tag{2.1}$$

median
$$\text{Median} = \begin{cases} \text{middle observation if } n \text{ odd;} \\ \text{average of middle two} \\ \quad \text{observations if } n \text{ even.} \end{cases} \tag{2.2}$$

mean absolute deviation
$$\text{MAD} = \frac{1}{n}\sum |Y_i - \bar{Y}| \tag{2.3}$$

mean squared deviation
$$\text{MSD} = \frac{1}{n}\sum (Y_i - \bar{Y})^2 \tag{2.4}$$

variance
$$S^2 = \frac{1}{n-1}\sum (Y_i - \bar{Y})^2 \tag{2.5}$$

standard deviation
$$S = \sqrt{S^2} = \sqrt{\frac{1}{n-1}\sum (Y_i - \bar{Y})^2}. \tag{2.6}$$

All summations are over the index i from 1 through n.

Of course, with much statistical software readily accessible, there
is usually no need to compute these statistics by hand. However,
it is important to understand the formulae behind them in order to
understand what they mean.

(1) Vehicle i	(2) Mileage M_i	(3) Deviation $(M_i - \bar{M})$	(4) $|M_i - \bar{M}|$	(5) $(M_i - \bar{M})^2$
1	19	−5.7	5.7	32.31
2	19	−5.7	5.7	32.31
3	20	−4.7	4.7	21.94
4	20	−4.7	4.7	21.94
5	20	−4.7	4.7	21.94
6	21	−3.7	3.7	13.57
7	21	−3.7	3.7	13.57
8	21	−3.7	3.7	13.57
9	22	−2.7	2.7	7.20
10	23	−1.7	1.7	2.84
11	24	−0.7	0.7	0.47
12	25	0.3	0.3	0.10
13	25	0.3	0.3	0.10
14	27	2.3	2.3	5.36
15	28	3.3	3.3	10.99
16	32	7.3	7.3	53.52
17	33	8.3	8.3	69.15
18	34	9.3	9.3	86.78
19	35	10.3	10.3	106.42
Sums	469	0.0	83.1	514.11

Mean	$\bar{M} = (\text{col 2 sum})/19 = 24.68$	using (2.1)
Median	$\text{Median} = (\text{col 2 middle observation}) = 23$	using (2.2)
Mean Absolute Deviation	$\text{MAD} = (\text{col 4 sum})/19 = 4.37$	using (2.3)
Mean Squared Deviation	$\text{MSD} = (\text{col 5 sum})/19 = 27.1$	using (2.4)
Variance	$S^2 = (\text{col 5 sum})/18 = 28.6$	using (2.5)
Standard Deviation	$S = \sqrt{S^2} = 5.34$	using (2.6)

Table 2-4: *Computation of the univariate statistics for the mileage of Japanese automobiles.*

Make	Vehicle	Mileage (mpg)	Price ($'000)
Mazda MPV V6	1	19	14.944
Nissan Van 4	2	19	14.799
Acura Legend V6	3	20	24.760
Mitsubishi Wagon 4	4	20	14.929
Nissan Axxess 4	5	20	13.949
Mitsubishi Sigma V6	6	21	17.879
Nissan Stanza 4	7	21	11.650
Mazda 929 V6	8	21	23.300
Nissan Maxima V6	9	22	17.899
Toyota Cressida 6	10	23	21.498
Nissan 240SX 4	11	24	13.249
Subaru Loyale 4	12	25	9.599
Mitsubishi Galant 4	13	25	10.989
Honda Prelude Si 4WS 4	14	27	13.945
Subaru XT 4	15	28	13.071
Mazda Protege 4	16	32	6.599
Honda Civic CRX Si 4	17	33	9.410
Subaru Justy 3	18	34	5.866
Toyota Tercel 4	19	35	6.488

Table 2-5: *Price and mileage for the Japanese automobiles listed in Table 2-1.*

2/3/2 Bivariate statistics

Table 2-5 shows the price and mileage for the Japanese automobiles given in Table 2-1. To prevent the computations from becoming cumbersome, we will deal with the price variable in units of thousands of dollars.

negative/positive relationships

When these data are plotted, as in Figure 2-5, it can be seen that a negative relationship exists between these two variables. By negative relationship we mean that as mileage increases, price tends to decrease. (A positive relationship would be similar to the height versus weight relationship—as height increases weight increases too.) Whenever we are dealing with two paired observations (e.g., price and mileage, height and weight, price and demand), it is of interest to examine and measure the extent of the relationship between the two variables.

Suppose we denote the two variables by X and Y. A statistic

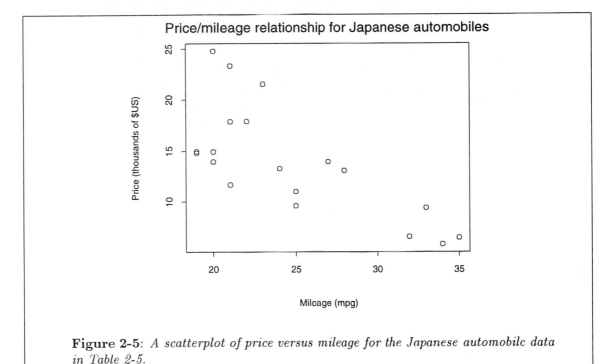

Figure 2-5: *A scatterplot of price versus mileage for the Japanese automobile data in Table 2-5.*

which indicates how two variables "co-vary" is called the *covariance* covariance and is defined as follows:

$$\text{Cov}_{XY} = \frac{1}{n-1} \sum_{i=1}^{n} (X_i - \bar{X})(Y_i - \bar{Y}) \tag{2.7}$$

where $\bar{X}$ and $\bar{Y}$ are the means of X and Y, respectively, and n is the number of observations on each variable.

For the price and mileage data in Table 2-5, the computations necessary for determining the covariance (Cov_{PM}) between price (P) and mileage (M) are shown in Table 2-6. First, the mean price ($\bar{P}$) and the mean mileage ($\bar{M}$) are computed using columns 2 and 3, respectively. Then deviations from the mean are calculated in columns 4 and 5, and column 8 gives the product of these two deviations. Summing the deviation products (column 8) and dividing by the degrees of freedom, $n - 1 = 18$, yields the desired covariance,

$$\text{Cov}_{PM} = -378.03/18 = -21.00.$$

(1) i	(2) M_i	(3) P_i	(4) $M_i - \bar{M}$	(5) $P_i - \bar{P}$	(6) $(M_i - \bar{M})^2$	(7) $(P_i - \bar{P})^2$	(8) $(M_i - \bar{M})(P_i - \bar{P})$
1	19	14.944	−5.68	1.01	32.31	1.01	−5.72
2	19	14.799	−5.68	0.86	32.31	0.74	−4.89
3	20	24.760	−4.68	10.82	21.94	117.12	−50.69
4	20	14.929	−4.68	0.99	21.94	0.98	−4.64
5	20	13.949	−4.68	0.01	21.94	0.00	−0.05
6	21	17.879	−3.68	3.94	13.57	15.53	−14.52
7	21	11.650	−3.68	−2.29	13.57	5.24	8.43
8	21	23.300	−3.68	9.36	13.57	87.65	−34.49
9	22	17.899	−2.68	3.96	7.21	15.69	−10.63
10	23	21.498	−1.68	7.56	2.84	57.15	−12.73
11	24	13.249	−0.68	−0.67	0.47	0.48	0.47
12	25	9.599	0.32	−4.34	0.10	18.83	−1.37
13	25	10.989	0.32	−2.95	0.10	8.70	−0.93
14	27	13.945	2.32	0.01	5.36	0.00	0.02
15	28	13.071	3.32	−0.87	10.99	0.75	−2.88
16	32	6.599	7.32	−7.34	53.52	53.86	−53.69
17	33	9.410	8.32	−4.53	69.15	20.50	−37.65
18	34	5.866	9.32	−8.07	86.78	65.16	−75.20
19	35	6.488	10.32	−7.45	106.42	55.50	−76.85
Sums	469	264.823	0.00	0.00	514.11	524.88	−378.03

Mean mileage $\qquad$ $\bar{M} = 469/19 = 24.68$ mpg

Mean price $\qquad$ $\bar{P} = 264.823/19 = 13.938$ thousands of dollars

Standard deviation of M $\qquad$ $S_M = \sqrt{514.11/18} = 5.34$

Standard deviation of P $\qquad$ $S_P = \sqrt{524.88/18} = 5.40$

Covariance between P and M $\qquad$ $\text{Cov}_{PM} = -378.03/18 = -21.00$

Correlation between P and M $\qquad$ $r_{PM} = \dfrac{\text{Cov}_{PM}}{S_P S_M} = \dfrac{-21.00}{(5.40)(5.34)} = -0.73$

Table 2-6: *Computations for determining the covariance and the correlation of the price and mileage data of Table 2-5.*

Note that the units of covariance are problematical. It is difficult to interpret thousands of dollar-miles per gallon. Hence the value of computing the correlation coefficient, described below. Note that the covariance between price and mileage is negative, but the magnitude of Cov_{PM} clearly depends on the units involved. If the mileage figures were converted to km per liter and the prices to dollars, the plot (Figure 2-5) would look the same but the covariance would be quite different.

The *correlation coefficient*, designated r, is a special covariance correlation measure that takes care of the scale problem just mentioned. If the covariance (Cov_{XY}) is divided by the two standard deviations $(S_X$ and $S_Y)$, then the units in the numerator and the denominator cancel out, leaving a dimensionless number, which is the correlation coefficient between X and Y. This is written as follows:

$$r_{XY} = \frac{\text{Cov}_{XY}}{S_X S_Y} = \frac{\sum (X_i - \bar{X})(Y_i - \bar{Y})}{\sqrt{\sum (X_i - \bar{X})^2}\sqrt{\sum (Y_i - \bar{Y})^2}} \qquad (2.8)$$

The effect of this scaling (dividing Cov_{XY} by S_X and S_Y) is to restrict the range of r_{XY} to the interval -1 to $+1$. No matter what the units of measurement for X and Y the correlation coefficient, r_{XY}, is always restricted to lie within that interval. More information about correlation is given in Sections 5/2/2 and 5/2/3.

For the data in Table 2-5 the computations involved in getting to the correlation coefficient are included in Table 2-6. Columns 6 and 7 are the squared deviations for height and weight, respectively, and can be used to determine the standard deviations S_P and S_M, using equation (2.6). Then the covariance between P and M can be divided by S_P and S_M to yield the correlation between price and mileage,

$$r_{PM} = \frac{-21.00}{(5.34)(5.40)} = -0.73. \qquad (2.9)$$

This summary number is readily interpretable. There is a correlation of -0.73 between price and mileage, which is negative and substantial. There is a strong negative association between price and mileage.

Covariance and especially correlation are the basic statistics for bivariate data sets, and for more extensive multivariate data sets. Care should be taken, however, to remember that these are measures of linear association between two variables, so that it is not appropriate (meaningful) to apply the correlation measure when there is a pronounced curvilinear relationship between the two variables. This point is amplified in Chapter 5.

In summary, the two "vital" statistics for bivariate data sets are

covariance

correlation

$$\text{Cov}_{XY} = \frac{1}{n-1}\sum(X_i - \bar{X})(Y_i - \bar{Y})$$

$$r_{XY} = \frac{\text{Cov}_{XY}}{S_X S_Y} = \frac{\sum(X_i - \bar{X})(Y_i - \bar{Y})}{\sqrt{\sum(X_i - \bar{X})^2}\sqrt{\sum(Y_i - \bar{Y})^2}}$$

In practice these calculations are done by computer.

2/3/3 Autocorrelation

The covariance and correlation coefficient are statistics (summary measures) that measure the extent of the linear relationship between two variables. As such, they can be used to identify *explanatory relationships*. Autocovariance and autocorrelation are comparable measures that serve the same purpose for a single time series.

autocovariance
autocorrelation

For example, if we compare Y_t (the observation at time t) with Y_{t-1} (the observation at time $t-1$), then we see how consecutive observations are related. The observation Y_{t-1} is described as "lagged" by one period. Similarly, it is possible to compare observations lagged by two periods, three periods, and so on.

lagged variable

Table 2-7 shows the beer series, which is a single time series over 56 months from January 1991 to August 1995. The observations Y_1, Y_2, ..., Y_{56} are observed at time periods 1, 2, ..., 56, respectively. If we lag the series by one period, as shown in column 3, then there will be 55 pairs of observations to compare. For these 55 overlapping observations we can compute the covariance and the correlation as if they were two separate series. However, since they are one and the same series (with a lag of one period) the summary measures are called autocovariance and autocorrelation.

Because the two series are almost the same, rather than use

the equations (2.7) and (2.8) to compute the autocovariance and autocorrelation, we normally use simpler formulas which give almost the same answers. We denote the autocovariance at lag k by c_k and the autocorrelation at lag k by r_k. Then define

$$c_k = \frac{1}{n} \sum_{t=k+1}^{n} (Y_t - \bar{Y})(Y_{t-k} - \bar{Y}) \qquad (2.10) \qquad \text{autocovariance}$$

$$\text{and} \qquad r_k = \frac{\displaystyle\sum_{t=k+1}^{n} (Y_t - \bar{Y})(Y_{t-k} - \bar{Y})}{\displaystyle\sum_{t=1}^{n}(Y_t - \bar{Y})^2} \qquad (2.11) \qquad \text{autocorrelation}$$

By way of illustration, consider the beer data and the calculations of autocovariance and autocorrelation in Table 2-7. The mean of *all* the data points in column 2 is $\bar{Y} = 149.30$, and the deviations in columns 4 and 5 are deviations from $\bar{Y}$. Column 6 is the squared deviations from column 4 and the sum of these squares is the denominator in equation (2.11). Column 7 is the column of deviation products (column 4 times column 5). The calculations, using (2.10) and (2.11), are given at the bottom of Table 2-7.

Using exactly similar procedures, the autocorrelations for lags two, three, and beyond can be obtained. The results for the beer data are as follows:

$$
\begin{array}{ll}
r_1 = 0.421 & r_8 = -0.156 \\
r_2 = 0.057 & r_9 = -0.008 \\
r_3 = -0.059 & r_{10} = 0.051 \\
r_4 = -0.188 & r_{11} = 0.374 \\
r_5 = -0.287 & r_{12} = 0.596 \\
r_6 = -0.424 & r_{13} = 0.303 \\
r_7 = -0.343 & r_{14} = 0.082 \\
\end{array}
$$

Notice that the autocorrelation at lag 12 is higher than for the other lags. This is due to the seasonal pattern in the data: the peaks tend to be 12 months apart and the troughs tend to be 12 months apart. Similarly, the autocorrelation at lag 6 is more negative than for the other lags because troughs tend to be 6 months behind peaks.

(1)	(2)	(3)	(4)	(5)	(6)	(7)
t	Y_t	Y_{t-1}	$(Y_t - \bar{Y})$	$(Y_{t-1} - \bar{Y})$	$(Y_t - \bar{Y})^2$	$(Y_t - \bar{Y})(Y_{t-1} - \bar{Y})$
1	164	—	14.70	—	215.99	—
2	148	164	−1.30	14.70	1.70	−19.16
3	152	148	2.70	−1.30	7.27	−3.51
4	144	152	−5.30	2.70	28.13	−14.30
5	155	144	5.70	−5.30	32.45	−30.21
6	125	155	−24.30	5.70	590.66	−138.44
⋮	⋮	⋮	⋮	⋮	⋮	⋮
53	151	127	1.70	−22.30	2.88	−37.84
54	130	151	−19.30	1.70	372.63	−32.75
55	119	130	−30.30	−19.30	918.31	584.97
56	153	119	3.70	−30.30	13.66	−112.01
Sums	8361				21135.84	8893.51

$$\text{Mean} \quad \bar{Y} = \frac{8361}{56} = 149.30$$

$$\text{Autocovariance lag 1} \quad c_1 = \frac{8893.51}{56} = 158.8$$

$$\text{Autocorrelation lag 1} \quad r_1 = \frac{8893.51}{21135.84} = 0.421$$

Table 2-7: *Computing the autocovariance and the autocorrelation using equations (2.10) and (2.11), and a lag of one period.*

autocorrelation function

correlogram

Together, the autocorrelations at lags 1, 2, ..., make up the *autocorrelation function* or ACF. Rather than scanning a list of numbers, it is much easier to plot the autocorrelations against the lag. Such a plot is known as a *correlogram* and helps us visualize the ACF quickly and easily. Figure 2-6 shows the ACF for the beer data. Here the seasonal pattern is seen very clearly.

A plot of the ACF is a standard tool in exploring a time series before forecasting. It provides a useful check for seasonality, cycles, and other time series patterns. In the exercises at the end of this chapter are some data sets that display various kinds of pattern (trend, seasonality, and cycles) and the autocorrelations for these

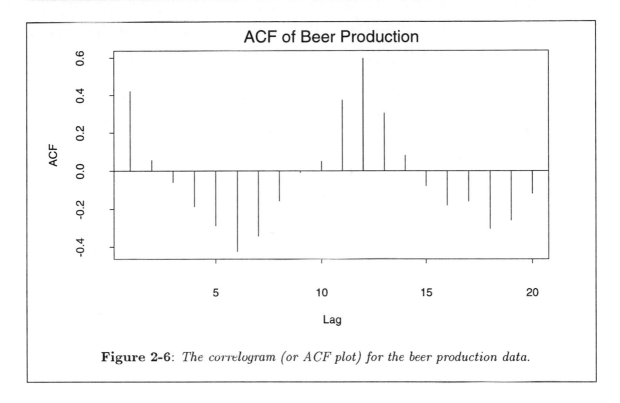

Figure 2-6: *The correlogram (or ACF plot) for the beer production data.*

series will be very helpful in verifying the pattern.

The ACF also helps us identify if previous values of the series contain much information about the next value, or whether there is little relationship between one observation and the next.

To sum up, much is to be learned about a single time series by examining the autocorrelations of the series with itself, lagged one period, two periods, and so on. The ACF plays a very important role in time series forecasting.

2/4 Measuring forecast accuracy

We now turn to another fundamental concern—how to measure the suitability of a particular forecasting method for a given data set. In most forecasting situations, accuracy is treated as the overriding criterion for selecting a forecasting method. In many instances, the word "accuracy" refers to "goodness of fit," which in turn refers to   goodness of fit
how well the forecasting model is able to reproduce the data that are

already known. To the consumer of forecasts, it is the accuracy of the *future* forecast that is most important.

In this section, a variety of measures of forecasting (or modeling) accuracy will be defined and in subsequent chapters these measures will be used in the context of worked examples.

To illustrate the computations involved, we will refer to the Australian monthly beer production. Table 2-8 shows the last 8 months of observations (January–August 1995). The second column shows forecasts for these values, obtained using a very simple method, by taking the average of each month over the past four years. So, for example, the forecast for January 1995 is the average production for January 1991, January 1992, January 1993, and January 1994.

Period t	Observation Y_t	Forecast F_t
1	138	150.25
2	136	139.50
3	152	157.25
4	127	143.50
5	151	138.00
6	130	127.50
7	119	138.25
8	153	141.50
9	—	140.50
10	—	167.25

Table 2-8: *The last eight beer production figures and forecasts obtained by taking the average of each month over the past four years.*

2/4/1 Standard statistical measures

If Y_t is the actual observation for time period t and F_t is the forecast for the same period, then the error is defined as

$$e_t = Y_t - F_t. \tag{2.12}$$

one-step forecast

Usually, F_t is calculated using data $Y_1, \ldots, Y_{t-1}$. It is a *one-step* forecast because it is forecasting one period ahead of the last observation used in the calculation. Therefore, we describe e_t as a *one-step forecast error*. It is the difference between the observation Y_t and the forecast made using all the observations up to but not including Y_t.

If there are observations and forecasts for n time periods, then there will be n error terms, and the following standard statistical measures can be defined:

$$ME = \frac{1}{n}\sum_{t=1}^{n} e_t \qquad (2.13) \qquad \text{mean error}$$

$$MAE = \frac{1}{n}\sum_{t=1}^{n} |e_t| \qquad (2.14) \qquad \text{mean absolute error}$$

$$MSE = \frac{1}{n}\sum_{t=1}^{n} e_t^2. \qquad (2.15) \qquad \text{mean squared error}$$

Table 2-9 illustrates the computation of these standard statistical measures.

Equation (2.12) can be used to compute the error for each period. These can then be averaged as in equation (2.13) to give the mean error. However, the ME is likely to be small since positive and negative errors tend to offset one another. In fact, the ME will only tell you if there is systematic under- or over-forecasting, called the forecast bias. It does not give much indication as to the size of the typical errors.

Therefore, the MAE is defined by first making each error positive by taking its absolute value, and then averaging the results. A similar idea is behind the definition of MSE. Here the errors are made positive by squaring each one, then the squared errors are averaged. The MAE has the advantage of being more interpretable and is easier to explain to non-specialists. The MSE has the advantage of being easier to handle mathematically (and so it is often used in statistical optimization).

Each of these statistics deals with measures of accuracy whose size depends on the scale of the data. Therefore, they do not facilitate comparison across different time series and for different time intervals. An error of 10 Ml when forecasting monthly beer production is quite different from an error of 10 Ml when forecasting

Period	Observation	Forecast	Error	Absolute Error	Squared Error
t	Y_t	F_t	$Y_t - F_t$	$|Y_t - F_t|$	$(Y_t - F_t)^2$
1	138	150.25	-12.25	12.25	150.06
2	136	139.50	-3.50	3.50	12.25
3	152	157.25	-5.25	5.25	27.56
4	127	143.50	-16.50	16.50	272.25
5	151	138.00	13.00	13.00	169.00
6	130	127.50	2.50	2.50	6.25
7	119	138.25	-19.25	19.25	370.56
8	153	141.50	11.50	11.50	132.25
Total			-29.75	83.75	1140.20

$$\text{ME} = -29.75/8 = -3.72 = \qquad \text{using equation (2.13)}$$
$$\text{MAE} = 83.75/8 = 10.47 = \qquad \text{using equation (2.14)}$$
$$\text{MSE} = 1140.20/8 = 142.52 = \qquad \text{using equation (2.15)}$$

Table 2-9: *Computations of the standard measures for the beer data.*

annual beer production or an error of 10 Ml when forecasting the water consumption of a city. To make comparisons like these, we need to work with relative or percentage error measures.

relative or percentage error

First we need to define a relative or percentage error as

$$\text{PE}_t = \left(\frac{Y_t - F_t}{Y_t} \right) \times 100. \tag{2.16}$$

Then the following two relative measures are frequently used:

mean percentage error

$$\text{MPE} = \frac{1}{n} \sum_{t=1}^{n} \text{PE}_t \tag{2.17}$$

mean absolute percentage error

$$\text{MAPE} = \frac{1}{n} \sum_{t=1}^{n} |\text{PE}_t| \tag{2.18}$$

Equation (2.16) can be used to compute the percentage error for any time period. These can then be averaged as in equation (2.17) to give the mean percentage error. However, as with the ME, the MPE is likely to be small since positive and negative PEs tend to offset one

Period t	Observation Y_t	Forecast F_t	Error $Y_t - F_t$	Percent Error $\left(\frac{Y_t-F_t}{Y_t}\right)100$	Absolute Percent Error $\left|\frac{Y_t-F_t}{Y_t}\right|100$
1	138	150.25	−12.25	−8.9	8.9
2	136	139.50	−3.50	−2.6	2.6
3	152	157.25	−5.25	−3.5	3.5
4	127	143.50	−16.50	−13.0	13.0
5	151	138.00	13.00	8.6	8.6
6	130	127.50	2.50	1.9	1.9
7	119	138.25	−19.25	−16.2	16.2
8	153	141.50	11.50	7.5	7.5
Total				−26.0	62.1

$$\text{MPE} = -26.0/8 = -3.3\% \qquad \text{using equation (2.17)}$$
$$\text{MAPE} = 62.1/8 = 7.8\% \qquad \text{using equation (2.18)}$$

Table 2-10: *Computations of the percentage measures for the beer data.*

another. Hence the MAPE is defined using absolute values of PE in equation (2.18). Table 2-10 shows how to compute the PE, MPE, and MAPE measures.

From the point of view of the ultimate user of forecasting, knowing that the MAPE of a method is 5% means a great deal more than simply knowing that the MSE is 183. However, the MAPE is only meaningful if the scale has a meaningful origin. For example, one would not use MAPE for assessing the accuracy of temperature forecasting since the common temperature scales (Fahrenheit and Celsius) have fairly arbitrary zero points. Difficulties also arise when the time series contains zeros, since the percentage error (2.16) cannot then be computed. (When the time series values are very close to zero, the computations involving PE can be meaningless.)

2/4/2 Out-of-sample accuracy measurement

The summary statistics described so far measure the goodness of fit of the model to *historical* data. Such fitting does not necessarily imply good forecasting. An MSE or MAPE of zero can always be obtained

over-fitting

in the fitting phase by using a polynomial of sufficiently high order. Over-fitting a model to a data series, which is equivalent to including randomness as part of the generating process, is as bad as failing to identify the systematic pattern in the data.

A second drawback of these measures of accuracy is that that different methods use different procedures in the fitting phase. For example, smoothing methods (Chapter 4) are highly dependent upon initial forecasting estimates; decomposition methods (Chapter 3) include the trend-cycle in the fitting phase as though it were known; regression methods (Chapter 5–6) minimize the MSE by giving equal weight to all observations; and Box-Jenkins methods (Chapter 7) minimize the MSE by a non-linear optimization procedure. Thus, comparison of such methods on a single criterion is of limited value.

test set
holdout set

These problems can be overcome by measuring true *out-of-sample* forecast accuracy. That is, the total data are divided into an "initialization" set and a "test" set or "holdout" set. Then, the initialization set is used to estimate any parameters and to initialize the method. Forecasts are made for the test set. Since the test set was not used in the model fitting, these forecasts are genuine forecasts made without using the values of the observations for these times. The accuracy measures are computed for the errors in the test set only.

2/4/3 Comparing forecast methods

comparing forecast methods

None of these measures give a good basis of comparison as to the gains in accuracy made by applying a specific forecasting method. Does a MSE of 5 or a MAPE of 3.2% indicate a good or bad forecasting performance? One basis for making such a comparison is to define some very simple naïve methods against which the performance of more sophisticated methods can be compared.

Naïve Forecast 1

We have found it useful to define two different naïve methods of forecasting for use as a basis in evaluating other methods in a given situation. The first is referred to as Naïve Forecast 1 or NF1. This method uses the most recent observation available as a forecast. Table 2-11 shows NF1 used to forecast the monthly beer production. Each forecast is produced by taking the value of the previous month's production. So the forecast for January 1995 is the production figure from December 1994, the forecast for February 1995 is the production

Period	Observation	NF1 Forecast	Absolute Error	Absolute Percent Error
t	Y_t	F_t	$\lvert Y_t - F_t \rvert$	$\left\lvert \dfrac{Y_t - F_t}{Y_t} \right\rvert 100$
1	138	182	44	31.9
2	136	138	2	1.5
3	152	136	16	10.5
4	127	152	25	19.7
5	151	127	24	15.9
6	130	151	21	16.2
7	119	130	11	9.2
8	153	119	34	22.2
Total			177	127.1

$$\text{MAE} = 177/8 = 22.1 \qquad \text{using equation (2.17)}$$
$$\text{MAPE} = 127.1/8 = 15.9\% \qquad \text{using equation (2.18)}$$

Table 2-11: *Computations of the percentage measures for the NF1 forecasts of the beer data.*

figure from January 1995, and so on.

The difference between the MAE or MAPE obtained from a more sophisticated method of forecasting and that obtained using NF1 provides a measure of the improvement attainable through use of that more sophisticated forecasting method. This type of comparison is much more useful than simply computing the MAPE or MAE of the first method, since it provides a basis for evaluating the relative accuracy of those results. In this case, the first forecasting method achieved a MAPE of 7.8% compared to about twice that for NF1 and a MAE of 10.5 Ml compared to 22.1 Ml for NF1. Clearly the first method provides much better forecasts.

A second naïve method of forecasting has also been found to be extremely useful as a basis for evaluating more formal forecasting methods. This method is referred to as Naïve Forecast 2 or NF2 and   Naïve Forecast 2 goes beyond NF1 in that it considers the possibility of seasonality in the series. Since seasonality often accounts for a substantial percentage of the fluctuation in a series, this method can frequently do much better than NF1 and yet is still a very simple straightforward approach. The procedure is to remove seasonality from the original data in order to obtain seasonally adjusted data. Once the seasonality has been removed, NF2 is comparable to NF1 in that it uses the most recent seasonally adjusted value as a forecast for the next seasonally adjusted value. In practice, NF2 allows one to decide whether or not the improvement obtained from going beyond a simple seasonal adjustment of the data is worth the time and cost involved.

2/4/4 Theil's U-statistic

The relative measures in the previous section all give equal weight to all errors in contrast to the MSE, which squares the errors and thereby emphasizes large errors. It would be helpful to have a measure that considers both the disproportionate cost of large errors and provides a relative basis for comparison with naïve methods. One measure that has these characteristics is the U-statistic developed by Theil (1966).

This statistic allows a relative comparison of formal forecasting methods with naïve approaches and also squares the errors involved so that large errors are given much more weight than small errors. The positive characteristic that is given up in moving to Theil's U-statistic as a measure of accuracy is that of intuitive interpretation. This difficulty will become more apparent as the computation of this statistic and its application are examined. Mathematically, Theil's U-statistic is defined as

Theil's U-statistic

$$U = \sqrt{\frac{\sum_{t=1}^{n-1}(\mathrm{FPE}_{t+1} - \mathrm{APE}_{t+1})^2}{\sum_{t=1}^{n-1}(\mathrm{APE}_{t+1})^2}} \qquad (2.19)$$

where $\mathrm{FPE}_{t+1} = \dfrac{F_{t+1} - Y_t}{Y_t}$ (forecast relative change)

and $\mathrm{APE}_{t+1} = \dfrac{Y_{t+1} - Y_t}{Y_t}$ (actual relative change).

Equation (2.19) is actually very straightforward, as can be seen

Period	Observation	Forecast	Numerator	Denominator
t	Y_t	F_t	$\left(\frac{F_{t+1}-Y_{t+1}}{Y_t}\right)^2$	$\left(\frac{Y_{t+1}-Y_t}{Y_t}\right)^2$
1	138	150.25	0.0006	0.0002
2	136	139.50	0.0015	0.0138
3	152	157.25	0.0118	0.0271
4	127	143.50	0.0105	0.0357
5	151	138.00	0.0003	0.0193
6	130	127.50	0.0219	0.0072
7	119	138.25	0.0093	0.0816
8	153	141.50	—	—
Total			0.0560	0.1849

$$\text{Theil's } U = \sqrt{\frac{0.0560}{0.1849}} = 0.550$$

Table 2-12: *Computations involved in determining Theil's U-statistic for the beer forecasts.*

by simplifying it to the form shown in (2.20). When the values of FPE_{t+1} and APE_{t+1} are substituted into equation (2.19), the result is

$$U = \sqrt{\frac{\sum_{t=1}^{n-1}\left(\frac{F_{t+1}-Y_t-Y_{t+1}+Y_t}{Y_t}\right)^2}{\sum_{t=1}^{n-1}\left(\frac{Y_{t+1}-Y_t}{Y_t}\right)^2}} = \sqrt{\frac{\sum_{t=1}^{n-1}\left(\frac{F_{t+1}-Y_{t+1}}{Y_t}\right)^2}{\sum_{t=1}^{n-1}\left(\frac{Y_{t+1}-Y_t}{Y_t}\right)^2}}.$$

$$(2.20)$$

Comparing the numerator of equation (2.20) with equation (2.18) shows that it is similar to what was defined previously as the MAPE of a given forecasting method. The denominator is equivalent to the numerator with F_{t+1} replaced by Y_t. So it is similar to the MAPE of NF1. Thus, the U-statistic is an accuracy measure that incorporates both concepts.

Table 2-12 shows how to compute Theil's U-statistic for the beer data.

Theil's U-statistic can be better understood by examining its interpretation. The value of the U-statistic given by equation (2.19) will be 0 only if $\text{FPE}_{t+1} = \text{APE}_{t+1}$ for $t = 1, 2, \ldots, n-1$. That in turn occurs only when the forecasts are exact (give 0 error). Alternatively, the U-statistic will have a value of 1 only when FPE_{t+1} is equal to 0. That would be the case only if the errors in the forecasting method were the same as those that would be obtained by forecasting no change at all in the actual values. That is comparable to assuming an NF1 approach. If FPE_{t+1} is in the opposite direction of APE_{t+1}, the U-statistic will be greater than unity since the numerator will be larger than the denominator. The ranges of the U-statistic can thus be summarized as follows:

$U = 1$: the naïve method is as good as the forecasting technique being evaluated.

$U < 1$: the forecasting technique being used is better than the naïve method. The smaller the U-statistic, the better the forecasting technique is relative to the naïve method.

$U > 1$: there is no point in using a formal forecasting method, since using a naïve method will produce better results.

2/4/5 ACF of forecast error

One other tool for analyzing forecast error needs to be mentioned. The autocorrelation function of the one-step forecast errors is very useful in determining if there is any remaining pattern in the errors (or residuals) after a forecasting model has been applied. This is not a measure of accuracy per se, but rather can be used to indicate if the forecasting method could be improved.

For example, suppose the naïve forecast method NF1 was used for the beer data. We analyze the forecast errors by a time plot and an ACF plot as shown in Figure 2-7.

Note that there is a pattern remaining in these errors—the January value is particularly low each year. Clearly, there is not what would be called a random set of errors. The autocorrelation statistics are sensitive to such patterns.

The ACF plot in the lower panel of Figure 2-7 tells a similar story. The autocorrelation at lag 12 is much larger than the other

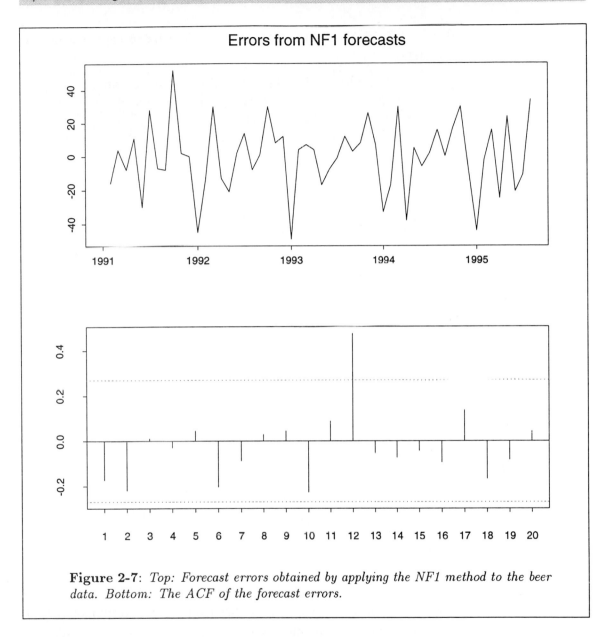

Figure 2-7: *Top: Forecast errors obtained by applying the NF1 method to the beer data. Bottom: The ACF of the forecast errors.*

autocorrelations. This shows there is some seasonal pattern in the error series (the low January values are 12 months apart).

It is important not to read too much into the other autocorrelations shown in Figure 2-7. With random series, no autocorrelations will be exactly zero, even if the series is entirely random. These small fluctuations around zero are quite acceptable and do not indicate there is information in the series which is not being captured by the forecasts.

It is useful to have a benchmark to determine if an autocorrelation is significantly large. A simple rule is to only consider autocorrelations that are larger than the *critical values* of $2/\sqrt{n}$ in magnitude. (Why this works will be discussed in Chapter 7.) For the beer data, $n = 56$, so the critical values are at $2/\sqrt{56} = 0.27$. Figure 2-7 shows the boundary as two horizontal lines at ± 0.27. Autocorrelations that fall within these boundaries can be safely ignored. Autocorrelations that fall outside the boundaries suggest there may be some additional information in the series which is not being captured by the forecast method.

ACF critical values

In this example, only the autocorrelation at lag 12 falls outside the critical values. This is another indication that there is some seasonality in the forecast errors, and that the forecast method could be improved. This is not surprising since the forecast method NF1 does not use the seasonal pattern in producing forecasts.

2/5 Prediction intervals

It is usually desirable to provide not only forecast values but accompanying uncertainty statements, usually in the form of *prediction intervals*. This is useful because it provides the user of the forecasts with "worst" or "best" case estimates and with a sense of how dependable the forecast is, and because it protects the forecaster from the criticism that the forecasts are "wrong." Forecasts cannot be expected to be perfect and intervals emphasize this.

prediction intervals

Prediction intervals are usually based on the MSE because it provides an estimate of the variance of the one-step forecast error. So the square root of the MSE is an estimate of the standard deviation of the forecast error. The usual assumption for constructing prediction intervals is that the forecast errors are normally distributed with zero mean. Under this assumption, an approximate prediction interval for the next observation is

$$\boxed{F_{n+1} \pm z\sqrt{\text{MSE}}.}$$

The value of z determines the width and probability of the prediction interval. For example, $z = 1.96$ gives a 95% prediction interval. That is, the interval has probability of 95% of containing the true value, as yet unknown.

For other percentages, different values of z can be used. The table below gives the most common values of z.

z	Probability
0.674	0.50
1.000	0.68
1.150	0.75
1.282	0.80
1.645	0.90
1.960	0.95
2.576	0.99

Other values of z are given in Table D of Appendix III. The rules of thumb given on page 32 are based on this table.

The September 1995 forecast for the beer data can be calculated as the average production for the previous four Septembers. This gives $F_{n+1} = 140.50$. Table 2-9 gives the MSE for the beer forecasts as 142.52. So a 90% prediction interval is

$$140.50 \pm 1.645\sqrt{142.52} = 140.50 \pm 19.64 = [120.86, 160.01].$$

That is, we can be 90% sure that the actual beer production figure for September 1995 will lie between 120.86 and 160.01 megaliters. (In fact, it was 144 megaliters.) A similar calculation gives the October 1995 forecast as 167.25 Ml with a 90% prediction interval of

$$167.25 \pm 1.645\sqrt{142.52} = 167.25 \pm 19.64 = [147.61, 186.89].$$

The actual figure for October was 166 Ml.

Although October is two periods ahead of the last observation, these are both *one-step* forecasts since the forecast method is based only on data from previous years. The forecast method treats the data from each month as separate series. That is why we could use the same MSE value in computing the prediction interval for October. If we had used the NF1 method, then the forecast for October would have been a two-step forecast, and the MSE would not have been valid for calculating a prediction interval.

This procedure only works for one-step forecasts since the MSE is based on one-step forecasts. For multi-step forecasts, we need to

h-step MSE

modify the MSE to be based on multi-step forecasts. One approach is to define the *h*-step MSE as

$$\text{MSE}_h = \frac{1}{n-h} \sum_{t=h+1}^{n} (e_t^{(h)})^2$$

where $e_t^{(h)}$ is the error from making an *h*-step forecast of the observation at time t. Then, if we assume the *h*-step forecast error is normally distributed with zero mean, we have the prediction interval

$$\boxed{F_{n+h} \pm z\sqrt{\text{MSE}_h}\,.}$$

Before calculating any prediction intervals in this way, the errors should be checked to ensure the assumptions of zero mean and normal distribution have been met.

2/6 Least squares estimates

In Chapter 1 we introduced two kinds of quantitative forecasting models: explanatory models and time series models. An explanatory model for GNP is of the form

$$\text{GNP} \quad = \quad f(\text{monetary and fiscal policies, inflation,}$$
$$\text{capital spending, imports, exports, error})$$

whereas a time series model is of the form

$$\text{GNP}_{t+1} = f(\text{GNP}_t, \text{GNP}_{t-1}, \text{GNP}_{t-2}, \text{GNP}_{t-3}, \dots, \text{error}).$$

random error

Neither model can be exact. That is why the error term is included on the right-hand sides of these equations. The error term represents variations in GNP that are not accounted for by the relationship f.

In both cases, what is observed as the output of the system is dependent on two things: the functional relationship governing the system (or the pattern, as it will be called from now on) and randomness (or error). That is,

$$\text{data} = \text{pattern} + \text{error}. \qquad (2.21)$$

The critical task in forecasting is to separate the pattern from the error component so that the former can be used for forecasting.

The general procedure for estimating the pattern of a relationship, whether explanatory or time series, is through fitting some functional form in such a way as to minimize the error component of equation (2.21). One form of this estimation is least squares. This approach is very old (developed first by Gauss in the 1800s) and is the one most widely used in classical statistics.

The name *least squares* is based on the fact that this estimation procedure seeks to minimize the sum of the squared errors in equation (2.21). The example shown below illustrates the basis of the least squares method. Its application to all types of functional forms (i.e., linear or non-linear) is analogous to that shown here.

least squares

Suppose that the manager of a supermarket wants to know how much a typical customer spends in the store. The manager might start by taking a sample of say 12 clients, at random, obtaining the results shown in Table 2-13.

From Table 2-13, it is clear that not all customers spend the same amount. Some of the variation might be explained through factors such as time of the day, day of the week, discounts offered, maximum or minimum amount of checks cashed, and so on, while part of the variation may be random or unexplainable. For purposes of this illustration, it will be assumed that no variation can be explained through explanatory or time series relationships. In such a case, the store manager faced with finding an appropriate estimator to describe

Client	Amount Spent ($)	Client	Amount Spent ($)
1	9	7	11
2	8	8	7
3	9	9	13
4	12	10	9
5	9	11	11
6	12	12	10

Table 2-13: *Sample expenditures for supermarket clients.*

		Estimate of $\hat{Y} = 7$		Estimate of $\hat{Y} = 10$		Estimate of $\hat{Y} = 12$	
Client	Amount spent	Error[a]	Error squared	Error	Error squared	Error	Error squared
1	9	2	4	−1	1	−3	9
2	8	1	1	−2	4	−4	16
3	9	2	4	−1	1	−3	9
4	12	5	25	2	4	0	0
5	9	2	4	−1	1	−3	9
6	12	5	25	2	4	0	0
7	11	4	16	1	1	−1	1
8	7	0	0	−3	9	−5	25
9	13	6	36	3	9	1	1
10	9	2	4	−1	1	−3	9
11	11	4	16	1	1	−1	1
12	10	3	9	0	0	−2	4
SSE (sum of squared errors)			144		36		84
MSE (mean squared error)			12		3		7

[a] Error = amount spent − estimated value.

Table 2-14: *Mean squared errors for estimates of client expenditure.*

the data may take a fixed value as an estimate. Having made this decision, the manager might decide to select an estimate in such a way as to minimize the mean (average) squared error. This could be done by trial and error. Suppose we denote the estimate by the symbol $\hat{Y}$. The manager tries values of $\hat{Y} = 7$, $\hat{Y} = 10$, and $\hat{Y} = 12$. The resulting mean squared errors are shown in Table 2-14.

From Table 2-14 it is clear that the squared error is least when the manager chooses 10 as the estimate. However, there may be a better estimate. Figure 2-8 shows the resulting MSEs for all estimates from 0 through 20, and it can be seen that the MSEs form a parabola. Furthermore, the minimum value on this parabola is indeed at the point where the estimate is 10. Thus, the minimum MSE will be achieved when the value of the estimate is 10, and we say that 10 is the least squares estimate of customer spending.

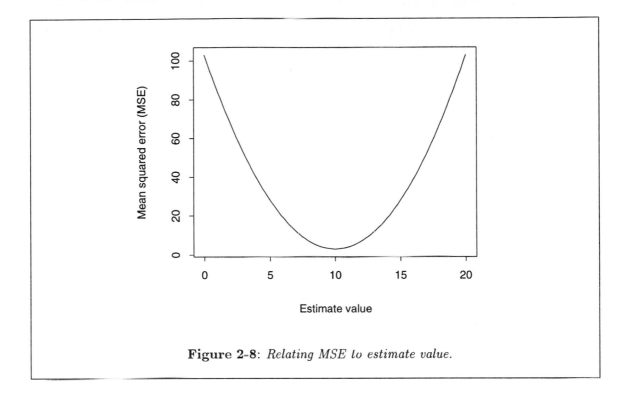

Figure 2-8: *Relating MSE to estimate value.*

Because Figure 2-8 is a mathematical function whose properties can be found exactly, it is not necessary to use trial and error to find the estimator that minimizes the MSE. Rather, this value can be found mathematically with the help of differentiation. The first step is to rewrite equation (2.21) so as to isolate the error on the left-hand side:

$$\text{error} = \text{data} - \text{pattern}. \tag{2.22}$$

As usual, the error will be denoted by e, the data by Y, and the estimate pattern by $\hat{Y}$. In addition, the subscript i ($i = 1, 2, 3, \ldots, 12$) will be added to denote the ith customer. Using this notation, equation (2.22) becomes: $e_i = Y_i - \hat{Y}$. Then the sum of squared errors is

$$\text{SSE} = \sum_{i=1}^{12} e_i^2 = \sum_{i=1}^{12} (Y_i - \hat{Y})^2 \tag{2.23}$$

and the mean squared error is

$$\text{MSE} = \frac{1}{12}\text{SSE} = \frac{1}{12}\sum_{i=1}^{12} (Y_i - \hat{Y})^2.$$

Now initially the value $\hat{Y}$ will not be known, but the store manager wants that value of $\hat{Y}$ which will minimize the sum of the squared errors (or, equivalently, to minimize the MSE).[4]

This can be found by taking the derivative of (2.23), setting it equal to zero, and solving for $\hat{Y}$, as follows:

$$\frac{d\,\text{SSE}}{d\,\hat{Y}} = -2\sum_{i=1}^{12}(Y_i - \hat{Y}) = 0$$

so that
$$\sum_{i=1}^{12}(Y_i - \hat{Y}) = 0$$

or
$$\sum_{i=1}^{12} Y_i - 12\hat{Y} = 0$$

which implies
$$\hat{Y} = \frac{1}{12}\sum_{i=1}^{12} Y_i = \bar{Y}. \qquad (2.24)$$

Solution (2.24) is easily recognized as the mean of the data, and it gives a value that minimizes the sum of the squared errors. Applying (2.24) to the store manager's data in Table 2-13 gives

$$\hat{Y} = \bar{Y} = \frac{1}{12}\sum_{i=1}^{12} Y_i = \frac{120}{12} = 10.$$

minimum MSE
estimate

This value is the minimum point of Figure 2-8. As a single point estimate of the pattern of the data, the mean fits the data as closely as possible, given the criterion of minimizing the MSE. While the mean is a somewhat simple estimate of the data in most situations, the procedure of least squares that was used to determine a MSE estimate can be applied no matter how complex or sophisticated the estimation situation is.

It is of course possible to minimize some other criterion (e.g., MAE) instead of minimizing the MSE. However, minimizing MAE is not as easy mathematically as minimizing the MSE. Also, squaring the

---

[4]Note that minimizing SSE (the sum of squared errors) is the "least squares" procedure. Dividing by n (which is 12 in the example given) gives the MSE. Thus minimizing the MSE is an exactly equivalent procedure.

errors magnifies (or gives more weight to) extreme values, and this result is attractive because large errors are less desirable than small errors. (Many cost relationships are quadratic in nature, suggesting the appropriateness of squaring.)

2/6/1 Discovering and describing relationships

If the measurable output of a system is viewed as data that include a pattern and some error, a major consideration in forecasting, whether explanatory or time series, is to identify and fit the most appropriate pattern (functional form) so as to minimize the MSE. The basic procedure is illustrated by comparing two different methods for forecasting the price of a Japanese automobile using the data for the 19 vehicles listed in Table 2-5.

The first method is simply to use the mean as a forecast (as was done for the store expenditure data). Table 2-15 gives the price data along with the forecasts and the resulting errors.

The forecasting model underlying Table 2-15 is

$$\hat{Y} = a. \tag{2.25}$$

That is, the forecasts are the same for all vehicles because we are not using other information about the vehicles. The value of a is estimated from the data to be equal to the mean of the data. Hence, $\hat{Y} = a = \bar{Y}$.

Using the mean as the estimate of the pattern might be acceptable if we had no other information about these vehicles. But we have already seen that price is correlated with mileage. We can use the mileage information to form a more accurate estimate of price than the mean. Figure 2-9 shows a straight line fitted to the price-mileage relationship. Notice that the errors (vertical distances from the points to the line) are smaller in this plot than the errors obtained using the mean as an estimate.

Using a straight line forecast model with mileage as the explanatory variable means

straight line model

$$\hat{Y} = a + b \times \text{mileage} \tag{2.26}$$

where a and b are suitably chosen values representing the intercept and slope of the line. The values of a and b can be chosen in the same

Price	Mean value	Error	Squared error
14.944	13.938	1.01	1.01
14.799	13.938	0.86	0.74
24.760	13.938	10.82	117.12
14.929	13.938	0.99	0.98
13.949	13.938	0.01	0.00
17.879	13.938	3.94	15.53
11.650	13.938	−2.29	5.24
23.300	13.938	9.36	87.65
17.899	13.938	3.96	15.69
21.498	13.938	7.56	57.15
13.249	13.938	−0.67	0.48
9.599	13.938	−4.34	18.83
10.989	13.938	−2.95	8.70
13.945	13.938	0.01	0.00
13.071	13.938	−0.87	0.75
6.599	13.938	−7.34	53.86
9.410	13.938	−4.53	20.50
5.866	13.938	−8.07	65.16
6.488	13.938	−7.45	55.50
Total 264.823	264.823	0.00	524.88

$$\bar{Y} = \frac{264.823}{19} = 13.938 \qquad \text{MSE} = \frac{524.88}{19} = 27.63$$

Table 2-15: *The mean as an estimate of the price of Japanese automobile.*

simple linear
regression

way as a was chosen in (2.25): that is, by minimizing the MSE. This procedure is known as *simple linear regression* and will be examined in detail in Chapter 5. The mechanics of how a and b are calculated are not important at this point.

For these data, the values of a and b which minimize the MSE are 32.1 and −0.735 respectively. So the forecast model is

$$\hat{Y} = 32.1 - 0.735 \times \text{mileage}. \qquad (2.27)$$

This line is shown in Figure 2-9.

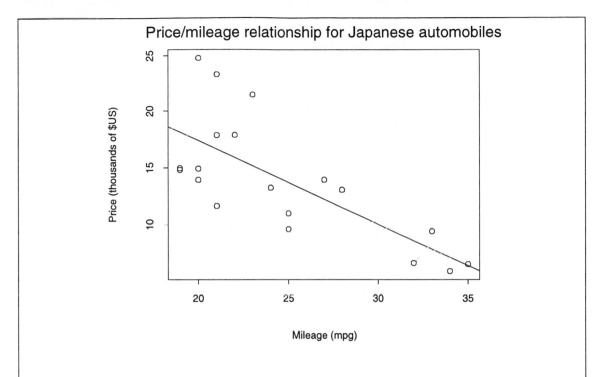

Figure 2-9: *Straight line estimate of vehicle price using mileage as an explanatory variable.*

It is important not to confuse an *explanatory* relationship (such as that between price and mileage) with a *causal* relationship. Of course, causal relationship higher mileage does not *cause* lower prices—both depend on other variables such as the size of the engine. The straight line forecast model (2.27) is used when we know the mileage of a vehicle and wish to predict its price.

For forecasting purposes, either the mean forecasting model or the straight line forecasting model can be used to predict the price of a Japanese automobile not listed. For example, if a vehicle has a mileage of 23 mpg, the mean gives a forecast of $13,938 while the straight line model gives a forecast of $[32.1 - 0.736(23)] \times 1,000 =$ $15,176. From historical data, one would expect the straight line model to be better since it had a smaller MSE value (13.00 compared with 27.63).

A little care must be taken in comparing MSE values (or any other measure of accuracy) from different models. More complicated

Price ($'000)	Mileage (mpg)	Forecast ($'000)	Error	Squared error
14.944	19	18.118	−3.174	10.072
14.799	19	18.118	−3.319	11.014
24.760	20	17.382	7.378	54.429
14.929	20	17.382	−2.453	6.019
13.949	20	17.382	−3.433	11.788
17.879	21	16.647	1.232	1.518
11.650	21	16.647	−4.997	24.971
23.300	21	16.647	6.653	44.261
17.899	22	15.912	1.987	3.949
21.498	23	15.176	6.322	39.962
13.249	24	14.441	−1.192	1.421
9.599	25	13.706	−4.107	16.866
10.989	25	13.706	−2.717	7.381
13.945	27	12.235	1.710	2.923
13.071	28	11.500	1.571	2.468
6.599	32	8.559	−1.960	3.840
9.410	33	7.823	1.587	2.517
5.866	34	7.088	−1.222	1.493
6.488	35	6.353	0.135	0.018

Sum of squared errors (SSE): 264.913

$$\text{MSE} = 246.913/19 = 13.00$$

Table 2-16: *Straight line estimate of vehicle price using mileage as explanatory variable. Straight line formula:* $\hat{Y} = 32.1 - 0.735(mileage)$.

models generally have smaller MSE values, even if they do not give more accurate forecasts. This is because they measure the goodness of fit of the model to historical data, rather than true out-of-sample forecasting performance. However, in this case the scatterplot (Figure 2-5) and negative correlation (Equation 2.9) both indicate that mileage should be included in the forecasting model. Also, the straight line model has only half the MSE of the mean model. Such a reduction is unlikely to be due to the additional complexity of the straight line model.

In general, there is no way that a statistical method can automatically determine the best pattern (functional form) to describe a given set of data. Rather, this decision must be based on judgment. Then a statistical method can be used to fit the specified pattern in such a way as to minimize the MSE.

2/7 Transformations and adjustments

Sometimes, adjusting the historical data will lead to a simpler and more interpretable forecasting model. In this section we deal with three kinds of adjustment: mathematical transformations (such as logarithms and square roots) are discussed in Section 2/7/1; adjustments to remove data variation due to the effects of the calendar are discussed in Section 2/7/2; and adjustments due to population changes and inflation are discussed in Section 2/7/3.

2/7/1 Mathematical transformations

Figure 2-10 shows monthly Australian electricity production data, the same data that were plotted in Figure 1-2a (p. 7). Notice that the size of the annual seasonal variation increases as the level of the series increases. At the start of the series, the total variation throughout the year was only about 300 million kwh, but in the most recent years, when the production is very high, the total variation is over 2,500 million kwh. Clearly any forecasts for these data must take account of the obvious increasing trend, the strong seasonal pattern, and this increasing variation with level. A mathematical transformation is a convenient method for accounting for the increasing variation.

mathematical transformation

One such transformation is the square root function. The top plot in Figure 2-11 shows the square roots of the electricity production data. The new data set was formed simply by taking the square root of each observation in the original data set. This mathematical transformation has helped in reducing the variation in the size of the annual cycles, making it easier to forecast these data than those shown in Figure 2-10.

square root transformation

Square roots are only one kind of transformation that can be

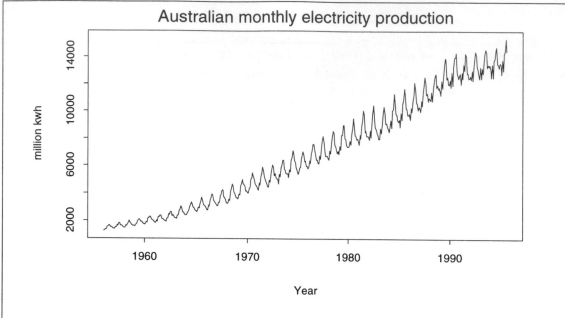

Figure 2-10: *Monthly Australian electricity production from January 1956 to August 1995. Note the increasing variation as the level of the series increases.*

used in this way. Many other transformations are possible, but in practice the square root and logarithm are most useful. Logarithms, in particular, are useful because they are more interpretable: changes in a log value are relative (percent) changes on the original scale.

Other useful transformations are given in Table 2-17. Here we denote the original observations as $Y_1, \ldots, Y_n$ and the transformed observations as $W_1, \ldots, W_n$. Figure 2-11 displays the electricity data transformed using some of the transformations given in Table 2-17, showing the effect of the increasing strength of the transformations.

power transformation   Each of the transformations in Table 2-17 is a member of the family of power transformations:

$$W_t = \begin{cases} -Y_t^p, & p < 0; \\ \log(Y_t), & p = 0; \\ Y_t^p, & p > 0. \end{cases} \qquad (2.28)$$

For $p = 1$ the transformation is simply $W_t = Y_t$, so this leaves the data alone. Choosing $p = \frac{1}{2}$ gives a square root and $p = -1$

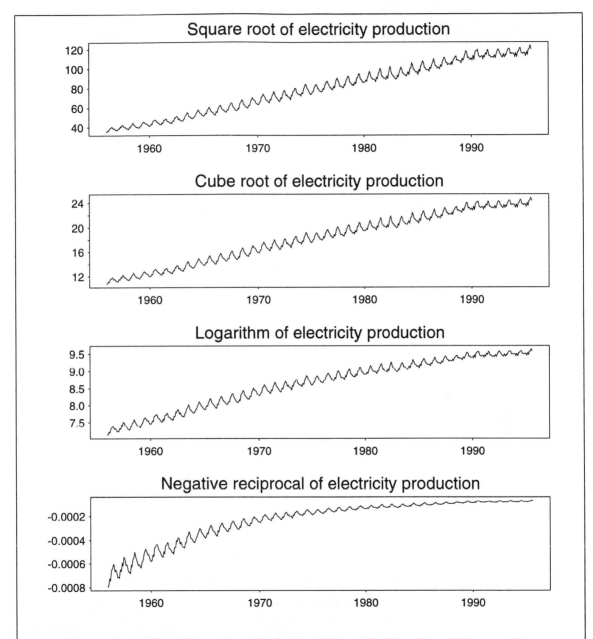

Figure 2-11: *Transformations of the electricity production data. Of these, either a square root, cube root, or a log transformation could be used to stabilize the variation to form a series which has variation approximately constant over the series.*

Square root	$W_t = \sqrt{Y_t}$	$\downarrow$
Cube root	$W_t = \sqrt[3]{Y_t}$	Increasing
Logarithm	$W_t = \log(Y_t)$	strength
Negative reciprocal	$W_t = -1/Y_t$	$\downarrow$

Table 2-17: *Mathematical transformations for stabilizing variation.*

gives the negative reciprocal. It might seem artificial to define the power transformation for $p = 0$ to be the logarithm, but it actually belongs there because Y_t^p for p close to zero behaves much like the logarithm. For $p < 0$, the negative of the power transformation is used so that all transformations result in increasing functions (i.e., the transformed variable increases as Y_t increases). The parameter p can be any number if the data are positive, but p must be greater than zero if the data have zeros. If the data have negative values, no power transformation is possible unless they are adjusted first by adding a constant to all values.

Forecasts are calculated on the transformed data rather than the original data. But since we are really interested in forecasts of the original data, not the transformed data, we must reverse the transformation (or *back-transform*) to obtain forecasts on the original scale. For example, the reverse of the square root function is the square function, the reverse of the logarithm function is the exponential function, and so on. Generally, the reverse power transformations are given by

back-transforming

$$Y_t = \begin{cases} (-W_t)^{1/p}, & p < 0; \\ \exp(W_t), & p = 0; \\ (W_t)^{1/p}, & p > 0. \end{cases}$$

For example, if we were to forecast the square root of the electricity data, we could obtain forecasts on the original scale by taking the square of the forecasts of the square root data.

It is preferable to choose a simple value of p to give a transformation such as those given in Table 2-17. Models and forecasts of a time series are relatively insensitive to the value of p chosen—nearby values of p will produce similar results. This is seen in Figure 2-11 where either $p = 1/2$, $p = 1/3$, or $p = 0$ could be used to stabilize the variation. Also, simple values of p such as 0, -1, or $1/2$ make the results much easier to interpret than a number like $p = 0.38463$. Very often it is found that no transformation (i.e., $p = 1$) is needed.

When the data have been transformed, then prediction intervals also need to be transformed back to the original scale. The simplest way to proceed is to apply the inverse transform to the end points of the prediction interval. So, if logarithms have been used, and the forecast on the log scale is F_{n+1} and the prediction interval is (L_{n+1}, U_{n+1}), then the forecast on the original scale is $e^{F_{n+1}}$ with the prediction interval $(e^{L_{n+1}}, e^{U_{n+1}})$. Note that these prediction intervals need not be symmetric around the forecast.

Empirical studies which have considered the merits of mathematical transformations have demonstrated that, for many series, transformation does not often have a major effect on forecast accuracy (Makridakis and Hibon, 1979; Makridakis et al., 1982; Meese and Geweke, 1984). This is because most forecast methods place more weight on the most recent data. Therefore the small annual variation earlier in the electricity series is unlikely to influence the forecasts very much. Only when the series is rapidly changing in variation will mathematical transformations make a large difference to the forecasts.

However, the MSE (and the other measures of accuracy) gives equal weight to all data and so prediction intervals will be affected by transformations. In calculating prediction intervals, it is assumed that the variation is approximately constant over the series.

2/7/2 Calendar adjustments

Some of the variation in a time series may be due to the variation in the number of days (or trading days) each month. It is a good idea to adjust for this known source of variation to allow study of other interesting features.

Month length can have quite a large effect, since length can differ by about $\frac{31-28}{30} = 10\%$. If this is not removed, it shows up as a seasonal effect, which may not cause problems with forecasts though it does make any seasonal pattern hard to interpret. It is

month length adjustment

easily adjusted for:

$$W_t = Y_t \times \frac{\text{no. of days in an average month}}{\text{no. of days in month } t}$$
$$= Y_t \times \frac{365.25/12}{\text{no. of days in month } t}.$$

Figure 2-12 shows monthly milk production per cow over a period of 14 years. Month length will, of course, affect the total monthly milk production of a cow. Figure 2-12 shows the milk production data adjusted for month length. The simpler pattern will lead to better forecasts and easier identification of unusual observations.

trading day
adjustment

Trading day adjustment is similar to month length adjustment but is not completely predictable. Trading days adjustments are often necessary because a given month may not have the same number of working, or trading, days in different years. In some industries such as retail sales and banks, this factor becomes very important, since it can have a significant influence on the level of sales. This source of variation occurs in monthly data when there is also a weekly cycle, since the proportions of the various days in a given month vary from year to year. For example, March may have four or five Sundays, and if Sunday is a non-trading day this must be accounted for. While the various proportions are completely predictable from the calendar (like month length adjustment) the effects of the various days are not predictable so this must be estimated.

In the simplest case, days are classified as either trading or non-trading days, and all trading days are assumed to have the same effect. In this case the adjustment is analogous to month length:

$$W_t = Y_t \times \frac{\text{no. of trading days in an average month}}{\text{no. of trading days in month } t}.$$

where Y_t has already been adjusted for month length and transformed if necessary. More complicated cases are discussed in Section 6/2/2.

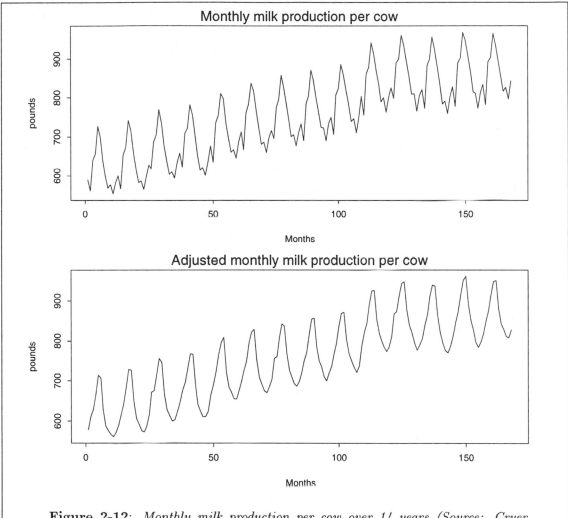

Figure 2-12: *Monthly milk production per cow over 14 years (Source: Cryer, 1986). The second graph shows the data adjusted for the length of month. This yields a simpler pattern enabling better forecasts and easier identification of unusual observations.*

2/7/3 Adjustments for inflation and population changes

adjusting for inflation

One obvious source of variation that afflicts time series is the effect of inflation or changes in population. For example, when forecasting the price of a new motor vehicle, it is essential to take into account the effect of inflation. A $15,000 vehicle this year is not the same as a $15,000 vehicle 10 years ago. The standard approach is to use equivalent value in 1990 dollars (for instance). Then the data are directly comparable and forecasts will not be affected by this additional source of variation.

adjusting for
population changes

Adjusting for population changes is similar. For example, when forecasting the number of public transport users in a city, it is preferable to take into account the effect of population changes. In this case, the data could be adjusted by the total *number* of people in the city. Rather than forecasting the total number of public transport users, it will probably be more accurate to forecast the *proportion* of people who are public transport users. Demographic studies are needed to provide forecasts of population and these can then be used to obtain forecasts of the number of public transport users in the future. A more refined approach would be to produce forecasts for different age groups and/or different socioeconomic groups.

Appendix 2-A
Notation for quantitative forecasting

Quantitative forecasts are based on data, or observations, that describe some factor of interest. In this book a single observed value will be represented by Y_t. (See Table 2-18.) This variable can be the actual number of units sold, the cost of production, the advertising budget, price per unit, gross national product, or any other event of interest, as long as it can be quantified. The objective of forecasting is to predict future values of Y. The individual forecasts will be denoted by F_t, or $\hat{Y}_t$, and the error by e_t, where the error is the difference between the actual value and the forecast value for observation i:

$$e_t = Y_t - \hat{Y}_t \qquad \text{or} \qquad e_t = Y_t - F_t.$$

In time series forecasting and in explanatory forecasting, when the data are taken at equal time intervals, n will denote the present time period, $n-1$ last period, $n-2$ two periods ago, and so on. A period can be a day, a week, a month, quarter, year, and so forth. The forecasts usually will be for future time periods such as $n+1$.

	Observed Values						Forecasted Values			
	Y_1	Y_2	Y_3	...	Y_{n-1}	Y_n				
Period t	1	2	3	...	$n-1$	n	$n+1$	$n+2$	...	$n+m$
Estimated values	$\hat{Y}_1$	$\hat{Y}_2$	$\hat{Y}_3$	...	$\hat{Y}_{n-1}$	$\hat{Y}_n$	$\hat{Y}_{n+1}$	$\hat{Y}_{n+2}$	...	$\hat{Y}_{n+m}$
or	F_1	F_2	F_3	...	F_{n-1}	F_n	F_{n+1}	F_{n+2}	...	F_{n+m}
Error	e_1	e_2	e_3	...	e_{n-1}	e_n				

$\uparrow$

Present

Table 2-18: *Notation used in time series forecasting.*

Appendix 2-B
Summation sign Σ

In order to simplify the manipulation of expressions involving the adding of many numbers, it is convenient to use a summation sign, Σ. The use of this sign and the elements of notation mentioned previously can be demonstrated using the data in Table 2-19.

Based on Table 2-19,

$$Y_t \quad \text{is the actual sales value,}$$
$$\hat{Y}_t \text{ or } F_t \quad \text{is the forecast values for sales, and}$$
$$e_t \quad \text{is the error or difference } Y_t - \hat{Y}_t.$$

If one wants the sum of the errors, it can be obtained from

$$e_1 + e_2 + e_3 + \cdots + e_{23} = \sum_{t=1}^{23} e_t$$
$$\text{or} \quad 3 - 3 - 2 - \cdots - 7 = -2.$$

Below and above the summation sign are the "limits" showing the variable which is indexing the sum (t) and the range of the summation (from 1 to 23). If it is obvious what the limits are, sometimes they are omitted.

The cumulative sales for the years 1985 through 1994 can be obtained from

$$\sum_{t=11}^{20} Y_t = Y_{11} + Y_{12} + Y_{13} + \cdots + Y_{20}$$
$$= 175 + 175 + 176 + \cdots + 251$$
$$= 2071.$$

	Period	No. of Units Sold				Period	No. of Units Sold		
Year	t	Actual	Forecast	Error	Year	t	Actual	Forecast	Error
1975	1	123	120	3	1986	12	175	173	2
1976	2	125	128	−3	1987	13	176	177	−1
1977	3	133	135	−2	1988	14	192	188	−4
1978	4	140	138	2	1989	15	199	195	−4
1979	5	144	148	−4	1990	16	210	215	5
1980	6	158	157	3	1991	17	225	230	5
1981	7	161	155	6	1993	18	230	236	−6
1982	8	160	168	−6	1993	19	238	242	−4
1983	9	163	168	−5	1994	20	251	248	3
1984	10	171	171	0	1995	21	259	255	4
1985	11	175	176	−1	1996	22	275	263	12
					1997	23	283	290	−7

Table 2-19: *Use of quantitative forecasting notation.*

The following rules apply to the use of summation signs:

1. $\sum_{t=1}^{n} \bar{Y} Y_t = \bar{Y} \sum_{t=1}^{n} Y_t$, where $\bar{Y}$ is the sample mean (therefore a constant) of the variable Y_t .

2. $\sum_{t=1}^{n} \bar{Y} = n\bar{Y}$.

3. $\sum_{t=1}^{n} (Y_t - \hat{Y}_t) = \sum_{t=1}^{n} Y_t - \sum_{t=1}^{n} \hat{Y}_t$.

4. $\sum_{t=1}^{n} (Y_t - \bar{Y}) = \sum_{t=1}^{n} Y_t - \sum_{t=1}^{n} \bar{Y} = \sum_{t=1}^{n} Y_t - n\bar{Y}$.

5. $\sum_{t=1}^{n} (Y_t - \bar{Y})^2 = \sum_{t=1}^{n} (Y_t^2 - 2\bar{Y} Y_t + \bar{Y}^2)$

$$= \sum_{t=1}^{n} Y_t^2 - 2\bar{Y} \sum_{t=1}^{n} Y_t + n\bar{Y}^2$$

$$= \sum_{t=1}^{n} Y_t^2 - n\bar{Y}^2$$

$$= \sum_{t=1}^{n} Y_t^2 - (\sum_{t=1}^{n} Y_t)^2 / n .$$

References and selected bibliography

ARMSTRONG, J.S. and F. COLLOPY (1992) Error measures for generalizing about forecasting methods: empirical comparisons (with discussion), *International Journal of Forecasting*, **8**, 69–111.

BIERMAN, H., C.P. BONINI, and W.H. HAUSMAN (1991) *Quantitative analysis for business decisions*, 8th ed., Homewood, Ill.: Richard D. Irwin.

CHATFIELD, C. (1993) Calculating interval forecasts (with discussion), *Journal of Business and Economic Statistics*, **11**, 121–144.

COGGER, K.O. (1979) "Time series analysis and forecasting with an absolute error criterion," in *TIMS Studies, Vol. 12, Forecasting*, S. Makridakis and S.C. Wheelwright, eds., Amsterdam: North-Holland, 89–102.

CONLEY, D.L., G.S. KRAHENBUHL, L.N. BURKETT, and A.L. MILLAR (1981) Physiological correlates of female road racing performance, *Research Quarterly Exercise Sport*, **52**, 441–448.

CONSUMER REPORTS (1990) Vol. 55, No. 4, Consumers Union, Mt Vernon, N.Y..

CRYER, J.D. (1986) *Time series analysis*, Belmont, Cal.: Duxbury Press.

FILDES, R. (1992) The evaluation of extrapolative forecasting methods (with discussion), *International Journal of Forecasting*, **8**, 81–111.

HOLLOWAY, C.A. (1979) *Decision making under uncertainty*, Englewood Cliffs, N.J.: Prentice-Hall.

KOOSIS, D.J. (1972) *Business statistics*, New York: John Wiley & Sons.

LOCKE, F.M. (1972) *Business mathematics*, New York: John Wiley & Sons.

MAKRIDAKIS, S. and M. HIBON. (1979) Accuracy of forecasting: an empirical investigation (with discussion), *Journal of the Royal Statistical Society A*, **142**, 97–145.

MAKRIDAKIS, S., A. ANDERSEN, R. CARBONE, R. FILDES, M. HIBON, R. LEWANDOWSKI, J. NEWTON, E. PARZEN, and R. WINKLER (1982) The accuracy of extrapolation (time series) methods: results of a forecasting competition, *Journal of Forecasting*, **1**, 111–153.

MCLAUGHLIN, R.L. (1975) The Real Record of the Economic Forecasters, *Business Economics*, **10**, No. 3, 28–36.

MEESE, R. and J. GEWEKE (1984) A comparison of autoregressive univariate forecasting procedures for macroeconomic time series, *Journal of Business and Economic Statistics*, **2**, 191–200.

MONTGOMERY, D.C., L.A. JOHNSON, and J.S. GARDINER (1990) *Forecasting and time series analysis*, 2nd ed., New York: McGraw-Hill.

NEWBOLD, P. and T. BOS (1994) *Introductory business forecasting*, 2nd ed., Cincinnati, Ohio: South-Western Publishing Co..

SPURR, W.A. and C.P. BONINI (1973) *Statistical analysis for business decisions*, revised ed., Homewood, Ill.: Richard D. Irwin.

STEECE, B.M. (1982) "The Evaluation of Forecasts," in *Handbook of Forecasting*, S. Makridakis and S.C. Wheelwright, eds., New York: John Wiley & Sons, 457–468.

THEIL, H. (1966) *Applied economic forecasting*, Amsterdam: North-Holland, 26–32.

RICE, J.A. (1995) *Mathematical statistics and data analysis*, 2nd ed., Belmont, Cal.: Duxbury Press.

WONNACOTT, T.H. and R.J. WONNACOTT (1990) *Introductory statistics for business and economics*, 4th ed., New York: John Wiley & Sons.

Exercises

2.1 Table 2-20 gives average monthly temperatures in Paris.

(a) What is your best estimate of the average temperature in June 1995?

(b) Make a time plot of the data. Is there any time pattern in the temperature readings?

	Jan	Feb	Mar	Apr	May	Jun	Jul	Aug	Sep	Oct	Nov	Dec
1994	7.6	7.1	8.3	11.5	13.7	17.2	18.5	19.7	15.1	8.9	8.5	8.5
1995	7.7	6.9	6.1	10.5	12.9							

Table 2-20: *Average monthly temperature in Paris (degrees Celsius).*

2.2 For each of the following series, what sort of time patterns would you expect to see?

(a) Monthly retail sales of computer disks for the past 10 years at your local store.

(b) Hourly pulse rate of a person for one week.

(c) Daily sales at a fast-food store for six months.

(d) Weekly electricity consumption for your local area over the past 10 years.

2.3 For each of the following series on the web page, make a graph of the data (using a computer package), describe the main features and, if transforming seems appropriate, do so and describe the effect.

(a) Monthly total of people on unemployed benefits in Australia (January 1956–July 1992).

(b) Daily morning temperature of a cow for 75 days.

(c) Number of lynx trapped annually in the McKenzie River district of northwest Canada (1821–1934).

(d) Monthly total of accidental deaths in the United States (January 1973–December 1978).

(e) Quarterly production of bricks (in millions of units) at Portland, Australia (March 1956–September 1994).

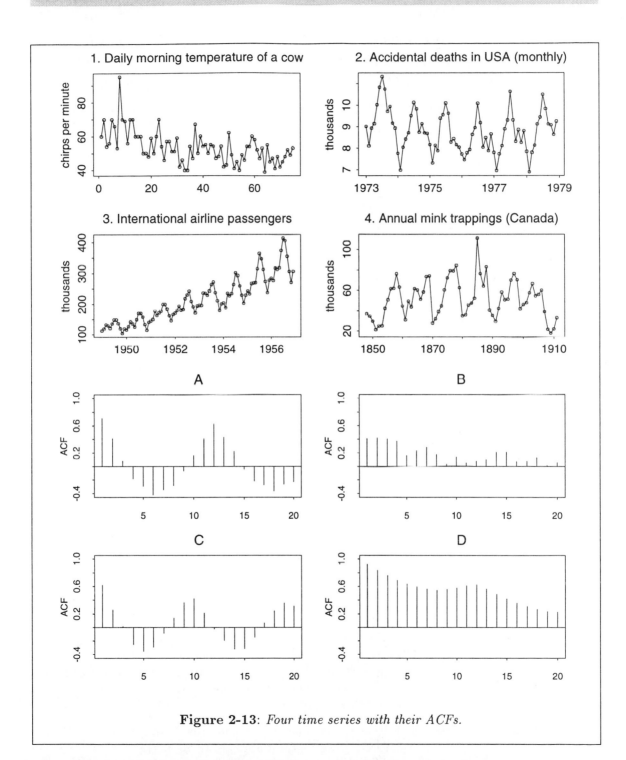

Figure 2-13: *Four time series with their ACFs.*

2.4 In the graphs on the previous page, four time series are plotted along with their ACFs. Which ACF goes with which time series?

2.5 Table 2-21 shows data on the performance of 14 trained female distance runners. The variables measured are the running time (minutes) in a 10 kilometer road race and the maximal aerobic power collected during the week following the run.

(a) Calculate the mean, median, MAD, MSD, and standard deviation for each variable.

(b) Which of these statistics give a measure of the center of data and which give a measure of the spread of data?

(c) Calculate the correlation of the two variables and produce a scatterplot of Y against X.

(d) Why is it inappropriate to calculate the autocorrelation of these data?

X	61.32	55.29	52.83	57.94	53.31	51.32	52.18	52.37	57.91	53.93	47.88	47.41	47.17	51.05
Y	39.37	39.80	40.03	41.32	42.03	42.37	43.93	44.90	44.90	45.12	45.60	46.03	47.83	48.55

Table 2-21: *Running times (Y) and maximal aerobic capacity (X) for 14 female runners. Source: Conley et al. (1981).*

2.6 Column 1 on the following page is the actual demand for product E15 over 20 months. Columns 2 and 3 are the one-month ahead forecasts according to two different forecasting models to be discussed in Chapter 4. (Method 1 gives forecasts from Table 4-4 and Method 2 gives forecasts from Table 4-6.)

(a) Plot the actual demand on a graph along with the forecasts from the two methods.

(b) For each method, compute the Mean Error, Mean Absolute Error, Mean Squared Error, Mean Percentage Error, and Mean Absolute Percentage Error using equations (2.13) through (2.18).

(c) Repeat Part (b) using columns 1 and 3 below. Which forecasting method appears to be better?

Period	(1) Actual Demand	(2) Method 1 Forecast	(3) Method 2 Forecast
1	139	157	170
2	137	145	162
3	174	140	157
4	142	162	173
5	141	149	164
6	162	144	158
7	180	156	166
8	164	172	179
9	171	167	177
10	206	169	180
11	193	193	199
12	207	193	202
13	218	202	211
14	229	213	221
15	225	223	232
16	204	224	235
17	227	211	225
18	223	221	232
19	242	222	233
20	239	235	243

2.7 Download the Dow Jones index from the web page and produce a time plot of the series using a computer package.

(a) Calculate the change in the index for each day by subtracting the value for the previous day. (This is known as "differencing" the data and is discussed in Chapter 6.)

(b) Forecast the change in the index for each of the next 20 days by taking the average of the historical changes.

(c) From these forecasts, compute forecasts for the original index for each of the 20 days.

(d) Add the forecasts to the graph.

(e) Show that the graphed forecasts are identical to extending the line drawn between the first and last observations.

		1950	32	1960	482	1970	5289	1980	11043
		1951	38	1961	814	1971	5811	1981	11180
		1952	39	1962	991	1972	6294	1982	10732
		1953	50	1963	1284	1973	7083	1983	11112
		1954	70	1964	1702	1974	6552	1984	11465
		1955	69	1965	1876	1975	6942	1985	12271
		1956	111	1966	2286	1976	7842	1986	12260
1947	11	1957	182	1967	3146	1977	8514	1987	12249
1948	20	1958	188	1968	4086	1978	9269	1988	12700
1948	29	1959	263	1969	4675	1979	9636	1989	13026

Table 2-22: *Japanese motor vehicle production (1947–1989) in thousands. Source: World motor vehicle data, Motor Vehicle Manufacturers Association of U.S. Inc., Detroit, 1991.*

2.8 Japanese motor vehicle production for 1947–1989 is given in Table 2-22.

(a) Plot the data in a time plot. What features of the data indicate a transformation may be appropriate?

(b) Transform the data using logarithms and do another time plot.

(c) Calculate forecasts for the transformed data for each year from 1948 to 1990 using Naïve Forecast 1.

(d) Compute the forecast errors and calculate the MSE and MAPE from these errors.

(e) Transform your forecast for 1990 back to the original scale by find the exponential of your forecast in (c). Add the forecast to your graph.

(f) From the graphs you have made, can you suggest a better forecasting method?

(g) The world motor vehicle market was greatly affected by the oil crisis in 1973–1974. How did it affect Japanese motor vehicle production? If this information could be included in the forecasts, how would it affect the values of the MSE and MAPE?

3

TIME SERIES DECOMPOSITION

Many forecasting methods are based on the concept that when an underlying pattern exists in a data series, that pattern can be distinguished from randomness by smoothing (averaging) past values. The effect of this smoothing is to eliminate randomness so the pattern can be projected into the future and used as the forecast. In many instances the pattern can be broken down (decomposed) into subpatterns that identify each component of the time series separately. Such a breakdown can frequently aid in better understanding the behavior of the series, which facilitates improved accuracy in forecasting.

Decomposition methods usually try to identify two separate components of the basic underlying pattern that tend to characterize economic and business series. These are the trend-cycle and the seasonal factors. The seasonal factor relates to periodic fluctuations of constant length that are caused by such things as temperature, rainfall, month of the year, timing of holidays, and corporate policies. The trend-cycle represents longer-term changes in the level of the series. The trend-cycle is sometimes separated into trend and cyclical components, but the distinction is somewhat artificial and most decomposition procedures leave the trend and cycle as a single component known as the trend-cycle.

trend-cycle

Decomposition assumes that the data are made up as follows:

time series
decomposition

$$\text{data} = \text{pattern} + \text{error}$$
$$= f(\text{trend-cycle, seasonality, error}).$$

Thus, in addition to the components of the pattern, an element of error or randomness is also assumed to be present. This error is assumed to be the difference between the combined effect of the two subpatterns of the series and the actual data. Therefore, it is often called the "irregular" or the "remainder" component.

There are several alternative approaches to decomposing a time series, all of which aim to isolate each component of the series as accurately as possible. The basic concept in such separation is empirical and consists of first removing the trend-cycle, then isolating the seasonal component. Any residual is assumed to be randomness which, while it cannot be predicted, can be identified. From a statistical point of view there are a number of theoretical weaknesses in the decomposition approach. Practitioners, however, have largely ignored these weaknesses and have used the approach with considerable success.

Decomposition methods are among the oldest approaches to time series analysis. They originated around the beginning of this century and were initiated from two different directions. First, it was recognized that to study the serial correlation within or between variable(s), any spurious correlation that might exist because of trend must be eliminated. As early as 1884, Poynting attempted to eliminate trend and some seasonal fluctuations by averaging prices over several years. Hooker (1901) followed Poynting's example, but was more precise in his methods for eliminating trend. His work was followed by Spencer (1904) and Anderson and Nochmals (1914), who generalized the procedure of trend elimination to include higher-order polynomials.

A second direction for work in this area originated with economists who worried about the impact of depressions and sought ways to predict them. They felt that the elements of economic activity should be separated so that changes in the business cycle could be isolated from seasonal and other changes. France appointed a committee that in 1911 presented a report analyzing the causes of the 1907 economic crisis. This group introduced the idea of leading and coincidental indicators and attempted to separate the trend from the cycle so that the movement of the latter could be followed.

In the United States this idea was expanded and the concept of constructing barometers of business activity was developed. Furthermore, an attempt to separate the seasonal fluctuation from the rest of the components was made as early as 1915 (Copeland). The process of decomposition, as it is known today, was introduced by Macauley (1930) who, in the 1920s, introduced the ratio-to-moving averages method that forms the basis of Census II. (For a summary article, see Burman, 1979.)

An impetus in the development of decomposition came with the introduction and widespread use of computers. Shiskin (1957) developed a computer program that could perform the needed computations easily and quickly. This gave rise to Census II, which has become the most widely used of the decomposition methods. Since that time, decomposition approaches have been used widely by both economists and business analysts.

More recently, the advantages of decomposition approaches have been recognized and efforts have been made to upgrade these approaches. These efforts have been in the direction of introducing statistical rigor into the approach without losing its intuitive appeal. (See Dagum, 1982; Cleveland, 1983.)

We introduce the ideas behind decomposition and seasonal adjustment in Section 3/2. A key step in all decomposition methods involves smoothing the original data. In Section 3/3 we describe moving average smoothers and their variations that are used in most decomposition methodology. An alternative smoother which is becoming increasingly popular is a local linear regression smoother; it is introduced in Section 3/4. The classical decomposition method, dating back to the 1920s, was once the most popular technique and still forms the basis for most other methods. Classical decomposition is discussed in Section 3/5. Today, the most popular method of decomposition is Census II, which lies behind a great many basic economic series used in the private and public sectors. We will study the latest variant of Census II (X-12-ARIMA) in Section 3/6. Then, in Section 3/7 we look at a relatively new decomposition method, STL, which is based on local linear regressions. Finally, in Section 3/8, we briefly review the role of time series decomposition in forecasting.

3/1 Principles of decomposition

3/1/1 Decomposition models

The general mathematical representation of the decomposition approach is:

$$Y_t = f(S_t, T_t, E_t) \qquad (3.1)$$

where Y_t is the time series value (actual data) at period t,
S_t is the seasonal component (or index) at period t,
T_t is the trend-cycle component at period t, and
E_t is the irregular (or remainder) component at period t.

The exact functional form of (3.1) depends on the decomposition method actually used. A common approach is to assume equation (3.1) has the additive form

additive
decomposition

$$Y_t = S_t + T_t + E_t.$$

That is, the seasonal, trend-cycle and irregular components are simply added together to give the observed series.

Alternatively, the multiplicative decomposition has the form

multiplicative decomposition

$$Y_t = S_t \times T_t \times E_t.$$

That is, the seasonal, trend-cycle and irregular components are multiplied together to give the observed series.

An additive model is appropriate if the magnitude of the seasonal fluctuations does not vary with the level of the series. But if the seasonal fluctuations increase and decrease proportionally with increases and decreases in the level of the series, then a multiplicative model is appropriate. Multiplicative decomposition is more prevalent with economic series because most seasonal economic series do have seasonal variation which increases with the level of the series. (See, for example, the electricity production data in Figure 2-10.)

Rather than choosing either an additive or multiplicative decomposition, we could use a transformation as discussed in Section 2/5/1. Very often the transformed series can be modeled additively, when the original data are not additive. Logarithms, in particular, turn a multiplicative relationship into an additive relationship, since if

$$Y_t = S_t \times T_t \times E_t,$$

then $\quad \log Y_t = \log S_t + \log T_t + \log E_t.$

So we can fit a multiplicative relationship by fitting an additive relationship to the logarithms of the data. Other transformations allow a decomposition which is somewhere between the additive and multiplicative forms.

A further decomposition method is *pseudo-additive decomposition* which takes the form

$$Y_t = T_t(S_t + E_t - 1).$$

This type of decomposition is useful in series where there is one month (or quarter) that is much higher or lower than all the other months (or quarters). For example, many European series take large dips in August when companies shut down for vacations. We will not discuss pseudo-additive decomposition in this book; Baxter (1994) describes it and its applications in detail.

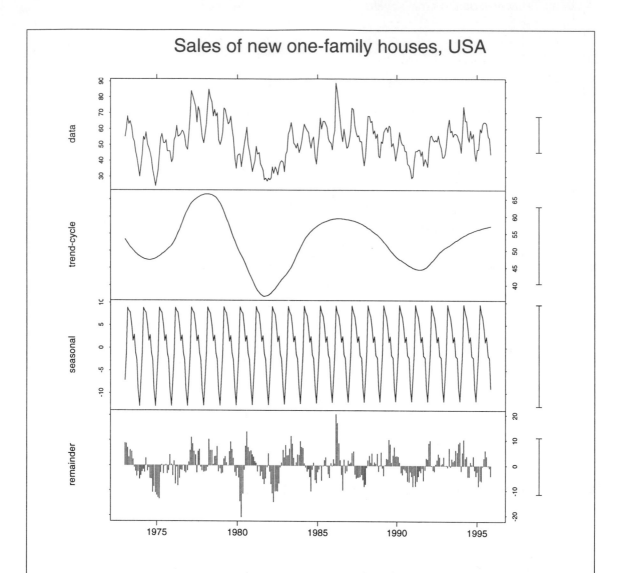

Figure 3-1: *Top: Monthly sales (in thousands) of new one-family houses sold in the United States since 1973. [Source: U.S. Census Bureau, Manufacturing and Construction Division.] The other panels give the components which, when added, make up the original data. The bars on the right-hand side show the different scales used in the plots; the bars represent the same length. The decomposition was computed using the STL method, described in Section 3/7.*

3/1/2 Decomposition graphics

Figure 3-1 shows an additive decomposition of monthly sales of new one-family houses sold in the United States since 1973. The original data are given in the top panel. This series shows both cyclical and seasonal behavior. The cyclical behavior is related to the economic health and confidence of the nation. The other panels in Figure 3-1 show estimates of the cyclical, seasonal, and irregular components. These were obtained by an additive decomposition using the STL method outlined in Section 3/6. When the three components (trend-cycle, seasonal, and irregular) are added together, the original data are obtained. This plot is known as a *decomposition plot* and is helpful in visualizing the decomposition procedure. Decomposition plots were introduced by Cleveland and Terpenning (1992).

decomposition plot

In this example, the seasonal component does not change much over time. The seasonal pattern at the start of the series is almost the same as the seasonal pattern at the end of the series. To see this more clearly, a *seasonal sub-series plot* is useful. This plot was also introduced by Cleveland and Terpenning (1992). Figure 3-2 shows the seasonal sub-series plot for the housing sales data. This is constructed by collecting together the values of the seasonal component in each month. First, the January values of the seasonal component are collected together to form the January sub-series. The mean of these is plotted as a horizontal line and the values of the sub-series are shown by the vertical lines emanating from the mean line. Each vertical line corresponds to one year. For this series, there is a very small increase in the seasonal component in January across the period of the time series. The other sub-series are similar. The largest changes in the seasonal pattern have occurred in May and December, and even these are small.

seasonal sub-series plot

Sub-series plots help in visualizing the overall seasonal pattern shown by the horizontal mean lines. In this example, we can see that house purchases are high in spring and summer months and lower in winter. Sub-series plots also show how the seasonal component is changing over time. We can see whether the change in any sub-series is large or small compared with the overall pattern of the seasonal component. In this example, the seasonal component of housing sales is stable in the sense that the changes in the monthly sub-series are small compared with the overall seasonal pattern.

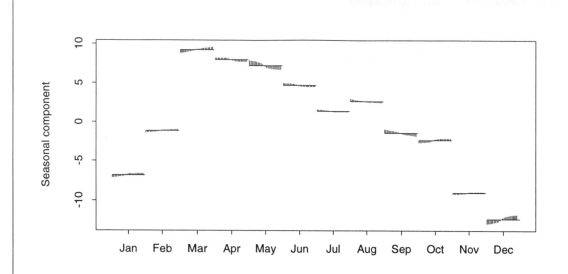

Figure 3-2: *Seasonal sub-series plot of the housing sales data. This shows the seasonal component plotted in Figure 3-1. For each month, the values of the seasonal component are collected together to form a sub-series. The mean of these values is shown as a horizontal line; the values of the sub-series are shown by the vertical lines emanating from the mean line. For this series, there is very little change in the seasonal component in any month.*

3/1/3 Seasonal adjustment

seasonal adjustment

A useful by-product of decomposition is that it provides an easy way to calculate seasonally adjusted data. For an additive decomposition, the seasonally adjusted data are computed by simply subtracting the seasonal component:

$$Y_t - S_t = T_t + E_t$$

leaving only trend-cycle and irregular components. For a multiplicative decomposition, the data are divided by the seasonal component to give seasonally adjusted data.

Most published economic series are seasonally adjusted because seasonal variation is typically not of primary interest. For example, for monthly unemployment we want to know whether an increase from one month to the next means a worsening in the economy. If the increase is due to the addition of a large number of school-leavers seeking work (a seasonal variation) we would not want to conclude the economy has weakened. The seasonally adjusted series show the data after any seasonal variation has been removed.

3/2 Moving averages

Table 3-1 lists three years of monthly sales of a shampoo product. The data are plotted in Figure 3-3. The series has no seasonal component, consisting only of a trend and an irregular component. Therefore, the decomposition of this series involves estimating only the trend-cycle.

The trend-cycle can be estimated by *smoothing* the series to reduce   smoothing the random variation. A range of smoothers is available, but we will begin with the simplest and oldest smoother, a moving average.   moving average

Moving averages provide a simple method for smoothing the "past history" data. In this section we consider several straightforward moving average methods, including simple moving averages, double moving averages, and weighted moving averages. In all cases the objective is to smooth past data to estimate the trend-cycle component.

Moving averages are a fundamental building block in all decomposition methods, and later we will apply the ideas introduced here to other aspects of the decomposition problem.

3/2/1 Simple moving averages

We wish to estimate the trend-cycle component at each observation. The idea behind moving averages is that observations which are nearby in time are also likely to be close in value. So taking an average

Year	Jan	Feb	Mar	Apr	May	Jun	Jul	Aug	Sep	Oct	Nov	Dec
1	266.0	145.9	183.1	119.3	180.3	168.5	231.8	224.5	192.8	122.9	336.5	185.9
2	194.3	149.5	210.1	273.3	191.4	287.0	226.0	303.6	289.9	421.6	264.5	342.3
3	339.7	440.4	315.9	439.3	401.3	437.4	575.5	407.6	682.0	475.3	581.3	646.9

Table 3-1: *Sales of shampoo (in liters) over a three-year period.*

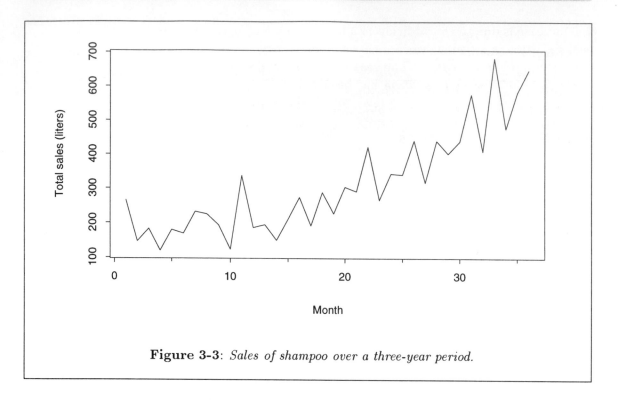

Figure 3-3: *Sales of shampoo over a three-year period.*

of the points near an observation will provide a reasonable estimate of the trend-cycle at that observation. The average eliminates some of the randomness in the data, leaving a smooth trend-cycle component.

We need to decide how many data points to include in each average. Suppose we use averages of three points, namely the observation at which we are calculating trend-cycle and the points on either side. This is called a moving average of order 3 or 3 MA smoother. For example, the trend-cycle for February of year 1 is estimated to be the average of the sales for January, February, and March of that year, namely

MA smoother

$$T_2 = \frac{1}{3}(Y_1 + Y_2 + Y_3) = (266.0 + 145.9 + 183.1)/3 = 198.3.$$

Generally, a moving average of order 3 centered at time t is

$$T_t = \frac{1}{3}(Y_{t-1} + Y_t + Y_{t+1}).$$

Table 3-2 shows how the 3 MA can be applied to each month of the first year of the shampoo data. Note that there is no estimate of

Month	Time period	Observed values (liters)	Three-month moving average 3 MA	Five-month moving average 5 MA
Jan	1	266.0	—	—
Feb	2	145.9	198.3	—
Mar	3	183.1	149.4	178.9
Apr	4	119.3	160.9	159.4
May	5	180.3	156.0	176.6
Jun	6	168.5	193.5	184.9
Jul	7	231.8	208.3	199.6
Aug	8	224.5	216.4	188.1
Sep	9	192.8	180.1	221.7
Oct	10	122.9	217.4	212.5
Nov	11	336.5	215.1	206.5
Dec	12	185.9	238.9	197.8
Jan	13	194.3	⋮	⋮
Feb	14	149.5		
⋮	⋮	⋮		

Table 3-2: *Calculation of 3 MA and 5 MA smoothers for the shampoo data.*

trend-cycle at time 1 since the observation before time period 1 is unavailable. The procedure can be applied to the entire three years of data to obtain the trend-cycle estimate shown in the upper panel of Figure 3-4.

The term "moving average" is used to describe this procedure because each average is computed by dropping the oldest observation and including the next observation. The averaging moves through the time series until the trend-cycle is computed at each observation for which all elements of the average are available. Note that the number of data points in each average remains constant and is centered on the observation for which the trend-cycle estimate is computed.

The number of points included in a moving average affects the smoothness of the resulting estimate. Figure 3-4 shows a moving average of order 5 or 5 MA applied to the same data and the resulting trend-cycle estimate is smoother than the 3 MA smoother. The 5

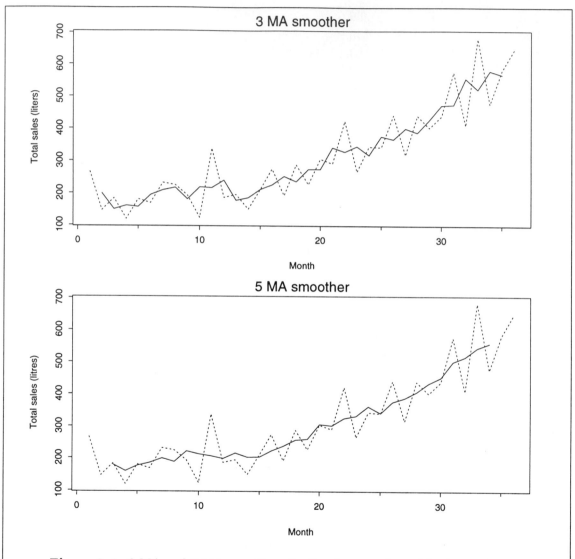

Figure 3-4: *3 MA and 5 MA smoothers for the shampoo data. The 3 MA smoother leaves too much randomness in the trend-cycle estimate. The 5 MA smoother is better, but the true trend-cycle is probably smoother still.*

MA smoother is simply the average of each observation with the two points on either side:

$$T_t = \frac{1}{5}(Y_{t-2} + Y_{t-1} + Y_t + Y_{t+1} + Y_{t+2}).$$

We define the *half-width* of a moving average as the number of   half-width points on either side which are included in the average, and we denote the half-width by m. So for a 3 MA, the half-width is $m = 1$ and for a 5 MA, the half-width is $m = 2$.

Simple moving averages can be defined for any odd order. A moving average of order k (or k MA) where k is an odd integer is defined as the average consisting of an observation and the $m = (k-1)/2$ points on either side so that

$$T_t = \frac{1}{k} \sum_{j=-m}^{m} Y_{t+j}. \qquad (3.2)$$

From Figure 3-4 it can be seen that the more observations included in the moving average (i.e., the larger the value of k), the smoother the resulting trend-cycle. However, even with a 5 MA, the fitted trend-cycle is still too rough. A much smoother curve, without the little bumps and wiggles, would be a more reasonable estimate; that would require a moving average of higher order.

Determining the appropriate length of a moving average is an important task in decomposition methods. As a rule, a larger number of terms in the moving average increases the likelihood that randomness will be eliminated. That argues for using as long a length as possible. However, the longer the length of the moving average, the more terms (and information) are lost in the process of averaging, since k data values are required for a k-term average. Also, longer-term moving average smoothers tend to smooth out the genuine bumps or cycles that are of interest.

In applying a k-term moving average, $m = (k-1)/2$ neighboring points are needed on either side of the observation. Therefore, it is not possible to estimate the trend-cycle close to the beginning and end of the series. The m terms lost in the beginning of the data are usually of little consequence, but those m lost in the end are critical, since they are the starting point for forecasting the cycle. Not only must the cyclical values for periods $t+1$, $t+2$, and so on, be estimated, but the values for periods t, $t-1$, $t-2$, ..., $t-m+1$ must also be estimated.

end point adjustment

To overcome the problem of missing values at the end of the data series, a shorter length moving average can be used. One approach is to take an average of the points that are available. For example, a 3 MA computed at time 1 would give $T_1 = (Y_1 + Y_2)/2$ since only these two observations are available. Thus we use a shorter length moving average at the ends of the data series and we adjust these averages to be centered around the point for which the trend-cycle is being estimated.

3/2/2 Centered moving averages

The simple moving average required an odd number of observations to be included in each average. This was to ensure that the average was centered at the middle of the data values being averaged.

But suppose we wish to calculate a moving average with an even number of observations. For example, to calculate a 4-term moving average or 4 MA for the shampoo data, the trend-cycle at time 3 could be calculated as

$$(266.0 + 145.9 + 183.1 + 119.3)/4 = 178.6$$
$$\text{or} \qquad (145.9 + 183.1 + 119.3 + 180.3)/4 = 157.2.$$

That is, should we include two terms on the left and one on the right of the observation, or one term on the left and two terms on the right? The center of the first moving average is at 2.5 (half a period early) while the center of the second moving average is at 3.5 (half a period late).

centered moving average

However, the average of the two moving averages is centered at 3, just where it should be. Therefore, this problem can be overcome by taking an additional 2-period moving average of the 4-period moving average. This *centered moving average* is denoted as 2×4 MA. The results of following this centering procedure are shown in Table 3-3, where column (5) is simply the average of two successive values of the 4 MA of column 4.

A centered moving average like the one described above can be expressed as a single but weighted moving average, where the weights

(1)	(2)	(3)	(4)	(5)
Month	Period	Data	4 MA	2×4 MA
Jan	1	266.0	—	—
Feb	2	145.9	178.6	—
Mar	3	183.1	157.2	167.9
Apr	4	119.3	162.8	160.0
May	5	180.3	175.0	168.9
Jun	6	168.5	201.3	188.1
Jul	7	231.8	204.4	202.8
Aug	8	224.5	193.0	198.7
Sep	9	192.8	219.2	206.1
Oct	10	122.9	209.5	214.4
Nov	11	336.5	209.9	209.7
Dec	12	185.9	216.6	213.2
Jan	13	194.3	⋮	⋮
Feb	14	149.5		
⋮	⋮	⋮		

Table 3-3: *Centered moving averages: The 2×4 MA is obtained by averaging two successive values of the 4 MA of column 3.*

for each period are unequal. The following notation is useful in discussing weighted and centered moving averages:

$$T_{2.5} = (Y_1 + Y_2 + Y_3 + Y_4)/4 \qquad (3.3)$$
$$T_{3.5} = (Y_2 + Y_3 + Y_4 + Y_5)/4. \qquad (3.4)$$

Averaging these two 4 MA smoothers gives

$$
\begin{aligned}
T_3'' &= \frac{T_{2.5} + T_{3.5}}{2} \\
&= \frac{1}{2}\left(\frac{Y_1 + Y_2 + Y_3 + Y_4}{4} + \frac{Y_2 + Y_3 + Y_4 + Y_5}{4}\right) \\
&= (Y_1 + 2Y_2 + 2Y_3 + 2Y_4 + Y_5)/8.
\end{aligned}
$$

So the first and last terms in this average have weights of $1/8 = 0.125$ and all other terms have weights of double that value, $1/4 = 0.25$. Therefore, a 2×4 MA smoother is equivalent to a weighted moving average of order 5.

So if this centered 4 MA was used with quarterly data, each quarter would be given equal weight. The ends of the moving average will apply to the same quarter in consecutive years. So each quarter receives the same weight with the weight for the quarter at the ends of the moving average split between the two years. It is this property that makes 2×4 MA very useful for estimating a trend-cycle in the presence of quarterly seasonality. The seasonal variation will be averaged out exactly when the moving average is computed. A slightly longer or a slightly shorter moving average will still retain some seasonal variation. An alternative to a 2×4 MA for quarterly data is a 2×8 or 2×12 which will also give equal weights to all quarters and produce a smoother fit than the 2×4 MA.

Generally, a $2 \times k$ MA smoother is equivalent to a weighted MA of order $k + 1$ with weights $1/k$ for all observations except for the first and last observations in the average, which have weights $1/2k$. For example, a 2×12 MA has weights

$$\frac{1}{12}[0.5, 1, 1, 1, 1, 1, 1, 1, 1, 1, 1, 0.5].$$

So this centered 12 MA could be used with monthly data, and each month would be given equal weight. Similarly, a 2×24 or 2×36 would give equal weights to all months and produce a smoother fit than the 2×12 MA.

The centered 4 MA and the centered 12 MA are frequently used for estimating a trend-cycle in quarterly and monthly seasonal data. Other moving averages tend to be contaminated by the seasonal variation. Figure 3-5 shows the new housing data with a 7 MA and a 2×12 MA. Notice how the 7 MA is tracking the seasonal variation whereas the 2×12 MA tracks the cycle without being contaminated by the seasonal variation.

Here, the trends near the ends of the series have been calculated by using shorter moving averages on the data that were available. A consequence of this is that the trend-cycle near the ends may be slightly contaminated by the seasonal variation. However, the effect does not seem to be particularly serious (in practice there are ways of avoiding such contamination).

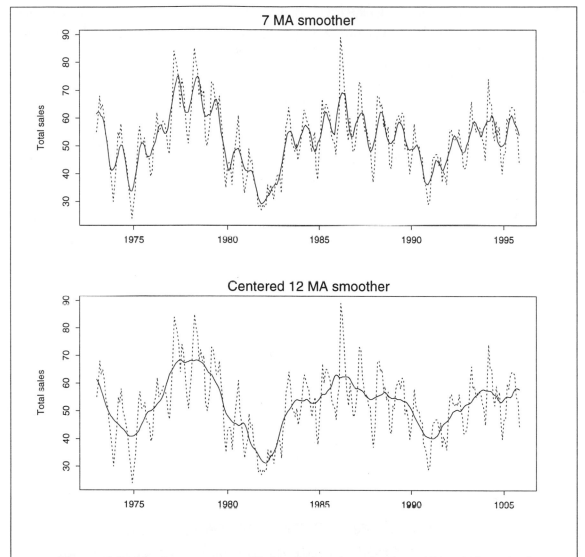

Figure 3-5: *Moving averages applied to the housing sales data. The 7 MA tracks the seasonal variation whereas the 2×12 MA tracks the cycle without being contaminated by the seasonal variation.*

3/2/3   Double moving averages

double moving
averages

The centered moving averages are an example of how a moving average can itself be smoothed by another moving average. Together, the smoother is known as a *double moving average*. In fact, any combination of moving averages can be used together to form a double moving average. For example, a 3×3 moving average is a 3 MA of a 3 MA. It is equivalent to a 5-period weighted moving average as shown by equations (3.5) through (3.10).

$$T_2 \; = \; (Y_1 + Y_2 + Y_3)/3 \quad \text{[a 3-months moving average of} \tag{3.5}$$
months 1, 2, and 3 (centered at period 2)]

$$T_3 \; = \; (Y_2 + Y_3 + Y_4)/3 \quad \begin{array}{l}\text{[like } T_2 \text{ but for months 2, 3, \&} \\ \text{4]}\end{array} \tag{3.6}$$

$$T_4 \; = \; (Y_3 + Y_4 + Y_5)/3 \tag{3.7}$$

$$T_5 \; = \; (Y_4 + Y_5 + Y_6)/3 \tag{3.8}$$
etc.

$$T_3'' \; = \; (T_2 + T_3 + T_4)/3 \quad \text{[a 3-months moving average of} \tag{3.9}$$
the moving averages (centered at period 3)]

Substituting (3.5), (3.6), and (3.7) into (3.9) gives

$$
\begin{aligned}
T_3'' \; &= \; \left(\frac{Y_1 + Y_2 + Y_3}{3} + \frac{Y_2 + Y_3 + Y_4}{3} + \frac{Y_3 + Y_4 + Y_5}{3} \right) \Big/ 3 \\
&= \; (Y_1 + 2Y_2 + 3Y_3 + 2Y_4 + Y_5)/9
\end{aligned}
\tag{3.10}
$$

Equation (3.10) is a 5-month weighted MA with weights of .1111, .2222, .3333, .2222, .1111 for the first, second, third, fourth, and fifth terms, respectively.

3/2/4   Weighted moving averages

weighted moving
average

In general, a weighted k-point moving average can be written as

$$T_t = \sum_{j=-m}^{m} a_j Y_{t+j} \tag{3.11}$$

where $m = (k-1)/2$ is the half-width and the weights are denoted by a_j. The simple k-point moving average given by (3.2) is a special

Name	a_0	a_1	a_2	a_3	a_4	a_5	a_6	a_7	a_8	a_9	a_{10}	a_{11}
3 MA	.333	.333										
5 MA	.200	.200	.200									
2 × 12 MA	.083	.083	.083	.083	.083	.083	.042					
3 × 3 MA	.333	.222	.111									
3 × 5 MA	.200	.200	.133	.067								
S15 MA	.231	.209	.144	.066	.009	-.016	-.019	-.009				
S21 MA	.171	.163	.134	.037	.051	.017	-.006	-.014	-.014	-.009	-.003	
H5 MA	.558	.294	-.073									
H9 MA	.330	.267	.119	-.010	-.041							
H13 MA	.240	.214	.147	.066	.000	-.028	-.019					
H23 MA	.148	.138	.122	.097	.068	.039	.013	-.005	-.015	-.016	-.011	-.004

S = Spencer's weighted moving average
H = Henderson's weighted moving average

Table 3-4: *Weight functions a_j for some common weighted moving averages.*

case of (3.11) where the weights are all set to $1/k$. For the weighted moving average to work properly, it is important that the total of the weights is one and that they are symmetric, that is $a_j = a_{-j}$.

The advantage of weighted averages is that the resulting smoothed trend-cycle is much smoother! Instead of observations entering and leaving the average abruptly, they can be slowly downweighted. There are many schemes for selecting appropriate weights. Kendall, Stuart, and Ord (1983, chapter 46) give details.

Some sets of weights are widely used and have been named after their proposers. For example, Spencer (1904) proposed a $5 \times 4 \times 4$ MA followed by a weighted 5-term moving average with weights $a_0 = 1$, $a_1 = a_{-1} = 3/4$, and $a_2 = a_{-2} = -3/4$. These values are not chosen arbitrarily, but because the resulting combination of moving averages can be shown to work well. Using similar calculations to those above, it can be shown that Spencer's MA is equivalent to the 15-point weighted moving average whose weights are $-.009$, $-.019$, $-.016$, .009, .066, .144, .209, .231, .209, .144, .066, .009, $-.016$, $-.019$, and $-.009$. Another Spencer's MA that is commonly used is the 21-point weighted moving average.

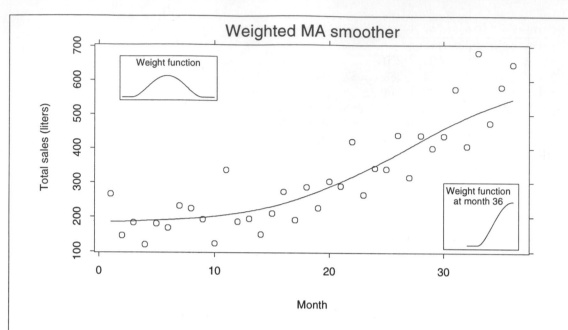

Figure 3-6: *A weighted 19-point MA applied to the shampoo data. The weights were calculated from the weight function shown at upper left. At the ends of the data a smaller number of observations were used in calculating the weighted average. For example, the weight function for calculating the smoothed trend-cycle at month 36 is shown at lower right.*

Henderson's weighted moving averages are also widely used. For example, Census Bureau methods (see Section 3/5) use Henderson's 5-, 7-, 9-, 13-, and 23-point weighted moving averages. The selection of a specific moving average is based upon the randomness present in the series—the greater the randomness, the larger the number of terms needed in the average.

weight function   The set of weights is known as the *weight function*. Table 3-4 shows some common weight functions. These are all symmetric, so $a_{-j} = a_j$.

Figure 3-6 shows a weighted 19-point moving average applied to the shampoo data, and the weight function used to compute the weights. The weights were calculated using the quartic function

$$Q(j, m) = \begin{cases} (1 - (j/m)^2)^2 & \text{for } -m < j < m; \\ 0 & \text{otherwise.} \end{cases} \qquad (3.12)$$

Then a_j is set to $Q(j,m)$ and scaled so the weights sum to one. Apart from the weights at the ends of the series, this means

$$a_j = \frac{Q(j,m)}{\displaystyle\sum_{i=-m}^{m} Q(i,m)}. \qquad (3.13)$$

For a 19-point moving average, $m = 9$. Using (3.12) and (3.13) we calculate the weights

$$a_j = (1 - j^2/81)^2/9.60 \qquad (3.14)$$

for $j = -9, -8, \ldots, 9$. At the ends of the data, a smaller number of observations are used in computing the fit. For example, at month 36 (the last in the series), only 10 observations are available (months 27, 28, ..., 36) and these are given the weights

$$a_j = (1 - j^2/81)^2/5.30$$

for $j = -9, -8, \ldots, 0$. A different divisor is used to ensure the weights sum to one. This weight function is shown at the lower right of the plot. So at month 36, the trend-cycle is estimated by a weighted average of only the last 10 observations. Because there is an increasing trend at this end of the data, the trend-cycle is underestimated by the weighted average. The estimated smooth trend-cycle curve "flattens" near the end, whereas the data suggest it should continue to climb. This bias is a feature of any moving average near the end of a data series which has trend, or where a data series has strong cyclic behavior. In the next section, we discuss a solution to this problem.

3/3 Local regression smoothing

We wish to extend the idea of moving averages to "moving lines." That is, instead of taking the average of the points, we may fit a straight line through these points and estimate the trend-cycle that way.

In Chapter 2, the least squares method of fitting a straight line was discussed. Recall that a straight trend line is represented by the equation $T_t = a + bt$. The two parameters, a and b, represent the intercept and slope respectively. The values of a and b can be found by minimizing the sum of squared errors where the errors are the differences between the data values of the time series and the corresponding trend line values. That is, a and b are the values that minimize the sum of squares

$$\sum_{t=1}^{n}(Y_t - a - bt)^2.$$

A straight-line trend is sometimes appropriate, but there are many time series where some curved trend is better. For example, the shampoo data plotted in Figure 3-3 do not follow a straight line.

local regression

Local regression is a way of fitting a much more flexible trend-cycle curve to the data. Instead of fitting a straight line to the entire data set, we fit a series of straight lines to sections of the data.

weighted sum of squares

The estimated trend-cycle at time t is $T_t = a + bt$ where a and b are chosen to minimize the weighted sum of squares

$$\sum_{j=-m}^{m} a_j(Y_{t+j} - a - b(t + j))^2. \tag{3.15}$$

Note that there is a different value of a and b for every value of t. In effect, a different straight line is fitted at each observation.

The calculation for trend-cycle at month 22 is shown in Figure 3-7. The steps involved are as follows.

Step 1 The number of points to be used in the weighted regression was chosen to be 19. The shaded area, centered on month 22, shows the 19 points to be used, nine on either side of month 22.

Step 2 The observations are assigned weights using the weight function shown in the upper right panel. This is exactly the same weight function as (3.14) which was used in Figure 3-6. The function has a maximum at month 22; the months closest to month 22 receive the largest weights and months further away receive smaller weights. The weights become zero at the boundaries of the shaded region. Months outside the shaded region receive zero weights, so they are excluded from the calculation.

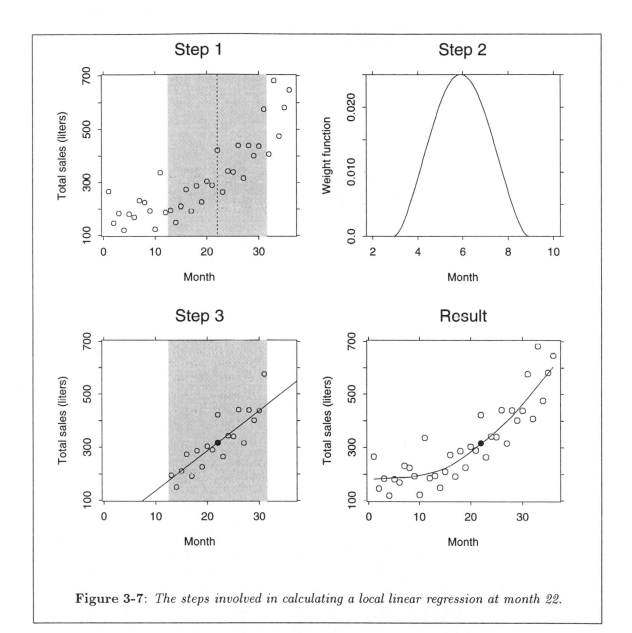

Figure 3-7: *The steps involved in calculating a local linear regression at month 22.*

Step 3 A line is fitted to the data using weighted least squares with the values of a and b chosen to minimize (3.15). The fit is shown in the lower left panel. The weights determine the influence each observation has on the fitting of the line. The estimate of trend-cycle for month 22 is shown by the filled circle.

The same calculations are carried out for each observation. The resulting trend-cycle estimates are joined together to form the line shown in the lower right panel. At the ends of the data, fewer observations are used in computing the fit.

Because a straight line is fitted to the data to estimate the trend-cycle, we do not have the same problem of bias at the end of the series which occurred with the moving average smoothers. This is the chief advantage of using local linear regression: it has smaller bias at the

bias reduction

ends and in areas where there is strong cyclic behavior.

smoothing
parameters

One parameter must be selected before fitting a local regression, the "smoothing parameter" k. The smoothing parameter is analogous to the order of a moving average—the larger the parameter, the smoother the resulting curve. This is illustrated in Figure 3-8 which shows three local regressions fitted to the shampoo sales data. In the top panel, k was set to 49 (or $m = 24$). Note that this is greater than the number of observations in the series. In this case, the calculation of weights is the same as for the ends of the series. The weights corresponding to available data are simply set to $Q(j, m)$ and scaled so the sum is one. The fitted trend-cycle is too straight because k is too large. The second panel shows the trend-cycle calculated with $k = 19$ as in Figure 3-7. In the bottom panel, k was set to 7 (or $m = 3$). Here the estimated trend-cycle is too rough; the local wiggles follow the randomness in the data rather than the underlying trend-cycle. The goal in choosing k is to produce a trend-cycle which is as smooth as possible without distorting the underlying pattern in the data. In this example, $k = 19$ is a good choice that follows the trend-cycle without undue wiggles.

3/3/1 Loess

"Loess" is an implementation of local linear smoothing, developed by Bill Cleveland and coworkers at AT&T Bell Laboratories. It is described in Cleveland and Devlin (1988) and Cleveland, Devlin, and

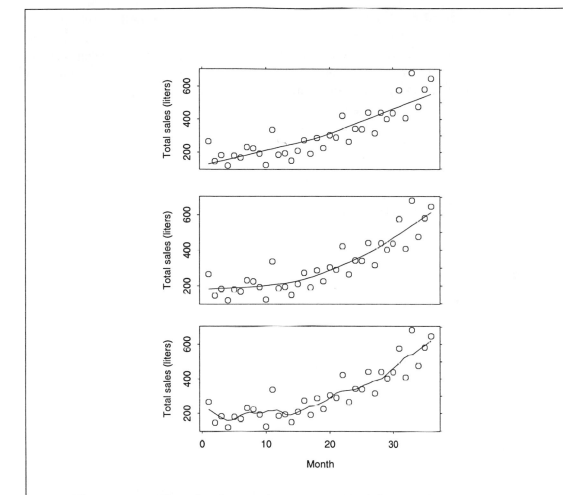

Figure 3-8: *Three local regression curves with different values of the smoothing parameter. From the top panel, the values of k are 49, 19, and 7.*

Cronoc (1988). It is widely used and is available in several software packages.

The heart of Loess is local linear smoothing but with some protection against extreme observations or outliers. An initial local regression is calculated as described in Figure 3-7. Then the irregular component is calculated using

$$\hat{E}_t = Y_t - \hat{T}_t.$$

These are simply the differences between each observation Y_t and the fitted curve $\hat{T}_t$. Then the local regression is calculated again, but this time the weights (a_j) are adjusted so that observations with large errors receive smaller weights than they did for the first estimate of the trend-cycle curve. A new irregular component is then found by subtracting the new estimate of T_t from the data. This procedure continues through further iterations, repeatedly smoothing the data, and at each iteration downweighting points where there is a large error value. The trend-cycle estimate $\hat{T}_t$ soon stabilizes, at which point there is no need for further iterations.

For many data sets, the resulting curve is almost identical to that obtained using the standard local linear regression. However, the two procedures may differ when there are one or more outliers. In this case, the Loess curve will be more robust to these unusual observations.

3/4 Classical decomposition

Decomposition methods can assume an additive or multiplicative model and can be of varying forms. For example, the decomposition method of simple averages assumes the additive model

$$Y_t = S_t + T_t + E_t \qquad (3.16)$$

whereas the ratio-to-trend method uses a multiplicative model

$$Y_t = S_t \times T_t \times E_t. \qquad (3.17)$$

The decomposition methods of simple averages and ratio-to-trend were used in the past mainly because of their computational simplicity. With the widespread introduction of computers, they have been improved and modified, but still form the building blocks of most decomposition algorithms.

classical
decomposition

Developed in the 1920s, the classical decomposition method was for many years the most commonly used decomposition procedure. This approach forms the basis for most of the modern decomposition methods which are examined later.

Section 3/4/1 describes the procedure for additive decomposition while Section 3/4/2 describes the procedure for multiplicative decomposition.

3/4/1 Additive decomposition

We will assume in this section that the time series is additive as described in equation (3.16), with seasonal period 12. The procedure for quarterly data is almost identical. Each step of the process is outlined below and applied to the new housing sales data described in Section 3/1.

A classical decomposition can be carried out using the following four steps.

Step 1 The trend-cycle is computed using a centered 12 MA. For the housing sales data, this is shown in the lower panel of Figure 3-5.

Step 2 The de-trended series is computed by subtracting the trend-cycle component from the data, leaving the seasonal and irregular terms. That is,

$$Y_t - T_t = S_t + E_t.$$

de-trended series

For the housing sales data, the de-trended series is plotted in the top panel of Figure 3-9.

Step 3 Once the trend-cycle component has been removed, the seasonal component is relatively easy to estimate. In classical decomposition, we assume the seasonal component is constant from year to year. So we only need to calculate one value for each month. The set of 12 values which are repeated to make up the seasonal component are known as the *seasonal indices*.

seasonal indices

We gather all the de-trended values for a given month and take the average. So the seasonal index for January is the average of all the de-trended values for January, and so on. The seasonal indices for the housing sales data are plotted in the lower panel of Figure 3-9. The seasonal component is constructed by stringing together the seasonal indices for each year of data.

Step 4 Finally, the irregular series E_t is computed by simply subtracting the estimated seasonality, trend, and cycle from the original data series.

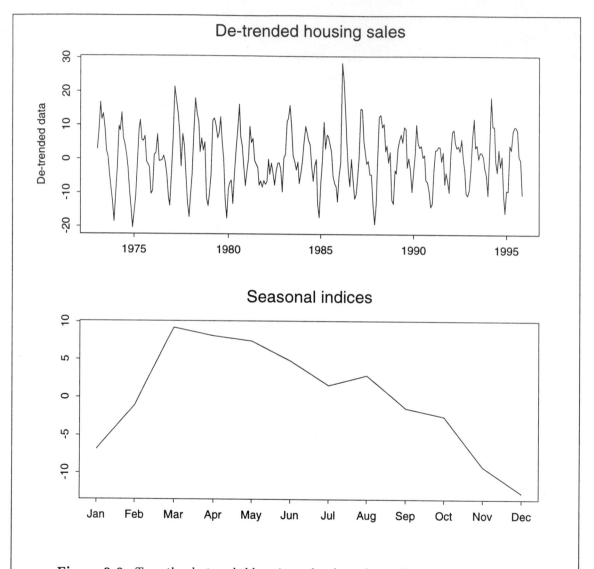

Figure 3-9: *Top: the de-trended housing sales data obtained by subtracting from the original data the trend-cycle component (2 × 12 MA) plotted in Figure 3-4. Bottom: the seasonal indices for the housing sales data.*

A time series decomposition is best visualized using a decomposition plot. The decomposition described above gives a very similar display to that in Figure 3-1, so we have omitted it.

3/4/2 Multiplicative decomposition

The multiplicative procedure is similar to the additive procedure except ratios are taken instead of differences. This method is often called the "ratio-to-moving averages" method.

ratio-to-moving averages

To illustrate the application of classical multiplicative decomposition, eight years of monthly data representing international airline passenger travel (in thousands) from 1949 through 1956 will be used. This is a classic data set in the time series literature, dating back to Brown (1963). The actual values for this data series are shown in Table 3-5 and plotted in Figure 3-10. Because the seasonal variation increases as the level of the series increases, we will decompose the series into its components using a multiplicative decomposition. (An additive decomposition of the logged data could also be used.)

Step 1 The trend-cycle T_t is computed using a centered 12 MA. The calculations necessary to obtain a 12-month centered MA are shown in columns 2 and 3 of Table 3-6. There are six values missing at the beginning and six values missing at the end because of the averaging procedure used.

Year	Jan	Feb	Mar	Apr	May	June	July	Aug	Sep	Oct	Nov	Dec
1949	112	118	132	129	121	135	148	148	136	119	104	118
1950	115	126	141	135	125	149	170	170	158	133	114	140
1951	145	150	178	163	172	178	199	199	184	162	146	166
1952	171	180	193	181	183	218	230	242	209	191	172	194
1953	196	196	236	235	229	243	264	272	237	211	180	201
1954	204	188	235	227	234	264	302	293	259	229	203	229
1955	242	233	267	269	270	315	364	347	312	274	237	278
1956	284	277	317	313	318	374	413	405	355	306	271	306

Table 3-5: *Actual data for international airline passenger travel. Total passengers (in thousands).*

		(1) Original data	(2) 12-month uncentered MA	(3) 12-month centered MA	(4) $100 \times (1)/(3)$ centered 12-month ratios
1949	Jan	112	—	—	—
	Feb	118	—	—	—
	Mar	132	—	—	—
	Apr	129	—	—	—
	May	121	—	—	—
	Jun	135	—	—	—
	Jul	148	126.667	126.792	116.727
	Aug	148	126.917	127.250	116.306
	Sep	136	127.583	127.958	106.285
	Oct	119	128.333	128.583	92.547
	Nov	104	128.833	129.000	80.620
	Dec	118	129.167	129.750	90.944
1950	Jan	115	130.333	131.250	87.619
	Feb	126	132.167	133.083	94.678
	Mar	141	134.000	134.917	104.509
	Apr	135	135.833	136.417	98.962
	May	125	137.000	137.417	90.964
	⋮	⋮	⋮	⋮	⋮

Centered 12-month seasonal ratios (original/moving average)

Year	Jan	Feb	Mar	Apr	May	Jun	Jul	Aug	Sep	Oct	Nov	Dec
1949	—	—	—	—	—	—	116.7	116.3	106.3	92.5	80.6	90.9
1950	87.6	94.7	104.5	99.0	91.0	107.4	120.6	118.7	108.4	89.6	75.2	90.5
1951	92.3	94.0	110.0	99.3	103.2	105.3	116.2	114.6	104.9	91.6	82.0	92.1
1952	93.4	96.7	102.1	94.6	94.5	111.3	116.1	121.2	103.4	92.6	81.7	90.9
1953	90.8	89.7	106.8	105.4	102.2	108.1	117.2	120.7	105.4	94.0	80.2	89.1
1954	89.5	81.6	101.2	97.0	99.3	111.0	125.6	120.1	104.8	91.5	80.1	89.1
1955	92.4	87.4	98.5	97.7	96.9	111.7	127.4	119.9	106.4	92.2	78.7	91.0
1956	91.6	88.1	99.5	97.3	98.0	114.3	—	—	—	—	—	—
Avg	91.1	90.3	103.2	98.6	97.9	109.9	120.0	118.8	105.6	92.0	79.8	90.5

Table 3-6: *Centered 12-month MA and ratios for the airline data.*

Figure 3-10: *Time plot of monthly international airline passenger traffic (in thousands) from 1949–1956.*

Step 2 The ratio of the data to these MA values are calculated as in column 4 of Table 3-6. Mathematically, these computations accomplish the following:

$$R_t = \frac{Y_t}{T_t} = \frac{S_t T_t E_t}{T_t} = S_t E_t. \qquad (3.18)$$

This is the ratio of actual-to-moving averages (thus the name of the method) and isolates the additional two components of the time series.

The de-trended values (R_t) are those shown in the lower part of Table 3-6. These are multiplied by 100 so they can be expressed as percentages.

Step 3 As with additive decomposition, the seasonal indices are estimated by taking averages of all the de-trended values for each month. These are given at the bottom of Table 3-6. The seasonal component S_t consists of eight copies of the seasonal

indices (one for each year) strung together. (That is, we assume
the seasonal component is constant from year to year.)

Step 4 The irregular series E_t is computed as the ratio of the data
to the trend and seasonal components:

$$E_t = \frac{Y_t}{S_t T_t}.$$

3/4/3 Variations on classical decomposition

The preceding procedures represent the simplest application of classical decomposition. In practice, there have been many variations to
these algorithms developed and used over the years. These are briefly
summarized here.

medial average

- In Step 3 (the calculation of seasonal indices), the simple averaging of values is often replaced by a *medial average*. This is
  the average calculated after the largest and smallest values have
  been excluded. Another alternative is to use a median. The
  advantage of medial averages or medians is that they protect
  against extreme months. They make the seasonal indices more
  robust.

- In many time series, the seasonal component is not stable
  but changes over time. A good example of this is electricity
  production data. Electricity demands have changed over time
  with such things as the spread of air-conditioning, the drop in
  oil-based heating, and the increase in high-powered electrical
  equipment in industry, contributing to the changing demand
  profile.   Therefore, it is inappropriate to estimate seasonal
  indices that are constant throughout the entire series. Instead,
  the seasonal component needs to adapt to the changes. This
  problem obviously becomes more important when decomposing
  long time series since there is greater scope for changes in the
  seasonal variation.

  Instead of taking a simple average (or medial average) of the de-
  trended values for each month, a moving average will allow such
  changes over time. That is, a moving average of the de-trended
  January values will give the January seasonal component, a

moving average of the de-trended February values will give the February seasonal component, and so on. Alternatively, the moving average can be replaced by a local linear regression computed for each of the 12 sets of de-trended monthly values.

3/5 Census Bureau methods

The Census II method has been developed by the U.S. Bureau of Census II
the Census. Julius Shiskin is considered the main contributor in the development of the early stages of the method. Census II has been used widely by the Bureau, other government agencies in the United States and elsewhere, and by an ever increasing number of businesses.

Census II has gone through several variations and refinements since 1955 when the first version was developed. The most widely used variants have been X-11 (Shiskin, Young, and Musgrave, 1967) and X-11
X-11-ARIMA developed by Statistics Canada (Dagum, 1988). The X-11-ARIMA
most recent variant is X-12-ARIMA (Findley et al., 1997) which is X-12-ARIMA
an extension of the X-11-ARIMA methodology. The underlying time series decomposition methodology has remained the same throughout this development, although the refinements allow a larger range of economic time series to be adequately seasonally adjusted. In this section, we describe the X-12-ARIMA variant of Census II.

Many of the steps in Census II decomposition involve the application of weighted moving averages to the data. Therefore, there is inevitable loss of data at the beginning and end of the series because of the averaging. Usually, the X-12-ARIMA method would use shorter weighted moving averages (called end-filters) to provide estimates for the observations at the beginning and end of the series. But X-12-ARIMA also provides the facility to extend the original series with forecasts to ensure that more of the observations are adjusted using the full weighted moving averages. (The initial values can also be forecast backward in time.) These forecasts are obtained using an ARIMA time series model (Section 7/8/4) or a regression model with ARIMA errors (Section 8/1).

Census II decomposition is usually multiplicative because most economic time series have seasonal variation which increases with the level of the series.

3/5/1 First iteration

As with all decomposition methods, Census II is aimed at making a separation of the seasonality from the trend-cycle and then isolating the randomness. The algorithm begins in a similar way to classical decomposition, and then proceeds through several iterations in which the estimated components are refined. The steps in each iteration are outlined below. We use the monthly airline passenger data of Table 3-5 to show the results of the first iteration.

Step 1 A 12-month centered moving average is applied to the original data giving a rough estimate of the trend-cycle. This is exactly the same as Step 1 of classical decomposition shown in Table 3-6. There are six values missing at the beginning because of the averaging procedure used. However, there are not six values missing at the end because the unobserved data for these months were forecast using an ARIMA model.

Step 2 The ratios of the original data to these MA values are calculated as in Step 2 of classical multiplicative decomposition.

Step 3 The ratios in the lower part of Table 3-6 include such random or unusual events as strikes and wars. The next task in Census II is to exclude such extreme values before finding estimates of the seasonal component.

extreme values

A separate 3×3 MA is applied to each month of the centered ratios of Table 3-6. The resulting values form a new series which is a rough estimate of the seasonal component. Now the centered ratios of Table 3-6 contain both the seasonal and irregular component. So dividing these by the estimated seasonal component, we obtain an estimate of the irregular component. Mathematically,

$$\frac{S_t E_t}{S_t} = E_t.$$

Large values of E_t indicate an extreme value in the original data. These extreme values are identified and the centered ratios of Table 3-6 are adjusted accordingly. This effectively eliminates any extreme values that do not fit the pattern of the rest of the data. The missing values at the beginning of the series are also replaced by estimates at this stage.

Step 4 The next step is to eliminate randomness by taking a 3×3 MA of each month of the year individually. This moving average is analogous to the one in Step 3 except that the modified data (with replaced extreme values and estimates for missing values) are used. Then the results are further adjusted to ensure they add up to approximately 1200 over any 12-month period. This calculation gives the values shown in Table 3-7.

Table 3-6 gives values equivalent to equation (3.18) and these include seasonality and randomness. Since randomness has been eliminated by replacing extreme values and smoothing through a 3×3 moving average, what remains in Table 3-7 is an estimate of the seasonal component.

Step 5 The original data are then divided by this preliminary seasonal component to obtain the preliminary seasonally adjusted series. These values contain only the trend-cycle and the irregular component. They can be written mathematically as:

$$\frac{Y_t}{S_t} = \frac{S_t T_t E_t}{S_t} = T_t E_t. \tag{3.19}$$

Step 6 The trend-cycle is then estimated by applying a weighted moving average to the preliminary seasonally adjusted values. In X-12-ARIMA, a Henderson's weighted average is used with the number of terms determined by the randomness in the series. (The greater the randomness, the longer the length of the moving average used.) For monthly series, either a 9-, 13-, or 23-term Henderson moving average is being selected depending upon the extent of the randomness in the series. For quarterly series, either a 5- or a 7-term Henderson moving average is being selected. (In this example, a 13-term Henderson moving average was selected.)

The rationale for applying this average is that the data given by equation (3.19) include trend-cycle and randomness. This moving average eliminates the randomness, providing a smooth

Year	Jan	Feb	Mar	Apr	May	Jun	Jul	Aug	Sep	Oct	Nov	Dec
1949	91.9	94.3	103.7	99.1	98.1	107.1	118.4	117.1	107.0	91.3	81.2	91.1
1950	92.0	94.0	103.5	99.0	98.1	107.4	118.1	117.5	106.6	91.4	81.5	91.2
1951	92.2	93.3	103.3	99.0	98.2	107.9	117.6	118.2	105.9	92.1	81.7	91.3
1952	92.1	92.1	102.7	98.5	98.4	109.0	118.2	119.6	105.3	92.6	81.6	90.9
1953	91.7	90.6	101.9	98.1	98.5	109.8	120.1	120.3	105.2	93.1	80.9	90.4
1954	91.3	89.3	100.8	97.6	98.4	111.0	123.1	120.7	105.5	92.5	80.2	90.0
1955	91.4	88.5	99.8	97.5	98.0	111.8	125.2	120.6	105.8	91.9	79.6	90.0
1956	91.5	88.1	99.2	97.3	97.8	112.7	126.1	120.7	105.9	91.4	79.4	90.0

Table 3-7: *Preliminary seasonal component.*

Year	Jan	Feb	Mar	Apr	May	Jun	Jul	Aug	Sep	Oct	Nov	Dec
1949	124.8	125.5	126.0	126.3	126.2	126.1	126.2	126.6	127.1	127.7	128.5	129.4
1950	130.3	131.3	132.4	134.0	136.2	138.6	140.9	142.9	144.5	146.2	148.4	151.9
1951	156.7	161.8	166.0	168.4	169.2	169.3	169.6	170.5	172.5	175.8	179.6	183.2
1952	185.7	187.3	188.4	189.6	191.0	193.1	196.1	199.5	202.8	205.4	208.4	212.6
1953	218.0	223.2	227.3	229.3	229.4	228.0	226.0	224.5	223.8	223.4	222.6	221.7
1954	221.7	223.4	226.8	231.3	235.8	239.5	242.2	244.1	246.3	249.1	252.5	256.5
1955	260.6	264.9	269.2	273.5	277.9	282.3	286.4	290.2	293.9	297.7	301.8	306.0
1956	310.5	314.8	318.8	322.5	325.8	328.6	331.1	333.3	335.2	337.0	339.0	341.2

Table 3-8: *Preliminary trend-cycle.*

Year	Jan	Feb	Mar	Apr	May	Jun	Jul	Aug	Sep	Oct	Nov	Dec
1949	90.4	93.7	105.5	99.5	96.8	106.7	118.1	118.0	106.9	92.2	81.2	91.3
1950	90.5	93.2	105.3	99.4	96.9	106.7	118.2	118.4	106.7	92.5	81.3	91.3
1951	90.7	92.3	104.9	99.0	97.3	107.0	118.8	119.0	106.3	92.6	81.4	91.1
1952	91.1	91.1	104.2	98.5	97.7	107.5	119.7	119.4	106.0	92.8	81.3	90.9
1953	91.5	89.9	103.2	98.1	97.9	108.6	120.8	120.1	105.7	92.7	81.2	90.7
1954	91.7	88.9	101.9	98.0	98.1	109.8	122.0	120.4	105.6	92.6	80.9	90.4
1955	91.7	88.4	100.9	97.9	98.1	111.1	123.1	120.5	105.6	92.1	80.6	90.1
1956	91.7	88.2	100.2	97.8	98.2	112.0	123.8	120.3	105.7	91.7	80.4	89.9

Table 3-9: *Seasonal component.*

curve that highlights the existence of a trend-cycle in the data. The resulting preliminary trend-cycle is given in Table 3-8.

Step 7 Now we have a new estimate of the trend-cycle, and we can repeat Step 2. New ratios are obtained by dividing the original data by the estimated trend-cycle leaving only the seasonal and irregular components remaining. These are called the final seasonal-irregular ratios and are given mathematically by

$$\frac{Y_t}{T_t} = \frac{T_t S_t E_t}{T_t} = S_t E_t \tag{3.20}$$

where T_t is the preliminary trend cycle estimated in Step 5. Applying a weighted moving average would normally cause the loss of several values at the beginning of the series and several at the end. To avoid this loss, each of the missing values is replaced by an estimated value.

Step 8 This is a repeat of Step 3 but using the new ratios computed in Step 7 and applying a 3×5 MA instead of a 3×3 MA.

Step 9 This is a repeat of Step 4 but using a 3×5 MA instead of a 3×3 MA. The resulting seasonal component is shown in Table 3-9.

Step 10 The same as Step 5 but using the seasonal component obtained in Step 9.

Step 11 The irregular component is obtained by dividing the seasonally adjusted data from Step 10 by the trend-cycle obtained in Step 6. Mathematically, the seasonally adjusted data are given by $T_t E_t$. So dividing by the trend-cycle T_t gives E_t, the irregular component.

Step 12 Extreme values of the irregular component are replaced as in Step 3. Then a series of modified data is obtained by multiplying the trend-cycle, seasonal component, and adjusted irregular component together. These modified data are exactly the same as the original data, but without the extreme values. For the airline data, 10 of the 96 values were adjusted.

Year	Jan	Feb	Mar	Apr	May	Jun	Jul	Aug	Sep	Oct	Nov	Dec
					Seasonal component							
1949	90.7	93.9	105.9	99.3	97.0	106.6	118.1	117.7	106.4	91.8	81.4	91.3
1950	90.8	93.4	105.8	99.1	97.2	106.7	118.1	118.2	106.2	92.0	81.4	91.3
1951	91.0	92.6	105.5	98.6	97.7	107.0	118.5	118.8	106.0	92.3	81.4	91.1
1952	91.3	91.3	104.8	98.2	98.2	107.7	119.2	119.4	105.8	92.5	81.3	90.8
1953	91.6	90.1	103.6	97.8	98.4	108.8	120.3	120.1	105.6	92.6	81.1	90.5
1954	91.7	89.1	102.3	97.7	98.5	110.0	121.4	120.4	105.6	92.6	80.9	90.3
1955	91.6	88.5	101.1	97.7	98.3	111.2	122.6	120.6	105.7	92.2	80.7	90.0
1956	91.6	88.2	100.2	97.7	98.2	112.0	123.4	120.5	105.9	91.9	80.5	89.9
					Trend component							
1949	124.9	125.4	125.8	126.1	126.2	126.2	126.4	126.7	127.1	127.6	128.3	129.1
1950	130.3	131.8	133.7	136.0	138.3	140.5	142.4	144.1	145.9	148.0	150.9	154.5
1951	158.4	162.2	164.9	166.4	167.0	167.4	168.2	169.9	172.6	176.0	179.3	182.0
1952	183.7	184.5	185.1	186.1	187.9	190.6	194.2	198.2	202.1	205.7	209.2	212.9
1953	217.0	221.0	224.3	226.3	227.2	227.1	226.3	225.3	224.4	223.8	223.4	223.4
1954	224.0	226.0	229.2	233.1	237.0	240.2	242.6	244.4	246.3	248.6	251.6	255.3
1955	259.5	263.9	268.2	272.5	276.8	281.1	285.3	289.5	293.6	297.9	302.2	306.1
1956	309.9	313.6	317.6	322.0	326.3	330.2	333.0	334.6	335.5	336.2	337.5	339.4
					Irregular component							
1949	98.9	100.2	99.1	103.1	98.9	100.3	99.2	99.2	100.5	101.6	99.6	100.1
1950	97.2	102.3	99.7	100.2	92.9	99.4	101.1	99.8	102.0	97.6	92.8	99.3
1951	100.6	99.9	102.4	99.3	105.4	99.3	99.8	98.6	100.6	99.7	100.0	100.2
1952	102.0	106.8	99.5	99.0	99.2	106.3	99.4	102.3	97.8	100.3	101.1	100.3
1953	98.6	98.4	101.5	106.1	102.4	98.4	97.0	100.6	100.0	101.8	99.3	99.4
1954	99.3	93.4	100.2	99.7	100.3	99.9	102.5	99.5	99.6	99.5	99.8	99.3
1955	101.8	99.8	98.5	101.1	99.2	100.8	104.1	99.4	100.5	99.7	97.2	100.8
1956	100.1	100.1	99.6	99.5	99.3	101.1	100.5	100.4	99.9	99.0	99.7	100.3

Table 3-10: *Final components for the airline series.*

3/5/2 Later iterations

These 12 steps are repeated two more times, but beginning with the modified data from Step 12 rather than the original data. On the final iteration, the 3×5 MA of Steps 8 and 9 is replaced by either a 3×3, 3×5, or 3×9 moving average, depending on the variability in the data. For the airline data, a 3×5 MA was chosen for the final iteration also.

The components obtained after the final iteration are given in Table 3-10. Note that the seasonal component and irregular component are usually given as percentages. Multiplying the three components together gives the original series. A decomposition plot showing each of these components is given in Figure 3-11 while Figure 3-12 shows the seasonal sub-series.

The final seasonally adjusted series is found by dividing the final seasonal component of Table 3-10 into the original data. This is equivalent to the product of the trend-cycle and irregular components.

After the basic components of the time series have been estimated, a series of diagnostic tests is used to determine whether or not the decomposition has been successful. These tests are not statistical in the rigorous mathematical sense, but are based on intuitive considerations. See Shiskin, Young, and Musgrave (1967), Lothian and Morry (1978), and Findley et al. (1990) for details.

diagnostic tests

An important characteristic of Census II is that the task of isolating randomness and seasonal factors is not done simultaneously as it is in most decomposition methods. The division of this task enlarges the computational requirements, but it also generally improves the accuracy.

It may well seem that the Census II method is very complicated because of the number of steps involved up to this point. However, the basic idea is really quite straightforward—to isolate the seasonal, trend-cycle, and irregular components one by one. The various steps and iterations are designed to refine and improve the estimate of each component.

3/5/3 Extensions to X-12-ARIMA

The X-12-ARIMA method has many additional features that are not described above. Two important additional features of X-12-ARIMA are (i) the ability to remove the effect of explanatory variables prior to decomposition and (ii) the large range of diagnostic tests available after decomposition.

Explanatory variables are particularly important since many sources of variation in the series can be removed in this manner. Some examples are listed below.

- Trading day adjustments can be made where there is a different

trading day adjustments

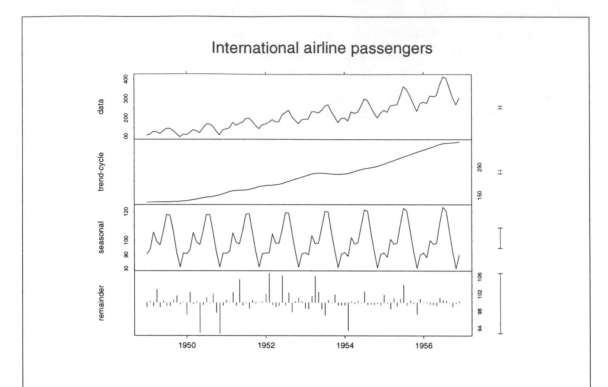

Figure 3-11: *The X-12-ARIMA multiplicative decomposition of the airline passenger data.*

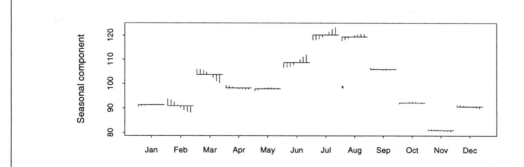

Figure 3-12: *A seasonal sub-series plot for the decomposition shown in Figure 3-11. The seasonal component for June, July, and August became larger over the period of the data, with corresponding falls in February and March.*

effect for each day of the week. In the airline data, trading days are not an important factor because their effects on airline schedules are largely random, owing to the fact that holidays vary from country to country.

- Outliers arise because of unusual circumstances such as major strikes. These effects can also be removed prior to decomposition.

- Other changes in the level of the series such as level shifts and temporary ramp effects can also be modeled.

Some examples of how these explanatory variables can be included in the decomposition are given in Findley and Monsell (1989).

Some other additional features are:

- missing values in the series can be estimated and replaced;   missing values

- the seasonal component can be forced to be constant over time (i.e., the same seasonal component for each year);

- holiday factors (such as Easter, Labor Day, and Thanksgiving)   holiday effects
can be estimated.

- automatic ARIMA model selection is available.

A more extensive discussion of X-12-ARIMA can be found in Findley et al. (1997).

3/6 STL decomposition

The STL decomposition method was proposed by Cleveland et al. in   STL decomposition
1990 as an alternative to Census II. The name "STL" is an acronym for "A Seasonal-Trend decomposition procedure based on Loess."

STL consists of a sequence of applications of the Loess smoother (Section 3/3/1) to give a decomposition that is highly resistant to extreme observations. One advantage of STL over other seasonal decomposition methods is that it is capable of handling seasonal time series where the length of seasonality is other than quarterly or monthly. In fact, any seasonal period greater than one is allowable.

Also, STL can be applied when the time series contains missing values, something other decomposition methods cannot handle easily.

Currently, only an additive version of the STL procedure is available. Multiplicative decomposition can be carried out by first transforming the data using logarithms.

Like Census II, STL is an iterative algorithm in which the estimates of the trend-cycle and seasonal components are progressively refined and improved. STL consists of two recursive procedures, one nested within the other. In each iteration of the inner loop, the seasonal and trend-cycle components are updated once. An iteration of the outer loop consists of one or two iterations of the inner loop followed by an identification of extreme values. Future iterations of the inner loop downweight the extreme values that were identified in the previous iteration of the outer loop. About 10 or 20 iterations of the outer loop are carried out in total.

3/6/1 Inner loop

We now describe the steps involved in a single iteration of the inner loop. Each iteration consists of a seasonal smoothing that updates the seasonal component followed by a trend-cycle smoothing which updates the trend-cycle component. The whole procedure must start with some initial estimate of the trend-cycle. This is set to be zero. That is, the procedure begins by assuming no trend at all. This poor estimate is quickly updated to something more reasonable after one iteration. As with the other decomposition methods, we will describe the procedure assuming we have monthly data.

Step 1 A de-trended series is computed by subtracting the trend estimate from the original data. That is,

$$Y_t - T_t = S_t + E_t.$$

Step 2 The de-trended values for each month are collected to form monthly sub-series. These twelve separate sub-series are each smoothed by a Loess smoother. The smoothed sub-series are glued back together to form a preliminary seasonal component. The Loess smoothers are extrapolated to estimate the seasonal component for a few months before and after the observed data.

Step 3 A $3 \times 12 \times 12$ moving average is applied to the preliminary seasonal component estimated in Step 2. The result is in turn smoothed by a Loess smoother of length 13 (one more than the seasonal period). The loss of values at the beginning and end of the series due to the weighted moving average was anticipated and overcome by the extrapolation of the seasonal component in Step 2. The purpose of this step is to identify any trend-cycle that may have contaminated the preliminary seasonal component in Step 2. If there is little trend-cycle in the preliminary seasonal component, the result of this smoothing will be a series with all values close to zero.

Step 4 The seasonal component is estimated as the difference between the preliminary seasonal component of Step 2 and the smoothed seasonal component of Step 3.

Step 5 A seasonally adjusted series is computed by subtracting the result of Step 4 from the original data. That is, $Y_t - S_t = T_t + E_t$.

Step 6 The seasonally adjusted series is smoothed by Loess to give the trend component, T_t.

3/6/2 Outer loop

The outer loop begins with one or two iterations of the inner loop. The resulting estimates of trend-cycle and seasonal components are then used to calculate the irregular component:

$$E_t = Y_t - T_t - S_t.$$

Large values of E_t indicate an extreme observation. These are identified and a weight calculated. That concludes the outer loop.

Future iterations of the inner loop use the weights in Steps 2 and 6 to downweight the effect of extreme values. Also, future iterations of the inner loop begin with the trend component from the previous iteration rather than starting with zero as in the very first iteration of the inner loop.

3/6/3 Choosing the STL parameters

Figure 3-1 shows the results of an STL decomposition applied to the housing data.

There are two smoothing parameters to select when using STL: the parameters for the Loess smoothers in Steps 2 and 6. The first is the seasonal smoothing parameter which determines how much change there will be in the seasonal indices from year to year. A small seasonal smoothing parameter will allow the seasonal component to change substantially from year to year, while a large seasonal smoothing parameter forces the seasonal component to change slowly from year to year. It is also possible to force the seasonal component to be identical across years.

The second smoothing parameter affects the smoothness of the trend calculated in Step 6. Again, a small parameter allows the trend to react to the variation in the data more than a large parameter will. It is important not to make the trend smoothing parameter too small or the seasonal variation might contaminate the trend component.

It is possible to have two or more trend-cycle components in an STL decomposition. This is useful when the user wishes to separate the trend-cycle into the long-term trend and a shorter-term cyclical component. There are also various other refinements in the computation of an STL decomposition which are discussed in Cleveland et al. (1990).

3/6/4 Comparing STL with X-12-ARIMA

X-12-ARIMA and STL are the two most sophisticated decomposition methods currently available. Their strengths and weaknesses and listed below.

- STL is less developed than X-12-ARIMA. For example, there are no publicly available versions of STL which handle trading day variation or calendar variation and there is no multiplicative option for STL.

- There are no seasonal adjustment diagnostics available with STL whereas there is a very large suite of well-developed diagnostics with X-12-ARIMA.

- STL is much more flexible than X-12-ARIMA in being able to handle trends of varying smoothness, missing values, and seasonality of period other than 4 or 12. But this flexibility also means the user has more decisions to make in specifying the two smoothing parameters.

- The calculations involved in STL are simpler than those for X-12-ARIMA, making it easier to extend the method to new situations.

- The estimate of trend for STL is unstable near the ends of the series (see the comments by Gray and Thomson in the discussion of Cleveland et al., 1990).

The computer source code for both X-12-ARIMA and STL is publicly available for other researchers to use and adapt.[1] Executable versions of X-12-ARIMA are available from the same Internet site. STL is also available as an option in the package S-plus.

3/7 Forecasting and decomposition

There have been many attempts to develop forecasts based directly on a decomposition. The individual components are projected into the future and recombined to form a forecast of the underlying series. Although this may appear a reasonable approach, in practice it rarely works well. The chief difficulty is in obtaining adequate forecasts of the components.

The trend-cycle is the most difficult component to forecast. It is sometimes proposed that it be modeled by a simple function such as a straight line or some other parametric trend model. But such models are rarely adequate. In the airline passenger example plotted in Figure 3-11, the trend-cycle does not follow any parametric trend model. But it does help identify "flat spots" and other features in the data which are not apparent from the time plot.

The other components are somewhat easier to forecast. The seasonal component for future years can be based on the seasonal

---

[1]STL code can be obtained from http://netlib.bell-labs.com/netlib/a/. X-12-ARIMA code can be obtained from ftp://ftp.census.gov/pub/ts/x12a/.

component from the last full period of data. But if the seasonal pattern is changing over time, this will be unlikely to be entirely adequate.

The irregular component may be forecast as zero (for additive decomposition) or one (for multiplicative decomposition). But this assumes that the irregular component is serially uncorrelated, which is often not the case. The decomposition of new one-family house sales (Figure 3-1) shows the irregular component with runs of positive or negative values. Clearly, if the irregular component at the end of the series is negative, it is more likely to be negative than zero for the first few forecasts, and so the forecasts will be too high.

One approach that has been found to work reasonably well is to forecast the seasonally adjusted data using Holt's method (Chapter 4), then adjust the forecasts using the seasonal component from the end of the data. Makridakis et al. (1982) found that forecasts obtained in this manner performed quite well compared with several other methods.

However, we prefer to use decomposition as a tool for understanding a time series rather than as a forecasting method in its own right. Time series decomposition provides graphical insight into the behavior of a time series. This can suggest possible causes of variation and help in identifying the structure of a series, thus leading to improved understanding of the problem and facilitating improved forecast accuracy. Decomposition is a useful tool in the forecaster's toolbox, to be applied as a preliminary step before selecting and applying a forecasting method.

References and selected bibliography

ANDERSON, O. and U. NOCHMALS (1914) The elimination of spurious correlation due to position in time or space, *Biometrika*, **10**, 269–276.

BAXTER, M.A. (1994) "A guide to seasonal adjustment of monthly data with X-11," 3rd ed., Central Statistical Office, United Kingdom.

BELL, W.R. and S.C. HILLMER (1984) Issues involved with the seasonal adjustment of economic time series, *Journal of Business and Economic Statistics*, **2**, 291–320.

BROWN, R.G. (1963) *Smoothing, forecasting and prediction of discrete time series*, Englewood Cliffs, N.J.: Prentice Hall.

BURMAN, J.P. (1979) Seasonal adjustment: A survey, *TIMS Studies in Management Sciences*, **12**, 45–57.

CLEVELAND, R.B., W.S. CLEVELAND, J.E. McRAE, and I. TERPENNING (1990) STL: A seasonal-trend decomposition procedure based on Loess (with discussion), *J. Official Statistics*, **6**, 3–73.

CLEVELAND, W.S. (1983) Seasonal and calendar adjustment, in *Handbook of statistics*, vol. 3., 39–72, ed. D.R. Brillinger and P.R. Krishnaiah. Elsevier Science Publishers B.V..

CLEVELAND, W.S. and S. DEVLIN (1988) Locally weighted regression: an approach to regression analysis by local fitting, *Journal of the American Statististical Association*, **74**, 596–610.

CLEVELAND, W.S., S. DEVLIN, and E. GROSSE (1988) Regression by local fitting: methods, properties and computational algorithms, *Journal of Econometrics*, **37**, 87–114.

CLEVELAND, W.S and I.J. TERPENNING (1992) Graphical methods for seasonal adjustment, *Journal of the American Statistical Association*, **77**, 52–62.

COPELAND, M.T. (1915) Statistical indices of business conditions, *Quarterly Journal of Economics*, **29**, 522–562.

DAGUM, E.B. (1982) Revisions of time varying seasonal filters, *Journal of Forecasting*, **1**, 20–28.

DAGUM, E.B. (1988) X-11-ARIMA/88 seasonal adjustment method: foundations and users manual, Statistics Canada.

DEN BUTTER, F.A.G. and M.M.G. FASE (1991) *Seasonal adjustment as a practical problem*, Amsterdam: North-Holland.

FINDLEY, D.F. and B.C. MONSELL (1989) Reg-ARIMA based pre-processing for seasonal adjustment, In *Analysis of data in time*, ed. A.C. Singe and P Whitridge, 117–123, Ottawa, Canada.

FINDLEY, D.F., B.C. MONSELL, H.B. SHULMAN, and M.G. PUGH (1990) Sliding spans diagnostics for seasonal and related adjustments, *Journal of the American Statistical Association*, **85**, 345–355.

FINDLEY, D.F, B.C. MONSELL, W.R. BELL, M.C. OTTO, and B.-C. CHEN (1997) New capabilities and methods of the X-12-ARIMA seasonal adjustment program, *Journal of Business and Economic Statistics*, to appear.

HOOKER, R.H. (1901) The suspension of the Berlin produce exchange and its effect upon corn prices, *Journal of the Royal Statistical Society*, **64**, 574–603.

KENDALL, M.G., A. STUART, and K. ORD (1983) *The advanced theory of statistics*, Vol 3. London: Charles Griffin.

LOTHIAN, J. and M. MORRY (1978) A test of quality control statistics for the X-11-ARIMA seasonal adjustment program, Research paper, Seasonal adjustment and time series staff, Statistics Canada.

MACAULEY, F.R. (1930) *The smoothing of time series*, National Bureau of Economic Research.

MAKRIDAKIS, S., A. ANDERSEN, R. CARBONE, R. FILDES, M. HIBON, R. LEWANDOWSKI, J. NEWTON, E. PARZEN, and R. WINKLER (1982) The accuracy of extrapolation (time series) methods: results of a forecasting competition, *Journal of Forecasting*, **1**, 111–153.

NEWBOLD, P. and T. BOS (1994) *Introductory business and economic forecasting*, 2nd ed., Cincinnati, Ohio: South-Western Publishing Co..

POYNTING, J.H. (1884) A comparison of the fluctuations in the price of wheat and in the cotton and silk imports into Great Britain, *Journal of the Royal Statistical Society*, **47**, 345–64.

"Rapport sur les indices des crises economiques et sur les mesures résultant de ces crises." (1911). Government report, Ministry of Planning, Paris, France.

SHISKIN, J. (1957) Electronic computers and business indicators, *National Bureau of Economic Research*, Occasional Paper 57.

——————— (1961) Tests and revisions of bureau of the census methods of seasonal adjustments, Bureau of the Census, Technical Paper No. 5.

SHISKIN, J., A.H. YOUNG, and J.C. MUSGRAVE (1967) The X-11 variant of the Census II method seasonal adjustment program, Bureau of the Census, Technical Paper No. 15.

SPENCER, J. (1904) On the graduation of the rates of sickness and mortality, *Journal of the Institute of Actuaries*, **38**, 334.

Exercises

3.1 The following values represent a cubic trend pattern mixed with some randomness. Apply a single 3-period moving average, a single 5-period moving average, a single 7-period moving average, a double 3×3 moving average, and a double 5×5 moving average. Which type of moving average seems most appropriate to you in identifying the cubic pattern of the data?

Period	Shipments	Period	Shipments
1	42	9	180
2	69	10	204
3	100	11	228
4	115	12	247
5	132	13	291
6	141	14	337
7	154	15	391
8	171		

3.2 Show that a 3×5 MA is equivalent to a 7-term weighted moving average with weights of 0.067, 0.133, 0.200, 0.200, 0.200, 0.133, and 0.067.

3.3 For quarterly data, an early step in seasonal adjustment often involves applying a moving average smoother of length 4 followed by a moving average of length 2.

   (a) Explain the choice of the smoother lengths in about two sentences.

   (b) Write the whole smoothing operation as a single weighted moving average by finding the appropriate weights.

3.4 Consider the quarterly electricity production for years 1–4:

Year	1	2	3	4
Q_1	99	120	139	160
Q_2	88	108	127	148
Q_3	93	111	131	150
Q_4	111	130	152	170

   (a) Estimate the trend using a centered moving average.

(b) Using an classical additive decomposition, calculate the seasonal component.

(c) Explain how you handled the end points.

3.5 The data in Table 3-11 represent the monthly sales of product A for a plastics manufacturer for years 1 through 5.

	1	2	3	4	5
Jan	742	741	896	951	1030
Feb	697	700	793	861	1032
Mar	776	774	885	938	1126
Apr	898	932	1055	1109	1285
May	1030	1099	1204	1274	1468
Jun	1107	1223	1326	1422	1637
Jul	1165	1290	1303	1486	1611
Aug	1216	1349	1436	1555	1608
Sep	1208	1341	1473	1604	1528
Oct	1131	1296	1453	1600	1420
Nov	971	1066	1170	1403	1119
Dec	783	901	1023	1209	1013

Table 3-11: *Monthly sales of product A for a plastics manufacturer (in 1,000s).*

(a) Plot the time series of sales of product A. Can you identify seasonal fluctuations and/or a trend?

(b) Use a classical multiplicative decomposition to calculate the trend-cycle and monthly seasonal indices.

(c) Do the results support the graphical interpretation from part (a)?

3.6 The following are the seasonal indices for Exercise **3.5** calculated by the classical multiplicative decomposition method.

	Seasonal Indices		Seasonal Indices
Jan	76.96	Jul	116.76
Feb	71.27	Aug	122.94
Mar	77.91	Sep	123.55
Apr	91.34	Oct	119.28
May	104.83	Nov	99.53
Jun	116.09	Dec	83.59

Assuming the trend in the data is $T_t = 894.11 + 8.85t$, where $t = 1$ is January of year 1 and $t = 60$ is December of year 5, prepare forecasts for the 12 months of year 6.

3.7 The sales data in Table 3-12 are for quarterly exports of a French company.

Year	Quarter	Period	Sales (thousands of francs)	Year	Quarter	Period	Sales (thousands of francs)
1	1	1	362	4	1	13	544
	2	2	385		2	14	582
	3	3	432		3	15	681
	4	4	341		4	16	557
2	1	5	382	5	1	17	628
	2	6	409		2	18	707
	3	7	498		3	19	773
	4	8	387		4	20	592
3	1	9	473	6	1	21	627
	2	10	513		2	22	725
	3	11	582		3	23	854
	4	12	474		4	24	661

Table 3-12: *Quarterly exports of a French company.*

(a) Make a time plot of the data. Note the pronounced seasonality.

(b) Use a classical multiplicative decomposition to estimate the seasonal indices and the trend.

(c) Comment on these results and their implications for forecasting.

3.8 Figure 3-13 shows the result of applying STL to the number of persons in the civilian labor force in Australia each month from February 1978 to August 1995.

(a) Say which quantities are plotted in each graph.

(b) Write about 3–5 sentences describing the results of the seasonal adjustment. Pay particular attention to the scales of the graphs in making your interpretation.

(c) Is the recession of 1991/1992 visible in the estimated components?

3.9 A company's six-monthly sales figures for a five-year period are given below (in millions of dollars).

	1992	1993	1994	1995	1996
Jan–June	1.09	1.10	1.08	1.04	1.03
July–Dec	1.07	1.06	1.03	1.01	0.96

(a) Obtain a trend estimate using a centered 2 MA smoother and compute the de-trended figures assuming an additive decomposition.

(b) Assuming the seasonality is not changing over time, calculate seasonally adjusted figures for 1996.

(c) Suppose several more years of data were available. Explain in about two sentences how the classical decomposition method could be modified to allow for seasonal effects changing over time.

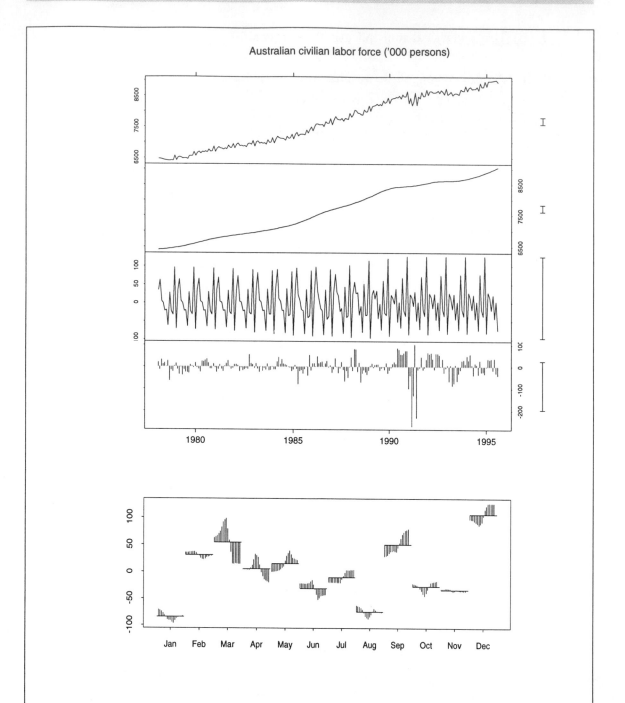

Figure 3-13: *STL decomposition of the number of persons in the civilian labor force in Australia each month from February 1978 to August 1995.*

4

EXPONENTIAL SMOOTHING METHODS

In Chapter 2 the mean was discussed as an estimator that minimizes the mean squared error (MSE). If the mean is used as a forecasting tool, then, as with all forecasting methods, optimal use requires a knowledge of the conditions that determine its appropriateness.

stationary
For the mean, the condition is that the data must be *stationary*, meaning that the process generating the data is in equilibrium around a constant value (the underlying mean) and that the variance around the mean remains constant over time.

Thus, if a time series is generated by a constant process subject to random error (or noise), then the mean is a useful statistic and can be used as a forecast for the next period(s). However, if the time series involves a trend (in an upward or downward direction), or a seasonal effect (strong sales of heating oil in winter months, for example), or both a trend and a seasonal effect, then the simple average is no longer able to capture the data pattern. In this chapter we consider a variety of smoothing methods that seek to improve upon the mean as the forecast for the next period(s).

Before discussing any particular methods, we introduce in Section 4/1 a general forecasting scenario and strategy for evaluating forecasting methods. This is used throughout the chapter when appraising and comparing methods.

averaging methods
The classification of the forecasting methods discussed in this chapter is done in Table 4-1 where two distinct groupings are evident. The group called "averaging methods" conform to the conventional understanding of what an average is—namely, equally weighted observations. Two examples from this class of methods are examined in Section 4/2.

exponential smoothing methods
The second group of methods applies an unequal set of weights to past data, and because the weights typically decay in an exponential manner from the most recent to the most distant data point, the methods are known as exponential smoothing methods. This is something of a misnomer since the methods are not smoothing the data in the sense of estimating a trend-cycle; they are taking a weighted average of past observations using weights that decay smoothly.

All methods in this second group require that certain parameters be defined, and these parameter values lie between 0 and 1. (These parameters will determine the unequal weights to be applied to past data.) The simplest exponential smoothing method is the single

Averaging methods

Simple average (4/2/1)

Moving averages (4/2/2)

Exponential smoothing methods

Single exponential smoothing
    one parameter (4/3/1)
    adaptive parameter (4/3/2)

Holt's linear method (4/3/3)
    (suitable for trends)

Holt-Winters' method (4/3/4)
    (suitable for trends and seasonality)

Pegels' classification (4/3/5)

Table 4-1: *A classification of smoothing methods.*

exponential smoothing (SES) method, for which just one parameter needs to be estimated. Another possibility is to allow the value of the parameter in SES to change over time in response to changes in the data pattern. This is known as adaptive SES and one variety to be discussed is known as Adaptive Response Rate Single Exponential Smoothing (ARRSES). Holt's method makes use of two different parameters and allows forecasting for series with trend. Holt-Winters' method involves three smoothing parameters to smooth the data, the trend, and the seasonal index. The exponential smoothing methods are discussed in Section 4/3.

Other exponential smoothing methods are possible and are discussed in Section 4/3/5. These methods are based on Pegels' (1969) classification of trend and seasonality patterns depending on whether they are additive or multiplicative. Patterns based on this classification are shown in Figure 4-1. For the practitioner of forecasting, the usage of an appropriate model is of vital importance. Clearly, an inappropriate forecasting model, even when optimized, will be inferior to a more appropriate model.

Pegels' classification

In Section 4/4 we apply all of the methods discussed in this chapter to a data set with both trend and seasonality, and compare the results. Finally, in Section 4/5 we look at some general issues in the practical implementation and use of exponential smoothing methods.

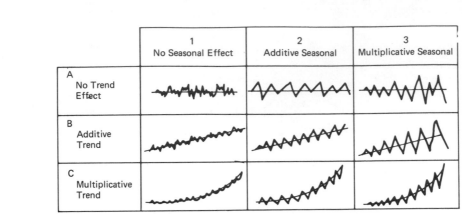

	1 No Seasonal Effect	2 Additive Seasonal	3 Multiplicative Seasonal
A No Trend Effect			
B Additive Trend			
C Multiplicative Trend			

(b) Patterns Based on Pegels' (1969) Classification

Figure 4-1: *Patterns based on Pegels' (1969) classification.*

4/1 The forecasting scenario

To set the stage, consider Figure 4-2, which presents the forecasting scenario. On the time scale we are standing at a certain point—called the point of reference—and we look backward over past observations and forward into the future. Once a forecasting model has been selected, we fit the model to the known data (by judicious choice of parameters and initializing procedures) and obtain the *fitted values*. For the known observations this allows calculation of *fitted errors*—a measure of goodness-of-fit of the model—and as new observations become available we can examine *forecasting errors*. The smoothing methods to be discussed in this chapter are mostly *recursive* in nature—moving through the known data period by period, as opposed to using all the past data in one "fitting" exercise.

Figure 4-3 describes a strategy for evaluating any forecasting methodology.

Stage 1 The time series of interest is divided into two parts (an "initialization set" and a "test set") so that an evaluation of a forecasting method can be conducted.

Stage 2 A forecasting method is chosen from a list of possible methods.

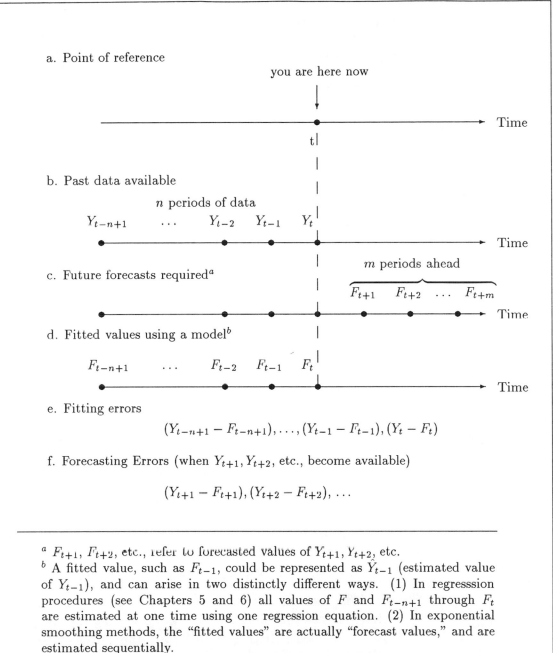

a. Point of reference

you are here now

Time

t|

b. Past data available

n periods of data

Y_{t-n+1} $\cdots$ Y_{t-2} Y_{t-1} Y_t

Time

c. Future forecasts required[a]

m periods ahead

F_{t+1} F_{t+2} $\cdots$ F_{t+m}

Time

d. Fitted values using a model[b]

F_{t-n+1} $\cdots$ F_{t-2} F_{t-1} F_t

Time

e. Fitting errors

$$(Y_{t-n+1} - F_{t-n+1}), \ldots, (Y_{t-1} - F_{t-1}), (Y_t - F_t)$$

f. Forecasting Errors (when Y_{t+1}, Y_{t+2}, etc., become available)

$$(Y_{t+1} - F_{t+1}), (Y_{t+2} - F_{t+2}), \ldots$$

---

[a] F_{t+1}, F_{t+2}, etc., refer to forecasted values of Y_{t+1}, Y_{t+2}, etc.
[b] A fitted value, such as F_{t-1}, could be represented as $\hat{Y}_{t-1}$ (estimated value of Y_{t-1}), and can arise in two distinctly different ways. (1) In regresssion procedures (see Chapters 5 and 6) all values of F and F_{t-n+1} through F_t are estimated at one time using one regression equation. (2) In exponential smoothing methods, the "fitted values" are actually "forecast values," and are estimated sequentially.

Figure 4-2: *The forecasting scenario.*

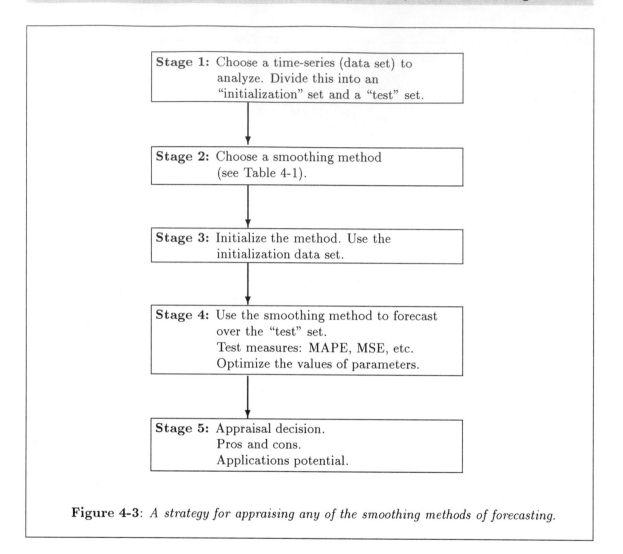

Figure 4-3: *A strategy for appraising any of the smoothing methods of forecasting.*

Stage 3 The initialization data set is used to get the forecasting
method started. Estimates of any trend components, seasonal
components, and parameter values are made at this stage.

Stage 4 The method is applied to the test set to see how well it
does on data that were not used in estimating the components
of the model. After each forecast, the forecasting error is
determined, and over the complete test set certain accuracy
measures are determined, as described in Chapter 2. This is
really an iterative phase. Since there is no guarantee that
the initial parameter values are optimal, this stage requires

modification of the initialization process and/or searching for the optimum values of parameters in the model.

Stage 5 Finally, the forecasting method is appraised as to its suitability for various kinds of data patterns (e.g., those shown in Figure 4-1) and the application potential is thereby made clearer.

4/2 Averaging methods

The "past history" data can be smoothed in many ways. In this section we consider two straightforward averaging methods, namely the mean (4/2/1) and simple moving averages (4/2/2). In both cases the objective is to make use of past data to develop a forecasting system for future periods.

4/2/1 The mean

The method of simple averages is simply to take the average of all observed data as the forecast. So

$$F_{t+1} = \frac{1}{t} \sum_{i=1}^{t} Y_i. \tag{4.1}$$

mean forecast

When a new observation, Y_{t+1}, becomes available, the forecast for time $t + 2$ is the new mean including the previously observed data plus this new observation:

$$F_{t+2} = \frac{1}{t+1} \sum_{i=1}^{t+1} Y_i. \tag{4.2}$$

When is this very simple method appropriate? Referring to the nine cells in Pegels' classification (Figure 4-1b), it is clear that only if the process underlying the observed Y values (i) has no noticeable trend, and (ii) has no noticeable seasonality will this simple averaging process produce good results. As the calculation of the mean is based on a larger and larger past history data set, it becomes more stable (from elementary statistical theory), assuming the underlying process is stationary.

What about data storage? It might seem that all the past data need to be stored for this procedure; but, in fact, only two items need be stored as time moves on. We can rewrite (4.2) in a recursive form:

recursive calculation

$$F_{t+2} = \frac{tF_{t+1} + Y_{t+1}}{t+1}.$$

So in carrying out the computations, only the most recent forecast and the most recent observations need to be stored. When forecasting a large number of series simultaneously (e.g., in inventory management), this saving becomes important.

The major impediment in using this simple method is the unlikely assumption that business time series are really based on an underlying "constant" process (cell A-1 in Pegels' table).

4/2/2 Moving averages

One way to modify the influence of past data on the mean-as-a-forecast is to specify at the outset just how many past observations will be included in a mean. The term "moving average" is used to describe this procedure because as each new observation becomes available, a new average can be computed by dropping the oldest observation and including the newest one. This moving average will then be the forecast for the next period. Note that the number of data points in each average remains constant and includes the most recent observations.

A moving average forecast of order k, or MA(k), is given by

moving average
forecast

$$F_{t+1} = \frac{1}{k} \sum_{i=t-k+1}^{t} Y_i.$$

This use of moving averages is slightly different from the use of moving averages in smoothing as described in the previous chapter. There we estimated the trend-cycle in a data series by taking an average of nearby points. Here we are forecasting the next observation by taking an average of the most recent observations. To avoid confusion, we use MA(k) to denote a moving average *forecast* of order k and k MA to denote a moving average *smoother* of order k.

Compared with the simple mean (of all past data) the moving average of order k has the following characteristics:

- it deals only with the latest k periods of known data,
- the number of data points in each average does not change as time goes on.

But it also has the following disadvantages:

- it requires more storage because all of the k latest observations must be stored, not just the average,
- it cannot handle trend or seasonality very well, although it can do better than the total mean.

Table 4-2 and Figure 4-4 illustrate the application of the technique of moving averages to the series of values for electric can opener shipments using both a three- and five-month moving average.

In Table 4-2 the MA(3) values in column 4 are based on the values for the previous three months. For example, the forecast for April (the fourth month) is taken to be the average of January, February, and March shipments.

$$\text{April's forecast} = (200 + 135 + 195)/3 = 176.7.$$

The last figure in column 4 is December's MA(3) forecast of 244.2 and is the average for September, October, and November.

Similarly, in column 5, the MA(5) averages are shown as forecasts for the next month ahead. The June forecast of 207.5 is the average of shipments made from January through May, and the December forecast of 203.5 is the average of months 7, 8, 9, 10, and 11. Clearly, as new values for shipments become known, the moving average can be easily recomputed.

From Figure 4-4 it can be seen that the more observations included in the moving average, the greater the smoothing effect. A forecaster must choose the number of periods (k) in a moving average. The two extreme cases are $k = 1$ and $k = n$.

MA(1) That is, a moving average of order 1—the last known data point (Y_t) is taken as the forecast for the next period $(F_{t+1} = Y_t)$. An example of this is "the forecast of tomorrow's closing price of IBM stock is today's closing price." This was called the naïve forecast (NF1) in Chapter 2.

(1) Month	(2) Time period	(3) Observed values (shipments)	(4) Three-month moving average	(5) Five-month moving average
Jan	1	200.0	—	—
Feb	2	135.0	—	—
Mar	3	195.0	—	—
Apr	4	197.5	176.7	—
May	5	310.0	175.8	—
Jun	6	175.0	234.2	207.5
Jul	7	155.0	227.5	202.5
Aug	8	130.0	213.3	206.5
Sep	9	220.0	153.3	193.5
Oct	10	277.5	168.3	198.0
Nov	11	235.0	209.2	191.4
Dec	12	—	244.2	203.5

Analysis of errors

Test periods:			4–11	6–11
Mean Error (ME)			17.71	−1.17
Mean Absolute Error (MAE)			71.46	51.00
Mean Absolute Percentage Error (MAPE)			34.89	27.88
Mean Square Error (MSE)			6395.66	3013.25
Theil's U-statistic			1.15	0.81

Table 4-2: *Forecasting electric can opener shipments using moving averages.*

MA(n) In this case, the mean of all observations is used as a forecast. So this is equivalent to the mean forecast method.

Note that use of a small value for k will allow the moving average to follow the pattern, but these MA forecasts will nevertheless trail the pattern, lagging behind by one or more periods. In general, the larger the order of the moving average—that is, the number of data points used for each average, the greater the smoothing effect.

Algebraically, the moving average can be written as follows:

$$F_{t+1} = \frac{Y_t + Y_{t-1} + \cdots + Y_{t-k+1}}{k}$$

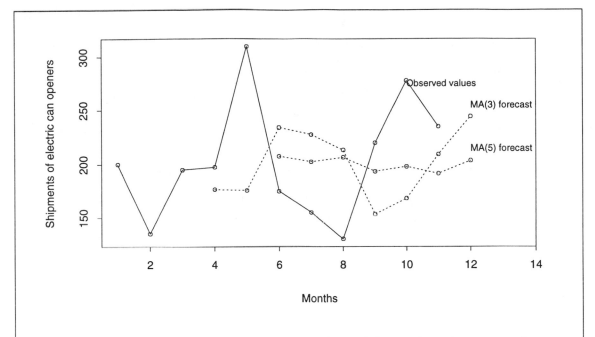

Figure 4-4: *Shipments of electric can openers: observed data and moving average forecasts.*

$$F_{t+2} = \frac{Y_{t+1} + Y_t + \cdots + Y_{t-k+2}}{k}.$$

Comparing F_{t+1} and F_{t+2}, it can be seen that F_{t+2} requires dropping the value Y_{t-k+1} and adding the value Y_{t+1} as it becomes available, so that another way to write F_{t+2} is

$$F_{t+2} = F_{t+1} + \frac{1}{k}(Y_{t+1} - Y_{t-k+1}) \qquad (4.3)$$

It can be seen from (4.3) that each new forecast (F_{t+2}) is simply an adjustment of the immediately preceding forecast (F_{t+1}). This adjustment is $(1/k)$th of the difference between Y_{t+1} and Y_{t-k+1}. Clearly if k is a big number, this adjustment is small, so that moving averages of high order provide forecasts that do not change very much.

In summary, an $MA(k)$ forecasting system will require k data points to be stored at any one time. If k is small (say 4), then the storage requirements are not severe although for many thousands of time series (say for inventories involving thousands of stockkeeping units) this can be a problem. In practice, however, the technique of moving averages as a forecasting procedure is not used often because

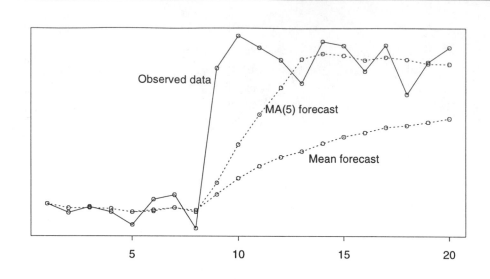

Figure 4-5: *Forecasts of data containing a level shift. Note that the mean of all past data does not catch up with the level shift, whereas the MA(5) forecast does correct for the shift after a few time periods.*

the methods of exponential smoothing (examined in Section 4/3) are generally superior.

breakdown of
assumptions

It is useful to consider how the forecasting method breaks down when the assumption of an underlying constant process is not met. As Figure 4-5 shows, when the underlying process is a step function (which is another way of saying the data undergo a sudden change at some point), then the mean used as a forecast for the next period is unable to catch up. However, the MA(5) method corrects its forecasts for the level shift after five periods. Similar tests of the behavior of the forecasts when the assumptions are not met can be carried out. As will be shown in Section 4/4, when the data series exhibits trend and seasonality, neither the mean as a forecast nor an MA forecast is appropriate.

4/3 Exponential smoothing methods

An obvious extension to the moving average method is forecasting by *weighted moving average*. With simple moving average forecasts, the mean of the past k observations was used as a forecast. This implies equal weights (equal to $1/k$) for all k data points. However, with forecasting, the most recent observations will usually provide the best guide as to the future, so we want a weighting scheme that has decreasing weights as the observations get older.

weighted MA

In this section we describe a class of methods that imply *exponentially decreasing* weights as the observations get older. Thus they are called *exponential smoothing* procedures. There is a variety of exponential smoothing methods. They all have in common the property that recent values are given relatively more weight in forecasting than the older observations.

exponentially decreasing weights

In the case of moving averages, the weights assigned to observations are a by-product of the particular MA system adopted. In exponential smoothing, however, there are one or more smoothing parameters to be determined explicitly, and these choices determine the weights assigned to observations, as will be indicated below.

4/3/1 Single exponential smoothing

Suppose we wish to forecast the next value of our time series Y_t which is yet to be observed. Our forecast is denoted by F_t. When the observation Y_t becomes available, the forecast error is found to be $Y_t - F_t$. The method of single exponential forecasting takes the forecast for the previous period and adjusts it using the forecast error. That is, the forecast for the next period is

$$F_{t+1} = F_t + \alpha(Y_t - F_t) \qquad (4.4)$$

single exponential forecast

where α is a constant between 0 and 1.

It can be seen that the new forecast is simply the old forecast plus an adjustment for the error that occurred in the last forecast. When α has a value close to 1, the new forecast will include a substantial adjustment for the error in the previous forecast. Conversely, when α is close to 0, the new forecast will include very little adjustment.

Thus, the effect of a large or small α is completely analogous (in an opposite direction) to the effect of including a small or a large number of observations when computing a moving average.

It should also be observed that these forecasts will always trail any trend in the actual data, since the most the method can do is adjust the next forecast for some percentage of the most recent error.

Equation (4.4) involves a basic principle of negative feedback, since it works much like the control process employed by automatic devices such as thermostats, automatic pilots, and so on. The past forecast error is used to correct the next forecast in a direction opposite to that of the error. There will be an adjustment until the error is corrected. It is the same principle that directs an automatic pilot device to an equilibrium course once a deviation (error) has taken place. This principle, simple as it may appear, plays an extremely important role in forecasting. If properly applied, it can be used to develop a self-adjusting process that corrects for forecasting error automatically.

Another way of writing (4.4) is

$$F_{t+1} = \alpha Y_t + (1 - \alpha)F_t. \qquad (4.5)$$

The forecast (F_{t+1}) is based on weighting the most recent observation (Y_t) with a weight value (α) and weighting the most recent forecast (F_t) with a weight of $1 - \alpha$.

Equation (4.5) is the general form used in exponential smoothing methods. It substantially reduces any storage problem, because it is no longer necessary to store all of the historical data or a subset of them (as in the case of the moving average). Rather, only the most recent observation, the most recent forecast, and a value for α must be stored.

The implications of exponential smoothing can be better seen if equation (4.5) is expanded by replacing F_t with its components as follows:

$$\begin{aligned} F_{t+1} &= \alpha Y_t + (1 - \alpha)[\alpha Y_{t-1} + (1 - \alpha)F_{t-1}] \\ &= \alpha Y_t + \alpha(1 - \alpha)Y_{t-1} + (1 - \alpha)^2 F_{t-1}. \end{aligned}$$

If this substitution process is repeated by replacing F_{t-1} by its components, F_{t-2} by its components, and so on, the result is

$$
\begin{aligned}
F_{t+1} = {} & \alpha Y_t + \alpha(1-\alpha)Y_{t-1} + \alpha(1-\alpha)^2 Y_{t-2} + \alpha(1-\alpha)^3 Y_{t-3} \\
& + \alpha(1-\alpha)^4 Y_{t-4} + \alpha(1-\alpha)^5 Y_{t-5} + \cdots + \alpha(1-\alpha)^{t-1} Y_1 \\
& + (1-\alpha)^t F_1.
\end{aligned} \tag{4.6}
$$

So F_{t+1} represents a weighted moving average of all past observations. Suppose $\alpha = 0.2$, 0.4, 0.6, or 0.8. Then the weights assigned to past observations would be as follows:

Weight assigned to:	$\alpha = 0.2$	$\alpha = 0.4$	$\alpha = 0.6$	$\alpha = 0.8$
Y_t	0.2	0.4	0.6	0.8
Y_{t-1}	0.16	0.24	0.24	0.16
Y_{t-2}	0.128	0.144	0.096	0.032
Y_{t-3}	0.1024	0.0864	0.0384	0.0064
Y_{t-4}	$(0.2)(0.8)^4$	$(0.4)(0.6)^4$	$(0.6)(0.4)^4$	$(0.8)(0.2)^4$

Notice that in each case, the weights for all past data sum approximately to one. If these weights are plotted as in Figure 4-6 it can be seen that they decrease exponentially, hence the name exponential smoothing.

The application of single exponential smoothing can be illustrated by using the electric can opener example given in Section 4/2/2. Table 4-3 and Figure 4-7 show the exponential smoothing results from electric can opener shipments using α values of 0.1, 0.5, and 0.9.

One can forecast with single exponential smoothing by using either equation (4.4) or (4.5). For example, in Table 4-3 the forecast for period 12 (December) when $\alpha = 0.1$ is computed as follows:

$$
F_{12} = \alpha Y_{11} + (1-\alpha)F_{11} = (0.1)(235.0) + (0.9)(202.3) = 205.6.
$$

Similarly, when $\alpha = 0.9$,

$$
F_{12} = (0.9)(235.0) + (0.1)(270.9) = 238.6.
$$

Note that the choice of α has considerable impact on the December forecast and the MAPE values for periods 2 through 11 range from 24.6% (for $\alpha = 0.1$) to 30.8% (for $\alpha = 0.9$). Single exponential smoothing requires little storage and few computations. It is therefore attractive when a large number of items require forecasting.

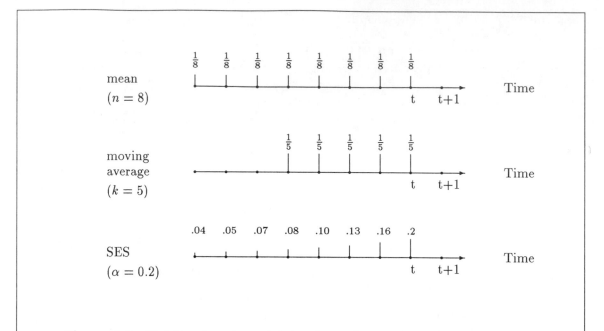

Figure 4-6: *Weights given to past data when a forecast is made at time t for the next period, using various forecasting procedures.*

initialization   One point of concern relates to the initializing phase of SES. For example, to get the SES forecasting system started we need F_1 because

$$F_2 = \alpha Y_1 + (1 - \alpha)F_1.$$

Since the value for F_1 is not known, we can use the first observed value (Y_1) as the first forecast $(F_1 = Y_1)$ and then proceed using equation (4.5). This is one method of initialization and is used in Table 4-3. Another possibility would be to average the first four or five values in the data set and use this as the initial forecast.

Note from equation (4.6) that the the last term is $(1 - \alpha)^t F_1$. So the *initial* forecast F_1 plays a role in *all* subsequent forecasts. But the weight attached to F_1 is $(1-\alpha)^t$ which is usually small. For example, if $t = 12$, then to four decimal places the weight is equal to

$$
\begin{aligned}
0.2824 & \quad \text{if } \alpha = .1 \\
0.0002 & \quad \text{if } \alpha = .5 \\
0.0000 & \quad \text{if } \alpha = .9
\end{aligned}
$$

Month	Time Period	Observed Values (shipments)	Exponentially Smoothed Values		
			$\alpha = 0.1$	$\alpha = 0.5$	$\alpha = 0.9$
Jan	1	200.0	—	—	—
Feb	2	135.0	200.0	200.0	200.0
Mar	3	195.0	193.5	167.5	141.5
Apr	4	197.5	193.7	181.3	189.7
May	5	310.0	194.0	189.4	196.7
Jun	6	175.0	205.6	249.7	298.7
Jul	7	155.0	202.6	212.3	187.4
Aug	8	130.0	197.8	183.7	158.2
Sep	9	220.0	191.0	156.8	132.8
Oct	10	277.5	193.9	188.4	211.3
Nov	11	235.0	202.3	233.0	270.9
Dec	12	—	205.6	234.0	238.6

Analysis of Errors
Test period: 2–11

Mean Error			5.56	6.80	4.29
Mean Absolute Error			47.76	56.94	61.32
Mean Absolute Percentage Error (MAPE)			24.58	29.20	30.81
Mean Square Error (MSE)			3438.33	4347.24	5039.37
Theil's U-statistic			0.81	0.92	0.98

Table 4-3: *Forecasting electric can opener shipments using exponential smoothing.*

Clearly, when a small value of α is chosen, the initial forecast plays a more prominent role than when a larger α is used. Also, when more data are available t is larger and so the weight attached to F_t is smaller. This type of initialization problem exists in all exponential smoothing methods. If the smoothing parameter α is not close to zero, the influence of the initialization process rapidly becomes of less significance as time goes by. However, if α is close to zero, the initialization process can play a significant role for many time periods ahead.

The smoothing effect of α can be seen in Figure 4-7. A large value of α (0.9) gives very little smoothing in the forecast, whereas

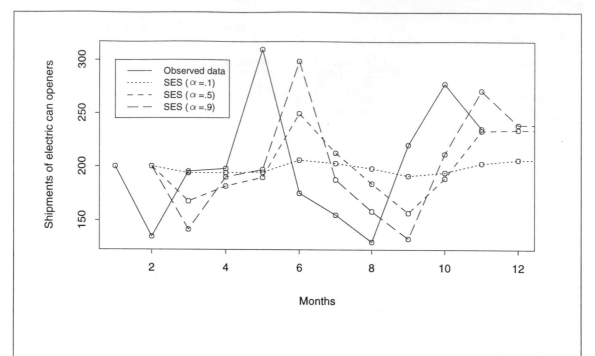

Figure 4-7: *Shipments of electric can openers: Actual and exponential smoothing forecasts.*

a small value of α (0.1) gives considerable smoothing. When $\alpha = 1$, (4.4) shows that exponential smoothing is equivalent to using the last observation as a forecast. That is, it is the same as NF1, the naïve forecast method 1.

optimization   Simple as exponential smoothing is, it does have its problems. One of these arises in trying to find an optimal value for α. Should we optimize to minimize MSE, MAPE, or some other measure? Suppose we try to minimize MSE. Unlike the mean, where this minimization occurs any time the average of a set of numbers is calculated, for exponential smoothing the minimum MSE must be determined through trial and error. A value for α is chosen, the MSE is computed over a test set, and then another α value is tried. The MSEs are then compared to find the α value that gives the minimum MSE. In the example of Table 4-3, using periods 2 through 11 as the test set,

$$MSE = 3438 \quad \text{when } \alpha = 0.1$$
$$MSE = 4347 \quad \text{when } \alpha = 0.5$$
$$MSE = 5039 \quad \text{when } \alpha = 0.9.$$

This wide range of MSE values indicates the important role of α in determining the resulting errors. Finding an α value that is close to the best possible generally requires only a few trials, since its value can be approximated by simply comparing a few MSE and α values. For the series in Table 4-3 it can be seen that the MSE decreases as α approaches 0. In fact,

$$\alpha = 0.05 \qquad \text{gives MSE} = 3301 \text{ and}$$
$$\alpha = 0.01 \qquad \text{gives MSE} = 3184.$$

The reason for this is that the data are almost random, so the smaller the value of α, the smaller the MSE.

One way to choose α is to calculate the MSE for a grid of values (e.g., $\alpha = 0.1, 0.2, \ldots, 0.9$), and choose the value that yields the smallest MSE value. Alternatively, this search for the optimal α can be carried out using a non-linear optimization algorithm.

It is customary to optimize the MSE because it is a smooth function of α and it is relatively easy to find the value of α which minimizes MSE. However, it is possible to optimize other measures of forecast error. For example, the optimum α could be different if the objective had been to minimize the MAPE.

It was also assumed that the forecast horizon was just one period ahead. For longer range forecasts, it is assumed that the forecast function is "flat." That is,   flat forecast function

$$F_{t+h} = F_{t+1}, \qquad h = 2, 3, \ldots .$$

A flat forecast function is used because single exponential smoothing works best for data which have no trend, no seasonality, or other underlying pattern. Interested readers should check Dalrymple and King (1981) for more on the issues relating to forecast horizon.

If there is a trend in the series, the forecasts lag behind the trend, farther behind for smaller α. Table 4-4 shows exponential smoothing forecasts (with α chosen to minimize MSE) applied to a series of inventory demand which has an increasing trend. Figure 4-8 shows the data with the forecasts. Notice that the forecasts tend to underestimate the data values. This is reflected in the large positive mean error of 10.24. Holt's smoothing (see Section 4/3/3 for a description) involves smaller errors and a correct extrapolation of the trend in the data.

	Period t	Observed data Y_t	SES forecasts F_t
	1	143	143.00
	2	152	143.00
	3	161	148.89
	4	139	156.81
	5	137	145.16
	6	174	139.82
	7	142	162.18
	8	141	148.98
	9	162	143.76
	10	180	155.69
	11	164	171.59
	12	171	166.63
Test	13	206	169.49
	14	193	193.37
	15	207	193.13
Set	16	218	202.20
	17	229	212.54
	18	225	223.31
	19	204	224.41
	20	227	211.06
	21	223	221.49
	22	242	222.48
	23	239	235.25
	24	266	237.70
	25		256.22
	26		256.22
	27		256.22
	28		256.22
	29		256.22
	30		256.22

Analysis of errors from period 10 to period 24

10.24	= Mean Error	6.57	= Mean Absolute Percentage Error
14.03	= Mean Absolute Error	1.01	= Theil's U-statistic
305.72	= Mean Square Error		

Table 4-4: *Application of exponential smoothing to inventory demand for product E15 with $\alpha = 0.654$ chosen by minimizing the MSE.*

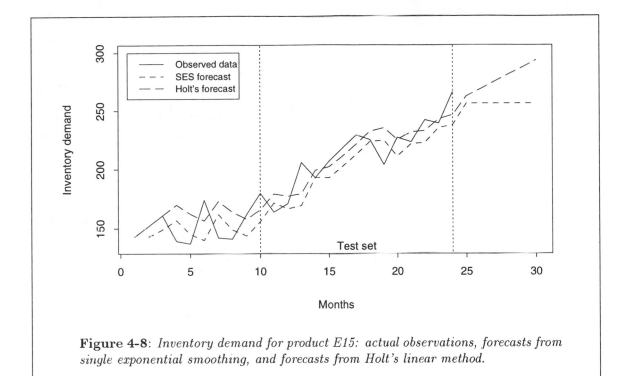

Figure 4-8: *Inventory demand for product E15: actual observations, forecasts from single exponential smoothing, and forecasts from Holt's linear method.*

In this example, we have used the first nine observations as the initialization set. Then period 10 to period 24 serve as the test set. The error measures are calculated on these periods. In Section 4/3/3 we will apply Holt's method which is more suitable for data with trend and compare the results over the same test period.

4/3/2 Single exponential smoothing: an adaptive approach

The SES forecasting method requires the specification of an α value and it has been shown that the MAPE and MSE measures depend on this choice. Adaptive-response-rate single exponential smoothing (ARRSES) may have an advantage over SES in that it allows the value of α to be modified, in a controlled manner, as changes in the pattern of data occur. This characteristic seems attractive when hundreds or even thousands of items require forecasting.

adaptive smoothing

The basic equation for forecasting with the method of ARRSES is similar to equation (4.5) except that α is replaced by α_t:

$$F_{t+1} = \alpha_t Y_t + (1 - \alpha_t) F_t \qquad (4.7)$$

$$\text{where} \quad \alpha_{t+1} = \left| \frac{A_t}{M_t} \right| \qquad (4.8)$$

$$A_t = \beta E_t + (1 - \beta) A_{t-1} \qquad (4.9)$$

$$M_t = \beta |E_t| + (1 - \beta) M_{t-1} \qquad (4.10)$$

$$E_t = Y_t - F_t \qquad (4.11)$$

β is a parameter between 0 and 1 and $|\ |$ denotes absolute values.

In equation (4.9) A_t denotes a smoothed estimate of forecast error, and is calculated as a weighted average of A_{t-1} and the last forecasting error E_t. Similarly, M_t denotes a smoothed estimate of the absolute forecast error, being calculated as a weighted average of M_{t-1} and the last absolute forecasting error $|E_t|$. Note that equations (4.9) and (4.10) both give SES estimates themselves. Equation (4.8) indicates that the value of α_t to be used for forecasting period $(t+2)$ is defined as an absolute value of the ratio of A_t and M_t. Instead of α_{t+1} we could have used α_t in equation (4.8). We prefer α_{t+1} because ARRSES is often too responsive to changes, thus using α_{t+1} we introduce a small lag of one period, which allows the system to "settle" a little and forecast in a more conservative manner.

initialization   Initialization of an ARRSES process is a little more complicated than for SES. For example, for the electric can opener shipments, we can initialize as follows:

$$F_2 = Y_1,$$
$$\alpha_2 = \alpha_3 = \alpha_4 = \beta = 0.2,$$
$$A_1 = M_1 = 0.$$

Then forecasts using the ARRSES method are as shown in Table 4-5.

The forecast for period 11, for example, is

$$
\begin{aligned}
F_{11} &= \alpha_{10} Y_{10} + (1 - \alpha_{10}) F_{10} \\
&= 0.228(277.5) + 0.772(201.6) = 218.9.
\end{aligned}
$$

Once the actual value for period 11 becomes known, α_t can be updated and used for the next period's calculations. This entails computing E_{11}, A_{11}, and M_{11} as follows:

Period	Observed value (shipments) Y_t	Forecast F_t	Error E_t	Smoothed error A_t	Absolute smoothed error M_t	α_t
1	200.0					
2	135.0	200.0	−65.0	−13.0	13.0	0.200
3	195.0	187.0	8.0	−8.8	12.0	0.200
4	197.5	188.6	8.9	−5.3	11.4	0.200
5	310.0	190.4	119.6	19.7	33.0	0.462
6	175.0	245.7	−70.7	1.6	40.6	0.597
7	155.0	203.5	−48.5	−8.4	42.1	0.040
8	130.0	201.5	−71.5	−21.0	48.0	0.199
9	220.0	187.3	32.7	−10.3	45.0	0.438
10	277.5	201.6	75.9	7.0	51.1	0.228
11	235.0	218.9	16.1	8.8	44.1	0.136
12	—	221.1	—	—	—	0.199

Table 4-5: *Forecasting electric can opener shipments using adaptive-response-rate single exponential smoothing.*

$$E_{11} = 235.0 - 218.9 = 16.1, \qquad \text{[using (4.11)]}$$
$$A_{11} = 0.2(16.1) + 0.8(7.0) = 8.8, \qquad \text{[using (4.9)]}$$
$$M_{11} = 0.2|16.1| + 0.8(51.1) = 44.1, \qquad \text{[using (4.10)]}$$
$$\text{and} \qquad \alpha_{12} = \left|\frac{8.8}{44.1}\right| = 0.199. \qquad \text{[using (4.8)]}$$

The forecast for period 12 can be computed using equation (4.7):

$$F_{12} = 0.136(235) + 0.864(218.9) = 221.1.$$

Note that the α_t values fluctuate quite significantly and, if a different initializing procedure had been adopted, a different series of α_t values would have been generated. Care should be taken in evaluating the fluctuations in α_t—and maybe curbing the extent of these changes. One way to control the changes in α_t is by controlling the value of β (the smaller the value of β the less will be the changes in α_t). Another way to do this is to put an upper bound on how much α_t is allowed to change from one period to the next.

Summing up, the ARRSES method is an SES method where the α value is systematically, and automatically, changed from period to

period to allow for changes in the pattern of the data. Although it may take one or two periods for α_t to catch up with changes in the data pattern, it will eventually do so. Thus, even if the forecasts from this method are somewhat inferior to those of single exponential smoothing with an optimal α, it may be preferable because it reduces the risk of serious errors and provides a system with minimal administrative worries. The fact that ARRSES is
automatic forecasting   completely automatic, in addition to having the other advantages of single exponential smoothing, makes it a useful method in practice when a large number of items are involved, and when the data are non-seasonal and show no trend. (Consult Gardner and Dannenbring (1980) for less favorable results using ARRSES.)

4/3/3   Holt's linear method

Holt (1957) extended single exponential smoothing to linear exponential smoothing to allow forecasting of data with trends. The forecast for Holt's linear exponential smoothing is found using two smoothing constants, α and β (with values between 0 and 1), and three equations:

Holt's linear forecasts

$$
\begin{align}
L_t &= \alpha Y_t + (1 - \alpha)(L_{t-1} + b_{t-1}), & (4.12)\\
b_t &= \beta(L_t - L_{t-1}) + (1 - \beta)b_{t-1}, & (4.13)\\
F_{t+m} &= L_t + b_t m. & (4.14)
\end{align}
$$

Here L_t denotes an estimate of the level of the series at time t and b_t denotes an estimate of the slope of the series at time t. Equation (4.12) adjusts L_t directly for the trend of the previous period, b_{t-1}, by adding it to the last smoothed value, L_{t-1}. This helps to eliminate the lag and brings L_t to the approximate level of the current data value. Equation (4.13) then updates the trend, which is expressed as the difference between the last two smoothed values. This is appropriate because if there is a trend in the data, new values should be higher or lower than the previous ones. Since there may be some randomness remaining, the trend is modified by smoothing with β the trend in the last period $(L_t - L_{t-1})$, and adding that to the previous estimate of the trend multiplied by $(1 - \beta)$. Thus, (4.13) is similar to the basic form of single smoothing given by equation (4.5) but applies to the updating of the trend. Finally, equation (4.14) is used to forecast ahead. The trend, b_t, is multiplied by the number of periods ahead to be forecast, m, and added to the base value, L_t.

Using the inventory demand data from Table 4-4, Table 4-6 shows the application of Holt's linear smoothing to a series with trend. The smoothing parameters α and β were chosen by minimizing the MSE over observations 1–24. The resulting forecasts are given in Figure 4-8.

The calculations involved can be illustrated by looking at the forecast for period 23, using $\alpha = 0.501$ and $\beta = 0.072$:

$$
\begin{aligned}
F_{23} &= L_{22} + b_{22}(1), && \text{[using (4.14)]} \\
\text{where} \quad L_{22} &= 0.501 Y_{22} + .499(L_{21} + b_{21}) && \text{[using (4.12)]} \\
&= 0.501(242) + .499(227.33 + 5.31) \\
&= 237.33, \\
b_{22} &= 0.072(L_{22} - L_{21}) + .928 b_{21} && \text{[using (4.13)]} \\
&= 0.072(237.33 - 227.33) + .928(5.31) \\
&= 5.64.
\end{aligned}
$$

Thus, $\quad F_{23} = 237.33 + 5.64(1) = 242.97.$

Similarly the forecast for period 24 is

$$
\begin{aligned}
F_{24} &= 240.98 + 5.50(1) = 246.48, \\
\text{since} \quad L_{23} &= 0.501(239) + 0.499(237.33 + 5.64) = 240.98 \\
\text{and} \quad b_{23} &= 0.072(240.98 - 237.33) + 0.928(5.64) = 5.50.
\end{aligned}
$$

Finally, the forecasts for periods 25 through 30 can be computed as

$$
\begin{aligned}
F_{25} &= 256.26 + 6.21(1) = 262.47, \\
F_{26} &= 256.26 + 6.210(2) = 268.68, \\
&\quad \cdots \\
F_{30} &= 256.26 + 6.21(6) = 293.51.
\end{aligned}
$$

The initialization process for Holt's linear exponential smoothing requires two estimates—one to get the first smoothed value for L_1 and the other to get the trend b_1. One alternative is to set $L_1 = Y_1$ and

$$ b_1 = Y_2 - Y_1 $$
$$ \text{or} \quad b_1 = (Y_4 - Y_1)/3. $$

	Period (t)	Observed data (Y_t)	Smoothing of data (L_t)	Smoothing of trend (b_t)	Forecast when m = 1 (F_t)	
	1	143	143.00	9.00	—	
	2	152	152.00	9.00	152.00	
	3	161	161.00	9.00	161.00	
	4	139	154.47	7.88	170.00	
	5	137	149.64	6.96	162.34	
	6	174	165.32	7.59	156.60	
	7	142	157.42	6.47	172.91	
	8	141	152.42	5.64	163.89	
	9	162	160.03	5.78	158.06	
	10	180	172.92	6.30	165.82	
	11	164	171.59	5.75	179.22	
	12	171	174.16	5.52	177.34	
Test	13	206	192.87	6.47	179.68	
	14	193	196.16	6.24	199.34	
	15	207	204.71	6.41	202.40	
Set	16	218	214.56	6.66	211.11	
	17	229	225.12	6.94	221.22	
	18	225	228.52	6.68	232.06	
	19	204	219.57	5.55	235.20	
	20	227	226.06	5.62	225.12	
	21	223	227.33	5.31	231.68	
	22	242	237.33	5.64	232.64	
	23	239	240.98	5.50	242.97	
	24	266	256.26	6.21	246.48	
	25				262.47	$(m = 1)$
	26				268.68	$(m = 2)$
	27				274.89	$(m = 3)$
	28				281.09	$(m = 4)$
	29				287.30	$(m = 5)$
	30				293.51	$(m = 6)$

Analysis of errors from period 10 to period 24

0.78	= Mean Error	5.45	= Mean Absolute Percentage Error
11.29	= Mean Absolute Error	0.78	= Theil's U-statistic
194.78	= Mean Square Error		

Table 4-6: *Application of Holt's two-parameter linear exponential smoothing to inventory demand data ($\alpha = 0.501$ and $\beta = 0.072$ chosen by minimizing the MSE).*

Another alternative is to use least squares regression on the first few values of the series for finding L_1 and b_1 (see Chapter 5).

The first alternative has been used in Table 4-6. When the data are well behaved it will not matter much, but the inventory data in Table 4-6 shows a dramatic drop from period 3 to 4. If this change $(Y_4 - Y_3)$ is involved in an initial slope estimate, it could take the forecasting system a long time to overcome the influence of such a large downward shift when the overall trend is upward.

As with single exponential smoothing, the weights α and β can be chosen by minimizing the value of MSE or some other criterion. optimization We could evaluate the MSE over a grid of values of α and β (e.g., each combination of $\alpha = 0.1, 0.2, \ldots, 0.9$ and $\beta = 0.1, 0.2, \ldots, 0.9$) and then select the combination of α and β which correspond to the lowest MSE. Alternatively, we could use a non-linear optimization algorithm. In the example of 4-6, such an algorithm identified the optimal values as $\alpha = 0.501$ and $\beta = 0.072$.

When the results are compared with those obtained using single exponential smoothing (Table 4-4), Holt's method outperforms SES on every measurement. This is not surprising since Holt's method is designed to handle trends whereas SES assumes the data have no underlying trend. Comparing the measures of forecast accuracy for Holt's method with those obtained using SES can give an idea of whether the additional complexity of Holt's method is justified.

Holt's method is sometimes called "double exponential smoothing." In the special case where $\alpha = \beta$, the method is equivalent to "Brown's double exponential smoothing."

4/3/4 Holt-Winters' trend and seasonality method

The set of moving average and exponential smoothing methods examined thus far in this chapter can deal with almost any type of data as long as such data are non-seasonal. When seasonality does exist, however, these methods are not appropriate on their own.

As an illustration, consider applying single exponential smoothing and Holt's method to the seasonal data in Table 4-7. These data are for quarterly exports of a French company over a six year period, and they are plotted in Figure 4-9.

Year	Quarter	Period	Sales (thous. of francs)	Year	Quarter	Period	Sales (thous. of francs)
1	1	1	362	4	1	13	544
	2	2	385		2	14	582
	3	3	432		3	15	681
	4	4	341		4	16	557
2	1	5	382	5	1	17	628
	2	6	409		2	18	707
	3	7	498		3	19	773
	4	8	387		4	20	592
3	1	9	473	6	1	21	627
	2	10	513		2	22	725
	3	11	582		3	23	854
	4	12	474		4	24	661

Table 4-7: *Quarterly sales data.*

Figure 4-10 shows the forecasts while Table 4-8 shows both the forecasts and and the errors (actual minus forecast) that result. It is easy to see in Table 4-8 that a systematic error pattern exists. The SES errors are all positive, except for negative values that occur every fourth period. (There is an exception at period 21, due to randomness.) The errors from Holt's method also show systematic seasonal patterns. Clearly such a data series requires the use of a seasonal method if the systematic pattern in the errors is to be eliminated. Holt-Winters' trend and seasonal smoothing is such a method.

The example in Table 4-8 raises the important concern of selecting the best smoothing method for a given data series. Using single exponential smoothing with an optimal parameter value of $\alpha = 0.464$ (chosen by minimizing the MSE), the MAPE and MSE measures are 13.19% and 8849, respectively, for the test set 10–24. If Holt's one-parameter linear exponential smoothing is used with optimal parameter values $\alpha = .065$ and $\beta = 0.334$, the MAPE and MSE values are 9.16% and 5090, respectively. There is some advantage

	Period	Actual	SES		Holt's method	
			Forecast	Error	Forecast	Error
	1	362	—	—	—	—
	2	385	362.00	23.00	385.00	0.00
	3	432	372.68	59.32	408.00	24.00
	4	341	400.22	−59.22	433.07	−92.07
	5	382	372.73	9.27	448.66	−66.66
	6	409	377.03	31.97	464.45	−55.45
	7	498	391.87	106.13	479.77	18.23
	8	387	441.14	−54.14	500.24	−113.24
	9	473	416.01	56.99	509.78	−36.78
	10	513	442.47	70.53	523.47	−10.47
	11	582	475.21	106.79	538.63	43.37
	12	474	524.79	−50.79	558.20	−84.20
Test	13	544	501.21	42.79	567.72	−23.72
	14	582	521.07	60.93	580.64	1.36
	15	681	549.36	131.64	595.20	85.80
Set	16	557	610.47	−53.47	617.06	−60.06
	17	628	585.65	42.35	628.21	−0.21
	18	707	605.31	101.69	643.22	63.78
	19	773	652.52	120.48	663.74	109.26
	20	592	708.45	−116.45	689.55	−97.55
	21	627	654.39	−27.39	699.90	−72.90
	22	725	641.67	83.33	710.27	14.73
	23	854	680.36	173.64	726.62	127.38
	24	661	760.97	−99.97	752.99	−91.99
	25		714.56		763.21	
	26		714.56		779.37	
	⋮		⋮		⋮	

Analysis of errors from period 10 to period 24

Mean Error	39.07	0.30
Mean Absolute Error	85.48	59.12
Mean Absolute Percentage Error (MAPE)	13.19	9.16
Mean Square Error (MSE)	8849.35	5090.26
Theil's U-statistic	0.96	0.69

Table 4-8: *Application of single exponential smoothing and Holt's method to quarterly sales data. Smoothing parameters were chosen by minimizing the MSE (SES: $\alpha = 0.464$; Holt's: $\alpha = 0.065$, $\beta = 0.334$).*

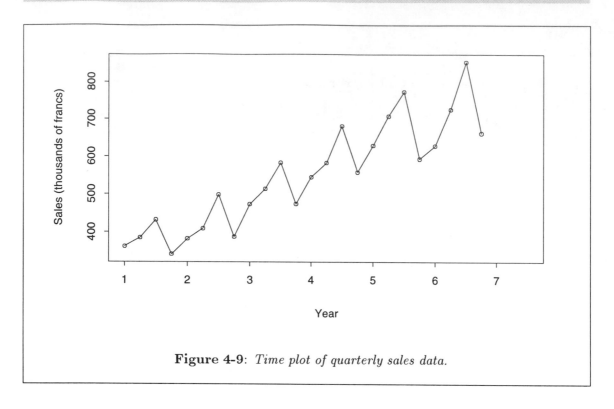

Figure 4-9: *Time plot of quarterly sales data.*

to using a method such as Holt's, which explicitly takes trend into account, but there is clearly room for improvement.

If the data have no trend or seasonal patterns, then moving averages or single exponential smoothing methods are appropriate. If the data exhibit a linear trend, Holt's linear method is appropriate. But if the data are seasonal, these methods, on their own, cannot handle the problem well. (Of course, the data could be deseasonalized first by some other procedure. See Chapter 3 for details.)

Holt-Winters' method   Holt's method was extended by Winters (1960) to capture seasonality directly. The Holt-Winters' method is based on three smoothing equations—one for the level, one for trend, and one for seasonality. It is similar to Holt's method, with one additional equation to deal with seasonality. In fact there are two different Holt-Winters' methods, depending on whether seasonality is modeled in an additive or multiplicative way.

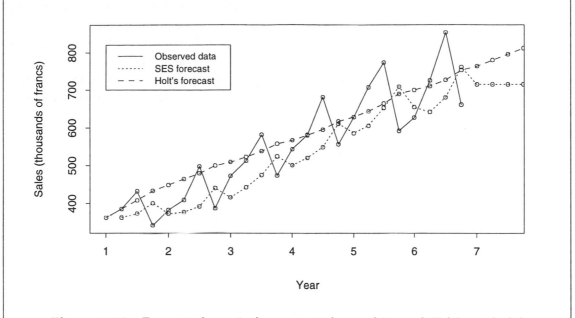

Figure 4-10: *Forecasts from single exponential smoothing and Holt's method for quarterly sales data. Neither method is appropriate for these data.*

Multiplicative seasonality

The basic equations for Holt-Winters' multiplicative method are as follows:

$$\text{Level:} \quad L_t = \alpha \frac{Y_t}{S_{t-s}} + (1-\alpha)(L_{t-1} + b_{t-1}) \quad (4.15)$$

$$\text{Trend:} \quad b_t = \beta(L_t - L_{t-1}) + (1-\beta)b_{t-1} \quad (4.16)$$

$$\text{Seasonal:} \quad S_t = \gamma \frac{Y_t}{L_t} + (1-\gamma)S_{t-s} \quad (4.17)$$

$$\text{Forecast:} \quad F_{t+m} = (L_t + b_t m)S_{t-s+m} \quad (4.18)$$

where s is the length of seasonality (e.g., number of months or quarters in a year), L_t represents the level of the series, b_t denotes the trend, S_t is the seasonal component, and F_{t+m} is the forecast for m periods ahead.

Equation (4.17) is comparable to a seasonal index that is found as a ratio of the current values of the series, Y_t, divided by the current single smoothed value for the series, L_t. If Y_t is larger than L_t, the ratio will be greater than 1, while if it is smaller than L_t, the ratio will be less than 1. Important to understanding this method is realizing that L_t is a smoothed (average) value of the series that does not include seasonality (this is the equivalent of saying that the data have been seasonally adjusted). The data values Y_t, on the other hand, do contain seasonality. It must also be remembered that Y_t includes randomness. In order to smooth this randomness, equation (4.17) weights the newly computed seasonal factor with γ and the most recent seasonal number corresponding to the same season with $(1 - \gamma)$. (This prior seasonal factor was computed in period $t - s$, since s is the length of seasonality.)

Equation (4.16) is exactly the same as Holt's equation (4.13) for smoothing the trend. Equation (4.15) differs slightly from Holt's equation (4.12) in that the first term is divided by the seasonal number S_{t-s}. This is done to deseasonalize (eliminate seasonal fluctuations from) Y_t. This adjustment can be illustrated by considering the case when S_{t-s} is greater than 1, which occurs when the value in period $t - s$ is greater than average in its seasonality. Dividing Y_t by this number greater than 1 gives a value that is smaller than the original value by a percentage just equal to the amount that the seasonality of period $t - s$ was higher than average. The opposite adjustment occurs when the seasonality number is less than 1. The value S_{t-s} is used in these calculations because S_t cannot be calculated until L_t is known from (4.15).

The data of Table 4-7 can be used to illustrate the application of Holt-Winters' method. With parameter values of $\alpha = 0.822$, $\beta = 0.055$, and $\gamma = 0.000$ chosen by minimizing the MSE, forecasts and related smoothed values are as shown in Table 4-9.

The computations involved in this method can be illustrated for period 24 as follows:

$$
\begin{aligned}
F_{24} &= [L_{23} + b_{23}(1)]S_{20} \qquad \text{[using (4.18)]} \\
&= (746.22 + 16.07).897 \\
&= 684.05
\end{aligned}
$$

	Period	Actual	Level	Trend	Seasonal	Forecast	
	t	Y_t	L_t	b_t	S_t	F_t	
	1	362	—	—	0.953	—	
	2	385	—	—	1.013	—	
	3	432	—	—	1.137	—	
	4	341	380.00	9.75	0.897	—	
	5	382	398.99	10.26	0.953	371.29	
	6	409	404.68	10.01	1.013	414.64	
	7	498	433.90	11.07	1.137	471.43	
	8	387	433.70	10.45	0.897	399.30	
	9	473	487.20	12.83	0.953	423.11	
	10	513	505.21	13.11	1.013	506.60	
	11	582	513.08	12.82	1.137	589.26	
	12	474	527.80	12.93	0.897	471.93	
Test	13	544	565.65	14.31	0.953	515.12	
	14	582	575.42	14.06	1.013	587.59	
	15	681	597.33	14.49	1.137	670.14	
Set	16	557	619.12	14.89	0.897	549.03	
	17	628	654.74	16.04	0.953	603.98	
	18	707	693.01	17.27	1.013	679.60	
	19	773	685.35	15.89	1.137	807.47	
	20	592	667.10	14.00	0.897	629.27	
	21	627	662.26	12.96	0.953	648.84	
	22	725	708.40	14.80	1.013	684.10	
	23	854	746.22	16.07	1.137	822.16	
	24	661	741.17	14.90	0.897	684.05	
	25				0.953	720.26	$(m = 1)$
	26				1.013	781.12	$(m = 2)$
	27					893.41	$(m = 3)$
	28					718.59	$(m = 4)$
	29					777.04	$(m = 5)$
	30					841.50	$(m = 6)$

Analysis of errors from period 10 to period 24

3.39	= Mean Error	3.13	= Mean Absolute Percentage Error
20.65	= Mean Absolute Error	0.25	= Theil's U-statistic
582.94	= Mean Square Error		

Table 4-9: *Application of Holt-Winters' linear and multiplicative seasonal exponential smoothing to quarterly sales data in Table 3-10. Smoothing parameters were chosen by minimizing the MSE ($\alpha = 0.822$, $\beta = 0.055$ and $\gamma = 0.00$).*

$$L_{24} = 0.822\frac{Y_{24}}{S_{20}} + 0.178(L_{23} + b_{23}) \qquad \text{[using (4.15)]}$$
$$= 0.822\frac{661}{0.897} + 0.178(746.22 + 16.07)$$
$$= 741.17$$
$$b_{24} = 0.055(L_{24} - L_{23}) + 0.945b_{23} \qquad \text{[using (4.16)]}$$
$$= 0.055(741.17 - 746.22) + 0.945(16.07)$$
$$= 14.90$$
$$S_{24} = 0.000\frac{Y_{24}}{L_{24}} + 1.00S_{20} \qquad \text{[using (4.17)]}$$
$$= 0.897.$$

Forecasts for periods 25, 26, 27, and 28, would then be:

$$F_{25} = [741.17 + 14.90(1)](0.953) = 720.26,$$
$$F_{26} = [741.17 + 14.90(2)](1.013) = 781.12,$$
$$F_{27} = [741.17 + 14.90(3)](1.137) = 893.41,$$
$$F_{28} = [741.17 + 14.90(4)](0.897) = 718.59.$$

initialization

As with all exponential smoothing methods, we need initial values of the components to start the algorithm. To initialize the Holt-Winters' forecasting method, we need initial values of the level L_t, the trend b_t, and the seasonal indices S_t. To determine initial estimates of the seasonal indices we need to use at least one complete season's data (i.e., s periods). Therefore we initialize trend and level at period s. The level is initialized by taking the average of the first season:

$$L_s = \frac{1}{s}(Y_1 + Y_2 + \cdots + Y_s).$$

Note that this is a moving average of order s and so will eliminate the seasonality in the data. To initialize trend, it is convenient to use two complete seasons (i.e., $2s$ periods) as follows:

$$b_s = \frac{1}{s}\left[\frac{Y_{s+1} - Y_1}{s} + \frac{Y_{s+2} - Y_2}{s} + \cdots + \frac{Y_{s+s} - Y_s}{s}\right]. \qquad (4.19)$$

(Each of these terms is an estimate of the trend over one complete season, and the initial estimate of b_s is taken as the average of s such terms.) Finally, the seasonal indices are initialized using the ratio of the first few data values to the mean of the first year so that

$$S_1 = \frac{Y_1}{L_s}, \quad S_2 = \frac{Y_2}{L_s}, \quad \ldots \quad S_s = \frac{Y_s}{L_s}.$$

Several other methods for initializing are also available.

The parameters α, β, and γ can be chosen to minimize MSE optimization or MAPE. An approach for determining these values is to use a non-linear optimization algorithm to find optimal parameter values. This is how the parameters were chosen in this example. With the increasing speed of computing, this method is now more feasible than it once was. However, if there are many data sets to handle, the computing time can still be considerable. Another approach is to use a grid search method to find optimal parameter values.

Additive seasonality

The seasonal component in Holt-Winters' method may also be treated additively, although this is less common. The basic equations for Holt-Winters' additive method are as follows:

$$
\begin{array}{lll}
\text{Level:} & L_t = \alpha(Y_t - S_{t-s}) + (1-\alpha)(L_{t-1} + b_{t-1}) & (4.20) \\
\text{Trend:} & b_t = \beta(L_t - L_{t-1}) + (1-\beta)b_{t-1} & (4.21) \\
\text{Seasonal:} & S_t = \gamma(Y_t - L_t) + (1-\gamma)S_{t-s} & (4.22) \\
\text{Forecast:} & F_{t+m} = L_t + b_t m + S_{t-s+m}. & (4.23)
\end{array}
$$

The second of these equations is identical to (4.16). The only differences in the other equations are that the seasonal indices are now added and subtracted instead of taking products and ratios.

The initial values for L_s and b_s are identical to those for the multiplicative method. To initialize the seasonal indices we use initialization

$$
S_1 = Y_1 - L_s, \quad S_2 = Y_2 - L_s, \quad \ldots \quad S_s = Y_s - L_s.
$$

4/3/5 Exponential smoothing: Pegels' classification

An important consideration in dealing with exponential smoothing methods having separate trend and seasonal aspects is whether or not the model should be additive (linear) or multiplicative (non-linear). Pegels (1969) has provided a simple but useful framework for discussing these matters (as already indicated in Figure 4-1) and his two-way classification is as follows:

Trend Component	Seasonal Component		
	1 (none)	2 (additive)	3 (multiplicative)
A (none)	A-1	A-2	A-3
B (additive)	B-1	B-2	B-3
C (multiplicative)	C-1	C-2	C-3

Converting Pegels' notation to that of this chapter, all nine exponential smoothing models can be summarized by the formulas:

$$L_t = \alpha P_t + (1 - \alpha)Q_t \qquad (4.24)$$
$$b_t = \beta R_t + (1 - \beta)b_{t-1} \qquad (4.25)$$
$$S_t = \gamma T_t + (1 - \gamma)S_{t-s} \qquad (4.26)$$

where P, Q, R, and T vary according to which of the cells the method belongs. Table 4-10 shows the appropriate values of P, Q, R, and T and the forecast formula for forecasting m periods ahead.

Note that cell A-1 describes the SES method and cell B-1 describes Holt's method. The additive Holt-Winters' method is given by cell B-2 and the multiplicative Holt-Winters' method is given by cell B-3.

To work through an example of one of the other cells, consider cell C-3, which refers to an exponential smoothing model that allows for multiplicative trend and multiplicative seasonality. From Table 4-10 and equations (4.24)–(4.26), we obtain the following formulas:

$$L_t = \alpha Y_t/S_{t-s} + (1 - \alpha)L_{t-1}b_{t-1}$$
$$b_t = \beta L_t/L_{t-1} + (1 - \beta)b_{t-1}$$
$$S_t = \gamma Y_t/L_t + (1 - \gamma)S_{t-s}$$

and if we wish to forecast m periods ahead, Table 4-10 shows that the forecast is:

$$F_{t+m} = L_t b_t^m S_{t+m-s} \,.$$

| Trend | Seasonal Component | | |
	1 (none)	2 (additive)	3 (multiplicative)
A (none)	$P_t = Y_t$ $Q_t = L_{t-1}$ $F_{t+m} = L_t$	$P_t = Y_t - S_{t-s}$ $Q_t = L_{t-1}$ $T_t = Y_t - L_t$ $F_{t+m} = L_t + S_{t+m-s}$	$P_t = Y_t/S_{t-s}$ $Q_t = L_{t-1}$ $T_t = Y_t/L_t$ $F_{t+m} = L_t S_{t+m-s}$
B (additive)	$P_t = Y_t$ $Q_t = L_{t-1} + b_{t-1}$ $R_t = L_t - L_{t-1}$ $F_{t+m} = L_t + mb_t$	$P_t = Y_t - S_{t-s}$ $Q_t = L_{t-1} + b_{t-1}$ $R_t = L_t - L_{t-1}$ $T_t = Y_t - L_t$ $F_{t+m} = L_t + mb_t$ $+ S_{t+m-s}$	$P_t = Y_t/S_{t-s}$ $Q_t = L_{t-1} + b_{t-1}$ $R_t = L_t - L_{t-1}$ $T_t = Y_t/L_t$ $F_{t+m} = (L_t + mb_t)S_{t+m-s}$
C (multiplicative)	$P_t = Y_t$ $Q_t = L_{t-1}b_{t-1}$ $R_t = L_t/L_{t-1}$ $F_{t+m} = L_t b_t^m$	$P_t = Y_t - S_{t-s}$ $Q_t = L_{t-1}b_{t-1}$ $R_t = L_t/L_{t-1}$ $T_t = Y_t - L_t$ $F_{t+m} = L_t b_t^m + S_{t+m-s}$	$P_t = Y_t/S_{t-s}$ $Q_t = L_{t-1}b_{t-1}$ $R_t = L_t/L_{t-1}$ $T_t = Y_t/L_t$ $F_{t+m} = L_t b_t^m S_{t+m-s}$

Table 4-10: *Formula for calculations and forecasting using the Pegels' classification scheme.*

4/4 A comparison of methods

A variety of methods has been presented in this chapter. In addition to these smoothing methods, many others have been proposed. Some of these involve extensive computations and are mathematically complicated, so they have not been adopted as practical methods.

A pragmatic question remains: How can a forecaster choose the "right" model for a data set? Human judgment has to be involved, but there are also some useful suggestions to make. A main objective is to decide on the nature of trend (if any) and seasonality (if any) and the strength of the random component. If the data are quarterly, for example, a time plot of the raw data might show the extent of trend, seasonality, and randomness (as in Figure 4-9).

Another approach for determining the patterns in the data is to study autocorrelations, a procedure that will be studied in detail in Chapter 8.

To round out the discussion of the major smoothing methods,

		ME	MAE	MSE	MAPE	auto-corr. r_1	Theil's U
1.	Mean of all past data	157.31	157.31	30546	23.78	0.82	1.81
2.	Moving average MA(4)	47.08	72.25	7365	10.92	0.23	0.90
3.	Pegels A-1 (SES) ($\alpha = 0.464$)	39.07	85.48	8849.35	13.19	−0.22	0.96
4.	Pegels A-2 ($\alpha = 0.621, \gamma = 1.000$)	26.17	36.34	1897.27	5.52	0.12	0.45
5.	Pegels A-3 ($\alpha = 1.000, \gamma = 1.000$)	16.27	23.34	800.27	3.59	0.09	0.31
6.	Pegels B-1 (Holt's) ($\alpha = 0.065, \beta = 0.334$)	0.30	59.12	5090.26	9.16	−0.19	0.69
7.	Pegels B-2 (additive Holt-Winters') ($\alpha = 0.353, \beta = 0.114, \gamma = 1.000$)	6.54	24.45	1137.77	3.77	0.33	0.35
8.	Pegels B-3 (multiplicative Holt-Winters') ($\alpha = 0.822, \beta = 0.055, \gamma = 0.000$)	3.39	20.65	582.94	3.13	0.15	0.25
9.	Pegels C-1 ($\alpha = 0.074, \beta = 0.591$)	−3.95	60.67	5398.80	9.47	−0.18	0.71
10.	Pegels C-2 ($\alpha = 0.449, \beta = 0.348, \gamma = 1.000$)	−7.19	29.77	1497.38	4.68	0.30	0.39
11.	Pegels C-3 ($\alpha = 0.917, \beta = 0.234, \gamma = 0.000$)	−9.46	24.00	824.75	3.75	0.17	0.29

Table 4-11: *A comparison of various smoothing methods applied to the data in Table 4-7.*

consider Table 4-11, which presents the results of 11 different analyses of the same data set (see Table 4-7). In fitting each model, parameters have been chosen by minimizing the MSE calculated using errors from periods 2 through 24 (5 through 24 for seasonal models).

The column headings indicate particular measures of "fit" (as described in Chapter 2). All these error measures refer to a "test set" defined as periods 10 through 24. The following points should be noted.

ME

- The ME (mean error) is not a very useful measure since positive and negative errors can cancel one another, as in Holt's method, which has the lowest ME but is clearly not a very good model for the data.

- The MAE (mean absolute error) or MSE are more useful mea- MAE
  sures than ME. MSE

- The MAPE (mean absolute percentage error) is another use- MAPE
  ful indicator but gives relative information as opposed to the
  absolute information in MAE or MSE.

- The minimum MSE (mean square error) is obtained for Pegels' optimal model
  cell B-3 method (row 8) when optimum values for the three
  parameters are determined. The same model also gives the
  minimum MAE and minimum MAPE values. This is not always
  the case and sometimes an alternative method might be chosen
  on the basis of MAPE, for example.

- The lag 1 autocorrelation (r_1) is a pattern indicator—it refers lag 1 ACF
  to the pattern of the errors. If the pattern is random, r_1 will
  be around 0. If there are runs of positive errors alternating
  with runs of negative errors, then r_1 is much greater than 0
  (approaching an upper limit of 1). If there are rapid oscillations
  in errors (from positive to negative), then r_1 is much less than
  0 (approaching a lower limit of -1). Note that a value near
  0 is not necessarily "best." For example, row 4 has r_1 smaller
  than the minimum MSE model in row 8. But the row 4 model
  (Pegels' A-2) does not include a trend component and is not a
  good model for these data.

- Theil's U-statistic (a compromise between absolute and relative Theil's U
  measures) is very useful. In row 1, $U = 1.81$, indicating a poor
  fit, far worse than the "naïve model," which would simply use
  last period's observation as the forecast for the next period. In
  row 3 the SES model is seen to be about as good as the naïve
  model. Row 8 shows Pegels' cell B-3 model to be far superior
  ($U = 0.25$).

In the final analysis, the choice of an appropriate forecasting method is of great importance and will be studied in more detail in Chapter 11.

4/5 General aspects of smoothing methods

Smoothing methods were first developed in the late 1950s by operations researchers. It is unclear whether Holt (1957) or Brown (1956) was the first to introduce exponential smoothing (see Cox, 1961, p. 414), or if perhaps it was Magee (1958) (see Muth, 1960, p. 299). Most of the important development work on exponential smoothing was completed in the late 1950s and published by the early 1960s. This work included that done by Brown (1956) and Holt (1957) and subsequent work by Magee (1958), Brown (1959), Holt et al. (1960), Winters (1960), Brown and Meyer (1961), and Brown (1963). Since that time, the concept of exponential smoothing has grown and become a practical method with wide application, mainly in the forecasting of inventories.

storage and cost
forecast accuracy

The major advantages of widely used smoothing methods are their simplicity and low cost. It is possible that better accuracy can be obtained using the more sophisticated methods of autoregressive/moving average schemes examined in Chapter 7 or the intuitively appealing decomposition methods discussed in Chapter 3. In fact, many exponential smoothing methods are special cases of the general class of autoregressive/moving average methods (see Section 7/8/5). However, when forecasts are needed for thousands of items, as is the case in many inventory systems, smoothing methods are often the only methods fast enough for acceptable implementation.

In instances of large forecasting requirements, even small things count. The computer time needed to make the necessary calculations must be kept at a reasonable level, and the method must run with a minimum of outside interference.

In implementing smoothing methods, there are three practical issues which need to be addressed: initialization, optimization, and prediction intervals.

4/5/1 Initialization

The reason initial values for the exponential smoothing methods are needed is that the methods are recursive equations, and so they need to start somewhere. This can be seen by examining the equation of single exponential smoothing

$$F_{t+1} = \alpha Y_t + (1 - \alpha) F_t$$

where Y_t is the most recent actual value, F_t is the latest forecast, F_{t+1} is the forecast for the next period, and α is the smoothing constant. When $t = 1$, we get

$$F_2 = \alpha Y_1 + (1 - \alpha) F_1.$$

In order to get a value for F_2, F_1 must be known. The value of F_1 should have been:

$$F_1 = \alpha Y_0 + (1 - \alpha) F_0.$$

Since Y_0 does not exist and F_0 cannot be found, this equation cannot be applied. Therefore, some alternative approach is needed to estimate the initial value of F_1.

In an analogous way, initial values are needed for any type of exponential smoothing; the number and type of values depend upon the particular exponential smoothing approach being used.

To some extent, the problem of an initial forecast value is academic. In practice, it arises only once for any series—when exponential smoothing is used for the very first time. But even the very first time that an exponential smoothing method is used the problem is more theoretical than real. When such a method is first applied, most managers will not think to use its forecasts immediately. Rather, the method will be used in parallel operation with whatever system, or manual approach, existed before. During this time, no matter what the initial values, there generally will be enough history built up for the method that self-adjustment will take place and good values will result independent of the starting value used.

The initialization methods discussed earlier in this chapter are simple and effective methods to start the recursive equations. But there are many other methods that have been proposed, most of which are summarized by Gardner (1985). Some of these are outlined below.

1. *Backcasting*: This is a method used in the Box-Jenkins methodology (see Box, Jenkins, and Reinsell, 1994, p. 218). It can also be applied to exponential smoothing methods. What it

backcasting

involves is to reverse the data series and start the estimation procedure from the latest (most recent) value and finish with the first (oldest) value. Doing so will provide forecasts and/or parameter estimates for the beginning of the data, which can be used as initial values when the data are forecast in the usual sequence (i.e., from the beginning to the end). Ledolter and Abraham (1984) discuss this approach in detail.

least squares
estimates

2. *Least squares estimates:* Initial values can also be calculated using ordinary least squares. For instance in single exponential smoothing, F_t can be found by averaging, say, 10 past values. In methods assuming a trend, a straight line can be fitted to the first few values and the values of the slope and intercept used for initial values.

decomposition

3. *Decomposition:* The decomposition methods of Chapter 3 may be applied to obtain initial estimates of the components.

A useful procedure is to specify high values for the smoothing parameters for the first part of the data. This will result in a fast adjustment in the various parameters and forecasts, and therefore the effect of not having optimal initial values will be minimal.

4/5/2 Optimization

All the exponential smoothing methods require specification of some smoothing parameters. These control how quickly the forecasts will react to changes in the data. Not long ago, the computer time needed to optimize these parameters was sufficiently great that methods involving more than one or two parameters were not widely used and values of the parameters were restricted to a small number of possibilities (e.g., 0.1, 0.3, 0.5, 0.7, and 0.9).

With the advent of much faster computing, it is relatively easy to choose optimal values of the parameters using a non-linear optimization algorithm. All good forecasting packages will give optimal parameter values automatically by minimizing the MSE. It is possible to optimize some other measurement of forecast error (such as MAE or MAPE) but the MSE tends to be easier to work with.

An alternative to worrying about optimal values is to find good initial estimates for the components L_t, b_t, and S_t, then specify small values for the parameters (around 0.1 to 0.2). The forecasting system will then react slowly but steadily to changes in the data. The disadvantage of this strategy is that it gives a low response system. However, this price is often worth paying to achieve long-term stability and to provide a general, low-cost method for forecasting all types of data.

4/5/3 Prediction intervals

The forecasts considered so far have been *point forecasts*; that is, single numbers that represent what we think the value of the series will be in the future. Sometimes, that is all that is required. But it is often desirable to have a measure of the uncertainty associated with that forecast.

point forecasts

The values of the measures of forecast accuracy such as MSE and MAPE give some guide to the uncertainty in forecasts, but they can be difficult to explain to others. A more intuitive method is to give a *prediction interval* which is a range in which the forecaster can be fairly sure that the true value lies.

prediction interval

Unfortunately, exponential smoothing methods do not allow the easy calculation of prediction intervals. One widely-used approach is to find a statistical model for which a particular exponential smoothing method is optimal. Then prediction intervals can be obtained from the statistical model. The equivalence between exponential smoothing methods and statistical models is discussed in Section 7/8/5.

However, there are a number of difficulties with this approach.

1. Exponential smoothing methods can be used even when the data do not satisfy the statistical model for which the method is optimal. In fact, exponential smoothing methods were developed as a widely applicable approach to forecasting a variety of time series. They were never intended to be optimal forecasts in the sense of an underlying statistical model.

2. The statistical models assume that the forecasting errors are uncorrelated and this is crucial in calculating prediction intervals, particularly intervals for forecasts more than one step ahead. Often, an exponential smoothing method will be applied

and give forecasting errors which are correlated. Then the prediction intervals are no longer valid.

3. For some exponential smoothing algorithms, the equivalent statistical model is not known.

For these reasons, care must be taken when using the prediction intervals computed by many computer packages. The forecast errors should be checked to ensure they satisfy the required assumptions (see Section 7/1).

References and selected bibliography

BOX, G.E.P., G.M. JENKINS, and G.C. REINSELL (1994) *Time series analysis: Forecasting and control*, 3rd ed., Englewood Cliffs, NJ: Prentice-Hall.

BROWN, R.G. (1956) "Exponential smoothing for predicting demand," presented at the tenth national meeting of the Operations Research Society of America, San Francisco, 16 November 1956.

_____ (1959) *Statistical forecasting for inventory control*, New York: McGraw-Hill.

_____ (1963) *Smoothing, forecasting and prediction*, Englewood Cliffs, N.J.: Prentice-Hall.

_____ and R.F. MEYER (1961) The fundamental theorem of exponential smoothing, *Operations Research*, **9**, No. 5, 673–685.

CHATFIELD, C. and M. YAR (1988) Holt-Winters' forecasting: some practical issues, *The Statistician*, **37**, 129–140.

COX, D.R. (1961) Prediction by exponentially weighted moving averages and related methods, *Journal of the Royal Statistical Society*, B **23**, No. 2, 414–422.

DALRYMPLE, D.J. and B.E. KING (1981) Selecting parameters for short-term forecasting techniques, *Decision Sciences*, **12**, 661–669.

GARDNER, E.S. (1985) Exponential smoothing: the state of the art, *Journal of Forecasting*, **4**, 1–28.

_____ and D.G. DANNENBRING (1980) Forecasting with exponential smoothing: some guidelines for model selection, *Decision Sciences*, **11**, 370–383.

GROFF, G.K. (1973) Empirical comparison of models for short-range forecasting, *Management Science*, **20**, No. 1, 22–31.

HOLT, C.C. (1957) Forecasting seasonal and trends by exponentially weighted moving averages, Office of Naval Research, Research Memorandum No. 52.

HOLT, C.C., F. MODIGLIANI, J.F. MUTH, and H.A. SIMON (1960) *Planning production inventories and work force*, Englewood Cliffs, N.J.: Prentice-Hall.

LEDOLTER, J. and B. ABRAHAM (1984) Some comments on the initialization of exponential smoothing, *Journal of Forecasting*, **3**, 79–84.

MAGEE, J.F. (1958) *Production planning and inventory control*, New York: McGraw-Hill.

MAKRIDAKIS, S. and S.C. WHEELWRIGHT (1978) *Interactive forecasting*, 2nd ed., San Francisco: Holden-Day.

MONTGOMERY, D.C., L.A. JOHNSON, and J.S. GARDINER (1990) *Forecasting and time series analysis*, 2nd ed., New York: McGraw-Hill.

MUTH, J.F. (1960) Optimal properties of exponentially weighted forecasts, *Journal of American Statistical Association*, **55**, 299–306.

PEGELS, C.C. (1969) Exponential forecasting: some new variations, *Management Science*, **12**, No. 5, 311–315.

WINTERS, P.R. (1960) Forecasting sales by exponentially weighted moving averages, *Management Science*, **6**, 324–342.

WOOD, D. and R. FILDES (1976) *Forecasting for business*, London: Longman.

Exercises

4.1 The Canadian unemployment rate as a percentage of the civilian labor force (seasonally adjusted) between 1974 and the third quarter of 1975 is shown below.

	Quarter	Unemployment Rate
1974	1	5.4
	2	5.3
	3	5.3
	4	5.6
1975	1	6.9
	2	7.2
	3	7.2

(a) Estimate unemployment in the fourth quarter of 1975 using a single moving average with $k = 3$.

(b) Repeat using single exponential smoothing with $\alpha = 0.7$.

(c) Compare your two estimates using the accuracy statistics.

4.2 The following data reflect the sales of electric knives for the period January 1991 through April 1992:

1991		1992	
Jan	19	Jan	82
Feb	15	Feb	17
Mar	39	Mar	26
Apr	102	Apr	29
May	90		
Jun	29		
Jul	90		
Aug	46		
Sep	30		
Oct	66		
Nov	80		
Dec	89		

Management wants to use both moving averages and exponential smoothing as methods for forecasting sales. Answer the following questions:

(a) What will the forecasts be for May 1992 using a 3-, 5-, 7-, 9-, and 11- month moving average?

(b) What will the forecasts be for May 1992 for exponential smoothing with α values of 0.1, 0.3, 0.5, 0.7, and 0.9?

(c) Assuming that the past pattern will continue into the future, what k and α values should management select in order to minimize the errors?

4.3 Using the single randomless series 2, 4, 6, 8, 10, 12, 14, 16, 18, and 20, compute a forecast for period 11 using:

(i) the method of single exponential smoothing,

(ii) Holt's method of linear exponential smoothing.

Find the optimal parameters in both cases.

(a) Which of the two methods is more appropriate? Why?

(b) What value of α did you use in (i) above? How can you explain it in light of equation (4.4)?

(c) What values of α and β did you use in (ii) above? Why?

4.4 The Paris Chamber of Commerce and Industry has been asked by several of its members to prepare a forecast of the French index of industrial production for its monthly newsletter. Using the monthly data given below:

(a) Compute a forecast using the method of moving averages with 12 observations in each average.

(b) Compute the error in each forecast. How accurate would you say these forecasts are?

(c) Now compute a new series of moving average forecasts using six observations in each average. Compute the errors as well.

(d) How do these two moving average forecasts compare?

Period	French index of industrial prod.	Period	French index of industrial prod.
1	108	15	98
2	108	16	97
3	110	17	101
4	106	18	104
5	108	19	101
6	108	20	99
7	105	21	95
8	100	22	95
9	97	23	96
10	95	24	96
11	95	25	97
12	92	26	98
13	95	27	94
14	95	28	92

4.5 The data in the following table show the daily sales of paperback books and hardcover books at the same store. The task is to forecast the next four days' sales for paperbacks and hardcover books.

(a) Use single exponential smoothing and compute the measures of forecasting accuracy over the test periods 11–30.

(b) Repeat using the method of linear exponential smoothing (Holt's method).

(c) Compare the error statistics and discuss the merits of the two forecasting methods for these data sets.

(d) Compare the forecasts for the two methods and discuss their relative merits.

(e) Study the autocorrelation functions for the forecast errors resulting from the two methods applied to the two data series. Is there any noticeable pattern left in the data?

Day	Paperbacks	Hardcovers	Day	Paperbacks	Hardcovers
1	199	139	16	243	240
2	172	128	17	225	189
3	111	172	18	167	222
4	209	139	19	237	158
5	161	191	20	202	178
6	119	168	21	186	217
7	195	170	22	176	261
8	195	145	23	232	238
9	131	184	24	195	240
10	183	135	25	190	214
11	143	218	26	182	200
12	141	198	27	222	201
13	168	230	28	217	283
14	201	222	29	188	220
15	155	206	30	247	259

4.6 Using the data in Table 4-5, examine the influence of different starting values for α and different values for β on the final value for α in period 12. Try using $\alpha = 0.1$ and $\alpha = 0.3$ in combination with β values of 0.1, 0.3, and 0.5. What role does β play in ARRSES?

4.7 Forecast the airline passenger series given in Table 3-5 two years in advance using whichever of the following methods seems most appropriate: single exponential forecasting, Holt's method, additive Holt-Winters method, and multiplicative Holt-Winters method.

4.8 Using the data in Table 4-7, use Pegels' cell C-3 to model the data. First, examine the equations that go along with this method (see Table 4-10), then pick specific values for the three parameters, and compute the one-ahead forecasts. Check the error statistics for the test period 10–24 and compare with the optimal results shown in Table 4-11. If you have access to a computer program to develop optimal values for the parameters, see if you can confirm the results in Table 4-11, for the appropriate method.

5

SIMPLE REGRESSION

5/1 Regression methods

In Chapters 3 and 4, two major classes of time series methods were examined: exponential smoothing and decomposition. Various methods within each class were presented—methods appropriate for different patterns of data and different conditions. The exponential smoothing methods were suggested to be appropriate for immediate or short-term forecasting when large numbers of forecasts are needed, such as at the operating level of a company. On the other hand, the decomposition methods were found to require more computations. In addition, they require the personal attention of the user, who must predict the cycle with only indirect help from information provided by the method. Thus the decomposition approach to forecasting requires more time and is therefore restricted to forecasting fewer items than the simpler smoothing models.

In this and the following chapter, another approach available to forecasters—that of explanatory methods—will be examined. It is one thing to forecast a single time series, it is quite another to come up with other variables that relate to the data series of interest and to develop a model that expresses the functional relationship among the variables.

Thus Chapter 5 introduces a new concept in the attempt to forecast: a forecast will be expressed as a function of a certain number of factors that influence its outcome. Such forecasts will not necessarily be time dependent. In addition, an explanatory model that relates output to inputs facilitates a better understanding of the situation and allows experimentation with different combinations of inputs to study their effect on the forecasts (the output). In this way, explanatory models can be geared toward intervention, influencing the future through decisions made today. More accurate forecasts also result as the influence of explanatory variables on the output can be estimated.

simple regression

Sometimes the forecaster will wish to predict one variable Y (e.g., sales) and have available one explanatory variable X (e.g., advertising expenditure). The objective is to develop an explanatory model relating Y and X. This is known as *simple regression* and will be discussed in this chapter. In other situations, there will be one variable to forecast (Y) and several explanatory variables ($X_1, X_2, \ldots, X_k$) and the objective will be to find a function that relates Y to all of the explanatory variables. This is *multiple regression* of Y on X_1 through X_k and will be handled in Chapter 6. Finally, in many situations there will be more than one variable to forecast and more than one explanatory variable, and indeed, sometimes the forecaster will even want to forecast some of the explanatory variables. Regression models that handle such situations often call for a set of equations (rather than a single equation) which are solved simultaneously, and this is known as *econometric modeling*. Section 6/6 deals briefly with this topic.

multiple regression

econometric modeling

The forecaster, then, must decide on how many variables to deal with, which one(s) will be forecast and which will be explanatory, and which functional form will be chosen. If the data are measured over time, then it will be called *time series regression*. If the data measurements are all taken at the same time, it will be referred to as *cross-sectional regression*. Even though cross-sectional regression does not deal with time explicitly, many important decisions affecting the future are made on the basis of such studies. In that sense it is proper to consider cross-sectional regression in a book on forecasting.

time series and cross-sectional regression

5/2 Simple regression

In this section the term "simple regression" will refer to any regression of a single Y variable (the forecast or dependent variable) on a single X variable (the explanatory or independent variable). The general situation will involve a set of n paired observations to be denoted:

forecast and explanatory variables

$$(X_i, Y_i) \quad \text{for } i = 1, 2, 3 \ldots, n.$$

The automobile data discussed in Chapter 2 were of this type where the price of the vehicle can be represented by Y and the mileage of the vehicle can be represented by X.

Another example is given in Table 5-1 and Figure 5-1. Here the forecast variable Y represents sales and the explanatory variable X is time. So this is an example of time series regression, whereas the automobile data involved cross-sectional regression.

In a scatterplot (see Section 2/1/3), each pair is plotted as a point and, by convention, Y values are plotted against the vertical axis and

scatterplot

Period	X_i	1	2	3	4	5	6	7	8	9	10
Sales	Y_i	30	20	45	35	30	60	40	50	45	65

Table 5-1: *Sales data over 10 time periods.*

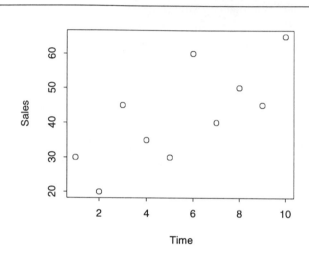

Figure 5-1: *A scatterplot of sales versus time (using data in Table 5-1).*

X values against the horizontal axis as shown in Figure 5-1. (Notice that when X is time, as in this example, a scatterplot is almost the same as a time plot except the points are not connected.)

We will consider a linear relationship between Y and X given by

$$Y = a + bX + e$$

where a is the intercept, b is the slope of the line, and e denotes the error (the deviation of the observation from the linear relationship).

5/2/1 Least squares estimation

The objective is to find values of a and b so the line $\hat{Y} = a + bX$ presents the "best fit" to the data.

As a way of introducing least squares estimation in this context, consider fitting two different straight lines through the points, as in

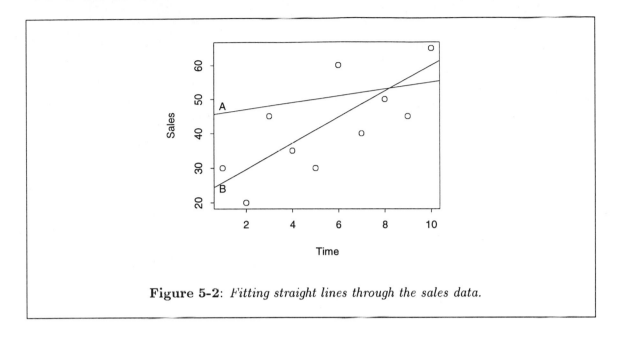

Figure 5-2: *Fitting straight lines through the sales data.*

Figure 5-2. Line A does not seem to do as well as line B in "fitting" the observed data. How can different lines be appraised in terms of goodness of fit?

Figure 5-3 indicates the standard way of evaluating goodness of fit. **goodness of fit** For each point (observation) in the plot, the error of fit can be defined as the vertical deviation between the observation and the fitted line, shown by the dotted lines in Figure 5-3.

These vertical deviations (or "errors") are denoted by

$$e_i = Y_i - \hat{Y}_i \qquad \text{where} \qquad \hat{Y}_i = a + bX_i.$$

The notation $\hat{Y}_i$ (pronounced "Y-hat") refers to the estimated value of Y_i if we only knew X_i.

What we are saying is that the observed values of Y are modeled in terms of a pattern and an error:

$$\left.\begin{array}{l} Y_i = \boxed{\text{pattern}} \quad + \text{error}, \\[2ex] Y_i = \boxed{a + bX_i} \quad + e_i, \\[2ex] Y_i = \hat{Y}_i \qquad\quad + e_i. \end{array}\right\} \tag{5.1}$$

The pattern is denoted by $\hat{Y}_i$ and the error by e_i.

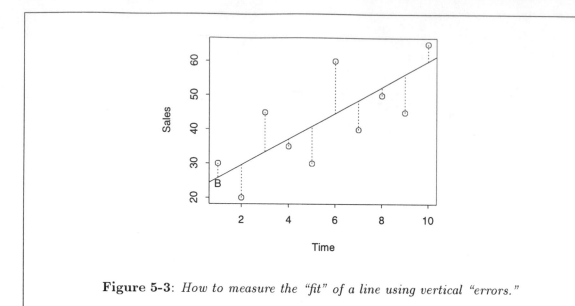

Figure 5-3: *How to measure the "fit" of a line using vertical "errors."*

sum of squares

To obtain an overall measure of "goodness of fit," we calculate the sum of the squared errors:

$$\text{SSE} = e_1^2 + e_2^2 + \cdots + e_n^2 = \sum_{i=1}^{n} e_i^2. \tag{5.2}$$

ordinary least squares

The line of best fit is chosen to be the one which yields the smallest value for this sum of the squared errors. This is known as *ordinary least squares* (OLS) estimation or just LS for short. Although there are other measures of "goodness of fit," the idea of minimizing the sum of squared errors is by far the most widely used in statistical estimation.

We can rewrite (5.2) to show that it is a function of a and b:

$$\sum_{i=1}^{n} e_i^2 = \sum_{i=1}^{n} (Y_i - \hat{Y}_i)^2 = \sum_{i=1}^{n} (Y_i - a - bX_i)^2.$$

Then we can use calculus to find the values of a and b which make this expression yield a minimum (see Appendix 5-A). The formula for determining the slope b is

LS estimate of slope

$$b = \frac{\sum_{i=1}^{n} (X_i - \bar{X})(Y_i - \bar{Y})}{\sum_{i=1}^{n} (X_i - \bar{X})^2} \tag{5.3}$$

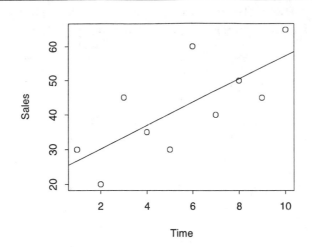

Figure 5-4: *The least squares (LS) line relating Sales (Y) to Time (X). The line has the equation $Y = 23.33 + 3.39X$.*

and the formula for determining the intercept a is

$$\boxed{a = \bar{Y} - b\bar{X}.}$$ (5.4)

LS estimate of intercept

In the case of the data in Table 5-1, the LS solution shown in Figure 5-4 is

$$Y = 23.33 + 3.39X.$$

Such computations are seldom done by hand anymore. Many hand calculators can perform simple regression analysis and all statistics packages and most spreadsheets can perform a simple regression analysis.

Example: Pulp shipments

Generally, the relationship between price and sales is negative, indicating that as price increases, sales decrease and vice versa. Figure 5-5 shows this relationship between world pulp price and shipments. The line fitted by least squares is shown on the scatterplot. Its equation is

$$S = 71.7 - 0.075P.$$

Pulp shipments (millions metric tons) S_i	World pulp price (dollars per ton) P_i
10.44	792.32
11.40	868.00
11.08	801.09
11.70	715.87
12.74	723.36
14.01	748.32
15.11	765.37
15.26	755.32
15.55	749.41
16.81	713.54
18.21	685.18
19.42	677.31
20.18	644.59
21.40	619.71
23.63	645.83
24.96	641.95
26.58	611.97
27.57	587.82
30.38	518.01
33.07	513.24
33.81	577.41
33.19	569.17
35.15	516.75
27.45	612.18
13.96	831.04

Table 5-2: *World pulp prices and shipments.*

The negative relationship is seen in the downward slope of -0.075. That is, when the price increases by one dollar, sales decrease, on average, by about 75 thousand metric tons. This is a time series regression, even though the X variable (P) is not time, since each observation is from a different period of time. That is, each of the variables forms a time series. In fitting the linear regression, we have ignored the time ordering of the data.

time series regression

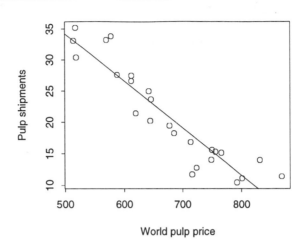

Figure 5-5: *A scatterplot of the data in Table 5-2. The relationship between world pulp price and pulp shipments is negative. As the price increases, the quantity shipped decreases. The fitted LS regression line has the equation $S = 71.7 - 0.075P$ where S denotes shipments and P denotes price.*

5/2/2 The correlation coefficient

It often occurs that two variables are related to each other, even though it might be incorrect to say that the value of one of the variables depends upon, or is influenced by, changes in the value of the other variable. In any event, a relationship can be stated by computing the correlation between the two variables. The coefficient of correlation, r, was introduced in Section 2/2/2 and is a relative measure of the linear association between two numerical variables. It can vary from 0 (which indicates no correlation) to ± 1 (which indicates perfect correlation). When the correlation coefficient is greater than 0, the two variables are said to be positively correlated (when one is large, the other is large), and when it is less than 0, they are said to be negatively correlated (when one is large, the other is small).

correlation

The correlation coefficient plays an important role in multivariate data analysis (i.e., whenever there are two or more variables involved) and has particularly strong ties with regression analysis. The reader is urged to develop an intuitive understanding of this coefficient.

The correlation between two variables X and Y is designated r_{XY} and for n paired observations the following formulas are relevant (these were discussed in Section 2/2/2):

mean of X

$$\bar{X} \;=\; \frac{1}{n}\sum_{i=1}^{n} X_i \tag{5.5}$$

mean of Y

$$\bar{Y} \;=\; \frac{1}{n}\sum_{i=1}^{n} Y_i \tag{5.6}$$

covariance between X and Y

$$\text{Cov}_{XY} \;=\; \frac{1}{n-1}\sum_{i=1}^{n}(X_i - \bar{X})(Y_i - \bar{Y}) \tag{5.7}$$

variance of X

$$S_X^2 = \text{Cov}_{XX} \;=\; \frac{1}{n-1}\sum_{i=1}^{n}(X_i - \bar{X})^2 \tag{5.8}$$

variance of Y

$$S_Y^2 = \text{Cov}_{YY} \;=\; \frac{1}{n-1}\sum_{i=1}^{n}(Y_i - Y)^2 \tag{5.9}$$

correlation between X and Y

$$r_{XY} \;=\; \frac{\text{Cov}_{XY}}{S_X S_Y} \tag{5.10}$$

where $S_X = \sqrt{S_X^2}$ and $S_Y = \sqrt{S_Y^2}$ are the standard deviations of X and Y, respectively. Note that the formula for r_{XY} is unchanged if X and Y are interchanged. So $r_{YX} = r_{XY}$.

The correlation coefficient can range from an extreme value of -1 (perfect negative correlation) through zero to an extreme value of $+1$ (perfect positive correlation). Figure 5-6 plots some artificial data that show various correlations. Each plot shows 100 observations.

Intuitively, the correlation tells us two things.

1. The sign of the correlation coefficient ($+$ or $-$) indicates the *direction* of the relationship between the two variables. If it is positive, they tend to increase and decrease together; if it is negative, one increases while the other decreases; if it is close to zero, they move their separate ways.

2. The magnitude of the correlation coefficient is a measure of the *strength* of the association—meaning that as the absolute value

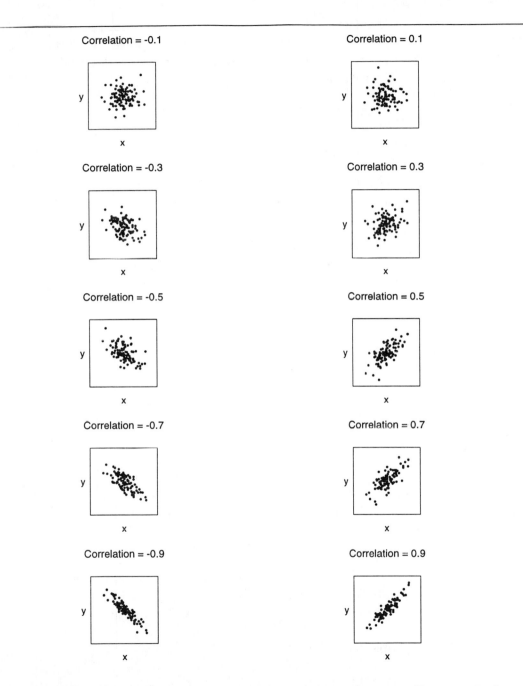

Figure 5-6: *Scatterplots corresponding to various correlation coefficients. Each plot shows 100 observations.*

of the correlation moves away from zero, the two variables are more strongly associated. Note, however, that there are some cautions that need to be observed, as described in the next section.

Examples

The sales and time data yield a correlation of $r_{XY} = 0.735$, indicating a moderately strong positive relationship between Sales and Time. As Time increased, Sales also increased—not perfectly so, but there was a strong tendency for this to happen.

The pulp price and shipments data have a correlation of $r_{PS} = -0.931$, indicating a very strong negative relationship between pulp price and pulp shipped. If the pulp price increases, the quantity of pulp shipped tends on average to decrease and vice versa.

5/2/3 Cautions in using correlation

The correlation coefficient is widely used in statistics and can be a very useful measure. However, certain cautions need to be observed. First, the correlation is a measure of *linear* association between two variables. If two variables are related in a non-linear manner, the correlation coefficient will not be able to do justice to the strength of the relationship. For example, in Figure 5-7, two variables X and Y are plotted to show that they have a very strong non-linear relationship, but their correlation coefficient is essentially zero.

non-linear
relationship

Second, when the sample size is small—meaning there are only a few pairs of data to use in computing the correlation—the sample r value is notoriously unstable. For example, if we consider the population of all adults in the world and have in mind that the correlation between height and weight is significantly positive, say $r_{HW} = 0.60$, then we can be surprised if we take a sample of $n = 10$ people and compute the correlation between height and weight for them. The sample r value can vary widely over the interval from -1 to $+1$. The message for the forecaster is that correlations based on small samples should be recognized as having a large standard error (i.e., they are unstable) and only when the sample size exceeds $n = 30$ do they become reasonably stable.

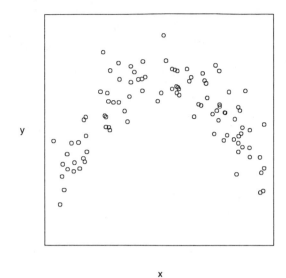

Figure 5-7: *The correlation coefficient does not help define a non-linear relationship. Here the correlation is 0.05 based on 100 observations.*

A third point about the correlation coefficient concerns the presence of extreme values. The value of r can be seriously affected by the presence of just one observation which lies away from the bulk of the data. We illustrate this important caution by referring to the "King Kong" effect in Figure 5-8.

King Kong effect on correlation

Suppose we are examining the relationship between height and weight for gorillas and we take a sample of size $n = 20$. Figure 5-8a shows a scatterplot for the height-weight pairings and the correlation turns out to be 0.527. Now if one gorilla, King Kong, is added to the sample, there is one large height and one large weight to add to the scatterplot, and the correlation increases to 0.940. Technically, what has happened here is that the height variable and the weight variable have become very skewed distributions, and skewness has a profound effect on the correlation coefficient. Sometimes, an extreme observation will make only one distribution skew, and then an r value of 0.5 might shift to an r value of 0.05.

effect of skewness on correlation

In the context of forecasting, the correlation coefficient is used very

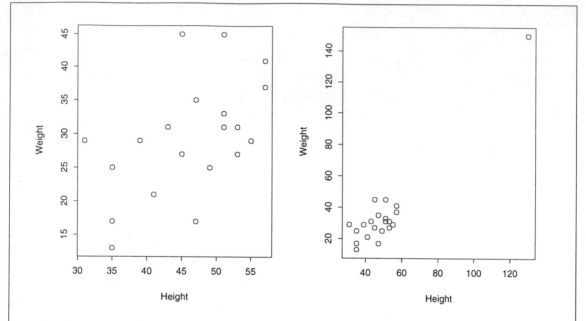

Figure 5-8: *The King Kong effect on r. The plot on the left has 20 points with correlation 0.527. The plot on the right has only one additional point, but has correlation 0.940.*

frequently. For example, in Chapter 7 the notion of autocorrelation forms the very basis for the time series methods discussed there. It is well to bear in mind that r values (whether they be regular correlations, autocorrelations, or cross-correlations) are unstable in small samples, are measures of linear association, and are seriously influenced by extreme values.

5/2/4 Simple regression and the correlation coefficient

Because there is a negative correlation between price and shipments of pulp (i.e., r_{PS} is negative), we know that if we raise the price we will tend to lower the quantity of pulp shipped, and vice versa. When we regress shipments on price, then we are able to estimate what the consumption will be for a given price. Clearly, the better the regression fit, the better will be the estimate obtained, and the linear regression fit will be better if there is a strong linear relationship (high correlation) between price and shipments. So we see that correlation and regression are intimately connected.

This relationship between correlation and regression can be established by examining the formulas used to determine the slope of a simple linear regression (5.3) and the formula used for computing the correlation coefficient (5.10). They are repeated here for ease of reference.

$$b = \frac{\sum_{i=1}^{n}(X_i - \bar{X})(Y_i - \bar{Y})}{\sum_{i=1}^{n}(X_i - \bar{X})^2} = \frac{\text{Cov}_{XY}}{S_X^2}$$

$$r_{XY} = \frac{\text{Cov}_{XY}}{S_X S_Y}$$

It is a simple matter to write an equation linking the slope and the correlation coefficient, as follows:

$$\boxed{b = \frac{\text{Cov}_{XY}}{S_X^2} = r_{XY}\frac{S_Y}{S_X}.} \tag{5.11}$$

Thus, the slope of the simple regression of Y on X is the correlation between X and Y multiplied by the ratio S_Y/S_X. (In passing, note that if we had been regressing X on Y, the slope of this regression line would be r_{XY} multiplied by the ratio S_X/S_Y.)

There is another important correlation to consider in regression. Once the regression model has been estimated—that is, the least squares estimates of the regression coefficients have been obtained—then all the known Y values can be compared with all the estimated Y values, using the regression line. The estimated Y values are designated $\hat{Y}$ and we have the identity

$$Y_i = (a + bX_i) + e_i = \hat{Y}_i + e_i.$$

There are now n pairs of values $(Y_i, \hat{Y}_i)$ and it is of great interest to know how these two values relate to each other. In regression, the correlation between Y and $\hat{Y}$ is usually designated R. Furthermore, it is customary to present this correlation in squared form, R^2, and this statistic is known as the *coefficient of determination*. R^2 is thus the squared correlation between the forecast variable Y and its estimated value, $\hat{Y}$. In general, R^2 can be defined as

coefficient of determination

$$R^2 = r_{Y\hat{Y}}^2 = \frac{\sum(\hat{Y}_i - \bar{Y})^2}{\sum(Y_i - \bar{Y})^2}. \tag{5.12}$$

For simple linear regression, the correlation between Y and $\hat{Y}$ is exactly the same as the correlation between Y and X. Therefore $R^2 = r^2_{Y\hat{Y}} = r^2_{XY}$.

The reason for presenting this correlation in squared form is that R^2 can be interpreted as *a proportion of the variation in Y which is explained by X*. The forecast variable Y has a certain amount of variability, defined by its variance, and the estimated $\hat{Y}$ values also have a certain amount of variance. The ratio of these two variances is R^2:

$$R^2 = \frac{\text{variance in the } \hat{Y} \text{ values}}{\text{variance in the } Y \text{ values}}.$$

Since the $\hat{Y}$ values are defined with reference to the estimated regression equation, this is often expressed as follows:

$$R^2 = \frac{\text{explained variance of } Y}{\text{total variance of } Y}.$$

Figure 5-9 helps to make this clearer. For any Y_i value there is a total deviation $(Y_i - \bar{Y})$ showing how far Y_i is from the mean of the

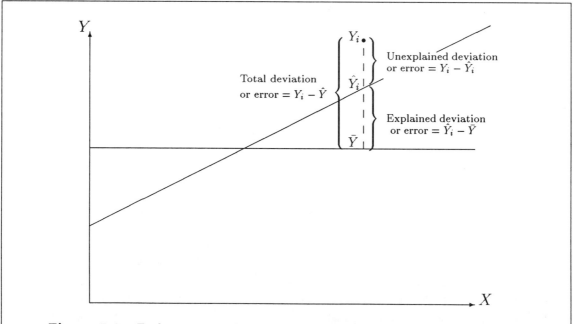

Figure 5-9: *Explanation of the partition of total deviation into explained and unexplained deviations (in the case of simple regression).*

Y values. This total deviation can be partitioned into two pieces, (i) an unexplained deviation $e_i = (Y_i - \hat{Y}_i)$, showing how far Y_i is from the regression line value, $\hat{Y}_i$, and (ii) an explained deviation $(\hat{Y}_i - \bar{Y})$, showing how far the regression value $\hat{Y}_i$ is from the mean of the $\bar{Y}$ values. In symbols, this partition is as follows:

$$(Y_i - \bar{Y}) \quad = \quad (Y_i - \hat{Y}_i) \quad + \quad (\hat{Y}_i - \bar{Y}).$$

| total deviation | unexplained deviation | explained deviation |

Then the squared deviations are given by

$$(Y_i - \bar{Y})^2 \quad = \quad \left[(Y_i - \hat{Y}_i) + (\hat{Y}_i - \bar{Y})\right]^2$$
$$= \quad (Y_i - \hat{Y}_i)^2 + (\hat{Y}_i - \bar{Y})^2 + 2(Y_i - \hat{Y}_i)(\hat{Y}_i - \bar{Y}).$$

Summing these over all data points gives

sums of squares

$$\sum(Y_i - \bar{Y})^2 \quad = \quad \sum(Y_i - \hat{Y}_i)^2 + \sum(\hat{Y}_i - \bar{Y})^2 + 2\sum(Y_i - \hat{Y}_i)(\hat{Y}_i - \bar{Y}).$$

The cross product term (the last term on the right) turns out to be exactly zero. Thus we have

$$\sum(Y_i - \bar{Y})^2 \quad = \quad \sum(Y_i - \hat{Y}_i)^2 \quad + \quad \sum(\hat{Y}_i - \bar{Y})^2$$

| total SS (SST) | unexplained SS (SSE) | explained SS (SSR) |

Note that unexplained deviations are actually the vertical errors, denoted by e_i. So the unexplained SS is the same as the sum of squared errors (SSE) given in equation (5.2). The label SSR for the explained SS stands for the "sum of squares from the regression."

So, the total sum of squares (SST) is equal to the sum of the unexplained sum of squares (SSE) and the explained sum of squares (SSR). If the explained SS is very nearly equal to the total SS, then the relationship between Y and X must be very nearly perfectly linear.

The coefficient of determination (R^2) can be expressed as the ratio of the explained SS to the total SS:

$$R^2 = \frac{\text{SSR}}{\text{SST}}.$$

Period	Sales	Estimated sales	Total deviation	Unexplained deviation	Explained deviation
X_i	Y_i	$\hat{Y}_i$	$Y_i - \bar{Y}$	$Y_i - \hat{Y}_i$	$\hat{Y}_i - \bar{Y}$
1	30	26.73	-12	3.27	-15.27
2	20	30.12	-22	-10.12	-11.89
3	45	33.52	3	11.48	-8.48
4	35	36.91	-7	-1.91	-5.09
5	30	40.30	-12	-10.30	-1.70
6	60	43.70	18	16.30	1.70
7	40	47.09	-2	-7.09	5.09
8	50	50.48	8	-0.48	8.48
9	45	53.88	3	-8.88	11.88
10	65	57.27	23	7.73	15.27
Sums of squares			1760	809.70	950.30
			SST	SSE	SSR

$$R^2 = 950.3/1760.0 = 0.540.$$

Table 5-3: *Calculation of R^2 for the Sales data.*

Examples

In the case of the Sales and Time data, the explained SS is 950.3 and the total SS is 1760.0 as shown in Table 5-3. Hence

$$R^2 = \frac{950.3}{1760} = 54.0\%.$$

Note that we could have also calculated R^2 as the square of r_{XY}: $R^2 = r_{XY}^2 = (0.735)^2 = 0.540$. So 54% of the variation in the Sales data can be "explained" by the straight line model with the Time variable. The remaining 46% of the variation is due to random fluctuation.

For the pulp data, the explained SS is 1357.2 and the total SS is 1566.2. Hence

$$R^2 = \frac{1357.2}{1566.2} = 86.7\%.$$

(Again, note that $R^2 = r_{PS}^2 = (-0.931)^2 = 0.867$.) In this case, 86.7% of the variation in the quantity of pulp shipped is explained by the linear relationship between pulp shipped and the changes in the world

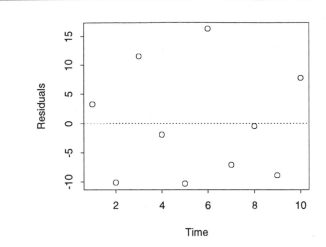

Figure 5-10: *Residual plot from the Sales/Time regression. The residuals e_i are plotted against the explanatory variable X_i. A good regression model will have residuals which are randomly scattered about 0, as seen here.*

pulp price. This is a stonger linear relation than that between Sales and Time.

5/2/5 Residuals, outliers, and influential observations

The errors (e_i) are also called the **residuals**. These are what we cannot explain with the regression line. After fitting a straight line through the data, it is helpful to examine the residuals to check that the fitted model is adequate and appropriate.   residuals

A useful plot for studying residuals is the scatterplot of residuals e_i against the explanatory variable X_i. This is known as a *residual plot.*   residual plot
Figure 5-10 shows the residuals from the regression of Sales on Time plotted against Time (the X variable). If the straight line regression is appropriate, the residuals should not be related to X_i. Therefore, the residual plot should show scatter in a horizontal band with no values too far from the band and no patterns such as curvature or increasing spread. The residual plot in Figure 5-10 shows no such patterns, and so the straight line regression can be considered appropriate.

Figure 5-11 shows the residual plot for the Pulp regression. In this

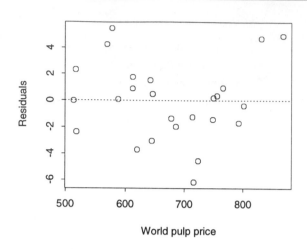

Figure 5-11: *Residual plot from the Pulp regression. Here the residuals show a V-shaped pattern. This indicates the straight line relationship was not appropriate for these data.*

case, the residuals do not form a horizontal band centered at zero. Instead, they tend to be positive at the edges of the plot (for small and large values of the X variable), but negative in the middle of the plot (for moderate values of the X variable). This may indicate that a straight line relationship was not the most appropriate model for these data. (It may also occur if an important variable has been omitted from the model.) It is easier to see this from the residual plot than from the original scatterplot in Figure 5-5. We will consider alternative (non-linear) relationships for these data in Section 5/4.

outliers

Outliers *are observations with large residuals.* Identifying outliers helps us to find observations which are different from the bulk of the observations, or which do not fit the linear pattern in some way. There are no outliers in the two examples considered here.

influential observations

Influential observations *are observations which have a great influence on the fitted equation.* If these observations were omitted, the position of the regression line would markedly change. An influential observation is usually an extreme observation in the X variable, lying away from the bulk of the X data. (See Figure 5-8 to visualize the influence of an extreme observation.) There are no influential observations in the two examples above.

An example of an influential observation in the Pulp example would be an observation with price $X = 1,000$ and shipments of $Y = 20$. This observation would not follow the pattern seen in the rest of the data (see Figure 5-5 on page 193). The fitted line would have a smaller slope and smaller intercept if such an observation were added to our data. Influential observations often have relatively small residuals, and so are usually not outliers.

Very often, interesting and useful information is gained by considering outliers and influential observations. But often they are omitted or ignored in statistical analysis. For example, the Antarctic ozone hole could have been detected much earlier if outliers had not been omitted. Satellites have been collecting atmospheric data for many years, but the software used to process the information rejected the extremely low values recorded near the South Pole as an aberration. It was not until ground-based instruments recorded ozone depletion in 1985 that the satellite data was reanalyzed. Then it was found that recorded ozone levels had begun falling in 1979. If the outliers had been investigated in the first analysis, this problem could have been detected much earlier.

Example: GDP and PCV sales

As a third example, consider the data listed in Table 5-4 and plotted in Figure 5-12. The regression line is

$$Y = -4.21 + 1.60X$$

where Y denotes the PCV sales and X denotes GDP. Hence, the PCV sales increase, on average, by 1.6% as GDP in Western Europe increases by 1%. A major consequence of such a relationship is the cyclical character of sales as they are related to GDP. In addition to the long-term trend of GDP (which contributes to increasing sales over time), it is also influenced by recessions and booms of various durations and strengths which increase or decrease the sales of PCV temporarily by an amount which on average is 1.6% greater or smaller than the corresponding percentage changes in GDP. The correlation of GDP and PCV sales is 0.949, so that $R^2 = (0.949)^2 = 0.901$. That is, that 90.1% of the variation in PCV sales is explained by the linear relationship with GDP.

GDP Western Europe (X)	PCV Industry Sales (Y)
7.90	8.45
7.92	8.52
7.91	8.25
7.96	8.58
7.98	8.58
8.01	8.63
8.05	8.74
8.06	8.70
8.06	8.61
8.07	8.59
8.09	8.77
8.11	8.80
8.14	8.79
8.17	8.83
8.19	8.91
8.23	8.97
8.27	8.97
8.29	9.04
8.30	9.05

Table 5-4: *Gross Domestic Product (GDP) and PCV industry sales for Western Europe for 19 consecutive years. Data have been transformed using logarithms.*

Figure 5-13 shows a residual plot for this regression. Here the residuals show no pattern indicating that the linear relationship was appropriate for these data. However, there is at least one outlier, and possibly three outliers. These highlight observations where the PCV sales were substantially less than that predicted by the linear relationship with GDP. These outliers are associated with the energy crisis (1973–1974) when gasoline prices increased substantially, forcing a steep price increase in PCV.

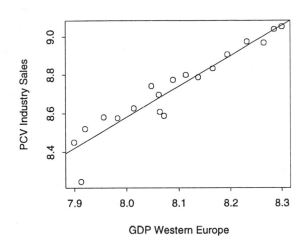

Figure 5-12: *Scatterplot and least squares regression line for the data in Table 5-3. The least squares line is $Y = -4.21 + 1.60X$ where Y denotes the PCV sales and X denotes GDP.*

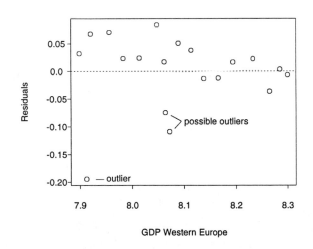

Figure 5-13: *Residual plot from the PCV/GDP regression. The lack of pattern in the residuals shows the straight line relationship was appropriate for these data. However, there is at least one outlier and possibly three outliers. These highlight unusual years where sales were substantially less than predicted by the linear relationship with GDP.*

5/2/6 Correlation and causation

causation

It is important to distinguish between correlation and causation. Two variables X and Y may be highly correlated, but an increase in X does not necessarily *cause* an increase in Y.

For example, suppose Y denotes the weekly total cans of cola sold nationally and X is the weekly number of deaths by drowning. Then X and Y are positively correlated, but no one would suggest that the number of drownings *causes* the sales of cola. Both X and Y increase together according to the weather. In summer, both drownings and cola sales increase, and in winter, they are both lower. In this case the temperature is a *lurking variable*.

lurking variable

In general a lurking variable is an explanatory variable which was not included in the regression but has an important effect on the forecast variable. It is correlated with both X and Y. In the exercises, there are several examples of a pair of variables which are correlated because they are both caused by a third lurking variable.

Even if X does have a direct causal effect on Y, there may be another variable Z which is correlated with X which also has a direct causal effect on Y. In this case Z is called a *confounding variable*.

confounding variable

For example, new car sales may depend both on advertising expenditure and on price. But if advertising expenditure goes up when the price is discounted, there is no way of telling which of the two variables is causing the subsequent increase in sales. Here advertising and price are confounded.

5/3 Inference and forecasting with simple regression

When we make a scatterplot of Y (forecast variable) against X (explanatory variable) and decide to define an equation relating Y to X, we are assuming that there is an underlying statistical model which we are estimating. Certain statistical tests can be conducted to test the significance of the overall regression equation, to test the individual coefficients in the equation, and to develop prediction intervals for any forecasts that might be made using the regression model.

In this section there will be only a brief introduction to regression as a statistical model (Section 5/3/1), then the F-test for overall significance of the regression model will be defined (Section 5/3/2), confidence intervals and t-tests for the individual slope and intercept coefficients will be defined (Sections 5/3/3 and 5/3/4), and finally, the regression equation will be used to forecast (Section 5/3/5).

The PCV data will be used to illustrate ideas throughout this section.

5/3/1 Regression as statistical modeling

In a nutshell, the simple linear regression model may be defined precisely as follows.

Regression model in theory

$$Y_i = \boxed{\alpha + \beta X_i} + \varepsilon_i, \qquad (5.13)$$

where Y_i and X_i represent the ith observations of the variables Y and X respectively, α and β are fixed (but unknown) parameters and ε_i is a random variable that is normally distributed with mean zero and having a variance σ_ε^2.

Note the formalities in a model of this type. The expression $\alpha + \beta X_i$ is the regression relationship—in this case a straight line—and α and β are called parameters (which are unknown, but if they were known they would be fixed numbers). There are several assumptions made about X_i and ε_i which are important: assumptions

1. The explanatory variable X_i takes values which are assumed to be either fixed numbers (measured without error), or they are random but uncorrelated with the error terms ε_i. In either case, the values of X_i must not be all the same.

2. The error terms ε_i are uncorrelated with one another.

3. The error terms ε_i all have mean zero and variance σ_ε^2, and have a normal distribution.

In contrast to the theoretical regression model, consider the regression model in practice. All the unknown parameters in the theoretical model have to be estimated. In place of α and β (unknown parameters) we have to find a and b (estimated statistics), and in place of σ_ε^2 (variance parameter for the theoretical error term) we have to determine s_e^2 (estimated variance of empirically defined errors).

Regression model in practice

$$Y_i = \boxed{a + bX_i} + e_i, \tag{5.14}$$

for $i = 1, 2, \ldots, n$, where a and b are estimates of α and β, and *are both random variables* and e_i is the estimated error (or residual) for the ith observation and is a random variable. The estimated variance of the errors is denoted by s_e^2.

---

estimate of error variance

The values of a and b are obtained using the LS equations (5.4) and (5.3) respectively. The value of s_e^2 is given by[1]

$$\boxed{s_e^2 = \frac{1}{n-2}\sum_{i=1}^{n} e_i^2 = \frac{1}{n-2}\sum_{i=1}^{n}(Y_i - \hat{Y}_i)^2}. \tag{5.15}$$

For the PCV data, the simplest theoretical model to be entertained is

$$Y = \alpha + \beta X + \varepsilon$$

where $\varepsilon \stackrel{d}{=} N(0, \sigma_\varepsilon^2)$. The practical model developed for this case was

$$Y_i = -4.21 + 1.60X_i + e_i$$

and the estimated variance of the errors is

$$s_e^2 = \frac{1}{19-2}(0.08081) = 0.00475.$$

If we measured GDP and PCV sales over a different time period, we would not expect to get exactly the same estimated regression line. The values of a and b will change with different sets of data. That is, a and b are random variables and this one line (where $a = -4.21$ and $b = 1.60$) is just one member of the family of lines that could have been obtained for this problem.

---

[1] Note that this equation is not quite the same as the sample variance of the residuals. The sample variance would have divisor $n-1$ whereas here we have used $n-2$. The sum of squared errors is divided by the degrees of freedom which can be defined as the number of data points minus the number of parameters estimated. In this case, we have estimated two parameters (α and β), so the degrees of freedom is two less than the total number of observations.

5/3/2 The F-test for overall significance

The simple regression model, $Y = \alpha + \beta X + \varepsilon$, has slope coefficient β. If this slope was zero, the regression line would be $Y = \alpha + \varepsilon$. In other words, knowing the X values would be of no consequence at all and there would be no relationship between Y and X. But we could still fit a straight line through the data and find a value for b which would not in general be exactly zero.

So, having fitted a regression line and obtained values for a and b, it is natural to ask if there is a *real* relationship between Y and X. The F-test allows us to test the significance of the overall regression model—to be able to answer the statistical question: Is there a significant relationship between Y and X?

significance of the regression

From Figure 5-14(a) it is clear that a linear relationship exists between Sales and Time. From Figure 5-14(b) there is a slight rising trend in consumption over time, but the variation around this trend is substantial. Thus, it is not obvious if the consumption really increases over time or if it an artifact of these data. From Figure 5-14(c) it seems that variable unit cost does not depend on how many units are produced. It would be helpful to have a statistical test that would aid the forecaster in deciding on the significance of the relationship between Y and X. The F-test is such a test.

The F statistic is defined as follows:

F statistic

$$
\begin{aligned}
F &= \frac{\text{explained MS}}{\text{unexplained MS}} \\
&= \frac{\text{explained SS/explained df}}{\text{unexplained SS/unexplained df}} \\
&= \frac{\sum(\hat{Y}_i - \bar{Y})^2/(m-1)}{\sum(Y_i - \hat{Y}_i)^2/(n-m)}
\end{aligned}
\tag{5.16}
$$

where MS = mean square, SS = sum of squares, df = degrees of freedom, and m = number of parameters (coefficients) in the regression equation.

Thus the F statistic is the ratio of two mean squares. The numerator refers to the variance that is explained by the regression, and the denominator refers to the variance of what is not explained

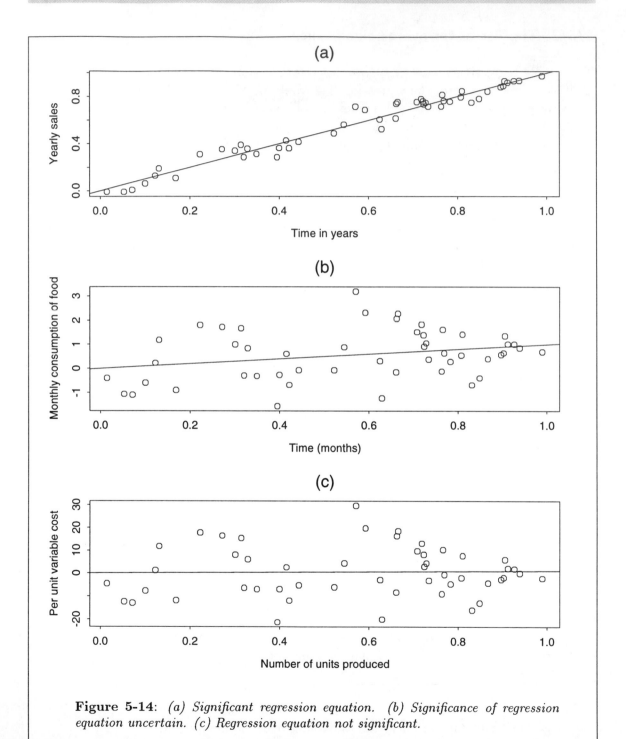

Figure 5-14: *(a) Significant regression equation. (b) Significance of regression equation uncertain. (c) Regression equation not significant.*

by the regression, namely the errors.

In fact, the F statistic in (5.16) is intimately connected to the definition of the coefficient of determination in (5.12). Thus it is easy to develop another computational formula for F, as follows:

$$F = \frac{R^2/(m-1)}{(1-R^2)/(n-m)}.$$

For the PCV data, using the computed $R^2 = .901$, we get:

$$F = \frac{.901/(2-1)}{(1-.901)/(19-2)} = \frac{.901}{.00582} = 154.7.$$

If the slope is significantly different from zero, then the regression will explain a substantial proportion of the variance, and so the F statistic will be large.

Most computer packages will also report the P-value along with the F statistic. The P-value gives the *probability of obtaining an F statistic as large as the one calculated for your data, if in fact the true slope is zero.* So, if the P-value is small, then the regression is significant. It is customary to conclude that the regression is significant if the P-value is smaller than 0.05, although this threshold is arbitrary.

P-value

Computer packages often present the calculation in the form of an analysis of variance (ANOVA) table in Table 5.5.

ANOVA table

Source	df	SS	MS	F	P
Regression	dfR $= m-1$	SSR	MSR $=$ SSR/dfR	MSR/MSE	P-value
Error	dfE $= n-m$	SSE	MSE $=$ SSE/dfE		
Total	dfT $=$ dfR+dfE	SST $=$ SSR+SSE			

Table 5-5: *Typical analysis of variance (ANOVA) table.*

Figure 5-5 shows a typical analysis of Variance (ANOVA) Table containing six columns: Source of Variation, degrees of freedom (df), sums of squares (SS), mean square (MS), the variance ratio or F statistic (F), and the P-value (P). There are two useful by-products of this analysis. First, the estimated variance of the errors, s_e^2, is given by MSE. Also, R^2 can easily be calculated as the ratio SSR/SST.

For the case of simple regression, there are two parameters (α and β) and so $m = 2$, and so for the PCV data, the linear regression model relating PCV sales to GDP would yield the following ANOVA table:

Source	df	SS	MS	F	P
Regression	1	0.735	0.735	154.72	0.000
Error	17	0.081	0.00475		
Total	18	0.816			

Here the P-value is very small indeed, less than 0.0005. This suggests very strongly that the relationship between PCV and GDP is significant. In other words, if the real slope β was zero, it is extremely unlikely that these data would have arisen.

When a computer package does not report the P-value, it is possible to calculate it from an F table. These show how large the F statistic must be before we can conclude that the regression is significant. To look up the F table, we need to know the degrees of freedom for the denominator and for the numerator. As noted above, for simple regression the df for the numerator is 1 and the df for the denominator is $n - 2 = 17$. The F table (Table C in Appendix III) for this combination of degrees of freedom give three critical values: 3.03, 4.45 and 8.40.

- If the F statistic is smaller than the first value, then the P-value is bigger than 0.10.
- If the F statistic is between the first value and the middle value, then the P-value is between 0.05 and 0.10.
- If the F statistic is between the middle value and the last value, then the P-value is between 0.01 and 0.05.

- If the F statistic is greater than the lower value then the P-value is smaller than 0.01.

In this case, the F statistic is 154.72 which is larger than all three critical values. So the P-value must be smaller than 0.01.

One point can be noted here concerning the F-test for overall significance of the regression line. In the case of simple regression, the F-test is really the same as testing the significance of the slope coefficient. In multiple regression (Chapter 6), the overall F-test is not the same as any one of the tests of significance for individual coefficients.

5/3/3 Confidence intervals for individual coefficients

In Section 5/3/1 it was pointed out that in the practical process of estimating the coefficients a and b, they must both be considered random variables. In other words, both a and b fluctuate from sample to sample.

The sampling distribution of a (the intercept coefficient) is a normal distribution with mean α and standard error:

$$\text{s.e.}(a) = \sigma_\epsilon \sqrt{\frac{1}{n} + \frac{\bar{X}^2}{\sum(X_i - \bar{X})^2}}. \qquad (5.17)$$

standard error of a

The sampling distribution of b (the slope coefficient) is a normal distribution with mean β and standard error:

$$\text{s.e.}(b) = \sigma_\epsilon \sqrt{\frac{1}{\sum(X_i - \bar{X})^2}}. \qquad (5.18)$$

standard error of b

In both these equations, the standard deviation of the errors (σ_ϵ) is unknown, but we can estimate it by

$$s_e = \sqrt{\frac{\sum(Y_i - \hat{Y}_i)^2}{n - 2}}.$$

standard deviation of errors

Using the PCV data (see Table 5-4), the following values are obtained:

Parameter	Estimate	s.e.
α	$a = -4.208$	1.040
β	$b = 1.599$	0.129

The standard errors are used to tell us how much the estimates are likely to fluctuate from sample to sample.

The best way of describing how much each estimate fluctuates is in the form of a confidence interval. We can obtain confidence intervals for the intercept and slope:

confidence intervals
for α & β

$$\alpha: \quad a \ \pm \ t^* \text{s.e.}(a)$$
$$\beta: \quad b \ \pm \ t^* \text{s.e.}(b).$$

Here t^* is a multiplying factor that depends on the number of observations used in the regression and the level of confidence required.

With the PCV data, 95% confidence intervals are obtained with $t^* = 2.11$. So the intervals are

$$-4.208 \pm 2.11(1.040) \ = \ -4.208 \pm 2.194 \ = \ [-6.40, -2.03]$$
$$1.599 \pm 2.11(0.129) \ = \ 1.599 \pm 0.270 \ = \ [1.33, 1.87].$$

That is, we can be 95% sure that the true value of α lies between -6.40 and -2.03 and we can be 95% sure that the true value of β lies between 1.33 and 1.87. The values of a and b represent our best estimates of the values of α and β.

The value of t^* is obtained from Table B in Appendix III. The degrees of freedom of a parameter estimate is the same as the degrees of freedom for the denominator in the F-test: the number of observations (n) minus the number of parameters estimated (m). For simple regression (with only one explanatory variable), $m = 2$.

For the PCV data, the degrees of freedom is $19 - 2 = 17$. This gives the row of the table. The relevant column is selected on the basis of the level of confidence required. For example, 90% confidence intervals would use $t^* = 1.74$ and 99% confidence intervals would use $t^* = 2.90$ (for 17 degrees of freedom). Generally, the larger the level of confidence, the larger the value of t^* and so the wider the interval.

5/3/4 t-tests for individual coefficients

A related idea is a t-test which is a test of whether a parameter is equal to zero. Two t-tests can be set up to test the intercept and slope values, as follows:

$$t_a = a/\text{s.e.}(a)$$ t statistic for a

$$t_b = b/\text{s.e.}(b).$$ t statistic for b

These statistics indicate if the values for a and b are significantly different from zero. For example, when the slope is significantly different from zero, the value of t_b will be large (in either the positive or negative direction depending on the sign of b).

Most computer packages will also report the P-values along with P-value
each of the t statistics. Each of these P-values is the *probability of obtaining a value of $|t|$ as large as the one calculated for your data, if in fact the parameter is equal to zero.* So, if a P-value is small, then the estimated parameter is significantly different from zero. As with F-tests, it is customary to conclude that an estimated parameter is significantly different from zero if the P-value is smaller than 0.05, although this threshold is arbitrary.

For the PCV data, the following values are obtained:

Parameter	Estimate	s.e.	t	P
α	$a = -4.208$	1.040	-4.0465	0.0008
β	$b = 1.599$	0.129	12.4387	0.0000

Both the P-values are small indicating that both parameters, the slope and the intercept, are highly significant—meaning significantly different from zero.

There is a direct relationship between confidence intervals and P-values. If the 95% confidence interval does not contain zero, then the P-value must be less than 0.05. Generally *if the $100\gamma\%$ confidence interval does not contain zero, the P-value must be less than $1 - \gamma$.*

For a simple regression (with one X variable), the P-value for the t-test of the slope b is exactly the same as the P-value for the F-test of the regression. Also, $F = t_b^2$. These tests are equivalent.

When a computer package does not report the P-value, it is possible to calculate it from t tables. These show how large the t statistic must be before we can conclude that the parameter is significant. Table B in Appendix III can be used to find a P-value given a t statistic. As with confidence intervals, the degrees of freedom is $n-2$ where n is the number of observations.

Considering the estimated parameters a and b separately is helpful, but it is worth remembering that they do not behave independently. They have a joint sampling distribution, and, in fact, there can be a strong correlation between a and b because the LS regression line goes through the mean of Y and the mean of X. If the mean of X is positive, then the correlation between a and b is negative: an increase in slope leads to a decrease in intercept, and vice versa. On the other hand, if the mean of X is negative, then the correlation between a and b is positive: an increase in slope leads to an increase in intercept, and vice versa.

5/3/5 Forecasting using the simple regression model

This is a book about forecasting. How does one use a regression model to forecast Y values? This translates into using new X values and asking what Y values are implied by these X values. We can compute point estimates for Y (i.e., single values, $\hat{Y}$) or interval estimates (prediction intervals). Given a particular new X value, designated X_0, the estimated regression model yields

point forecast
$$\boxed{\hat{Y}_0 = a + bX_0}$$

as the expected value of Y given X_0. However, since a and b are both random variables (fluctuating from sample to sample), and since there is some random error in every observation, we do not expect the new observation Y_0 to be exactly $\hat{Y}_0$.

How far it may vary is measured by its standard error given by

standard error of forecast
$$\boxed{\text{s.e.}(\hat{Y}_0) = s_e\sqrt{1 + \frac{1}{n} + \frac{(X_0 - \bar{X})^2}{\sum(X_i - \bar{X})^2}}}. \quad (5.19)$$

(The sum on the right-hand side is over all the n known X values.)

Note in equation (5.19) that the only item to change on the right-hand side is X_0, the new X value. If this value equals the mean of the n known X values, then equation (5.19) yields the lowest possible value for the standard error of the mean forecast. As X_0 moves away from $\bar{X}$, the standard error increases.

Example

To illustrate the points made above, consider the PCV example once again. The LS regression solution is

$$Y_i \text{ (PCV sales)} = -4.21 + 1.60 X_i \text{ (GDP).}$$

and the F-test ($F = 154.7$, with 1 and 17 df) was highly significant. The linear regression equation significantly improves upon the use of the mean alone as a forecast of PCV sales. In other words, knowing the GDP in Western Europe helps to estimate sales much better than if GDP were ignored.

Now suppose that decision makers in the PCV industry need to forecast what the sales of PCV would be if GDP were 7.5, 8.0, or 8.5. The first thing they could do is substitute these values into the regression equation and get estimates of sales as follows:

$$7.78 \quad \text{when the GDP is } 7.5$$
$$8.58 \quad \text{when the GDP is } 8.0$$
$$9.38 \quad \text{when the GDP is } 8.5$$

Equation (5.19) can be used to determine the standard errors of forecasts for individual values. In this example, we have $\bar{X} = 8.09$, $\sum(X_i - \bar{X})^2 = 0.288$, and $s_e^2 = 0.00475$ so that $s_e = \sqrt{0.00475} = 0.0689$. So we have the general formula:

$$\text{s.e.}(\hat{Y}_0) = (0.0689)\sqrt{1 + \frac{1}{19} + \frac{(X_0 - 8.09)^2}{0.288}}.$$

where the only item to be defined is the new GDP value (X_0) of interest. For the three values of GDP under consideration, the standard errors are

$$\text{s.e.}(Y_0) = 0.1036 \text{ when the GDP is } 7.5$$
$$\text{s.e.}(Y_0) = 0.0716 \text{ when the GDP is } 8.0$$
$$\text{s.e.}(Y_0) = 0.0881 \text{ when the GDP is } 8.5$$

Note that the middle one is smaller than the others because GDP of 8.0 is much closer to the mean of the observed GDP values than either 7.5 or 8.5.

These standard errors can then be used to obtain prediction intervals for the future sales of PCV. The general formula for a prediction interval is

prediction interval

$$\boxed{Y_0 \pm t^* \text{s.e.}(Y_0).}$$
(5.20)

The value of t^* is exactly the same as that used in confidence intervals for individual parameters. So the value of t^* is obtained from Table B in Appendix III. The row is chosen by the degrees of freedom $(n-2)$ and the column is chosen by the percentage interval required.

For these three GDP values of interest, the degrees of freedom is $19 - 2 = 17$, and for 90% prediction intervals we use $t^* = 1.74$. So we obtain the following 90% prediction intervals:

$$7.78 \pm 1.74(0.1036) \ = \ 7.78 \pm 0.180 \ = \ [7.60, 7.96]$$
$$8.58 \pm 1.74(0.0716) \ = \ 8.58 \pm 0.125 \ = \ [8.46, 8.71]$$
$$9.38 \pm 1.74(0.0881) \ = \ 9.38 \pm 0.153 \ = \ [9.23, 9.53]$$

These prediction intervals are shown in Figure 5-15 along with the observed data. The prediction intervals are symmetric about the point estimates and the range of the prediction interval increases as the new X_0 value (price in this instance) moves away from the mean $(\bar{X})$.

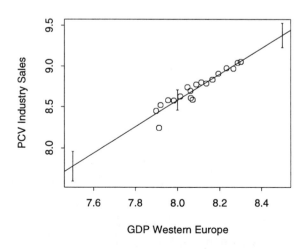

Figure 5-15: *Prediction intervals for GDP of 7.5, 8.0 and 8.5. The prediction intervals are smallest near the average GDP, and get larger as we move away from the average GDP.*

There is an obvious danger in forecasting beyond the range of the data. We identified a straight line relationship for these data when GDP lay between about 7.9 and 8.3. But in extrapolating the line beyond that range, we are assuming that the linear relationship holds for a wider range of GDP. If the relationship is not linear for GDP less than 7.9 or GDP greater than 8.3, then the forecast and prediction interval obtained for a GDP outside the data range may be a long way from the true value of PCV sales. It is safest to make predictions for values of GDP within the range of the data, or not too far outside that range.

danger of extrapolation

5/4 Non-linear relationships

We discovered in Figure 5-11 that the relationship between pulp shipments and world pulp price was non-linear. Although we had fitted a linear relationship in Figure 5-5, the residual plot from the fitted model showed a straight line relationship was not appropriate. We can write the non-linear relationship as

$$\text{shipments} = f(\text{price}) \qquad \text{or} \qquad S = f(P).$$

This equation states that the level of shipments is a function of price, and that future values of shipments may be forecast by identifying this price relationship.

Figure 5-16 shows the data with a non-linear relationship fitted to the observations. We could use the fitted line to forecast the pulp shipments at any given price. The non-linear relationship fitted to the pulp data was found using a local regression (see Section 5/4/3).

There are an infinite variety of non-linear functions. Some of the simplest non-linear functions have been given names. Figure 5-17 shows a variety of functional relationships that could exist between Y and X.

5/4/1 Non-linearity in the parameters

An important technical distinction needs to be made between linear and non-linear regression models. All regression models are written as equations linking the forecast and explanatory variables. For

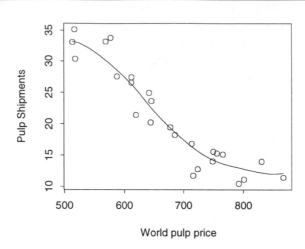

Figure 5-16: *A scatterplot of the pulp data with a non-linear relationship shown. This was estimated using a local regression.*

example, $Y = 1.5 + 2.5X$ expresses Y as a function of X. When this equation is written in its general form, $Y = \alpha + \beta X$, where α and β are the two parameters, we can make two statements about it. First, Y is a linear function of X—because if we plot Y against X it will turn out to be a straight line, and second, this equation is linear in the parameters.

"Linear in the parameters" means that once you give a value to X, the parameters occur as variables raised to the power 1 and in additive form. For example $Y = \alpha + \beta X$ is linear in the parameters α and β. If X is given a value, say 2, then the resulting equation is $Y = \alpha + 2\beta$, a linear function of the parameters. On the other hand, $Y = ce^{\beta X + \alpha}$ is not linear in the parameters. If X is given the value 2, the resulting equation is $Y = ce^{\alpha + 2\beta}$ which is not a linear function of the parameters. In Figure 5-17, functions (i), (iii), and (iv) are linear in the parameters but function (ii) is non-linear in the parameters.

The reason for making this distinction between linear and non-linear in the parameters is of computational interest. It is relatively easy to estimate the coefficients of a regression equation when it is linear *in the parameters*. It is much more difficult if the equation is not linear in the parameters. Whether it is linear or non-linear *in the variables* is of less importance.

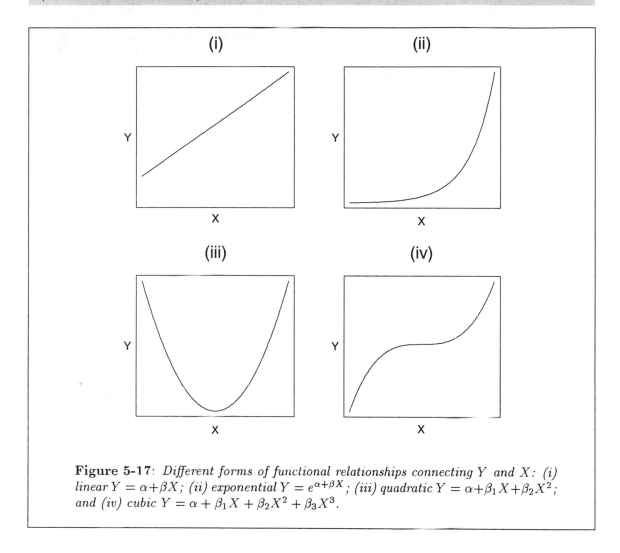

Figure 5-17: *Different forms of functional relationships connecting Y and X: (i) linear $Y = \alpha + \beta X$; (ii) exponential $Y = e^{\alpha+\beta X}$; (iii) quadratic $Y = \alpha + \beta_1 X + \beta_2 X^2$; and (iv) cubic $Y = \alpha + \beta_1 X + \beta_2 X^2 + \beta_3 X^3$.*

Having selected a particular function, it becomes necessary to estimate, from the known data pairs, the values of the parameters in the function. If the function is linear in the parameters, the principle of LS can be applied directly and expressions for the parameter estimates can be found using calculus.

For functions which are non-linear in the parameters, it is much more difficult. For example, Figure 5-17(ii), if it is not transformed in any way, would pose difficulties in solving for α and β (since these parameters occur in the exponent of e). It is possible to solve such a problem by non-linear LS, but the methodology is iterative and often cannot guarantee that the global LS error fit will be obtained.

5/4/2 Using logarithms to form linear models

However, it should be noted that many non-linear functions can be transformed into linear functions. A few simple cases can illustrate the point. Consider

$$W = AB^X. \tag{5.21}$$

Equation (5.21) relates variable W to variable X and a plot of W versus X would be non-linear. Our concern is with the parameters A and B, which appear as a product (therefore not linear) and B is raised to a power other than 1 (therefore not linear). To fit this curve to a set of data pairs (W, X) would require an iterative procedure, unless logarithms are taken of both sides:

$$\log W = \log A + (\log B)X.$$

Substituting $Y = \log W$, $\alpha = \log A$ and $\beta = \log B$ gives

$$Y = \alpha + \beta X. \tag{5.22}$$

Equation (5.22) is now a simple linear relationship since the function is linear in α and β. (It is also linear in X.) Thus we can use simple LS regression on equation (5.22), solve α and β, and then recover A and B via antilogarithms to get the parameter estimates for equation (5.21).

A second example of a non-linear function of parameters is that of Figure 5-17(ii):

$$W = e^{\alpha + \beta X}. \tag{5.23}$$

Taking logarithms to base e of both sides yields

$$\begin{aligned} \log_e W &= (\alpha + \beta X)\log_e e \\ &= \alpha + \beta X \qquad (\text{since } \log_e e = 1). \end{aligned}$$

Substituting $Y = \log_e W$ gives $Y = \alpha + \beta X$ which is now in linear form, so that α and β can be estimated directly. Using these values in equation (5.23) allows W to be predicted (estimated) for any known value of X.

5/4/3 Local regression

Local regression smoothing was discussed in Section 3/4 and used to estimate the trend-cycle of a time series. The same technique can be used for regression to estimate a non-linear relationship.

In linear regression, we fit a straight line $Y = a + bX$. The parameters, a and b, are found by minimizing the sum of squares

$$\sum_{i=1}^{n}(Y_i - a - bX_i)^2.$$

Local regression is a way of fitting a much more flexible curve to the data. Instead of fitting a straight line to the entire data set, we fit a series of straight lines to sections of the data. The resulting curve is our non-linear relationship.

The situation was simpler in Chapter 3 since there the explanatory variable was always time which was equally spaced. Here our explanatory variable could be anything and observations are not always equally spaced.

The estimated curve at the point X is $Y = a + bX$ where a and b are chosen to minimize the weighted sum of squares

weighted sum of squares

$$\sum_{j=1}^{n} w_j(X)(Y_j - a - bX_j)^2. \qquad (5.24)$$

Here $w_j(X)$ represents the weights. Note that there is a different value of a and b for every value of X, and that X may take values other than the observed $X_1, \ldots, X_n$.

To find the values of $w_j(X)$, we first define the distances between X and all the observed X_i. Let $\Delta_j(X) = |X_j - X|$ be the distance from X to X_j. Then we choose the largest distance we wish to include in the calculation. This is called the bandwidth h. The weights are then defined using a weight function. For example, we could use the quartic function

$$w_j(X) = \begin{cases} (1 - (\Delta_j(X)/h)^2)^2 & \text{for } -h < \Delta_j(X) < h; \\ 0 & \text{otherwise.} \end{cases}$$

(The weights must also be scaled so that they sum to one.) This gives positive weight to the points with X_i value no more than h from X and zero weights elsewhere. The points closest to X receive the largest weights.

The calculation for the value of the curve at $X = 700$ is shown in Figure 5-18. The steps involved are as follows.

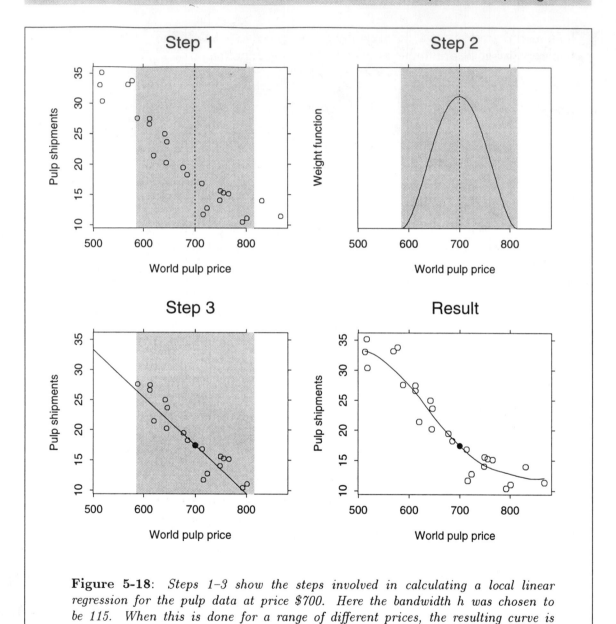

Figure 5-18: *Steps 1–3 show the steps involved in calculating a local linear regression for the pulp data at price $700. Here the bandwidth h was chosen to be 115. When this is done for a range of different prices, the resulting curve is shown at lower right.*

Step 1 The bandwidth to be used in the weighted regression was chosen to be $h = 115$. The shaded area, centered at $X = 700$, shows all points with X_i value within 115 from 700 (i.e., between 585 and 815). Eighteen points fall within this range.

Step 2 The observations are assigned weights using the weight function shown in the upper right panel. The function has a maximum at $X = 700$; the observations with price close to 700 receive the largest weights and observations with price further away receive smaller weights. The weights become zero at the boundaries of the shaded region. Observations outside the shaded region receive zero weights, so they are excluded from the calculation.

Step 3 A line is fitted to the data using weighted least squares with the values of a and b chosen to minimize (5.24). The fit is shown in the lower left panel. The weights determine the influence each observation has on the fitting of the line. The estimate of the relationship at $X = 700$ is shown by the filled circle.

The same calculations are carried out for many different values of X. The number of points included in the calculation will vary with X. The resulting estimates are joined together to form the line shown in the lower right panel.

One parameter must be selected before fitting a local regression, the bandwidth (or smoothing parameter) h. This is chosen in the same way as the smoothing parameter for estimating a trend-cycle. The goal is to choose h to produce a relationship which is as smooth as possible without distorting the underlying pattern in the data. In this example, $h = 115$ is a good choice that appears to follow the non-linear relationship without undue wiggles.

Appendix 5-A
Determining the values of a and b

Assume there are n pairs of data points denoted by

$$(X_1, Y_1), \ldots, (X_n, Y_n).$$

Then the regression equation $\hat{Y}_i = a + bX_i$ can be estimated so as to minimize the sum of the squared deviations.

Defining $e_i = Y_i - \hat{Y}_i$, the sum of squared deviations is

$$\sum_{i=1}^{n} e_i^2 = \sum_{i=1}^{n}(Y_i - \hat{Y}_i)^2 = \sum_{i=1}^{n}(Y_i - a - bX_i)^2.$$

Applying calculus,

$$\frac{\partial \sum e_i^2}{\partial a} = -2\sum(Y_i - a - bX_i) = 0 \qquad (5.25)$$

$$\frac{\partial \sum e_i^2}{\partial b} = -2\sum X_i(Y_i - a - bX_i) = 0. \qquad (5.26)$$

From (5.25)

$$-\sum Y_i + na + b\sum X_i = 0$$

and so

$$a = \frac{1}{n}\left(\sum Y_i - b\sum X_i\right) = \bar{Y} - b\bar{X}. \qquad (5.27)$$

From (5.26)

$$-\sum X_i Y_i + a\sum X_i + b\sum X_i^2 = 0. \qquad (5.28)$$

Substituting the value of a from (5.27) into (5.28) and solving for b yields

$$b = \frac{n\sum X_i Y_i - \sum X_i \sum Y_i}{n\sum X_i^2 - (\sum X_i)^2}. \qquad (5.29)$$

After some algebraic manipulation, this can be shown to be equivalent to

$$b = \frac{\sum(X_i - \bar{X})(Y_i - \bar{Y})}{\sum(X_i - \bar{X})^2} \qquad (5.30)$$

Thus, the values of a and b in (5.27) and (5.30) correspond to the points where the first derivatives of (5.25) and (5.26) are zero; that is, where the sum of the squared errors is at a minimum.

Since the value of b is known through (5.30), it can be substituted into (5.27) to get a. The solution point for a and b is indeed where $\sum e_i^2$ is at a minimum, as can be verified by computing the second derivatives, and showing that

$$\frac{\partial^2 \sum e_i^2}{\partial a^2} > 0 \qquad \text{and} \qquad \frac{\partial^2 \sum e_i^2}{\partial b^2} > 0.$$

References and selected bibliography

CLEVELAND, W.S. (1993) *Visualizing data*, Summit, N.J.: Hobart Press.

INTRILIGATOR, M.D., R.G. BODKIN and C. HSIAO (1996) *Econometric models, techniques, and applications*, 2nd ed., Englewood Cliffs, N.J.: Prentice-Hall.

JOHNSTON, J (1984) *Econometric methods*, 3rd ed., New York: McGraw-Hill.

MENDENHALL, W. and T. SINCICH (1996) *A second course in statistics: regression analysis*, 5th ed., Englewood Cliffs, N.J.: Prentice Hall.

PINDYCK, R.S., and D.L. RUBENFELD (1991) *Econometric models and economic forecasts*, 3rd ed., New York: McGraw-Hill.

"Regression as a Forecasting Aid" (1973) *Boston: Intercollegiate Case Clearing House*, 9-173-147.

SPURR, W.A., and C.P. BONINI (1967) *Statistical analysis for business decisions*, Homewood, Ill.: Irwin.

WONNACOTT, T.H. and R.J. WONNACOTT (1990) *Introductory statistics for business and economics*, 4th ed., New York: John Wiley & Sons.

Exercises

5.1 (a) Below are three scatterplots. Guess whether the correlation is closest to ± 0.2, ± 0.7, or ± 1.

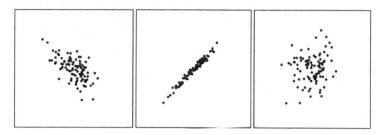

(b) If the correlation coefficient is -0.75, below-average values of one variable tend to be associated with below-average values of the other variable. True or false? Explain.

(c) A study finds an association between the number of new houses built and average weekly earnings (AWE). Should you conclude that AWE causes new houses? Or can you explain the association between AWE and new houses in some other way?

(d) A positive correlation between inflation and unemployment is observed. Does this indicate a causal connection or can it be explained in some other way?

(e) A survey in 1960 showed a correlation of $r = -0.3$ between age and educational level for persons aged over 25. How can you explain the negative correlation?

5.2 Suppose the following data represent the total costs and the number of units produced by a company.

Total Cost	Y	25	11	34	23	32
Units Produced	X	5	2	8	4	6

(a) Determine the linear regression line relating Y to X.

(b) Compute the F statistic and its associated P-value, and the 95% confidence intervals for the slope and intercept.

(c) Calculate r_{XY}, $r_{Y\hat{Y}}$, and R^2. Check that $r_{XY} = r_{Y\hat{Y}}$ and $R^2 = r_{Y\hat{Y}}^2$.

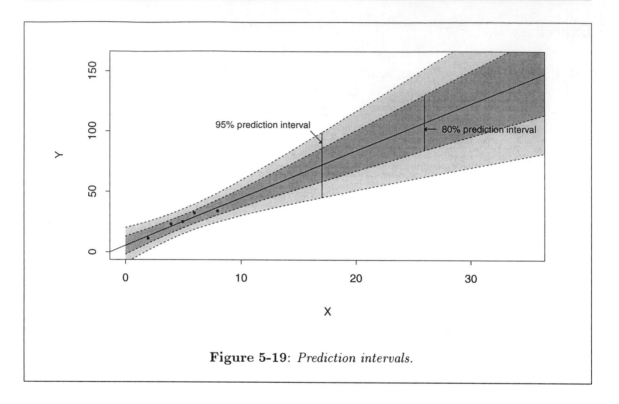

Figure 5-19: *Prediction intervals.*

(d) Figure 5-19 shows the prediction intervals corresponding to the above data. Interpret the meaning of the different lines.

5.3 Skin cancer rates have been steadily increasing over recent years. It is thought that this may be due to ozone depletion. The following data are ozone depletion rates in various locations and the rates of melanoma (a form of skin cancer) in these locations.

Ozone dep (%)	5	7	13	14	17	20	26	30	34	39	44
Melanoma (%)	1	1	3	4	6	5	6	8	7	10	9

(a) Plot melanoma against ozone depletion and fit a straight line regression model to the data.

(b) Plot the residuals from your regression against ozone depletion. What does this say about the fitted model?

(c) What percentage of the variation in rates of melanoma is explained by the regression relationship?

(d) In 1993, scientists discovered that 40% of ozone was depleted in the region of Hamburg, Germany. What would you expect to be the rate of melanoma in this area? Give a prediction interval.

(e) Explain the assumptions and limitations in your prediction. What other factors may play a role?

5.4 Data on the test scores of various workers and their subsequent production ratings are shown in the table below.

Worker	Test score X	Production rating Y	Worker	Test score X	Production rating Y
A	53	45	K	54	59
B	36	43	L	73	77
C	88	89	M	65	56
D	84	79	N	29	28
E	86	84	O	52	51
F	64	66	P	22	27
G	45	49	Q	76	76
H	48	48	R	32	34
I	39	43	S	51	60
J	67	76	T	37	32

Table 5-6: *Scores on manual dexterity test and production ratings for 20 workers.*

(a) Plot these data on a graph with test score as the X-axis and production rating as the Y-axis.

(b) Compute the coefficients of the linear regression of Y on X, and examine the significance of the relationship.

(c) If a test score was 80, what would be your forecast of the production rating? What is the standard error of this forecast?

(d) Determine the 95% confidence interval for the slope coefficient in the regression equation.

(e) Determine the 95% prediction interval for the Y values corresponding to the X values of 20, 40, 60, and 80. If possible, construct a graph similar to that in Figure 5-19.

5.5 Electricity consumption was recorded for a small town on 12 randomly chosen days. The following maximum temperatures (degrees Celsius) and consumption (megawatt-hours) were recorded for each day.

Day	1	2	3	4	5	6	7	8	9	10	11	12
Mwh	16.3	16.8	15.5	18.2	15.2	17.5	19.8	19.0	17.5	16.0	19.6	18.0
temp	29.3	21.7	23.7	10.4	29.7	11.9	9.0	23.4	17.8	30.0	8.6	11.8

(a) Plot the data and find the regression model for Mwh with temperature as an explanatory variable. Why is there a negative relationship?

(b) Find the correlation coefficient, r.

(c) Produce a residual plot. Is the model adequate? Are there any outliers or influential observations?

(d) Use the model to predict the electricity consumption that you would expect for a day with maximum temperature 10° and a day with maximum temperature 35°. Do you believe these predictions?

5.6 Figure 5-8 (p. 198) presents the King Kong data set and shows how strong the influence of one outlier can be in determining the correlation coefficient.

(a) Imagine that the King Kong data added to the 20 normal gorillas were $H = 130$ and $W = 45$ (a very skinny King Kong!) and recompute r_{HW}.

(b) Imagine that the King Kong data were $H = 40$ and $W = 150$ (a short fat King Kong!) and recompute r_{HW}.

(c) What can you conclude generally about the impact of such outliers on r?

5.7 Table 5-7 gives the winning times (in seconds) for the men's 400 meters final in each Olympic Games from 1896 to 1996.

(a) Plot the winning time against the year. Describe the main features of the scatterplot.

(b) Fit a regression line to the data. Obviously the winning times have been decreasing, but at what *average* rate per year?

(c) Plot the residuals against the year. What does this indicate about the suitability of the fitted line?

1896	54.2	1924	47.6	1956	46.7	1980	44.60
1900	49.4	1928	47.8	1960	44.9	1984	44.27
1904	49.2	1932	46.2	1964	45.1	1988	43.87
1908	50.0	1936	46.5	1968	43.8	1992	43.50
1912	48.2	1948	46.2	1972	44.66	1996	43.49
1920	49.6	1952	45.9	1976	44.26		

Table 5-7: *Winning times (in seconds) for the men's 400 meters final in each Olympic Games from 1896 to 1996.*

(d) Predict the winning time for the men's 400 meters final in the 2000 Olympics. Give a prediction interval for your forecast. What assumptions have you made in these calculations?

5.8 The data in Table 5-8 concern the monthly sales figures of a shop which opened in January 1987 and sells gifts, souvenirs, and novelties. The shop is situated on the wharf at a beach resort town in Queensland, Australia. The sales volume varies with the seasonal population of tourists. There is a large influx of visitors to the town at Christmas and for the local surfing festival, held every March since 1988. Over time, the shop has expanded its premises, range of products, and staff.

(a) Produce a time plot of the data and describe the patterns in the graph. Identify any unusual or unexpected fluctuations in the time series.

(b) Explain why it is necessary to take logarithms of these data before fitting a model.

(c) Calculate total sales each year and find the logarithms of these sales. Plot these against the year and fit a linear regression line to these data.

(d) Use your regression model to predict the logarithm of the total annual sales for 1994, 1995, and 1996. Produce prediction intervals for each of your forecasts.

(e) Transform your predictions and intervals to obtain predictions and intervals for the raw data.

	1987	1988	1989	1990	1991	1992	1993
Jan	1664.81	2499.81	4717.02	5921.10	4826.64	7615.03	10243.24
Feb	2397.53	5198.24	5702.63	5814.58	6470.23	9849.69	11266.88
Mar	2840.71	7225.14	9957.58	12421.25	9638.77	14558.40	21826.84
Apr	3547.29	4806.03	5304.78	6369.77	8821.17	11587.33	17357.33
May	3752.96	5900.88	6492.43	7609.12	8722.37	9332.56	15997.79
Jun	3714.74	4951.34	6630.80	7224.75	10209.48	13082.09	18601.53
Jul	4349.61	6179.12	7349.62	8121.22	11276.55	16732.78	26155.15
Aug	3566.34	4752.15	8176.62	7979.25	12552.22	19888.61	28586.52
Sep	5021.82	5496.43	8573.17	8093.06	11637.39	23933.38	30505.41
Oct	6423.48	5835.10	9690.50	8476.70	13606.89	25391.35	30821.33
Nov	7600.60	12600.08	15151.84	17914.66	21822.11	36024.80	46634.38
Dec	19756.21	28541.72	34061.01	30114.41	45060.69	80721.71	104660.67

Table 5-8: *Monthly sales figures for a souvenir shop on the wharf at a beach resort town in Queensland, Australia.*

(f) Consider how you might split each annual forecast into monthly forecasts of sales, allowing for the seasonal pattern in sales volume.

5.9 Table 5-9 shows data from poultry farmers on the percentage mortality of their birds. The farmers use two different types of bird denoted here by Type A and Type B. They are concerned that the Type B birds have a higher mortality than the Type A birds.

(a) Produce a scatterplot of the two variables. Fit a linear regression model to the data with the percentage of Type A birds as the explanatory variable and the percentage mortality as the forecast variable. Show the fitted line on your graph.

(b) Use a t-test to see if the slope of the line is significantly different from zero. Also give a 95% confidence interval for the slope coefficient. Are the farmers' concerns justified?

(c) What is the expected percentage mortality for a farmer using all Type A birds? Give a prediction interval for your answer. Repeat for a farmer using all Type B birds.

X	Y	X	Y	X	Y	X	Y	X	Y	X	Y
75.1	4.87	75.5	6.86	83.6	7.97	42.8	4.68	100.00	3.87	64.9	5.34
86.5	6.56	100.0	4.97	100.0	6.72	100.0	6.97	100.00	6.90	100.0	5.09
72.1	4.84	100.0	7.65	89.6	5.83	100.0	5.25	64.54	7.76	100.0	4.22
89.8	4.87	72.4	4.17	100.0	6.84	100.0	8.86	100.00	7.69	100.0	6.39
80.2	4.07	80.9	6.54	100.0	4.36	100.0	7.34	94.62	7.86	100.0	5.08
75.6	4.16	77.6	3.31	100.0	6.51	100.0	4.15	100.00	8.93	100.0	8.02
78.2	3.50	100.0	5.03	63.1	3.81	100.0	5.06	37.5	7.79	100.0	6.93
86.9	7.11	84.9	6.70	100.0	4.47	65.4	3.88	100.0	6.09	65.9	4.38
60.0	8.89	79.2	5.07	100.0	5.68	63.5	3.80	100.0	11.26	100.0	8.10
93.1	4.68	85.6	4.82	100.0	4.08	85.6	5.90	100.0	14.96	100.0	11.18
83.5	5.62	96.9	7.40	100.0	3.58	78.18	6.20	100.0	5.32	100.0	3.72
73.3	3.98	87.0	5.56	59.1	5.20	63.30	5.70	100.0	5.07	100.0	4.33
80.4	4.84	36.6	3.39	100.0	5.42	74.76	8.36	100.0	4.82	100.0	3.77
85.0	4.07	100.0	4.21	68.9	3.72	33.89	5.80	100.0	5.18	100.0	4.86
60.2	4.30	50.0	3.24	100.0	5.81	86.65	4.85	100.0	5.03	100.0	6.04
60.1	3.62	95.5	3.62	100.0	4.55	64.65	5.58	100.0	5.80	95.0	4.87
86.5	8.35	100.0	5.68	100.0	6.21	100.00	7.62	100.0	7.03	66.7	4.31
78.2	4.55	100.0	4.46	100.0	8.44	78.81	11.45	100.0	4.63	53.3	4.25
64.8	6.06	100.0	4.43	100.0	5.04	89.75	3.86	92.7	4.85	98.2	5.89
77.6	9.52	100.0	3.22	0.0	3.92	69.61	6.32	100.0	7.23	100.0	5.87
57.4	5.40	100.0	4.42	100.0	3.72	100.00	4.86	100.0	8.15	100.0	7.04
92.3	4.75	100.0	7.08	100.0	4.44	68.25	5.58	100.0	5.60	64.9	4.73
81.4	3.73	100.0	5.04	100.0	4.39	90.61	4.97	100.0	4.77	100.0	7.47
72.1	4.05	100.0	7.58	100.0	6.17	100.00	4.64	100.0	4.87	70.1	7.96
70.8	3.86	100.0	4.73	100.0	5.41	2.72	6.29	100.0	5.74	100	8.92
79.9	6.65	100.0	5.24	100.0	7.63	100.00	4.84	100.0	6.98	100	6.65

Table 5-9: *Mortality data for 156 Victorian poultry farms collected in the period August 1995–July 1996. The percentage mortality (birds that died during breeding period) is denoted by Y and the percentage of Type A birds is given by X.*

(d) What proportion of variation in mortality can be ascribed to bird type?

(e) One poultry farmer tells you that he tends to use higher proportions of Type A birds in summer because they are better adapted to the Australian heat. How does this information alter your interpretation of the results?

City	Average price (cents per thousand cubic feet)	Consumption per customer (thousand cubic feet)
Amarillo	30	134
Borger	31	112
Dalhart	37	136
Shamrock	42	109
Royalty	43	105
Texarkana	45	87
Corpus Christi	50	56
Palestine	54	43
Marshall	54	77
Iowa Park	57	35
Palo Pinto	58	65
Millsap	58	56
Memphis	60	58
Granger	73	55
Llano	88	49
Brownsville	89	39
Mercedes	92	36
Karnes City	97	46
Mathis	100	40
La Pryor	102	42

Table 5-10: *Price and per capita consumption of natural gas in 20 towns in Texas.*

5.10 Table 5-10 shows a data set consisting of the demand for natural gas and the price of natural gas for 20 towns in Texas in 1969.

(a) Are these cross-sectional or time series data?

(b) Plot these data on a graph with consumption as the Y-axis and price as the X-axis.

(c) The data are clearly not linear. Two possible non-linear models for the data are given below

exponential model

piecewise linear model

$$Y_i = \exp(a + bX_i + e_i)$$

$$Y_i = \begin{cases} a_1 + b_1 X_i + e_i & \text{when } X_i \leq 60 \\ a_2 + b_2 X_i + e_i & \text{when } X_i > 60. \end{cases}$$

The second model divides the data into two sections, depending on whether the price is above or below 60 cents per 1,000 cubic feet. The parameters a_1, a_2, b_1, b_2 can be estimated by simply fitting a linear regression to each of the two groups of data.

Can you explain why the slope of the fitted line should change with X_i?

(d) Fit the two models and find the coefficients, and residual variance in each case. For the first model, use (5.15) to estimate the residual variance. But for the second model, because there are four parameters, the residual degrees of freedom is $n - 4$. So the residual variance σ_ε^2 can be estimated using the following equation (similar to (5.15))

$$s_e^2 = \frac{1}{n-4} \sum_{i=1}^{n} e_i^2.$$

(e) For each model, find the value of R^2 and produce a residual plot. Comment on the adequacy of the two models.

(f) If you have access to a suitable computer package, fit a local linear regression to these data. You will need to try several bandwidths and select the one which looks most appropriate. What does the fitted curve suggest about the two models?

(g) For prices 40, 60, 80, 100, and 120 cents per 1,000 cubic feet, compute the forecasted per capita demand using the best model of the two above.

(h) Compute the standard errors for each of the forecasts, and 95% prediction intervals. [If using the second model, use $n-4$ degrees of freedom in obtaining the multiplying factor t^*.] Make a graph of these prediction intervals and discuss their interpretation.

6

MULTIPLE REGRESSION

6/1 Introduction to multiple linear regression

Simple regression, as discussed in Chapter 5, is a special case of multiple regression. In multiple regression there is one variable to be predicted (e.g., sales), but there are two or more explanatory variables. The general form of multiple regression is

multiple regression model

$$Y = b_0 + b_1 X_1 + b_2 X_2 + \cdots + b_k X_k + e.$$

Thus if sales were the variable to be forecast, several factors such as GNP, advertising, prices, competition, R&D budget, and time could be tested for their influence on sales by using regression. If it is found that these variables do influence the level of sales, they can be used to predict future values of sales.

Case Study: Mutual savings bank deposits

To illustrate the application of multiple regression in a forecasting context, data from a mutual savings bank study will be examined throughout the chapter. These data refer to a mutual savings bank in a large metropolitan area. In 1993 there was considerable concern within the mutual savings banks because monthly changes in deposits were getting smaller and monthly changes in withdrawals were getting bigger. Thus it was of interest to develop a short-term forecasting model to forecast the changes in end-of-month (EOM) balance over the next few months. Table 6-1 shows 60 monthly observations (February 1988 through January 1993) of end-of-month balance (in column 2) and a plot of these EOM values is shown in Figure 6-1. Note that there was strong growth in early 1991 and then a slowing down of the growth rate since the middle of 1991.

Also presented in Table 6-1 are the composite AAA bond rates (in column 3) and the rates on U.S. Government 3-4 year bonds (in column 4). It was hypothesized that these two rates had an influence on the EOM balance figures in the bank.

Now of interest to the bank was the *change* in the end-of-month balance and so *first differences* of the EOM data in Table 6-1 are shown as column 2 of Table 6-2. These differences, denoted D(EOM) in subsequent equations are plotted in Figure 6-2, and it is clear that the bank was facing a volatile situation in the last two years or so.

(1) Month	(2) (EOM)	(3) (AAA)	(4) (3-4)	(1) Month	(2) (EOM)	(3) (AAA)	(4) (3-4)
1	360.071	5.94	5.31	31	380.119	8.05	7.46
2	361.217	6.00	5.60	32	382.288	7.94	7.09
3	358.774	6.08	5.49	33	383.270	7.88	6.82
4	360.271	6.17	5.80	34	387.978	7.79	6.22
5	360.139	6.14	5.61	35	394.041	7.41	5.61
6	362.164	6.09	5.28	36	403.423	7.18	5.48
7	362.901	5.87	5.19	37	412.727	7.15	4.78
8	361.878	5.84	5.18	38	423.417	7.27	4.14
9	360.922	5.99	5.30	39	429.948	7.37	4.64
10	361.307	6.12	5.23	40	437.821	7.54	5.52
11	362.290	6.42	5.64	41	441.703	7.58	5.95
12	367.382	6.48	5.62	42	446.663	7.62	6.20
13	371.031	6.52	5.67	43	447.964	7.58	6.03
14	373.734	6.64	5.83	44	449.118	7.48	5.60
15	373.463	6.75	5.53	45	449.234	7.35	5.26
16	375.518	6.73	5.76	46	454.162	7.19	4.96
17	374.804	6.89	6.09	47	456.692	7.19	5.28
18	375.457	6.98	6.52	48	465.117	7.11	5.37
19	375.423	6.98	6.68	49	470.408	7.16	5.53
20	374.365	7.10	7.07	50	475.600	7.22	5.72
21	372.314	7.19	7.12	51	475.857	7.36	6.04
22	373.765	7.29	7.25	52	480.259	7.34	5.66
23	372.776	7.65	7.85	53	483.432	7.30	5.75
24	374.134	7.75	8.02	54	488.536	7.30	5.82
25	374.880	7.72	7.87	55	493.182	7.27	5.90
26	376.735	7.67	7.14	56	494.242	7.30	6.11
27	374.841	7.66	7.20	57	493.484	7.31	6.05
28	375.622	7.89	7.59	58	498.186	7.26	5.98
29	375.461	8.14	7.74	59	500.064	7.24	6.00
30	377.694	8.21	7.51	60	506.684	7.25	6.24

Table 6-1: *Bank data: end-of-month balance (in thousands of dollars), AAA bond rates, and rates for 3-4 year government bond issues over the period February 1988 through January 1993.*

The challenge to the forecaster is to forecast these rapidly changing EOM values.

In preparation for some of the regression analyses to be done in this chapter, Table 6-2 designates D(EOM) as Y, the forecast variable, and shows three explanatory variables X_1, X_2, and X_3. Variable X_1 is

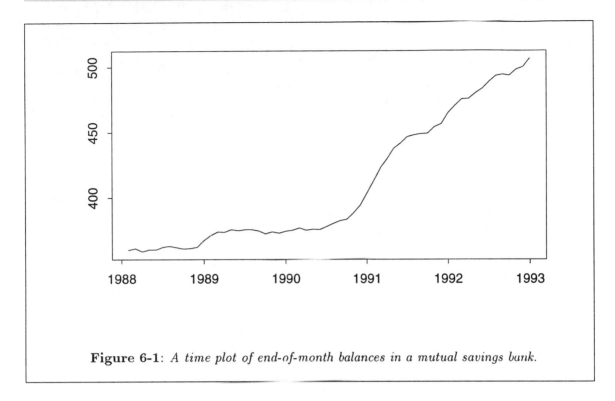

Figure 6-1: *A time plot of end-of-month balances in a mutual savings bank.*

the AAA bond rates from Table 6-1, but they are now shown *leading* the D(EOM) values. Similarly, variable X_2 refers to the rates on 3-4 year government bonds and they are shown *leading* the D(EOM) values by one month. Finally, variable X_3 refers to the first differences of the 3-4 year government bond rates, and the timing for this variable *coincides* with that of the D(EOM) variable.

Referring to the numbers in the first row of Table 6-2, they are explained as follows:

$$1.146 = (\text{EOM balance Mar. 1988}) - (\text{EOM balance Feb. 1988})$$
$$5.94 = \text{AAA bond rate for Feb. 1988}$$
$$5.31 = \text{3-4 year government bond rate for Feb. 1988}$$
$$0.29 = (\text{3-4 rate for Mar. 1988}) - (\text{3-4 rate for Feb. 1988})$$

(Note that the particular choice of these explanatory variables is not arbitrary, but rather based on an extensive analysis that will not be presented in detail here.)

For the purpose of illustration in this chapter, the last six rows

t Month	Y D(EOM)	X_1 (AAA)	X_2 (3-4)	X_3 D(3-4)	t Month	Y D(EOM)	X_1 (AAA)	X_2 (3-4)	X_3 D(3-4)
1	1.146	5.94	5.31	0.29	31	2.169	8.05	7.46	−0.37
2	−2.443	6.00	5.60	−0.11	32	0.982	7.94	7.09	−0.27
3	1.497	6.08	5.49	0.31	33	4.708	7.88	6.82	−0.60
4	−0.132	6.17	5.80	−0.19	34	6.063	7.79	6.22	−0.61
5	2.025	6.14	5.61	−0.33	35	9.382	7.41	5.61	−0.13
6	0.737	6.09	5.28	−0.09	36	9.304	7.18	5.48	−0.70
7	−1.023	5.87	5.19	−0.01	37	10.690	7.15	4.78	−0.64
8	−0.956	5.84	5.18	0.12	38	6.531	7.27	4.14	0.50
9	0.385	5.99	5.30	−0.07	39	7.873	7.37	4.64	0.88
10	0.983	6.12	5.23	0.41	40	3.882	7.54	5.52	0.43
11	5.092	6.42	5.64	−0.02	41	4.960	7.58	5.95	0.25
12	3.649	6.48	5.62	0.05	42	1.301	7.62	6.20	−0.17
13	2.703	6.52	5.67	0.16	43	1.154	7.58	6.03	−0.43
14	−0.271	6.64	5.83	−0.30	44	0.116	7.48	5.60	−0.34
15	2.055	6.75	5.53	0.23	45	4.928	7.35	5.26	−0.30
16	−0.714	6.73	5.76	0.33	46	2.530	7.19	4.96	0.32
17	0.653	6.89	6.09	0.43	47	8.425	7.19	5.28	0.09
18	−0.034	6.98	6.52	0.16	48	5.291	7.11	5.37	0.16
19	−1.058	6.98	6.68	0.39	49	5.192	7.16	5.53	0.19
20	−2.051	7.10	7.07	0.05	50	0.257	7.22	5.72	0.32
21	1.451	7.19	7.12	0.13	51	4.402	7.36	6.04	−0.38
22	−0.989	7.29	7.25	0.60	52	3.173	7.34	5.66	0.09
23	1.358	7.65	7.85	0.17	53	5.104	7.30	5.75	0.07
24	0.746	7.75	8.02	−0.15	54	4.646	7.30	5.82	0.08
25	1.855	7.72	7.87	−0.73	55	1.060	7.27	5.90	0.21
26	−1.894	7.67	7.14	0.06	56	−0.758	7.30	6.11	−0.06
27	0.781	7.66	7.20	0.39	57	4.702	7.31	6.05	−0.07
28	−0.161	7.89	7.59	0.15	58	1.878	7.26	5.98	0.02
29	2.233	8.14	7.74	−0.23	59	6.620	7.24	6.00	0.24
30	2.425	8.21	7.51	−0.05					

Table 6-2: *Bank data: monthly changes in balance as forecast variable and three explanatory variables. (Data for months 54–59 to be ignored in all analyses and then used to check forecasts.)*

in Table 6-2 will be ignored in all the analyses that follow, so that they may be used to examine the accuracy of the various forecasting models to be employed. By the end of the chapter we will forecast the D(EOM) figures for periods 54–59, and will be able to compare them with the known figures not used in developing our regression model.

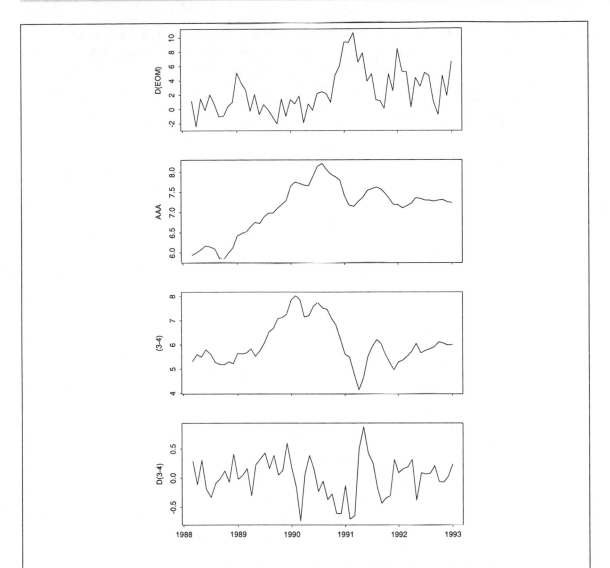

Figure 6-2: *(a) A time plot of the monthly change of end-of-month balances at a mutual savings bank. (b) A time plot of AAA bond rates. (c) A time plot of 3-4 year government bond issues. (d) A time plot of the monthly change in 3-4 year government bond issues. All series are shown over the period February 1988 through January 1993.*

The bank could forecast Y (the D(EOM) variable) on the basis of X_1 alone, or on the basis of a combination of the X_1, X_2, and X_3 variables shown in columns 3, 4, and 5. So Y, the forecast variable, is a function of one or more of the explanatory variables (also called regressors or independent variables). Although several different forms of the function could be written to designate the relationships among these variables, a straightforward one that is linear and additive is

$$Y = b_0 + b_1 X_1 + b_2 X_2 + b_3 X_3 + e, \qquad (6.1)$$

$$\begin{aligned}
\text{where } Y &= \text{D(EOM)}, \\
X_1 &= \text{AAA bond rates}, \\
X_2 &= \text{3-4 rates}, \\
X_3 &= \text{D(3-4) year rates}, \\
e &= \text{error term}.
\end{aligned}$$

From equation (6.1) it can readily be seen that if two of the X variables were omitted, the equation would be like those handled previously with simple linear regression (Chapter 5). Just as the method of least squares was used in Chapter 5 to estimate the coefficients b_0 and b_1 in simple regression, so it may be used to estimate b_0, b_1, b_2, and b_3 in the equation above.

Time plots of each of the variables are given in Figure 6-2. These show the four variables individually as they move through time. Notice how some of the major peaks and troughs line up, implying that the variables may be related.

Scatterplots of each combination of variables are given in Figure 6-3. These enable us to visualize the relationship between each pair of variables. Each panel shows a scatterplot of one of the four variables against another of the four variables. The variable on the vertical axis is the variable named in that row; the variable on the horizontal axis is the variable named in that column. So, for example, the panel in the top row and second column is a plot of D(EOM) against AAA. Similarly, the panel in the second row and third column is a plot scatterplot matrix of AAA against (3–4). This figure is known as a *scatterplot matrix* and is a very useful way of visualizing the relationships between the variables.

Note that the mirror image of each plot above the diagonal is given below the diagonal. For example, the plot of D(EOM) against AAA given in the top row and second column is mirrored in the second row and first column with a plot of AAA against D(EOM).

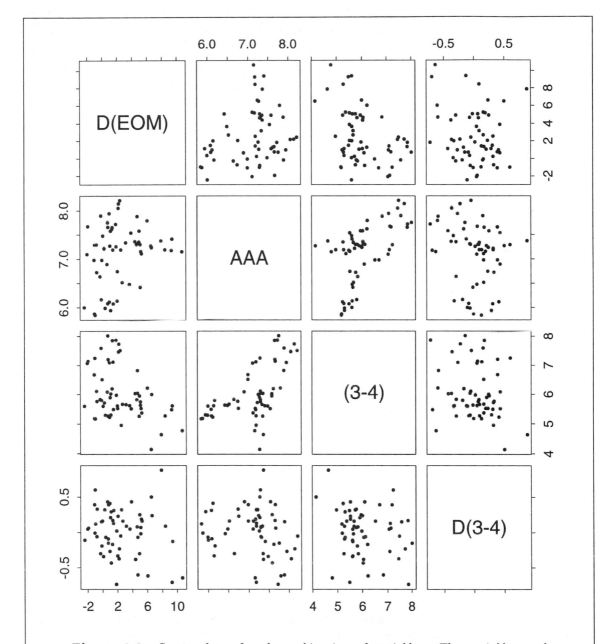

Figure 6-3: *Scatterplots of each combination of variables. The variable on the vertical axis is the variable named in that row; the variable on the horizontal axis is the variable named in that column. This scatterplot matrix is a very useful way of visualizing the relationships between each pair of variables.*

collinearity

Figure 6-3 shows that there is a weak linear relationship between D(EOM) and each of the other variables. It also shows that two of the explanatory variables, AAA and (3-4), are related linearly. This phenomenon is known as *collinearity* and means it may be difficult to distinguish the effect of AAA and (3-4) on D(EOM).

6/1/1 Multiple regression model: theory and practice

In Section 5/3/1, simple linear regression was presented as a formal statistical model. We do so now for the general multiple linear regression model.

Regression model in theory

$$Y_i = \boxed{\beta_0 + \beta_1 X_{1,i} + \cdots + \beta_k X_{k,i}} + \varepsilon_i, \qquad (6.2)$$

where $Y_i, X_{1,i}, \ldots, X_{k,i}$ represent the ith observations of each of the variables $Y, X_1, \ldots, X_k$ respectively, $\beta_0, \beta_1, \ldots, \beta_k$ are fixed (but unknown) parameters and ε_i is a random variable that is normally distributed with mean zero and having a variance σ_ε^2.

Note in (6.2) that the form of the regression model (i.e., the part enclosed by the small rectangle) is linear in the coefficients. The exponent of every coefficient is 1—that is, linear—and this means that estimates of the coefficients can be obtained by direct calculation using the least squares (LS) method. The shape of the function relating Y to the several X variables is no longer quite so easy to describe. If there is only one X variable in (6.2), then the shape of the underlying function is a straight line. If there are two variables, then Y is mapped into a plane (above the axes formed by the two X variables). If there are more than two explanatory variables in (6.2), then we say Y is mapped into a hyperplane (meaning a higher dimensional surface).

assumptions

As with simple regression, there are several assumptions made about X_i and ε_i which are important:

1. The explanatory variables $X_1, \ldots, X_k$ take values which are assumed to be either fixed numbers (measured without error), or they are random but uncorrelated with the error terms ε_i. In either case, the values of X_j $(j = 1, 2, \ldots, k)$ must not be all the same.

2. The error terms ε_i are uncorrelated with one another.

3. The error terms ε_i all have mean zero and variance σ_ε^2, and have a normal distribution.

These assumptions are discussed in more detail in Section 6/1/6.

Now in practice, the task of regression modeling is to estimate the unknown parameters of the model (6.2), namely, $\beta_0, \beta_1, \ldots, \beta_k$, and σ_ε^2. From a known data set (such as in Table 6-2), the LS procedure can be applied to determine $b_0, b_1, \ldots, b_k$ and an estimate of σ_ε^2. Thus the pragmatic form of the statistical regression model is as follows.

Regression model in practice

$$Y_i = \boxed{b_0 + b_1 X_{1,i} + \cdots + b_k X_{k,i}} + e_i, \qquad (6.3)$$

for $i = 1, 2, \ldots, n$, where $b_0, b_1, \ldots, b_k$ are estimates of $\beta_0, \beta_1, \ldots, \beta_k$ and are all random variables, and e_i is the estimated error (or residual) for the ith observation and is a random variable. The estimated variance of the errors is denoted by s_c^2.

Note that the coefficients in the model are no longer fixed as they were in (6.2). From sample to sample the b-coefficients fluctuate, giving rise to a statistical family of regression surfaces.

For the bank data in Table 6-2—using only the first 53 rows—the model in equation (6.1) can be solved using least squares to give

$$\hat{Y} = -4.34 + 3.37(X_1) - 2.83(X_2) - 1.96(X_3). \qquad (6.4)$$

Note that a "hat" is used over $\hat{Y}$ to indicate that this is an estimate of Y, not the *observed* Y. This estimate $\hat{Y}$ is based on the three explanatory variables only. The difference between the observed Y and the estimated $\hat{Y}$ tells us something about the "fit" of the model, and this discrepancy is called the residual (or error):

$$e_i = \underset{\underset{\text{(observed)}}{\uparrow}}{Y_i} - \underset{\underset{\substack{\text{(estimated using} \\ \text{regression model)}}}{\uparrow}}{\hat{Y}_i} \qquad \text{residual}$$

6/1/2 Solving for the regression coefficients

A computer program would normally be used to solve for the coefficients in a multiple regression model. However, it is important to get a good understanding of what is behind the method. The practitioner proposes a model for the data; for example,

$$Y_i = \boxed{b_0 + b_1 X_{1,i} + b_2 X_{2,i} + b_3 X_{3,i}} + e_i$$

$$= \boxed{\hat{Y}_i} + e_i.$$

least squares
estimation

The method of least squares is used to find the minimum sum of squares of the error terms—that is, find b_0, b_1, b_2 and b_3 to minimize

$$S = \sum_{i=1}^{n} e_i^2$$

$$= \sum_{i=1}^{n} (Y_i - \hat{Y}_i)^2$$

$$= \sum_{i=1}^{n} (Y_i - b_0 - b_1 X_{1,i} - b_2 X_{2,i} - b_3 X_{3,i})^2.$$

Readers with a calculus background will recognize that this problem is solved by taking partial derivatives of S with respect to each of the unknown coefficients b_0, b_1, b_2, and b_3, setting these derivatives equal to zero, and solving a set of four equations in four unknowns to get estimated values for b_0, b_1, b_2 and b_3.

The solution to the bank data has already been shown in equation (6.4). Consider the first observation vector in Table 6-2:

$$Y_1 = 1.146, \quad X_{1,1} = 5.94, \quad X_{2,1} = 5.31, \quad X_{3,1} = 0.29.$$

$$\text{Then} \quad \hat{Y}_1 = -4.34 + 3.37(5.94) - 2.83(5.31) - 1.96(0.29)$$
$$= 0.086 \quad \text{using (6.4)}$$
$$e_1 = Y_1 - \hat{Y}_1$$
$$= 1.146 - 0.086 = 1.060.$$

We have found the residual (or error) for the first Y value. Proceeding in this manner through all of the first 53 rows of Table 6-2 we can determine the sum of the squared errors to be

$$S = \sum_{i=1}^{53} e_i^2 = 219.60.$$

(1) Period	(2) Y	(3) $\hat{Y}$	(4) $Y - \hat{Y}$	(5) $\hat{Y} - \bar{Y}$	(6) $Y - \bar{Y}$	(7) $(Y - \hat{Y})^2$	(8) $(\hat{Y} - \bar{Y})^2$	(9) $(Y - \bar{Y})^2$
1	1.146	0.086	1.06	−2.34	−1.28	1.12	5.46	1.63
2	−2.443	0.253	−2.70	−2.17	−4.87	7.27	4.71	23.69
3	1.497	0.009	1.49	−2.41	−0.93	2.21	5.83	0.86
4	−0.132	0.417	−0.55	−2.01	−2.56	0.30	4.03	6.53
5	2.025	1.129	0.90	−1.29	−0.40	0.80	1.68	0.16
⋮	⋮	⋮	⋮	⋮	⋮	⋮	⋮	⋮
49	5.192	3.774	1.42	1.35	2.77	2.01	1.82	7.66
50	0.257	3.183	−2.93	0.76	−2.17	8.56	0.58	4.70
51	4.402	4.124	0.28	1.70	1.98	0.08	2.89	3.91
52	3.173	4.209	−1.04	1.79	0.75	1.07	3.19	0.56
53	5.104	3.859	1.25	1.43	2.68	1.55	2.06	7.18
Sums	128.465	128.465	0.00	0.00	0.00	219.60 SSE	280.38 SSR	499.99 SST

Table 6-3: *Bank data: showing the original Y, the fitted $\hat{Y}$, and the residual $(Y - \hat{Y})$. The remaining columns show the calculation of the residual sum of squares and R^2.*

This number is the lowest it can be when Y is regressed linearly on X_1, X_2, and X_3. It is the LS solution for these explanatory variables.

Details of this computation are shown in Table 6-3, along with other information to be used later. Column 2 shows the original Y values, D(EOM). Column 3 gives the $\hat{Y}$ values based on equation (6.4), and column 4 is the list of errors of fit. Note three things: (1) the column sums for columns 2 and 3 are the same—which also indicates that the means of Y and $\hat{Y}$ are the same; (2) the sum of the residuals in column 4 is zero—as it will always be for LS fitting of linear regression models (unless the intercept b_0 is omitted); and (3) because of (1) and (2) above, it will also be true that the sums on columns 5 and 6 will be zero.

6/1/3 Multiple regression and the coefficient of determination

In Table 6-3, column 2 gives the observed Y values and column 3 gives the estimated values $\hat{Y}$, based on the fitted regression model (6.4). The correlation between Y and $\hat{Y}$ can be computed using equation

coefficient of
determination

(5.12) and turns out to be $r_{Y\hat{Y}} = 0.749$. The square of this correlation is called the coefficient of determination:

$$R^2 = r_{Y\hat{Y}}^2 = (0.749)^2 = 0.561.$$

multiple correlation
coefficient

R itself is known as the *multiple correlation* coefficient, and is the correlation between a forecast variable Y and an estimate of Y based on multiple explanatory variables.

To compute R^2 another way, the form is the same as for simple regression:

$$R^2 = \frac{\sum(\hat{Y}_i - \bar{Y})^2}{\sum(Y_i - \bar{Y})^2} = \frac{\text{explained SS}}{\text{total SS}} = \frac{\text{SSR}}{\text{SST}} \qquad (6.5)$$

where SS means sum of squared deviations.

For the bank data, referring to Table 6-3, the R^2 value can be computed using equation (6.5) as follows:

$$R^2 = \frac{280.38}{499.99} = 0.561.$$

As with simple regression, R^2 has a useful interpretation as the proportion of variance accounted for (explained) by the explanatory variables $X_1, X_2, \ldots, X_k$.

6/1/4   The F-test for overall significance

After estimating the coefficients of a regression model to determine the $\hat{Y}$ values, there will be a set of errors of fit—such as $e_i = (Y_i - \hat{Y}_i)$ for the ith observation. Figure 5-9 shows that one way to discuss errors of fit is to partition the discrepancy $(Y_i - \bar{Y})$ into two parts:

$$(Y_i - \bar{Y}) = (Y_i - \hat{Y}_i) + (\hat{Y}_i - \bar{Y}).$$

In Section 5/2/4 it was shown that if such a partition is made for all Y_i values, and if each part in the partition is squared, then the following relation among the sums of squared deviations holds:

sums of squares

$$\sum(Y_i - \bar{Y})^2 \quad = \quad \sum(Y_i - \hat{Y}_i)^2 \quad + \quad \sum(\hat{Y}_i - \bar{Y})^2.$$

$$\begin{array}{ccc} \uparrow & \uparrow & \uparrow \\ \text{total SS} & \text{unexplained SS} & \text{explained SS} \\ \text{(SST)} & \text{(SSE)} & \text{(SSR)} \end{array}$$

Furthermore, the degrees of freedom for this partition satisfy the relation

$$\text{total df} = \text{unexplained df} + \text{explained df.}$$

If we are dealing with k explanatory variables, X_1 through X_k, then there will be $k + 1$ coefficients, b_0 through b_k, and the degrees of freedom for each part of the partition are calculated as follows: degrees of freedom

total:	dfT	$= n - 1$	(no. obsns. -1)
explained:	dfR	$= k$	(no. coefficients -1)
unexplained:	dfE	$= n - k - 1$	(no. obsns. $-$ no. coefficients).

It is now possible to construct an overall F-test to check on the statistical significance of the regression model. Since an F statistic is defined as the ratio of two variances (or "mean squares" as statisticians often call them), we have to convert "sums of squares" to "mean squares" as follows: mean squares

total:	MST	$=$ SST / dfT
explained:	MSR	$=$ SSR / dfR
unexplained:	MSE	$=$ SSE / dfE

The F statistic that tests the significance of the regression model F statistic
is

$$F = \frac{\text{MSR}}{\text{MSE}} = \frac{\sum(\hat{Y} - \bar{Y})^2/k}{\sum(Y - \hat{Y})^2/(n - k - 1)}. \tag{6.6}$$

Note that this F-test is sensitive to the relative strengths of the numerator and denominator. If the unexplained MS (the variance of the errors) is large, then the regression model is not doing well, and F becomes smaller. If the explained MS is large relative to the unexplained MS, then F becomes larger. Looking up an F table, we can make a decision as to the significance of the regression model.

As mentioned in Section 5/3/2 there is a close connection between R^2 and F, so that in the case of multiple regression we can write

$$\boxed{F = \frac{R^2/k}{(1 - R^2)/(n - k - 1)}.} \tag{6.7}$$

Just as with simple regression, computer packages often present the calculation in the form of an analysis of variance (ANOVA) table   ANOVA table
as shown in Table 6-4. Note that R^2 and F are easily obtained from

Source	df	SS	MS	F	P
Regression	dfR = k	SSR	MSR = SSR/dfR	MSR/MSE	P-value
Error	dfE = $n - k - 1$	SSE	MSE = SSE/dfE		
Total	dfT = dfR+dfE	SST = SSR+SSE			

Table 6-4: *Typical analysis of variance (ANOVA) table.*

this table. The F value is given in the column headed **F** and R^2 is simply the ratio SSR/SST.

For the bank problem, the ANOVA table is given below.

Source	df	SS	MS	F	P
Regression	3	280.38	93.46	20.85	0.000
Error	49	219.60	4.48		
Total	52	499.99			

We could also have calculated F using (6.7):

$$F = \frac{(0.561)/3}{(1 - 0.561)/49} = 20.85.$$

P-value

The P-value in the ANOVA table is very small, less than 0.0005. This suggests very strongly that the three variables are accounting for a significant part of the variation in Y. The ANOVA table does not show if all of the three variables are important, or which of the three is most important. But it does show that there is some relationship between D(EOM) and the three variables.

When a computer package does not report the P-value, it is possible to calculate it from an F table using the same procedure as in simple regression. For multiple regression, the F statistic has k degrees of freedom for the numerator and $n-k-1$ degrees of freedom for the denominator.

Looking up the F table for (3, 49) df, it is found that only 0.01 (or 1%) of the area under the F distribution lies to the right of $F = 4.22$. Since the computed F value for the bank data is 20.85, we can conclude that this is a highly significant regression model. That is, the explanatory variables explain a significant amount of the variability in the change in end-of-month deposits at this mutual savings bank. And we can also say that the coefficient of determination (R^2) is highly significant.

6/1/5 Individual coefficients: confidence intervals and t-tests

Before getting into this section it is advisable to appreciate the merits of computing

1. the simple correlation coefficients between all pairs of explanatory variables (i.e., X_1, X_2, ..., X_k);
2. the simple correlation coefficients between the forecast variable Y and each of the X variables in turn; and
3. the coefficient of determination, R^2, for the linear regression model.

The first set of correlations is helpful in selecting appropriate explanatory variables for a regression model (see Section 6/3) and, at a deeper level of analysis, is critical for examining multicollinearity (see Section 6/4). The second set indicates how each explanatory variable, on its own, relates to Y, and R^2 indicates the extent to which a linear combination of the X variables can explain the variability in Y.

After examining the overall significance of the regression model it is sometimes useful to study the significance of individual regression coefficients. There is one very important point to bear in mind.

> A t-test on an individual coefficient is a test of its significance *in the presence of all other explanatory variables.*

So confidence intervals for each coefficient are computed in the presence of the other explanatory variables. Multiple regression makes use of the interdependence of the explanatory variables to model Y. It is improper to treat individual coefficients as if they could stand alone (except in the very special case where all explanatory variables are uncorrelated with each other).

For each regression coefficient b_j we can determine a standard error (a measure of the stability of the coefficient), calculate its confidence interval, and assess its significance in the regression equation. If the particular term has no real effect in the regression equation, then (given the normality and constancy assumptions in the regression model—see Section 6/1/1) it is known that t, defined by the following equation, has a t-distribution with $(n - k - 1)$ df:

t-test

$$t = \frac{b_j}{\text{se}(b_j)}, \qquad\qquad (6.8)$$

$$
\begin{aligned}
\text{where}\quad b_j &= \text{estimated } j\text{th coefficient,}\\
\text{and}\quad \text{se}(b_j) &= \text{standard error of } b_j.
\end{aligned}
$$

Thus, using equation (6.8) for each regression coefficient, we can do a formal statistical test of the significance of that coefficient. This is a test of whether the explanatory variable in question is helping significantly in the prediction of Y—*in the presence of the other explanatory variables.*

In the case of the bank data and the linear regression of D(EOM) on (AAA), (3-4), and D(3-4), the full output from a regression program included the following information:

Term	Coeff.	Value	se of b_j	t	*P*-value
Constant	b_0	−4.3391	3.2590	−1.3314	0.1892
AAA	b_1	3.3722	0.5560	6.0649	0.0000
(3-4)	b_2	−2.8316	0.3895	−7.2694	0.0000
D(3-4)	b_3	−1.9648	0.8627	−2.2773	0.0272

Note that for each estimated coefficient, there is a standard error, a t value, and a P-value. We can use the P-value to assess the effect of each variable.

Consider the coefficient b_1 for the variable (AAA). The P-value is very small indeed—to four decimal places it is essentially zero. From this we conclude that the estimated b_1-coefficient is very significantly different from zero. The (AAA) variable is a significant explanatory variable in the presence of the other two explanatory variables. Similarly, the coefficients b_2 and b_3, for (3-4) and D(3-4), respectively, are highly significant, in the presence of the other two explanatory variables.

Since the overall F-test indicated a significant regression line (in Section 6/1/4), it was to be expected that at least one of the t-tests would also be significant. (However, the converse is not necessarily true.) In the case of the bank data, D(EOM) has a significant relationship to (AAA), (3-4), and D(3-4), but as we will see, there is room for considerable improvement still.

To calculate confidence intervals for the individual coefficients, *confidence intervals* we can use the standard errors given in the table above. Hence, a confidence interval for β_j is

$$\boxed{b_j \pm t^* \text{s.e.}(b_j).}$$

The multiplying factor, t^*, can be obtained from Table B in Appendix III and depends on n (the number of observations used in the regression), k (the number of explanatory variables included), and the level of confidence required. The df (degrees of freedom) of a parameter estimate is $n - k - 1$, the same as the df for the t-test.

For the bank regression, the df $= 53 - 3 - 1 = 49$. The df gives the row of the table and the relevant column is selected on the basis of the level of confidence required. There is no row for 49 df in the table. We can take the row closest to 49 df (i.e., the row for 40 df), or we can interpolate between the 40 df and 60 df rows, or we can use a computer to find the exact value for 49 df. Whichever of these methods we choose will have little impact on the result. In this case, 95% confidence intervals would use $t^* = 2.01$ and 99% confidence intervals would use $t^* = 2.68$ (for 49 df). The following table gives 95% intervals for the regression parameters.

Constant	$-4.34 \pm 2.01(3.26)$	=	[-10.89,	2.21]
AAA	$3.37 \pm 2.01(0.56)$	=	[2.25,	4.49]
(3-4)	$-2.83 \pm 2.01(0.39)$	=	[-3.61,	-2.05]
D(3-4)	$-1.96 \pm 2.01(0.86)$	=	[-3.70,	-0.23]

As with simple regression, there is a direct relationship here between confidence intervals and P-values. If the 95% confidence interval does not contain zero, then the P-value must be less than 0.05. Generally *if the 100γ% confidence interval does not contain zero, the P-value must be less than $1 - \gamma$.*

There are two additional aspects to consider in dealing with tests of individual coefficients. First, the *stability of the regression coefficients* depends upon the intercorrelation among the explanatory variables.

Given two explanatory variables, X_1 and X_2, the higher the correlation between them the more unstable will be the two coefficients (b_1 and b_2) determined for these variables. In the case of more than two explanatory variables the situation is similar but more subtle—in the sense that even without large correlations it is possible to have very unstable coefficients—and Section 6/3 will discuss this matter in more detail.

The second aspect to consider is the *estimated correlations among the regression coefficients themselves.* It will be remembered that in the practical regression model the coefficients b_0 through b_k are all random variables—that is, they fluctuate from sample to sample and have a joint probability distribution. Hence it is possible to determine the correlations among the coefficients. Many computer programs do not automatically provide this information, but it is very helpful. For example, in the previous chapter (Section 5/3/4) it was noted that the slope and the intercept are always going to be correlated because an LS regression line goes through the mean of Y and the mean of X.

In multiple regression, the situation is more complicated, but if, for instance, two coefficients b_3 and b_5 are found to be significantly correlated (positive or negative), then the investigator should be warned that individual t-tests on b_3 and b_5 should not be considered in isolation of each other. The two coefficients are dependent on each other.

Table 6-5 shows the correlations among the explanatory and forecast variables in the bank example. None of the explanatory variables has a particularly high correlation with the Y value D(EOM), and the explanatory variables themselves do not correlate very highly

	Y D(EOM)	X_1 (AAA)	X_2 (3-4)	X_3 D(3-4)
Y = D(EOM)	1.000	0.257	−0.391	−0.195
X_1 = (AAA)	0.257	1.000	0.587	−0.204
X_2 = (3-4)	−0.391	0.587	1.000	−0.201
X_3 = D(3-4)	−0.195	−0.204	−0.201	1.000

Table 6-5: *Bank data: the correlations among the forecast and explanatory variables.*

	b_0	b_1	b_2	b_3
b_0	1.000	−0.799	−0.035	−0.208
b_1	−0.799	1.000	−0.569	0.108
b_2	−0.035	−0.569	1.000	0.103
b_3	−0.208	0.108	0.103	1.000

Table 6-6: *Bank data: the interrelatedness among the regression coefficients.*

($r_{X_1 X_2} = 0.587$ is the biggest). We suspect no multicollinearity problem (see Section 6/4) and the correlations $r_{X_1 Y}$, $r_{X_2 Y}$, and $r_{X_3 Y}$ would tend to suggest that these three explanatory variables together will not be able to explain a lot of the variance in Y. They *do* combine to explain 53% (R^2), it is a significant contribution (F-test), and all three coefficients are significantly different from zero (t-tests), but more can be done.

Finally, Table 6-6 shows how the regression coefficients themselves are interrelated. Note how all three coefficients, b_1, b_2, and b_3, correlate negatively with the constant b_0. There is an analogy here to the simple regression case—tilt a hyperplane "up" and the constant goes "down." Note, too, that b_1 and b_2 correlate −0.569. The variables X_1 and X_2 correlate 0.587 and their coefficients correlate −0.569. Thus it is necessary to interpret these two variables *jointly*. Increase b_1 and there would, in general, be a decrease in b_2, and vice versa. These considerations are obviously very important in forecasting.

6/1/6 The assumptions behind multiple linear regression models

The theoretical regression model described in Section 6/1/1 makes certain assumptions, so that the practical application of such a model requires the user to examine these assumptions in the context of the problem at hand. There are four basic assumptions:

1. model form
2. independence of residuals
3. homoscedasticity
4. normality of residuals.

If each of these assumptions is valid for the data set at hand, then the multiple linear regression model may be a good one, providing useful forecasts. But if the errors show any kind of pattern, then the model is not incorporating all the useful information in the data set.

The full implications of each assumption can only be appreciated in conjunction with a thorough understanding of the statistical theory behind regression, but the following practical points can be made.

model form

1. With regard to "model form," the assumption refers to the form of the relationship between the forecast variable and the explanatory variables. If the assumed form is incorrect, then the forecasts may be inaccurate and the F-test, t-tests, and confidence intervals are not strictly valid any longer. Often a more appropriate model form (e.g., a non-linear model) can be found and the model reestimated.

independence

2. The "independence of residuals" assumption is also tied directly to the validity of the F- and t-tests, R^2, and confidence intervals. If the residuals are not independent, the use of the F- and t-tests and confidence intervals is not strictly valid and the estimates of the coefficients may be unstable. We will examine this assumption in Section 6/2/1. When the independence assumption is violated, it can be corrected using the approach discussed in Section 8/1.

homoscedasticity

3. Homoscedasticity is a word used for the "constant variance" assumption. The regression model assumes that the residuals have the same variance throughout. Once again the impact of this assumption is on the validity of the statistical tests (F and t) and confidence intervals associated with the formal regression model. For many time series (e.g., passenger traffic on airlines, monthly withdrawals at a savings bank) the raw data itself show multiplicative trend and/or seasonality, and if regression models are used in such cases, the equal variance assumption for residuals might well be violated. When this assumption is violated, the problem is called "heteroscedasticity," or changing variance. When the residuals show heteroscedasticity, the problem can often be corrected using a mathematical transformation (see Section 2/6/1).

4. Many regression models assume a normal distribution for the   normal errors
   error term. This makes no difference to the estimates of the
   coefficients, or the ability of the model to forecast. But it
   does affect the F- and t-tests and confidence intervals. This
   is not such a serious assumption in that residuals are the
   result of many unimportant factors acting together to influence
   the forecast variable, and the net effect of such influences is
   often reasonably well modeled by a normal distribution. If the
   assumption is seriously violated, it is inappropriate to do the
   significance testing. Sometimes a mathematical transformation
   (Section 2/6/1) can help in correcting this problem.

One assumption of the regression model that has not been treated
above is the statement that the explanatory variables are fixed—
that is, measured without error. This is patently false in real-world
settings. Econometricians have dealt with this subject in great detail
and the interested reader should pursue the topic in Judge et al.,
(1988).

Apart from the assumption of independent residuals, each of these
assumptions can be examined by producing appropriate plots of
residuals.

Figure 6-4 shows four plots of the residuals after fitting the model

$$D(EOM) = -4.34 + 3.37(AAA) - 2.83(3\text{-}4) - 1.96(D(3\text{-}4)).$$

These plots help examine the linearity and homoscedasticity assumptions.

The bottom right panel of Figure 6-4 shows the residuals (e_i)
against the fitted values ($\hat{Y}_i$). The other panels show the residuals
plotted against the explanatory variables. Each of the plots can be
interpreted in the same way as the residual plot for simple regression
(see Section 5/2/5). The residuals should not be related to the fitted
values or the explanatory variables. So each residual plot should show
scatter in a horizontal band with no values too far from the band and
no patterns such as curvature or increasing spread. All four plots in
Figure 6-4 show no such patterns.

If there is any curvature pattern in one of the plots against an
explanatory variable, it suggests that the relationship between Y and
X variable is non-linear (a violation of the linearity assumption). The

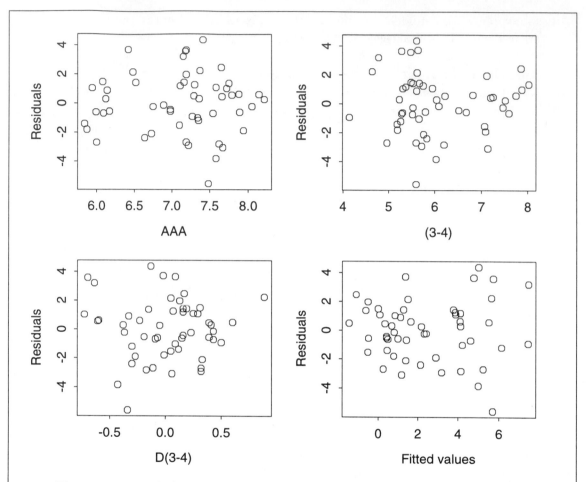

Figure 6-4: *Bank data: plots of the residuals obtained when D(EOM) is regressed against the three explanatory variables AAA, (3-4), and D(3-4). The lower right panel shows the residuals plotted against the fitted values (e_i vs $\hat{Y}_i$). The other plots show the residuals plotted against the explanatory variables (e_i vs $X_{j,i}$).*

plot of residuals against fitted values is to check the assumption of homoscedasticity and to identify large residuals (possible outliers). For example, if the residuals show increasing spread from left to right (i.e., as $\hat{Y}$ increases), then the variance of the residuals is not constant.

It is also useful to plot the residuals against explanatory variables which were *not included* in the model. If such plots show any pattern, it indicates that the variable concerned contains some valuable predictive information and it should be added to the regression model.

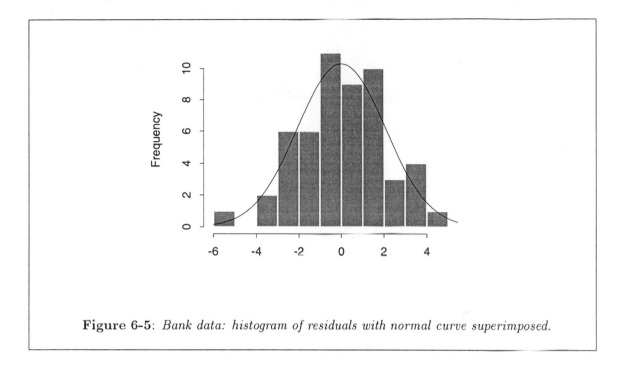

Figure 6-5: *Bank data: histogram of residuals with normal curve superimposed.*

To check the assumption of normality, we can plot a histogram of the residuals. Figure 6-5 shows such a histogram with a normal curve superimposed. The histogram shows the number of residuals obtained within each of the intervals marked on the horizontal axis. The normal curve shows how many observations one would get on average from a normal distribution. In this case, there does not appear to be any problem with the normality assumption.

There is one residual (with value −5.6) lying away from the other values which is seen in the histogram (Figure 6-5) and the residuals plots of Figure 6-4. However, this residual is not sufficiently far from the other values to warrant much close attention.

6/2 Regression with time series

With time series regression there are some additional problems that need to be addressed.

- There is a possible lack of independence in the residuals which needs to be examined (Section 6/2/1).

- We may need to allow for time-related effects such as trend, seasonality, or trading day variation (Section 6/2/2).

- When forecasting the Y variable, we need to first have forecasts for each of the explanatory variables (Section 6/5).

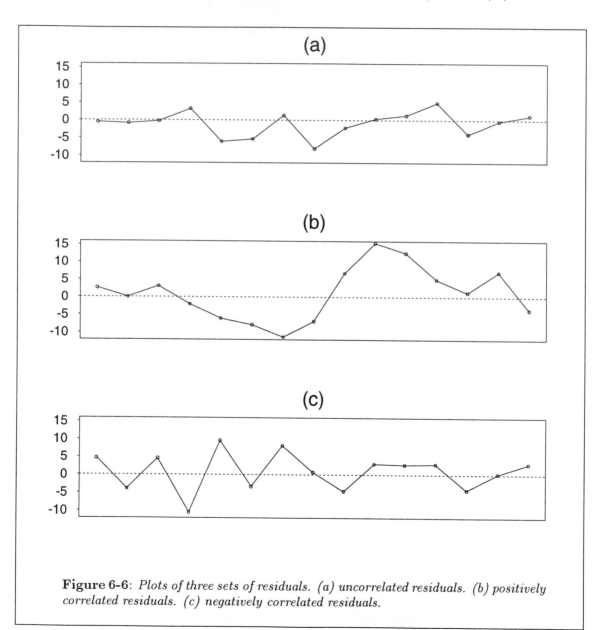

Figure 6-6: *Plots of three sets of residuals. (a) uncorrelated residuals. (b) positively correlated residuals. (c) negatively correlated residuals.*

6/2/1 Checking independence of residuals

Figure 6-6 shows time plots for three series of artificial residuals, only one of which is independent. Panel (a) shows a series of independent (unpatterned) residuals. Note that we may well see "pattern" in Figure 6-6(a), especially when successive points are joined, but this perception of a pattern is clearly stronger for panel (b). In Figure 6-6(b), the errors tend to stay negative longer than expected (if they were truly random) and then stay positive longer than expected. The third set (c) shows another residual pattern—a see-saw or zigzag effect. The errors seem to flip back and forth between being positive and negative. The residuals shown in panels (b) and (c) are not independent—they show *autocorrelation* (or *serial correlation*) which means each residual is affected by the previous one. Panel (b) shows positive autocorrelation (each residual is positively correlated with the previous one) and panel (c) shows negative autocorrelation (each residual is negatively correlated with the previous one).

serial correlation

It is also possible to have correlation between residuals more than one time period apart. For example, if the data are seasonal but the seasonality has not been included in the model, there may be correlation at the seasonal lag.

The top panel in Figure 6-7 shows a time plot of the residuals from the bank data model. There may be a slight seasonal pattern here. Notice the peaks around January of each year. This suggests there may be some seasonality in the residual series, which we should allow for in our model.

An alternative approach to checking for autocorrelation is to compute the autocorrelation function or ACF and plot it as a correlogram (see Section 2/2/3). The bottom panel in Figure 6-7 shows the ACF of the same residuals from the bank model. This shows clearly there is a problem with autocorrelation, particularly at lag 12 (the seasonal lag). There are also significant correlations at some other lags.

The horizontal bands shown on the correlogram (Figure 6-7) are at $\pm\frac{2}{\sqrt{n}} = \pm 0.27$ since $n = 53$. These provide a rough guide as to the significance of each correlation. But more accurate tests are available. Here, we will look only at the Durbin-Watson test for autocorrelation at lag 1. This is not as restrictive as it sounds since autocorrelation at lag 1 is the most common form, and if there is autocorrelation at lag 1, there is often correlation at other lags too.

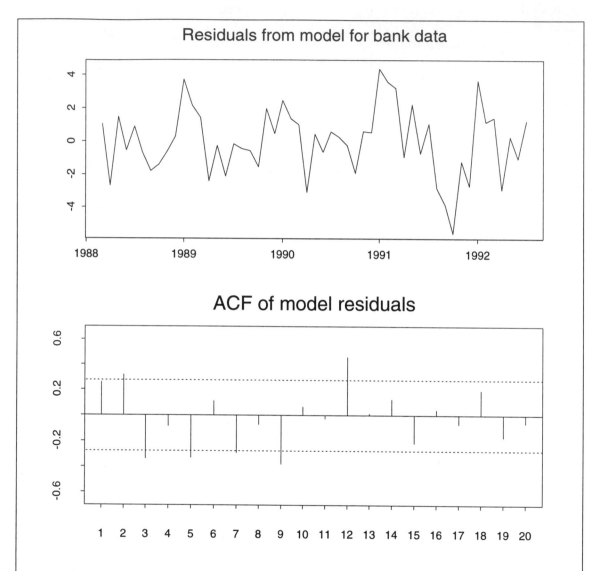

Figure 6-7: *Bank data: top—a time plot of the residuals when D(EOM) is regressed against the three explanatory variables (AAA), (3-4), and D(3-4); bottom—the ACF of the residuals.*

Time	(1) Error	(2) Squared error	(3)	(4)
t	e_t	e_t^2	$e_t - e_{t-1}$	$(e_t - e_{t-1})^2$
1	-0.60	0.36		
2	-0.90	0.81	-0.30	0.09
3	-0.30	0.09	0.60	0.36
4	3.20	10.24	3.50	12.25
5	-6.10	37.21	-9.30	86.49
6	-5.40	29.16	0.70	0.49
7	1.30	1.69	6.70	44.89
8	-8.10	65.61	-9.40	88.36
9	-2.20	4.84	5.90	34.81
10	0.30	0.09	2.50	6.25
11	1.30	1.69	1.00	1.00
12	4.90	24.01	3.60	12.96
13	-4.00	16.00	-8.90	79.21
14	-0.40	0.16	3.60	12.96
15	1.20	1.44	1.60	2.56
SS		193.40		382.68

$$DW = \frac{382.68}{193.40} = 1.979$$

Table 6-7: *Computation of the Durbin-Watson statistic for the residuals plotted in Figure 6-6(a).*

The Durbin-Watson statistic is defined by:

$$DW = \frac{\sum_{t=2}^{n}(e_t - e_{t-1})^2}{\sum_{t=1}^{n} e_t^2} \qquad (6.9) \qquad \text{Durbin-Watson statistic}$$

The numerator takes differences between successive errors, squares these differences, and adds them up. The denominator is simply the sum of the squared errors. Table 6-7 indicates how these calculations can be made for the artificial data plotted in Figure 6-6(a). Column 2 contains the squared errors and column 3 contains the successive error differences. For example, the first column 3 entry is determined as follows:

$$e_2 - e_1 = (-0.90) - (-0.60) = -0.30.$$

The Durbin-Watson statistic is computed by taking the ratio of the totals of columns 2 and 3 of Table 6-7:

$$DW = \frac{382.68}{193.40} = 1.979.$$

For data sets (b) and (c) in Figure 6-6, the DW statistic is computed to be 0.706 and 3.140, respectively. Note the following:

- When there is a distinct slow-moving pattern to the errors—as in case (b)—successive error differences tend to be small and the DW statistic will be small.

- When there is a distinct fast-moving (zigzag) pattern—as in case (c)—the successive error differences tend to be large and the DW statistic will be large.

As a matter of fact, the DW statistic ranges in value from 0 through 4, with an intermediate value of 2. The theory behind this statistic is complicated (see Appendix 6-A for some details), but it is readily usable in a practical setting. For the random errors in Table 6-7 the DW statistic is near 2. For set (b) the DW value is less than one—indicating positive autocorrelation (i.e., successive errors tend to have a positive relationship). And for set (c), DW = 3.14, indicating negative autocorrelation (i.e., successive errors tend to be negatively related).

Actually, the DW statistic is very close to $2(1 - r^2)$ where r is the autocorrelation at lag one. However it is useful to consider DW as well as lag one autocorrelation because DW can be tested using the Durbin-Watson test described in Appendix 6-A.

Returning now to the bank example and the set of residuals in Figure 6-7, the Durbin-Watson statistic is computed to be

$$DW = 1.48 \qquad \text{(for Figure 6-7 residuals)}.$$

This value is less than 2, and indicates that there is some positive lag one autocorrelation remaining in the errors. (Note that DW is a measure of the autocorrelation at lag one only—it cannot detect autocorrelations at higher lags.) Because there is still some pattern in the residuals, we can improve on the bank forecasting model.

6/2/2 Time-related explanatory variables

We can create new explanatory variables to allow various time-related features of our data to be included in the regression model. The most common applications of this idea are described below.

Time If we wish to include a linear time trend in our regression   linear trend
model, we can create an explanatory variable X_j which takes
values equal to the times of observation.

Seasonal dummy variables One way to handle seasonality is to   dummy variable
assume that the seasonal component is unchanging from year
to year and to model it by a collection of dummy (or indicator)
variables each of which has only two allowable values, 0 or 1. For   indicator variable
example, if we have monthly data, we may define the following
11 monthly variables:

$D_1 = 1$ if the month is Jan. and zero otherwise;
$D_2 = 1$ if the month is Feb. and zero otherwise;
$\vdots$
$D_{11} = 1$ if the month is Nov. and zero otherwise.

Each of these dummy variables is equivalent to a new explanatory variable. Note that if we had used 12 dummy variables for the 12 monthly periods, we would encounter the problem of multicollinearity (discussed in Section 6/4). Instead, we use *one less than the number of periods*. The general rule is: *use $(s-1)$ dummy variables to denote s different periods.* So quarterly data can be handled similarly but with only three dummy variables.

The coefficients associated with these variables reflect the average difference in the forecast variable between those months and the omitted month. So the coefficient associated with D_1 is a measure of the effect of January on the forecast variable compared to December. If some other month had been chosen as the base period, the regression values would look different, but still tell the same story.

An example of seasonal dummy variables with the bank data is given later in this section.

trading day variation

Trading day variation Sales data often vary according to the day of the week. So to forecast monthly sales figures, we need to take into account the number of Mondays, Tuesdays, etc. in each month. Similarly, many stores do their bookkeeping on Friday afternoons so that the number of Fridays in a month will affect the monthly sales figures.

One approach is to set up variables denoting the number of times each day of the week occurs in each month. That is,

T_1 = the number of times Monday occurred in that month;

T_2 = the number of times Tuesday occurred in that month;

$$\vdots$$

T_7 = the number of times Sunday occurred in that month.

The regression coefficients for the trading day variables give a measure of the trading day effect for each of the seven days.

This model is easily modified to allow for a variety of trading situations. For example, if there is never any trade on Sundays, we would exclude the Sunday term from the model.

Bell and Hillmer (1983) suggest an alternative approach which leads to more stable estimates.

holiday effects

Variable holiday effects The effect of Christmas on monthly sales data is easily handled because Christmas always occurs in December. So the method of seasonal dummy variables will include the effect of Christmas in the December component.

Easter is more difficult because it is not always in the same month, sometimes occurring in March and sometimes in April. Similarly, the Chinese New Year can occur in different months.

One approach is to define a dummy variable for Easter:

$V = 1$ if any part of the Easter period falls in that month and zero otherwise.

Then the coefficient associated with V represents the average increase in the forecast variable due to Easter. More complicated Easter models can be defined by allowing for the number of days of pre-Easter sales in each month (see Bell and Hillmer, 1983).

Interventions We have seen how seasonal components and variable holiday effects can be modeled using dummy variables. Dummy variables can be much more widely useful to model a great variety of possible events.

One application is to model interventions. An *intervention* occurs when there is some outside influence at a particular time which affects the forecast variable. For example, the introduction of seat belts may have caused the number of road fatalities to undergo a level shift downward. We can define a dummy variable consisting of 0's before the introduction of seat belts and 1's after that month. Then the regression coefficient measures the effect of the seat belt introduction. This assumes that the effect occurred instantly. If the effect of seat belt legislation resulted in a continuous decrease in road fatalities as more people began to use them, we would need to use a different explanatory variable allowing for such a decrease rather than a simple level shift.

interventions

Dummy variables can be used in many contexts to denote special events. However, the analyst should beware of using too many dummy variables; each new dummy variable is a new explanatory variable, requiring another regression coefficient to be estimated and thereby losing one degree of freedom for the error term.

The modeling of interventions is discussed in Section 8/3.

Advertising expenditure Sales may be able to be modeled as a function of advertising expenditure. Since the effect of advertising lasts for some time beyond the actual advertising campaign, we need to include several weeks (or months) advertising expenditure in the model:

$A_1 =$ advertising expenditure for the previous month;

$A_2 =$ advertising expenditure for two months previously;

$\vdots$

$A_m =$ advertising expenditure for m months previously.

Since we would expect the effect of advertising to tail off over time, it is common to require the coefficients associated with these variables to decrease. This type of model is discussed in more detail in Section 8/2.

	D(EOM)	(AAA)	(3-4)	D(3-4)	D_1	D_2	D_3	D_4	D_5	D_6	D_7	D_8	D_9	D_{10}	D_{11}
1	1.146	5.94	5.31	0.29	1	0	0	0	0	0	0	0	0	0	0
2	−2.443	6.00	5.60	−0.11	0	1	0	0	0	0	0	0	0	0	0
3	1.497	6.08	5.49	0.31	0	0	1	0	0	0	0	0	0	0	0
4	−0.132	6.17	5.80	−0.19	0	0	0	1	0	0	0	0	0	0	0
5	2.025	6.14	5.61	−0.33	0	0	0	0	1	0	0	0	0	0	0
6	0.737	6.09	5.28	−0.09	0	0	0	0	0	1	0	0	0	0	0
7	−1.023	5.87	5.19	−0.01	0	0	0	0	0	0	1	0	0	0	0
8	−0.956	5.84	5.18	0.12	0	0	0	0	0	0	0	1	0	0	0
9	0.385	5.99	5.30	−0.07	0	0	0	0	0	0	0	0	1	0	0
10	0.983	6.12	5.23	0.41	0	0	0	0	0	0	0	0	0	1	0
11	5.092	6.42	5.64	−0.02	0	0	0	0	0	0	0	0	0	0	1
12	3.649	6.48	5.62	0.05	0	0	0	0	0	0	0	0	0	0	0
13	2.703	6.52	5.67	0.16	1	0	0	0	0	0	0	0	0	0	0
14	−0.271	6.64	5.83	−0.30	0	1	0	0	0	0	0	0	0	0	0
15	2.055	6.75	5.53	0.23	0	0	1	0	0	0	0	0	0	0	0
16	−0.714	6.73	5.76	0.33	0	0	0	1	0	0	0	0	0	0	0
17	0.653	6.89	6.09	0.43	0	0	0	0	1	0	0	0	0	0	0
18	−0.034	6.98	6.52	0.16	0	0	0	0	0	1	0	0	0	0	0
19	−1.058	6.98	6.68	0.39	0	0	0	0	0	0	1	0	0	0	0
20	−2.051	7.10	7.07	0.05	0	0	0	0	0	0	0	1	0	0	0
21	1.451	7.19	7.12	0.13	0	0	0	0	0	0	0	0	1	0	0
22	−0.989	7.29	7.25	0.60	0	0	0	0	0	0	0	0	0	1	0
23	1.358	7.65	7.85	0.17	0	0	0	0	0	0	0	0	0	0	1
24	0.746	7.75	8.02	−0.15	0	0	0	0	0	0	0	0	0	0	0
25	1.855	7.72	7.87	−0.73	1	0	0	0	0	0	0	0	0	0	0
26	−1.894	7.67	7.14	0.06	0	1	0	0	0	0	0	0	0	0	0
27	0.781	7.66	7.20	0.39	0	0	1	0	0	0	0	0	0	0	0
28	−0.161	7.89	7.59	0.15	0	0	0	1	0	0	0	0	0	0	0
29	2.233	8.14	7.74	−0.23	0	0	0	0	1	0	0	0	0	0	0
30	2.425	8.21	7.51	−0.05	0	0	0	0	0	1	0	0	0	0	0
31	2.169	8.05	7.46	−0.37	0	0	0	0	0	0	1	0	0	0	0
32	0.982	7.94	7.09	−0.27	0	0	0	0	0	0	0	1	0	0	0
33	4.708	7.88	6.82	−0.60	0	0	0	0	0	0	0	0	1	0	0
34	6.063	7.79	6.22	−0.61	0	0	0	0	0	0	0	0	0	1	0
35	9.382	7.41	5.61	−0.13	0	0	0	0	0	0	0	0	0	0	1
36	9.304	7.18	5.48	−0.70	0	0	0	0	0	0	0	0	0	0	0
37	10.690	7.15	4.78	−0.64	1	0	0	0	0	0	0	0	0	0	0
38	6.531	7.27	4.14	0.50	0	1	0	0	0	0	0	0	0	0	0
39	7.873	7.37	4.64	0.88	0	0	1	0	0	0	0	0	0	0	0
40	3.882	7.54	5.52	0.43	0	0	0	1	0	0	0	0	0	0	0
41	4.960	7.58	5.95	0.25	0	0	0	0	1	0	0	0	0	0	0
42	1.301	7.62	6.20	−0.17	0	0	0	0	0	1	0	0	0	0	0
43	1.154	7.58	6.03	−0.43	0	0	0	0	0	0	1	0	0	0	0
44	0.116	7.48	5.60	−0.34	0	0	0	0	0	0	0	1	0	0	0
45	4.928	7.35	5.26	−0.30	0	0	0	0	0	0	0	0	1	0	0
46	2.530	7.19	4.96	0.32	0	0	0	0	0	0	0	0	0	1	0
47	8.425	7.19	5.28	0.09	0	0	0	0	0	0	0	0	0	0	1
48	5.291	7.11	5.37	0.16	0	0	0	0	0	0	0	0	0	0	0
49	5.192	7.16	5.53	0.19	1	0	0	0	0	0	0	0	0	0	0
50	0.257	7.22	5.72	0.32	0	1	0	0	0	0	0	0	0	0	0
51	4.402	7.36	6.04	−0.38	0	0	1	0	0	0	0	0	0	0	0
52	3.173	7.34	5.66	0.09	0	0	0	1	0	0	0	0	0	0	0
53	5.104	7.30	5.75	0.07	0	0	0	0	1	0	0	0	0	0	0
54	4.646	7.30	5.82	0.08	0	0	0	0	0	1	0	0	0	0	0
55	1.060	7.27	5.90	0.21	0	0	0	0	0	0	1	0	0	0	0
56	−0.758	7.30	6.11	−0.06	0	0	0	0	0	0	0	1	0	0	0
57	4.702	7.31	6.05	−0.07	0	0	0	0	0	0	0	0	1	0	0
58	1.878	7.26	5.98	0.02	0	0	0	0	0	0	0	0	0	1	0
59	6.620	7.24	6.00	0.24	0	0	0	0	0	0	0	0	0	0	1

Table 6-8: *Bank data: showing the addition of 11 dummy variables to handle seasonality.*

The bank data with seasonal dummy variables

Since the bank data is monthly, we will use 11 dummy variables, as shown in Table 6-8. Note that, since Y here is D(EOM), and the first observation is the difference for March 1988–Feb. 1988, dummy variable D_1 really refers to a (March–Feb.) change, not a specific month. Note, too, that for the twelfth data row, all 11 dummy variables have the value zero—so this set of 11 dummy variables identifies all 12 change periods.

Running a regression model on the data in Table 6-8 shows a big improvement over the simpler model analyzed previously. The results are as follows:

The Regression Equation is:

$$\hat{Y} = -2.20 + 3.3X_1 - 2.8X_2 - 1.7X_3 - 0.4D_1 - 4.5D_2 - 1.3D_3$$
$$- 3.1D_4 - 1.4D_5 - 3.0D_6 - 3.7D_7 - 4.7D_8 - 1.9D_9$$
$$-2.5D_{10} + 1.4D_{11}. \tag{6.10}$$

The full output from a regression program included the following information.

Term		Coeff. (b_j)	se of b_j	t	P-value
	Constant	−2.1983	1.9894	−4.1762	0.0002
X_1	AAA	3.2988	0.3248	10.1580	0.0000
X_2	(3-4)	−2.7524	0.2289	−12.0250	0.0000
X_3	D(3-4)	−1.7308	0.5535	−3.1271	0.0034
D_1	(Mar-Feb)	−0.4403	0.8211	−0.5362	0.5949
D_2	(Apr-Mar)	−4.5125	0.8322	−5.4221	0.0000
D_3	(May-Apr)	−1.3130	0.8551	−1.5355	0.1329
D_4	(Jun-May)	−3.1493	0.8377	−3.7593	0.0006
D_5	(Jul-Jun)	−1.3833	0.8269	−1.6729	0.1026
D_6	(Aug-Jul)	−3.0397	0.8675	−3.5042	0.0012
D_7	(Sep-Aug)	−3.7102	0.8650	−4.2893	0.0001
D_8	(Oct-Sep)	−4.6966	0.8640	−5.4362	0.0000
D_9	(Nov-Oct)	−1.8684	0.8634	−2.1641	0.0368
D_{10}	(Dec-Nov)	−2.4762	0.8832	−2.8036	0.0079
D_{11}	(Jan-Dec)	1.4419	0.8694	1.6585	0.1055

Comparing this equation with the solution in equation (6.4), the following results are obtained.

	Current model with seasonal dummies	Earlier model without seasonal dummies
R^2	0.887	0.561
MSE	1.49	4.48
F	21.27	20.85
df	(14,38)	(3,49)
P	0.0000	0.0000
DW	0.71	1.48

The proportion of variance in Y, explained by regressing on these 14 explanatory variables, is now 88.7% (R^2), instead of just 56.1%. The mean square error has dropped considerably, from 4.48 to 1.49. The F values, in an absolute sense, are not very different, but there has been a shift in the degrees of freedom (from denominator to numerator), which makes the numerator more stable. In other words, the F value for the current model (with seasonal dummy variables) is more significant than for the earlier model.

Also note that the Durbin-Watson statistic gives more cause for concern now (DW $= 0.72$) than it did earlier (DW $= 1.48$). There is not nearly as much unexplained error left in the current model, but what there is, is still patterned. There is strong evidence of positively autocorrelated errors. This point will be elaborated on in the next section.

Figure 6-8 shows the residuals from the new model. This is on the same scale as Figure 6-7 so that a comparison can be made more easily. The improvement is clear. There is no longer evidence of seasonality and the residuals are generally smaller, but the autocorrelation at lags one and two appears even stronger than before. This is because we have taken out the seasonal variation making it easier to identify other patterns such as autocorrelation. The use of dummy variables to denote seasonality has resulted in a significantly improved bank model. We will discuss methods for including autocorrelation in the regression model in Section 8/1.

6/3 Selecting variables

Developing a regression model for real data is never a simple process, but some guidelines can be given. Whatever the situation is (and we will illustrate this section with the bank data), experts in the

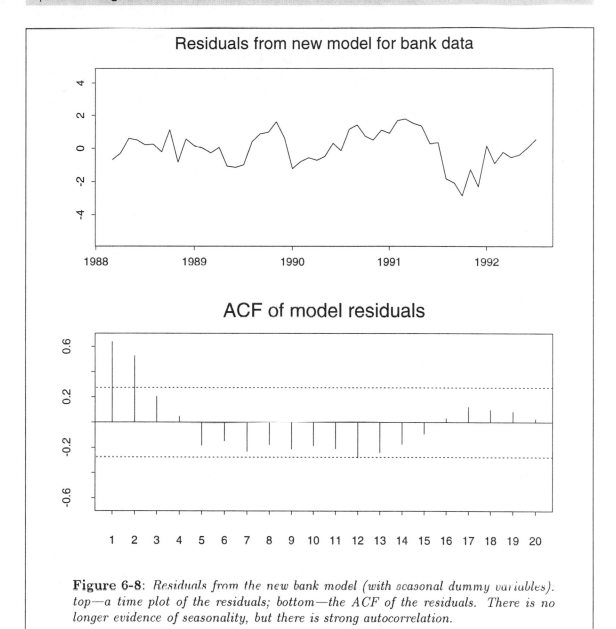

Figure 6-8: *Residuals from the new bank model (with seasonal dummy variables):*
top—a time plot of the residuals; bottom—the ACF of the residuals. There is no
longer evidence of seasonality, but there is strong autocorrelation.

general area will have to be called upon for counsel. For a defined
forecast variable, Y, it will be necessary to draw up a "long list" of
variables that impact on Y—this will be a set of potential explanatory
variables. The "long list" will usually be reduced to a "short list" by
various means, and a certain amount of creativity is essential. The

shape of the model (or the functional form for the regression model) will gradually be decided upon in conjunction with the development of the "short list," and finally, the parameters of the model will be estimated using data collected for that purpose. In this section, we describe briefly how the bank problem was handled.

6/3/1 The long list

Based on (i) hunches of experts and other knowledgeable people, (ii) availability of data, and (iii) practical time and cost constraints, it was decided that end-of-month balances in a mutual savings bank were conceivably related to (or depended on) the following 19 economic variables:

1. U.S. Gross Demand Deposits
2. First Gross Demand Deposits
3. U.S. Personal Income
4. Northeast Personal Income
5. Massachusetts Personal Income
6. N.H. Personal Income
7. Rates for Three-Month Bills
8. Rates for 3-4 Year Government Issues
9. Rates for AAA Bonds
10. U.S. Negotiable CDs
11. First Negotiable CDs
12. U.S. Mutual Savings Bank Savings
13. First Mutual Savings Bank Savings
14. Massachusetts Mutual Savings Bank Savings
15. N.H. Mutual Savings Bank Savings
16. U.S. Consumer Price Index
17. U.S. Savings and Loan Index
18. First Savings and Loan Index
19. National Personal Income

In addition, since the EOM data set (Table 6-1) was a monthly time series, some other variables were being kept in mind—namely, "time" and "seasonal indices." The model "shape" was to be a simple linear (in the coefficients) function, with the possibility that a non-linear trend line would have to be accommodated.

6/3/2 The short list

There are many proposals regarding how to select appropriate variables for a final model. Some of these are straightforward, but not recommended:

- Plot Y against a particular explanatory variable (X_j) and if it shows no noticeable relationship, drop it.
- Look at the intercorrelations among the explanatory variables (all of the potential candidates) and every time a large correlation is encountered, remove one of the two variables from further consideration; otherwise you might run into multicollinearity problems (see Section 6/4).
- Do a multiple linear regression on all the explanatory variables and disregard all variables whose t values are very small (say $|t| < 0.05$).

Although these approaches are commonly followed, none of them is reliable in finding a good regression model.

Some proposals are more complicated, but more justifiable:

- Do a best subsets regression (see Section 6/3/3).
- Do a stepwise regression (see Section 6/3/4).
- Do a principal components analysis of all the variables (including Y) to decide on which are key variables (see Draper and Smith, 1981).
- Do a distributed lag analysis to decide which leads and lags are most appropriate for the study at hand.

Quite often, a combination of the above will be used to reach the final short list of explanatory variables and the functional form that seems most justified.

For the bank forecasting problem, the 19 potential candidates for explanatory variables were reduced to a short list of just four using a principal components analysis:

   7. Rates for Three-Month Bills
   8. Rates for 3-4 Year Government Issues
   9. Rates for AAA Bonds
 10. U.S. Negotiable CDs

Next, to study the relevance of lags or leads, the matrix of explanatory variables ($n = 60$ rows and 4 columns—X_1, X_2, X_3, X_4) was

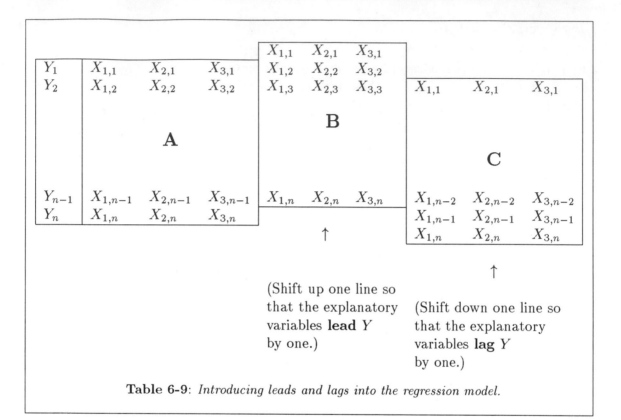

Table 6-9: *Introducing leads and lags into the regression model.*

shifted one period ahead of Y and one period behind Y, as indicated in Table 6-9. The original data matrix is designated A. The data block labeled B is the data for the explanatory variables shifted up one line (i.e., one time period)—so that "leads" can be evaluated—and data block C shows how data for the explanatory variables can be shifted down one period—so that "lags" can be evaluated. Note that the first observation and last observation cannot now be used in the regression model since a full set of explanatory variables do not exist for these cases. If necessary, further leads and lags can be built up in this manner (but each lead or lag will result in one more observation being unavailable).

Sometimes we may wish to use the first differences of some of the explanatory variables as additional explanatory variables in block A. In this case, it will not be possible to use the lag 1 variables because of the problem of multicollinearity discussed in Section 6/4.

For the bank data, since the Y variable was itself a first difference D(EOM), it makes sense to use first differences rather than lags of the chosen (short-list) explanatory variables. Thus instead of just four explanatory variables in data block A, eight explanatory variables were used:

$$\begin{array}{cccc} \text{(3 month)} & \text{(3-4 yr)} & \text{(AAA)} & \text{(CPI)} \\ \text{and} \quad \text{D(3 months)} & \text{D(3-4 yr)} & \text{D(AAA)} & \text{D(CPI)} \end{array}$$

With these eight explanatory variables, leads of 1 and 2 periods, lags of 2 periods (but not 1 period), seasonal dummy variables, and a time trend, the total number of candidates for explanatory variables is 44:

1. four short-list explanatory variables
2. four first differences from (1)
3. 1-period leads on the eight variables in (1) and (2)
4. 2-period leads on the eight variables in (1) and (2)
5. 2 period lags on the eight variables in (1) and (2)
6. 11 seasonal dummy variables
7. 1 time variable

6/3/3 Best subsets regression

Ideally, we would like to calculate all possible regression models using our set of 44 candidate explanatory variables and choose the best model among them. There are two problems here. First it may not be feasible to compute all the models because of the huge number of combinations of variables that is possible. Second, how do we decide what is best?

We will consider the second problem first. A naïve approach to selecting the best model would be to find the model which gives the largest value of R^2. In fact, that is the model which contains *all* the explanatory variables! Every additional explanatory variable will result in an *increase* in R^2. Clearly not all of these explanatory variables should be included. So maximizing the value of R^2 is not an appropriate method for finding the best model.

The problem is that R^2 does not take into account degrees of freedom. To overcome this problem, an *adjusted* R^2 is defined, as   adjusted R^2
follows:

$$\bar{R}^2 \;=\; 1 - (1 - R^2)\frac{(\text{total df})}{(\text{error df})}$$

$$\;=\; 1 - (1 - R^2)\frac{n-1}{n-k-1} \qquad (6.11)$$

where n is the number of observations and k is the number of explanatory variables in the model.

Note that $\bar{R}^2$ is referred to as "adjusted R^2" or "R-bar-squared," or sometimes as "R^2, corrected for degrees of freedom."

For the bank data,

$$\bar{R}^2 = 1 - (1 - 0.561)\frac{53-1}{53-3-1} = 0.534$$

when the seasonal dummy variables are excluded and

$$\bar{R}^2 = 1 - (1 - 0.887)\frac{53-1}{53-14-1} = 0.845$$

when the seasonal dummy variables are included. So, using $\bar{R}^2$ as a measure, the second model is still much better.

There are other measures which, like $\bar{R}^2$, can be used to find the best regression model. Some computer programs will output several possible measures. Apart from $\bar{R}^2$, the most commonly used measures are Mallow's C_p statistic and Akaike's AIC statistic (see Draper and Smith, 1981; Judge et al., 1988).

We can compare the $\bar{R}^2$ values for all the possible regression models and select the model with the highest value for $\bar{R}^2$. We have 44 possible explanatory variables and we can use anywhere between 0 and 44 of these in our final model. That is a total of $2^{44} = 18$ trillion possible regression models! Even using modern computing facilities, it is impossible to compute that many regression models in a person's lifetime. So we need some other approach. Clearly the problem can quickly get out of hand without some help. To select the best explanatory variables from among the 44 candidate variables, we need to use stepwise regression (discussed in the next section).

For a smaller number of explanatory variables, it is possible to compute all possible regression models. We will consider a restricted set of 17 variables for the bank problem:

$$Y = D(EOM) \text{ [as in Table 6-2]}$$
$$X_1 = (AAA)_{-1} \text{ [as in Table 6-2]}$$
$$X_2 = (3\text{-}4)_{-1} \text{ [as in Table 6-2]}$$
$$X_3 = D(3\text{-}4)_0 \text{ [as in Table 6-2]}$$
$$D_1 = \text{dummy variable for a (Mar}-\text{Feb) change}$$
$$D_2 = \text{dummy variable for a (Apr}-\text{Mar) change}$$
$$\vdots$$
$$D_{11} = \text{dummy variable for a (Jan}-\text{Dec) change}$$
$$X_4 = \text{time}$$
$$X_5 = (\text{time})^2$$
$$X_6 = (\text{time})^3$$

The last three allow for up to a cubic trend with the variable "time" as the number of months (i.e., column (1) of Table 6-1).

Many computer programs have facilities for identifying the best subsets of the explanatory variables when the number of explanatory variables is not too large. That is, the best models with only one explanatory variable are identified, the best models with two explanatory variables are identified, and so on. Table 6-10 shows the results from a best subsets regression analysis for the bank data. The three best models of each size are given in the table. The first column gives k, the number of explanatory variables in the model. An x indicates the variable has been included. Models can be compared using the $\bar{R}^2$ value in the right-hand column. The best model overall is marked with an asterisk ($*$) and has $\bar{R}^2 = 0.858$. As noted previously, the best model with respect to R^2 is the model containing all 17 explanatory variables.

The final model from the best subsets regression includes the three original variables (X_1, X_2 and X_3), 10 of the 11 seasonal variables (all but D_1), and $(\text{time})^3$ (X_6). In fact, it makes no sense to include a *cubic* time term without the linear and quadratic terms. When this constraint is made, the model chosen is identical except that the cubic term (X_6) is replaced by a linear term (X_4). The resulting model has $\bar{R}^2 = 0.856$.

So our final regression model is as follows:

k	AAA X_1	(3-4) X_2	D(3-4) X_3	Mar D_1	Apr D_2	May D_3	Jun D_4	Jul D_5	Aug D_6	Sep D_7	Oct D_8	Nov D_9	Dec D_{10}	Jan D_{11}	t X_4	t^2 X_5	t^3 X_6	R^2	$\bar{R}^2$
1															x			0.277	0.263
1																x		0.258	0.244
1																	x	0.215	0.200
2	x	x																0.514	0.495
2		x													x			0.415	0.392
2														x	x			0.379	0.354
3	x	x												x				0.620	0.597
3	x	x		x														0.586	0.560
3	x	x									x							0.564	0.537
4	x	x		x										x				0.677	0.650
4	x	x			x									x				0.677	0.650
4	x	x	x											x				0.670	0.642
5	x	x			x						x			x				0.726	0.697
5	x	x		x	x									x				0.722	0.692
5	x	x	x		x									x				0.721	0.691
6	x	x	x		x						x			x				0.778	0.749
6	x	x		x	x						x			x				0.761	0.730
6	x	x	x	x	x									x				0.753	0.720
7	x	x	x		x					x	x			x				0.808	0.779
7	x	x	x	x	x						x			x				0.800	0.769
7	x	x	x		x		x				x			x				0.795	0.763
8	x	x	x		x		x		x		x			x				0.831	0.800
8	x	x	x		x			x	x		x			x				0.825	0.793
8	x	x	x	x	x				x		x			x				0.824	0.792
9	x	x	x		x		x		x	x	x			x				0.854	0.823
9	x	x	x	x	x		x		x		x			x				0.842	0.809
9	x	x	x		x		x		x		x		x	x				0.840	0.806
10	x	x	x		x		x		x	x	x		x	x				0.868	0.836
10	x	x	x		x		x		x	x	x			x			x	0.862	0.829
10	x	x	x		x		x		x	x	x			x		x		0.862	0.829
11	x	x	x		x		x		x	x	x		x	x			x	0.877	0.844
11	x	x	x		x		x		x	x	x		x	x		x		0.877	0.844
11	x	x	x		x		x		x	x	x	x	x	x				0.875	0.842
†12	x	x	x		x		x		x	x	x	x	x	x			x	0.886	0.852
12	x	x	x		x		x		x	x	x	x	x	x		x		0.885	0.851
12	x	x	x		x		x		x	x	x	x	x	x	x			0.882	0.847
13	x	x	x		x		x		x	x	x	x	x	x	x		x	0.890	0.853
13	x	x	x		x	x	x		x	x	x	x	x	x			x	0.889	0.852
13	x	x	x		x		x	x	x	x	x	x	x	x			x	0.889	0.852
*14	x	x	x		x	x	x	x	x	x	x	x	x	x			x	0.896	**0.858**
14	x	x	x		x	x	x	x	x	x	x	x	x	x		x		0.896	0.858
14	x	x	x		x	x	x	x	x	x	x	x	x	x	x			0.895	0.856
15	x	x	x	x	x	x	x	x	x	x	x	x	x	x			x	0.897	0.856
15	x	x	x	x	x	x	x	x	x	x	x	x	x	x		x		0.897	0.856
15	x	x	x		x	x	x	x	x	x	x	x	x	x	x	x		0.897	0.855
16	x	x	x	x	x	x	x	x	x	x	x	x	x	x	x	x		0.898	0.852
16	x	x	x	x	x	x	x	x	x	x	x	x	x	x	x		x	0.898	0.852
16	x	x	x	x	x	x	x	x	x	x	x	x	x	x		x	x	0.897	0.852
17	x	x	x	x	x	x	x	x	x	x	x	x	x	x	x	x	x	0.898	0.848

Table 6-10: *Best subset analysis for the bank data. The model marked * is the best model overall. The model marked † is the model selected using stepwise regression.*

The Regression Equation is:

$$\hat{Y} = -6.2 + 4.4X_1 - 3.2X_2 - 1.7X_3 - 4.4D_2 - 1.2D_3 - 3.0D_4$$
$$- 1.2D_5 - 3.0D_6 - 3.5D_7 - 4.5D_8 - 1.7D_9 - 2.3D_{10} + 1.6D_{11}$$
$$- 0.04(\text{time}). \hspace{3cm} (6.12)$$

The full output from a regression program included the following information.

Term		Coeff. (b_j)	se of b_j	t	P-value
	Constant	−6.1525	2.7476	−4.9404	0.0000
X_1	AAA	4.3925	0.6874	6.3901	0.0000
X_2	(3-4)	−3.2230	0.3466	−9.2999	0.0000
X_3	D(3-4)	−1.6893	0.5343	−3.1617	0.0031
D_2	(Apr–Mar)	−4.4136	0.6758	−6.5310	0.0000
D_3	(May–Apr)	−1.2279	0.7044	−1.7433	0.0894
D_4	(Jun–May)	−2.9812	0.6817	−4.3732	0.0001
D_5	(Jul–Jun)	−1.1753	0.6692	−1.7563	0.0871
D_6	(Aug–Jul)	−2.9832	0.7231	−4.1255	0.0002
D_7	(Sep–Aug)	−3.5119	0.7120	−4.9326	0.0000
D_8	(Oct–Sep)	−4.4730	0.7098	−6.3020	0.0000
D_9	(Nov–Oct)	−1.6645	0.7088	−2.3484	0.0242
D_{10}	(Dec–Nov)	−2.3400	0.7337	−3.1895	0.0029
D_{11}	(Jan–Dec)	1.6342	0.7170	2.2794	0.0283
X_4	time	−0.0417	0.0235	−1.7743	0.0840

Comparing this model with the previous two models fitted, we obtain the following results.

	Best regression model	Model with all seasonal dummies	First model without seasonal dummies
R^2	0.895	0.887	0.561
$\bar{R}^2$	0.856	0.845	0.534
MSE	1.39	1.49	4.48
F	23.06	21.27	20.85
df	(14,38)	(14,38)	(3,49)
P	0.0000	0.0000	0.0000
DW	0.82	0.71	1.48

Ten of the 11 seasonal dummy variables were entered and all but two show very significant t values. Since these variables do not correlate very highly with one another, the individual t-tests can be interpreted readily.

Clearly there is a lot of significant seasonality in the D(EOM) measures. How do we isolate the seasonality effects? Suppose we concentrate on the (April–March) change, which means rows 2, 14, 26, 38, and 50. For each of these rows the second dummy variable $D_2 = 1$ and all others are zero. Putting these values into the regression equation (6.12), we get

$$D(EOM) = -6.2 + 4.4X_1 - 3.2X_2 - 1.7X_3 - 4.4(1) - 0.04(\text{time}).$$

Note that the dummy variable D_2 has the effect of changing the constant term only. The new constant is

$$-6.2 - 4.4 = -1.8 \quad \text{(for April - Mar.)}$$

seasonal indices

Repeating this procedure systematically for 12 possible changes, we could determine the seasonality indices for each change. This will be an exercise at the end of the chapter.

The F value (with 14 and 38 df) for this analysis is 23.06, which is again very significant, as expected, and the MSE is 1.39 which is the lowest yet obtained. Additional improvements in the model are unlikely to come easily.

At this stage it is necessary to check again that the assumptions of the model are satisfied by plotting the residuals. In fact, the residual plots are almost identical to those given in Figures 6-4 and 6-8 and so are not reproduced here.

business cycles

Perhaps the only remaining bothersome aspect of the model is the obvious presence of positive autocorrelation in the residuals. The DW statistic has a value 0.82, which indicates positive autocorrelation. The time plot of residuals (similar to Figure 6-8) also gives evidence of the pattern remaining in the residuals. Underlying many economic time series is the presence of business cycles of one kind or another, and often such cycles are established by default. In other words, after everything reasonable is done to model systematic aspects of a Y variable, the residual pattern may be "random noise" plus a "business cycle aspect." Chapter 8 deals with this problem in the general context of regression models with correlated residuals.

One consequence of autocorrelation in the residuals (discussed in Section 8/1/1) is that the F-test and t-tests above may not be valid as they rely on the residuals being uncorrelated. Similarly, the computation of $\bar{R}^2$ in determining the best model may be affected by the autocorrelation. Therefore, the identified model should not be considered the final solution, but the best found so far. Applying the methods of Chapter 8 to the bank data may lead to further improvements.

6/3/4 Stepwise regression

Stepwise regression is a method which can be used to help sort out the relevant explanatory variables from a set of candidate explanatory variables when the number of explanatory variables is too large to allow all possible regression models to be computed.

The book by Draper and Smith (1981) has an excellent treatment of the main kinds of stepwise regression in use today. Three such approaches are:

1. Stepwise forward regression,
2. Stepwise backward regression,
3. Stepwise forward-with-a-backward-look regression.

The first method has several variations of its own, one of which is as follows. From among the potential explanatory variables, pick the one that has the highest correlation with Y. Determine the residuals from this regression, and think of these residuals as a new set of Y values. From among the remaining explanatory variables, pick the one that correlates most highly with these residuals. Continue this process until no remaining explanatory variable has a significant relationship with the last set of residuals.

The stepwise backward method also has several variations. One is to start with a regression including all the variables—assuming this is possible—and weeding out that variable that is least significant in the equation (as measured by the t value). Then, with this variable out, another regression solution is run, and the next variable to remove is determined, and so on.

Neither the stepwise forward nor the stepwise backward method is guaranteed to produce the optimal pair of explanatory variables, or triple of explanatory variables, and so on. There is, in fact, only one sure way of doing this—do all possible regressions! Since this is impractical we often have to rely on less than perfect answers, and the third method is of considerable value.

The reason for the name "stepwise forward-with-a-backward-look" is explained below.

Step 1: Find the best single variable (X_{1*}).

Step 2: Find the best pair of variables (X_{1*} together with one of the remaining explanatory variables—call it X_{2*}).

Step 3: Find the best triple of explanatory variables (X_{1*}, X_{2*} plus one of the remaining explanatory variables—call the new one X_{3*}).

Step 4: From this step on, the procedure checks to see if any of the earlier introduced variables might conceivably have to be removed. For example, the regression of Y on X_{2*} and X_{3*} might give better $\bar{R}^2$ results than if all three variables X_{1*}, X_{2*}, and X_{3*} had been included. At step 2, the best pair of explanatory variables had to include X_{1*}, by step 3, X_{2*} and X_{3*} could actually be superior to all three variables.

Step 5: The process of (a) looking for the next best explanatory variable to include, and (b) checking to see if a previously included variable should be removed, is continued until certain criteria are satisfied. For example, in running a stepwise regression program, the user is asked to enter two "tail" probabilities:
    1. the probability, P_1, to "enter" a variable, and
    2. the probability, P_2, to "remove" a variable.
When it is no longer possible to find any new variable that contributes at the P_1 level to the $\bar{R}^2$ value, or if no variable needs to be removed at the P_2 level, then the iterative procedure stops.

With all the procedures mentioned in the preceding sections, a forecaster can spend a lot of time trying various combinations of variables—original measures, first differences, lags, leads, and so on—there really is no substitute for a little creativity and a lot of "feeling" for the subject matter under consideration.

Application to the bank data

To complete the bank example, we will do a stepwise regression on the same restricted set of variables considered in the previous section.

Step	AAA X_1	(3-4) X_2	D(3-4) X_3	Mar D_1	Apr D_2	May D_3	Jun D_4	Jul D_5	Aug D_6	Sep D_7	Oct D_8	Nov D_9	Dec D_{10}	Jan D_{11}	t X_4	t^2 X_5	t^3 X_6	R^2	$\bar{R}^2$
1																x		0.277	0.263
2		x														x		0.415	0.392
3		x													x	x		0.521	0.491
4	x	x													x	x		0.622	0.590
5	x	x														x		0.620	0.597
6	x	x			x											x		0.677	0.650
5	x	x			x					x						x		0.726	0.697
6	x	x	x		x					x						x		0.778	0.749
7	x	x	x		x				x	x						x		0.808	0.779
8	x	x	x		x	x			x	x						x		0.831	0.800
9	x	x	x		x	x	x		x	x						x		0.854	0.823
10	x	x	x		x	x	x		x	x			x			x		0.868	0.836
11	x	x	x		x	x	x		x	x			x			x	x	0.877	0.844
12	x	x	x		x	x	x		x	x		x	x			x	x	0.886	0.852

Table 6-11: *Bank data: a final stepwise regression analysis of 17 explanatory variables.*

The stepwise results are given in Table 6-11. For this run the probability to enter and remove a variable was set at 0.10. Note that as the procedure unfolds, the $\bar{R}^2$ values steadily increase—even when a variable is removed at step 5. At the end of the analysis $\bar{R}^2 = 0.852$. Different computer packages may give slightly different results from those in Table 6-11—there are several different parameters which control the stepwise regression algorithm.

The final model from the stepwise regression is almost the same as that for the best subsets regression except the seasonal variables D_3 and D_5 have been omitted. The value of $\bar{R}^2 = 0.852$ which is almost as good as 0.858 obtained in Table 6-10, but achieved with far fewer computations.

6/4 Multicollinearity

If two vectors (columns of data) point in the same direction, they can be called collinear. In regression analysis, multicollinearity is the name given to any one or more of the following conditions:

- Two explanatory variables are perfectly correlated (and therefore, the vectors representing these variables are collinear).

- Two explanatory variables are highly correlated (i.e., the correlation between them is close to $+1$ or -1).

- A linear combination of some of the explanatory variables is highly correlated with another explanatory variable.

- A linear combination of one subset of explanatory variables is highly correlated with a linear combination of another subset of explanatory variables.

unstable
computations

The reason for concern about this issue is first and foremost a computational one. If perfect multicollinearity exists in a regression problem, it is simply not possible to carry out the LS solution. If nearly perfect multicollinearity exists, the LS solutions can be affected by round-off error problems in some calculators and some computer packages. There are computational methods that are robust enough to take care of all but the most difficult multicollinearity problems (see Draper and Smith, 1981), but not all packages take advantage of these methods.

unstable coefficients

The other major concern is that the stability of the regression coefficients is affected by multicollinearity. As multicollinearity becomes more and more nearly perfect, the regression coefficients computed by standard regression programs are therefore going to be (a) unstable—as measured by the standard error of the coefficient, and (b) unreliable—in that different computer programs are likely to give different solution values.

Multicollinearity is not a problem unless either (i) the individual regression coefficients are of interest, or (ii) attempts are made to isolate the contribution of one explanatory variable to Y, *without* the influence of the other explanatory variables. Multicollinearity will not affect the ability of the model to predict.

A common but incorrect idea is that an examination of the inter-correlations among the explanatory variables can reveal the presence or absence of multicollinearity. While it is true that a correlation very close to $+1$ or -1 does suggest multicollinearity, it is not true (unless there are only two explanatory variables) to infer that multicollinearity does not exist when there are no high correlations between any pair of explanatory variables. This point will be examined in the next two sections.

6/4/1 Multicollinearity when there are two explanatory variables

If Y is being regressed on X_1 and X_2, multicollinearity[1] means that the correlation between X_1 and X_2 is perfect (or very nearly so). Thus, in this case, multicollinearity can be detected by looking at the correlation between the explanatory variables and making a decision as to what constitutes nearly perfect multicollinearity. From a computational point of view $r_{X_1X_2} = 0.99$ may give no trouble, but from a practical point of view this would undoubtedly be viewed as a serious case of multicollinearity.

The practical concern is with the standard error of the two regression coefficients, b_1 and b_2. The formula for the calculation of the standard errors of b_1 and b_2 has the following form:

$$se_b = \frac{v_e^*}{1 - r_{X_1X_2}^2}$$

where v_c^* is related to the error variance. Clearly, as $r_{X_1X_2}$ approaches $+1$ or -1, the denominator approaches the value zero. Dividing by a number that approaches zero means exploding the standard error. If the standard error of a coefficient is very large, then the analyst cannot put much faith in the value of the coefficient.

6/4/2 Multicollinearity when there are more than two explanatory variables

As mentioned in the introduction to this section, multicollinearity becomes increasingly difficult to detect as the number of explanatory variables increases. To illustrate the point, consider Table 6-12, which presents a data matrix for a forecast variable Y (quarterly sales) and four seasonal dummy variables, D_1 through D_4. (We can disregard the fact that these are dummy variables—they are simply four explanatory variables.) The lower part of Table 6-12 also gives the correlation matrix for all the variables. Concentrating on the correlations among the four explanatory variables themselves,

---

[1] Actually, when there are only two explanatory variables, there is no need to use the word "*multi*collinear." Two explanatory variables are merely "collinear" or not.

Y	D_1	D_2	D_3	D_4
86	1	0	0	0
125	0	1	0	0
167	0	0	1	0
65	0	0	0	1
95	1	0	0	0
133	0	1	0	0
174	0	0	1	0
73	0	0	0	1
96	1	0	0	0
140	0	1	0	0
186	0	0	1	0
74	0	0	0	1
104	1	0	0	0
148	0	1	0	0
205	0	0	1	0
84	0	0	0	1
107	1	0	0	0
155	0	1	0	0
220	0	0	1	0
87	0	0	0	1

The Correlation Matrix

	Y	D_1	D_2	D_3	D_4
Y	1.000	-0.364	0.178	0.818	-0.632
D_1	-0.364	1.000	-0.333	-0.333	-0.333
D_2	0.178	-0.333	1.000	-0.333	-0.333
D_3	0.818	-0.333	-0.333	1.000	-0.333
D_4	-0.632	-0.333	-0.333	-0.333	1.000

Table 6-12: *Quarterly data and seasonal dummy variables showing the correlations among the dummy variables and Y.*

notice that they are all the same and all reasonably small (-0.333)—certainly not big enough to make anyone think of multicollinearity. Yet, if a regression run is attempted for the model

$$Y = b_0 + b_1 D_1 + b_2 D_2 + b_3 D_3 + b_4 D_4,$$

the computer program should reject the data. This occurs because the set of four dummy variables represents perfect multicollinearity since

$$1 - (D_1 + D_2 + D_3) = D_4$$

so that it is theoretically impossible to compute the regression solution. The correct regression model is obtained by leaving out one dummy variable or the constant b_0.

It is not only seasonal indices which cause multicollinearity problems. In many financial analyses, a large number of financial ratios and indices are used, and many of them depend on one another in various ways. The fact of the matter is that cases of perfect (or nearly so) multicollinearity have occurred, and will continue to occur, as analysts depend more and more on large data bases with literally thousands of potential variables to choose from.

6/5 Multiple regression and forecasting

The main objective of this book is to examine forecasting models and then to critique their practical use. Regression models can be very useful in the hands of a creative forecaster, but there are two distinct phases to consider. The first is actually developing and fitting a model (which has been the subject matter of the current chapter so far), and the second is to do some actual forecasting with the model. We now concentrate on this second phase.

For any forecast to be made, a set of values for the future values of the explanatory variables has to be provided. These are then put into the regression equation and a predicted value $\hat{Y}$ is obtained. To decide how much faith to put in this value of $\hat{Y}$, equation (6.13) is used to evaluate the standard error of the forecast.

In Chapter 5, equation (5-19) defined the standard error of forecast for $\hat{Y}$. For the general case of multiple linear regression, the standard error formula has to be given in matrix algebra terms, as follows:

$$\text{s.e.}(\hat{Y}_0) = s_e \sqrt{1 + c'(X'X)^{-1}c}, \qquad (6.13)$$

standard error of forecast

where c is the vector $[1\ X_1^*\ X_2^*\ \ldots\ X_k^*]'$ of new values for the explanatory variables, X is the matrix of order n by $k+1$, where the first column is a set of ones and the other columns are the vectors of explanatory variables.

Equation (6.13) (and similarly, equation (5-19)) is based on the assumption that the explanatory variables are measured without error. When forecasts of Y are made, they depend on future values of the explanatory variables, $X_1^*, X_2^*, \ldots, X_k^*$. In the case of regression models for time series data, future values of the explanatory variables often have to be forecast themselves, and so *are* subject to error. Hence, the standard error formulas underestimate the actual forecast errors.

6/5/1 Example: cross-sectional regression and forecasting

Table 6-13 displays some meteorological data. The objective of this analysis is to find out if upper atmosphere water vapor content is related to measurements that can be made on the ground. It is expensive to send weather balloons aloft to get direct measurement of Y (water vapor), so that if the explanatory variables (X_1, X_2, X_3, X_4, and X_5) can "explain" a significant amount of the variation in Y, a useful model will be provided. The explanatory variables in this instance are pressure (X_1), temperature (X_2), dew point (X_3), and the wind vector is resolved into an east-west component (X_4) and a north-south component (X_5).

Using $n = 299$ daily observations on these six variables, a multiple linear regression model was estimated as follows:

$$Y = 23.725 - 0.228X_1 - 0.024X_2 + 0.182X_3 - 0.006X_4 - 0.006X_5,$$
$$(6.14)$$

and the standard deviation of the residuals was $s_e = 0.622$.

Suppose now that a prediction is to be made on the basis of the following set of ground control values:

$$X_1^* = 1005, \ X_2^* = 22.0, \ X_3^* = 13.0, \ X_4^* = 10, \ X_5^* = 10.$$

Substituting these values in equation (6.14) gives a prediction $\hat{Y}$ (of water vapor content) of 2.595. Using equation (6.13), the standard error of this prediction will be 0.636.

prediction interval   In order to give 95% prediction limits on the $\hat{Y}$ forecast, we add and subtract 1.96 times the standard error to 2.595, as follows:

$$2.595 \pm 1.96[0.636] = 2.595 \pm 1.247 = [1.35, 3.84].$$

The regression run gave an R^2 of 0.665, so that it is not surprising to find a large prediction interval for $\hat{Y}$. A lot of the variance in $\hat{Y}$ is not being explained by the regression.

X_1 Day	X_2 Pressure	X_3 Temp	X_4 Dew Pt.	X_5 Wind E-W	X_6 Wind N-S	Y Water Vapor
1	1013.3	24.7	15.0	0.00	25.00	2.65
2	1011.6	24.8	17.0	12.86	15.32	2.63
3	1009.4	26.5	19.4	7.87	21.61	4.95
4	1003.1	29.6	20.1	20.78	12.00	4.49
5	1006.6	25.7	19.5	0.00	7.00	3.17
6	1006.5	25.0	20.1	8.21	22.55	3.88
7	1016.9	21.6	16.3	0.00	12.00	3.90
8	1011.8	24.7	18.0	9.58	26.31	3.51
9	1010.3	25.9	18.3	0.00	20.00	3.90
10	1013.6	25.6	18.7	6.89	5.79	3.47
11	1005.4	27.9	21.9	5.81	15.97	5.53
12	1013.4	25.8	20.0	3.13	17.73	3.48
13	1009.6	26.2	20.2	11.28	4.10	4.35
14	1013.0	24.8	21.5	0.00	26.00	4.38
15	1009.8	27.7	20.6	10.00	17.32	4.39
16	1005.9	26.2	22.0	3.13	17.73	5.02
17	1011.0	23.9	22.0	1.03	2.82	4.77
18	1003.7	28.1	23.4	12.21	14.55	5.36
19	1001.4	23.0	18.5	5.36	4.50	3.85
...	...	...	...	...	...	...
293	1011.3	26.0	16.4	6.16	16.91	2.94
294	1012.4	23.6	21.0	6.93	4.00	4.28
295	1013.0	22.4	15.0	1.56	8.86	4.14
296	1013.3	22.6	19.4	0.00	0.00	4.31
297	1015.6	23.4	20.3	3.08	8.46	4.13
298	1007.2	27.5	22.0	14.78	17.62	3.64
299	1003.0	32.0	19.4	3.13	17.73	3.42

Table 6-13: *Meteorological data: water vapor in the upper atmosphere is the forecast variable.*

6/5/2 Example: time series regression and forecasting

For the bank example (see Table 6-8) and the regression model (6.12), the data setup is as follows:

Period	D(EOM)	(AAA)	(3-4)	D(3-4)
52	Jun '72–May '72	May '72	May '72	Jun '72–May '72
53	Jul '72–Jun '72	Jun '72	Jun '72	Jul '72–Jun '72
	(Data for D(EOM) assumed unknown from here on)			
54	Aug '72–Jul '72	Jul '72	Jul '72	Aug '72–Jul '72
55	Sep '72–Aug '72	Aug '72	Aug '72	Sep '72–Aug '72
56	Oct '72–Sep '72	Oct '72	Oct '72	Oct '72–Sep '72
57	Nov '72–Oct '72	Nov '72	Nov '72	Nov '72–Oct '72
58	Dec '72–Nov '72	Dec '72	Dec '72	Dec '72–Nov '72
59	Jan '73–Dec '72	Jan '73	Jan '73	Jan '73–Dec '72

The objective is to forecast D(EOM) for periods 54, 55, ..., 59 (six-month forecast). It becomes crucial to consider the timing of the availability of the data. For example, when will the value of D(EOM) for (July 1992–June 1992) be known? Maybe after the first few days into August 1992. When will the June 1992 rates be known for (AAA) and (3-4)? And when will D(3-4) for (July 1992–June 1992) be available? Answers to these questions will determine how difficult it will be to forecast D(EOM) for period 54.

The equation for forecasting D(EOM) for period 54 is

$$D(EOM)_{54} = -6.2 + 4.4(AAA)_{54} - 3.2(3\text{-}4)_{54} - 1.7D(3\text{-}4)_{54} - 3.0 - 0.04(54).$$

The second last term (-3.0) arises because the only seasonal dummy variable which is not zero is D_6 and takes the value 1 (see Table 6-8) with coefficient -3.0. Therefore, if the time point of reference is, for example, August 5, 1992, the data

$(AAA)_{54}$ for (July 1992) will already be known,

$(3\text{-}4)_{54}$ for (July 1992) will already be known,

$D(3\text{-}4)_{54}$ for (August 1992–July 1992) will not be known.

The last variable, $D(3\text{-}4)_{54}$, will have to be forecast. Any of the methods in Chapter 4 might well be tried until a "best" forecast for (3-4) rates for August 1992 can be obtained. Then D(3-4) for period 54 will be calculable.

For period 55, none of the three explanatory variable values will be known as of August 5, 1992. They will all have to be forecast.

(1)	(2)	(3)	(4)	(5)	(6)	(7)	(8)
		Period	Period	Period	Period	Period	Period
Label		54	55	56	57	58	59
X_1	$(AAA)_{-1}$	7.298	7.305	7.307	7.309	7.311	7.313
X_2	$(3\text{-}4)_{-1}$	5.820	5.848	5.883	5.918	5.952	5.987
X_3	$D(3\text{-}4)_0$	0.028	0.035	0.035	0.034	0.035	0.034
D_2	Apr–Mar	0	0	0	0	0	0
D_3	May–Jun	0	0	0	0	0	0
D_4	Jun–May	0	0	0	0	0	0
D_5	Jul–Jun	0	0	0	0	0	0
D_6	Aug–Jul	1	0	0	0	0	0
D_7	Sep–Aug	0	1	0	0	0	0
D_8	Oct–Sep	0	0	1	0	0	0
D_9	Nov–Oct	0	0	0	1	0	0
D_{10}	Dec–Nov	0	0	0	0	1	0
D_{11}	Jan–Dec	0	0	0	0	0	1
Time		54	55	56	57	58	59
D(EOM)		1.863	1.221	0.114	2.779	1.959	5.789

Table 6-14: *Bank data: forecast values of the explanatory variables obtained using Holt's method.*

Similarly, for any future time period, the values of (3-4) and (AAA) will have to be forecast first, and only then can the regression equation be used. All the dummy variables and the (time) variable in (6.12) present no problem—they are constants.

Table 6-14 shows the forecasts which are needed. Columns (3) through (8) are the time periods 54 through 59, for which forecasts of D(EOM) are required. In row 1, dealing with $(AAA)_{-1}$—that is, AAA bond rates lagged one period—the regression equation will require values for periods 54 through 59. The $(AAA)_1$ value for period 54 is already known (it is 7.30) because $(AAA)_1$ leads D(EOM) by one period. The other values for $(AAA)_1$ have to be estimated (forecast). To do this, Holt's method of exponential smoothing (see Section 4/3/3) was used and the 5-period ahead forecasts using this method are shown in Table 6-14. (Note that no attempt has been made to do the best job of forecasting the explanatory variables. It is one of the exercises to improve upon the procedure illustrated in this section.)

Similarly, for row 2, dealing with $(3\text{-}4)_{-1}$—that is, rates for 3-4 year government issues—the value for period 54 is already known (it is 5.82) and the other values have to be forecast. Again using Holt's method to provide these forecasts, we determine the values shown in the rest of row 2. The row 3 data in Table 6-14 are the set of first differences for the (3-4) data. Note that it was actually necessary to forecast six periods ahead for the (3-4) data so as to get the last D(3-4) value of 0.034 in row 3 of Table 6-14.

The rows dealing with the dummy variables are straightforward. For example, the first four dummy variables (chosen in the best subsets procedure leading to equation (6.12)) take on the value 0 for all periods 54 through 59. All other dummy variables have one value that is 1 and all other values zero, as shown in Table 6-14. Finally, for the linear trend term, the values in Table 6-14 are simply (54), (55), ..., (59).

In the very last row of Table 6-14 are the forecasts for D(EOM) for periods 54 through 59 obtained using equation (6.12) with the values of explanatory variables given in the table. For example, under column (2), for period 54 (which refers to the change period Aug. 1992 minus July 1992) the forecast of D(EOM) is 1.863. This is obtained by substituting the values in column 3 into equation (6.12) as follows:

$$
\begin{aligned}
1.863 \;=\; & -6.15 + 4.39(7.298) - 3.22(5.820) - 1.69(0.028) - 4.41(0) \\
& - 1.23(0) - 2.98(0) - 1.18(0) - 2.98(1) - 3.51(0) \\
& - 4.47(0) - 1.66(0) - 2.34(0) + 1.63(0) - 0.042(54).
\end{aligned}
$$

From the bank's point of view, if it is August 5, 1992 and the value of D(EOM) for (July 1992–June 1992) is known, then they can expect an increase of $1,863 in end-of-month balance by the end of August. This is what the forecast says.

Similarly, the other forecasts can be used to get an idea of the changes in (EOM) that can be expected in future months. Since the regression method allows the forecaster to provide prediction intervals around any given forecast, we now use equation (6.13) to obtain 90% prediction intervals for the forecasts. Table 6-15 and Figure 6-9 show the results. Note that five out of the six actual values for these periods fall within the intervals for $\hat{Y}$.

Period	True value Y	Forecast $\hat{Y}$	Standard Error	90% Prediction Interval
54	4.646	1.86	1.42	$[-0.47\,,\,4.20\,]$
55	1.060	1.22	1.40	$[-1.09\,,\,3.53\,]$
56	-0.758	0.11	1.41	$[-2.20\,,\,2.43\,]$
57	4.702	2.78	1.42	$[\ 0.44\,,\,5.12\,]$
58	1.878	1.96	1.44	$[-0.42\,,\,4.33\,]$
59	6.620	5.79	1.44	$[\ 3.42\,,\,8.16\,]$

Table 6-15: *Predictions and prediction intervals for the bank forecasts for periods 54 through 59 using the regression model in equation (6.12).*

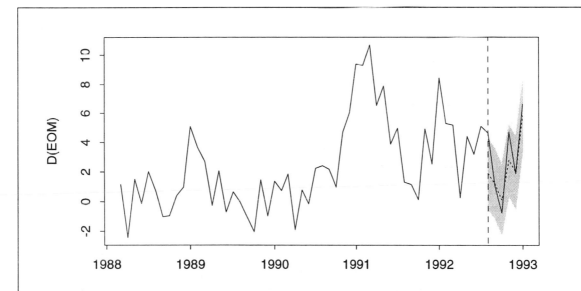

Figure 6-9: *Predictions for the bank data as given in Table 6-15. The solid line shows the actual data, the dotted line shows the forecasts. The 90% intervals are shown as the shaded region.*

6/5/3 Recapitulation

From the previous section it is clear that if a regression model involved a explanatory variable that leads the forecast variable by two periods, say, then two forecasts of $\hat{Y}$ can be made without having to forecast the explanatory variables. There are two values of the explanatory variable in hand already. Whenever $\hat{Y}$ is being forecast further ahead, then the explanatory variables must also be forecast, and the forecast values $(\hat{Y})$ are subject to additional uncertainty which is not reflected in the forecast intervals.

Dummy variables can be used effectively to handle seasonality or special events or both. In the cases mentioned above, the dummy variables affected only the constant term (the intercept), but they can be used to influence the slope coefficients as well.

Regression packages are widely available, so that the computational grind is minimal, but forecasters should be aware that not all computer programs are equally good. Some are robust with respect to roundness of errors—others are not. Some are sensitive to near-collinearity problems—others are not. Some provide information on the correlations among the explanatory variables and the correlations among the regression coefficients—others do not. Some allow for graphical output—others do not. In our opinion, it is worthwhile making sure a comprehensive regression package is available for the model-building process described in this chapter.

Since explanatory variables often have to be predicted before the forecast variable can be predicted, it is important to get good forecasts for these explanatory variables. Many firms buy the services of forecasting houses to get such forecasts, and, often, corporate planners will buy econometric forecasts which will then be passed down to the business units of the company for their forecasting and planning models. Much has been written on the relative merits of econometric forecasts—and the performance of such forecasts over time—but some major companies make use of them as inputs for other models (e.g., regression models at the business unit level).

Regression analysis is a powerful method and the most commonly used approach to model the effect of explanatory variables on the forecast variable.

6/6 Econometric models

In the same way that simple regression is a special case of multiple regression, the latter is a special case of econometric models. While multiple regression involves a single equation, econometric models can include any number of simultaneous multiple regression equations. The term "econometric models" will be used in this book to denote systems of linear equations involving several *interdependent variables*. It should be noted that this is not the only usage of the term "econometrics," since there are those who use it as a general term to cover simple, multiple, and systems of multiple regression equations. The more limited definition used in this chapter appears to be the most common usage at this time.

The objective of this section is not to provide the level of detailed information needed to fully utilize these models, but to review the main ideas and concepts underlying econometric models and present the main advantages and difficulties involved.

6/6/1 The basis of econometric modeling

Regression analysis assumes that each of the explanatory variables included in the regression equation is determined by outside factors; that is, they are exogenous to the system. In economic or organizational relationships, however, such an assumption is often unrealistic. To illustrate this point, one can assume that sales $= f(\text{GNP, price, advertising})$. In regression, all three explanatory variables are assumed to be exogenously determined; they are not influenced by the level of sales itself. This is a fair assumption as far as GNP is concerned, which, except for very large corporations, is not influenced directly by the sales of a single firm. However, for price and advertising there is unlikely to be a similar absence of influence. For example, if the per unit cost is proportional to sales volume, different levels of sales will result in higher or lower per unit costs.

Furthermore, advertising expenditures will certainly influence the per unit price of the product offered, since production and selling costs influence the per unit price. The price in turn influences the magnitude of sales, which can consequently influence the level of advertising. These interrelationships point to the mutual interdependence among the variables of such an equation. Regression analysis is incapable of dealing with such interdependence as part of the explanatory model.

Instead we can use a system of simultaneous equations that can deal with the interdependence among the variables. For example, these interdependencies might be represented by the following simple econometric model:

$$\text{sales} = f(\text{GNP, price, advertising})$$
$$\text{production cost} = f(\text{number of units produced, inventories,}$$
$$\text{labor costs, material cost})$$
$$\text{selling expenses} = f(\text{advertising, other selling expenses})$$
$$\text{advertising} = f(\text{sales})$$
$$\text{price} = f(\text{production cost, selling expenses, administrative overhead, profit}).$$

In place of one regression equation expressing sales as a function of three explanatory variables, the set of five simultaneous equations above expresses sales and the explanatory variables as functions of each other plus other exogenous factors.

The basic premise of econometric modeling is that everything in the real world depends upon everything else. Changing A not only affects A and its immediate system, but also the environment in general. The practical question is, of course, where to stop considering these interdependencies. One could develop an almost infinite number of interdependent relationships, but data collection, computational limitations, and estimation problems restrict one in practice to a limited number of relationships. In addition, the marginal understanding, or forecasting accuracy, does not increase in proportion to the effort required to include an additional variable or equation after the first few. In econometric models, a major decision is determining how much detail to include, since more detail inevitably means more complexity.

In an econometric model one is faced with many tasks similar to those in multiple regression analysis. These tasks include:

1. determining which variables to include in each equation (specification);
2. determining the functional form (i.e., linear, exponential, logarithmic, etc.) of each of the equations;
3. estimating in a simultaneous manner the parameters of all the equations;

4. testing the statistical significance of the results;

5. checking the validity of the assumptions involved.

Steps 2, 4, and 5 do not differ in their basic approach from those of multiple regression, and therefore will not be discussed further in this chapter. However, it should be mentioned that there is usually not much choice on Step 2, and Step 4 is seldom pursued rigorously, in practice. Furthermore, in practice, Step 3 is not often done in a simultaneous manner.

6/6/2 The advantages and drawbacks of econometric methods

The main advantage of econometric models lies in their ability to deal with interdependencies. If a government, for example, would like to know the results of a 10% tax reduction aimed at stimulating a recessionary economy, it has few alternatives other than econometric models. A tax cut will have direct and immediate effects on increasing personal disposable income and probably decreasing government revenues. It will also tend to influence inflation, unemployment, savings, capital spending, and so on. Each of these will in turn influence personal disposable income and therefore taxes of subsequent years. Through a series of chain reactions, the 10% decrease will affect almost all economic factors and business revenues. These interdependencies must be considered if the effect of the tax cut is to be accurately predicted. (However, it must be remembered that while an econometric model may provide useful insights, the "effects" it captures will be those built into it.)

Econometric models are valuable tools for increasing the understanding of the way an economic system works and for testing and evaluating alternative policies. These goals, however, are somewhat different from forecasting. Complex econometric models do not always give better forecasts than simpler time series approaches. It is important to distinguish between econometric models used for policy analysis and econometric models used for forecasting. They are two different things.

Econometric models for forecasting are generally much simpler and involve fewer equations than those designed for policy study. The main purpose of forecasting versions is to derive values for the explanatory variables so that they do not have to be estimated. For example, in the simple econometric model given above, two of the variables (price and advertising) can be estimated internally. Thus there is no need to specify their values in order to forecast sales. GNP, on the other hand, still needs to be specified because it is determined outside or exogenously.

Whether intended for policy or forecasting purposes, econometric models are considerably more difficult to develop and estimate than using alternative statistical methods. The difficulties are of two types:

1. technical aspects, involved in specifying the equations and estimating their parameters, and
2. cost considerations, related to the amount of data needed and the computing and human resources required.

In the final analysis, the question is whether the extra burden required for developing and running an econometric model justifies the costs involved. It is the authors' experience that the answer is *yes* if the user is a government, *maybe* if it is a large organization interested in policy considerations, and *probably not* if it is a medium or small organization, or if the econometric model is intended for forecasting purposes only. The above guidelines do not apply to buying the services of one of the several econometric models available commercially. Generally, the cost of using such services is only a small fraction of that of developing and operating one's own econometric model. But even the forecasting accuracy of such models must be considered against cheaper or free alternatives (e.g., the cost-free forecasts provided by central banks, governmental organizations, or OECD).

One of the major weaknesses of econometric models is the absence of a set of rules that can be applied across different situations. This makes the development of econometric models highly dependent upon the specific situation and requires the involvement of a skilled and experienced econometrician. Such skills are expensive, increasing forecasting costs. Finally, once a model is developed, it cannot be left to run on its own with no outside interference. Continuous monitoring of the results and updating for periodic changes are needed. These disadvantages have limited the application of econometrics to forecasting, even in large organizations.

Appendix 6-A
The Durbin-Watson statistic

The Durbin-Watson (DW) statistic tests the hypothesis that there is no lag one autocorrelation present in the residuals. Like the F-test and t-tests, the computed value of the Durbin-Watson test is compared with the corresponding values from Table F of Appendix III. If there is no autocorrelation, the DW distribution is symmetric around 2, its mean value.

The test is based on the five regions shown in Figure 6-10. These are computed using the two values (DW_L and DW_U) which are read from the row of the DW table that corresponds to the degrees of freedom of the data.

The five intervals are:

1. less than DW_L

2. between DW_L and DW_U

3. between DW_U and $4 - DW_U$

4. between $4 - DW_U$ and $4 - DW_L$

5. more than $4 - DW_L$

If the computed value of DW is either in interval 1 or 5, the existence of autocorrelation is indicated. If DW is in interval 3, no autocorrelation is present. If it is in either 2 or 4, the test is inconclusive as to whether autocorrelation exists.

For example, if there are three explanatory variables and 30 observations, then

$$DW_L = 1.21 \quad \text{and} \quad DW_U = 1.65.$$

If DW is less than 1.21 or more than

$$4 - DW_L = 41.21 = 2.79,$$

303

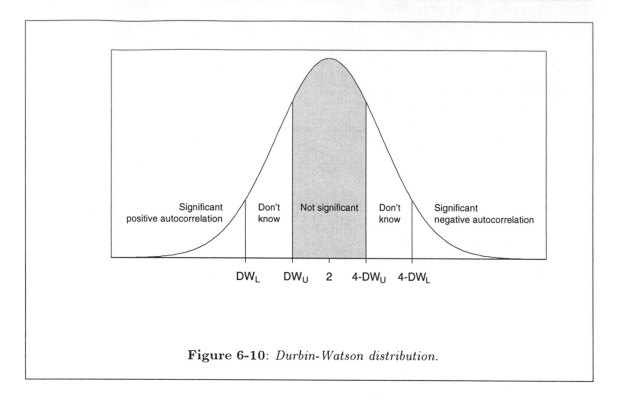

Figure 6-10: *Durbin-Watson distribution.*

there is autocorrelation. If DW is between 1.65 and $4 - DW_U = 2.35$, there is no autocorrelation. If DW is between 1.21 and 1.65 or between 2.35 and 2.79, the test is inconclusive.

It should be noted that when there is no prior knowledge of the sign of the serial correlation, two-sided tests may be made by combining single-tail tests. Thus by using the 5% values of DW_L and DW_U from Table F in Appendix III, a two-sided test at the 10% level is obtained.

References and selected bibliography

BELL, W.R. and S.C. HILLMER (1983) Modeling time series with calendar variation, *Journal of the American Statistical Association*, **78**, 526–534.

CLEVELAND, W.S. (1993) *Visualizing data*, Summit, N.J.: Hobart Press.

COOLEY, W.W. and P.R. LOHNES (1971) *Multivariate data analysis*, New York: John Wiley & Sons.

DRAPER, N.R. and H. SMITH (1981) *Applied regression analysis*, 2nd ed., New York: John Wiley & Sons.

JOHNSTON, J. (1984) *Econometric Methods*, 3rd ed., New York: McGraw-Hill.

JUDGE, G.G., R.C. HILL, W.E. GRIFFITHS, H. LÜTKEPOHL, and T.-C. LEE (1988) *Introduction to the theory and practice of econometrics*, 2nd ed, New York: John Wiley & Sons.

KMENTA, J. (1986) *Elements of Econometrics*, 3rd ed., New York: Macmillan.

MANSFIELD, E. (1994) *Statistics for business and economics: methods and applications*, 5th ed., Norton.

MENDENHALL, W. and T. SINCICH (1996) *A second course in statistics: regression analysis*, 5th ed., Englewood Cliffs, N.J.: Prentice-Hall.

MONTGOMERY, D.C. and E.A. PECK (1992) *Introduction to linear regression analysis*, 2nd ed., New York: John Wiley & Sons.

PINDYCK, R.S. and D.L. RUBENFELD (1991) *Econometric models and economic forecasts*, 3rd ed., New York: McGraw-Hill.

WONNACOTT, T.H. and R.J. WONNACOTT (1990) *Introductory statistics for business and economics*, 4th ed., New York: John Wiley & Sons.

Exercises

6.1 Table 6-16 presents some of the computer output from a regression analysis.

   (a) How many observations were involved?

   (b) What would be the value of $\bar{R}^2$?

   (c) Is the overall regression significant?

   (d) Which coefficients are significantly different from zero (i.e., have P-value less than 0.05)?

   (e) What should be done next?

Variable	Coefficient	Standard Error	t
Constant	357835.	30740.7	11.6404
1	1007.43	524.846	1.91947
2	56089.2	43008.2	-1.30415
3	21165.1	34096.0	0.62075
4	88410.9	35825.1	-2.46785
5	22488.2	35428.0	0.63476
6	35399.5	34087.5	-1.03849
7	21218.7	33351.4	-0.63622
8	122709.	36535.8	-3.35859
9	3048.89	30339.1	-0.10049
10	57311.0	37581.1	-1.52500
11	70596.2	38493.5	-1.83398
12	184778.	36655.7	-5.04089
13	0.417727	0.00684181	6.10550
14	0.216098	0.00653552	-3.30651
15	0.297009	0.00334643	8.87541
16	0.00119271	0.00337776	0.35311
17	0.00685211	0.00326835	-2.09650

$R^2 = 0.943$ $s = 3850.12$

DF for numerator $= 16$ DF for denominator $= 30$

F value $= 31.04$ Durbin-Watson statistic $= 2.27202$

Table 6-16: *Results of regression run.*

6.2 The Texas natural gas data in Table 5-10 show gas consumption (C) and price (P). In Exercise 5.10, two regression models were fitted to these data: a linear regression of log C on P and a piecewise linear regression of C on P.

(a) Now try what is known as a quadratic regression with

$$\hat{C} = b_0 + b_1 P + b_2 P^2.$$

Compare this with the previous results. Check the $\bar{R}^2$ value, the t values for the coefficients, and consider which of the three models makes most sense.

(b) For the quadratic regression compute prediction intervals for forecasts of consumption for various prices, for example, $P = 20$, 40, 60, 80, 100, and 120 cents per 1,000 cubic feet [using (6.13)].

(c) What is the correlation between P and P^2? Does this suggest any general problem to be considered in dealing with polynomial regressions—especially of higher orders?

6.3 The regression analysis resulting in equation (6.12) was used to forecast the change in end-of-month balance for a bank for the next six time periods (periods 54 through 59). See Section 6/5/2 for details. However, since we originally omitted the known values for D(EOM) for these periods, it is possible to examine the usefulness of the regression model.

(a) Compare the forecasts with the actuals (Table 6-15) and determine the MAPE and other summary statistics for these forecasts.

(b) It was necessary to forecast (AAA) and (3-4) rates for future periods before it was possible to get forecasts for D(EOM). Holt's linear exponential smoothing method was used in Section 6/5/2 to do this. However, this is not necessarily the best choice and no attempt was made to optimize the parameter values. Try finding a better method to forecast these (AAA) and (3-4) rates, and then recompute the forecasts for D(EOM) according to the scheme laid out in Table 6-14.

(c) Compare your new forecasts with the actual D(EOM) values in Table 6-15 and compute the MAPE and other statistics to show the quality of the forecasts. How well do your new forecasts compare with those in Table 6-14?

X_1	7	11	11	3	2	3	21	1	11	10
X_2	26	52	55	71	31	54	47	40	66	68
X_3	60	20	22	6	44	22	26	34	12	14
Y	78	104	109	102	74	93	115	83	113	109

Table 6-17: *Cement composition and heat data. X_1, X_2, and X_3 denote percentages by weight of three components in the cement mixture, and Y denotes the heat evolved in calories per gram of cement.*

6.4 Table 6-17 shows the percentages by weight of three components in the cement mixture, and the heat emitted in calories per gram of cement.

(a) Regress Y against the three components and find confidence intervals for each of the three coefficients.

(b) Carry out an F-test for the regression model. What does the P-value mean?

(c) Plot the residuals against each of the explanatory variables. Does the model appear satisfactory?

(d) What proportion of the variation in Y is explained by the regression relationship?

(e) Which of the three components cause an increase in heat and which cause a decrease in heat? Which component has the greatest effect on the heat emitted?

(f) What would be the heat emitted for cement consisting of $X_1 = 10$, $X_2 = 40$, and $X_3 = 30$? Give a 90% prediction interval.

6.5 The data set in Table 6-18 shows the dollar volume on the New York plus American Stock Exchange (as the explanatory variable X) and the dollar volume on the Boston Regional Exchange (as the forecast variable Y).

(a) Regress Y on X and check the significance of the results.

(b) Regress Y on X and t (time) and check the significance of the results.

(c) Plot the data (Y against X) and join up the points according to their timing—that is, join the point for $t = 1$ to the point for $t = 2$, and so on. Note that the relationship between Y and X changes over time.

Month (t)	New York and American Stock Exchanges (X)	Boston Stock Exchange (Y)
Jan 1967	10581.6	78.8
Feb 1967	10234.3	69.1
Mar 1967	13299.5	87.6
Apr 1967	10746.5	72.8
May 1967	13310.7	79.4
Jun 1967	12835.5	85.6
Jul 1967	12194.2	75.0
Aug 1967	12860.4	85.3
Sep 1967	11955.6	86.9
Oct 1967	13351.5	107.8
Nov 1967	13285.9	128.7
Dec 1967	13784.4	134.5
Jan 1968	16336.7	148.7
Feb 1968	11040.5	94.2
Mar 1968	11525.3	128.1
Apr 1968	16056.4	154.1
May 1968	18464.3	191.3
Jun 1968	17092.2	191.9
Jul 1968	15178.8	159.6
Aug 1968	12774.8	185.5
Sep 1968	12377.8	178.0
Oct 1968	16856.3	271.8
Nov 1968	14635.3	212.3
Dec 1968	17436.9	139.4
Jan 1969	16482.2	106.0
Feb 1969	13905.4	112.1
Mar 1969	11973.7	103.5
Apr 1969	12573.6	92.5
May 1969	16566.8	116.9
Jun 1969	13558.7	78.9
Jul 1969	11530.9	57.4
Aug 1969	11278.0	75.9
Sep 1969	11263.7	109.8
Oct 1969	15649.5	129.2
Nov 1969	12197.1	115.1

Table 6-18: *Monthly dollar volume of sales (in millions) on Boston Stock Exchange and combined New York and American Stock Exchanges. Source: McGee and Carleton (1970) "Piecewise regression," Journal of the American Statistical Association, 65, 1109–1124.*

6.6 Equations (6.10) and (6.12) give two regression models for the mutual savings bank data.

(a) From equation (6.10) compute a set of seasonal indices by examining the constant term in the regression equation when just one dummy variable at a time is set equal to 1, with all others set to 0. Finally, set all dummy variables to 0 and examine the constant term.

(b) Repeat this procedure using equation (6.12) and compare the two sets of seasonal indices.

(c) The use of dummy variables requires that some time period is regarded as "base period" (the period for which all the dummy variables have zero value). In equations (6.10) and (6.12) the twelfth-period was chosen as base. Rerun the regression model of equation (6.10) using some other period as the base. Then recompute the seasonal indices and compare them with those in part (a) above.

6.7 A company which manufactures automotive parts wishes to model the effect of advertising on sales. The advertising expenditure each month and the sales volume each month for the last two years are given in Table 6-19.

(a) Fit the regression model $Y_t = a + bX_t + e_t$ where Y_t denotes sales, X_t denotes advertising, and e_t is the error.

(b) Calculate the Durbin–Watson statistic and show that there is significant autocorrelation in the residuals.

t	X	Y	t	X	Y	t	X	Y	t	X	Y
1	25	92.8	7	5	79.9	13	15	85.4	19	15	89.1
2	0	79.2	8	5	81.1	14	5	80.5	20	20	90.9
3	15	84.5	9	15	86.4	15	10	83.5	21	25	92.7
4	10	83.0	10	15	86.3	16	25	92.5	22	15	88.1
5	20	88.1	11	5	79.9	17	15	89.5	23	0	79.5
6	10	83.9	12	20	86.6	18	5	83.6	24	5	82.9

Table 6-19: *Sales volume (Y) and advertising expenditure (X) data for an automotive parts company.*

7

THE BOX-JENKINS METHODOLOGY FOR ARIMA MODELS

ARIMA models

Autoregressive / Integrated / Moving Average (ARIMA) models have been studied extensively. They were popularized by George Box and Gwilym Jenkins in the early 1970s, and their names have frequently been used synonymously with general ARIMA models applied to time series analysis and forecasting. Box and Jenkins (1970) effectively put together in a comprehensive manner the relevant information required to understand and use univariate time series ARIMA models. The theoretical underpinnings described by Box and Jenkins (1970) and later by Box, Jenkins, and Reinsell (1994) are quite sophisticated, but it is possible for the non-specialist to get a clear understanding of the essence of ARIMA methodology.

In this chapter, we have four main purposes:

1. introduction of the various *concepts* useful in time series analysis (and forecasting);
2. description of the *statistical tools* that have proved useful in analyzing time series;
3. definition of some general *notation* (proposed by Box and Jenkins, 1970) for dealing with general ARIMA models;
4. illustrations of how the concepts, statistical tools, and notation can be combined to model and forecast a wide variety of time series.

As indicated in preceding chapters, application of a general class of forecasting methods involves two basic tasks: *analysis* of the data series and *selection* of the forecasting model (i.e., the specific methods within that class) that best fits the data series. Thus in using a smoothing method, analysis of the data series for seasonality aids in selection of a specific smoothing method that can handle the seasonality (or its absence). A similar sequence of analysis and selection is used in working with decomposition methods and regression methods. Thus, it will come as no surprise that the same two tasks of analysis and model selection occur again in this chapter. The first three sections of this chapter will focus on the task of analysis. The subsequent sections will concentrate on model selection and applications of the models to forecasting.

After plotting the time series, the major statistical tool is the autocorrelation coefficient, r_k, which describes the relationship between various values of the time series that are lagged k periods apart. Autocorrelations and related tools are considered in Section 7/1.

Section 7/2 looks at techniques to make a time series stationary—an essential step for the analysis and modeling of time series. ARIMA models are introduced in Section 7/3 and some of their properties are considered.

The basis of the Box-Jenkins approach to modeling time series is summarized in Figure 7-1 and consists of three phases: identification, estimation and testing, and application. In this chapter, each of the three phases of Figure 7-1 will be examined and practical examples illustrating the application of the Box-Jenkins methodology to univariate time series analysis will be given. Identifying an appropriate ARIMA model is considered in Section 7/4 and estimating the parameters of the model is the subject of Section 7/5. Section 7/6 discusses methods for refining the selected ARIMA model and Section 7/7 uses the techniques of Section 7/1 to test that the chosen model is appropriate. Finally, the model can be applied in forecasting as described in Section 7/8.

7/1 Examining correlations in time series data

In this section we concentrate on certain analyses that can be applied to an empirical time series to determine its statistical properties. These techniques will later be applied to gain insight as to what kind of formal forecasting model might be appropriate.

7/1/1 The autocorrelation function

The key statistic in time series analysis is the autocorrelation coefficient (or the correlation of the time series with itself, lagged by 1, 2, or more periods). This was introduced in Section 2/2/3. Recall the formula

autocorrelation

$$
r_k = \frac{\displaystyle\sum_{t=k+1}^{n} (Y_t - \bar{Y})(Y_{t-k} - \bar{Y})}{\displaystyle\sum_{t=1}^{n} (Y_t - \bar{Y})^2}.
\qquad (7.1)
$$

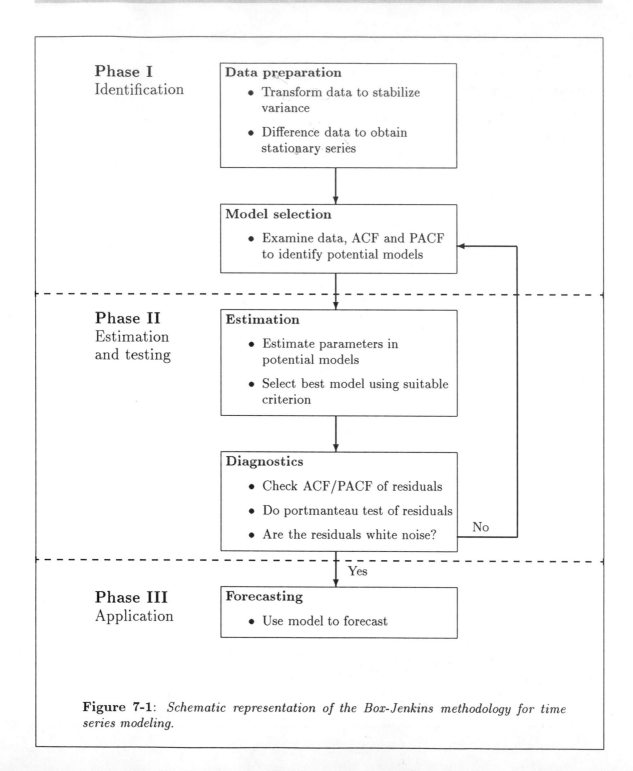

Figure 7-1: *Schematic representation of the Box-Jenkins methodology for time series modeling.*

Period	Value	Period	Value	Period	Value
1	23	13	86	25	17
2	59	14	33	26	45
3	36	15	90	27	9
4	99	16	74	28	72
5	36	17	7	29	33
6	74	18	54	30	17
7	30	19	98	31	3
8	54	20	50	32	29
9	17	21	86	33	30
10	36	22	90	34	68
11	89	23	65	35	87
12	77	24	20	36	44

Table 7-1: *Time series with 36 values.*

Then r_1 indicates how successive values of Y relate to each other, r_2 indicates how Y values two periods apart relate to each other, and so on. Together, the autocorrelations at lags 1, 2, ..., make up the *autocorrelation function* or ACF. Plots of the ACF were used in Sections 2/2/3 and 6/2/1.

autocorrelation function (ACF)

Consider the time series consisting of the 36 observations in Table 7-1 and plotted in Figure 7-2. This series was constructed using uncorrelated random numbers between 0 and 100. Suppose, however, that this fact were not known. It could be determined by applying autocorrelation analysis. For uncorrelated data, we would expect each autocorrelation to be close to zero. Figure 7-3 shows the autocorrelation coefficients for the data in Table 7-1, for time lags of $1, 2, 3, \ldots, 10$.

The autocorrelation function is a valuable tool for investigating properties of an empirical time series, as will become clear in the pages that follow. However, the statistical theory underlying r_k is quite complicated, and in some cases intractable. For the special case of a "white noise" series (see Section 7/1/2), the sampling theory of r_k is known and can be used to practical advantage.

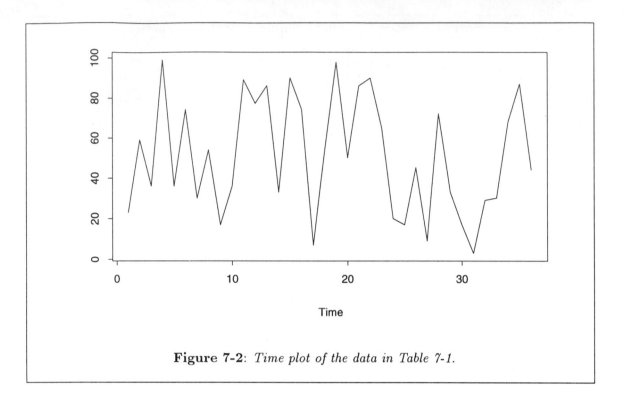

Figure 7-2: *Time plot of the data in Table 7-1.*

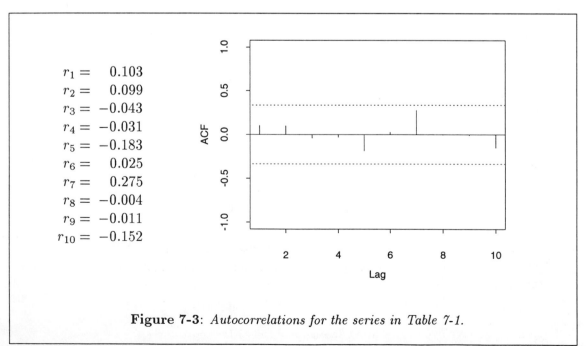

$r_1 = 0.103$
$r_2 = 0.099$
$r_3 = -0.043$
$r_4 = -0.031$
$r_5 = -0.183$
$r_6 = 0.025$
$r_7 = 0.275$
$r_8 = -0.004$
$r_9 = -0.011$
$r_{10} = -0.152$

Figure 7-3: *Autocorrelations for the series in Table 7-1.*

7/1/2 A white noise model

Equation (7.2) is a simple random model where observation Y_t is made up of two parts, an overall level, c, and a random error component, e_t, which is uncorrelated from period to period:

$$\boxed{Y_t = c + e_t}.$$ (7.2)

The data in Table 7-1 were obtained from this model. It is often called a "white noise" model—a terminology which comes from engineering.   white noise

The white noise model is fundamental to many techniques in time series analysis. In fact, we have already used it in earlier chapters. Any good forecasting model should have forecast errors which follow a white noise model (see Section 2/4/5).

7/1/3 The sampling distribution of autocorrelations

With a time series which is white noise, the sampling theory of r_k is known and so the properties of the ACF can be studied for this model.

One way of approaching this problem is to study the r_k values one at a time and to develop a standard error formula to test whether a particular r_k is significantly different from zero.

Theoretically, all autocorrelation coefficients for a series of random numbers must be zero. But because we have finite samples, each of the sample autocorrelations will not be exactly zero. It has been shown by Anderson (1942), Bartlett (1946), Quenouille (1949), and others, that the autocorrelation coefficients of white noise data have a sampling distribution that can be approximated by a normal curve with mean zero and standard error $1/\sqrt{n}$ where n is the number of   standard error observations in the series. This information can be used to develop tests of hypotheses similar to those of the F-test and the t-tests examined in Chapters 5 and 6.

For example, 95% of all sample autocorrelation coefficients must lie within a range specified by the mean plus or minus 1.96 standard errors.[1]   Since the mean is zero and the standard error is $1/\sqrt{n}$

---

[1]The value of 1.96 is found by looking at Table A, Appendix III, of areas under the normal curve. Since it is close to 2, it is often approximated by 2.

for white noise, we expect about 95% of all sample autocorrelation coefficients to be within $\pm 1.96/\sqrt{n}$. If this is not the case, the series is probably not white noise. For this reason, it is common to plot lines at $\pm 1.96/\sqrt{n}$ when plotting the ACF. These limits are known as the *critical values*.

critical values

In Table 7-1, $n = 36$ and so the standard error is $1/\sqrt{36} = 0.167$. This means that the limits for the autocorrelations are at $\pm 1.96/\sqrt{36} = \pm 0.327$. These limits are shown on Figure 7-3. All 10 autocorrelation coefficients lie within these limits, confirming what in this case was already known—the data are white noise.

The concept of a sampling distribution is of critical importance in time series analysis. The autocorrelation coefficient corresponding to a time lag of seven periods in Figure 7-3 is 0.275. This value is different from zero because of the effect of chance. The sampling distribution provides guidelines as to what is chance and what constitutes a significant relationship. The value of 0.275 is not significantly different from zero. However, if this value had been obtained for 360 observations instead of 36, the standard error would have been only 0.053 and the limits would have been ± 0.103, instead of ± 0.327. This means that, on average, the autocorrelations would be smaller than ± 0.103 in 95 out of every 100 times. In that case an r_7 of 0.275 would have indicated the presence of a pattern every seven time lags (or periods), since it would have fallen outside the limits. Of course, with 360 random values, it would be very unlikely to observe such a high r value. In summary, the sampling distribution and standard error allow us to interpret the results from autocorrelation analysis so that we can distinguish what is pattern from what is randomness, or white noise, in our data.

7/1/4 Portmanteau tests

Rather than study the r_k values one at a time, an alternative approach is to consider a whole set of r_k values, say the first 15 of them (r_1 through r_{15}) all at one time, and develop a test to see whether the set is significantly different from a zero set. Tests of this sort are known as *portmanteau tests*.

portmanteau tests

A common portmanteau test is the Box-Pierce test which is based on the Box-Pierce Q statistic:

$$Q = n \sum_{k=1}^{h} r_k^2$$

Box-Pierce Q statistic

where h is the maximum lag being considered and n is the number of observations in the series. Usually $h \approx 20$ is selected. Some packages will give the Q statistic for several different values of h.

Clearly, if each r_k is close to zero, Q will be relatively small whereas if some r_k values are large (either positive or negative), the Q statistic will be relatively large. The Box-Pierce test was designed by Box and Pierce (1970) for testing the residuals from a forecast model. If the residuals are white noise, the statistic Q has a chi-square (χ^2) distribution with $(h - m)$ degrees of freedom where m is the number of parameters in the model which has been fitted to the data. The value of Q can be compared with the chi-square table (Table E of Appendix III) to assess if it is significant.

chi-square distribution

The test can easily be applied to raw data, when no model has been fitted, by simply setting $m = 0$.

For the r_k values in Figure 7-3, the Box-Pierce Q statistic is computed as follows:

$$Q = 36 \sum_{k=1}^{10} r_k^2 = 5.62.$$

Here we have used $h = 10$ and, since the data in Table 7-1 were not modeled in any way, $m = 0$. Hence, we look up the chi-square value of 5.62 (in Table E of Appendix III) with 10 degrees of freedom. In the row corresponding to 10 df, we see that the probability of obtaining a chi-square value as large or larger than 5.62 is more than 0.1. So we conclude that the set of r_k values is not significantly different from a null set.

An alternative portmanteau test is the Ljung-Box test due to Ljung and Box (1978). They argued that the alternative statistic

$$Q^* = n(n+2) \sum_{k=1}^{h} (n-k)^{-1} r_k^2$$

Ljung-Box Q^* statistic

has a distribution closer to the chi-square distribution than does the

Q statistic. For the r_k values in Figure 7-3,

$$Q^* = 36(38) \sum_{k=1}^{10} \frac{1}{36-k} r_k^2$$

$$= 36(38) \left[\frac{1}{35} r_1^2 + \frac{1}{34} r_2^2 + \cdots + \frac{1}{26} r_{10}^2 \right]$$

$$= 7.22.$$

chi-square
distribution

If the data are white noise, the Ljung-Box Q^* statistic has exactly the same distribution as the Box-Pierce Q statistic, namely a chi-square distribution with $(h-m)$ degrees of freedom. Comparing $Q^* = 5.93$ with Table E of Appendix III (df=10) shows it is not significant.

It is normal to conclude the data are not white noise if the value of Q (or Q^*) lies in the extreme 5% of the right-hand tail of the χ^2 distribution. (That is, the value of Q or Q^* is greater than the value given in the column of Table E headed 0.05.) Unfortunately, these tests sometimes fail to reject poorly fitting models. Care should be taken not to accept a model on the basis of portmanteau tests alone.

7/1/5 The partial autocorrelation coefficient

In regression analysis, if the forecast variable Y is regressed on explanatory variables X_1 and X_2, then it might be of interest to ask how much explanatory power does X_1 have if the effects of X_2 are somehow *partialled out* first. Typically, this means regressing Y on X_2, getting the residual errors from this analysis, and finding the correlation of the residuals with X_1. In time series analysis there is a similar concept.

partial
autocorrelations

Partial autocorrelations are used to measure the degree of association between Y_t and Y_{t-k}, when the effects of other time lags— $1, 2, 3, \ldots, k-1$—are removed.

The value of this can be seen in the following simple example. Suppose there was a significant autocorrelation between Y_t and Y_{t-1}. Then there will also be a significant correlation between Y_{t-1} and Y_{t-2} since they are also one time unit apart. Consequently, there will be a correlation between Y_t and Y_{t-2} because both are related to Y_{t-1}. So to measure the real correlation between Y_t and Y_{t-2}, we need to *take out* the effect of the intervening value Y_{t-1}. This is what partial autocorrelation does.

The partial autocorrelation coefficient of order k is denoted by α_k partial
and can be calculated by regressing Y_t against $Y_{t-1}, \ldots, Y_{t-k}$:   autocorrelation

$$Y_t = b_0 + b_1 Y_{t-1} + b_2 Y_{t-2} + \cdots + b_k Y_{t-k}. \qquad (7.3)$$

This is an unusual regression because the explanatory variables on the right-hand side are previous values of the forecast variable Y_t. These are simply time-lagged values of the forecast variable, and therefore the name *autoregression* (AR) is used to describe equations of the   autoregression
form of (7.3).

The partial autocorrelation, α_k, is the estimated coefficient b_k from this multiple regression. Note that the first partial autocorrelation is always equal to the first autocorrelation. Varying the number of terms on the right-hand side of (7.3) will give the partial autocorrelations for different values of k. (Actually, there are fast algorithms for computing partial autocorrelations rather than computing the regression in (7.3).)

It is usual to plot the partial autocorrelation function or PACF.   PACF
The PACF of the data in Table 7-1 is plotted in Figure 7-4.

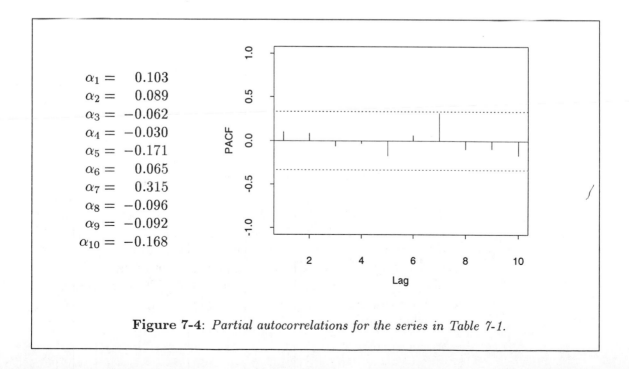

$$\alpha_1 = 0.103$$
$$\alpha_2 = 0.089$$
$$\alpha_3 = -0.062$$
$$\alpha_4 = -0.030$$
$$\alpha_5 = -0.171$$
$$\alpha_6 = 0.065$$
$$\alpha_7 = 0.315$$
$$\alpha_8 = -0.096$$
$$\alpha_9 = -0.092$$
$$\alpha_{10} = -0.168$$

Figure 7-4: *Partial autocorrelations for the series in Table 7-1.*

As with the ACF, the partial autocorrelations should all be close to zero for a white noise series. Quenouille (1949) showed that if the time series is white noise, then the estimated partial autocorrelations are approximately independent and normally distributed with a standard

critical values

error $1/\sqrt{n}$. Hence, the same critical values of $\pm 1.96/\sqrt{n}$ can be used with a PACF to assess if the data are white noise.

7/1/6 Recognizing seasonality in a time series

seasonality

Seasonality is defined as a pattern that repeats itself over fixed intervals of time. The sales of heating oil, for example, are high in winter and low in summer, indicating a 12-month seasonal pattern. If the pattern is a consistent one, the autocorrelation coefficient at lag 12 months will have a high positive value indicating the existence of seasonality. If it were not significantly different from zero, it would indicate that months one year apart are uncorrelated with no consistent pattern emerging from one year to the next. Such data would not be seasonal.

seasonal lags

In general, seasonality can be found by identifying a large autocorrelation coefficient or a large partial autocorrelation coefficient at the seasonal lag. Often autocorrelations at multiples of the seasonal lag will also be significant. So for monthly data, large autocorrelations might also be seen at lag 24 and even lag 36.

In Chapter 6, we detected seasonality in the residuals from the model for the bank data by plotting the ACF in Figure 6-7 (p. 266). The peak at lag 12 demonstrated the existence of seasonality which led to an improved model later in Chapter 6.

7/1/7 Example: Pigs slaughtered

Figure 7-5 shows the monthly total number of pigs slaughtered in the state of Victoria, Australia, from January 1990 through August 1995. It is very difficult from the time plot to detect any seasonality, or other pattern in the data. However, the ACF shows some significant autocorrelation at lags 1, 2, and 3, and the PACF shows significant partial autocorrelation at lags 1 and 3. These show that the series is not a white noise series.

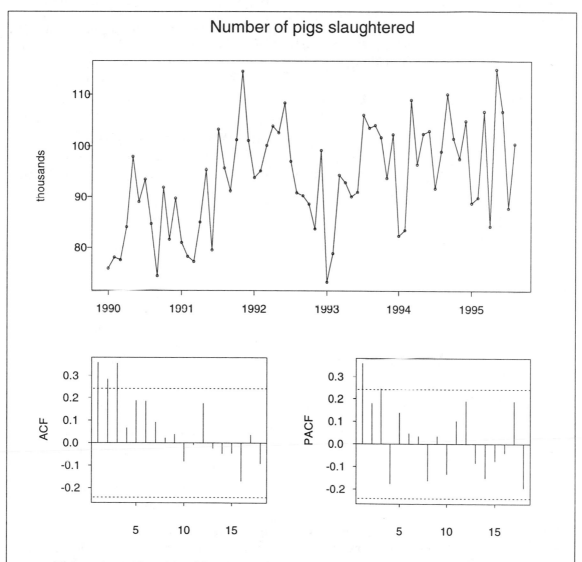

Figure 7-5: *Top: Monthly total number of pigs slaughtered in the state of Victoria, Australia, from January 1990 through August 1995. (Source: Australian Bureau of Statistics.) Bottom: ACF and PACF of these data.*

The autocorrelation at lag 12 is also relatively large although not significant. This may indicate some slight seasonality in the series, although it is not strong enough to draw a positive conclusion.

The Box-Pierce test for $h = 15$ gives the result $Q = 31.3$ and the Ljung-Box test for $h = 15$ gives $Q^* = 34.1$. As these are based on the raw data we set $m = 0$ and compare these figures to a chi-squared distribution with 15 degrees of freedom. Table E of Appendix III shows that these results are both significant and we can conclude that the data are not white noise. The value of $Q = 31.3$ is significant at $p = 0.01$ and $Q^* = 34.1$ is significant at $p = 0.005$. This means that for white noise data, there is less than a 1% chance of obtaining a value of Q as high as 31.3 and less than a 0.5% chance of obtaining a value of Q^* as high as 34.1.

7/2 Examining stationarity of time series data

stationarity

Recall that *stationarity* means that there is no growth or decline in the data. The data must be roughly horizontal along the time axis. In other words the data fluctuate around a constant mean, independent of time, and the variance of the fluctuation remains essentially constant over time. For a formal definition of *stationarity*, see Box, Jenkins, and Reinsell (1994), p. 23.

We can usually assess stationarity using a time plot.

1. If a time series is plotted and there is no evidence of a change in the mean over time (e.g., Figure 7-6(a)), then we say the series is stationary in the mean.
2. If the plotted series shows no obvious change in the variance over time, then we say the series is stationary in the variance.

non-stationary in mean
non-stationary in variance

Figure 7-6(b) shows a typical data series that is non-stationary in the mean—the mean of the series changes over time. Figure 7-6(c) shows a time series that is non-stationary in both mean and variance. The mean wanders (changes over time), and the variance (or standard deviation) is not reasonably constant over time.

The visual plot of a time series is often enough to convince a forecaster that the data are stationary or non-stationary. The autocorrelation plot can also readily expose non-stationarity in the mean. The autocorrelations of stationary data drop to zero relatively

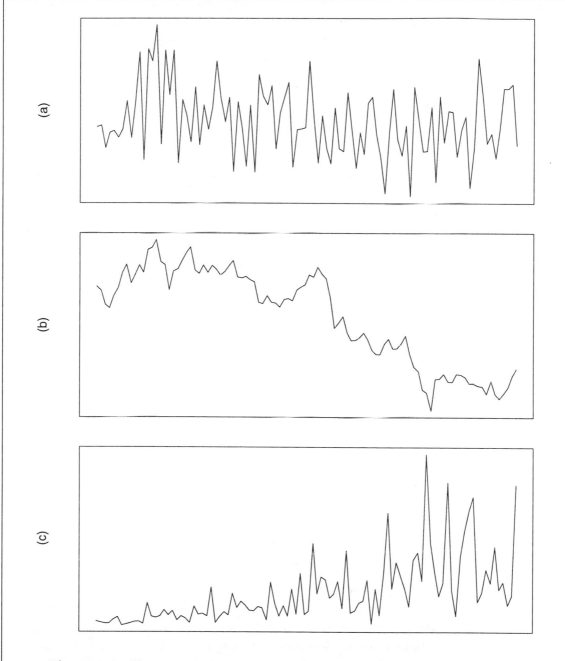

Figure 7-6: *Illustrations of time series data, showing (a) a series stationary in the mean; (b) a series non-stationary in the mean; and (c) a series non-stationary in the mean and variance. In each case, n = 100.*

quickly, while for a non-stationary series they are significantly different from zero for several time lags. When represented graphically, the autocorrelations of non-stationary data decrease slowly as the number of time lags increases.

ACF of
non-stationary data

Figure 7-7 shows the Dow-Jones index over 251 trading days. The time plot shows that it is non-stationary in the mean. The ACF also displays a typical pattern for a non-stationary series, with a slow decrease in the size of the autocorrelations. The autocorrelation for one time lag, r_1, is very large and positive. The autocorrelation for two time lags is also large and positive, but not as large as r_1, because the random error component has entered the picture twice. In general, r_k for non-stationary data will be relatively large and positive, until k gets big enough so that the random error components begin to dominate the autocorrelation. The PACF shown in Figure 7-7 is also typical of a non-stationary series with a large spike close to 1 at lag 1.

7/2/1 Removing non-stationarity in a time series

Trends, or other non-stationary patterns in the level of a series, result in positive autocorrelations that dominate the autocorrelation diagram. Therefore it is important to remove the non-stationarity, so other correlation structure can be seen before proceeding with time series model building. One way of removing non-stationarity is through the method of *differencing*. We define the differenced series as the *change* between each observation in the original series:

$$\boxed{Y_t' = Y_t - Y_{t-1}}.$$

The differenced series will have only $n-1$ values since it is not possible to calculate a difference Y_1' for the first observation.

Taking the first difference of the Dow-Jones data shown in Figure 7-7 gives the series of day-to-day changes shown Figure 7-8. Now the series looks just like a white noise series, with almost no autocorrelations or partial autocorrelations outside the 95% limits. (The ACF at lag 6 is just outside the limits, but it is acceptable to have about 5% of spikes fall a short distance beyond the limits due to chance.) The Box-Pierce Q statistic takes the value of 27.1 and the Ljung-Box Q^* statistic is equal to 28.4 for these data when $h = 24$ and $m = 0$.

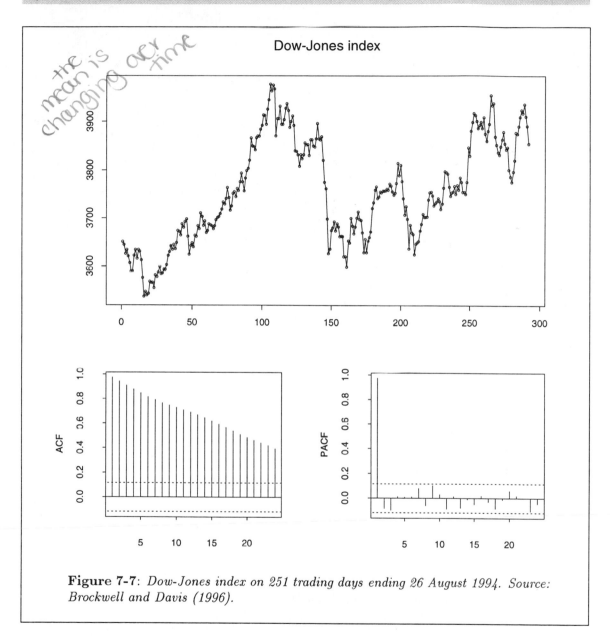

Figure 7-7: *Dow-Jones index on 251 trading days ending 26 August 1994. Source: Brockwell and Davis (1996).*

Compared to a chi-square distribution with 24 degrees of freedom, neither of these is significant.

Taking differences has transformed the data into a stationary series which resembles white noise, showing that the *daily change* in the Dow-Jones index is essentially a random amount uncorrelated with previous days.

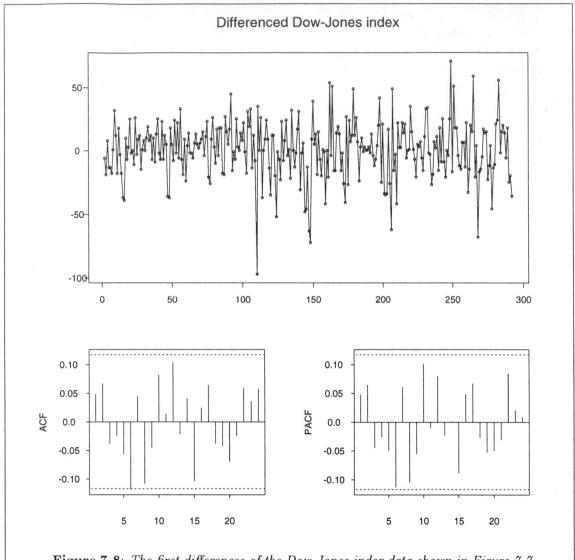

Figure 7-8: *The first differences of the Dow-Jones index data shown in Figure 7-7. These data are now stationary and resemble white noise.*

Taking first differences is a very useful tool for removing non-stationarity. However, occasionally the differenced data will not appear stationary and it may be necessary to difference the data a second time:

second-order
differences

$$Y_t'' = Y_t' - Y_{t-1}' = (Y_t - Y_{t-1}) - (Y_{t-1} - Y_{t-2}) = Y_t - 2Y_{t-1} + Y_{t-2}.$$

Y_t'' is referred to as the series of second-order differences. This series will have $n - 2$ values. In practice, it is almost never necessary to go beyond second-order differences, because real data generally involve non-stationarity of only the first or second level.

7/2/2 A random walk model

If we denote the Dow-Jones index by Y_t, then Figure 7-8 suggests that a suitable model for the data might be

$$Y_t - Y_{t-1} = e_t$$

where e_t is white noise. This can be rewritten as

$$\boxed{Y_t = Y_{t-1} + e_t}. \qquad (7.4)$$

This model is very widely used for non-stationary data and is known as a "random walk" model. Figure 7-6(b) shows another random walk series. Random walks typically have long periods of apparent trends up or down which can suddenly change direction unpredictably. They are commonly used in analyzing economic and stock price series.

random walk

7/2/3 Tests for stationarity

There have been several statistical tests developed to determine if a series is stationary. These are also known as *unit root tests*. The most widely-used such test is the Dickey-Fuller test.

unit root tests
Dickey-Fuller test

To carry out the test, we estimate the regression model

$$Y_t' = \phi Y_{t-1} + b_1 Y_{t-1}' + b_2 Y_{t-2}' + \cdots + b_p Y_{t-p}' \qquad (7.5)$$

where Y_t' denotes the differenced series $Y_t - Y_{t-1}$. The number of lagged terms in the regression, p, is usually set to be about 3. Then if the original series, Y_t, needs differencing, the estimated value of ϕ will be close to zero. If Y_t is already stationary, the estimated value of ϕ will be negative.

The value of ϕ is estimated from the regression (7.5) using ordinary least squares. If differencing is required, then the assumptions behind the t-test for ϕ are no longer valid. Instead, the value of ϕ must be compared using tables provided by Fuller (1976). If the parameter is significant, then the series being tested can be considered stationary. See Dickey, Bell, and Miller (1986) for more information on the Dickey-Fuller test.

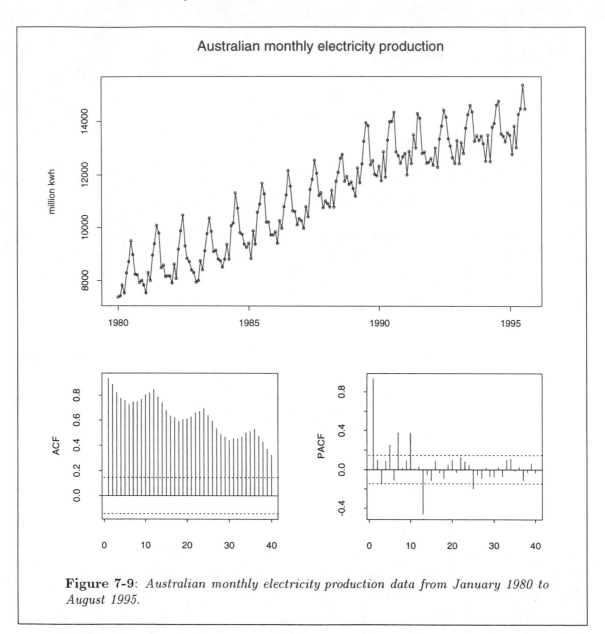

Figure 7-9: *Australian monthly electricity production data from January 1980 to August 1995.*

7/2/4 Seasonal differencing

With seasonal data which is non-stationary, it may be appropriate
to take *seasonal differences*. A seasonal difference is the difference   seasonal differences
between an observation and the corresponding observation from the
previous year. So for monthly data having an annual 12-month
pattern, we let

$$\boxed{Y_t' = Y_t - Y_{t-12}}.$$

In general, the seasonally differenced series, Y_t', is the change between
observations separated by s time periods, where s is the number of
seasons. For monthly data $s = 12$, for quarterly data $s = 4$, and so on.
As with first differences, the differencing can be repeated to obtain
second-order seasonal differencing, although this is rarely needed.

A clear illustration of a non-stationary seasonal series is the electricity production data plotted in Figure 7-9. A longer version of
the same series was considered in Section 2/7/1. Note that the
188 monthly figures show a trend and a very pronounced seasonal
pattern. The autocorrelations illustrate clearly that (i) the series
is non-stationary (the values of r_k stay large and positive), and (ii)
the series is seasonal (the values of r_{12}, r_{24}, and r_{36} are all larger
than their adjacent autocorrelations). The PACF also shows the
seasonality with a large spike at lag 12.

Figure 7-10 shows the seasonally differenced series. The data
plotted are the change in electricity production between months of
consecutive years. The series is now much closer to being stationary.
The seasonality is also much less obvious, although still present as
shown by spikes at lags 12, 24, and 36 in the PACF.

The remaining non-stationarity in the mean can be removed with
a further first difference. The resulting series is shown in Figure 7-11.
If $Y_t' = Y_t - Y_{t-12}$ denotes the seasonally differenced series, then the
series plotted in Figure 7-11 is

$$\begin{aligned}
Y_t^* &= Y_t' - Y_{t-1}' \\
&= (Y_t - Y_{t-12}) - (Y_{t-1} - Y_{t-13}) \\
&= Y_t - Y_{t-1} - Y_{t-12} + Y_{t-13}.
\end{aligned} \qquad (7.6)$$

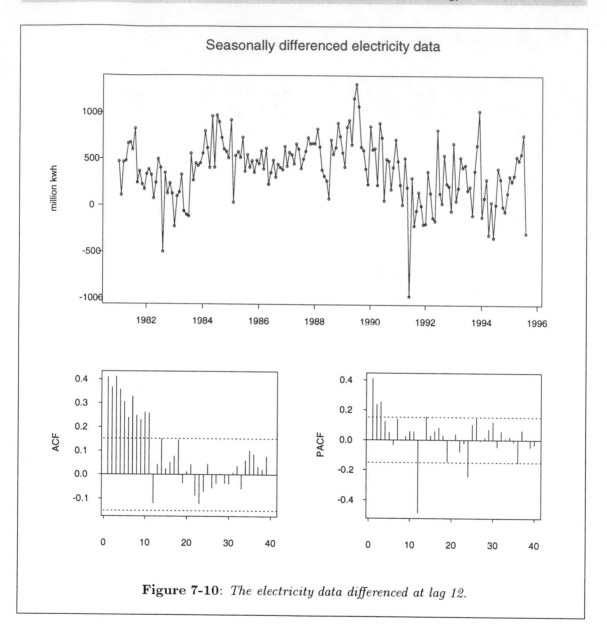

Figure 7-10: *The electricity data differenced at lag 12.*

When both seasonal and first differences are applied, it makes no difference which is done first—the result will be the same. However, we recommend that seasonal differencing be done first because sometimes the resulting series will be stationary and there will be no need for a further first difference.

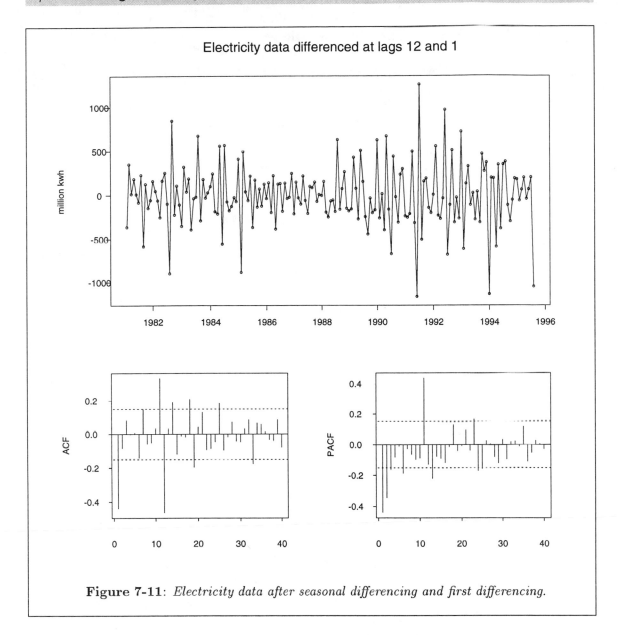

Figure 7-11: *Electricity data after seasonal differencing and first differencing.*

It is important that if differencing is used, the differences are interpretable. For example, first differences are the change between one observation and the next and seasonal differences are the change from one year to the next. But taking lag 3 differences for yearly data, for example, results in a model which cannot be sensibly interpreted.

7/2/5 Backshift notation

backward shift operator

A very useful notational device is the backward shift operator, B, which is used as follows:

$$\boxed{BY_t = Y_{t-1}} \,. \tag{7.7}$$

In other words, B, operating on Y_t, has the effect of shifting the data back one period. Two applications of B to Y_t shifts the data back two periods, as follows:

$$B(BY_t) = B^2 Y_t = Y_{t-2} \,. \tag{7.8}$$

For monthly data, if we wish to shift attention to "the same month last year," then B^{12} is used, and the notation is $B^{12}Y_t = Y_{t-12}$.

first difference

The backward shift operator is convenient for describing the process of *differencing*. A first difference can be written as

$$Y_t' = Y_t - Y_{t-1} = Y_t - BY_t = (1 - B)Y_t \,. \tag{7.9}$$

second-order difference

Note that a first difference is represented by $(1 - B)$. Similarly, if second-order differences (i.e., first differences of first differences) have to be computed, then:

$$
\begin{aligned}
Y_t'' &= (Y_t' - Y_{t-1}') \\
&= (Y_t - Y_{t-1}) - (Y_{t-1} - Y_{t-2}) \\
&= Y_t - 2Y_{t-1} + Y_{t-2} \\
&= (1 - 2B + B^2)Y_t \\
&= (1 - B)^2 Y_t \,.
\end{aligned}
\tag{7.10}
$$

Note that the second-order difference is denoted $(1 - B)^2$. (It is important to recognize that a *second-order difference* is not the same as a *second difference*, which would be denoted $1 - B^2$; similarly, a twelfth difference would be $1 - B^{12}$, but a twelfth-order difference would be $(1 - B)^{12}$.)

dth-order difference

In general, a dth-order difference can be written as

$$(1 - B)^d Y_t \,.$$

A seasonal difference followed by a first difference can be written as

$$(1 - B)(1 - B^s)Y_t \,. \tag{7.11}$$

The "backshift" notation is convenient because the terms can be multiplied together to see the combined effect. For example (7.11) can be expanded to give

$$(1-B)(1-B^s)Y_t = (1-B-B^s+B^{s+1})Y_t = Y_t - Y_{t-1} - Y_{t-s} + Y_{t-s-1}.$$

For monthly data, $s = 12$ and we obtain the same result as in (7.6).

7/3 ARIMA models for time series data

In Chapters 5 and 6 we discussed regression models of the form   *regression*

$$Y = b_0 + b_1X_1 + b_2X_2 + \cdots + b_pX_p + e, \qquad (7.12)$$

where Y is the forecast variable, X_1 through X_p are the explanatory variables, b_0 through b_p are the linear regression coefficients, and e is the error term. In equation (7.12), $X_1, X_2, \ldots, X_p$ can represent any factors such as GNP, advertising, prices, money supply, and so on.

Suppose, however, that these variables are defined as $X_1 = Y_{t-1}$, $X_2 = Y_{t-2}, X_3 = Y_{t-3}, \ldots, X_p = Y_{t-p}$. Equation (7.12) then becomes

$$Y_t = b_0 + b_1Y_{t-1} + b_2Y_{t-2} + \cdots + b_pY_{t-p} + e_t. \qquad (7.13)$$

Equation (7.13) is still a regression equation, but differs from (7.12) in that the right-hand side variables of (7.12) are different explanatory variables, while those of (7.13) are previous values of the forecast variable Y_t. These are simply time-lagged values of the forecast variable, and therefore the name *autoregression* (AR) is used to   *autoregression* describe equations of the form of (7.13). In fact, equations of this sort have already been used in (7.3) and (7.5).

One question that arises from considering equation (7.13) is why autoregression should be treated differently from ordinary regression models (Chapters 5 and 6). The answer is twofold:

1. In autoregression the basic assumption of independence of the error (residual) terms can easily be violated, since the explanatory (right-hand side) variables in equation (7.13) usually have a built-in dependence relationship.
2. Determining the number of past values of Y_t to include in equation (7.13) is not always straightforward.

Just as it is possible to regress against past values of the series, there is a time series model which uses past *errors* as explanatory variables:

$$Y_t = b_0 + b_1 e_{t-1} + b_2 e_{t-2} + \cdots + b_q e_{t-q} + e_t. \qquad (7.14)$$

moving average

Here, explicitly, a dependence relationship is set up among the successive error terms, and the equation is called a *moving average* (MA) model.

The phrase *moving average* in this time series terminology should not be confused with the same phrase in Chapters 3 and 4. The model in (7.14) is called a moving average because it is defined as a moving average of the error series, e_t. In Chapters 3 and 4, we considered moving averages of the *observations*, Y_t. In this and subsequent chapters, *moving average* is used only in reference to a model of the form of (7.14).

ARMA models

Autoregressive (AR) models can be effectively coupled with moving average (MA) models to form a general and useful class of time series models called autoregressive moving average (ARMA) models. However, they can only be used when the data are stationary. This class of models can be extended to non-stationary series by allowing differencing of the data series. These are called autoregressive inte-

ARIMA models

grated moving average (ARIMA) models. Box and Jenkins (1970) popularized ARIMA models.

ARIMA notation

There is a huge variety of ARIMA models. The general non-seasonal model is known as ARIMA(p, d, q):

AR: $p =$ order of the autoregressive part
I: $d =$ degree of first differencing involved
MA: $q =$ order of the moving average part.

white noise

The two models we have already seen can be written in this notation. A white noise model is classified as ARIMA$(0,0,0)$ because there is no AR aspect to it (Y_t does not depend on Y_{t-1}), there is no differencing involved, and there is no MA part (Y_t does not depend on

random walk

e_{t-1}). Similarly, a random walk model is classified as ARIMA$(0,1,0)$ because it has no AR or MA aspects and involves one difference.

Note that if any of p, d, or q are equal to zero, the model can also be written in a shorthand notation by dropping the unused parts of the model. For example, an ARIMA(2,0,0) can be written as AR(2) because there is no differencing (the I part) and no moving average (MA) part. Similarly, an ARIMA(1,0,1) can also be written as ARMA(1,1); an ARIMA(0,1,1) can also be written as IMA(1,1); and so on.

7/3/1 An autoregressive model of order one

Equation (7.15) shows the basic form of an ARIMA(1,0,0) or AR(1) model. Observation Y_t depends on Y_{t-1}, and the value of the autoregressive coefficient ϕ_1 is restricted to lie between -1 and $+1$:

$$Y_t = c + \phi_1 Y_{t-1} + e_t .\qquad (7.15)$$

ARIMA(1,0,0) or AR(1)

Figure 7-12(a) shows an illustrative ARIMA(1,0,0) data series with the equation

$$Y_t = 3 + 0.7 Y_{t-1} + e_t$$

where e_t is normally distributed with mean 0 and variance 1.

The time plot of an AR(1) model varies with the parameter ϕ_1. For example, when $\phi_1 = 0$, Y_t is equivalent to a white noise series (compare equation (7.2)). When $\phi_1 - 1$, Y_t is equivalent to a random

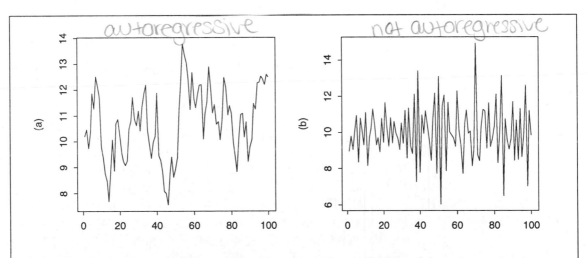

Figure 7-12: *Illustrations of time series data, showing (a) a first-order autoregressive model—ARIMA(1,0,0); and (b) a first-order moving average model—ARIMA(0,0,1). In both cases, n = 100.*

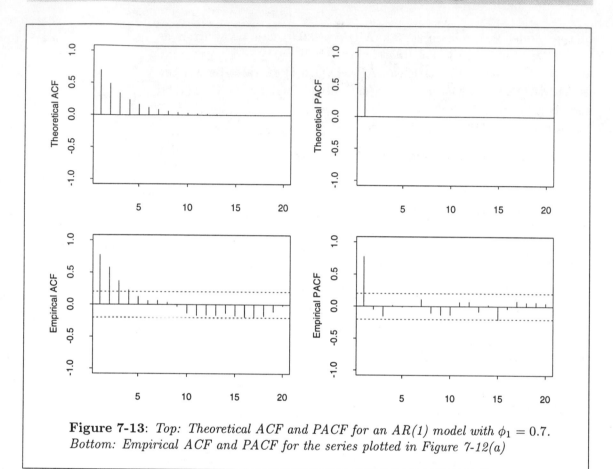

Figure 7-13: *Top: Theoretical ACF and PACF for an AR(1) model with $\phi_1 = 0.7$. Bottom: Empirical ACF and PACF for the series plotted in Figure 7-12(a)*

walk series (compare equation (7.4)). The example shown in Figure 7-12) is somewhere between these two extremes. For negative values of ϕ_1, the series tends to oscillate between postive and negative values.

The top two plots in Figure 7-13 show the theoretical ACF and PACF for an AR(1) model with $\phi_1 = 0.7$. Note that the autocorrelations decay exponentially and that there is only one non-zero partial autocorrelation at lag 1. In reality, we do not know the order of the ARIMA model. However, we can use the ACF and PACF to infer (*identify*) an AR(1) model when (i) the autocorrelations are exponentially decaying and (ii) there is a single significant partial autocorrelation. The bottom two plots in Figure 7-13 show the *empirical* ACFs of the data plotted in Figure 7-12(a). The computed autocorrelations do decay exponentially, but because of the error component, they do not die out to zero as do the theoretical autocorrelations on the top of

model identification

Figure 7-13. Similarly, there is one dominant partial autocorrelation, but also some random non-zero partial autocorrelations. In fact, the fifteenth partial autocorrelation is, by chance, close to the critical value denoting statistical significance.

7/3/2 A moving average model of order one

Equation (7.16) gives an MA(1) model or ARIMA(0,0,1) to be general. Observation Y_t depends on the error term e_t and also the previous error term e_{t-1}, with coefficient $-\theta_1$:

$$Y_t = c + e_t - \theta_1 e_{t-1} \ . \qquad (7.16)$$

ARIMA(0,0,1) or MA(1)

The value of the coefficient θ_1 is restricted to lie between -1 and $+1$. Note the minus sign on the coefficient θ_1 in (7.16). This is a convention for ARIMA models. Figure 7-12(b) shows an example of an ARIMA(0,0,1) model with the equation

$$Y_t = 10 + e_t - 0.7 e_{t-1}$$

where e_t is normally distributed with mean 0 and variance 1.

The top two plots in Figure 7-14 show the theoretical ACF and PACF for an MA(1) model with $\theta_1 = 0.7$. Note that there is only one non-zero autocorrelation at lag 1 and that the partial autocorrelations decay exponentially. The bottom two plots show the corresponding empirical results for the series plotted in Figure 7-12(b).

7/3/3 Higher-order autoregressive models

In general, a pth-order AR model is defined as follows:

$$Y_t = c + \phi_1 Y_{t-1} + \phi_2 Y_{t-2} + \cdots + \phi_p Y_{t-p} + e_t, \qquad (7.17)$$

ARIMA(p,0,0) or AR(p)

$$\begin{aligned}
\text{where } c \ &= \ \text{constant term,} \\
\phi_j \ &= \ j\text{th autoregressive parameter,} \\
e_t \ &= \ \text{the error term at time } t.
\end{aligned}$$

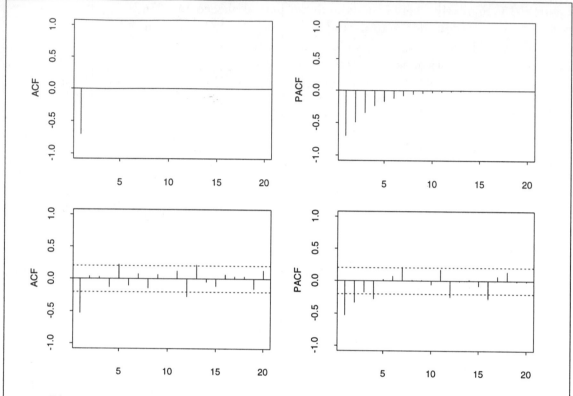

Figure 7-14: *Top: Theoretical ACF and PACF for an MA(1) model with $\theta_1 = 0.7$. Bottom: Empirical ACF and PACF for the series plotted in Figure 7-12(b)*

parameter restrictions   There are specific restrictions on the allowable values of the autoregressive parameters. For $p = 1$, $-1 < \phi_1 < 1$. For $p = 2$, the following three conditions must all be met:

$$-1 < \phi_2 < 1 \qquad \phi_2 + \phi_1 < 1 \qquad \phi_2 - \phi_1 < 1.$$

More complicated conditions hold for $p \geq 3$.

Using the backward shift symbol, B, equation (7.17) can be rewritten as

$$\left.\begin{array}{rcl} Y_t - \phi_1 Y_{t-1} - \cdots - \phi_p Y_{t-p} &=& c + e_t \\[2mm] (1 - \phi_1 B - \cdots - \phi_p B^p) Y_t &=& c + e_t \end{array}\right\} \qquad (7.18)$$

or

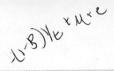

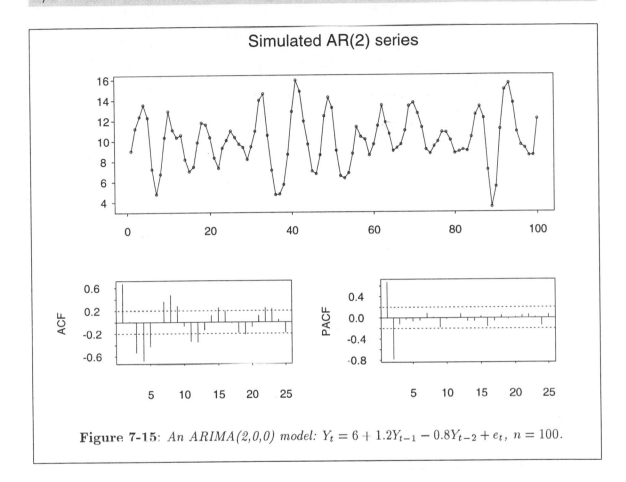

Figure 7-15: *An ARIMA(2,0,0) model*: $Y_t = 6 + 1.2Y_{t-1} - 0.8Y_{t-2} + e_t$, $n = 100$.

A great variety of time series are possible with autoregressive models. Figure 7-15 shows one example, an AR(2) model with the following equation:

$$Y_t = 6 + 1.2Y_{t-1} - 0.8Y_{t-2} + e_t,$$

where e_t was generated from a normal distribution with mean zero and variance 1. Note that for the AR(2) model, the autocorrelations die out in a damped sine-wave manner and that there are exactly two significant partial correlations.

In general, the ACF of an AR(p) model with $p \geq 2$ can show exponential decay or damped sine-wave patterns. The partial autocorrelations of an AR(p) model are zero beyond lag p.

Process	ACF	PACF
AR(1)	Exponential decay: on positive side if $\phi_1 > 0$ and alternating in sign starting on negative side if $\phi_1 < 0$.	Spike at lag 1, then cuts off to zero: spike positive if $\phi_1 > 0$, negative if $\phi_1 < 0$.
AR(p)	Exponential decay or damped sine-wave. The exact pattern depends on the signs and sizes of $\phi_1, \ldots, \phi_p$.	Spikes at lags 1 to p, then cuts off to zero.
MA(1)	Spike at lag 1 then cuts off to zero: spike positive if $\theta_1 < 0$, negative if $\theta_1 > 0$.	Exponential decay: on negative side if $\theta_1 > 0$ and alternating in sign starting on positive side if $\theta_1 < 0$.
MA(q)	Spikes at lags 1 to q, then cuts off to zero.	Exponential decay or damped sine-wave. The exact pattern depends on the signs and sizes of $\theta_1, \ldots, \theta_q$.

Table 7-2: *Expected patterns in the ACF and PACF for simple AR and MA models.*

7/3/4 Higher-order moving average models

The general MA model of order q can be written as follows:

ARIMA(0,0,q)
or MA(q)

$$Y_t = c + e_t - \theta_1 e_{t-1} - \theta_2 e_{t-2} - \cdots - \theta_q e_{t-q}, \qquad (7.19)$$

$$\text{where } c \;=\; \text{constant term,}$$
$$\theta_j \;=\; j\text{th moving average parameter,}$$
$$e_{t-k} \;=\; \text{the error term at time } t - k.$$

parameter restrictions The same restrictions that were required for AR models are also required for MA models. Therefore, for $q = 1$, we require $-1 < \theta_1 < 1$. For $q = 2$, the following three conditions must all be met:

$$-1 < \theta_2 < 1 \qquad \theta_2 + \theta_1 < 1 \qquad \theta_2 - \theta_1 < 1.$$

More complicated conditions hold for $q \geq 3$.

In the backshift notation, (7.19) can be written

$$Y_t = c + (1 - \theta_1 B - \theta_2 B^2 - \cdots - \theta_q B^q)e_t.$$

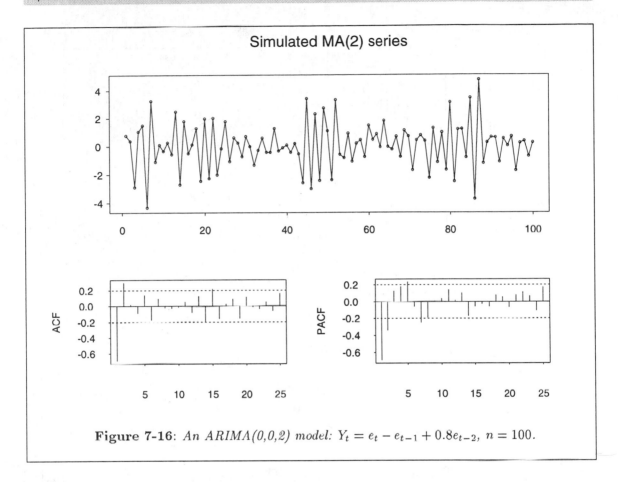

Figure 7-16: *An ARIMA(0,0,2) model:* $Y_t = e_t - e_{t-1} + 0.8e_{t-2}$, *n* = 100.

A wide variety of time series can be produced using moving average models. Figure 7-16 shows one example defined by the model

$$Y_t = e_t - e_{t-1} + 0.8e_{t-2}.$$

Note there are two non-zero autocorrelations and that the partial autocorrelations decay in a damped sine-wave manner. This is exactly the reverse of what is seen for an AR(2) model. In general, the autocorrelations of an MA(q) model are zero beyond lag q. If $q \geq 2$, the PACF can show exponential decay or damped sine-wave patterns.

Table 7-2 summarizes the ACF and PACF patterns for pure AR and pure MA models.

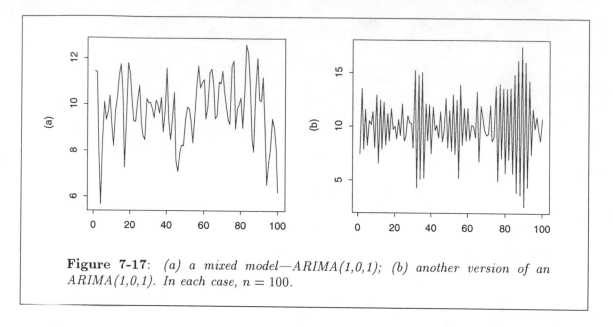

Figure 7-17: *(a) a mixed model—ARIMA(1,0,1); (b) another version of an ARIMA(1,0,1). In each case, n = 100.*

7/3/5 Mixtures: ARMA models

The basic elements of AR and MA models can be combined to produce a great variety of models. For example, equation (7.20) combines a first-order AR model and a first-order MA model. This is called an ARMA(1,1) or ARIMA(1,0,1) model:

ARIMA(1,0,1)
or ARMA(1,1)

$$Y_t = c + \phi_1 Y_{t-1} + e_t - \theta_1 e_{t-1} \, . \qquad (7.20)$$

Here, Y_t depends on one previous Y_{t-1} value and one previous error term e_{t-1}. The series is assumed stationary in the mean and in the variance. Figure 7-17(a) gives one example of an artificially generated ARIMA(1,0,1) series, where $\phi_1 = 0.3$, $\theta_1 = -0.7$, and $c = 7$. Figure 7-17(b) gives another example of an ARIMA(1,0,1) model, where $\phi_1 = -0.8$, $\theta_1 = 0.8$, and $c = 18$. In both cases, e_t is normal with mean 0 and variance 1. Note how different the two ARIMA(1,0,1) models can be.

Using the backshift notation, the ARIMA(1,0,1) is written

$$(1 - \phi_1 B)Y_t \;=\; c + (1 - \theta_1 B)e_t \, .$$
$$\uparrow \qquad\qquad\qquad \uparrow$$
$$\text{AR(1)} \qquad\qquad \text{MA(1)}$$

An ARMA model with higher-order terms is written

$$Y_t = c + \phi_1 Y_{t-1} + \cdots + \phi_p Y_{t-p} + e_t - \theta_1 e_{t-1} - \cdots - \theta_q e_{t-q}$$

or

$$(1 - \phi_1 B - \cdots - \phi_p B^p)Y_t = c + (1 - \theta_1 B - \cdots - \theta_q B^q)e_t .$$

$$(7.21)$$

ARIMA(p,0,q)
or ARMA(p,q)

The same parameter restrictions apply here as for pure AR and pure MA models.

parameter restrictions

7/3/6 Mixtures: ARIMA models

If non-stationarity is added to a mixed ARMA model, then the general ARIMA(p, d, q) model is obtained. The equation for the simplest case, ARIMA(1,1,1), is as follows:

$$(1 - \phi_1 B) \quad (1 - B)Y_t \;=\; c + (1 - \theta_1 B)e_t$$

$$\uparrow \qquad\qquad \uparrow \qquad\qquad\qquad \uparrow$$

$$\text{AR(1)} \qquad \text{First} \qquad\qquad \text{MA(1)}$$

$$\text{difference}$$

$$(7.22)$$

Notice the use of the backward shift operator to describe (i) the first difference, (ii) the AR(1) portion of the model, and (iii) the MA(1) aspect.

The general ARIMA(p, d, q) model yields a tremendous variety of patterns in the ACF and PACF, so that it is unwise to state rules for identifying general ARIMA models. However, the simpler AR(p) and MA(q) models do provide some identifying features that can help a forecaster zero in on a particular ARIMA model identification. It is also helpful to know that several different models might yield almost the same quality forecasts, so that the process of identification is not quite like looking for a needle in a haystack.

In practice, it is seldom necessary to deal with values p, d, or q that are other than 0, 1, or 2. It is perhaps remarkable that such a small range of values for p, d, or q can cover a tremendous range of practical forecasting situations.

7/3/7 Seasonality and ARIMA models

seasonal ARIMA
models

One final complexity to add to ARIMA models is seasonality. In exactly the same way that *consecutive* data points might exhibit AR, MA, mixed ARMA, or mixed ARIMA properties, so data separated by a whole season (i.e., a year) may exhibit the same properties.

ARIMA notation

The ARIMA notation can be extended readily to handle seasonal aspects, and the general shorthand notation is

$$
\text{ARIMA}\ \underbrace{(p, d, q)}_{\displaystyle\uparrow}\ \underbrace{(P, D, Q)_s}_{\displaystyle\nwarrow}
$$

$$
\begin{pmatrix} \text{Non-seasonal} \\ \text{part of the} \\ \text{model} \end{pmatrix} \begin{pmatrix} \text{Seasonal} \\ \text{part of} \\ \text{the model} \end{pmatrix}
$$

where $s =$ number of periods per season.

The algebra is simple but can get lengthy, so for illustrative purposes consider the following general $\text{ARIMA}(1, 1, 1)(1, 1, 1)_4$ model:

$$
(1 - \phi_1 B)(1 - \Phi_1 B^4)(1 - B)(1 - B^4)Y_t = (1 - \theta_1 B)(1 - \Theta_1 B^4)e_t.
$$

$$
\begin{pmatrix} \text{Non-seasonal} \\ \text{AR(1)} \end{pmatrix} \quad \begin{pmatrix} \text{Non-seasonal} \\ \text{difference} \end{pmatrix} \quad \begin{pmatrix} \text{Non-seasonal} \\ \text{MA(1)} \end{pmatrix}
$$

$$
\begin{pmatrix} \text{Seasonal} \\ \text{AR(1)} \end{pmatrix} \quad \begin{pmatrix} \text{Seasonal} \\ \text{difference} \end{pmatrix} \quad \begin{pmatrix} \text{Seasonal} \\ \text{MA(1)} \end{pmatrix}
$$

All the factors can be multiplied out and the general model written as follows:

$$
\begin{aligned}
Y_t = \ & (1 + \phi_1)Y_{t-1} - \phi_1 Y_{t-2} + (1 + \Phi_1)Y_{t-4} \\
& - (1 + \phi_1 + \Phi_1 + \phi_1\Phi_1)Y_{t-5} + (\phi_1 + \phi_1\Phi_1)Y_{t-6} \\
& - \Phi_1 Y_{t-8} + (\Phi_1 + \phi_1\Phi_1)Y_{t-9} - \phi_1\Phi_1 Y_{t-10} \\
& + e_t - \theta_1 e_{t-1} - \Theta_1 e_{t-4} + \theta_1\Theta_1 e_{t-5}.
\end{aligned} \tag{7.23}
$$

In this form, once the coefficients ϕ_1, Φ_1, θ_1, and Θ_1 have been estimated from the data, equation (7.23) can be used for forecasting.

Note that the constant term has been omitted for clarity. If Y_t is replaced by $(Y_t - \mu)$, where μ is the mean of the Y values, then a constant term would ultimately appear on the right-hand side of equation (7.23).

The seasonal part of an AR or MA model will be seen in the seasonal lags of the PACF and ACF. For example, the seasonal MA model ARIMA$(0,0,0)(0,0,1)_{12}$ will show a spike at lag 12 in the ACF but no other significant spikes. The PACF will show exponential decay in the seasonal lags; that is, at lags $12, 24, 36, \ldots$. Similarly an ARIMA$(0,0,0)(1,0,0)_{12}$ (a seasonal AR model) will show exponential decay in the seasonal lags of the ACF, and a single significant spike at lag 12 in the PACF.

seasonal lags

7/4 Identification

There is such a bewildering variety of ARIMA models, it can be difficult to decide which model is most appropriate for a given set of data. The following steps outline an approach to this problem.

1. Plot the data. Identify any unusual observations. Decide if a transformation is necessary to stabilize the variance. If necessary, transform the data to achieve stationarity in the variance.

2. Consider if the (possibly transformed) data appear stationary from the time plot and the ACF and PACF. If the time plot shows the data scattered horizontally around a constant mean, or equivalently, the ACF and PACF drop to or near zero quickly, it indicates that the data are stationary. If the time plot is not horizontal, or the ACF and PACF do not drop to zero, non-stationarity is implied.

3. When the data appear non-stationary, they can be made stationary by differencing. For non-seasonal data, take first differences of the data. For seasonal data, take seasonal differences of the data. Check that these appear stationary. If they are still non-stationary, take the first differences of the differenced data. For most practical purposes a maximum of two differences will transform the data into a stationary series.

4. When stationarity has been achieved, examine the autocorrelation to see if any pattern remains. There are three possibilities to consider.

(a) Seasonality may suggest itself—autocorrelations and/or partial autocorrelations at the seasonal lags are large and significantly different from zero.

(b) AR or MA models may be revealed—the pattern of autocorrelations and partial autocorrelations will indicate a possible model. If there are no significant autocorrelations after lag q, a MA(q) model may be appropriate. If there are no significant partial autocorrelations after lag p, an AR(p) model may be appropriate.

(c) If there is no clear MA or AR model suggested, a mixture model may be necessary. (How to determine the order of the model will be discussed in Section 7/6.)

We will illustrate this approach through three examples.

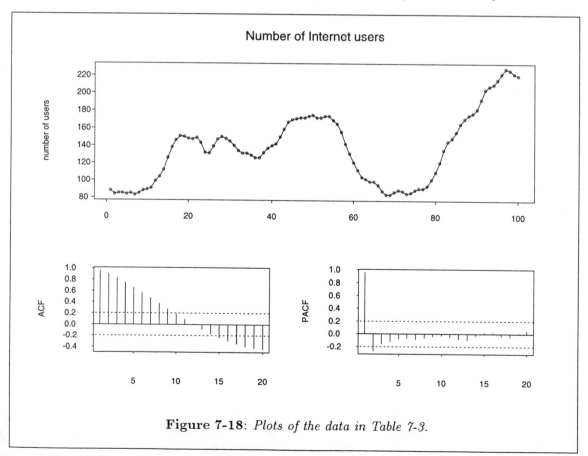

Figure 7-18: *Plots of the data in Table 7-3.*

Minute	Users	Minute	Users	Minute	Users	Minute	Users
1	88	26	139	51	172	76	91
2	84	27	147	52	172	77	91
3	85	28	150	53	174	78	94
4	85	29	148	54	174	79	101
5	84	30	145	55	169	80	110
6	85	31	140	56	165	81	121
7	83	32	134	57	156	82	135
8	85	33	131	58	142	83	145
9	88	34	131	59	131	84	149
10	89	35	129	60	121	85	156
11	91	36	126	61	112	86	165
12	99	37	126	62	104	87	171
13	104	38	132	63	102	88	175
14	112	39	137	64	99	89	177
15	126	40	140	65	99	90	182
16	138	41	142	66	95	91	193
17	146	42	150	67	88	92	204
18	151	43	159	68	84	93	208
19	150	44	167	69	84	94	210
20	148	45	170	70	87	95	215
21	147	46	171	71	89	96	222
22	149	47	172	72	88	97	228
23	143	48	172	73	85	98	226
24	132	49	174	74	86	99	222
25	131	50	175	75	89	100	220

Table 7-3: *The number of users logged on to an Internet server each minute over 100 minutes.*

7/4/1 Example 1: A non-seasonal time series

Table 7-3 contains the number of users logged onto an Internet server each minute over a 100-minute period. Figure 7-18 shows an initial analysis of the data. The autocorrelation plot gives indications of non-stationarity, and the data plot makes this clear too. The first partial autocorrelation is very dominant and close to 1—also showing the non-stationarity. So we take first differences of the data and reanalyze.

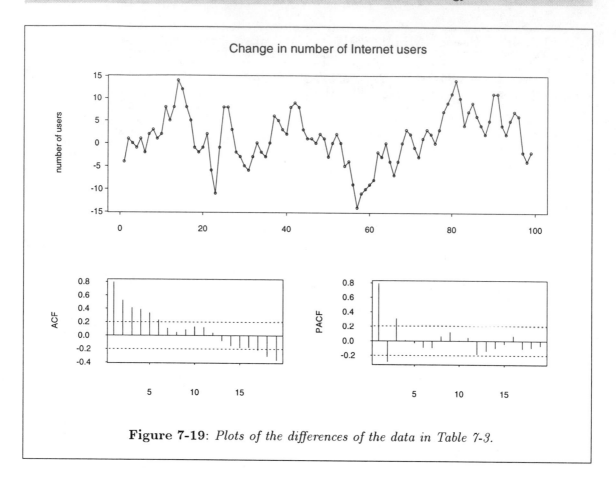

Figure 7-19: *Plots of the differences of the data in Table 7-3.*

Figure 7-19 shows the results. Now autocorrelations show a mixture of an exponential decay and sine-wave pattern and there are three significant partial autocorrelation. This suggests an AR(3) model is operating.

So, for the original series, we have identified an ARIMA(3,1,0) model. That is, the model to be examined has the following form:

$$(1 - \phi_1 B - \phi_2 B^2 - \phi_3 B^3)(1 - B)Y_t = e_t.$$

In terms of the Box-Jenkins stages (Figure 7-1), the identification of a tentative model has been completed.

Period	Observation	Period	Observation	Period	Observation
1	562.674	41	701.108	81	742.000
2	599.000	42	790.079	82	847.152
3	668.516	43	594.621	83	731.675
4	597.798	44	230.716	84	898.527
5	579.889	45	617.189	85	778.139
6	668.233	46	691.389	86	856.075
7	499.232	47	701.067	87	938.833
8	215.187	48	705.777	88	813.023
9	555.813	49	747.636	89	783.417
10	586.935	50	773.392	90	828.110
11	546.136	51	813.788	91	657.311
12	571.111	52	766.713	92	310.032
13	634.712	53	728.875	93	780.000
14	639.283	54	749.197	94	860.000
15	712.182	55	680.954	95	780.000
16	621.557	56	241.424	96	807.993
17	621.000	57	680.234	97	895.217
18	675.989	58	708.326	98	856.075
19	501.322	59	694.238	99	893.268
20	220.286	60	772.071	100	875.000
21	560.727	61	795.337	101	835.088
22	602.530	62	788.421	102	934.595
23	626.379	63	889.968	103	832.500
24	605.508	64	797.393	104	300.000
25	646.783	65	751.000	105	791.443
26	658.442	66	821.255	106	900.000
27	712.906	67	691.605	107	781.729
28	687.714	68	290.655	108	880.000
29	723.916	69	727.147	109	875.024
30	707.183	70	868.355	110	992.968
31	629.000	71	812.390	111	976.804
32	237.530	72	799.556	112	968.697
33	613.296	73	843.038	113	871.675
34	730.444	74	847.000	114	1006.852
35	734.925	75	941.952	115	832.037
36	651.812	76	804.309	116	345.587
37	676.155	77	840.307	117	849.528
38	748.183	78	871.528	118	913.871
39	810.681	79	656.330	119	868.746
40	729.363	80	370.508	120	993.733

Table 7-4: *Industry sales for printing and writing paper (in thousands of French francs). January 1963–December 1972.*

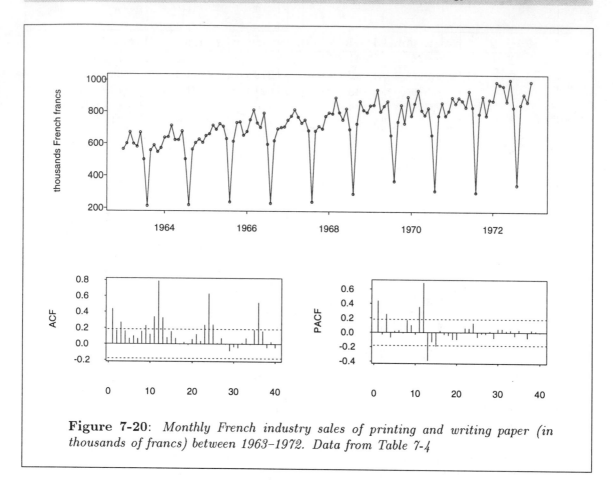

Figure 7-20: *Monthly French industry sales of printing and writing paper (in thousands of francs) between 1963–1972. Data from Table 7-4*

7/4/2 Example 2: A seasonal time series

Table 7-4 shows the monthly industry sales (in thousands of francs) for printing and writing paper between the years 1963 and 1972. Figure 7-20 shows the very clear seasonal pattern in the data plot and a general increasing trend. The autocorrelations are almost all positive, and the dominant seasonal pattern shows clearly in the large values or r_{12}, r_{24}, and r_{36}.

The evidence of Figure 7-20 suggests taking a seasonal difference. The seasonally differenced data also appear non-stationary (a plot of these is not shown) and so the series is differenced again at lag 1. The twice differenced series is shown in Figure 7-21. The twice differenced data appear to be stationary, and a lot of the dominant seasonal spikes have disappeared.

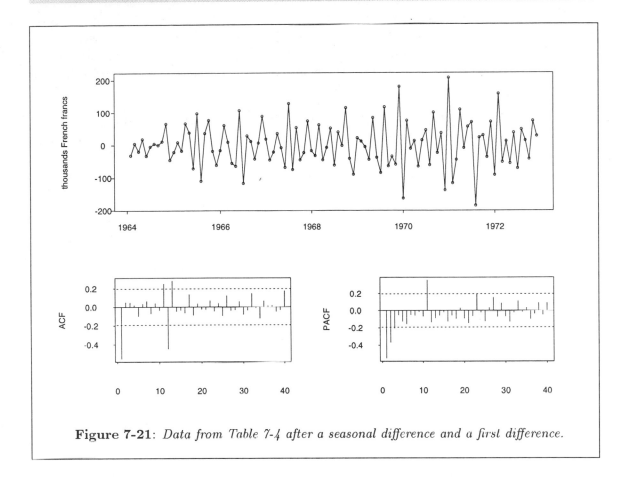

Figure 7-21: *Data from Table 7-4 after a seasonal difference and a first difference.*

So we have identified the model to be an $\text{ARIMA}(p, 1, q)(P, 1, Q)_{12}$ where values for p, q, P, and Q are yet to be determined. From the PACF in Figure 7-21, note the exponential decay of the first few lags—suggesting a non-seasonal MA(1) model. This suggests setting $q = 1$ and $p = 0$. In the ACF, the value r_1 is significant—reinforcing the non-seasonal MA(1) model—and r_{12} is significant—suggesting a seasonal MA(1) model. With a little imagination the PACF can be used to support this seasonal MA(1) model, and we end up with the tentative identification:

$$\text{ARIMA}(0, 1, 1)(0, 1, 1)_{12}$$

$$\text{or} \quad \underbrace{(1 - B)}_{\substack{\uparrow \\ \text{Non-seasonal} \\ \text{difference}}} \underbrace{(1 - B^{12})}_{\substack{\uparrow \\ \text{Seasonal} \\ \text{difference}}} Y_t = \underbrace{(1 - \theta_1 B)}_{\substack{\uparrow \\ \text{Non-seasonal} \\ \text{MA(1)}}} \underbrace{(1 - \Theta_1 B^{12})}_{\substack{\uparrow \\ \text{Seasonal} \\ \text{MA(1)}}} e_t.$$

airline model

Note that this model is sometimes called the "airline model" because it was applied to international airline data by Box and Jenkins (1970). It is one of the most commonly used seasonal ARIMA models.

7/4/3 Example 3: A seasonal time series needing transformation

As a final example in this section, consider the data in Table 7-5, which show the monthly shipments of a company that manufactures pollution equipment. They are plotted in Figure 7-22. It can be seen clearly that the fluctuations increase as one moves from left to right on the graph. Until December 1989, the value of shipments was low and so were the fluctuations. From December 1989 until March 1991, shipments increased and so did their variations from one month to the next. The same pattern continues until 1995 when both shipments and fluctuations are largest. This variation in the magnitude of the

non-stationarity in variance

fluctuations with time is referred to as non-stationarity in the variance of the data. It must be corrected (i.e., a stationary variance achieved) before fitting an ARIMA model to the series.

transformation

The main approach for achieving stationarity in variance is through a logarithmic or power transformation of the data (see Section 2/7/1). Figure 7-23 shows the logarithm of the data. It is clear that the

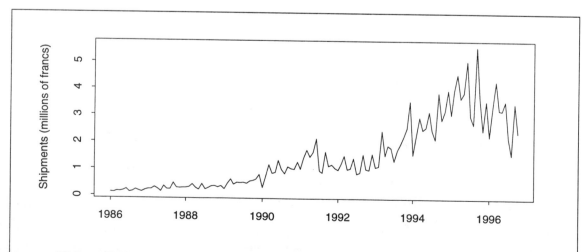

Figure 7-22: *Monthly shipments of pollution equipment. Data from Table 7-5. The data need transforming to stabilize the variance.*

Period	Observation	Period	Observation	Period	Observation
1	122.640	44	459.024	87	2411.628
2	120.888	45	543.120	88	1510.224
3	164.688	46	567.648	89	1876.392
4	147.168	47	613.200	90	1792.296
5	171.696	48	791.904	91	1307.868
6	228.636	49	305.724	92	1705.572
7	124.392	50	713.064	93	1945.596
8	155.928	51	1156.320	94	2219.784
9	217.248	52	829.572	95	2528.136
10	176.076	53	865.488	96	3534.660
11	142.788	54	1318.380	97	1546.140
12	196.224	55	971.484	98	2246.064
13	228.636	56	817.308	99	2930.220
14	234.768	57	1079.232	100	2462.436
15	319.740	58	1013.532	101	2551.788
16	241.776	59	986.376	102	3140.460
17	151.548	60	1264.068	103	2437.032
18	352.152	61	997.764	104	2109.408
19	239.148	62	1415.616	105	3853.523
20	233.892	63	1709.952	106	2840.868
21	471.288	64	1443.648	107	3164.112
22	290.832	65	1619.724	108	3946.380
23	284.700	66	2120.796	109	3044.976
24	291.708	67	923.304	110	3957.768
25	287.328	68	860.232	111	4552.571
26	315.360	69	1639.872	112	3651.167
27	417.852	70	1106.388	113	3861.408
28	288.204	71	1161.576	114	5048.388
29	225.132	72	1034.556	115	2990.664
30	430.992	73	960.972	116	2677.056
31	229.512	74	1214.136	117	5566.103
32	296.964	75	1492.704	118	3661.680
33	355.656	76	991.632	119	2435.280
34	367.920	77	1025.796	120	3550.428
35	317.112	78	1399.848	121	2215.404
36	359.160	79	818.184	122	3312.156
37	249.660	80	865.488	123	4289.771
38	455.520	81	1547.892	124	3218.424
39	607.068	82	1003.020	125	3193.020
40	425.736	83	960.972	126	3542.544
41	494.064	84	1568.040	127	2169.852
42	486.180	85	1065.216	128	1536.504
43	494.064	86	1107.264	129	3454.944
				130	2351.184

Table 7-5: *Monthly shipments of pollution equipment from January 1986 through October 1996 (in thousands of French francs).*

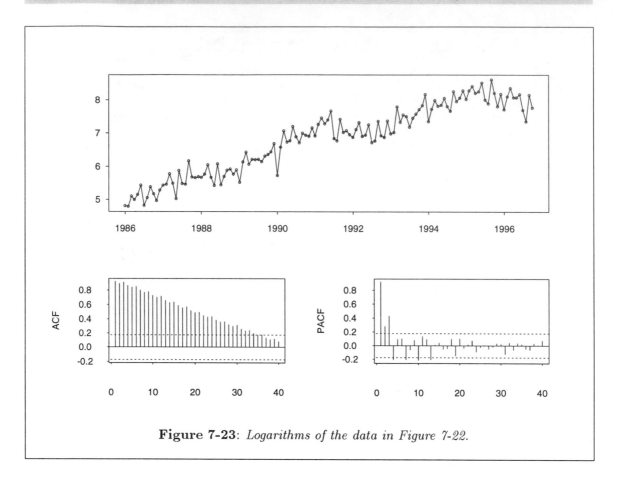

Figure 7-23: *Logarithms of the data in Figure 7-22.*

magnitude of the fluctuations in the logarithmic transformed data does not vary with time. Even the fluctuations in the very beginning of the series are not much different from those at the end. Thus one can say that the logarithmic transformation has achieved a series that is stationary in its variance. Once this stationarity in variance is achieved, an ARIMA model can be fitted.

The logged data are clearly non-stationary and require differencing. In this case, there is no strong seasonality, and so we take a first difference rather than a seasonal difference. The differenced and logged series is shown in Figure 7-24. There are significant spikes at lags 1 and 2 in the PACF indicating an AR(2) might be a feasible non-seasonal component. The single spike at lag 12 in the PACF indicates a seasonal AR(1) component. Therefore, for the logged data, a tentative model would be

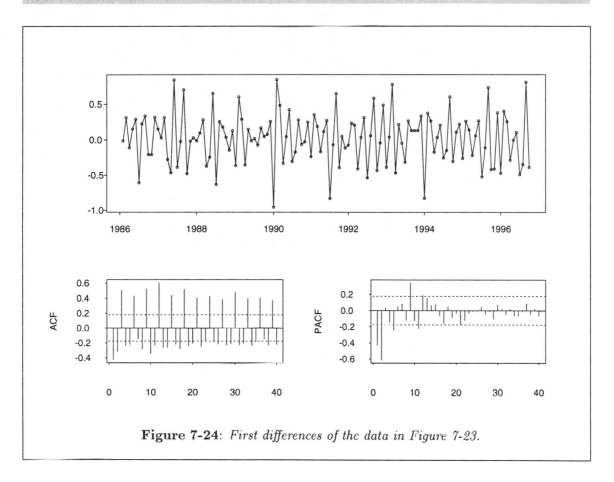

Figure 7-24: *First differences of the data in Figure 7-23.*

$$\text{ARIMA}(2,1,0)(1,0,0)_{12}$$

$$\text{or} \quad \underbrace{(1 - \phi_1 B - \phi_2 B^2)}_{\substack{\uparrow \\ \text{Non-seasonal} \\ \text{AR}(2)}} \underbrace{(1 - \Phi_1 B^{12})}_{\substack{\uparrow \\ \text{Seasonal} \\ \text{AR}(1)}} \underbrace{(1 - B)}_{\substack{\uparrow \\ \text{Non-seasonal} \\ \text{difference}}} Y_t = e_t.$$

7/4/4 Recapitulation

The process of identifying a Box-Jenkins ARIMA model requires experience and good judgment, but there are some helpful guiding principles.

1. *Make the series stationary.* An initial analysis of the raw data can quite readily show whether the time series is stationary in the mean and the variance. Differencing, (non-seasonal and/or seasonal) will usually take care of any non-stationarity in the mean. Logarithmic or power transformations will often take care of non-stationary variance.

2. *Consider non-seasonal aspects.* An examination of the ACF and PACF of the stationary series obtained in Step 1 can reveal whether a MA or AR model is feasible.

3. *Consider seasonal aspects.* An examination of the ACF and PACF at the seasonal lags can help identify AR and MA models for the seasonal aspects of the data, but the indications are by no means as easy to find as in the case of the non-seasonal aspects. For quarterly data, the forecaster should try to see the pattern of r_4, r_8, r_{12}, r_{16}, and so on, in the ACF and PACF. For monthly data, it is seldom possible to examine very many autocorrelations for lags in multiples of 12. Thus r_{12}, r_{24}, and possibly r_{36} may be available—but these are all that can be used.

7/5 Estimating the parameters

Having made a tentative model identification (Section 7/4), the AR and MA parameters, seasonal and non-seasonal, have to be determined in the best possible manner. For example, suppose the class of model identified is ARIMA $(0, 1, 1)$. This is a family of models depending on one MA coefficient θ_1:

$$(1 - B)Y_t = (1 - \theta_1 B)e_t \,.$$

We want the best estimate of θ_1 to fit the time series that is being modeled.

least squares   The method of least squares can be used for ARIMA models, just as with regression (see Sections 5/2/1 and 6/1/2). However, for models involving an MA component (i.e., where $q > 0$), there is unfortunately no simple formula that can be applied to obtain the estimates as there is in regression. Instead an iterative method must be used. A preliminary estimate is chosen and a computer program refines the estimate iteratively until the sum of squared errors is minimized.

Another method which is frequently used is *maximum likelihood.* The *likelihood* of a set of data is denoted by L and is proportional to the probability of obtaining the data given the model. Thus it is a measure of the plausibility of observing our actual sample of observations given a particular set of parameter values. The method of maximum likelihood finds the values of the parameters which maximize the likelihood L. Like least squares estimates, these estimates must be found iteratively. Maximum likelihood estimation is usually favored by statisticians because it has some desirable statistical properties (see Box, Jenkins, and Reinsell, 1994, p. 225).

maximum likelihood estimation

Computer programs for fitting ARIMA models will automatically find appropriate initial estimates of the parameters and then successively refine them until the optimum values of the parameters are found using either the least squares or maximum likelihood criterion.

The statistical assumptions underlying the general ARIMA model allow some useful summary statistics to be computed after optimum coefficient values have been estimated. For example, for each coefficient there will be a standard error for that coefficient. From the parameter estimate and its standard error, a test for significance can be computed.

standard error

For example 1 in Section 7/4/1, an ARIMA(3,1,0) model was identified:

$$Y_t' = \phi_1 Y_{t-1}' + \phi_2 Y_{t-2}' + \phi_3 Y_{t-3}' + e_t$$

where $Y_t' = Y_t - Y_{t-1}$. Using maximum likelihood estimation, the following information was produced by the computer program.

Parameter	Estimate	Std. Error	Z	P
ϕ_1	1.151	0.096	12.03	0.0000
ϕ_2	-0.661	0.136	-4.87	0.0000
ϕ_3	0.341	0.095	3.58	0.0003
σ^2	9.66			

Hence, the estimated model is

$$(Y_t - Y_{t-1}) = 1.151(Y_{t-1} - Y_{t-2}) - 0.661(Y_{t-2} - Y_{t-3})$$
$$+ 0.341(Y_{t-3} - Y_{t-4}) + e_t. \qquad (7.24)$$

The parameter σ^2 is the variance of the residuals, e_t. The model (7.24) can be rewritten

$$Y_t = 2.151Y_{t-1} - 1.812Y_{t-2} + 1.002Y_{t-3} - 0.341Y_{t-4} + e_t. \quad (7.25)$$

Note that this model now looks like an AR(4) model. However, the parameters for (7.25) do not satisfy the conditions necessary to give a stationary series.

P-value

The P-value in the above table gives a method of testing the significance of each parameter separately. The Z value gives the ratio of the estimate to its standard error. The P-values are calculated using a two-sided z-test from the normal probability table (Table A, Appendix III). For example, the P-value for ϕ_1 is obtained by finding the probability of a normal variable being greater than 12.03 or less than -12.03. The table shows that the probability is zero (to four decimal places). As usual, we consider the test to be significant if the P-value is small (less than 0.05). In this case, all parameters are highly significant (all P-values are very small) showing each of the three terms in the model is required. If any of these parameters had not been significant, we may have been able to improve the model by dropping the corresponding terms from the model.

7/6   Identification revisited

Having estimated an ARIMA model, it is necessary to revisit the question of identification to see if the selected model can be improved. There are three aspects of model identification that can arise at this point in the modeling process.

1. Some of the estimated parameters may have been insignificant (their P-values may have been larger than 0.05). If so, a revised model with the insignificant terms omitted may be considered.

2. The ACF and PACF provide some guidance on how to select pure AR or pure MA models. But mixture models are much harder to identify. Therefore it is normal to begin with either a pure AR or a pure MA model. Now it may be worth considering *ARMA models* extending the selected model to a mixed ARMA model.

3. There may have been more than one plausible model identified, and we need a method to determine which of them is preferred.

Because of these considerations, it is common to have several competing models for the series and we need a method for selecting the best of the models. A plausible criterion for choosing the best ARIMA model might appear to be to choose the model which gives the smallest sum of squared errors or the largest value for the likelihood. Unfortunately, this approach will not always work—often the MSE can be made smaller and the likelihood made larger simply by increasing the number of terms in the model.

This is analogous to the problem of selecting a regression model by maximizing the R^2 value. The R^2 value can always be increased by adding another explanatory variable. In the regression context, the solution to the problem was to adjust the value of R^2 to include a penalty for the number of terms in the regression model (see Section 6/3/3). For ARIMA models, the solution is very similar: the likelihood is penalized for each additional term in the model. **penalized likelihood** If the extra term does not improve the likelihood more than the penalty amount, it is not worth adding. The most common penalized likelihood procedure is the AIC.

Let $m = p + q + P + Q$ be the number of terms estimated in the model. Then we can choose the values of p, q, P, and Q by minimizing Akaike's Information Criterion or AIC: **Akaike's Information Criterion (AIC)**

$$\boxed{AIC = -2 \log L + 2m} \qquad (7.26)$$

where L denotes the likelihood. The AIC was proposed by Akaike (1974).

There are several modifications to the AIC that are also used including the Schwarz BIC (Bayesian Information Criterion) and FPE **Schwarz BIC** (Final prediction error). See Brockwell and Davis (1996) for details. **FPE**

Because not all computer programs produce the AIC or the likelihood L, it is not always possible to find the AIC for a given model. However, a useful approximation to the AIC is obtained via the approximation

$$-2 \log L \approx n(1 + \log(2\pi)) + n \log \sigma^2$$

where σ^2 is the variance of the residuals and n is the number of observations in the series. All computer programs will produce the value of σ^2 so the AIC can be found approximately using the formula

$$\boxed{AIC \approx n(1 + \log(2\pi)) + n \log \sigma^2 + 2m}. \qquad (7.27)$$

Sometimes the first term above is omitted because it is the same value for all models. Note that the AIC does not have much meaning by itself. It is only useful in comparison to the AIC value for another model fitted to the same data set.

You may wish to consider several models with AIC values close to the minimum. A difference in AIC values of 2 or less is not regarded as substantial and you may wish to choose a simpler model either for simplicity, or for the sake of getting a better model fit.

7/6/1 Example 1: Internet usage

We previously identified that a first difference makes this non-seasonal series stationary. Therefore, we need consider only ARIMA$(p,1,q)$ models. It is feasible to compute all such models for small values of p and q. Table 7-6 shows the AIC values for these models. The ARIMA$(3,1,0)$ selected initially is still the best model since it has the smallest AIC value. Note that some models were not able to be estimated. The computer program used was unable to find appropriate parameter estimates using the iterative maximum likelihood algorithm. This probably means those models are not suitable and so it is not a cause of much concern.

7/6/2 Example 2: Sales of printing/writing paper

The estimated model for this series is the ARIMA$(0,1,1)(0,1,1)_{12}$:

$$(1 - B)(1 - B^{12})Y_t = (1 - 0.840B)(1 - 0.636B^{12})e_t.$$

Both parameters are very significant with P-values less than 0.0001.

We considered a large number of other ARIMA models and compared their performance using the AIC. Some of the models fitted are shown in Table 7-7, including the best 10 models according to their AIC values. The ARIMA$(0,1,1)(0,1,1)_{12}$ model initially selected has the lowest AIC value. But note that seven of the other top 10 models have a larger likelihood value than this model and that the model with the largest likelihood value is the ARIMA$(0,1,3)(0,1,1)_{12}$ model. However, the AIC shows that the gain by including the two additional MA terms is not sufficient to justify their inclusion. In this case, the model with the minimum MSE is also the model with the minimum AIC.

	$q=0$	$q=1$	$q=2$	$q=3$	$q=4$	$q=5$
$p=0$	628.99	547.81	517.87	518.27	517.38	516.86
$p=1$	527.24	512.30	514.25	512.58	513.10	514.28
$p=2$	520.18	514.29	–	–	–	–
$p=3$	509.99	511.94	513.92	515.14	–	–
$p=4$	511.93	510.87	–	–	–	–
$p=5$	513.86	–	–	–	–	515.76

Table 7-6: *AIC values for ARIMA(p,1,q) models fitted to the computer usage data of Table 7-3.*

Model	$\log(L)$	m	AIC	MSE
ARIMA$(0,1,1)(0,1,1)_{12}$	-556.914	2	1117.827	1916.2
ARIMA$(1,1,1)(0,1,1)_{12}$	-556.423	3	1118.845	1920.4
ARIMA$(0,1,2)(0,1,1)_{12}$	-556.441	3	1118.881	1921.0
ARIMA$(0,1,1)(0,1,2)_{12}$	-556.902	3	1119.803	1933.1
ARIMA$(0,1,1)(1,1,1)_{12}$	-556.906	3	1119.811	1933.5
ARIMA$(0,1,3)(0,1,1)_{12}$	-556.381	4	1120.762	1937.4
ARIMA$(1,1,1)(1,1,1)_{12}$	-556.417	4	1120.834	1938.2
ARIMA$(0,1,1)(1,1,0)_{12}$	-561.968	2	1127.936	2126.6
ARIMA$(1,0,1)(0,1,2)_{12}$	-556.415	4	1120.830	1962.2
ARIMA$(1,1,1)(1,1,0)_{12}$	-561.481	3	1128.962	2129.5
ARIMA$(1,1,0)(0,1,1)_{12}$	-569.463	2	1142.925	2439.1
ARIMA$(0,1,1)(0,1,0)_{12}$	-572.632	1	1147.264	2608.8
ARIMA$(1,1,0)(1,1,0)_{12}$	-574.552	2	1153.103	2703.5
ARIMA$(1,1,0)(0,1,0)_{12}$	-584.846	1	1171.691	3296.9

Table 7-7: *Some ARIMA models for the paper sales data of Table 7-4. The first 10 listed are the best models according to their AIC values. The last four are listed for later comparisons.*

7/7 Diagnostic checking

residuals

Although our selected model may appear to be the best among those models considered, it is also necessary to do diagnostic checking to verify that the model is adequate. This is done by studying the residuals to see if any pattern remains unaccounted for. It is not as straightforward to compute the residuals of an ARIMA model as it is for a regression model. However, these are always produced as part of the algorithm for estimating an ARIMA model.

For a good forecasting model, the residuals left over after fitting the model should be simply white noise. Therefore, if the ACF and PACF of the residuals are obtained, we would hope to find no significant autocorrelations and no significant partial autocorrelations.

For example, in Example 2 (relating to the data in Table 7-4), the residuals from the fitted $ARIMA(0, 1, 1)(0, 1, 1)_{12}$ model are analyzed in Figure 7-25. Since both a non-seasonal and a seasonal difference were applied to the 120 original data points, there are only 107 residuals to examine. In general, the number of residuals will be $n - d - sD$, where n = number of observations, d and D are the degrees of non-seasonal and seasonal differencing, respectively, and s is the number of observations per season. In Example 2, $107 = 120 - 1 - (12)1$.

outliers

It is normal in such plots to standardize (or scale) the residuals so they have variance equal to one. This makes it easier to spot outliers. Any residual smaller than -3 or greater than 3 is an outlier and may be worth investigating. There are no outliers in Figure 7-25. None of the ACF or PACF spikes is outside the limits, also suggesting the residual series is white noise.

portmanteau test

A portmanteau test (Section 7/1/4) can also be applied to the residuals as an additional test of fit. In this case $Q^* = 12.86$ for $h = 24$. Because the model had two parameters, we compare this value to the χ^2 distribution with $24 - 2 = 22$ degrees of freedom (see Table E of Appendix III). The value of Q^* is not significant, showing the residuals can be considered a white noise series.

So each of these tests suggest the model is adequate and there is no need to consider further refinement of the model.

If the portmanteau test had been significant, then the model would

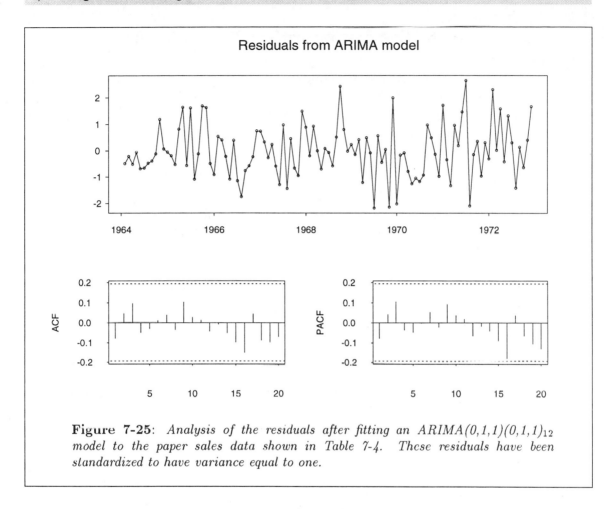

Figure 7-25: *Analysis of the residuals after fitting an ARIMA(0,1,1)(0,1,1)$_{12}$ model to the paper sales data shown in Table 7-4. These residuals have been standardized to have variance equal to one.*

have been inadequate. In this case, we would need to go back and consider other ARIMA models. The pattern of significant spikes in the ACF and PACF of the residuals may suggest how the model can be improved. For example, significant spikes at the seasonal lags suggest adding a seasonal component to the chosen model. Significant spikes at small lags suggest increasing the non-seasonal AR or MA components of the model.

Any new models will need their parameters estimated and their AIC values computed and compared with other models. Usually the model with the smallest AIC will have residuals which resemble white noise. Occasionally, it might be necessary to adopt a model with not quite the smallest AIC value, but with better behaved residuals.

7/8 Forecasting with ARIMA models

7/8/1 Point forecasts

The notation used throughout this chapter is compact and convenient. An ARIMA$(0, 1, 1)(0, 1, 1)_{12}$ model is described as

$$(1 - B)(1 - B^{12})Y_t = (1 - \theta_1 B)(1 - \Theta_1 B^{12})e_t, \qquad (7.28)$$

for example.   However, in order to use an identified model for forecasting, it is necessary to expand the equation and make it look like a more conventional regression equation. For the model above, the form is

$$Y_t = Y_{t-1} + Y_{t-12} - Y_{t-13} + e_t - \theta_1 e_{t-1} - \Theta_1 e_{t-12} + \theta_1 \Theta_1 e_{t-13}. \quad (7.29)$$

In order to use this equation to forecast 1 period ahead—that is, Y_{t+1}—we increase the subscripts by one, throughout:

$$Y_{t+1} = Y_t + Y_{t-11} - Y_{t-12} + e_{t+1} - \theta_1 e_t - \Theta_1 e_{t-11} + \theta_1 \Theta_1 e_{t-12}. \quad (7.30)$$

The term e_{t+1} will not be known because the expected value of future random errors has to be taken as zero, but from the fitted model it will be possible to replace the values e_t, e_{t-11}, and e_{t-12} by their empirically determined values—that is, the residuals for times t, $t - 11$, and $t - 12$ respectively. Of course, as we forecast further and further ahead, there will be no empirical values for the e terms after a while, and so their expected values will all be zero.

For the Y values, at the start of the forecasting process, we will know the values Y_t, Y_{t-11}, and Y_{t-12}. After a while, however, the Y values in equation (7.30) will be forecasted values rather than known past values.

By way of illustration, consider the ARIMA$(0,1,1)(0,1,1)_{12}$ fitted to the paper sales data of Example 2 (from Table 7-4). This model will be used to forecast two years ahead. Recall the fitted model is

$$(1 - B)(1 - B^{12})Y_t = (1 - 0.840B)(1 - 0.636B^{12})e_t$$

or

$$Y_t = Y_{t-1} + Y_{t-12} - Y_{t-13} + e_t - 0.840e_{t-1} - 0.636e_{t-12} + 0.534e_{t-13}.$$
$$(7.31)$$

Month	Period t	Sales Y_t	Error e_t
$\vdots$	$\vdots$	$\vdots$	$\vdots$
Apr 71	100	875.000	41.14
May 71	101	835.088	8.28
Jun 71	102	934.595	61.85
Jul 71	103	832.500	112.83
Aug 71	104	300.000	-88.66
Sep 71	105	791.443	-5.91
Oct 71	106	900.000	14.80
Nov 71	107	781.729	-40.67
Dec 71	108	880.000	12.81
Jan 72	109	875.024	-12.85
Feb 72	110	992.968	98.03
Mar 72	111	976.804	0.98
Apr 72	112	968.697	67.20
May 72	113	871.675	-17.36
Jun 72	114	1006.852	55.98
Jul 72	115	832.037	13.01
Aug 72	116	345.587	-59.64
Sep 72	117	849.528	5.98
Oct 72	118	913.871	-26.62
Nov 72	119	868.746	17.02
Dec 72	120	993.733	70.88

Table 7-8: *The industry paper sales data (from Table 7-4) and the residuals after fitting an ARIMA(0,1,1)(0,1,1)$_{12}$.*

Now in order to forecast period 121, equation (7.31) would have to be written as

$$\hat{Y}_{121} = Y_{120} + Y_{109} - Y_{108} + \hat{e}_{121} - 0.840e_{120} - 0.636e_{109} + 0.534e_{108}.$$

The value of e_{121} is not known, so we have replaced it by $\hat{e}_{121} = 0$. Table 7-8 shows some of the residuals for the paper sales data of Example 2. The period number is given in Column 2, the known observations are shown in Column 3, and the residual (or error, e_t) is given in Column 4. Using values from this table, the forecast for

Month	Period t	Forecast $\hat{Y}_t$	Lower limit	Upper limit
Jan 1973	121	944.2212	860.8496	1027.593
Feb 1973	122	992.9713	908.5420	1077.401
Mar 1973	123	1028.5496	943.0757	1114.024
Apr 1973	124	978.2355	891.7295	1064.741
May 1973	125	928.1504	840.6246	1015.676
Jun 1973	126	1018.4610	929.9271	1106.995
Jul 1973	127	865.2814	775.7507	954.812
Aug 1973	128	423.7038	333.1873	514.220
Sep 1973	129	891.9768	800.4851	983.468
Oct 1973	130	976.4427	883.9862	1068.899
Nov 1973	131	906.2744	812.8630	999.686
Dec 1973	132	995.2867	900.9300	1089.643
Jan 1974	133	983.6404	879.6629	1087.618
Feb 1974	134	1032.3906	926.8370	1137.944
Mar 1974	135	1067.9689	960.8623	1175.076
Apr 1974	136	1017.6548	909.0174	1126.292
May 1974	137	967.5697	857.4229	1077.717
Jun 1974	138	1057.8803	946.2444	1169.516
Jul 1974	139	904.7006	791.5953	1017.806
Aug 1974	140	463.1230	348.5671	577.679
Sep 1974	141	931.3960	815.4076	1047.384
Oct 1974	142	1015.8619	898.4585	1133.265
Nov 1974	143	945.6936	826.8921	1064.495
Dec 1974	144	1034.7060	914.5225	1154.889

Table 7-9: *Forecasts and 95% prediction intervals for the paper sales data of Table 7-4 using an ARIMA(0,1,1)(0,1,1)$_{12}$ model.*

period 121 can be calculated as follows:

$$\begin{aligned}
\hat{Y}_{121} &= 993.73 + 875.02 - 880.00 + 0 - 0.840(70.88) \\
&\quad - 0.636(-12.85) + 0.534(12.81) \\
&= 944.22.
\end{aligned}$$

For period 122, the forecast is

$$\begin{aligned}
\hat{Y}_{122} &= \hat{Y}_{121} + Y_{110} - Y_{109} \\
&\quad + \hat{e}_{122} - 0.840\hat{e}_{121} - 0.636e_{110} + 0.534e_{109}
\end{aligned}$$

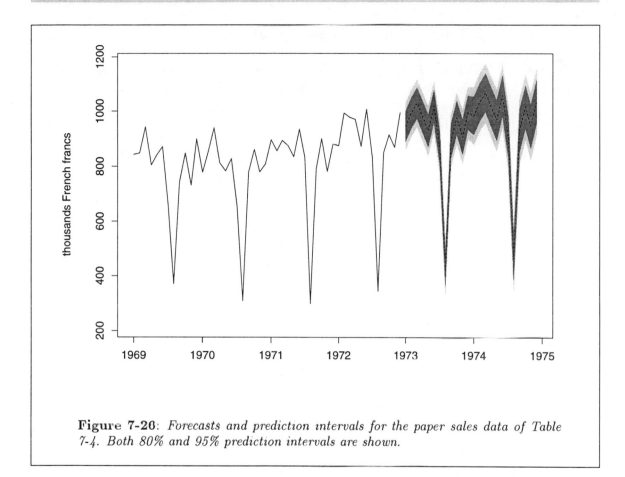

Figure 7-26: *Forecasts and prediction intervals for the paper sales data of Table 7-4. Both 80% and 95% prediction intervals are shown.*

$$
\begin{aligned}
= \quad & 944.22 + 992.97 - 875.02 \\
& + 0 - 0.840(0) - 0.636(98.03) + 0.534(-12.85) \\
= \quad & 992.97.
\end{aligned}
$$

Table 7-9 shows forecasts for the next 24 months, along with a 95% prediction interval for each forecast. Figure 7-26 shows these forecasts and intervals along with 80% prediction intervals. As we forecast with a longer and longer lead-time, the prediction intervals increase steadily in size. These prediction intervals can be difficult to calculate by hand, and are usually done using a computer package. The calculations involved assume the residuals are uncorrelated and normally distributed.

prediction intervals

7/8/2 Out-of-sample forecasting

out-of-sample
forecasting

There are several reasons why genuine out-of-sample forecasting may not be as accurate as the prediction intervals suggest. First, in computing the prediction intervals, the uncertainty in the parameter estimates has not been accounted for. Consequently, the intervals are narrower than they should be. This is a problem peculiar to ARIMA models as the mathematics becomes too difficult to allow the additional uncertainty to be included. The prediction intervals for regression models computed in Chapters 5 and 6 did allow for the parameter estimation.

assumptions

A second reason for forecast inaccuracy is that the ARIMA model contains several assumptions which may not be met. One of the most important assumptions is that the historical patterns of our data will not change during the forecast period. If the model assumptions are true, the forecasts obtained are optimal. However, for business series, actual out-of-sample forecast accuracy from ARIMA models is often worse than is indicated by the prediction limits, because the patterns of real data series can and do change during the periods we are forecasting.

holdout set

A more realistic way of assessing a model's accuracy is to use a holdout set (Section 2/4/2). That is, some of the data at the end of the series are omitted before the models are estimated. Then the models are compared on the basis of how well they forecast the data which have been withheld rather than how well they forecast the same data which has been used for modeling. For example, if we hold out the last 12 months of the paper sales data of Example 2 and refit the models using the remaining data, a different picture emerges. Because we are comparing the models on their genuine forecasting ability, we can simply compare their MSE performance on the holdout set. There is no need to consider the likelihood or AIC values.

Table 7-10 shows some of the ARIMA models from Table 7-7, this time compared according to their ability to forecast the final 12 months of the series. Note that the previously selected model actually performs rather worse than several other models in this comparison. Also the best performing model is a simple MA(1) applied to the differenced data. It is common for simpler models to perform best in an out-of-sample comparison (see Chapter 11 for more details).

Model	MSE
ARIMA$(0,1,1)(0,1,0)_{12}$	2691.5
ARIMA$(1,1,0)(1,1,0)_{12}$	2704.7
ARIMA$(1,1,0)(0,1,0)_{12}$	2826.0
ARIMA$(0,1,1)(0,1,1)_{12}$	2837.1
ARIMA$(1,1,0)(0,1,1)_{12}$	2878.5

Table 7-10: *The best few ARIMA models for the paper sales data of Table 7-4 according to their MSE values based on a holdout sample of 12 months.*

7/8/3 The effect of differencing on forecasts

Differencing a series can have a great effect on the forecasts. It is important to understand how the forecasts will be affected by the differencing as it may influence the decision as to how many differences to take. Although models with different degrees of differencing may perform similarly over the historical data, the behavior of the forecasts can vary greatly. The following comments summarize the behavior of the forecasts under different model conditions as the forecast horizon increases.

Undifferenced data
> Forecasts from undifferenced data will converge to the mean of the historical data if a constant term has been included in the model. Otherwise, the forecasts will converge to zero. In either case, the forecast variances will converge to the variance of the historical data. Therefore prediction intervals will also converge.

Data differenced once at lag 1
> If a constant term has not been included, the forecasts will converge to the value of the last observation. If a constant term has been included, the long-range forecasts will follow a linear trend where the slope of the trend is equal to the fitted constant. In either case, the forecast variances will increase in proportion to the forecast horizon. So prediction intervals will diverge.

linear trend

Data differenced twice at lag 1

quadratic trend

If a series has been differenced twice and no constant fitted, the long-range forecasts will follow a linear trend extrapolating the trend at the end of the data series. If a constant has been fitted, the long-range forecasts will follow a quadratic trend. In either case, the forecast variances will diverge very quickly (faster than for single differencing). So prediction intervals will also diverge quickly.

Seasonally differenced data

The effect of seasonal differencing is similar. In particular, if a series has been seasonally differenced and first differenced, the forecasts will behave in a similar manner to data which have been differenced twice at lag 1, except that the forecasts will also show seasonality.

Clearly, we do not want large prediction intervals and so differencing should be done as few times as necessary. If it is unreasonable to assume the forecast variances diverge linearly or quadratically, then differencing is probably inappropriate for the problem. An alternative to differencing is to remove the trend and seasonality by estimating them directly as described in Section 8/1.

7/8/4 ARIMA models used in time series decomposition

In the Census Bureau decomposition procedures (see Section 3/5), an ARIMA model is often used to forecast the series before decomposition. This reduces bias at the ends of the series. The X-11-ARIMA procedure and the X-12-ARIMA procedure both use an ARIMA model in this way.

The user can specify an appropriate model or let the computer program automatically select a model.

If automatic selection is used, one of five predetermined models will be applied. These were chosen on the basis of testing a large number of economic series (Dagum, 1988) and should provide reasonable forecasts for most economic series. The five models are given in the table below.

$$
\begin{array}{ll}
\text{ARIMA}(0,1,1)(0,1,1)_s & \text{with log transformation} \\
\text{ARIMA}(0,1,2)(0,1,1)_s & \text{with log transformation} \\
\text{ARIMA}(2,1,0)(0,1,1)_s & \text{with log transformation} \\
\text{ARIMA}(0,2,2)(0,1,1)_s & \text{with log transformation} \\
\text{ARIMA}(2,1,2)(0,1,1)_s & \text{with no transformation}
\end{array}
$$

7/8/5 Equivalances with exponential smoothing models

It is possible to show that the forecasts obtained from some exponential smoothing models (Chapter 4) are identical with forecasts from particular ARIMA models (see McKenzie, 1984, 1986; Yar and Chatfield, 1990; Chatfield and Yar, 1991).

- The simple exponential smoothing forecasts are equivalent to   SES forecasts
  those from an ARIMA(0,1,1) model. The moving average
  parameter, θ, is equivalent to $1 - \alpha$ where α is the smoothing
  parameter.

- Holt's linear method is equivalent to an ARIMA(0,2,2) model.   Holt's method
  The moving average parameters are $\theta_1 = 2 - \alpha - \alpha\beta$ and $\theta_2 =$
  $\alpha - 1$ where α and β are the two smoothing parameters.

- Holt-Winters' additive method gives forecasts equivalent to an   Holt-Winters' method
  ARIMA$(0, 1, s+1)(0, 1, 0)_s$ model. There are several parameter
  restrictions because the ARIMA model has $s + 1$ parameters
  whereas the Holt-Winters' method uses only three parameters.

- Holt-Winters' multiplicative method has no equivalent ARIMA
  model.

Many computer packages use these equivalences to produce prediction intervals for exponential smoothing. However, see our comments on this in Section 4/5/3.

References and selected bibliography

ABRAHAM, B. and LEDOLTER, J. (1983) *Statistical methods for forecasting*, New York: John Wiley & Sons.

AKAIKE, H. (1974) A new look at statistical model identification, *IEEE transactions on automatic control*, **AC-19**, 716–723.

ANDERSON, R.L. (1942) Distribution of the serial correlation coefficient, *Annals of Mathematical Statistics*, **13**, 1–13.

BARTLETT, M.S. (1946) On the theoretical specification of sampling properties of autocorrelated time series, *Journal of the Royal Statistical Society*, Series B., **8**, 27.

BOWERMAN, B.L. and O'CONNELL, R.T. (1987) *Time series forecasting*, 2nd ed., Belmont, Cal.: Duxbury Press.

BOX, G.E.P. and G.M. JENKINS (1970) *Time series analysis: Forecasting and control*, San Francisco: Holden-Day.

BOX, G.E.P., G.M. JENKINS, and G.C. REINSELL (1994) *Time series analysis: Forecasting and control*, 3rd ed., Englewood Cliffs, N.J.: Prentice-Hall.

BOX, G.E.P. and D.A. PIERCE (1970) Distribution of the residual autocorrelations in autoregressive-integrated moving-average time series models, *Journal of the American Statistical Association*, **65**, 1509–1526.

BROCKWELL, P.J. and R.A. DAVIS (1996) *An introduction to time series and forecasting*, New York: Springer-Verlag.

CHATFIELD, C. (1996) *The analysis of time series: an introduction*, 5th ed., London: Chapman and Hall.

CHATFIELD, C. and M. YAR (1991) Prediction intervals for multiplicative Holt-Winters, *International Journal of Forecasting*, **7**, 31–37.

CHOI, B. (1992) *ARMA model identification*, Berlin: Springer-Verlag.

CLEARY, J.P. and H. LEVENBACH (1982) *The professional forecaster*, Belmont, Cal.: Lifetime Learning Publications.

CRYER, J.D. (1986) *Time series analysis*, Belmont, Cal.: Duxbury Press.

DAGUM, E.B. (1988) X-11-ARIMA/88 seasonal adjustment method: foundations and users manual, Statistics Canada.

DICKEY, D.A. and W.A. FULLER (1979) Distribution of the estimators for autoregressive time series with a unit root, *Journal of the American Statistical Association*, **74**, 427–431.

DICKEY, D.A., W.R. BELL, and R.B. MILLER (1986) Unit roots in time series models: tests and implications, *American Statistician*, **40**, 12–26.

FULLER, W.A. (1976) *Introduction to statistical time series*, New York: John Wiley & Sons.

GRANGER, C.W.J. (1989) *Forecasting in business and economics*, 2nd ed., New York: Academic Press.

GRANGER, C.W.J. and P. NEWBOLD (1986) *Forecasting economic time series*, 2nd ed., New York: Academic Press.

HANNAN, E.J. (1963) The estimation of seasonal variation in economic time series, *Journal of the American Statistical Association*, **58**, 31–44.

HARVEY, A.C. (1993) *Time series models*, 2nd ed., New York: Harvester-Wheatsheaf.

JANACEK, G. and SWIFT, L. (1993) *Time Series: forecasting, simulation, applications*, New York: Ellis Horwood.

KENDALL, M.G. (1976) *Time series*, 2nd ed., London: Griffin.

LJUNG, G.M. and G.E.P. BOX (1978) On a measure of lack of fit in time series models, *Biometrika*, **65**, 297–303.

MAKRIDAKIS, S. and S. WHEELWRIGHT (1978) *Interactive forecasting*, 2nd ed., San Francisco: Holden-Day.

——————— (1979) *Forecasting*, TIMS Studies in Management Science, vol. 12. Amsterdam: North-Holland.

McLEOD, A.I. (1978) On the distribution of residual autocorrelations in Box-Jenkins models, *Journal of the Royal Statistical Society*, Series B, **40**, No. 3, 296–302.

McKENZIE, E. (1984) General exponential smoothing and the equivalent ARIMA process, *Journal of Forecasting*, **3**, 333–344.

——————— (1986) Error analysis for Winters' additive seasonal forecasting system, *International Journal of Forecasting*, **2**, 373–382.

MONTGOMERY, D.C., L.A. JOHNSON, and J.S. GARDINER (1990) *Forecasting and time series analysis*, 2nd ed., New York: McGraw-Hill.

NELSON, C.R. (1973) *Applied time series analysis for managerial forecasting*, San Francisco: Holden-Day.

PANKRATZ, A. (1983) *Forecasting with univariate Box–Jenkins models: concepts and cases*, New York: John Wiley & Sons.

QUENOUILLE, M.H. (1949) The joint distribution of serial correlation coefficients, *Annals of Mathematical Statistics*, **20**, 561–71.

THOMOPOULOS, N.T. (1980) *Applied forecasting methods*, Englewood Cliffs, N.J.: Prentice-Hall.

YAR, M. and C. CHATFIELD (1990) Prediction intervals for the Holt-Winters' forecasting procedure, *International Journal of Forecasting*, **6**, 127–137.

Exercises

7.1 Figure 7-3 shows the ACF for 36 random numbers, and Figure
7-27 shows the ACFs for 360 random numbers and for 1,000
random numbers.

    (a) Explain the differences among these figures. Do they all
indicate the data are white noise?

    (b) Why are the critical values at different distances from the
mean of zero? Why are the autocorrelations different in
each figure when they each refer to white noise?

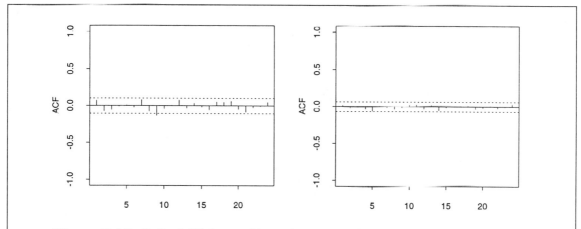

Figure 7-27: *Left: ACF for a white noise series of 360 numbers. Right: ACF for
a white noise series of 1,000 numbers.*

7.2 A classic example of a non-stationary series is the daily closing
IBM stock prices. Figure 7-28 shows the analysis of $n = 369$
daily closing prices for IBM stock. Explain how each plot
shows the series is non-stationary and should be differenced.

7.3 The data below are from a white noise series with a standard
normal distribution (mean zero and variance one). (Read left
to right.)

0.01	1.38	0.53	1.58	1.32	1.04	0.33	-0.20	1.90	0.72
-0.27	-1.43	-1.15	-0.07	1.69	0.28	0.01	0.94	-2.10	0.09
0.91	1.76	0.84	-1.13	0.92	1.67	-1.03	-1.71	1.18	-0.59

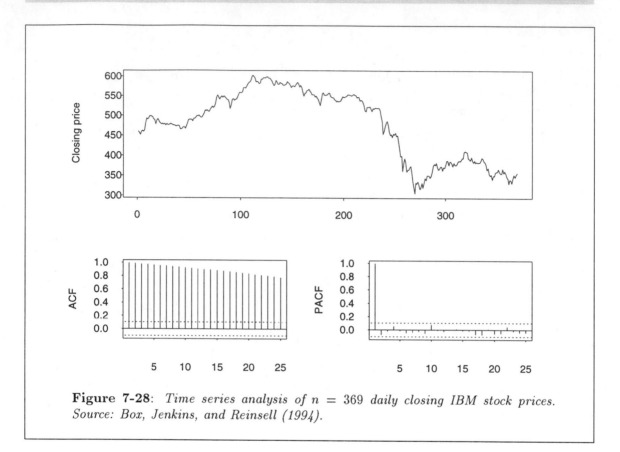

Figure 7-28: *Time series analysis of* $n = 369$ *daily closing IBM stock prices. Source: Box, Jenkins, and Reinsell (1994).*

(a) Using the normal random numbers of the table, generate data from an AR(1) model with $\phi_1 = 0.6$. Start with $Y_0 = 0$.

(b) Generate data from an MA(1) model with $\theta_1 = -0.6$. Start with $Z_0 = 0$.

(c) Produce a time plot for each series. What can you say about the differences between the two models?

(d) Generate data from an ARMA(1,1) model with $\phi_1 = 0.6$ and $\theta_1 = -0.6$. Start with $Y_0 = 0$ and $Z_0 = 0$.

(e) Generate data from an AR(2) model with $\phi_1 = -0.8$ and $\phi_2 = 0.3$. Start with $Y_0 = Y_{-1} = 0$. Generate data from an MA(2) model with $\theta_1 = -0.8$ and $\theta_2 = 0.3$. Start with $Z_0 = Z_{-1} = 0$. Graph the two series and compare them.

4737	5117	5091	3468	4320	3825	3673	3694	3708	3333
3367	3614	3362	3655	3963	4405	4595	5045	5700	5716
5138	5010	5353	6074	5031	5648	5506	4230	4827	3885

Table 7-11: *The number of strikes in the United States from 1951–1980. Read left to right. Source: Brockwell and Davis (1996).*

7.4 Consider Table 7-11 which gives the number of strikes in the United States from 1951–1980.

(a) By studying appropriate graphs of the series, explain why an ARIMA(0,1,1) model seems appropriate.

(b) Should you include a constant in the model? Explain.

(c) Write this model in terms of the backshift operator.

(d) Fit the model using a computer package and examine the residuals. Is the model satisfactory?

(e) Forecast three times ahead by hand. Check your forecasts with forecasts generated by the computer package.

(f) Create a plot of the series with forecasts and prediction intervals for the next three periods shown.

7.5 Figure 7-29 shows the data for Manufacturer's stocks of Evaporated and Sweet Condensed Milk (case goods) for the period January 1971 through December 1980.

(a) Describe the time plot.

(b) What can you learn from the ACF graph?

(c) What can you learn from the PACF graph?

(d) Figure 7-30 shows an analysis of the differenced data $(1 - B)(1 - B^{12})Y_t$—that is, a first-order non-seasonal differencing ($d = 1$) and a first-order seasonal differencing ($D = 1$). What model do these graphs suggest?

(e) Write the model in terms of the backshift operator, and then without using the backshift operator.

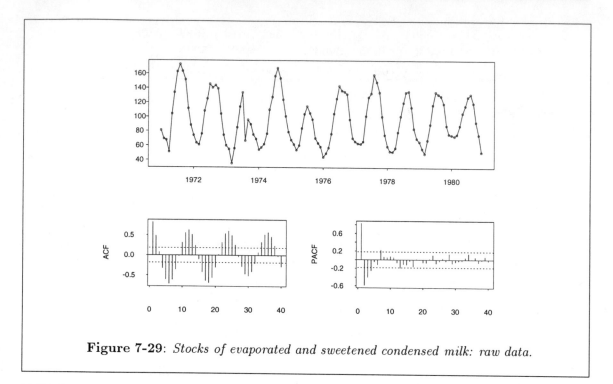

Figure 7-29: *Stocks of evaporated and sweetened condensed milk: raw data.*

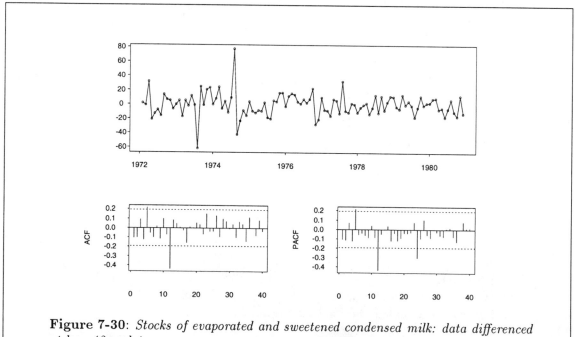

Figure 7-30: *Stocks of evaporated and sweetened condensed milk: data differenced at lags 12 and 1.*

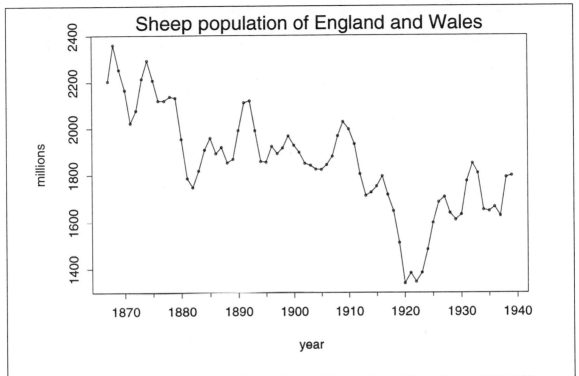

Figure 7-31: *Sheep population (in millions) of England and Wales from 1867–1939. (Source: Kendall, 1976.)*

7.6 The sheep population of England and Wales from 1867–1939 is graphed in Figure 7-31. Assume you decide to fit the following model:

$$Y_t = Y_{t-1} + \phi_1(Y_{t-1} - Y_{t-2}) + \phi_2(Y_{t-2} - Y_{t-3}) + \phi_3(Y_{t-3} - Y_{t-4}) + e_t$$

where e_t is a white noise series.

(a) What sort of ARIMA model is this (i.e., what are p, d, and q)?

(b) By examining Figure 7-32, explain why this model is appropriate.

(c) The last five values of the series are given below:

Year	1935	1936	1937	1938	1939
Millions of sheep	1648	1665	1627	1791	1797

Given the estimated parameters are $\phi_1 = 0.42$, $\phi_2 = -0.20$, and $\phi_3 = -0.30$, give forecasts for the next three years (1940–1942).

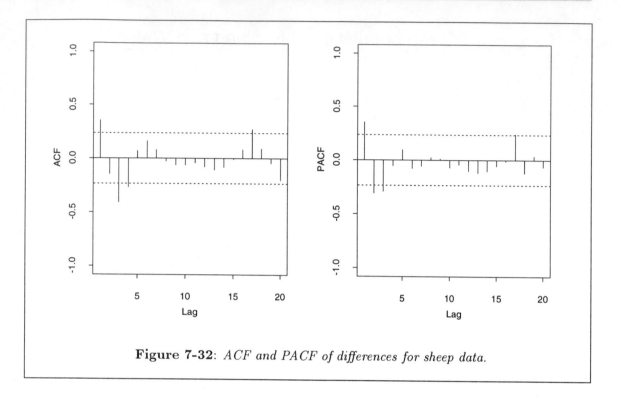

Figure 7-32: *ACF and PACF of differences for sheep data.*

7.7 Figure 7-33 shows the annual bituminous coal production in the United States from 1920 to 1968. You decide to fit the following model to the series:

$$Y_t = c + \phi_1 Y_{t-1} + \phi_2 Y_{t-2} + \phi_3 Y_{t-3} + \phi_4 Y_{t-4} + e_t$$

where Y_t is the coal production in year t and e_t is a white noise series.

(a) What sort of ARIMA model is this (i.e., what are p, d, and q)?

(b) Explain why this model was chosen.

(c) The last five values of the series are given below:

t (**year**)	1964	1965	1966	1967	1968
Y_t (**million tons net**)	467	512	534	552	545

The estimated parameters are $c = 146.1$, $\phi_1 = 0.891$, $\phi_2 = -0.257$, $\phi_3 = 0.392$, $\phi_4 = -0.333$. Give forecasts for the next three years (1969–1971).

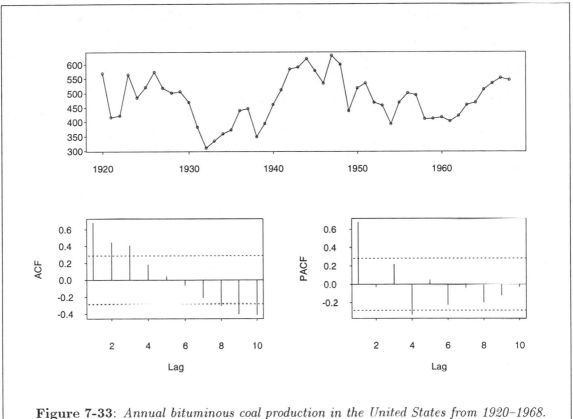

Figure 7-33: *Annual bituminous coal production in the United States from 1920–1968.*

7.8 Table 7-12 shows the total net generation of electricity (in billion kilowatt hours) by the U.S. electric industry (monthly for the period 1985–1996). In general there are two peaks per year: in mid-summer and mid-winter.

(a) Examine the 12-month moving average of this series to see what kind of trend is involved.

(b) Do the data need transforming? If so, find a suitable transformation.

(c) Are the data stationary? If not, find an appropriate differencing which yields stationary data.

(d) Identify a couple of ARIMA models that might be useful in describing the time series. Which of your models is the best according to their AIC values?

1985	227.86	198.24	194.97	184.88	196.79	205.36	226.72	226.05	202.50	194.79	192.43	219.25
1986	217.47	192.34	196.83	186.07	197.31	215.02	242.67	225.17	206.69	197.75	196.43	213.55
1987	222.75	194.03	201.85	189.50	206.07	225.59	247.91	247.64	213.01	203.01	200.26	220.50
1988	237.90	216.94	214.01	196.00	208.37	232.75	257.46	267.69	220.18	210.61	209.59	232.75
1989	232.75	219.82	226.74	208.04	220.12	235.69	257.05	258.69	227.15	219.91	219.30	259.04
1990	237.29	212.88	226.03	211.07	222.91	249.18	266.38	268.53	238.02	224.69	213.75	237.43
1991	248.46	210.82	221.40	209.00	234.37	248.43	271.98	268.11	233.88	223.43	221.38	233.76
1992	243.97	217.76	224.66	210.84	220.35	236.84	266.15	255.20	234.76	221.29	221.26	244.13
1993	245.78	224.62	234.80	211.37	222.39	249.63	282.29	279.13	236.60	223.62	225.86	246.41
1994	261.70	225.01	231.54	214.82	227.70	263.86	278.15	274.64	237.66	227.97	224.75	242.91
1995	253.08	228.13	233.68	217.38	236.38	256.08	292.83	304.71	245.57	234.41	234.12	258.17
1996	268.66	245.31	247.47	226.25	251.67	268.79	288.94	290.16	250.69	240.80		

Table 7-12: *Total net generation of electricity by the U.S. electric industry (monthly data for the period January 1985–October 1996). Read left to right. Source: National Energy Information Center.*

(e) Estimate the parameters of your best model and do diagnostic testing on the residuals. Do the residuals resemble white noise? If not, try to find another ARIMA model which fits better.

(f) Forecast the next 24 months of generation of electricity by the U.S. electric industry. See if you can get the latest figures from your library (or on the web at **www.eia.doe.gov**) to check on the accuracy of your forecasts.

7.9 Table 7-13 shows monthly employment figures for the motion picture industry (SIC Code 78) for 192 months from Jan. 1955 through Dec. 1970. This period covers the declining months due to the advent of TV and then a recovery.

(a) How consistent is the seasonal pattern? Examine this question using several different techniques, including decomposition methods (Chapter 4) and autocorrelations for lags up to 36 or 48.

(b) Split the data set into two parts, the first eight years (96 months) and the second eight years (96 months) and do Box-Jenkins identification, estimation, and diagnostic testing for each part separately. Is there any difference between the two identified models?

t	Y_t	t	Y_t	t	Y_t	t	Y_t
1	218.20	49	183.70	97	167.20	145	179.50
2	217.90	50	184.90	98	165.00	146	179.90
3	224.70	51	188.40	99	168.80	147	181.70
4	236.40	52	197.00	100	175.00	148	191.70
5	238.70	53	199.20	101	177.90	149	199.10
6	240.80	54	201.60	102	183.70	150	205.50
7	241.90	55	204.30	103	187.20	151	212.00
8	241.30	56	206.80	104	189.30	152	213.10
9	240.40	57	203.20	105	183.40	153	203.30
10	233.40	58	195.90	106	177.30	154	193.40
11	226.60	59	190.90	107	172.30	155	190.30
12	219.40	60	185.30	108	171.40	156	181.50
13	215.80	61	184.00	109	164.90	157	176.00
14	213.80	62	183.40	110	164.40	158	176.80
15	220.80	63	181.70	111	166.90	159	182.20
16	234.50	64	188.40	112	174.20	160	191.20
17	236.00	65	191.60	113	177.50	161	197.60
18	232.50	66	194.50	114	183.60	162	201.40
19	233.80	67	198.10	115	189.50	163	208.00
20	233.20	68	200.40	116	191.60	164	210.20
21	232.60	69	196.30	117	185.10	165	206.30
22	226.90	70	189.10	118	181.90	166	200.50
23	217.90	71	185.10	119	175.40	167	202.20
24	212.30	72	182.60	120	174.20	168	200.10
25	208.80	73	179.70	121	172.70	169	194.80
26	209.30	74	178.50	122	168.20	170	192.30
27	212.80	75	181.50	123	171.40	171	192.60
28	208.80	76	190.10	124	177.00	172	199.00
29	211.70	77	190.50	125	182.60	173	207.70
30	214.10	78	193.70	126	191.40	174	215.80
31	214.70	79	195.70	127	200.80	175	219.90
32	216.20	80	195.10	128	201.20	176	221.70
33	218.50	81	192.40	129	195.60	177	214.30
34	213.60	82	185.90	130	188.40	178	211.50
35	206.00	83	178.80	131	184.80	179	206.40
36	198.90	84	175.80	132	187.30	180	204.60
37	194.70	85	169.70	133	182.40	181	196.80
38	193.60	86	169.30	134	176.20	182	190.80
39	195.40	87	172.30	135	178.90	183	188.50
40	203.00	88	180.80	136	182.20	184	196.50
41	204.30	89	183.10	137	184.90	185	204.70
42	203.80	90	182.90	138	195.30	186	211.70
43	205.90	91	186.10	139	198.50	187	216.80
44	207.60	92	189.30	140	200.90	188	217.30
45	205.90	93	183.80	141	195.60	189	212.80
46	198.70	94	179.00	142	187.60	190	206.60
47	189.70	95	172.50	143	183.70	191	203.90
48	186.70	96	171.10	144	184.20	192	202.90

Table 7-13: *Employment figures in the motion picture industry (SIC Code 78) for the period Jan. 1955 through Dec. 1970. Source: "Employment and Earnings, U.S. 1909–1978," published by the Department of Labor, 1979.*

(c) For the first 96 months (1955 through 1962) use the ARIMA model obtained in (b) above to forecast the next 12 months ahead. How do these forecasts relate to the actuals?

(d) For the last 96 months (1963 through 1970) use the model obtained in (b) above to forecast the next 12 months ahead. Compare your forecast with the actual figures given below.

Year	J	F	M	A	M	J	J	A	S	O	N	D
1971	194.5	187.9	187.7	198.3	202.7	204.2	211.7	213.4	212.0	203.4	199.5	199.3

(e) In general, when there is a reasonably long time series such as this one, and there is a clear long-term cycle (shown by plotting a 12-month moving average, for instance) what should the forecaster do? Use all the data? Use only the last so-many years? If the object is to forecast the next 12 months ahead?

7.10 Figure 7-34 shows the analysis of 107 months of U.S. sales of new one-family houses for the period Jan. 1987 through Nov. 1995. (A longer version of this series was also analyzed in Chapter 4.) Figure 7-35 shows the analysis of the seasonal differences of these data.

(a) What can you say about seasonality of the data?

(b) What can you say about trend in the time series?

(c) What does the one large partial autocorrelation in Figure 7-35 suggest?

(d) What would your next step be if you were trying to develop an ARIMA model for this time series? Can you identify a model on the basis of Figures 7-34 and 7-35? Would you want to do some more analyses, and if so, what would they be?

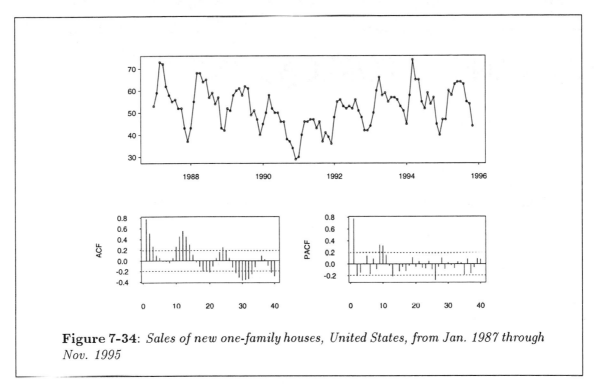

Figure 7-34: *Sales of new one-family houses, United States, from Jan. 1987 through Nov. 1995*

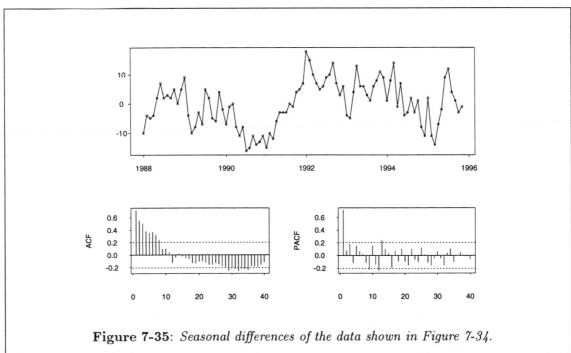

Figure 7-35: *Seasonal differences of the data shown in Figure 7-34.*

8
ADVANCED FORECASTING MODELS

The ARIMA models examined in the previous chapter dealt with *single* time series and did not allow the inclusion of other information in the models and forecasts. But very often there is other information which can assist in forecasting the series of interest. There may be information about holidays, or strikes, or changes in the law, or some other external variables which would assist in developing more accurate forecasts. In this chapter we extend the ARIMA models of Chapter 7 to allow other series and other external information to be included in the models.

The first approach to this problem is given in Section 8/1 where we combine a multiple regression model from Chapter 6 with an ARIMA model from Chapter 7. The resulting model is a regression with ARIMA errors and provides all the advantages of regression with the powerful time series features of an ARIMA model.

regression with ARIMA errors

Section 8/2 extends the regression model with ARIMA errors to allow the explanatory variables to be included in the model using a more general and powerful method. These are dynamic regression models (or transfer function models).

dynamic regression models

A special case of the dynamic regression model occurs when the explanatory variable represents an intervention. That is, a one-off event which impacts the time series of interest (e.g., a strike or a war or the introduction of new legislation). This is such an important case that it deserves separate study and is discussed in Section 8/3.

intervention analysis

For each of the models discussed in Sections 8/1 through 8/3, it is assumed that the explanatory variable affects the forecast variable, but that it is not affected itself by the forecast variable. That is, there is no feedback between the variables. When this assumption is invalid, a multivariate time series model is required. Multivariate autoregressive models are covered in Section 8/4.

multivariate autoregressive models

All of the above models may be written in the form of a "state space" model. This general formulation provides a unified way of handling computations as well as providing a vehicle for some new forecasting methods. State space models are introduced in Section 8/5.

state space models

Sections 8/6 and 8/7 introduce two relatively recent developments in forecasting methodology. Section 8/6 describes some non-linear time series models, and neural network forecasting is introduced in Section 8/7.

non-linear time series neural networks

Some of the models discussed here require a considerable amount of computation in going through the stages of identification, estimation, diagnostic checking, and finally, forecasting. Forecasters using these methods should not fall into the same trap as econometricians who, during the 1960s, seemed to think that the more complex their forecasting models, the more accurate they would be. It is important to assess forecast accuracy for all models used, by applying the techniques discussed in Chapter 2. Often, simpler models will perform better than the more complicated models when out-of-sample predictions are made.

8/1 Regression with ARIMA errors

In Chapter 6 we considered regression models of the form

$$\boxed{Y_t = b_0 + b_1 X_{1,t} + \cdots + b_k X_{k,t} + N_t}. \tag{8.1}$$

That is, Y_t is modeled as a function of the k explanatory variables $X_{1,t}, \ldots, X_{k,t}$. The error term in equation (8.1) is N_t. One of the key assumptions in Chapter 6 was that N_t was an uncorrelated series, that is, it was "white noise." We looked at methods for determining if N_t was uncorrelated in Section 6/2/1. In this section we consider

autocorrelated errors   fitting models of the form (8.1) where N_t contains autocorrelations.

The method we will adopt is to combine the ARIMA models of Chapter 7 to handle the autocorrelations with the regression models of Chapter 6 to describe the explanatory relationship. The resulting model is a regression model with ARIMA errors. Equation (8.1) still holds but N_t is modeled as an ARIMA process.

For example, if N_t is an ARIMA(1,1,1) model, (8.1) may be written

$$Y_t \;=\; b_0 + b_1 X_{1,t} + \cdots + b_k X_{k,t} + N_t \tag{8.2}$$
$$\text{where} \qquad (1 - \phi_1 B)(1 - B)N_t = (1 - \theta_1 B)e_t \tag{8.3}$$

and e_t is a white noise series.

errors
residuals

We need to be careful here in distinguishing N_t from e_t. We will refer to N_t as the *errors* and e_t as the *residuals*. In ordinary regression, N_t is assumed to be white noise and so $N_t = e_t$. Therefore we have tended to use "errors" and "residuals" interchangeably. However, in this chapter they will, in general, be different.

Note that if we difference all the variables in (8.2) we obtain

$$Y_t' = b_1 X_{1,t}' + \cdots + b_k X_{k,t}' + N_t'.$$

This is now a regression with an ARMA(1,1) error since $N_t' = (1 - B)N_t$ is modeled as an ARMA(1,1) process. In general, any regression with an ARIMA error can be rewritten as a regression with an ARMA error by differencing all variables with the same differencing operator as in the ARIMA model.

8/1/1 Modeling procedure

There are two main problems with applying ordinary least squares estimation to a regression problem with autocorrelated errors.

least squares estimation

1. The resulting estimates are no longer the best way to compute the coefficients as they do not take account of the time-relationships in the data.

2. The standard errors of the coefficients are incorrect when there are autocorrelations in the errors. They are most likely too small. This also invalidates the t-tests and F-test and prediction intervals.

The second problem is more serious than the first because it can lead to misleading results. If the standard errors obtained using the usual ordinary least squares estimation are smaller than they should be, some explanatory variables may appear to be significant when, in fact, they are not. This is known as "spurious regression."

spurious regression

So regression with autocorrelated errors needs a different approach from that described in Chapter 6. Instead of ordinary least squares estimation we can use either generalized least squares estimation or maximum likelihood estimation. Generalized least squares estimates are obtained by minimizing

generalized least squares estimation

$$G = \sum_{i=1}^{n} \sum_{j=1}^{n} w_i w_j N_i N_j$$

where w_i and w_j are weights based on the pattern of autocorrelations. Note that instead of only summing the squared errors, we also sum the cross-products of the errors. Maximum likelihood estimation is more complicated but results in very similar estimates.

maximum likelihood estimation

Generalized least squares estimation only works for stationary errors. That is, N_t must follow an ARMA model. Computer programs which fit regression models with ARMA errors will calculate the weights automatically, provided one first specifies the ARMA model for the error series, N_t. The difficulty is that until the model is fitted there is no way of examining the N_t series to determine an appropriate ARMA model. However, an approximate ARMA model may be chosen first as a *proxy model* and the errors examined. Then a more appropriate ARMA model can be selected and the whole regression model refitted. One approach is to first specify a proxy low-order AR model for the errors—an AR(1) or AR(2) for example. This will capture most autocorrelations in the data so that a more appropriate ARMA model may be chosen later.

proxy model

If a non-stationary model is required for the errors, then the model can be estimated by first differencing all the variables and then fitting a regression with an ARMA model for the errors.

Therefore we have the following modeling procedure (based on Pankratz, 1991).

---

1. Fit the regression model with a proxy AR(1) or AR(2) model for errors.
2. If the errors from the regression appear to be non-stationary, and differencing appears appropriate, then difference the forecast variable and all explanatory variables. Then fit the model using the same proxy model for errors, this time using differenced variables.
3. If the errors now appear stationary, identify an appropriate ARMA model for the error series, N_t.
4. Refit the entire model using the new ARMA model for the errors.
5. Check that the e_t residual series looks like white noise.

This procedure is demonstrated in the following two examples.

1964	1702	1971	5811	1978	9269	1985	12271
1965	1876	1972	6294	1979	9636	1986	12260
1966	2286	1973	7083	1980	11043	1987	12249
1967	3146	1974	6552	1981	11180	1988	12700
1968	4086	1975	6942	1982	10732	1989	13026
1969	4675	1976	7842	1983	11112		
1970	5289	1977	8514	1984	11465		

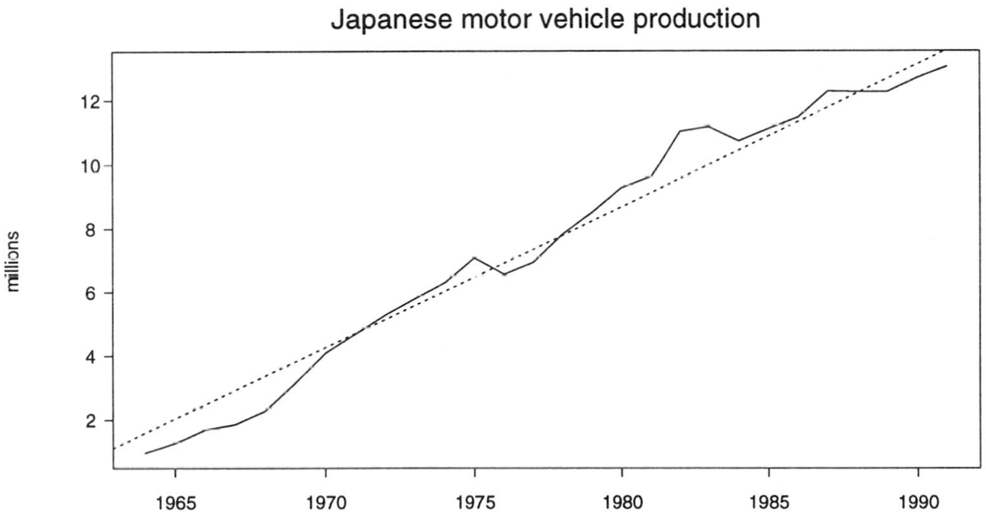

Japanese motor vehicle production

Figure 8-1: *Japanese annual motor vehicle production, 1964–1989. Source: World motor vehicle data, Motor Vehicle Manufacturers Association of U.S. Inc., Detroit, 1991.*

8/1/2 Example: Japanese motor vehicle production

One common application of the regression with ARIMA errors model is where the explanatory variable represents time. This is sometimes used as an alternative to eliminating a trend by differencing.

time trend

For example, consider the Japanese annual motor vehicle production (1964–1989) given in Figure 8-1. We will fit a linear trend model to these data:

$$Y_t = a + bX_t + N_t$$

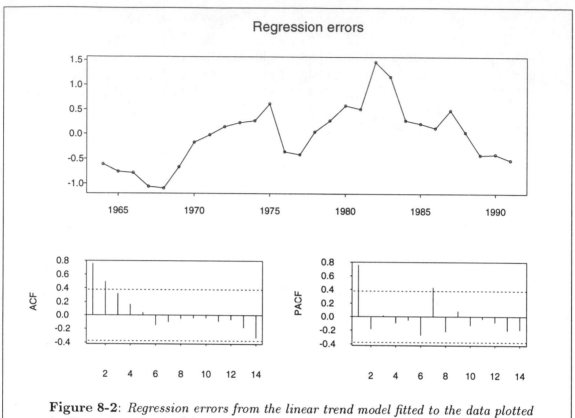

Figure 8-2: *Regression errors from the linear trend model fitted to the data plotted in Figure 8-1. An AR(1) model is a clear choice for these errors.*

where $X_t = t - 1963$. The fitted line is shown on the graph. In estimating these coefficients we used a proxy AR(1) model for the errors, N_t.

The regression errors, $N_t = Y_t - a - bX_t$, are shown in Figure 8-2. These appear stationary and so we proceed to Step 3. The single spike in the PACF and exponential decay in the ACF show that an AR(1) will be the best model. So the full model is

$$Y_t = a + bX_t + N_t \qquad \text{where} \quad N_t = \phi_1 N_{t-1} + e_t$$

and e_t is a white noise series.

Because the model for N_t happened to be the same as the proxy used in Step 2, there is no need to reestimate the model in Step 4. The parameter estimates are shown below along with statistics to test their significance.

Parameter		Estimate	Standard Error	Z	P-value
AR(1)	ϕ_1	0.736	0.152	4.84	0.000
Intercept	a	1662.	504.1	3.30	0.010
Slope	b	463.6	32.31	14.35	0.000

Finally, we need to check that the residuals (e_t) from our model look like a white noise series; the tools introduced in Section 7/1 may be used. In this case, all tests are passed (details not shown).

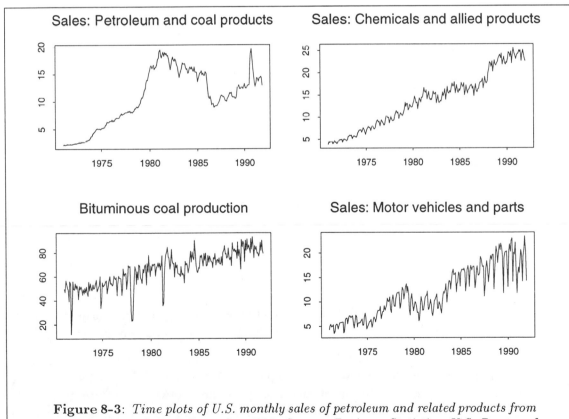

Figure 8-3: *Time plots of U.S. monthly sales of petroleum and related products from January 1971 through December 1991. Source: Business Statistics, U.S. Bureau of Economic Analysis.*

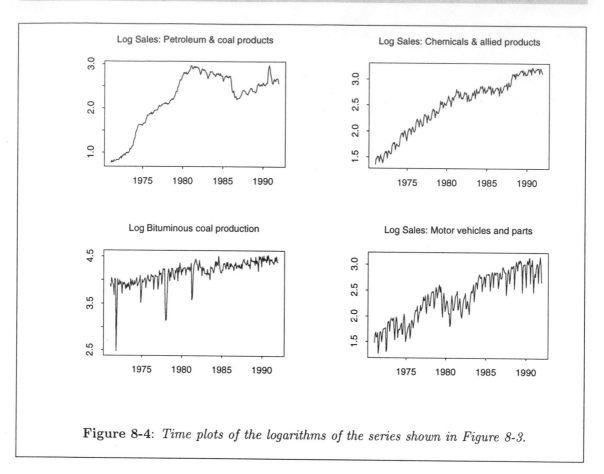

Figure 8-4: *Time plots of the logarithms of the series shown in Figure 8-3.*

8/1/3 Example: Sales of petroleum and coal products

Figure 8-3 shows four time series concerning U.S. monthly sales of petroleum and related products from January 1971 through December 1991. It is clear that the variation in at least three of the series increases with the level of the series. Therefore, we transform the data using logarithms to stabilize the variance. The transformed data are in Figure 8-4. The variances now appear to be roughly constant.

We begin by studying the relationship between the four variables. Figure 8-5 shows a scatterplot matrix of the four transformed series. Clearly there is much interdependence between the four series. We are interested here in predicting petroleum sales using the other three series. Therefore we fit a multiple regression model

$$Y_t = b_0 + b_1 X_{1,t} + b_2 X_{2,t} + b_3 X_{3,t} + N_t$$

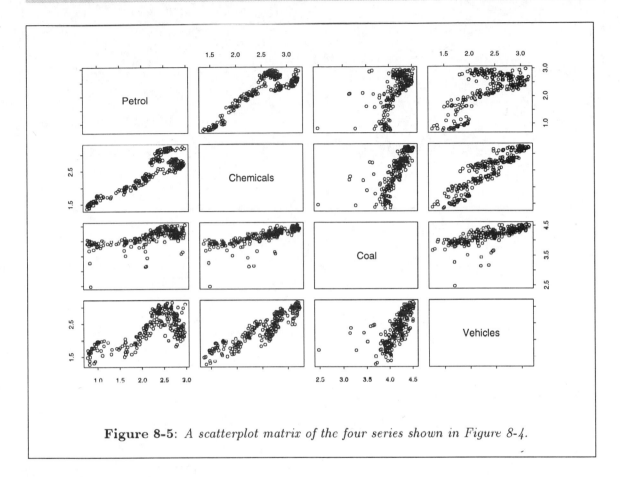

Figure 8-5: *A scatterplot matrix of the four series shown in Figure 8-4.*

where Y_t denotes the log of petroleum sales, $X_{1,t}$ denotes the log of chemical sales, $X_{2,t}$ denotes the log of coal production and $X_{3,t}$ denotes the log of motor vehicle and parts sales. Following the procedure outlined above, we assume N_t is a low-order AR process for now. Because the data are seasonal, we will use an ARIMA$(1,0,0)(1,0,0)_{12}$ model as a proxy for the errors. Having estimated the coefficients, we compute the errors as

$$N_t = Y_t - b_0 - b_1 X_{1,t} - b_2 X_{2,t} - b_3 X_{3,t}.$$

The series was clearly non-stationary and so we differenced the four data series and refitted the model. Our regression model is now

$$Y'_t = b_1 X'_{1,t} + b_2 X'_{2,t} + b_3 X'_{3,t} + N'_t$$

where $Y'_t = Y_t - Y_{t-1}$, $X'_{1,t} = X_{1,t} - X_{1,t-1}$ and so on. In fitting this model we assumed N'_t was an ARIMA$(1,0,0)(1,0,0)_{12}$ process. Note that we have now dropped the constant term. This could have

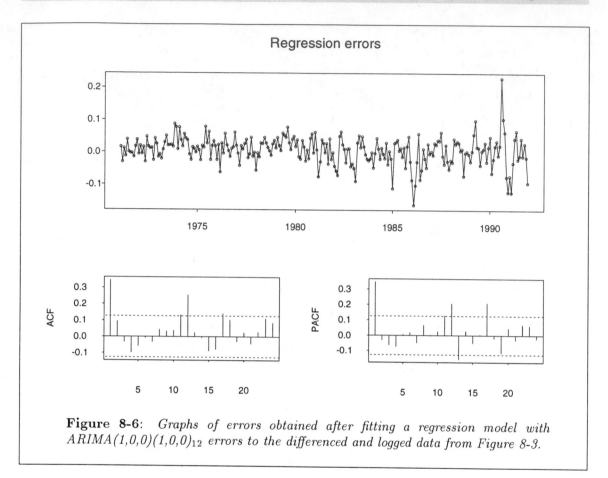

Figure 8-6: *Graphs of errors obtained after fitting a regression model with ARIMA(1,0,0)(1,0,0)$_{12}$ errors to the differenced and logged data from Figure 8-3.*

been included but would have resulted in forecasts with a linear trend which was felt to be inappropriate.

This new error series is

$$N_t' = Y_t' - b_1 X_{1,t}' - b_2 X_{2,t}' - b_3 X_{3,t}'$$

which is shown in Figure 8-6. This time the errors appear to be stationary and we can attempt to identify an appropriate model for the error series. The large spikes at lags 1 and 12 in the ACF and PACF suggest that an ARIMA(0,0,1)(0,0,1)$_{12}$ or an ARIMA(1,0,0)(1,0,0)$_{12}$ model may be appropriate. These and several other models were tried. According to the AIC values, the best model for N_t' is an ARIMA(1,0,0)(1,0,0)$_{12}$. So our full model is

$$Y_t' = b_1 X_{1,t}' + b_2 X_{2,t}' + b_3 X_{3,t}' + N_t'$$

where $(1 - \Phi_1 B^{12})(1 - \phi_1 B)N_t' = e_t.$

Again, by coincidence, the model for N_t' happened to be the same as the proxy used in Step 2, and there is no need to reestimate the model in Step 4. The parameter estimates are shown below along with statistics to test their significance.

Parameter		Estimate	Standard Error	Z	P-value
AR(1)	ϕ_1	0.362	0.060	6.03	0.000
Seasonal AR(1)	Φ_1	0.289	0.064	4.53	0.000
Log Chemicals	b_1	0.258	0.054	4.79	0.000
Log Coal	b_2	-0.026	0.012	-2.12	0.034
Log Vehicles	b_3	-0.015	0.020	-0.75	0.453

This shows that the motor vehicles and parts variable is not having a significant effect and can be dropped from the model. We refit the model with this variable omitted to obtain the following results.

Parameter		Estimate	Standard Error	Z	P-value
AR(1)	ϕ_1	0.366	0.059	6.16	0.000
Seasonal AR(1)	Φ_1	0.286	0.064	4.50	0.000
Log Chemicals	b_1	0.235	0.044	5.31	0.000
Log Coal	b_2	-0.027	0.012	-2.17	0.030

Finally, we need to check that the residuals from our model look like a white noise series. Figure 8-7 shows the residuals (e_t) from the final model. With no spikes outside the limits in the ACF and PACF figures, the model does appear to have adequately described the data. Plots of the residuals against the explanatory variables and fitted values can also be useful in assessing the model as with ordinary regression models (see Section 6/1/6).

We can rewrite the final model in terms of the undifferenced (but logged) data as

$$Y_t = b_1 X_{1,t} + b_2 X_{2,t} + N_t$$

where $\qquad (1 - \Phi_1 B^{12})(1 - \phi_1 B)(1 - B)N_t = e_t.$

That is, a regression with an ARIMA$(1,1,0)(1,0,0)_{12}$ error series. In terms of the untransformed data, our model is

$$\boxed{\text{Petrol}_t = \text{Chemicals}_t^{b_1} \text{Coal}_t^{b_2} e^{N_t}}.$$

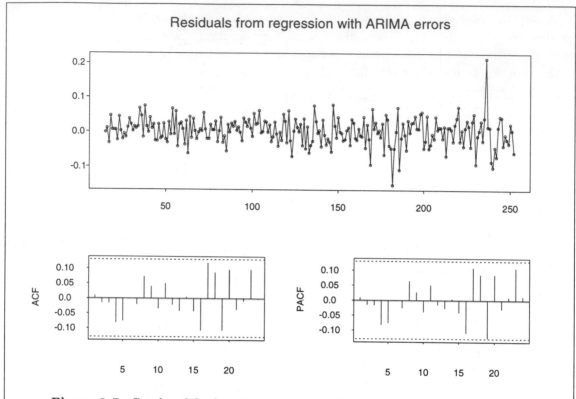

Figure 8-7: *Graphs of final residuals obtained after fitting a regression model with ARIMA(1,1,0)(1,0,0)$_{12}$ errors to the logged data from Figure 8-3.*

8/1/4 Forecasting

To forecast a regression model with ARIMA errors, we need to forecast the regression part of the model and the ARIMA part of the model and combine the results. So for the petroleum example, our forecast of Y_{t+h} is

$$\hat{Y}_{t+h} = b_1\hat{X}_{1,t+h} + b_2\hat{X}_{2,t+h} + \hat{N}_{t+h}. \tag{8.4}$$

To compute this equation we require future values of all explanatory variables and a forecast of the ARIMA error. The ARIMA error can be forecast using the methods discussed in Chapter 7.

forecasting
explanatory variables

When future values of the explanatory variables are unknown (as in the Petroleum example), they need to be forecast themselves and the forecasts fed into (8.4) to obtain forecasts of $\hat{Y}_{t+h}$. Where macroeconomic variables are used as explanatory variables, forecasts

may be obtained from specialist bureaus, trade or government organizations. In other cases, separate forecasting models may need to
be developed for predicting the explanatory variables.

Where an explanatory variable is known into the future, we have
no need to develop a separate forecasting model. This occurs most
frequently when a dummy variable (or indicator variable) is used or
when time is used as an explanatory variable. For example, in the
Japanese motor vehicle example we know the value of X_t into the
future, so we can plug the values into (8.4) to obtain forecasts of Y.
Figure 8-8 shows forecasts along with 95% prediction intervals for
this example.

It is interesting to compare the forecasts obtained in this way with
those obtained after removing the linear trend by first-differencing.   differencing
After differencing, the resulting data looked like white noise. So
an alternative model for these data is an ARIMA(0,1,0): $Y_t = a +
Y_{t-1} + e_t$. The forecasts from this model are shown at the bottom of
Figure 8-8. Notice that the forecasts are almost identical, but that
the prediction intervals increase in width more rapidly. Prediction   prediction intervals
intervals will usually be narrower for models with an explicit linear
trend rather than first differencing. However, the forecasts assume
that the linear trend will continue into the future, at least as far
as the longest forecast horizon. In the case of the Japanese motor
vehicle production, this is not an unreasonable assumption. But in
many data sets, the historical trend may not be expected to continue,
in which case differencing is to be preferred.

These prediction intervals are calculated by combining the effects
of the regression and ARIMA parts to the model. There are four
sources of variation which ought to be accounted for in the prediction   sources of variation
intervals:

1. the variation due to the error series N_t;
2. the variation due to the error in forecasting the explanatory
   variables (where necessary);
3. the variation due to estimating the regression part of the model;
4. the variation due to estimating the ARIMA part of the model.

Unfortunately, calculating the prediction intervals to allow for all
four sources of variation would involve tedious and time-consuming
calculations and so this is rarely done. Usually one of two approaches
is implemented, both of which ignore two of the sources of variation.
The "regression approach" is to ignore the error from points 2. and 4.

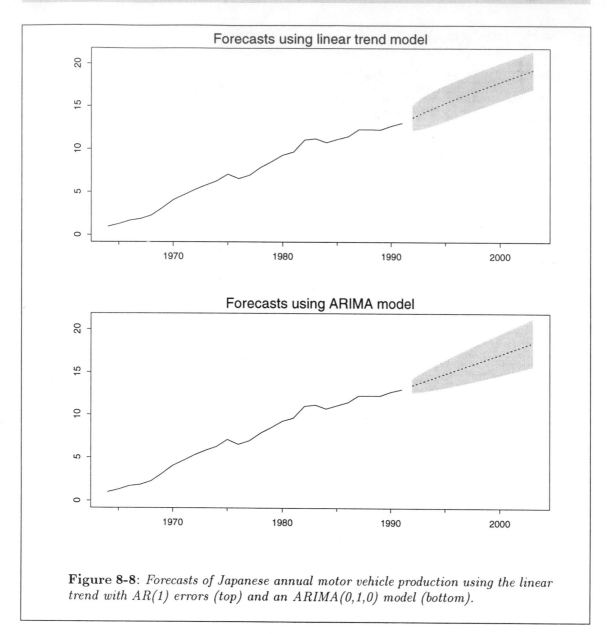

Figure 8-8: *Forecasts of Japanese annual motor vehicle production using the linear trend with AR(1) errors (top) and an ARIMA(0,1,0) model (bottom).*

above (see Judge et al., 1988). Alternatively, if ARIMA models are used to forecast the explanatory variables, then dynamic regression modeling provides prediction intervals which allow for the error from points 1. and 2. but not 3. and 4. (see Section 8/2/5). Whichever approach is followed, the prediction intervals for $\hat{Y}_{t+h}$ will, in general, be too narrow.

8/2　Dynamic regression models

Sometimes the effect of a change in an explanatory variable (X_t) does not show up in the forecast variable (Y_t) instantaneously, but is distributed across several time periods. Consider the following examples.

1. The effect of rainfall on stream flow is not instantaneous; it takes some time for the rain to find its way into the stream. So we would model the daily stream flow (Y_t) as a function of the past few days rainfall $(X_t, X_{t-1}, X_{t-2}, \ldots)$.

2. The effect of an advertising campaign lasts for some time beyond the end of the campaign. Monthly sales figures (Y_t) may be modeled as a function of the advertising expenditure in each of the past few months, that is $X_t, X_{t-1}, X_{t-2}, \ldots$.

3. Let the number of letters mailed at a post office on day t be X_t and the number of letters delivered by the post office on day t be Y_t. Clearly Y_t will be a function of $X_t, X_{t-1}, X_{t-2}, \ldots$.

4. The impact of new breeding stock (X_t) on the size of the herd (Y_t) will be distributed over several time periods.

In each of these cases, there is an output time series, called Y_t, which is influenced by an input time series, called X_t. The whole system is a dynamic system. In other words, the input series X_t exerts its influence on the output series over several *future* time periods. The objective of dynamic regression modeling is to determine a parsimonious model relating Y_t to X_t and N_t. Note that the main objective in this kind of modeling is to identify the role of a *leading*　leading indicator *indicator* (the input series) in determining the variable of interest (the output series).

8/2/1　Lagged explanatory variables

The model should include not only the explanatory variable X_t, but also previous values of the explanatory variable, $X_{t-1}, X_{t-2}, \ldots$. Thus, we write the model as

$$Y_t = a + \nu_0 X_t + \nu_1 X_{t-1} + \nu_2 X_{t-2} + \cdots + \nu_k X_{t-k} + N_t \qquad (8.5)$$

where N_t is an ARIMA process.

t	Y	X	t	Y	X	t	Y	X	t	Y	X
1	12.0	15	10	28.0	36	19	30.5	33	28	30.6	40
2	20.5	16	11	24.0	40	20	28.0	62	29	32.3	49
3	21.0	18	12	15.5	3	21	26.0	22	30	29.5	7
4	15.5	27	13	17.3	21	22	21.5	12	31	28.3	52
5	15.3	21	14	25.3	29	23	19.7	24	32	31.3	65
6	23.5	49	15	25.0	62	24	19.0	3	33	32.2	17
7	24.5	21	16	36.5	65	25	16.0	5	34	26.4	5
8	21.3	22	17	36.5	46	26	20.7	14	35	23.4	17
9	23.5	28	18	29.6	44	27	26.5	36	36	16.4	1

Table 8-1: *Sales volume (Y) and advertising expenditure (X) for a dietary weight control product. Sales are measured in equivalent serving units, advertising is measured in dollars. Source: Blattberg and Jeuland (1981).*

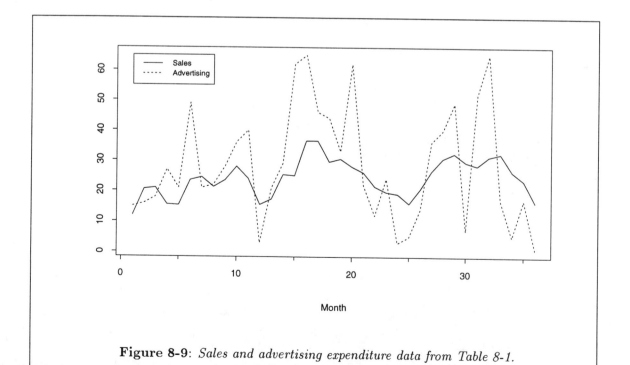

Figure 8-9: *Sales and advertising expenditure data from Table 8-1.*

For example, consider the two time series in Table 8-1 which are plotted in Figure 8-9. These data were reported in Blattberg and Jeuland (1981) and concern the sales volume (Y) and advertising expenditure (X) for a dietary weight control product.

We will model the sales series as a regression against the advertising expenditure from the current month and the past few months. The resulting equation is

$$Y_t = 13.7 + 0.13X_t + 0.15X_{t-1} + 0.05X_{t-2} + 0.04X_{t-3} - 0.0007X_{t-4} + N_t.$$

Notice how the effect of advertising on sales is positive and drops off over time as one would expect. Because the error series N_t may be correlated, we used a low-order autoregressive model for the errors when estimating this equation.

The values of ν_0 through ν_4 are called the *impulse response weights* (or transfer function weights). The coefficient ν_i is a measure of how Y_t responds to a change in X_{t-i}. However, the lagged explanatory variables are usually collinear so that caution is needed in attributing much meaning to each coefficient. It is important to also note that after some time, the effect of advertising will become so small that it will be swamped by the random error. Hence, the negative sign for ν_4 does not mean that advertising has a reverse effect after four months. Instead, the effect is so small that it is indistinguishable from zero and the coefficient came out negative by chance.

impulse response weights

Equation (8.5) can be written as follows:

$$
\begin{aligned}
Y_t &= a + \nu_0 X_t + \nu_1 X_{t-1} + \nu_2 X_{t-2} + \cdots + \nu_k X_{t-k} + N_t \\
&= a + (\nu_0 + \nu_1 B + \nu_2 B^2 + \cdots + \nu_k B^k)X_t + N_t \\
&= a + \nu(B)X_t + N_t.
\end{aligned}
\tag{8.6}
$$

Note the various ways in which this equation can be written, the last being the shorthand notation. $\nu(B)$ is called the *transfer function* since it describes how a change in X_t is transferred to Y_t.

transfer function

We will call models of the form (8.6) *dynamic regression models* because they involve a dynamic relationship between the response and explanatory variables. This term was applied to these models by Pankratz (1991) and it has since been used by others and some software packages. Earlier writers call the model a *transfer function model* following the terminology of Box and Jenkins (1970). In the case that N_t is a white noise process, economists refer to the model as a *distributed lag model*.

dynamic regression model

transfer function model

distributed lag model

Dynamic regression models allow current and past values of the explanatory variable, X, to influence the forecast variable, Y. However, Y is not allowed to influence X. If this is not appropriate, a more general multivariate model may be better (see Section 8/4).

8/2/2 Koyck model

An important dynamic regression model is the Koyck model, developed by Koyck (1954). We suppose that the effect of X decreases exponentially over time. Therefore, let

$$Y_t = a + \omega(X_t + \delta X_{t-1} + \delta^2 X_{t-2} + \cdots + \delta^k X_{t-k}) + N_t$$

where $|\delta| < 1$. The coefficient of X_{t-k} is $\nu_k = \omega\delta^k$ which will be close to zero for large k because δ is smaller than one in absolute value. This model is sometimes used in modeling the response of sales to advertising expenditure since advertising in month t will have a decreasing effect over future months.

The transfer function has the special form

$$\nu(B) \; = \; \omega(1 + \delta B + \delta^2 B^2 + \cdots + \delta^k B^k).$$

Notice that

$$
\begin{aligned}
(1 - \delta B)\nu(B) \;\; &= \;\; \omega(1 - \delta B)(1 + \delta B + \delta^2 B^2 + \cdots + \delta^m B^m) \\
&= \;\; \omega(1 + \delta B + \delta^2 B^2 + \cdots + \delta^k B^k \\
&\qquad\quad - \delta B - \delta^2 B^2 - \cdots - \delta^k B^k - \delta^{k+1} B^{k+1}) \\
&= \;\; \omega(1 - \delta^{k+1} B^{k+1}) \\
&\approx \;\; \omega \text{ if } k \text{ is large.}
\end{aligned}
$$

So we can write

$$\boxed{\nu(B) \approx \frac{\omega}{1 - \delta B}}.$$

Thus we have replaced the transfer function by a more parsimonious form.

8/2/3 The basic forms of the dynamic regression model

The dynamic regression model is written in two general forms. The first form is as follows:

$$Y_t = a + \nu(B)X_t + N_t, \qquad (8.7)$$

where Y_t = the forecast variable or output series;
X_t = the explanatory variable or input series;
N_t = the combined effects of all other factors influencing Y_t (called the "noise"); and
$\nu(B) = (\nu_0 + \nu_1 B + \nu_2 B^2 + \cdots + \nu_k B^k)$, where k is the order of the transfer function.

The input and output series should be appropriately transformed (to take care of non-stationary variance), differenced (to take care of non-stationary means), and possibly seasonally adjusted (to make for simpler models).

The order of the transfer function is k (being the longest lag of X used) and this can sometimes be rather large (and therefore not parsimonious). For this reason, the dynamic regression model is also written in a more parsimonious form in the same way as we wrote the Koyck model in a simpler form:

$$Y_t = a + \frac{\omega(B)}{\delta(B)} X_{t-b} + N_t \qquad (8.8)$$

Notes

where
$$\omega(B) = \omega_0 - \omega_1 B - \omega_2 B^2 - \cdots - \omega_s B^s,$$
$$\delta(B) = 1 - \delta_1 B - \delta_2 B^2 - \cdots - \delta_r B^r,$$
$$Y_t = \text{the forecast variable,}$$
$$X_t = \text{the explanatory variable}$$

and r, s, and b are constants.

The two expressions, $\omega(B)$ and $\delta(B)$, replace the $\nu(B)$ expression in equation (8.7). The purpose of rewriting the model in this way is to find a simpler, more parsimonious, way of writing the transfer function. This reduces the number of parameters to estimate, making more efficient use of the data (reducing the degrees of freedom) and so producing more accurate forecasts.

Why is equation (8.8) considered to be more parsimonious? The reason is that the values of r and s are usually going to be much smaller than the value k in equation (8.7). For example, in the Koyck model, $r = 1$ and $s = 0$ so that there are fewer parameters than for (8.7) where we would have needed a large value of k to capture the decaying effect of advertising.

As a second example, suppose $\omega(B) = (1.2 - 0.5B)$ and $\delta(B) = (1 - 0.8B)$. Then

$$
\begin{aligned}
\frac{\omega(B)}{\delta(B)} &= \frac{(1.2 - 0.5B)}{(1 - 0.8B)} \\
&= (1.2 - 0.5B)(1 - 0.8B)^{-1} \\
&= (1.2 - 0.5B)(1 + 0.8B + 0.8^2 B^2 + 0.8^3 B^3 + \cdots) \\
&= 1.2 + 0.46B + 0.368B^2 + 0.294B^3 + 0.236B^4 + \cdots \\
&= \nu(B).
\end{aligned}
$$

In other words, the $\nu(B)$ function, corresponding to the ratio of $\omega(B)$ to $\delta(B)$, would have an infinite number of terms, and therefore an infinite number of ν-weights. This is a case where $r = 1$ (the order of the δ function), $s = 1$ (the order of the ω function), and k is very large. So equation (8.8) is a more parsimonious representation.

In equation (8.8), note that the subscript for X is $(t - b)$. What this means is that there is a delay of b periods before X begins to influence Y. So X_t influences Y_{t+b} first, or X_{t-b} influences Y_t first. When $b > 0$, X is often called a "leading indicator" since X_t is leading Y_t by b time periods.

It is straightforward to extend the dynamic regression model to include several explanatory variables:

$$
Y_t = a + \sum_{i=1}^{m} \frac{B^{b_i} \omega_i(B)}{\delta_i(B)} X_{i,t} + N_t \qquad (8.9)
$$

$$
\text{where} \quad \omega_i(B) = \omega_{i,0} - \omega_{i,1}B - \cdots - \omega_{i,s_i} B^{s_i} \qquad (8.10)
$$

$$
\delta_i(B) = 1 - \delta_{i,1}B - \cdots - \delta_{i,r_i} B^{r_i} \qquad (8.11)
$$

and N_t is an ARIMA process. The dynamic regression model (8.9) is a general model which includes many simpler models as special cases including multiple regression, regression with ARIMA errors, and ARIMA models.

8/2/4 Selecting the model order

We wil keep things simple by assuming there is just one explanatory variable. So our full model is

$$Y_t = a + \frac{\omega(B)}{\delta(B)} X_{t-b} + N_t \qquad (8.12)$$

$$\text{where} \quad \begin{aligned} \omega(B) &= \omega_0 - \omega_1 B - \omega_2 B^2 - \cdots - \omega_s B^s, \\ \delta(B) &= 1 - \delta_1 B - \delta_2 B^2 - \cdots - \delta_r B^r, \end{aligned}$$

and N_t is an ARIMA process.

In selecting the form of the model, we need to determine the values of r, s, and b, and the values of p, d, and q in the ARIMA(p, d, q) model for N_t. If the data are seasonal, we may need to also find the order of the seasonal part of the ARIMA model.

There are two methods which are used to select r, s, and b. The older and more complicated method is due to Box and Jenkins (1970) and uses prewhitening and cross-correlations. It is a difficult method to use, particularly with more than one explanatory variable. The method used in this book is known as the "linear transfer function" or LTF method and is described in detail by Pankratz (1991).

LTF identification method

The LTF method follows a similar approach to that described in Section 8/1 for fitting a regression model with ARIMA errors. The general procedure is as follows.

Step 1 The first step in identifying the appropriate dynamic regression model is to fit a multiple regression model of the form

$$Y_t = a + \nu_0 X_t + \nu_1 X_{t-1} + \nu_2 X_{t-2} + \cdots + \nu_k X_{t-k} + N_t$$

where k is sufficiently large so the model captures the longest time-lagged response that is likely to be important. Since the form of the noise is relatively unimportant at this stage, it is convenient to use a low-order proxy AR model for N_t.

Step 2 If the errors from the regression appear to be non-stationary, and differencing appears appropriate, then difference Y and X. Fit the model again using a low-order autoregressive model for the errors, this time using differenced variables.

Step 3 If the errors now appear stationary, identify an appropriate transfer function for $\nu(B)$. That is, the values of b, r, and s must be selected. The value of b is the number of periods before X_t influences Y_t. The value of s (the order of $\omega(B)$) controls the number of transfer function coefficients before they begin to decay. The value of r (the order of $\delta(B)$) controls the decay pattern.

The following rules may be used to select values for b, r, and s.

1. The dead time, b, is equal to the number of ν-weights that are not significantly different from zero. That is, we look for a set of approximately zero-valued ν-weights (ν_0, ν_1, ν_{b-1}).

2. The value of r determines the decay pattern in the remaining ν-weights.

no decay
   - If there is no decay pattern at all, but a group of spikes followed by a cutoff to zero, then choose $r = 0$.

exponential decay
   - If there is simple exponential decay (perhaps after some ν-weights that do not decay), then $r = 1$.

complex decay
   - If the ν-weights show a more complex decay pattern (e.g., damped sine-wave decay), then $r = 2$.

3. The value of s is the number of non-zero ν-weights before the decay.

Step 4 The next step is to calculate the errors from the regression model

$$N_t = Y_t - a - \nu_0 X_t - \nu_1 X_{t-1} - \cdots - \nu_k X_{t-k}$$

and identify an appropriate ARMA model for the error series. The techniques of Chapter 7 may be used.

Step 5 Refit the entire model using the new ARMA model for the errors and the transfer function model for X.

Step 6 Finally, we need to check that the fitted model is adequate by analyzing the residuals e_t to see if they are significantly
diagnostic tests
different from a white noise series. The usual diagnostic tests can be used. Note that a wrong dynamic regression model may induce significant autocorrelations in the residual series. If the residuals show any problems, it is good practice to reconsider the appropriateness of the transfer function as well as the error model.

The only new part of this procedure is identifying an appropriate transfer function model for $\nu(B)$ in Step 3. Also, the estimation in Step 5 is only available in software with facilities for handling dynamic regression models (see Appendix I).

Example: Sales and advertising

The data in Table 8-1 will be used to illustrate the process. We have already completed Step 1 by fitting a multiple regression model to these data with lagged values of X_t in Section 8/2/1. The fitted model was

$$Y_t = 13.7+0.13X_t+0.15X_{t-1}+0.05X_{t-2}+0.04X_{t-3}-0.0007X_{t-4}+N_t.$$
$$(8.13)$$

In fitting this model, it was assumed that N_t was an AR(1) process. Figure 8-10 shows some information which was also produced by the computer program used to fit the model. The model yields an MSE of 11.47 and an AIC value of 84.16. It is of interest to query whether the dynamic regression methodology can improve upon this result.

Parameter	Estimate	s.e.	Z	P-value
a	13.715	3.010	4.56	0.0000
ν_0	0.1311	0.033	4.00	0.0001
ν_1	0.1508	0.034	4.90	0.0002
ν_2	0.0497	0.034	1.31	0.1888
ν_3	0.0371	0.034	0.53	0.5933
ν_4	-0.0007	0.035	-0.02	0.9848

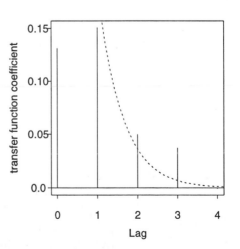

Figure 8-10: *Estimates of the transfer function coefficients in (8.13) and their significance. The coefficients are plotted and the decay shown by the dashed line.*

The errors from this model do appear to be stationary (graphs not shown) and so we can proceed to Step 3 of the modeling procedure. The dynamic regression model that we will study for these observations is

$$Y_t = a + \frac{\omega(B)}{\delta(B)} X_{t-b} + N_t.$$

From the P-values in Figure 8-10, it is clear that there is no delay—the first significant coefficient is at lag 0. So we set $b = 0$. This is to be expected with an advertising/sales relationship. Figure 8-10 shows that the coefficients begin to decay at lag 1. So we set $s = 1$. They appear to decay exponentially as shown by the dashed line in Figure 8-10. Hence we also set $r = 1$.

Moving to Step 4, Figure 8-11 shows the error series, N_t, from the fitted regression model. The single significant spikes in the ACF and PACF suggest either an AR(1) or an MA(1) model. The MA(1) model has a smaller AIC value and so we will adopt that as the model for the errors.

Now the full model is

$$Y_t = a + \frac{\omega_0 - \omega_1 B}{1 - \delta_1 B} X_t + N_t$$

$$\text{where} \qquad N_t = e_t - \theta e_{t-1}.$$

We proceed to Step 5 and estimate the parameters. This is normally done using a maximum likelihood procedure. In this case we obtain the following values:

$$a = 14.19, \quad \omega_0 = 0.12, \quad \omega_1 = -0.13, \quad \delta_1 = 0.30, \quad \theta = -0.73.$$

The model can now be written as

$$Y_t = 14.19 + \frac{0.12 + 0.13B}{1 - 0.30B} X_t + (1 + 0.73B)e_t. \qquad (8.14)$$

The final task is to check the residuals in Step 6. This is identical to what is done in ARIMA modeling as described in Section 7/7 and so we omit the details here. In this example, the residuals pass all tests for white noise.

The dynamic regression model (8.14) has an MSE of 9.5 and an AIC of 82.08. On both counts it is a superior model to (8.13).

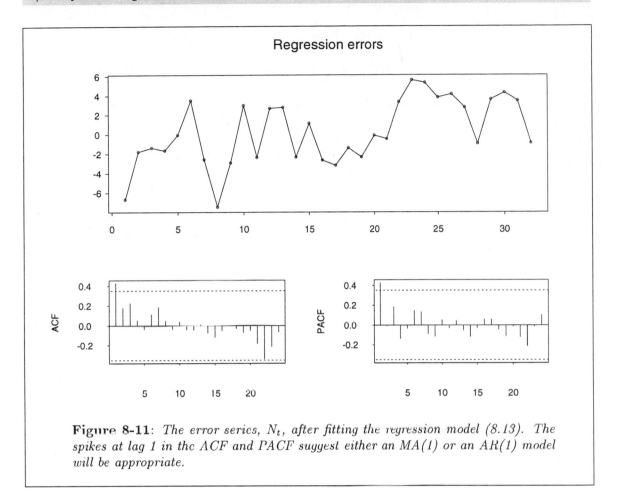

Figure 8-11: *The error series, N_t, after fitting the regression model (8.13). The spikes at lag 1 in the ACF and PACF suggest either an MA(1) or an AR(1) model will be appropriate.*

8/2/5 Forecasting

Once the model has been identified, and all the parameters have been estimated, the *forecasting version* of the equation needs to be determined. We first write the model (8.8) in a single line by replacing N_t by its operator form:

$$Y_t = a + \frac{\omega(B)}{\delta(B)}X_{t-b} + \frac{\theta(B)}{\phi(B)}e_t \qquad (8.15)$$

where e_t is white noise. (We have assumed that N_t has a stationary ARMA model here. If this is not the case, all variables can be differenced first.) Then (8.15) is multiplied throughout by the product of

$\delta(B)$ and $\phi(B)$, and we get

$$\delta(B)\phi(B)Y_t = \delta(B)\phi(B)a + \phi(B)\omega(B)X_{t-b} + \delta(B)\theta(B)e_t. \quad (8.16)$$

The various difference operators are then multiplied together, terms are collected, and all terms except Y_t are moved to the right-hand side of the equation. For example, with (8.14) we obtain:

$$
\begin{aligned}
Y_t &= a + \frac{\omega_0 - \omega_1 B}{1 - \delta_1 B}X_t + (1 - \theta B)e_t \\
(1 - \delta_1 B)Y_t &= a(1 - \delta_1) + (\omega_0 - \omega_1 B)X_t + (1 - \delta_1 B)(1 - \theta B)e_t \\
Y_t &= a(1 - \delta_1) + \delta_1 Y_{t-1} + \omega_0 X_t - \omega_1 X_{t-1} \quad\quad (8.17) \\
&\quad + e_t - (\delta_1 + \theta_1)e_{t-1} + \delta_1 \theta e_{t-2}.
\end{aligned}
$$

Knowing the values of the parameters, past values of Y, X, and e, and future values of X, this equation can be used to determine Y values for future periods.

In the advertising/sales example, X is advertising and therefore not random but under the control of the company. Therefore the effects of various future advertising strategies on sales could be examined by feeding the planned future advertising expenditure into the forecasting equation.

forecasting
explanatory variables

Where X is random, it is common to forecast X as an ARIMA process and to feed the forecasts of X obtained in this way into the forecasting equation. In the advertising/sales example, if we treat advertising as random then it may be modeled using an MA(1). Figure 8-12 shows forecasts of the sales series using (8.17) with the values of X forecast using an MA(1) model.

prediction intervals

Computer packages which have facilities for dynamic regression modeling will produce prediction intervals for forecasts automatically. The computational details are too complicated to be covered here, but are explained in Pankratz (1991). Note that the prediction intervals will not allow for the uncertainty in estimation of the transfer function or ARIMA error model. However, if the explanatory variable is forecast using an ARIMA model, the additional variation associated with this forecast (but not the estimation of the ARIMA model) can be included in the prediction intervals.

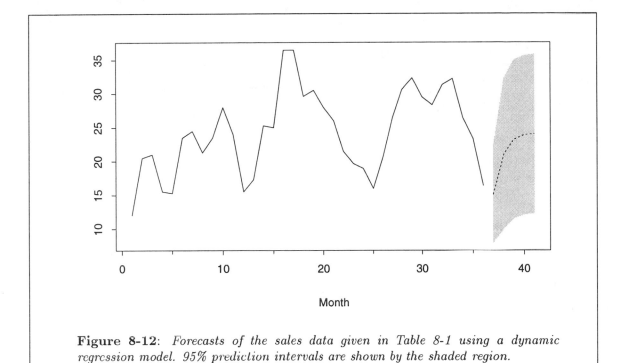

Figure 8-12: *Forecasts of the sales data given in Table 8-1 using a dynamic regression model. 95% prediction intervals are shown by the shaded region.*

8/2/6 Example: Housing starts

The data shown in the top plot of Figure 8-13 are the number of housing starts in the United States from January 1983 to October 1989. We wish to develop a forecasting model for these data using construction contracts and mortgage interest rates as possible dynamic regression variables. These variables are also shown in Figure 8-13. Both housing starts and construction contracts are seasonal because construction declines in the wet and cold weather. The plot of construction contracts appears to increase steadily over time, whereas the plot of housing starts shows a steady pattern for several years and then declines slightly after 1986. This could be because the construction contracts data have not been adjusted for inflation. It may also reflect a tendency for new houses to be increasing in size.

Because private housing starts make up one component of total construction contracts, it is expected that these two series are positively related. It is also reasonable to expect that interest rates are negatively related to housing starts as lower mortgage rates might

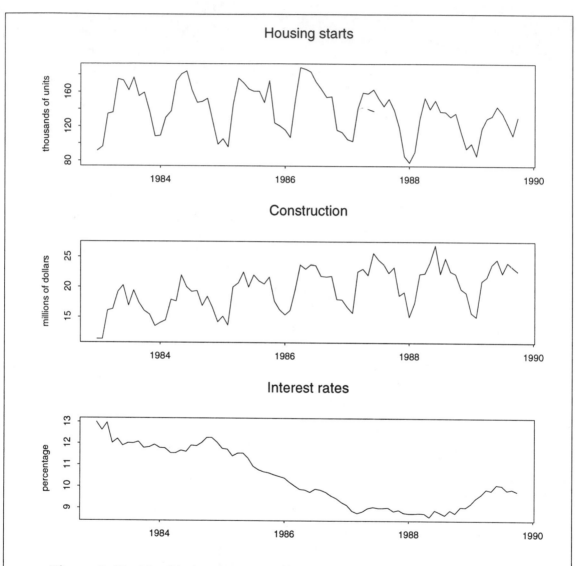

Figure 8-13: *Monthly housing starts (thousands of units), construction contracts (millions of dollars), and average new home mortgage rates from January 1983 to October 1989. Source: Survey of Current Business, U.S. Department of Commerce, 1990.*

foster investment in building. There may be some months of delay after a change in construction or mortgage rates before we would see a consequential change in housing starts. We will allow up to nine months lag for interest rates and up to six months for construction.

So in Step 1 we fit the model

$$Y_t = a + v_0 X_t + v_1 X_{t-1} + \cdots + v_6 X_{t-6} + b_0 Z_t + b_1 Z_{t-1} + \cdots + b_9 Z_{t-9} + N_t \tag{8.18}$$

where X denotes construction and Z denotes the interest rate. An AR(1) proxy model was used for N_t.

We will use the last 12 months of data as a holdout set on which to evaluate the forecasting ability of models. Therefore only data up to October 1988 was used in fitting the model. The estimated parameters for the initial model are given in Table 8-2. The errors for the fitted model appear stationary, so we proceed to Step 3 in identifying an appropriate dynamic regression model for the data.

Parameter	Value	s.e.	Z	P
a	163.94	54.75	2.99	0.003
v_0	−6.27	0.71	−8.81	0.000
v_1	3.74	0.74	5.07	0.000
v_2	−1.60	0.74	−2.16	0.031
v_3	−1.30	0.70	−1.85	0.064
v_4	−1.02	0.77	−1.33	0.184
v_5	1.85	0.74	2.50	0.013
v_6	−0.42	0.73	−0.58	0.562
b_0	−6.96	9.81	−0.71	0.478
b_1	−2.32	11.70	−0.20	0.843
b_2	6.68	11.84	0.56	0.573
b_3	−19.26	12.13	−1.59	0.112
b_4	−2.94	12.11	−0.24	0.808
b_5	27.58	12.99	2.12	0.034
b_6	−28.26	12.28	−2.30	0.021
b_7	4.49	10.05	0.45	0.655
b_8	16.45	8.64	1.90	0.057
b_9	5.14	7.66	0.67	0.502

Table 8-2: *Estimated parameters for the initial model for the housing starts data given in (8.18).*

The P-values in Table 8-2 suggest that the construction figures up to a lag of five months may be useful explanatory variables and the interest rates between five and eight months may be useful explanatory variables. There is no evidence of exponential or sinusoidal decay in the coefficients. The ACF and PACF of the disturbance term, N_t, suggest an AR(1) model might be appropriate. Therefore we fit the model

$$Y_t = a + (\nu_0 + \nu_1 B + \cdots + \nu_5 B^5) X_t + B^5 (b_0 + b_1 B + b_2 B^2 + b_3 B^3) Z_t + N_t$$

where $N_t = \phi N_{t-1} + e_t$. The mean absolute error (MAE) for the holdout set was 11.87 compared to 12.67 for model (8.18). Further exploration of related models showed that the model

$$Y_t = a + (\nu_0 + \nu_1 B + \nu_2 B^2) X_t + B^3 (b_0 + b_1 B + \cdots + b_5 B^5) Z_t + N_t$$

is better, giving a MAE of 9.84 on the holdout set.

forecast accuracy

A common mistake is to think that sophisticated models with explanatory variables produce better forecasts than some simple models. In this example, an ARIMA$(2,0,0)(1,0,0)_{12}$ gives a MAE of 9.10 and Winters additive method gives a MAE of 9.22, yet neither of these models takes construction or interest rates into account. However, sophisticated models allow us to better explain the variation in the variable we want to predict.

8/3   Intervention analysis

Figure 8-14 shows the monthly total number of deaths and serious injuries on roads in the United Kingdom from January 1975 to December 1984. In February 1983, new legislation came into force requiring seat belts to be worn. It appears from the graph that this had an immediate and successful impact on reducing fatalities and serious injuries.

intervention

The new legislation is an example of an *intervention*—a one-off event which has an impact on the forecast variable. We can model the effect of the intervention using a special case of a dynamic regression model. The impact may be instantaneous or it may be spread over a period of time. However, the intervention is assumed to occur at one time period only.

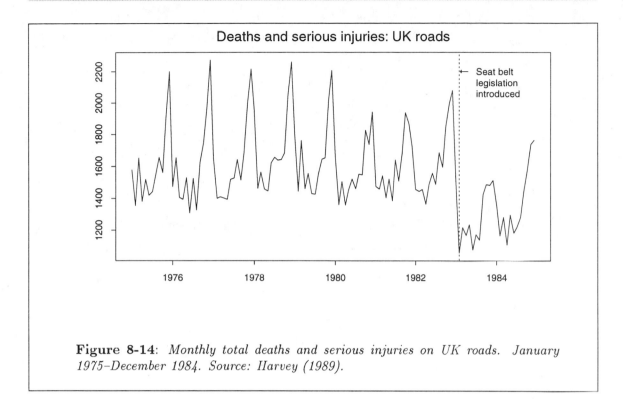

Figure 8-14: *Monthly total deaths and serious injuries on UK roads. January 1975–December 1984. Source: Harvey (1989).*

Intervention analysis is useful if we wish to measure the precise impact of the intervention, or if we wish to forecast the series allowing for the effect of the intervention. It was made widely known through an article entitled "Intervention analysis with applications to economic and environmental problems," in which Box and Tiao (1975) suggest an approach for handling this problem in a dynamic regression framework. Their approach is aimed at answering questions such as "How will sales be affected if the price is increased by 20%?" or "How will sales be affected if a promotional campaign is started on July 1?" These types of questions are concerned not only with the time at which the change occurred, but also with the transition period between the old equilibrium level and the new equilibrium level.

8/3/1 Step-based interventions

The simplest forms of interventions are step functions. That is where we expect the intervention to result in a sudden and lasting drop or rise in the forecast variable.

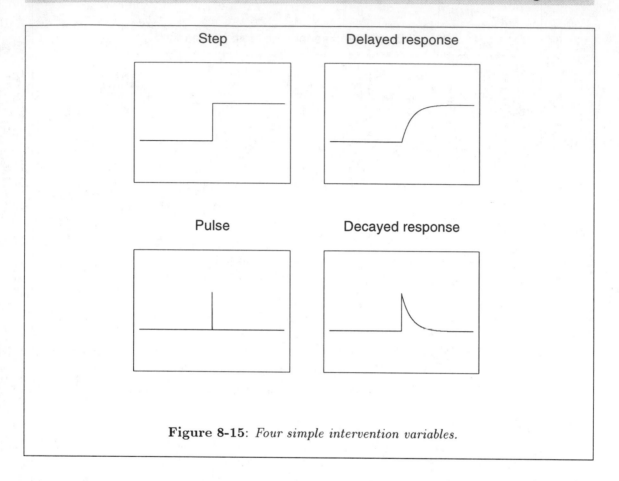

Figure 8-15: *Four simple intervention variables.*

Suppose the intervention occurred at time u. Then we can define the dummy variable as

step function

$$X_t = \begin{cases} 0 & t < u \\ 1 & t \geq u \end{cases} \qquad (8.19)$$

which is zero before the intervention and one after the intervention. This is called a "step intervention" because the graph of X_t against t resembles a step. It is shown at the top left of Figure 8-15.

For example, we can model the effect of the new seat belt law on the series in Figure 8-14 using this dummy variable with u corresponding to February 1983. The model is then

$$Y_t = a + \omega X_t + N_t \qquad (8.20)$$

where N_t is an ARIMA model. The value of ω represents the size of the drop in the monthly total number of deaths and serious injuries.

The approach to fitting an intervention model is identical to that for regression with ARIMA errors. We use a low-order autoregressive proxy model for N_t and fit equation (8.20). The errors were non-stationary and so we seasonally difference both Y_t and X_t and refit the model (without the constant). After examining the resulting errors, N_t', we select an ARIMA$(1,0,1)(0,0,1)_{12}$ model. So our full model is

$$Y_t = \omega X_t + N_t$$

where N_t is an ARIMA$(1,0,1)(0,1,1)_{12}$ process. We expect ω to be negative since the number of deaths and injuries should *fall* with the introduction of seat belts. The estimated value of ω is -306.2 with standard error 41.4. That is, seat belts have reduced the number of deaths and serious injuries by about 306 people per month. A 95% confidence interval for ω is

$$\omega \pm 1.96 \times \text{s.e.}(\omega) = -306.2 \pm 1.96(41.4) = [-387.3, -225.1].$$

In some circumstances an intervention will yield a rise or fall in the forecast variable, but not instantaneously. To model a delayed rise or drop in the forecast variable we use the following transfer function:

$$\nu(B) = \frac{\omega}{1 - \delta B} X_t \qquad \text{delayed response}$$

where X_t is the step variable (8.19). The shape of the resulting intervention response is shown at the top right of Figure 8-15. The value of δ determines the rate at which the level shift occurs. The ultimate size of the level shift is $\omega/(1 - \delta)$.

Other models can also be defined using the step variable with different transfer functions. So the general form of the model is

$$Y_t = a + \frac{\omega(B)}{\delta(B)} X_t + N_t. \qquad (8.21)$$

Intervention models which are based on the step function assume that the effect of the intervention is lasting.

8/3/2 Pulse-based interventions

Some interventions have a temporary effect on the series and the series will eventually return to a "steady state." In these cases, we use intervention models based on a pulse function rather than a step function. Again assuming the intervention occurred at time u, we define the pulse variable

pulse functions

$$X_t = \begin{cases} 0 & t \neq u \\ 1 & t = u. \end{cases} \tag{8.22}$$

That is, X_t is zero everywhere, except at the point of intervention where it takes the value one.

A simple pulse intervention is obtained by

$$Y_t = a + \omega X_t + N_t.$$

That is, the intervention affects the response at the point of intervention but nowhere else. The shape of the intervention response in this case is shown at the bottom left of Figure 8-15. This might be useful to model unusual one-off events such as industrial strikes, or outliers due to other causes.

For an intervention which has an immediate impact but then decays away slowly, we can define the model

decayed response

$$Y_t = a + \frac{\omega}{1 - \delta B} X_t + N_t.$$

The shape of this intervention is given at the bottom right of Figure 8-15. The value of ω gives the size of the immediate increase in Y_t and δ determines the rate of decay.

Again, other intervention models can be defined using using the pulse variable and the general form of the model is the same as (8.21) but with X_t representing the pulse variable (8.22).

8/3/3 Further reading

Mixtures of step- and pulse-based interventions allow more complicated response functions to be modeled. See Box and Tiao (1975), McCleary and Hay (1980), and Pankratz (1991) for details of these more complicated intervention models. Other interesting applications of intervention analysis may be found in the following papers.

- Montgomery and Weatherby (1980) considered the effect of the Arab oil embargo using a delayed response model.

- Wichern and Jones (1977) analyzed the impact of the American Dental Association's endorsement of Crest toothpaste on the market share of Crest and Colgate dentrifice.

- Atkins (1979) considered the number of traffic accidents on the freeways in British Columbia, and used intervention analysis to tease out the influence of three changes—compulsory auto insurance, a company strike, and a change in insurance companies' policies—on the number of accidents.

- Ledolter and Chan (1996) also looked at traffic accidents and focused on the effect of a change in the speed limit on the rural interstate highway system in Iowa.

8/3/4 Intervention models and forecasting

Intervention models are useful in explaining the effect of an intervention and so they help improve forecast accuracy *after* an intervention. However, they are of limited value in forecasting the effect of an intervention *before* it occurs as we cannot estimate (because of the lack of data) the parameters of the intervention model.

8/4 Multivariate autoregressive models

The data in Figure 8-16 concern quarterly capital expenditures and capital appropriations for U.S. manufacturing between 1953 and 1974. Both series have been seasonally adjusted. It is expected that appropriations might lead expenditures since funds must be appropriated before expenditures occur, and since capital construction projects take time to complete. On the other hand, after large expenditure, appropriations will often be reduced for a few months. So we might expect both variables to be influencing each other. This is known as *feedback*. In these circumstances, a dynamic regression model is not appropriate because it only allows the explanatory variable to influence the forecast variable, not vice-versa. feedback

   Before introducing an appropriate model for these data, we will make the variables stationary. Figure 8-16 shows both non-stationary mean and variance. We can stabilize the variance with a logarithmic

	Y_1	Y_2		Y_1	Y_2		Y_1	Y_2		Y_1	Y_2
1953	2072	1767		2140	2201	1964	3136	4123		6631	7595
	2077	2061		2012	2233		3299	4656		6828	7436
	2078	2289	1959	2071	2690		3514	4906	1970	6645	6679
	2043	2047		2192	2940		3815	4344		6703	6475
1954	2062	1856		2240	3127	1965	4040	5080		6659	6319
	2067	1842		2421	3131		4274	5539		6337	5860
	1964	1866	1960	2639	2872		4565	5583	1971	6165	5705
	1981	2279		2733	2515		4838	6147		5875	5521
1955	1914	2688		2721	2271	1966	5222	6545		5798	5920
	1991	3264		2640	2711		5406	6770		5921	5937
	2129	3896	1961	2513	2394		5705	5955	1972	5772	6570
	2309	4014		2448	2457		5871	6015		5874	7087
1956	2614	4041		2429	2720	1967	5953	6029		5872	7206
	2896	3710		2516	2703		5868	5975		6159	8431
	3058	3383	1962	2534	2992		5573	5894	1973	6583	9718
	3309	3431		2494	2516		5672	5951		6961	10921
1957	3446	3613		2596	2817	1968	5543	5952		7449	11672
	3466	3205		2572	3153		5526	5723		8093	12199
	3435	2426	1963	2601	2756		5750	6351	1974	9013	12865
	3183	2330		2648	3269		5761	6636		9752	14985
1958	2697	1954		2840	3657	1969	5943	6799		10704	16378
	2338	1936		2937	3941		6212	7753		11597	12680

Table 8-3: *Seasonally adjusted quarterly capital expenditure (Y_1) and appropriations (Y_2) in U.S. manufacturing, 1953–1974. (Millions of current dollars.) Source: Judge et al. (1988).*

transformation, and create stationary data by differencing.   The resulting data are shown in Figure 8-17.

Let E_t denote the expenditure and A_t denote the appropriations at time t. These are the series in Figure 8-16. Then we define the series in Figure 8-17 as

$$Y_{1,t} = \log(E_t) - \log(E_{t-1}) = \log(E_t/E_{t-1})$$
$$Y_{2,t} = \log(A_t) - \log(A_{t-1}) = \log(A_t/A_{t-1}).$$

We suppose each series is a function of its own past and the past of

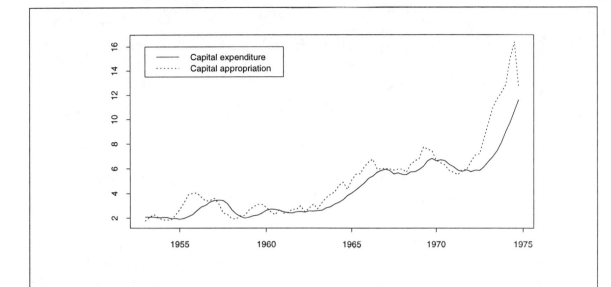

Figure 8-16: *Time plots of data given in Table 8-3. Quarterly capital expenditures and appropriations for U.S. manufacturing (1953–1974).*

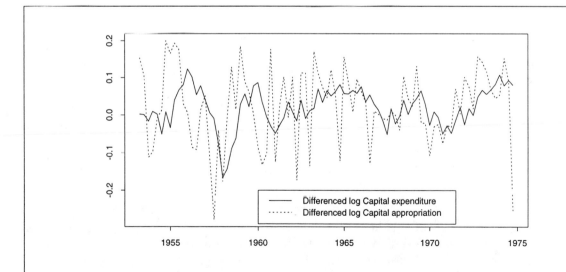

Figure 8-17: *The two series in Figure 8-16 after taking logarithms to stabilize the variance and differencing to give a stationary mean.*

the other series:

$$
\begin{aligned}
Y_{1,t} &= \phi_{111}Y_{1,t-1} + \phi_{112}Y_{1,t-2} + \cdots + \phi_{11p}Y_{1,t-p} \\
&\quad + \phi_{121}Y_{2,t-1} + \phi_{122}Y_{2,t-2} + \cdots + \phi_{11p}Y_{2,t-p} + e_{1,t} \\
Y_{2,t} &= \phi_{211}Y_{1,t-1} + \phi_{212}Y_{1,t-2} + \cdots + \phi_{21p}Y_{1,t-p} \\
&\quad + \phi_{221}Y_{2,t-1} + \phi_{222}Y_{2,t-2} + \cdots + \phi_{21p}Y_{2,t-p} + e_{2,t}
\end{aligned}
$$

The coefficients here need three subscripts: the first tells which variable is on the left-hand side; the second tells which variable the coefficient is attached to on the right-hand side; the third refers to the lag-length.

In general, we have K series and each one is related to its own past and the past of each of the other $K-1$ series in the group. This model is known as a *multivariate (or vector) autoregressive model*. It is possible to also introduce lagged error terms on the right-hand side of the model to give a multivariate ARMA model. However, we will restrict our discussion to the simpler AR model.

multivariate autoregressive model

It is easier to write the model using matrices. For $K = 2$, we define vectors of observations and errors

$$
\mathbf{Y}_t = \begin{bmatrix} Y_{1,t} \\ Y_{2,t} \end{bmatrix}, \qquad \mathbf{e}_t = \begin{bmatrix} e_{1,t} \\ e_{2,t} \end{bmatrix},
$$

and group the coefficients into matrices

$$
\Phi_1 = \begin{bmatrix} \phi_{111} & \phi_{121} \\ \phi_{211} & \phi_{221} \end{bmatrix}, \quad \Phi_2 = \begin{bmatrix} \phi_{112} & \phi_{122} \\ \phi_{212} & \phi_{222} \end{bmatrix}, \dots, \Phi_p = \begin{bmatrix} \phi_{11p} & \phi_{12p} \\ \phi_{21p} & \phi_{22p} \end{bmatrix}.
$$

Then the model can be written as

$$
\boxed{\mathbf{Y}_t = \Phi_1 \mathbf{Y}_{t-1} + \Phi_2 \mathbf{Y}_{t-2} + \cdots + \Phi_p \mathbf{Y}_{t-p} + \mathbf{e}_t.} \tag{8.23}
$$

AIC

The appropriate order of the model can be chosen using Akaike's Information Criterion (AIC) as for univariate models (see Section 7/6). Recall the formula

$$
\text{AIC} = -2 \log L + 2m
$$

where L is the likelihood of the model and m is the number of parameters estimated. In this case, $m = pK^2$.

For the capital expenditure and appropriation data, the following AIC values are obtained.

Model order (p)	0	1	2	3	4	5
AIC	-911.2	-992.6	-1011.8	-1018.8	-1019.7	-1014.5
Model order (p)	6	7	8	9	10	
AIC	-1010.8	-1016.3	-1013.1	-1011.4	-1007.7	

Since the smallest of these is for $p = 4$, we select the multivariate AR(4) model for these data. The estimated model is

$$
\mathbf{Y}_t = \begin{bmatrix} Y_{1,t} \\ Y_{2,t} \end{bmatrix} = \begin{bmatrix} 0.260 & 0.097 \\ 0.434 & 0.144 \end{bmatrix} \begin{bmatrix} Y_{1,t-1} \\ Y_{2,t-1} \end{bmatrix}
$$

$$
+ \begin{bmatrix} 0.101 & 0.138 \\ -0.807 & 0.026 \end{bmatrix} \begin{bmatrix} Y_{1,t-2} \\ Y_{2,t-2} \end{bmatrix}
$$

$$
+ \begin{bmatrix} 0.207 & 0.143 \\ 0.196 & 0.152 \end{bmatrix} \begin{bmatrix} Y_{1,t-3} \\ Y_{2,t-3} \end{bmatrix} \tag{8.24}
$$

$$
+ \begin{bmatrix} -0.124 & 0.675 \\ -0.284 & 0.126 \end{bmatrix} \begin{bmatrix} Y_{1,t-4} \\ Y_{2,t-4} \end{bmatrix} + \begin{bmatrix} e_{1,t} \\ e_{2,t} \end{bmatrix}.
$$

Suppose there was no feedback so the relationship between the **feedback** variables was only one-way. For example, suppose $Y_{2,t}$ did not depend on past values of $Y_{1,t}$ but $Y_{1,t}$ did depend on past values of $Y_{2,t}$. Then we would expect the lower left corner of each of these matrices to be close to zero. (For the alternative one-way relationship, it would be the upper right corner of the matrices which would show small values.) This provides a method for testing if the full multivariate model is worth using. If a one-way relationship is discovered, a dynamic regression model could be used instead. In this case, there are some large values in both the upper right and lower left corners of the matrices, showing we need the full multivariate model.

Forecasts are obtained easily by dropping the error term. Then the next few values of both series can be predicted using (8.24) in exactly the same way as for univariate AR models. Figure 8-18 shows forecasts for the next 12 periods for the capital expenditure and appropriation data, along with 90% prediction intervals.

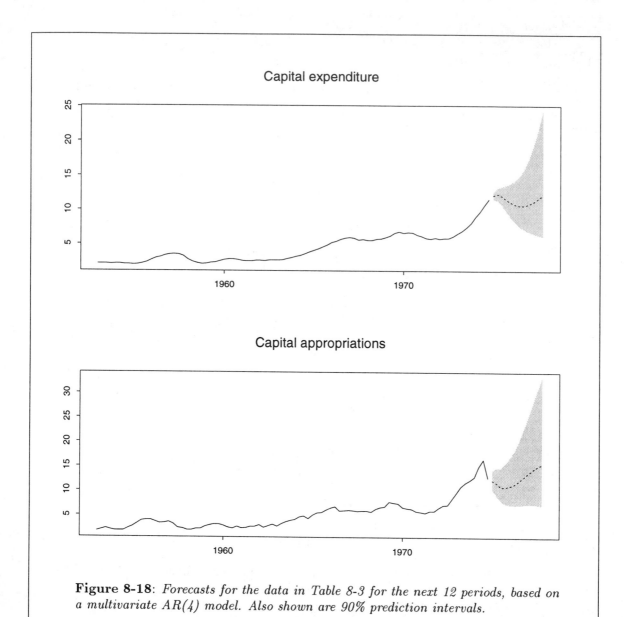

Figure 8-18: *Forecasts for the data in Table 8-3 for the next 12 periods, based on a multivariate AR(4) model. Also shown are 90% prediction intervals.*

8/5 State space models

The state space formulation assumes that the forecast variable Y_t can be expressed as a linear function of some random variables $X_{1,t}$, $X_{2,t}$, ..., $X_{d,t}$. So we write

$$Y_t = h_1 X_{1,t} + h_2 X_{2,t} + \cdots + h_d X_{d,t} + z_t.$$

The variables $X_{1,t}, \ldots, X_{d,t}$ are called the state variables. These are **state variables** not necessarily observed. We can write this equation in matrix form:

$$\boxed{Y_t = H\boldsymbol{X}_t + z_t} \qquad (8.25) \quad \text{observation equation}$$

where $\boldsymbol{X}_t$ is a multivariate time series with the state variables as components and H is a matrix consisting of one row with elements $h_1, \ldots, h_d$. Equation (8.25) is known as the "observation equation."

It is assumed that the state $\boldsymbol{X}_t$ depends on the previous state:

$$\boxed{\boldsymbol{X}_t = F\boldsymbol{X}_{t-1} + G\boldsymbol{e}_t} \qquad (8.26) \quad \text{state equation}$$

where $\boldsymbol{e}_t$ consists of white noise components and the matrices F and G consist of parameters for the model. Equation (8.26) is called the "state equation." Notice that it is almost the same as a multivariate AR(1) model except that it is for the state variable rather than the observed time series, and there is an additional matrix G.

Together, equations (8.25) and (8.26) form a *state space model*. The state space model for a multivariate time series $\boldsymbol{Y}_t$ is written in exactly the same way except both Y_t and z_t are replaced by vectors.

8/5/1 Some forecasting models in state space form

Although this formulation may not look similar to any model we have previously looked at, all of the time series and regression models we have considered can be expressed in "state space form." Even the most complex dynamic regression model with ARIMA errors has a state space counterpart which gives exactly the same forecasts. We will look at three examples to demonstrate how general the state space formulation is.

An AR(2) model would normally be written as

AR(2) model
$$Y_t = \phi_1 Y_{t-1} + \phi_2 Y_{t-2} + a_t$$

where a_t represents white noise. If we define $X_{1,t} = Y_t$ and $X_{2,t} = Y_{t-1}$, then we can write

$$\boldsymbol{X}_t = \begin{bmatrix} \phi_1 & \phi_2 \\ 1 & 0 \end{bmatrix} \boldsymbol{X}_{t-1} + \begin{bmatrix} a_t \\ 0 \end{bmatrix}$$

and $\quad Y_t = [1 \ 0]\boldsymbol{X}_t.$

This is now in state space form with

$$F = \begin{bmatrix} \phi_1 & \phi_2 \\ 1 & 0 \end{bmatrix}, G = \begin{bmatrix} 1 & 0 \\ 0 & 1 \end{bmatrix}, H = [1 \ 0], \boldsymbol{e}_t = \begin{bmatrix} a_t \\ 0 \end{bmatrix} \text{ and } z_t = 0.$$

In this case, the state consists of consecutive observations of the Y_t series.

Any ARIMA model can be written in state space form. See Brockwell and Davis (1996) for details.

As a second example, we define a random walk observed with error:

$$X_t = X_{t-1} + e_t \tag{8.27}$$
$$Y_t = X_t + z_t.$$

The first equation is a random walk while the second shows the observed time series is equal to the random walk series with some additional random error. This model is already in state space form with $F = G = H = 1$. In this example, the state is not observed. The forecasts obtained using this state space model are almost identical with those obtained using single exponential smoothing (see Harvey, 1989). In Section 7/8/5 we noted that single exponential smoothing was equivalent to forecasting with an ARIMA(0,1,1) model. So this random walk with error model is also equivalent to an ARIMA(0,1,1) model.

Finally, consider a regression model with one explanatory variable and AR(1) errors. Normally we would write this as

$$Y_t = a + bW_t + N_t, \qquad \text{where} \quad N_t = \phi N_{t-1} + a_t$$

where W_t denotes the explanatory variable and a_t denotes white noise. To express this in state space form, we define the state $\boldsymbol{X}_t$

to consist of the three elements a, b, and $N_t - z_t$. (Note that none of these is observable.) Then we can write

$$Y_t = \begin{bmatrix} 1 & W_t & 1 \end{bmatrix} X_t + z_t$$

$$X_t = \begin{bmatrix} 1 & 0 & 0 \\ 0 & 1 & 0 \\ 0 & 0 & \phi \end{bmatrix} X_{t-1} + \begin{bmatrix} 0 \\ 0 \\ \phi z_{t-1} \end{bmatrix}.$$

Check that this state space model gives the required equations when expanded.

8/5/2 State space forecasting

Writing time series models in state space form allows their properties to be studied in a common mathematical framework. It also means computer programs can use the same code for fitting a number of different models. But it does not help us forecast any better because the range of models available is not extended by the new framework.

However, there are some useful automatic forecasting algorithms   automatic forecasting
which are based on the state space formulations. The most widely used procedure is due to Akaike (1976) and can handle either univariate or multivariate data. It performs the following five steps.

1. It fits a sequence of multivariate autoregressive models for lags   multivariate
   0 to 10. For each model, the AIC is calculated and the model   autoregression
   with the smallest AIC value is selected for use in subsequent
   steps.

2. It tries to improve the fit of the selected AR model by adding
   moving average terms and removing some of the autoregressive
   terms.

3. The best of the revised models is then approximated by a state
   space model with fewer parameters.

4. The parameters of the state space model are estimated.

5. Forecasts for the model are produced.

Note that this procedure assumes that the variables are stationary. If this is not the case, they must first be transformed and differenced until they are stationary.

This procedure was applied to the data in Table 8-3. The best multivariate AR model found in Step 1 was that given in (8.24). The final model computed in Step 4 is given below.

$$
\boldsymbol{Y}_t \;=\; \underset{H}{\begin{bmatrix} 1 & 0 & 0 & 0 \\ 0 & 1 & 0 & 0 \end{bmatrix}} \boldsymbol{X}_t
$$

$$
\boldsymbol{X}_t \;=\; \underset{F}{\begin{bmatrix} 0 & 0 & 1 & 0 \\ 0 & 0 & 0 & 1 \\ -0.195 & 0.090 & 0.984 & 0.163 \\ -1.110 & 0.016 & 0.837 & 0.332 \end{bmatrix}} \boldsymbol{X}_{t-1} + \underset{G}{\begin{bmatrix} 1 & 0 \\ 0 & 1 \\ 0.270 & 0.095 \\ 0.259 & 0.100 \end{bmatrix}} \boldsymbol{e}_t
$$

Note that this state space model involves a bivariate observation $\boldsymbol{Y}_t$. The state vector $\boldsymbol{X}_t$ consists of four elements: the first two elements are the observations of expenditure and appropriations for time t; the second two elements are one-step forecasts of expenditure and appropriations at time $t+1$. The forecasts obtained by this model are very similar to those given in Figure 8-18 and so are not plotted here.

State space forecasting is not widely used because of the complexity of the mathematical theory underlying the model. However, it is useful and easy to use and probably deserves to be more widely applied than it is. One need not understand the mathematical theory of state space methodology to use it productively. Where state space methods have been used in forecasting competitions, they have produced mixed results (see Granger and McCollister, 1978; Makridakis et al., 1982). See also Chapter 11.

Apart from the Akaike approach to state space modeling there are several other approaches which are used. Structural models (Harvey, 1989) are a general class of models handling trend and seasonality which can be represented in state space form. In fact, the random walk with error model (8.27) is the simplest of Harvey's structural models. An advantage of structural models is that they are easily interpretable, unlike most state space models and ARIMA models. Janacek and Swift (1993) provide an introduction to structural models and Andrews (1994) explores their forecasting performance compared to other approaches.

Dynamic linear models are another model family based on the state space form. For these models, the state comprises components for trend and seasonal terms and so they are more interpretable than the general state space model. They rely on Bayesian ideas for their interpretation. Pole, West, and Harrison (1994) provide an introduction and discuss their application.

8/5/3 The value of state space models

There are several reasons why state space models are useful.

1. Kalman (1960) and Kalman and Bucy (1961) developed a general set of recursive equations to handle the forecasting. These are usually called the "Kalman recursion equations" or the "Kalman filter." The equations also enable easy calculation of the one-step forecast errors and the likelihood. So provided a model can be written in state space form, the calculations can all be carried out using the Kalman recursion equations. This unified framework for computation simplifies the development of forecasting packages because a wide range of models can be handled within the same code.

   Kalman recursion equations

2. State space models are easy to generalize. For example, we generalized simple exponential smoothing to allow the parameters to be changing over time (the adaptive response model). This can also be handled in the state space framework and can be done for *any* state space model. So, for example, it would be possible to use a dynamic regression model where the parameters of the ARIMA error changed over time.

3. The state space formulation makes it easier to handle missing values within a time series.

8/6 Non-linear models

Almost all of the models considered so far in this book have been *linear*. That is, the forecast models can all be expressed as a linear combination of past observations, errors, and explanatory variables. However, there are some features which occur in real data that cannot

asymmetric cycles

outliers

be captured by linear models. For example, linear models cannot model asymmetric cycles where the average number of observations on the up-cycle is different from the average number of observations on the down-cycle. Nor can they model series containing occasional bursts of outlying observations.

The only non-linear forecasting methods which we have covered so far are the adaptive response exponential smoothing method and state space models where the parameters are allowed to change over time. But neither of these is designed to cope with the features usually associated with non-linear time series.

Non-linear modeling became popular in the 1980s with the introduction of several non-linear equations of the form

$$Y_t = f(Y_{t-1}, Y_{t-2}, \ldots, Y_{t-p}) + g(Y_{t-1}, Y_{t-2}, \ldots, Y_{t-p})e_t \qquad (8.28)$$

where Y_t denotes the observed (stationary) time series, e_t is a white noise series, and f and g are functions of past observations in the series. If $g = 1$ and f is a linear function, (8.28) gives an ordinary linear $\mathrm{AR}(p)$ model. With f and g non-linear functions, a wide variety

threshold models
exponential
autoregressive models
ARCH models

of models can be obtained. For example, threshold models (Tong, 1983, 1990), exponential autoregressive models (Ozaki, 1980), and ARCH models (Engle, 1982) are all of this form.

We will consider just one example given by Tiao and Tsay (1994). They apply a threshold autoregressive model to quarterly U.S. GNP data from 1947 to 1991. The data are first transformed using logarithms and then differenced. They model the resulting series by four separate autoregressive models depending on the values of the previous two observations. The full model is

$$Y_t = \begin{cases} -0.015 - 1.076Y_{t-1} + 0.0062e_t & \text{regime 1} \\ -0.006 + 0.630Y_{t-1} - 0.756Y_{t-2} + 0.0132e_t & \text{regime 2} \\ 0.006 + 0.438Y_{t-1} + 0.0094e_t & \text{regime 3} \\ 0.004 + 0.443Y_{t-1} + 0.0082e_t & \text{regime 4} \end{cases}$$

where the regimes are defined as follows:

$$
\begin{aligned}
&\text{regime 1:} \quad Y_{t-1} \le Y_{t-2} \le 0; \\
&\text{regime 2:} \quad Y_{t-1} > Y_{t-2} \text{ but } Y_{t-2} \le 0; \\
&\text{regime 3:} \quad Y_{t-1} \le Y_{t-2} \text{ but } Y_{t-2} > 0; \\
&\text{regime 4:} \quad Y_{t-1} > Y_{t-2} > 0.
\end{aligned}
$$

These four regimes represent four different stages in the economic cycle. The first regime denotes a recession period in which the economy changes from contraction to an even worse recession; the second regime is where the economy is in contraction but improving; the third regime is where the economy is expanding but declining; and the fourth regime denotes an expansion period in which the economy is expanding and becoming stronger. Within each regime is a simple linear AR(1) or AR(2) model. The combination of models allows us to fit more complicated patterns than is possible with linear autoregressive models.

De Gooijer and Kumar (1992) highlight several practical difficulties in using non-linear models for forecasting including the calculation of multi-step ahead forecasts and prediction intervals. However, the approach given by Hyndman (1995) has now largely overcome this problem.

The big problem which has not been resolved so far is when do non-linear models forecast more accurately than simple linear ones. Non-linear models (and other statistically sophisticated models) clearly fit past data better, but empirical research has shown (see Chapter 11) that they often do not predict the future more accurately.

One of the interesting features of non-linear models is they can give rise to chaotic behavior. Chaos is the characteristic of time series where values may appear to be random and non-periodic, but are actually the result of a completely deterministic process. Typically, a small change in an observation will affect future observations with exponentially increasing magnitude. (With linear time series, a small change in an observation will die out quickly.) This has serious consequences for the forecastability of the time series.

chaos

For further reading on non-linear forecasting, see Tong (1990), De Gooijer and Kumar (1992), Casdagli and Eubank (1992), and Granger and Teräsvirta (1993).

8/7 Neural network forecasting

Artificial neural networks are based on simple mathematical models of the way brains are thought to work. When applied to time series, they provide a non-linear forecasting method. Neural network forecasting generally requires a much larger number of observations than the other methods discussed in this book, but it also allows more flexible and complicated models to be fitted.

Forecasters using neural network methods have adopted terminology quite different from that used with other methods, which has led to some confusion. For example, instead of a "model," we have a "network." Instead of "parameters," networks have "weights." Instead of talking about "estimating parameters," neural network forecasters talk about "training the network."

network
weights
training

A neural network can be thought of as a network of neuron-like units organized in layers. The bottom layer consists of a set of input units and the top layer consists of a set of output units. The units in each layer are linked to units in higher layers.

A number of ingredients are needed to specify a neural network:

network architecture
- its "architechure" (the number of layers and units in the network and the way units are connected);

activation functions
- its "activation functions" (that describe how each unit combines inputs to give an output);

cost function
- the "cost function" (a measure of forecast accuracy such as MSE);

training algorithm
- a "training" algorithm to find parameter values which minimize the cost function.

To explain this notation, consider a simple linear AR(p) model which can be described using a neural network. Figure 8-19 shows a typical neural network diagram for the linear AR(p) model. The input layer gives the variables which act as inputs to the network, in this case the past p observations. The output layer (forecasts) is obtained by a linear function of the inputs, shown by the connecting lines. The weights attached to each input are the parameters $\phi_1, \ldots, \phi_p$. These are selected in the neural network framework by a "learning" or "training algorithm" which minimizes a cost function such as MSE.

hidden units

The power of neural networks comes about with the inclusion of additional intermediate layers consisting of non-linear hidden units between the inputs and outputs. A simple example is shown in Figure 8-20 which shows a network containing only one hidden layer. Here the inputs are connected to a layer of non-linear hidden units which

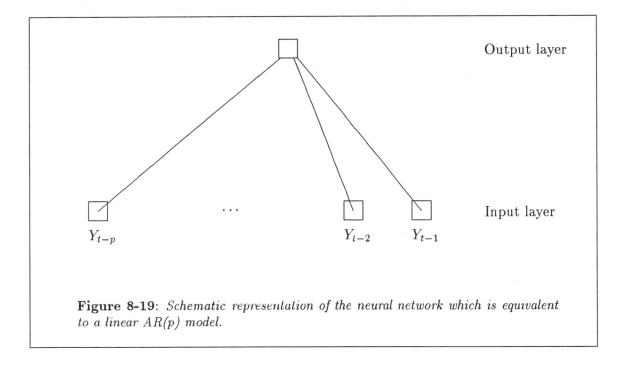

Figure 8-19: *Schematic representation of the neural network which is equivalent to a linear AR(p) model.*

are connected to one linear output unit. It is also possible to define a network with non-linear inputs and outputs.

The response of a unit is called its "activation value." A common choice for a non-linear activation function is a combination of a linear function of the inputs followed by a non-linear "squashing" function known as a "sigmoid." For example, the inputs into a hidden unit in Figure 8-20 can be linearly combined to give

$$Z = b + \sum_{i=1}^{p} w_i Y_{t-i}$$

which, in turn, is an input into the non-linear function

$$S(Z) = \frac{1}{1 + e^{-aZ}}. \qquad \text{sigmoid}$$

One benefit of the sigmoid function is that it reduces the effect of extreme input values, thus providing some degree of robustness to the network. In this example, the parameters are a, b and $w_1, \ldots, w_p$. The resulting values of $S(Z)$ for each of the hidden units in Figure 8-20 are then combined using a linear function to give an output (or forecast).

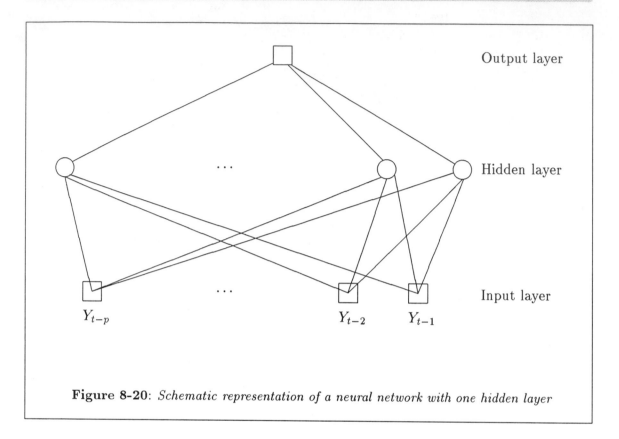

Figure 8-20: *Schematic representation of a neural network with one hidden layer*

This neural network is equivalent to a non-linear autoregression model

$$Y_t = f(Y_{t-1}, \ldots, Y_{t-p}) + e_t.$$

However, the form of the non-linear function f is not apparent from the neural network.

The input layer of a network usually consists of as many reasonable explanatory variables as possible in addition to lagged values of the time series. For seasonal data, the general practice is to have as many lagged inputs as there are periods in the season. The number of units in the output layer corresponds to the number of variables to be forecast.

Many forecasting networks have only one hidden layer. However, more complicated networks have also been used. For details, see Weigend and Gershenfeld (1994), Weigend, Huberman, and Remulhart (1990), and Vemuri and Rogers (1994).

A disadvantage of neural network methods is that they do not allow much understanding of the data because there is no explicit model. They provide a "black box" approach to forecasting. On the other hand, they may work in situations where an explicit model-based approach fails. In fact, much of their promise comes from the hope that they can adapt to irregularities and unusual features in the time series of interest.

black box forecasting

The practical application of artificial neural networks in forecasting has been marked by great hope and hype. It is too early to say whether neural network methods will live up to their alleged potential as a powerful and largely automatic approach to non-linear forecasting. There has been some research in comparing neural network techniques with more conventional forecasting methods. See Tang, de Almeida, and Fishwick (1991) and Hill et al. (1994) for details. The indications so far are that neural network techniques sometimes perform better than competing methods, but not always.

References and selected bibliography

ANDREWS, R.L. (1994) Forecasting performance of structural time series models, *Journal of Business and Economic Statistics*, **12**, 129–133.

AKAIKE, H. (1976) Canonical correlation analysis and information criterion, *System identification: advances and case studies*, Mehra and Lainiotis, eds., New York: Academic Press.

ATKINS, S.M. (1979) Case study on the use of intervention analysis applied to traffic accidents, *Journal Operations Research Society*, **30**, No. 7, 651–659.

BLATTBERG, R.C. and A.P. JEULAND (1981) A micromodeling approach to investigate the advertising-sales relationship, *Management Science*, **27**, 988–1005.

BOX, G.E.P. and G.M. JENKINS (1970) *Time series analysis forecasting and control*, 1st ed., San Francisco: Holden-Day.

BOX, G.E.P., G.M. JENKINS, and G.C. REINSELL (1994) *Time series analysis: Forecasting and control*, 3rd ed., Englewood Cliffs, N.J.: Prentice-Hall.

BOX, G.E.P. and G.C. TIAO (1975) Intervention analysis with applications to economic and environmental problems, *Journal of the American Statistical Association*, **70**, No. 349, 70–79.

BROCKWELL, P.J. and R.A. DAVIS (1996) *An introduction to time series and forecasting*, New York: Springer-Verlag.

CASDAGLI, M. and S. EUBANK (eds.) (1992) *Nonlinear modeling and forecasting*, Reading, Mass.: Addison-Wesley.

DE GOOIJER, J. and K. KUMAR (1992) Some recent developments in non-linear time series modelling, testing, and forecasting, *Journal of Forecasting*, **8**, 135–156.

ENGLE, R.F. (1982) Autoregressive conditional heteroscedasticity with estimates of the variance of U.K. inflation, *Econometrica*, **50**, 987–1008.

GRANGER, C.W.J. and G. McCOLLISTER (1978) "Comparison of selected series by adaptive, Box-Jenkins, and state space methods," ORSA/TIMS meeting, Los Angeles, Summer 1978.

GRANGER, C.W.J. and T. TERÄSVIRTA (1993) *Modeling nonlinear economic relationships*, New York: Oxford University Press.

HARVEY, A.C. (1989) *Forecasting, structural time series models and the Kalman filter*, Cambridge: Cambridge University Press.

HILL, T., L. MARQUEZ, M. O'CONNOR, and W. REMUS (1994) Artificial neural network models for forecasting and decision making, *International Journal of Forecasting*, **10**, 5–15.

HYNDMAN, R.J. (1995) Highest density forecast regions for non-linear and non-normal time series models, *Journal of Forecasting*, **14**, 431–441.

JANACEK, G. and SWIFT, L. (1993) *Time series: forecasting, simulation, applications*, New York: Ellis Horwood.

JUDGE, G.G., R.C. HILL, W.E. GRIFFITHS, H. LÜTKEPOHL, and T.-C. LEE (1988) *Introduction to the theory and practice of econometrics*, 2nd ed, New York: John Wiley & Sons.

KALMAN, R.E. (1960) A new approach to linear filtering and prediction problems, *Journal of Basic Engineering*, **D82**, March, 35–44.

KALMAN, R.E. and R.S. BUCY. (1961) New results in linear filtering and prediction theory, *Journal of Basic Engineering*, **D83**, March, 95–107.

KOEHLER, A.B. and E.S. MURPHREE (1988) A comparison of results from state space forecasting with forecasts from the Makridakis competition, *International Journal of Forecasting*, 4, 45–55.

KOYCK, L.M. (1954) *Distributed lags and investment analysis*, Amsterdam: North-Holland.

LEDOLTER, J. and K.S. CHAN (1996) Evaluating the impact of the 65 mph maximum speed limit on Iowa rural interstates, *American Statistician*, **50**, 79–85.

LÜTKEPOHL, H. (1991) *Introduction to multiple time series*, New York: Springer-Verlag.

MAKRIDAKIS, S., A. ANDERSEN, R. CARBONE, R. FILDES, M. HIBON, R. LEWANDOWSKI, J. NEWTON, E. PARZEN, and R. WINKLER (1982) The accuracy of extrapolation (time series) methods: results of a forecasting competition, *Journal of Forecasting*, **1**, 111–153.

McCLEARY, R. and R.A. HAY, JR. (1980) *Applied time series analysis for the social sciences*, Beverly Hills, Cal.: Sage Publications.

MONTGOMERY, D.C. and G. WEATHERBY. (1980) Modeling and forecasting time series using transfer function and intervention methods, *AIIE Transactions*, December, 289–307.

MORRISON, F. (1991) *The art of modeling dynamic systems: forecasting for chaos, randomness, and determinism*, Wiley-Interscience, New York: John Wiley & Sons.

OZAKI, T. (1980) Non-linear time series models for non-linear random vibrations, *Journal of Applied Probability*, **17**, 84–93.

PANKRATZ, A. (1991) *Forecasting with dynamic regression models*, New York: John Wiley & Sons.

POLE, A., M. WEST, and J. HARRISON (1994) *Applied Bayesian forecasting and time series analysis*, New York: Chapman and Hall.

PRIESTLEY, M.B. (1988) *Non-linear and non-stationary time series analysis*, London: Academic Press.

TANG, Z., C. DE ALMEIDA, and P.A. FISHWICK (1991) Time series forecasting using neural networks vs. Box-Jenkins methodology, *Simulation*, **57**, 303–310.

TIAO, G.C. and R.S. TSAY (1994) Some advances in non-linear and adaptive modeling in time series, *Journal of Forecasting*, **13**, 109–131.

TONG, H. (1983) *Threshold models in non-linear time series analysis*, Lecture notes in statistics, **21**, New York: Springer-Verlag.

——————————— (1990) *Non-linear time series: a dynamical system approach*, Oxford: Oxford University Press.

VEMURI, V. RAO and R.D ROGERS(eds.) (1994) *Artificial neural networks: forecasting time series*, Los Alamitos, Cal.: IEEE Computer Society Press.

WEI, W.W.S. (1990) *Time series analysis, univariate and multivariate methods*, Reading, MA: Addison-Wesley.

WEIGEND, A.S. and N.A. GERSHENFELD (eds.) (1994) *Time series prediction: forecasting the future and understanding the past*, Santa Fe Institute Studies in the Sciences of Complexity, Proc. Vol. XV. Reading, Mass.: Addison-Wesley.

WEIGEND, A.S., B.A. HUBERMAN, and D.E. REMULHART (1990) Predicting the future: a connectionist approach, *International Journal of Neural Systems*, **1**, 193–209.

WEST, M. and J. HARRISON (1989) *Bayesian forecasting and dynamic models*, Berlin: Springer-Verlag.

WICHERN, D.W. and R.H. JONES (1977) Assessing the impact of market disturbances using intervention analysis, *Management Science*, **24**, No. 3, 329–337.

Exercises

8.1 Consider the problem in Exercise 6.7. We fitted a regression model

$$Y_t = a + bX_t + N_t$$

where Y_t denotes sales, X_t denotes advertising and showed that N_t had significant autocorrelation.

(a) Refit the regression model with an AR(1) model for the errors. How much difference does the error model make to the estimated parameters?

(b) Plot the ACF and PACF of the errors to verify that an AR(1) model for the errors is appropriate.

8.2 (a) Fit a linear regression model with an AR(1) proxy model for error to the Lake Huron data given in Table 8-4 using the year as the explanatory variable.

(b) Using the ACF and PACF of the errors, identify and estimate an appropriate ARMA model for the error. Write down the full regression model and explain how you arrived at this model.

10.38	11.86	10.97	10.80	9.79	10.39	10.42	10.82	11.40	11.32
11.44	11.68	11.17	10.53	10.01	9.91	9.14	9.16	9.55	9.67
8.44	8.24	9.10	9.09	9.35	8.82	9.32	9.01	9.00	9.80
9.83	9.72	9.89	10.01	9.37	8.69	8.19	8.67	9.55	8.92
8.09	9.37	10.13	10.14	9.51	9.24	8.66	8.86	8.05	7.79
6.75	6.75	7.82	8.64	10.58	9.48	7.38	6.90	6.94	6.24
6.84	6.85	6.90	7.79	8.18	7.51	7.23	8.42	9.61	9.05
9.26	9.22	9.38	9.10	7.95	8.12	9.75	10.85	10.41	9.96
9.61	8.76	8.18	7.21	7.13	9.10	8.25	7.91	6.89	5.96
6.80	7.68	8.38	8.52	9.74	9.31	9.89	9.96		

Table 8-4: *Level of Lake Huron in feet, 1875–1972. Read from left to right. Data reduced by 570 feet, so that the true levels were 580.38, 581.86, etc. Source: Brockwell and Davis (1996).*

8.3 Electricity consumption is often modeled as a function of temperature. Temperature is measured by daily heating degrees and cooling degrees. Heating degrees is 65°F minus the average daily temperature when the daily average is below 65°F; otherwise it is zero. This provides a measure of our need to heat ourselves as temperature falls. Cooling degrees measures our need to cool ourselves as the temperature rises. It is defined as the average daily temperature minus 65°F when the daily average is above 65°F; otherwise it is zero. Let Y_t denote the monthly total of kilowatt-hours of electricity used, let $X_{1,t}$ denote the monthly total of heating degrees, and let $X_{2,t}$ denote the monthly total of cooling degrees.

Pankratz (1991) fits the following model to a set of such data:

$$Y_t' = b_0 + b_1 X_{1,t}' + b_2 X_{2,t}' + N_t$$

where $\quad (1 - B)(1 - B^{12})N_t = \dfrac{1 - \theta_1 B}{1 - \phi_{12}B^{12} - \phi_{24}B^{24}} e_t$

and $Y_t' = \log(Y_t)$, $X_{1,t}' = \sqrt{X_{1,t}}$ and $X_{2,t}' = \sqrt{X_{2,t}}$.

(a) What sort of ARIMA model is identified for N_t? Explain how the statistician would have arrived at this model.

(b) The estimated coefficients are

Parameter	Estimate	s.e.	Z	P-value
b_1	0.0077	0.0015	4.98	0.000
b_2	0.0208	0.0023	9.23	0.000
θ_1	0.5830	0.0720	8.10	0.000
ϕ_{12}	−0.5373	0.0856	-6.27	0.000
ϕ_{24}	−0.4667	0.0862	-5.41	0.000

Explain what the estimates of b_1 and b_2 tell us about electricity consumption.

(c) Describe how this model could be used to forecast electricity demand for the next 12 months.

(d) Explain why the N_t term should be modeled with an ARIMA model rather than modeling the data using a standard regression package. In your discussion, comment on the properties of the estimates, the validity of the standard regression results, and the importance of the N_t model in producing forecasts.

8.4 Box, Jenkins, and Reinsell (1994) fit a dynamic regression model to data from a gas combustion chamber. The two variables of interest are the volume of methane entering the chamber (X_t in cubic feet per minute) and the percentage concentration of carbon dioxide emitted (Y_t). Each variable is measured once every 9 seconds. Their model is

$$Y_t = \frac{(-0.53 + 0.37B + 0.51B^2)B^3}{1 - 0.57B} X_t + \frac{1}{1 - 1.53B + 0.63B^2} e_t.$$

(a) What are the values of b, r, and s for the transfer function?

(b) What sort of ARIMA model is used for the errors?

(c) What are the values of the coefficients ω_0, ω_1, ω_2, δ_1, δ_2, θ_1, θ_2, ϕ_1, and ϕ_2?

(d) If the methane input was increased, how long would it take before the carbon dioxide emission is affected?

8.5 Sketch the graph of the impulse response weights for the following transfer functions:

(a) $Y_t = 2(1 - 0.5B)B^2 X_t$

(b) $Y_t = \dfrac{3B}{1 - 0.7B} X_t$

(c) $Y_t = \dfrac{1 - 0.5B}{1.2 - 0.8B} X_t$

(d) $Y_t = \dfrac{1}{1 - 1.1B + 0.5B^2} X_t.$

t	1	2	3	4	5	6	7	8	9	10	11	12	13	14	15
X_t	50	90	50	30	80	80	30	70	60	10	40	20	40	20	10
t	16	17	18	19	20	21	22	23	24	25	26	27	28	29	30
X_t	30	60	70	40	70	10	30	30	40	30	100	60	90	60	100

Table 8-5: *An input series, X_t, for Exercise 8.6.*

8.6 An input (explanatory) time series X_t is shown in Table 8-5.

(a) Using equation (8.5), generate three output time series Y_t corresponding to the three sets of transfer function weights below.

	v_1	v_2	v_3	v_4	v_5	v_6	v_7
Set 1	0.2	0.4	0.3	0.1	0.0	0.0	0.0
Set 2	0.0	0.2	0.4	0.3	0.1	0.0	0.0
Set 3	0.0	0.0	0.2	0.5	0.4	0.2	0.1

Assume that N_t is normally distributed white noise with mean 0 and standard deviation 1. Values for N_t may be generated by a computer program or obtained from Table G in Appendix III. How many Y_t values can you calculate for each set?

(b) Now generate data with the same input data from Table 8-5 and the following transfer functions.

4. $r = 1$, $s = 0$, $b = 1$ with $\omega_0 = 2.0$ and $\delta_1 = 0.7$.

5. $r = 0$, $s = 2$, $b = 0$ with $\omega_0 = 1.2$, $\omega_1 = -2.0$, $\omega_2 = 0.8$.

Again, assume N_t is white noise with mean 0 and standard deviation 1.

8.7 Table 8-6 gives the total monthly takings from accommodation and the total room nights occupied at hotels, motels, and guest houses in Victoria, Australia, between January 1980 and June 1995. Table 8-7 gives quarterly CPI values for the same period and the same region.

(a) Use the data in Table 8-6 to calculate the average cost of a night's accommodation in Victoria each month.

(b) Estimate the monthly CPI using the data in Table 8-7.

(c) Produce time series plots of both variables and explain why logarithms of both variables need to be taken before fitting any models.

(d) Follow the modeling procedure in Section 8/2 to fit a dynamic regression model. Explain your reasoning in arriving at the final model.

(e) Forecast the average price per room for the next twelve months using your fitted model. (Hint: You will need to find forecasts of the CPI figures first.)

		Jan	Feb	Mar	Apr	May	Jun	Jul	Aug	Sep	Oct	Nov	Dec
1980	R	277.0	260.6	291.6	275.4	275.3	231.7	238.8	274.2	277.8	299.1	286.6	232.3
	C	7.7	7.5	8.3	7.8	7.9	6.6	7.0	8.2	8.2	9.1	9.0	7.1
1981	R	294.1	267.5	309.7	280.7	287.3	235.7	256.4	289.0	290.8	321.9	291.8	241.4
	C	8.9	8.5	9.8	8.8	9.2	7.4	8.3	9.7	9.7	10.8	9.8	7.9
1982	R	295.5	258.2	306.1	281.5	283.1	237.4	274.8	299.3	300.4	340.9	318.8	265.7
	C	9.8	9.0	10.5	9.5	9.7	8.1	10.1	11.1	11.2	12.6	12.2	9.9
1983	R	322.7	281.6	323.5	312.6	310.8	262.8	273.8	320.0	310.3	342.2	320.1	265.6
	C	11.8	11.1	12.6	11.9	11.9	10.0	10.8	12.9	12.5	13.8	13.1	10.5
1984	R	327.0	300.7	346.4	317.3	326.2	270.7	278.2	324.6	321.8	343.5	354.0	278.2
	C	12.9	12.9	14.4	12.7	13.3	11.0	11.9	14.1	14.4	14.9	15.7	12.0
1985	R	330.2	307.3	375.9	335.3	339.3	280.3	293.7	341.2	345.1	368.7	369.4	288.4
	C	14.3	14.2	17.4	15.1	15.3	12.6	14.0	16.6	16.7	17.6	18.3	13.6
1986	R	341.0	319.1	374.2	344.5	337.3	281.0	282.2	321.0	325.4	366.3	380.3	300.7
	C	15.8	16.1	18.6	17.3	17.0	13.9	15.2	17.8	18.0	19.4	21.8	16.2
1987	R	359.3	327.6	383.6	352.4	329.4	294.5	333.5	334.3	358.0	396.1	387.0	307.2
	C	19.2	19.5	22.0	20.0	19.2	16.9	20.0	20.4	21.8	25.0	25.8	19.4
1988	R	363.9	344.7	397.6	376.8	337.1	299.3	323.1	329.1	347.0	462.0	436.5	360.4
	C	22.6	24.1	26.9	24.9	23.3	20.3	22.3	23.7	24.3	31.7	32.2	25.4
1989	R	415.5	382.1	432.2	424.3	386.7	354.5	375.8	368.0	402.4	426.5	433.3	338.5
	C	28.6	28.7	30.9	31.4	29.1	26.3	28.9	28.9	31.0	33.4	35.9	25.8
1990	R	416.8	381.1	445.7	412.4	394.0	348.2	380.1	373.7	393.6	434.2	430.7	344.5
	C	31.2	31.7	36.2	32.0	32.1	28.1	31.1	31.9	32.0	36.6	38.1	28.1
1991	R	411.9	370.5	437.3	411.3	385.5	341.3	384.2	373.2	415.8	448.6	454.3	350.3
	C	32.9	30.7	35.4	33.7	31.6	27.9	32.2	32.3	35.3	37.2	39.6	28.4
1992	R	419.1	398.0	456.1	430.1	399.8	362.7	384.9	385.3	432.3	468.9	442.7	370.2
	C	33.9	33.7	38.3	34.6	32.7	29.5	32.0	33.2	36.7	38.6	38.1	29.8
1993	R	439.4	393.9	468.7	438.8	430.1	366.3	391.0	380.9	431.4	465.4	471.5	387.5
	C	35.6	33.2	38.9	34.8	37.2	29.7	32.2	32.1	36.3	38.4	40.8	31.3
1994	R	446.4	421.5	504.8	492.1	421.3	396.7	428.0	421.9	465.6	525.8	499.9	435.3
	C	36.2	35.1	44.1	39.3	34.1	32.4	36.3	36.8	40.5	46.0	43.9	37.2
1995	R	479.5	473.0	554.4	489.6	462.2	420.3						
	C	40.7	42.0	49.2	42.3	40.8	37.6						

Table 8-6: *Total monthly takings (C in thousands of Australian dollars) and total room nights occupied (R in thousands) from accommodation at hotels, motels, and guest houses in Victoria from January 1980 through June 1995. Source: Australian Bureau of Statistics.*

45.2	46.6	47.5	48.5	49.6	50.7	51.8	54.1	54.8	56.1	58.1	59.6
60.9	62.6	63.6	65.5	65.1	65.3	66.3	67.1	67.9	69.9	71.4	72.6
74.6	75.7	77.7	80.0	81.5	82.8	84.3	85.7	87.0	88.6	89.9	91.5
92.7	95.2	97.3	99.2	100.7	102.7	103.5	106.6	106.1	106.8	107.6	108.4
108.3	108.2	107.9	108.2	109.5	110.1	110.5	110.8	111.2	112.0	112.2	113.1
115.0	116.2										

Table 8-7: *Quarterly CPI (consumer price index) for Victoria, Q1 1980–Q2 1995. Read from left to right. Source: Australian Bureau of Statistics.*

55	56	48	46	56	46	59	60	53	58	73	69	72	51	72	69	68	69	79	77
53	63	80	65	78	64	72	77	82	77	35	79	71	73	77	76	83	73	78	91
70	88	88	85	77	63	91	94	72	83	88	78	84	78	75	75	86	79	76	87
66	73	62	27	52	47	65	59	77	47	51	47	49	54	58	56	50	54	45	66
39	51	39	27	39	37	43	41	27	29	27	26	29	31	28	38	37	26	31	45
38	33	33	25	24	29	37	35	32	31	28	40	31	37	34	43	38	33	28	35

Table 8-8: *Daily perceptual speed scores for a schizophrenic patient. A new drug was introduced on day 61. Read left to right. Source: McCleary and Hay (1980)*

8.8 The data in Table 8-8 are the daily scores achieved by a schizophrenic patient on a test of perceptual speed. The patient began receiving a powerful tranquilizer (chlorpromazine) on the sixty-first day and continued receiving the drug for the rest of the sample period. It is expected that this drug would reduce perceptual speed.

(a) Produce a time plot of the data showing where the intervention occurred.

(b) Fit an intervention model with a step function intervention to the series. Write out the model including the ARIMA model for the errors.

(c) What does the model say about the effect of the drug?

(d) Fit a new intervention model with a delayed response to the drug. Which model fits the data better? Are the forecasts from the two models very different?

(e) Construct an ARIMA model ignoring the intervention and compare the forecasts with those obtained from your preferred intervention model. How much does the intervention affect the forecasts?

(f) If the level of drug given varied from day-to-day, how could you modify your model to allow for this?

8.9 Consider the regression model fitted in Exercise **8.7** concerning the cost of tourist accommodation and the CPI.

(a) Let Y_t denote the log of the average room rate and X_t denote the log of the CPI. Suppose these form a bivariate time series. Both series were differenced and a bivariate AR(12) model was fitted to the differenced data. The order of the model was chosen by minimizing the AIC statistic. Write down the form of the fitted model.

(b) The first three coefficient matrices were

$$\Phi_1 = \begin{bmatrix} -0.38 & 0.15 \\ 0.04 & -0.07 \end{bmatrix}, \quad \Phi_2 = \begin{bmatrix} -0.37 & 0.13 \\ 0.04 & -0.05 \end{bmatrix}$$

$$\text{and} \quad \Phi_3 = \begin{bmatrix} -0.20 & 0.15 \\ 0.06 & 0.12 \end{bmatrix}.$$

Writing Y_t as a function of $Y_{t-1}, Y_{t-2}, \ldots$ and $X_{t-1}, X_{t-2}, \ldots$, what are the coefficients of Y_{t-1}, Y_{t-2}, X_{t-1}, and X_{t-2}?

(c) In no more than half a page, discuss the differences between this model and that considered in Exercise **8.7**. You should include mention of the assumptions in each model and explain which approach you think is most appropriate for these data.

8.10 (a) Write an AR(3) model in state space form.

(b) Write an MA(1) model in state space form. (Hint: Set $F = 0$.)

(c) Show that Holt's method (Section 4/3/3) can be written in the following "error feedback form":

$$L_t = L_{t-1} + b_{t-1} + \alpha e_t$$
$$b_t = b_{t-1} + \beta \alpha e_t$$

where $e_t = Y_t - L_{t-1} - b_{t-1}$. Use this result to find a state space form of Holt's method with state vector containing L_t and b_t.

(d) Give two reasons why you might want to use the state space form of these models rather than the usual form.

9

FORECASTING THE LONG-TERM

technological
forecasting

Forecasting the long-term requires a different approach from that described in the previous six chapters, since in the long run many things can and do happen that substantially change established patterns and/or existing relationships. This renders our forecasts both inaccurate and misleading and is why, in the past, a specialized area called "technological forecasting" existed. Technology is not the only factor affecting the long run, however. And many of the tools and techniques advocated in technological forecasting did not provide more accurate predictions about the long-term and have been, in consequence, abandoned. Today, we prefer to simply talk about "forecasting the long-term." In this chapter, such forecasting will be based on three aspects: (a) identifying and extrapolating mega trends going back in time as far as necessary; (b) using analogies; and (c) constructing scenarios to consider future possibilities, particularly their affect on the business environment and on businesses themselves. We begin by showing the dangers of mere extrapolation when the real mega trend is not properly identified.

9/1 Cycles versus long-term trends: forecasting copper prices

R-squared

extrapolation

Figure 9-1 shows monthly copper prices (in constant 1997 dollars) for 28 consecutive months. The downward trend is obvious. Constant prices were about \$5.5 at the beginning of the graph and \$2.5 at the end, a decrease of around 50%. Moreover, as the R^2 (a measure of how well the downward sloping exponential curve fits the historical data— the monthly copper prices) of the model (the negative exponential curve shown in Figure 9-1) is 0.974, we may feel fairly comfortable about extrapolating such a downward trend to future periods. In addition, our uncertainty, based on these 28 data points, is very low as R^2 is close to 1 and the variance of the model fitting errors is small. For instance, by extrapolating the trend of Figure 9-1, we arrive at a forecast for Month 36 of \$2 per kg while a pessimistic/optimistic (i.e., 95%) prediction interval around such a forecast is in the \$1.8 to \$2.2 range. Similarly, for Month 49 the forecast is \$1.42 with a pessimistic/optimistic prediction interval in the range of \$1.28 to \$1.57 per kg.

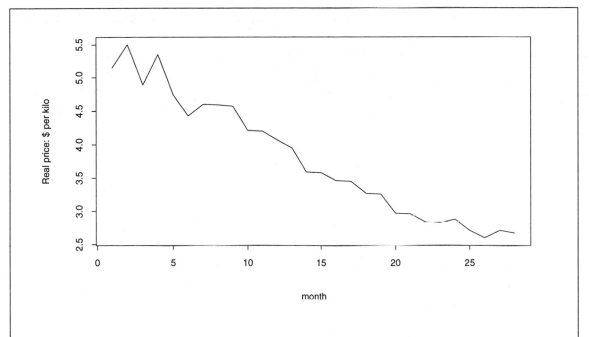

Figure 9-1: *Monthly copper prices for 28 consecutive months (in constant 1997 dollars).*

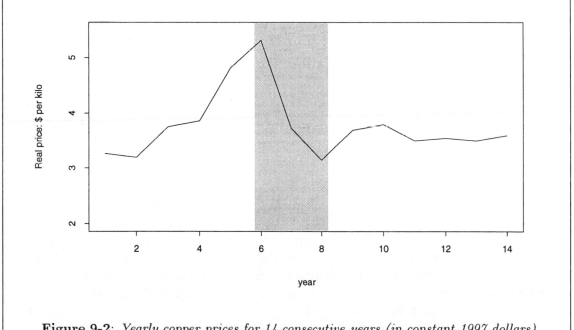

Figure 9-2: *Yearly copper prices for 14 consecutive years (in constant 1997 dollars).*

Figure 9-2 shows real copper prices for 14 years and indicates that they are constant, not declining. Which of the two figures is correct? Comparing their R^2 values would lead one to think Figure 9-1 is to be preferred to Figure 9-2 since its R^2 is 0.974, versus 0.007 for Figure 9-2. Moreover, the model implied in Figure 9-1 is based on 28 points while Figure 9-2 uses 14 points only. However, the prices shown in Figure 9-1 are monthly, and consist of a small part (the shaded region) of the yearly data displayed in Figure 9-2. Logic dictates, therefore, that measures of accuracy should be set aside, concluding instead that real copper prices are constant.

Figure 9-3, which contains 43 years of data, suggests a different picture: increasing copper prices (the 14 yearly data of Figure 9-2 are simply the part shown in the shaded region of Figure 9-3). The R^2 of the data shown in Figure 9-3 is 0.743.

What can a copper firm conclude from these graphs? As the highest R^2 is found in Figure 9-1, the model that best fits past data is the one shown in Figure 9-1. Logic dictates, however, that yearly data should be trusted more than monthly ones, irrespective of the value of R^2—meaning that the model of Figure 9-3 should be preferred. But even if we assume that the best model is that related to Figure 9-3, can its increasing trend be used to make an important strategic investment decision for opening, say, a new copper mine that will cost more than \$1 billion? After all, 43 years is a very long period (most executives complain that their data do not go back more than 5 to 10 years) and the fit of the model shown in Figure 9-3 is pretty good—its R^2 is 0.743. Our confidence, therefore, about extrapolating the exponential trend of copper prices to future years should be pretty good. (For example, its forecast for 10 years later is \$5.66 per kg, with a pessimistic/optimistic prediction interval of between \$4.12 and \$7.80 per kg.)

Long-wave cycle

Kondradieff cycle

In real life, however, 43 years of data may not represent a long enough period to draw any conclusions about the long-term trend in copper prices. Long-wave (Kondradieff) cycles—often observed in economic data series—can last for more than 60 years. It is possible, therefore, that what seems to be an upward trend for 43 years is, in effect, the rising part of a Kondradieff cycle. This is the case for the data shown in Figure 9-3, which includes the upward increase of the long-wave cycle that started in 1932 and ended in 1974. The full cycle that started in 1932 can be seen in Figure 9-4, which shows copper

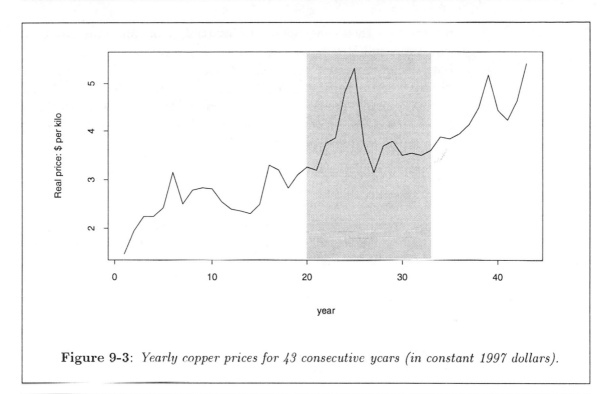

Figure 9-3: *Yearly copper prices for 43 consecutive years (in constant 1997 dollars).*

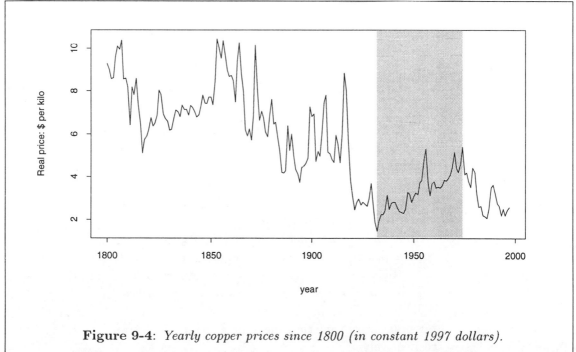

Figure 9-4: *Yearly copper prices since 1800 (in constant 1997 dollars).*

prices since 1800 (an *appropriate* starting time since the effects of
the Industrial Revolution started at about this time) and displays
both an exponentially decreasing trend and many cycles of various
durations and lengths. (The 43 years of Figure 9-3 are simply the
part of Figure 9-4 shown in the shaded region, from 1932 to 1974; it
is not clear that the downward decline of such a cycle that started in
1974 has ended as yet.)

Even though the R^2 relating to Figure 9-4 is 0.618, smaller than
the 0.743 of Figure 9-3 and even smaller than the 0.974 of Figure 9-1,
we will have to conclude that real copper prices are not increasing in
the long run, as Figure 9-3 suggests, or decreasing at the rate implied
in Figure 9-1. Instead, they are decreasing in the exponential fashion
and the rate shown in Figure 9-4. This means that Figures 9-1,
9-2, and 9-3 have little value for strategists apart from illustrating,
beyond the slightest doubt, the dangers of making long-term forecasts
starting period   without selecting an appropriate starting data set for the problem
being analyzed. In fact, any conclusion drawn from Figures 9-1, 9-2,
or 9-3 can be highly misleading and must not be used for basing
strategic or other long-term decisions that require accurate prediction
of long-term copper prices on which, for instance, capital expansion
plans would be based. This conclusion implies a fundamental change
in our approach to forecasting as well as its use for long-term planning
and strategic decisions. Unless we are certain that we use a plausible
starting period (as with Figure 9-4), we cannot be confident about
our extrapolations or our ability to distinguish long-wave cycles from
long-term trends.

long-term planning   Successful strategy and effective long-term planning (e.g., capital
budgeting) require figuring out the implication of long trends and
distinguishing such trends from the various cycles associated with
them. In fact, the farther the copper prices move away from the
long-term trend, as is the case in Figure 9-3, the greater the chance
that there will be a regression toward, and possibly below, the long-
term trend. This has happened in Figure 9-4, which shows that
copper prices, well above the long-term declining trend in 1974, have
fallen below such a trend in the past several years. Based on Figure
9-4 we can forecast the long-term copper prices (in constant 1997
dollars) as $2.48 in the year 2000 and $2.40 in the year 2005, with
pessimistic/optimistic ranges of $1.41 to $4.35 and $1.37 to $4.22,
respectively.

9/1/1 Forecasting IBM's sales

Extrapolating long-term trends is dangerous even when shorter periods are involved and micro series are utilized. For instance, in 1984 John Opel, IBM's chairman, announced that the sales of his firm, $50 billion at the time, would double to $100 billion by 1990, while its profits would continue their exponential growth. Figure 9-5(a) shows IBM's sales between 1954 and 1984, while Figure 9-5(b) displays its profits. Extrapolating the historical growth of IBM's sales for 1990 results in $110 billion sales, $10 billion more than Opel's 1984 forecast—which could, therefore, be considered conservative since it underestimated the straightforward extrapolation of IBM's past sales.

Based on such forecasts IBM hired more than 100,000 new personnel in order to provide its existing and new customers with the high-quality service it was much acclaimed for and which constituted the foundations for its strong competitive advantage. Things did not turn out as expected, however. Figures 9-5(c) and (d) show, in addition to the 1954 to 1984 era, IBM's sales and profits since 1984. In 1996, its sales were only $72 billion ($28 billion below the $100 billion predicted for 1990) while it incurred losses of more than $13 billion in 1991, 1992, and 1993. Moreover, its work force was, by the end of 1996, at about half its 1986/87 peak of 430,000.

IBM's management assumed that the business environment and IBM itself would not change in the following six years and felt justified, therefore, in extrapolating historical patterns and basing its overall strategy and expansion plans on forecasts from such extrapolation. The belief that the best model fitting the past data guarantees the most accurate forecast for the future, however, is not correct for three reasons. First, if nothing changes, the future will be deterministic, as straightforward extrapolation is trivial and can be done by everyone—including IBM's existing as well as new competitors, who would also make plans to expand and take for themselves as large a part of the growing pie as possible. But inevitably, the changing environment lure of high growth and big profits creates overcapacity, intensifies competition, and results in price wars that diminish profits or even bring losses. Second, yearly growth rates in the 15 to 20% range may be possible for a small or medium sized company but become exceedingly difficult for a $50 billion giant (the size of IBM in 1984), since 16% growth meant an $8 billion yearly increase, more than the

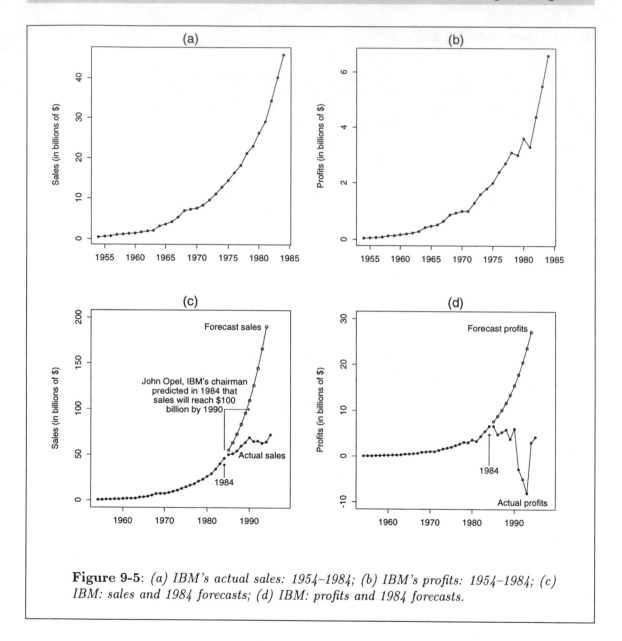

Figure 9-5: *(a) IBM's actual sales: 1954–1984; (b) IBM's profits: 1954–1984; (c) IBM: sales and 1984 forecasts; (d) IBM: profits and 1984 forecasts.*

revenues of all but a few dozen of 1984's largest firms. Finally, even if IBM's revenues had managed to grow, it is highly unlikely that its profits would have grown equally well. John Opel and IBM ignored these simple forecasting principles that apply to long-term predictions and instead extrapolated established trends, not wanting to believe that such trends could change in the future.

9/2 Long-term mega economic trends

Although long-term economic trends can also change, it is not likely that they will do so because, by definition, they have lasted for a very long time, being the outcome of the economic system of free competition. Such trends can, therefore, be extrapolated with a reasonable degree of certainty unless we have reasons to believe that the present economic system will change in some fundamental manner during the future.

In the long run, the price, excluding inflation, of most standardized (commodity type) products or services decreases. The decrease, first observed for agricultural products, has continued for practically all standardized products and services (Makridakis, 1990). Figure 9-6 displays real wheat prices since 1264, and clearly shows their considerable decrease since around 1800, when the effects of the Industrial Revolution began to impact the agriculture economy. Since then, real wheat prices have behaved very much like the copper prices shown in Figure 9-4. Both have been declining exponentially, in

decrease in real prices

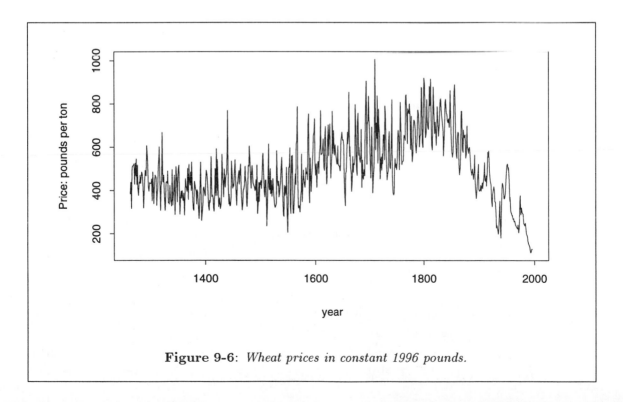

Figure 9-6: *Wheat prices in constant 1996 pounds.*

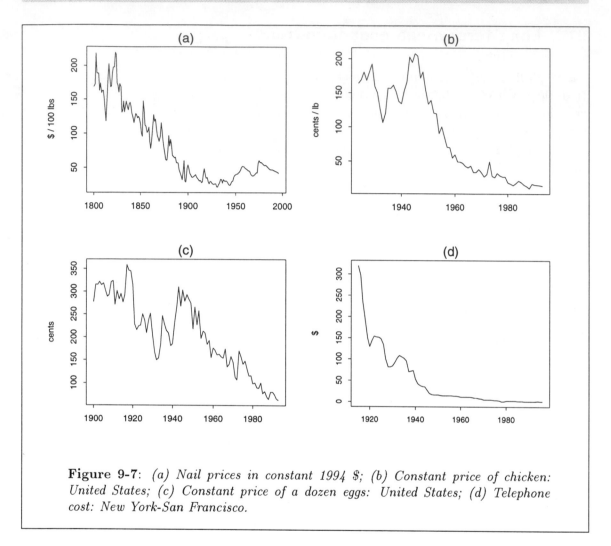

Figure 9-7: *(a) Nail prices in constant 1994 \$; (b) Constant price of chicken: United States; (c) Constant price of a dozen eggs: United States; (d) Telephone cost: New York-San Francisco.*

real terms, because supply has increased above demand (although the population increased sixfold between 1800 and 1997, increasing demand considerably), thus forcing real prices to drop. The same is true with virtually all standardized products/services. See Figures 9-7(a) to (d).

The long-term decrease in real prices implies that firms must continuously improve their productivity, through technological and/or organizational innovation, in order to be capable of decreasing their costs and real prices continuously; this is at least true for firms producing standardized products/services. Moreover, there is little doubt that such a decline will continue in the future. It may even accelerate through the impact of the Information Revolution (see below) now underway.

Since the beginning of the Industrial Revolution real income has been increasing, although its increase is characterized by cyclical fluctuations. Figure 9-8 shows real wages in England since 1264 and clearly indicates that real income has been increasing exponentially (the scale of Figure 9-8(b) is exponential), first from around 1625 until 1725 under the impact of the Agricultural Revolution, and second since about 1800 under the impact of the Industrial Revolution. As real wages increase, so does real GNP or wealth, which has been growing exponentially since at least 1800.

real income increasing

9/2/1 Cycles of various durations and depths

The prices, income, and buying power graphs displayed in Figures 9-4, and 9-6 to 9-7 exhibit strong deviations, some more than others, around the long-term trend; these deviations, or cycles, can present a considerable challenge for both forecasters and planners/strategists. Unfortunately, however, cycles cannot be predicted quantitatively, as their length and depth are not constant. As Slutsky (1937) has pointed out, cycles are the outcome of cumulative random errors of the following form:

cycles

$$Y_t = \sum e_t \qquad (9.1)$$

where the errors e_t are independent and normally distributed (i.e., white noise) terms, with a mean of zero and a constant variance. That is, expression (9.1) represents the summation of random happenings, or errors, over time and considering their cumulative impact. Expression (9.1) is often referred to as a random walk (see Section 7/2/2).

white noise

random walk

Figure 9-9 shows four graphs generated by expression (9.1). Figure 9-9(a) includes two graphs. One displays the cycles of copper prices (the difference between the actual copper prices and their long-term trend from Figure 9-4); the other displays the series, among 10 generated by expression (9.1), that has the highest correlation to the copper price cycles found (after the trend has been removed) from Figure 9-4. The obvious resemblance (see Figure 9-9(a)) between the copper price cycles and the series generated through expression

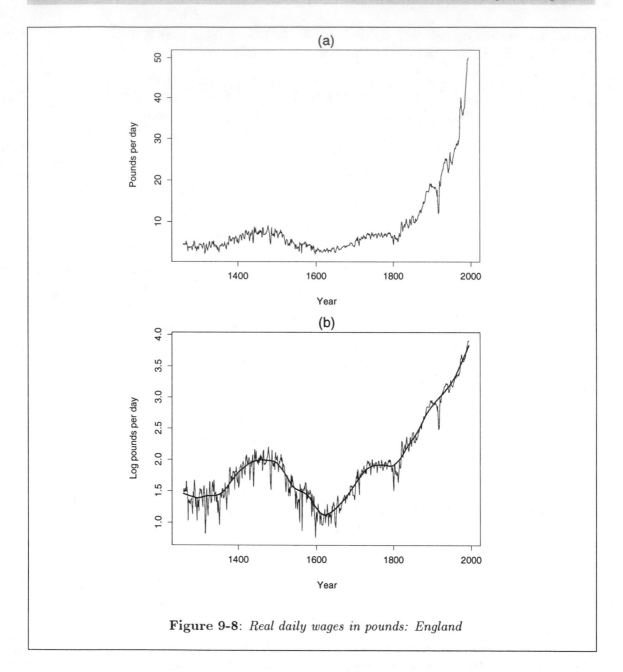

Figure 9-8: *Real daily wages in pounds: England*

(9.1) in Figure 9-9(d) is striking, suggesting that copper cycles can be thought of as the outcome of random forces whose influence is being accumulated over time. The curve in Figure 9-9(b) suggests that the cumulative effect of random fluctuations can result in strong cyclical

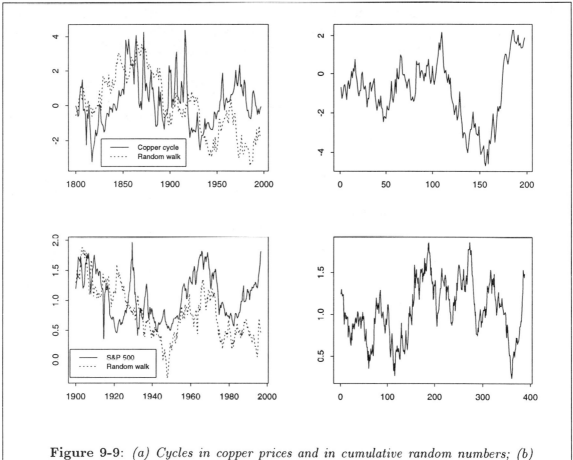

Figure 9-9: *(a) Cycles in copper prices and in cumulative random numbers; (b) Cycles in cumulative random numbers "0-200"; (c) Cycles in the S&P 500 and in cumulative random numbers; (d) Cycles in cumulative random numbers "0-400."*

patterns; these can make us believe, in an illusory manner (Langer, 1975), that there are underlying factors behind them when there is nothing more than chance happenings whose effect cumulates over time. Figure 9-9(c) shows the cycles in the quarterly values (in real terms) of the S&P 500 index as well as the best (the one with the highest correlation to the S&P 500 index) of the 10 series generated by expression (9.1). Finally, Figure 9-9(d) shows another series (selected also among 10 trials) that illustrates a strong cyclical pattern.

Y_t, as presented by expression (9.1), is a random walk and is characterized by our inability to predict its next turning point. Many

economic and business series behave like random walks, making the
most appropriate forecast, for any future value of Y_t, the most recent
actual value available (the "naïve forecast") or,

$$\hat{Y}_{t+i} = Y_t. \tag{9.2}$$

Expression (9.2) suggests that the best forecast for the future is the
current value of the series.

Figure 9-9(a) and 9-9(c) suggest that copper prices, and the quarterly S&P 500 index, once the long-term trend has been excluded,
are random walks, which cannot be predicted unless additional non-
quantitative information is available (e.g., inside information about
the market or capacity utilization rates, the power of cartels to
limit production, etc.). The random walk character of economic and
business series explains why sophisticated models, which identify and
extrapolate short- and medium-term trends, are not more accurate
(Fildes and Makridakis, 1995; see Chapter 11) than methods that
assume no trend (e.g., single exponential smoothing) or that slow
down its continuation (e.g, damped exponential smoothing). It is
highly unlikely that such cycles, and the uncertainty associated with
them, will disappear in the future. Hence, long-term forecasting must
accept both the great consistency of long-term trends and the high
extent of uncertainty (because we cannot predict their turning points
statistically) involved given the considerable fluctuations (cycles)
around such trends.

9/2/2 Implications of extrapolating long-term trends

Table 9-1 shows the effects of a 1% decline in real prices, a 2.8%
increase in the index of industrial production (IIP), a 1.8% increase
in the per capita GNP, and the corresponding improvement in buying
power. These percentages are close to the historical averages that
have prevailed in developed countries since around 1800. The table
also shows the population of the earth, assuming that its growth in
developing countries will follow the same pattern as that of developed
ones. Table 9-2 shows the same variables except for prices, which are
assumed to decline by an average of 2% per year (it is more difficult to
estimate the price declines as they will be affected by the forthcoming
technologies of the Information Revolution) instead of the 1% used
in Table 9-1.

	1890	1990	2000	2015	2050	2090
IIP (index of industrial production)	6	100	132	200	524	1582
Real GNP	17	100	120	156	292	595
Real prices	270	100	90	78	55	37
Buying power	6	100	133	200	530	1608
Earth population	30	100	120	145	240	250
Over 65: developed	4%	12%	14%	17%	24%	24%
Over 65: developing	2%	4%	5%	6%	14%	21%

Table 9-1: *The cumulative effect of growth rates: prices = −1%, per capita IIP = 2.8%, GNP = 1.8% (assuming that developing countries' population growth will follow the same pattern as that of developed ones)*

	1890	1990	2000	2015	2050	2090
IIP (index of industrial production)	6	100	132	200	524	1582
Real GNP	17	100	120	156	292	595
Real prices	725	100	82	60	30	13
Buying power	2	100	146	260	973	4577
Earth population	30	100	120	145	240	250
Over 65: developed	4%	12%	14%	17%	24%	24%
Over 65: developing	2%	4%	5%	6%	14%	21%

Table 9-2: *The cumulative effect of growth rates: prices = −2%, per capita IIP = 2.8%, GNP = 1.8% (assuming that developing countries' population growth will follow the same pattern as that of developed ones)*

The effects of cumulative growth are phenomenal. Buying power, 6 in 1890, becomes 100 in 1990, 133 in 2000, 200 in 2015, and 1608 in 2090; that is 16 times higher than in 1990 and 260 higher than in 1890. When average price decreases are assumed to be 2% (see Table 9-2), the effects are even more spectacular: buying power will be 146 in 2000, 260 in 2015, and 4577 in 2090—more than a 45-fold increase in a mere 100 years.

If the trends shown in Table 9-1 or 9-2 continue, excluding unforeseen disasters, we are about to enter into an era of full material abundance, first for Western countries and later for developing ones, where the buying of goods and services, at least standardized ones, will be done with a very small percentage of our income. The obvious implications are that people will easily own everything they need and will seek *new* products and in particular *additional* services on which to spend their increasing real income. In such an environment the biggest challenge will be to identify and quickly bring to market *novel* products and provide *extra* services to satisfy the needs of consumers who will already own practically everything available they may want.

Furthermore, this challenge will have to be met in the expectation of falling prices, which will require continuous productivity improvements so that firms will be able to survive. Success and high profits will then have to come from technological or other innovations, and from using these innovations to open new markets and satisfy new customer needs, as nearly all existing ones will have already been saturated. Success will therefore require forecasting to identify *emerging future technologies* and/or *needs* and/or *markets* rather than from past success or imitating what others have been doing well in the past.

Tables 9-1 and 9-2 highlight the opportunities (high buying power, big increases in demand in developing nations), concerns (need for continuous productivity improvements, innovation and creativity), and problems (pollution, potential social conflict between the rich and poor, a graying population in developed countries), which could be turned into business opportunities. Businesspeople will have to study these and similar trends carefully and debate alternative scenarios of how they will affect their specific country, industry, and firms. It is through such a debate that collective organizational foresight can be developed; this suggests a critical role for forecasting and forecasters.

9/3 Analogies

lack of data

Extrapolating long-term trends is limited by the fact that in many instances no, or little, historical information is available, much less data series going back to 1800. In such cases analogies can be used, allowing forecasters to make predictions based on similar situations for which past data, or accumulated experience, are available.

Analogies are used in the short-term for forecasting the implications of special events or competitive actions based on similar past examples. They are used in the medium-term for assessing the length and depth of, say, recessions by relating the current recession to all those post World War II. Similarly, they are utilized in the longer-term to predict the sales of new products or services based upon past demand for similar ones.

In this section the approach of analogies will be applied to forecasting or, more correctly, assessing the impact of computers and tele-communications (C&T), the engines behind what is referred to as the Information Revolution. In addition, the analogy between five important inventions of the Industrial Revolution and corresponding ones of the Information Revolution is explored.

9/3/1 The Information versus the Industrial Revolution

The arrival of the Information Revolution has been heralded since the late 1960s, although all predictions about its profound changes have *not* materialized as yet. Even today there are widespread complaints that white-collar productivity has not improved (Roach, 1988; 1991) despite huge advancements and substantial investments in computers and tele-communications. The critical question is whether or not the Information Revolution is on target and when precisely it will lead to significant benefits and far-reaching changes similar to those of the Industrial Revolution.

Information
Revolution

Experience with long-term forecasts has demonstrated the existence of three phases. First, predictions over the very long-term are often accurate, even though they do not have much value since the timing of their arrival is not specified. Back in 1260, for instance, Roger Bacon predicted:

> "Machines may be made by which the largest ships, with only one man steering them, will be moved faster than if they were filled with rowers; wagons may be built which move with incredible speed and without the aid of beasts; flying machines can be constructed in which a man ... may beat the air with wings like a bird ... machines will make it possible to go to the bottom of the seas."

Similarly, Leonardo da Vinci, Francis Bacon, Jules Verne, H.G. Wells, Aldous Huxley, and Arthur Clarke have made some quite astonishingly accurate predictions but without specifying the time of their occurrence (invention) or when they could be exploited for economically useful results.

In the second phase, when a new invention first appears, few people are capable of believing its value and the extent to which it can and will affect us. For example, at the beginning of the century few could predict the potential importance and widespread usage of cars, electrical appliances, telephones, radios, televisions, and so forth. Even in the early 1950s, the chairman of IBM was predicting a maximum demand for computers of no more than 100 (there are more than 100 million today) while the president of Intel was, in the early 1980s, forecasting a maximum demand for 50,000 personal computers.

Finally, euphoria prevails once the new technology has started spreading; scientists associated with the new technology, firms or individuals attempting to sell it, and technology zealots overpredict the timing and the benefits that the new technology will bring. Proponents of robots predicted, for instance, that these would be used to do *all* repetitive and routine tasks by the end of this century. It is important, therefore, not to be unduly influenced by the over-overpessimism   pessimism of disbelievers or the overoptimism of proponents. This overoptimism   is where analogies can play a significant role in helping us assess

Mechanical Power		Computer Power	
1712	Newcomen's steam engine	1946	ENIAC computer
1784	Watt's double action steam engine	1950s	IBM's business computers
1830	Electricity	1971	Time sharing
1876	Otto's internal combustion engine	1973	Microprocessor
1890	Cars	1970s	Electronic data processing (EDP)
1901	Electricity in homes	1977	Apple's computer
1914	Continuous production lines	1980s	Computers with modems
1919	Electricity in 1/3 of homes	1993	Personal computer in 1/3 of homes
Widespread use of:			
1950s	Electrical appliances	200?	Computers/communications
1960s	Cars	200?	Tele-services/shopping
1970s	Long distance telephones	200?	Tele-work
200?	Unattended factories	200?	Expert systems

Table 9-3: *From steam engines to unattended factories and from the ENIAC computer to expert systems*

forthcoming technologies and predict when their value and benefits will start becoming practical and economical. Table 9-3 shows some analogous events of the Industrial and Information Revolutions (for more information, see Makridakis, 1995) in an attempt to increase our ability to more accurately predict the changes brought by the latter.

Newcomen developed the first workable steam engine in the early eighteenth century. It took more than 200 years before Henry Ford used such an invention for building a practical and useful car that the majority of people could afford to buy, and another half a century before cars would substantially change our mode of life. Similarly, it took more than 90 years between the time electricity was invented and its widespread use by firms to substantially improve productivity. It has been estimated that it took more than 20 years at the beginning of our century before the considerable investments in electricity paid off (David, 1993).

Therefore, if technological developments in computers and tele-communications continue, and if the analogies displayed in Table 9-3 are valid, we will be entering, by the end of this century or the beginning of the next, a period when major productivity improvements from C&T will be achieved. By 2015 the Information Revolution should have provided firms with as much productivity improvement as those of the Industrial Revolution today (Makridakis, 1990). The implications are obviously far-reaching, although it may take some time before their full impact becomes widespread (see Section 9/4).

9/3/2 Five major inventions of the Industrial Revolution and their analogs

Table 9-4 shows five important technologies of the Industrial Revolution. Contributing significantly to changing the way people lived and the organization, management, and running of firms, each has achieved virtually 100% penetration in most developed countries. The obvious reason is that people want them and are willing to pay to obtain them; once luxuries, they have become necessities. It is interesting to consider analogous technologies of the Information Revolution once it will have come into full swing.

Industrial Revolution

Automobiles	Trains, trucks, tractors, boats, airplanes
Electricity	Batteries
Electrical appliances	Programmable, rechargeable
Telephones	Cordless, mobile
Television	VCR, cable, remote control

Table 9-4: *Five inventions that have contributed significant changes to our lives*

Electricity: Computer networks will be able to deliver computer power everywhere; increasingly, smaller sized computers can be connected to these networks allowing unlimited access to a great variety of services. Information can, therefore, become instantly available whenever and wherever it is needed, as electricity is today.

Electrical appliances: Software and groupware will become easy to use, providing high value in ways that are not yet clear. Much as the importance of electrical appliances was not obvious in the past, software likely will find whole new areas of application. As electrical appliances permit us to do a great variety of manual tasks much more easily and efficiently, so will software and groupware, for all aspects relating to information and its processing.

Automobiles: Instead of the physical freedom of choice that cars allow us because they let us go anywhere at any time, computers and tele-communications will permit us to achieve similar results but without having to be physically present. They will allow us to have person-to-person interaction (e.g., through tele-conferencing or tele-work/shopping) "virtually." Our freedom of choice will, therefore, increase considerably beyond that provided by cars.

Telephones: Computers and modern tele-communications augment the voice transmission capabilities of telephones in many ways. As all information can be digitized, computers will provide unheralded possibilities for all sorts of communications. "Information superhighways" will permit, for example, cheap tele-conferencing via personal computers; that will allow the customized buying of products directly from any manufacturer anywhere in the world, the obtaining of any kind of service, or the completion of work by people far away. The Internet, intranets, extranets, and similar types of networks will permit unlimited access to any information and/or person, any place in the world at any convenient time for those involved, for the mere cost of a local telephone connection.

Television: As information superhighways allow the carrying of images, music, sound, data, and any other type of information to any household, the possibilities grow limitless, not only for entertainment but also for all kinds of related leisure activities, from reading a rare book to viewing the entire work of Picasso, touring the Acropolis in Athens, or seeing any concert or theater play, current or old, anywhere in the world. In addition, the integration of communications and computers will permit a high degree of interactivity and customization of exactly what one wants when it is wanted.

The analogy of the Industrial and the Information Revolutions as well as the analyses of the development of electricity, appliances, automobiles, telephones, or television can provide useful starting points for predicting changes to come, while avoiding the bias of under-estimating the extent of such forthcoming changes—as did the famous French economist Jean-Baptiste Say, who wrote in 1843:

"No machine will ever be able to perform what even the worst of horses can—the service of carrying people and goods through the bustle and throng of a great city." (Say, 1843, p. 170.)

Long-term forecasting requires, therefore, an open mind so that a realistic and accurate picture of what is to come can be formed, debated, and once crystallized, used to develop foresight. This foresight is, in turn, indispensable for planning the long-term and formulating realistic strategies to anticipate forthcoming major changes and prepare organizations to adapt to such changes as painlessly and successfully as possible.

9/4   Scenario building

As the future is not predetermined, scenarios are attempts to visualize a number of possible futures and consider their implications. Scenarios are based in part on objective information (such as by extrapolating mega trends or by drawing analogies like the one between the Industrial and Information Revolutions), and in part on subjective interpretations and specific assumptions about critical aspects of the future. A major purpose of scenarios is to challenge conventional thinking and avoid extrapolating into the future in a linear fashion; they represent tools around which careful thinking can be centered and major issues debated so a consensus of those involved emerges.

In the remainder of this chapter several likely scenarios are presented and their implications discussed.   They all build on the extrapolation of mega trends and the analogy that the Information Revolution will bring changes of about equal magnitude and consequence to the industrial one.

9/4/1   Businesses: gaining and/or maintaining competitive advantages

overcapacity

At present, overcapacity prevails in nearly all industries except those producing luxury or some high tech products or offering personalized, high quality services. Such overcapacity drives real prices down and provides consumers with a large choice of products and services. As it is highly likely that present trends will continue, overcapacity will also prevail in the future, in particular when population growth slows down or stops. Moreover, computers and tele-communications (C&T) will continue to make the dissemination of information instant and practically free no matter where on earth such information or the person needing it is located.

competition

In this open environment competition will be fierce, further exaggerating the consequences of overcapacity. The question that cannot be answered at present is the extent to which prices will keep falling. Scenarios will even have to consider zero prices (as in commercial TV) or well-below costs (as when buying magazines or newspapers), along with the cost and pricing structure of C&T products. In that structure, the marginal cost of additional units is insignificant in comparison to R&D expenditures—for example, the cost of selling a computer program can be practically zero if sales are made through the Internet, yet development costs can be huge. Will C&T products be given away to "hook" customers to whom firms can sell new versions of the programs and additional services—including advertising for new products/services? Who will determine and/or control the standards? What will be the extent of integrating various C&T technologies and equipment? These questions cannot be answered at present, making future predictions difficult and raising the need for scenarios. Clearly, new challenges, problems, opportunities, dangers, players, and rules will continuously emerge.

As all routine, repetitive, and standard tasks and decisions will be automated, gaining and/or maintaining competitive advantages will require innovative and motivated employees. Will firms become like advertising agencies, where the critical factor is the creative talent of key people? Alternatively, will innovative/creative thinking be bought or subcontracted? But if creative talent can be bought/subcontracted, where would a firm's competitive advantages come from if everything, including creative talent, could be bought on the outside? Perhaps creativity will become the scarce resource—the major, if not single, factor determining success. In such a scenario only firms that can best map the creative potential of their employees will be capable of gaining and/or maintaining competitive advantage.

creativity

The role and value of creativity

A $5,000 top-of-the line multimedia notebook computer weighing less than 3 kg is worth today about the same as 10,000 kg of potatoes. Producing potatoes requires few skills and can be achieved at quantities greater than the demand for all the potatoes people can eat. Competition is, therefore, fierce, forcing prices downward and reducing farmers' profit margins. Designing, producing, and selling top-line notebook computers, on the other hand, require considerable skills and creativity, which are not readily available except at a dozen firms in a few developed countries, while potatoes can be grown practically everywhere. The inability to produce as many top-line notebook computers as demanded permits firms to charge high prices and realize big profit margins. High value added always comes from products or services whose demand is greater than their supply, and laptops/potatoes are no exception.

automation   Since the Industrial Revolution the widespread use of machines has brought *dramatic* improvements in productivity and huge increases in the production of both agricultural and industrial goods. Simultaneously, it resulted in considerable cost and, consequently, price reductions, which increased the demand for these goods. As the pace of technological innovation has accelerated, so has automation, further increasing productivity and production and slashing costs and prices at an exponential rate. Finally, as technology has become relatively cheaper *and* more readily available, it is being employed to a great extent throughout the world, creating overcapacity in practically all industries producing or offering standardized goods or services.

By extrapolating established trends, there is little doubt that in 10 to 15 years down the road superautomation will be widespread and the production of all standardized goods and the rendering of all standardized services will be done with few or no people, at quantities as high above demand as agricultural products stand today. At that time the only products/services that will not be in great oversupply will be new or unique ones. The ability to supply such products/services is bound, therefore, to become the single most important factor determining success and creating wealth to nations, firms, and/or individuals. In such an environment the most critical concerns will be (a) how firms become "creative" and (b) how to cultivate and best exploit their creative potential to gain and/or maintain competitive advantages. However, as benchmarking will be practiced on a grand scale and as information will be instantly disseminated on a global basis, it will be relatively easy for competitors to quickly identify and imitate successful, creative ideas, making it difficult to prolong success unless creativity can be continuously maintained.

creative thinking   Creativity requires novel thinking that can produce useful results. If creativity, or the thinking process needed to achieve it, could be standardized, it would become mundane, and "creativity" would be raised to a higher level that would still demand originality. A major challenge for organizations will therefore be how to enter this above-average category and stay there, knowing that their competitors will also strive to be as creative as possible. Another challenge will be how to change the present mentality in organizations, which rewards conformity and encourages traditional thinking, to one that values originality. If firms do not prepare themselves to become creative they will have no choice but to remain in markets/industries characterized by overcapacity and diminishing profit margins. Scenarios taking into consideration the role and value of creativity will need to be considered so that firms can debate the consequences involved and be proactive in changing themselves to better prepare for the future.

9/4/2 Jobs, work, and leisure time

Because automation will eliminate nearly all repetitive and routine tasks (both manual and mental), the type of jobs available will be fundamentally changed. On the one hand, there will be jobs requiring *jobs* a high level of mental skills, both personal and interpersonal, and/or talents. On the other hand, there will be jobs that provide personal services but which require few or no special skills/talents—cleaning the streets or collecting the garbage, for instance. The former type of jobs are at present much higher paid and provide more satisfaction than the latter. This raises two questions. Will there be enough jobs of the first type to satisfy the demand of the majority of the working population? And who does the dull, uninteresting jobs— particularly if we consider a full-abundance society where food and basic necessities could be available to almost everyone? The supply and demand in the job market may shift considerably if the pool of skillful/talented workers becomes global, while the great majority of low skill/talent jobs require physical presence and will have to be, therefore, local. Scenarios built around these issues need to be constructed so that their implications can be debated.

A related question is the division between work and leisure time. *work and leisure* If we assume that a great number of people will only work when their job is interesting and satisfying, then work itself may become a hobby, indistinguishable from leisure activities. Great artists and scientists as well as highly successful professionals work long hours not because they are obliged to do so but because they enjoy their work and gain significant pleasure from the accomplishments it brings. At the same time, those doing boring, uninteresting jobs will wish to work as little as possible, having a lot of free time for leisure activities. How precisely the job market and the nature of work will evolve and what the implications will be for businesses, and society in general, is not obvious; thus, again, the need for debate and scenarios.

9/4/3 Physical versus tele-interactions: extent and speed of acceptance

There is no doubt that tele-communications and multimedia comput-ers will open brand-new possibilities that will fundamentally change (as the Industrial Revolution did) all aspects of our societies (work, education, shopping, and entertainment), especially as the cost of C&T becomes increasingly lower. The hotly debated question is whether or not people will opt for using multimedia technologies (including tele-conferencing) on a grand scale, choosing to shop and obtain services, work, entertain themselves, and communicate through "tele-means" rather than physically. The answer depends upon the value and cost as well as the inconvenience of each alter-native, where the social pleasure of physical interaction is one of the factors added to "value."

tele-shopping

If tele-shopping is done directly from the manufacturer, prices can be substantially lower since all intermediaries are avoided. Moreover, if buying can be done through the manufacturer of one's choice, no matter where in the world it may be located, the choices available will be practically infinite.

tele-services

Whatever is true for products is even more so for services. Once a multimedia computer terminal is connected to a network that pro-vides access to service firms around the world, there are no constraints or limits to tele-services—which can extend beyond traditional ones to include education and even medical diagnosis. In the realm of entertainment, C&T networks will allow for essentially unlimited choices and a high degree of interactivity and personalization of what one chooses to watch or play, individually or with others. Moreover, entertainment can move into directions neither fully understood nor explored.   Interactive games played by people located far away, gambling at home, and virtual reality simulations will be possible in the future, for example.

tele-work

Tele-work is less straightforward. It is clear, however, that with tele-conferencing and computer-conducted meetings, efficiency can be greatly improved without the need of participants being co-located; data and information can be displayed, minutes kept, action steps verified, and various decisions and their implications viewed and debated.   Moreover, as the cost of such tele-work lessens, firms using these new technologies will be at a competitive advantage over traditional ones relying on extensive office space to conduct their business.

Although it is not possible to predict the exact percentage of people who will work, shop/obtain services, educate, and entertain themselves mostly at home, we can safely assume that the penetration of multimedia computers connected to at least one national and probably one global network in the year 2015 will extend to nearly all households in advanced countries. Moreover, buying standardized products and obtaining standardized services as well as getting all types of entertainment through the computer network will be commonplace, as the cost of using C&T will have become insignificant and the prices of tele-shopping/services and tele-entertainment will be lower than those of alternatives.

What is unknown is how quickly people will adopt the available technology and whether or not by the year 2015 there will be one-third or five-sixths of the population that use tele-means to shop/obtain services, work, and entertain themselves. Similarly it is not known whether one-third or five-sixths of knowledge transfer will be done through multimedia programs versus through a teacher talking in front of his or her students. However, if the use of tele-means has not become widespread by 2015, it will be so by 2025 or 2035. It is a matter of time, making it necessary for individuals, firms, and governments to start considering the implications involved and build alternative scenarios of how a future of practically free computers and tele-communications would look like.

References and selected bibliography

DAVID, P. (1993) Investment in electricity and payoffs, *Stanford Working Paper*, Stanford University.

FILDES, R. and S. MAKRIDAKIS (1995) The impact of empirical accuracy studies on time series analysis and forecasting, *International Statistical Review*, **63**(3), 289–308.

GROVE, A.S. (1996) *Only the paranoid survive: how to exploit the crisis points that challenge every company and career*, New York: Currency Doubleday.

HALAL, W.E. and M.D. KULL (1996) "1996 Delphi forecast of emerging technologies: a biennial survey of expert opinion," Working Paper, Department of Management Science, George Washington University.

HAMEL, G. and C.K. PRAHALAD (1994) *Competing for the future: breakthrough strategies for seizing control of your industry and creating the markets of tomorrow*, Boston: Harvard Business School Press.

HUSS, W.R. (1988) A move towards scenario analysis, *International Journal of Forecasting*, 4, 377–388.

JOHNSON, P. (1991) *The birth of the modern: world society 1815–1830*, London: Weidenfeld and Nicolson.

LANGER, E.J. (1975) The illusion of control, *Journal of Personality and Social Psychology*, **32**(2), 311–328.

MAKRIDAKIS, S. (1990) *Forecasting, planning and strategy for the 21st century*, New York: Free Press.

——————— (1995) The forthcoming information revolution: its impact on society and firms, *Futures*, **27**, 799–821.

ROACH, S.S. (1988) Technology and the services sector: the hidden competitive challenge, *Technological Forecasting and Social Change*, **34**, 4.

——————— (1991) Services under siege—the restructuring imperative, *Harvard Business Review*, September–October.

SAY, J.-B. (1843) *Cours complet d'economie politique pratique*, Paris: Atheneo.

SCHOEMAKER, P.J.H. (1995) Scenario planning: a tool for strategic thinking, *Sloan Management Review*, 25–39.

SLUTSKY, E. (1937) The summation of random causes as the source of cyclic processes, *Econometrica*, **5**, 105–146.

VAN DER HEIJDEN, K. (1996) *Scenarios: the art of strategic conversation*, Chichester: John Wiley & Sons.

WACK, P. (1985) Scenarios: uncharted waters ahead, *Harvard Business Review*, **55**, 73–89.

Exercises

9.1 Build a scenario about the future implications of the following new inventions:

    (a) There have been several computer programs developed recently that recognize continuous speech and turn it into written text in a computer word processing program.

    (b) In 1997, an IBM computer program (Deep Blue) beat the world chess champion (Kasparov).

    (c) Today one can buy a PC running at 266Mhz and having 32 megabytes of RAM memory and 3 gigabytes of disk memory, plus many other powerful characteristics, for under $1,500. (In 1968 an electrical calculator which would only perform the four basic arithmetic functions used to cost $1,000–$4,000 in 1997 prices.)

9.2 Today one can buy a color photocopier which can also be used as a color computer printer, as a plain paper color fax machine and as a scanner. The price of this all-inclusive machine is under $1,000. Such a machine together with the powerful $3,000 computer mentioned above are all that one needs to work from home, in particular since the computer also includes a modem and can connect to the Internet.

Comment on the implication of this for the future of tele-work.

9.3 Consider the price trends in computers and office equipment. A computer whose speed was a fraction of a Mhz and which had only 8,000 words of RAM memory cost $10,000 in 1968 ($40,000 in 1997 prices). Similarly, a thermo-paper fax machine, or black-and-white photocopier cost more than $1,000 a decade ago.

Comment on the implication of these price trends for the future of tele-work.

9.4 In Johnson (1991), the following quote is said to have been made by Samuel Taylor in 1801. Comment on this quote.

> Samuel Taylor, of Fox & Taylor, flatly refused to believe that machinery could replace skilled craftsmen. He insisted that the existing method was perfect: "I have no hope of anything better ever being discovered, and I am convinced there cannot be."

Comment also on the following two quotes:

> "There is no reason for any individual to have a computer in their home."
>
> > Ken Olson, 1977. Chairman and CEO, DEC.

> "Digital Television defies the laws of physics."
>
> > Senior CBS Executive, 1991.

10

JUDGMENTAL FORECASTING AND ADJUSTMENTS

The statistical forecasting methods presented in Chapters 3 to 8 allow us to extrapolate established patterns and/or existing re- lationships in order to predict their continuation, assuming that such patterns/relationships will *not* change during the forecasting phase. At the same time, because changes can and do occur, these must be detected as early as possible to avoid large, usually costly, forecasting errors.

extrapolation

detecting changes

However, when changes are detected, or if we can know when they are about to occur, human judgment is the only viable alternative for predicting both their extent and their implications on forecasting. Human judgment is also needed to incorporate inside information and knowledge, as well as managers' experience, about the future. Before using our judgment for improving forecasting accurately, however, we must understand its biases and limitations along with its major advantages. Doing so allows us to combine the information from our statistical predictions with those of our judgment (Clemen, 1989) by exploiting the advantages of both while avoiding their drawbacks.

human judgment

10/1 The accuracy of judgmental forecasts

Although we make innumerable forecasts every day (for both our organizations and our personal lives), we expend little effort in evaluating them to find ways of improving their accuracy. The reason is simple: we do not want to be held responsible if our forecasts go wrong. However, unless we get feedback about the accuracy of our predictions, it is not likely that we can improve our performance when making similar forecasts in the future. Because judgmental forecasts are much more common than statistical ones (see Chapter 11), not only can we not ignore them, but we must also be willing to accept that judgmental forecasting errors cannot be entirely avoided; we will be better off if we can accept such errors while learning as much as possible from them so we can improve our ability to forecast more accurately in the future.

The accuracy of judgmental forecasts is, on average, inferior to statistical ones. This is because our judgment is often characterized by considerable biases and limitations. In the following sections the available evidence that compares judgmental to statistical forecasts is presented (see also the bibliography for this and subsequent chapters).

We will also see that the accuracy of our judgmental predictions can be improved by using some generally simple statistical models; the cost of such models is, moreover, significantly less than that of the people making the forecasts. The challenge for forecasters, therefore, is to avoid the limitations posed by their judgment by combining the best aspects of statistical methods with those of their judgment while avoiding its biases. This chapter explores that challenge and suggests specific steps for dealing with it.

10/1/1 The accuracy of forecasts in financial and other markets

A large number of forecasts are made virtually every day on the stock, bond, interest, foreign exchange, and futures markets. As the purpose of buying and selling in these markets is to maximize profits, it is straightforward to evaluate the accuracy of these market forecasts either directly (as in the case of investment newsletters, which provide advice about the market and/or specific stocks), or indirectly, that is, when investment managers and analysts buy and/or sell stocks, bonds, etc., for themselves or their clients.

The advice of newsletters for investments

newsletters

In a comprehensive study of 237 investment strategies recommended by newsletters over a period of 13 years (1980 to 1992), Graham and Harvey (1995) conclude the following about the accuracy of these strategies:

1. Only 22.8% of newsletters have average returns higher than a passive portfolio of equity and cash with the same volatility. Indeed, some recommendations are remarkably poor. For example, the (once) high profile *Granville Market Letter-Traders* has produced an average annual loss of 0.4% over the past 13 years. This compares to a 21.1% average annual gain on the Standard and Poor's 500 price index.

2. Consistent with mutual funds studies, we find that poor performance is far more persistent than good performance.

3. Most of our tests focus on the ability of newsletters to call the direction of the market, that is, market timing.

We find little evidence that equity weights increase before future positive market returns or decrease before negative ones. We find no evidence that the investment letters as a group have any knowledge over and above the common level of predictability.

4. The bottom line is that very few newsletters can "beat" the S&P 500. In addition, few can beat the market forecasts derived from a statistical representation of publicly available information. There is no evidence that the letters can time the market (forecast direction). Consistent with mutual funds studies, "winners" rarely win again and "losers" often lose again.

Investment newsletters have, therefore, no value for those seeking an accurate forecast of financial markets (or better, their advice produces consistent losses). A random selection of stocks outperforms the advice of more than three-quarters of the investment newsletters written by supposedly knowledgeable professionals.

Professionally managed investment funds

If investment newsletters provide only "advice" for investment decisions, professional managers of investment funds make actual ones by investing many billions in the stock, bond, and other markets. Their performance is not satisfactory. Figure 10-1 shows the percentage of professional managers who, over a period of three, five, and ten years, have beaten the S&P 500 index, or the benchmark master bond index. This percentage is always below 50%, indicating that these managers have not done better than someone selecting stocks and bonds randomly—that is, if the managers had used the random walk model in Chapter 7:

$$\hat{Y}_{t+h} = Y_t . \qquad (10.1)$$

The random walk approach uses the most recent actual value as the forecast for the next period. It captures the notion that the next observation is equally likely to be greater than or less than the most recent actual value.

The same conclusion can be drawn from Figure 10-2, which shows the average return of professionally managed funds versus

investment funds

random walk

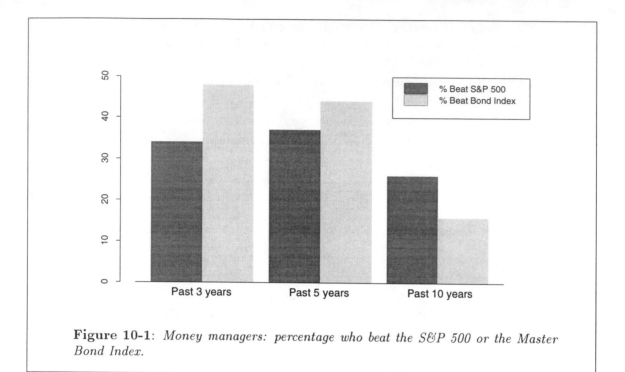

Figure 10-1: *Money managers: percentage who beat the S&P 500 or the Master Bond Index.*

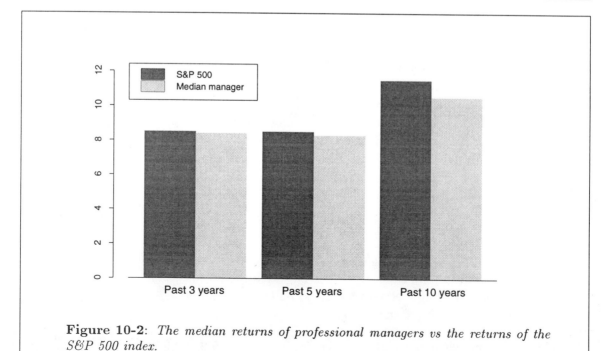

Figure 10-2: *The median returns of professional managers vs the returns of the S&P 500 index.*

those of the S&P index. The median of professional managers consistently underperforms this index by a significant amount. Investors would have been better off (richer), on average, therefore, had they chosen their stocks and bonds randomly, using (10.1), rather than paying the "experts" to do so.

Finally, Table 10-1 shows the performance of various types of mutual funds in 1994 and over the 1984–1994 period. No mutual fund did better than the market average in 1994 or over the 1984–1994 period, with the one exception in 1994, when the losses of municipal bond mutual funds were smaller (−5.18% versus −5.6%) than those of the municipal bond index. Glassman (1997) provides several reasons why professional managers do not outperform random selections of various investment instruments. One of the most important reasons is that the

Type of fund	1994 total return	1984–1994 average annual return
Aggressive growth stocks	−3.1%	13.4%
Growth stock	−2.1%	12.8%
Growth and income stock	−1.5%	11.8%
S&P 500 index	1.3%	14.4%
International stock	−2.9%	15.7%
Morgan Stanley foreign stock index	7.8%	17.6%
Government bond	−3.6%	8.3%
Treasury bond	−4.1%	8.2%
Lehman Bros. government bond index	−3.4%	9.6%
Municipal bond	−5.2%	8.4%
Lehman Bros. municipal bond index	−5.6%	9.4%

Table 10-1: *The performance of mutual funds. Do mutual funds with their professional managers beat the market?: Their 1994 and 1984–1994 performance.*

			Returns				
	1988	1989	1990	1991	1992	1993	Total
Garzarelli	−13.1	22.5	−7.2	31.5	7.7	5.0	41.9
Ave. fund	15.7	25.1	−6.1	36.7	9.1	4.8	85.3
S&P 500	16.6	31.7	−3.1	30.5	7.6	4.9	88.2

Table 10-2: *Superstar (guru) Elaine Garzarelli predicted the 1987 stock market crash. She was extremely bullish on stocks early in 1994. She was fired by Lehman Brothers on October 27, 1994, for poor performance.*

managers' objective is not to maximize investors' returns but rather their own bonuses, which are related to how much better they do than the market average. This objective encourages them to take too many risks and buy and sell stocks with timing that shows above-average returns.

Talented forecasters and investment gurus

gurus

stock market crash

In October 1987, one week before the stock market collapse that sunk the S&P index by 40%, Elaine Garzarelli, a stock market analyst, gained considerable fame by having advised her clients to sell their stocks. Doing so saved them millions of dollars and made Garzarelli a celebrity. Subsequently, she started an investment fund whose performance, until she was fired in July 1994, can be seen in Table 10-2. Garzarelli's fund underperformed the market consistently and by a large factor. It also did worse than the average investment fund by less than half. Her "foresight" in predicting the October 1987 crash did not extend beyond this single event, since she obviously missed the subsequent ups and downs of the market (see Table 10-2). The performance of her fund lost many millions of dollars for her clients, who would have been much better off had they selected their stocks at random. Her past success was not a good predictor of her future performance.

Some investment gurus have consistently outperformed the market. But they represent a tiny exception, confirming the rule that past above-average performance does not indicate such performance will continue in the future. Obviously, if there are many investors, some will do better than average

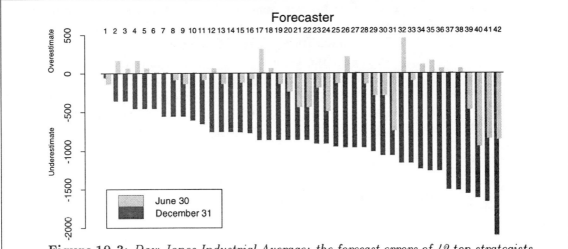

Figure 10-3: *Dow Jones Industrial Average: the forecast errors of 42 top strategists (made in late December 1995 for 30 June 1996 and 31 December 1996).*

because of pure chance. However, even top forecasters make huge mistakes, as can be seen in Figure 10-3, which lists forecast errors in predicting the Dow Jones Industrial Average. The forecasts of these top strategists for major Wall Street investment firms were made in late December 1995 for June 30, 1996 and December 31, 1996. Strategists underestimated the DJIA at the end of 1996: six of them by over 1500 points, one by close to 2300 points; and the majority did so for June 30, though by smaller amounts.

Other evidence points to the same conclusion. All markets where information is widely disseminated and that cannot be influenced by a few players behave like random walks, making it impossible to predict them more accurately than by using today's price as the best possible forecast—that is, expression (10.1) (the naïve forecast). This conclusion has serious impli-   naïve forecast
cations for investing, yet the majority of investors are unwilling to accept either the conclusion or its implications.

Understanding the reasons for such unwillingness helps us evaluate the role and value of judgmental forecasting. We do not want to accept the considerable empirical evidence telling us that the most profitable way of investing in the various markets is to select stocks, bonds, futures contracts, etc., randomly because we do not like the uncertainty implied by the naïve model (10.1). In addition, we tend to be convinced that some "expert" can do better than a random selection, and that belief will both reduce our uncertainty and generate a better-than-average return. This belief, or bias, is, however, without merit, and if we manage to avoid it we can improve the profits from our investments, or at least reduce our losses, while not having to pay anyone for providing us a service of negative value.

10/1/2 Non-investment type forecasts

Although empirical evidence concerning judgmental forecasts for areas other than investments is not as plentiful, the conclusion is similar: the accuracy of these forecasts is, on average, inferior to statistical ones. In this section the evidence from salespeople, management, and "expert" predictions are presented.

Salespeople forecasts

salespeople forecasts

"Salesmen" forecasts were once very popular, since salespeople, being close to customers, are presumably in a position to know about forthcoming changes in the marketplace. Empirical evidence (Walker and McClelland, 1991; Winklhofer et al., 1996) has shown, however, that salespeople's forecasts are notoriously inaccurate. Worse, they fluctuate considerably depending upon the mood of the moment and whether the last few sales calls were successful or not. In addition, salespeople are often rewarded when they sell above some target, which is itself usually determined by some type of "forecasting." Thus, they have an interest in setting low targets that can be easily achieved or exceeded, thereby receiving a bonus. At the same time, sales managers want to set high sales targets to motivate their salespeople. So they adjust the sales force estimates upward, thereby confusing objective forecasts with the attainment of desired targets. Finally, salespeople determine how sales are doing at present in their own territory rather than how they will do in the future when conditions may be different. For all these reasons, their judgmental predictions are not the most appropriate means to decide about the overall future sales of firms.

Management forecasts

Managers, unlike salespeople, have a more global picture of the firm, its market(s), and the economy. However, they are often overoptimistic about the firm's future or the products they are responsible for (see the example of Elco Electronics below); managers rarely forecast decreasing sales or predict that products will fail, for instance. Managers are also not the appropriate forecasters to assess competitive threats or the impact of new technologies that might make their products obsolete. Hence, their forecasts are usually no more accurate than those of statistical methods, whose major advantage is objectivity. This does not mean that managers or salespeople cannot make accurate predictions (see Walker and McClelland, 1991) or that they do not possess valuable information that could greatly improve a firm's ability to predict the future correctly. Rather, they are overoptimistic and do not separate personal or political interests from the best way for achieving the most accurate predictions, as was shown to be true in the Walker and McClelland (1991) study, which also illustrated the inferiority of management forecasts when compared with statistical models.

management forecasts

Eurotunnel forecasts

The actual cost of building the Eurotunnel was more than twice the original estimate while its intended date of opening was missed by almost two years. This is the usual pattern for similar forecasts of big projects, whose costs and completion times are seriously underestimated while potential revenues are exaggerated. In the case of Eurotunnel, it was estimated in 1986 that 16.5 million passengers would use its rail services during the first year of operation. This forecast was reduced to 13 million in 1993, and subsequently cut to 6 million in 1994. The actual number of passengers during the first full year of operation (1995) was only 3 million (half the number predicted in 1994 and less than 20% of the initial 1986 forecast). At the beginning of 1996, the most optimistic forecast was 10 million passengers by the end of the decade.

big project forecasts

"Expert" forecasts

expert forecasts

There is significant empirical evidence comparing "expert" forecasts with those of statistical models. In nearly all cases (Dawes, 1988; Hogarth and Makridakis, 1981; Kahneman et al., 1982; Meehl, 1954) where the data can be quantified, the predictions of the models are superior to those of the expert. The implications of these findings, as well as those mentioned above, have critical consequences if the objective is to improve forecasting accuracy and reduce the uncertainty of our predictions. We humans are not good forecasters, sometimes for good reasons (imagine a product manager predicting that his or her new product will fail: the obvious course of action would be to not launch the product at all). Our judgment is influenced by a number of biases and other limitations that influence the way we forecast and, therefore, decrease the accuracy of our predictions. These biases are described next.

10/2   The nature of judgmental biases and limitations

memory limitations

Most of us are well aware of the limitations of our memory; we know we cannot remember everything, so we take concrete steps to avoid negative consequences. We write down, for example, the names of people and businesses in alphabetical order, along with their addresses and phone numbers, in a booklet or electronic organizer for easy retrieval. Doing so, however, does not imply that our memory is deficient; on the contrary, the human memory is of enormous value. But its vast capacity would be filled in days if everything were indiscriminately stored, so a crucial task is determining what is important to remember and what can be ignored. The more our memory is relieved of the burden of storing trivial facts, the greater its capacity to store and easily retrieve more important information.

Yet, while we accept the deficiencies and limitations of our memory (and thus jot down what we want to remember later on), we rarely do anything to remedy the deficiencies of our judgment (Hogarth and Makridakis, 1981)—mainly because we are unwilling to accept that our judgment can be faulty or biased. Because judgmental biases are almost never presumed to exist, it is extremely important to expose them: empirical evidence clearly demonstrates their existence and their negative, damaging consequences. Judgmental biases do not imply stupidity, however; their presence is clearly discernible among highly intelligent people. Rather, they result from the way the mind operates and reflect its attempts to reconcile conflicting objectives.

10/2/1 Judgmental biases in forecasting

Imagine that you work for Elco Electronics, a company with some 2,000 employees, as the product manager for laser printers. Accounting for about 40% of Elco's revenues, these printers can also be used as fax machines, scanners, and photocopiers. Competition in the laser printer market is fierce, from both new entrants at home and imports primarily from Pacific Rim countries. As product manager, you must decide how many units of each of 10 models of printers to produce and ship to distributors, and whether or not to invest in new plant and equipment. Making those decisions requires forecasting.

Figure 10-4 shows Elco's sales of laser printers since 1992. Al-

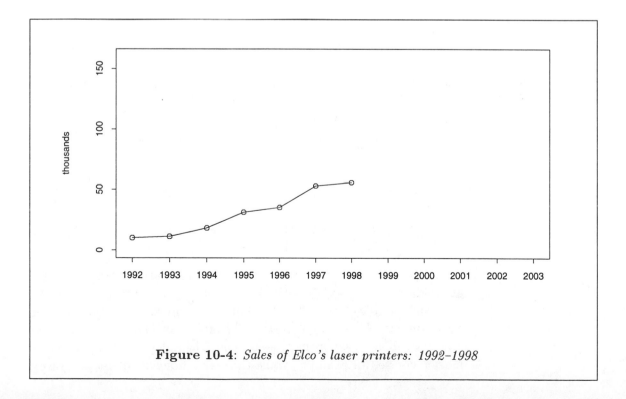

Figure 10-4: *Sales of Elco's laser printers: 1992–1998*

though sales have seen a healthy increase in the past, your concern is the future. You must make a unit sales forecast (in addition to price, competition, and so on) for next year and for five years from now. What will, in your opinion, be the forecast for 1999 and 2003, including a low, pessimistic sales figure and a high, optimistic one?

Year	Low (pessimistic) Forecast	Most likely Forecast	High (optimistic) Forecast
1999	——————	——————	——————
2003	——————	——————	——————

Table 10-3: *Forecast the sales of laser printers for 1999 and 2003 (consult Figure 10-4)*

straight-line extrapolation

In fact, there is no right or wrong forecast in predicting the sales of laser printers. If a third party (like yourself) were asked to forecast Elco's sales, he or she would most likely predict a straight-line extrapolation from the past to the future. Thus, the most likely forecast, around which most answers will hover, is about 65,000 units for 1999 and 99,000 units for 2003. That is because it is assumed that what has happened in the past will continue to happen in the future; the various factors causing sales to go up or down will cancel themselves out as Elco and its competitors make moves and countermoves that effectively neutralize each other. This is the approach used by people making judgmental forecasts when no additional inside information is available, and when personal or political considerations are not at stake. In practice, such an approach, although mechanistic, seems to work better than alternatives. Interestingly enough, forecasts of the statistical technique of trend extrapolation provide very similar numbers as third parties who are asked to make judgmental predictions concerning Elco's sales.

What is important, however, is how the forecasts change if people are told that the data in Figure 10-4 represent a new (or, alternatively, a mature or old) product. As shown in Figure 10-5, the answers vary widely, which demonstrates how often we ignore concrete data and instead forecast using stereotypes (the sales of a new product must increase, for example, while those of an old one must decrease).

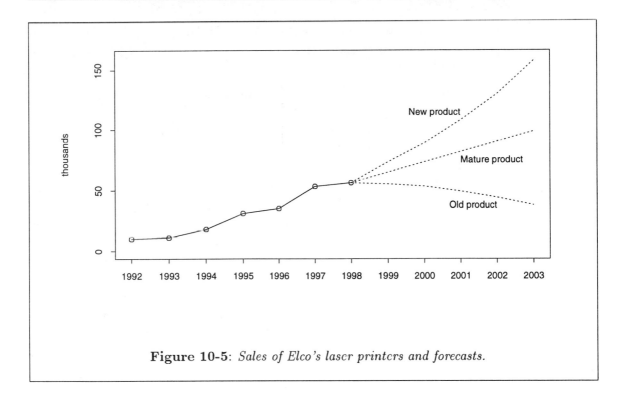

Figure 10-5: *Sales of Elco's laser printers and forecasts.*

In fact, the differences in the forecasts for new, mature, and old products (in particular for 2003) are enormous, highlighting the need to exclude judgmental biases while forecasting. After all, it cannot be automatically assumed that sales will increase in more than a straight line simply because a product is new—particularly in the personal computer industry where the life cycle of products rarely exceeds a couple of years, making a seven-year-old product not a new but an extremely old one. Yet this type of mistake is constantly made by people who are asked to predict the sales at Elco.

One author gave the same data in Figure 10-4 to a group of product managers who were told that the information represented the past sales of a product from their company. They extrapolated the figures to show an exponential increase similar to the one of "new product" in Figure 10-5. However, another group of managers of the same company, provided with the same information but told that it related to a product belonging to their major *competitor*, forecast an exponential decline, similar to the one of "old product" in Figure 10-5! Obviously, such differences in forecasting are caused by personal considerations, springing from optimism or wishful thinking, and have little or nothing to do with an objective assessment of future conditions.

Finally, all respondents who saw Figure 10-4 considerably underestimated the uncertainty involved (the estimation of the interval between high and low forecasts). This was true in particular for 2003, when sales could be a great deal lower than the lowest interval and much higher than the highest interval specified by the respondents. Many things can happen over five years, but respondents consistently underestimated future uncertainty regardless of their position (MBA students, middle managers, top managers) or their background (MBAs, engineers, fine art students; financial, marketing, or general managers). Assuming a linear trend, a realistic estimate, based on statistical theory, of the low and high sales value for 1999 is from 50,000 to 79,000 units. For 2003, the same figures are from 78,000 to 119,000 units. The vast majority of people estimated these intervals to be less than half of those postulated by statistical theory, which, it must be added, estimates its intervals assuming that the established pattern will *not* change.

prediction intervals

10/2/2 Dealing with judgmental biases

The entire subject of judgmental biases could take many volumes to treat thoroughly and cannot, therefore, be covered in this chapter in detail (see Kahneman and Tversky, 1979). Thus, we intend to discuss those aspects of judgmental biases that most critically and directly affect forecasting.

inconsistency

Inconsistency, a human bias with serious negative consequences, refers to changing our minds (or decisions) when there is no need to do so. Consider a production manager who must forecast how much to manufacture for each of 10 products in the coming month. Bowman (1963), back in the 1950s, found that production managers' forecasts (and actual decisions) about how much to produce fluctuated from month to month for no apparent good reason. Indeed, simply by making decisions consistent, forecasting accuracy and profitability improved. Bowman's findings have been reproduced in a great number of studies (Hogarth and Makridakis, 1981), and the conclusion is always the same: repetitive, routine forecasts (and decisions in general) can be improved if inconsistency is removed. People, however, are often unable or unwilling to apply the same criteria or procedures when making similar decisions. Sometimes they forget; other times they are influenced by their mood of the day (think of a forecast made the morning after a quarrel with one's partner and a sleepless night). Other times people might be bored and want to try something new. Finally, they might believe that conditions have changed when they actually have not.

Production managers are not the only ones whose decisions are inconsistent. Meehl (1954), in a small but influential book, concluded that decision rules using a few variables predict better than people, mostly because the models can consistently apply the same decision criteria, while people are inconsistent in their choice of factors on which to base their decisions. Meehl's conclusions have been confirmed by hundreds of additional studies. Decision rules in the form of simple statistical models have been found to outperform expert judges when repetitive, routine decisions were involved (Dawes, 1988). These decisions included medical diagnoses, psychological predictions about people's personality traits, selection of students to be admitted to colleges or universities, predicting future earnings of companies, and so forth. There is hardly any evidence showing that expert decision makers do better than decision rules. Obviously, these studies refer to repetitive, routine decisions, but even then the conclusions are surprising, as in the case of medical diagnosis. Garland (1960), for instance, reported a study in which experienced X-ray specialists failed, about 30% of the time, to recognize the presence of lung disease that was definitely visible on the X-ray film. Similarly, studies found that radiologists changed their minds about 20% of the time *when given the same X-ray on two different occasions.*

Inconsistency can be avoided by formalizing the decision-making process (today this is called building expert systems). This would require deciding, first, which factors are important to consider in making a certain repetitive decision; second, how such factors should be weighted (one might be twice as important as another or vice versa); and third, what objective should be optimized. The usefulness of decision rules derives from the fact that several people can be involved in determining them, thus making it possible to select the best factors, an optimal weighting scheme, and the most viable objective(s). Since the rule will be used again and again, it makes sense to devote significant effort and resources to coming up with the best one

expert systems

decision rules

possible. The rule can subsequently be applied on a routine basis, freeing considerable human resources and contributing to improving forecasting accuracy or, more generally, decision making.

Consider, for instance, whether or not a purchase by a Visa cardholder should be approved. Doing so on a case-by-case basis takes numerous credit officers and becomes an expensive operation. Now consider finding all important factors that credit officers use to decide whether or not to approve a credit request. Since many officers can be consulted and a great deal of effort can be devoted to the process, the most relevant factors can be found and included in a statistical model, which would determine if such factors are indeed important and how much weight should be given to each. A decision rule will thus be established, allowing a clerk to enter the required information and let the model reach a decision. As the objective is to minimize fraudulent purchases, an expert system can be built and credit officers would be consulted only in the exceptional case, where the model indicates a gray area and cannot decide. With such a system fewer officers are required and decisions are consistent and objective. Equally important, the decisions can be evaluated after the fact in ways that can help further improve the model, if necessary.

Given today's computer technology and tele-communications capabilities, decision models of the type just described can be economically developed and profitably applied on a routine basis. Visa has indeed applied such decision-making models with considerable improvements in efficiency and profits. Similar decision rules can be applied when making judgmental forecasts.

monitoring

Obviously, decision rules cannot be used indefinitely. The environment changes, as does competition; new objectives might be set and so on. Thus, the effectiveness of decision rules must be monitored constantly to make sure they are still appropriate. That means learning must be introduced into the expert system; otherwise, we run the risk of applying obsolete rules. Too much consistency can be as dangerous as inconsistency, for it excludes learning and leads to another bias, conservatism.

This is precisely the problem with biases: in trying to avoid one we might cultivate another. A bias in this case exists precisely because our minds must ensure consistency but must also allow for learning. The challenge facing all of us, therefore, is to be consistent while at the same time introduce mechanisms to ensure learning and eventually changes in the decision rules to adapt to new conditions. For forecasters this is a critical challenge, in particular for long-term predictions, where learning is infrequent and changes abound.

Can biases be avoided if decisions are made in groups? Unfortunately not—in fact, evidence suggests that groups amplify bias (Janis, 1972) by introducing groupthink, a phenomenon that develops when group members become supportive of their leader and each other, thus avoiding conflict and dissent during their meetings. Moreover, group decisions are more risky, as responsibility for the decisions taken cannot be attributed to any single individual.

groupthink

Table 10-4 describes those biases we have found (through our experience of working with companies, our research work, and relevant findings in the forecasting literature) to be of critical importance for forecasting and future-oriented decision making in general. It also provides suggestions to help prevent or mitigate their impact.

common biases

A prominent example of one such bias, recency (remembering recent events more vividly, which consequently influences our judgment to a greater extent than less recent events), concerns oil prices between 1965 and 1988. During that period basic economic facts were ignored and many mistakes made as organizations and governments overreacted to the latest price levels and made decisions assuming that such prices (or the trends involved) would last forever. This turned out to be wrong both before 1973, when they were going down, and between 1974 and 1981, when they were increasing at a steep pace. If all the information about oil prices (see Figure 10-6) had been used, it would have suggested that real oil prices would remain constant in the long-term. This was true both before 1974 and now. Thus, it should have been assumed that the deviations around the long-term trend would be temporary and that the market would return to its long-term equilibrium captured by the oil price's mega trend (see Chapter 9). In reality this has happened, even though oil prices skyrocketed from $14.2 in 1973 to $64.7 seven years later. As Figure 10-6 shows, oil prices in 1997 were very close to the long-term, mega trend of such prices.

Type of bias	Description of bias	Ways of avoiding or reducing the negative impact of bias
Inconsistency	Being unable to apply the same decision criteria in similar situations	• Formalize the decision-making process • Create decision making rules to be followed
Conservatism	Failing to change (or changing slowly) one's own mind in light of new information/evidence	• Monitor for changes in the environment and build procedures to take actions when such changes are identified
Recency	Having the most recent events dominate those in the less recent past, which are downgraded or ignored	• Realize that cycles exist and that not all ups or downs are permanent • Consider the fundamental factors that affect the event of interest
Availability	Relying upon specific events easily recalled from memory to the exclusion of other pertinent information	• Present complete information • Present information in a way that points out all sides of the situation being considered
Anchoring	Being unduly influenced by initial information which is given more weight in the forecasting process	• Start with objective information (e.g., forecasts) • Ask people to discuss the types of changes possible; ask the reasons when changes are proposed
Illusory correlations	Believing that patterns are evident and/or two variables are causally related when they are not	• Verify statistical significance of patterns. • Model relationships, if possible, in terms of changes

Table 10-4: *Common biases in forecasting and proposed ways of avoiding or reducing their negative impact.*

Type of bias	Description of bias	Ways of avoiding or reducing the negative impact of bias
Search for supportive evidence	Gathering facts that lead toward certain conclusions and disregarding others that threaten them	• Induce disconfirming evidence • Introduce role of devil's advocate
Regression effects	Persistent increases (or decreases) might be due to chance rather than a genuine trend.	• One needs to explain that if the errors are random, the apparent trend is unlikely to continue.
Attribution of success and failure	Believing success is attributable to one's skills while failure to bad luck, or someone else's error. This inhibits learning as it does not allow recognition of one's mistakes	• Do not punish mistakes, instead encourage people to accept their mistakes and make them public so they and others can learn to avoid similar mistakes in the future. (This is how Japanese companies deal with mistakes.)
Optimism, wishful thinking	People's preferences for future outcomes affect their forecasts of such outcomes	• Have forecasts made by a disinterested third party • Have more than one person independently make the forecasts
Underestimating uncertainty	Excessive optimism, illusory correlation, and the need to reduce anxiety result in underestimating future uncertainty	• Estimate uncertainty objectively. Consider many possible future events by asking different people to come up with unpredictable situations/events
Selective perception	Seeing problems in terms of one's own background and experience	• Ask people with different backgrounds and experience to independently suggest solutions

Table 10-4 continued: *Common biases in forecasting and proposed ways of avoiding or reducing their negative impact.*

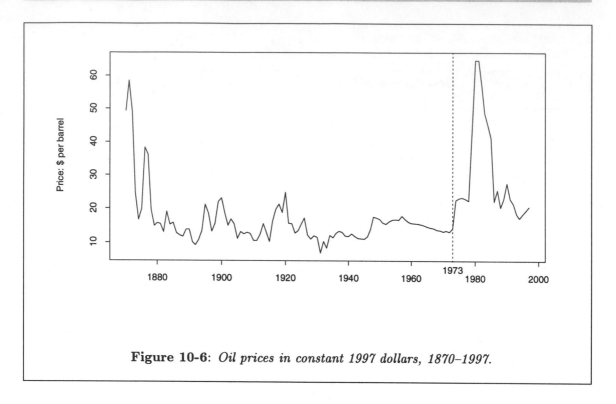

Figure 10-6: *Oil prices in constant 1997 dollars, 1870–1997.*

10/2/3 Conventional wisdom

conventional wisdom

Another type of judgmental bias that can threaten decision-making effectiveness is unfounded beliefs or conventional wisdom. We believe, for instance, that the more information we have, the more accurate our decisions will be. Empirical evidence does not support such a belief, however. Instead, more information merely seems to increase our confidence that we are right without necessarily improving the accuracy of our decisions. This is a finding reached by Oskamp (1965) and many other researchers, who warn against devoting energy and resources to gathering a lot of information. In reality, the information found is usually redundant and provides little additional value, if not being outright harmful since it increases our confidence about the future.

discriminating
information

Another example of conventional wisdom we are willing to accept is that we can discriminate between useful and irrelevant information. Empirical research indicates that this is rarely the case. In experiments, subjects supplied with "good" and "bad" information are not capable of distinguishing between the two. In addition, the irrelevant information is often used, decreasing decision-making effectiveness particuarly if the relevant information is of a quantitative nature and the irrelevant is qualitative (most people seem to weight "verbal" information more heavily than numbers).

Table 10-5 summarizes relevant conventional wisdom, including the two examples already offered. It also lists the evidence available through empirical and laboratory studies. As with the biases discussed, the conventional wisdom listed in Table 10-5 can greatly influence our forecasts and decisions in general. It is, therefore, important to avoid negative consequences by establishing procedures aimed at minimizing their impact through the use of empirical findings listed in Table 10-5.

10/3 Combining statistical and judgmental forecasts

The big challenge in arriving at accurate forecasts is to utilize the *best* aspects of statistical predictions while exploiting the value of knowledge and judgmental information, while also capitalizing on the experience of top and other managers. In the remainder of this chapter we describe an approach one of the authors has been using in many firms, which exploits the advantages of both judgmental and statistical forecasts while avoiding their drawbacks. The example involves coming up with budget forecasts, but it is applicable to other situations requiring predictions.

10/3/1 Arriving at final forecasts during a budget meeting

In annual budget meetings, usually held in October or November, budget meetings the major objective is to decide how much sales will grow in the following year. Based on such growth, many other decisions are made about how resources should be allocated and long-range plans implemented; hence, considerable effort is devoted to forecasting overall sales growth rate as accurately as possible.

There are conflicting interests of those participants in the budget meeting, however, with marketing executives usually opting for a

Conventional Wisdom	Empirical Findings
1. The more information we have, the more accurate the decision.	The amount of information does not improve the accuracy of decisions, instead it increases our confidence that our decision will be correct.
2. We can distinguish between useful and irrelevant information.	Irrelevant information can be the cause of reducing the accuracy of our decisions.
3. The more confident we are about the correctness of our decision, the more accurate our decision will be.	There is *no* relationship between how confident one is and how accurate his or her decision is.
4. We can decide rationally when it is time to quit.	We feel we have invested too much to quit, although the investment is a sunk cost.
5. Monetary rewards and punishments contribute to better performance.	Human behavior is too complex to be motivated by monetary factors alone.
6. We can assess our chances of succeeding or failing reasonably well.	We are overly optimistic and tend to downgrade or ignore problems and difficulties.
7. Experience and/or expertise improve accuracy of decisions.	In many repetitive, routine decisions, experience and/or expertise do *not* contribute more value to future-oriented decisions.
8. We really know what we want, and our preferences are stable.	Slight differences in a situation can change our preferences (e.g., most people prefer a half-full to a half-empty glass of water).

Table 10-5: *Conventional wisdom versus empirical findings*

higher growth and production executives for lower. In a typical budget meeting the final growth rate represents the outcome of a bargaining process, which sometimes has little to do with forecasting (see Walker and McClelland, 1991) and much more to do with the relative power of each executive participating in the meeting, his or her ability to persuade the others, personality, and political considerations, the opinion of the CEO, and tradeoffs to minimize conflict. It becomes important, therefore, to provide a solid, objective base and a systematic procedure to forecast next year's growth rate as accurately as possible. For this to become possible the influence of judgmental biases and other nonobjective considerations must be minimized.

Anchoring the initial forecast objectively

Anchoring is a judgmental bias that develops if someone starts with an initial growth rate forecast that may not be realistic but which serves as an anchor that keeps the final forecast close to it. This anchoring effect becomes even more serious if the chairman and CEO start by specifying a growth forecast for next year: the discussion focuses on (anchors) such a forecast and does not consider alternatives far away from it. To avoid this bias and even use it for beneficial purposes, everyone in the meeting can be given a folder in advance that contains historical information about the economy, industry, and firm; this information is extrapolated, providing objective forecasts for the economy, industry, and firm.

anchoring

It is also made clear that these forecasts will only be valid if, and only if, the future will be a continuation of the past. However, participants are told that it is fairly certain that changes are likely to occur and that they, in the group, are in the best position to assess the magnitude and consequences of the changes.

The participants are asked, therefore, to use their knowledge of the market and competition as well as their experience and inside information about next year to estimate the *extent* to which the objective forecast of the growth rate *ought to be changed,* and to write down the factors involved. That is, the participants are *not* asked to make a forecast from scratch; rather, they are instructed to modify the statistical one, which is, therefore, used as an anchor to prevent predictions that may not be grounded in the firm's objective past performance and prevailing economic/industry conditions. At the same time, participants are asked to provide which reasons they believe will be responsible for whatever modification they are proposing to the statistical, objective predictions. Finally, they write down their forecasts anonymously so that they will not influence each other by their rank or functional position.

All forecasts have, as such, the same weight and are all anchored around objective, statistical predictions. To facilitate and clarify the process, a form similar to Table 10-6 is provided to each participant to fill in anonymously after he or she has read the background information provided in the folder. Once the forms are collected, their results are tabulated, summarized, and presented to participants before the discussion starts.

Three observations can be made from our experience with the use of these forms. First, participants are indeed anchored to the statistical, objective forecasts, which are changed only if there are strong reasons to believe doing so is necessary. Second, factors that some participants consider to increase sales are considered by other participants to decrease sales; thus, these factors can be disregarded unless subsequent discussion can prove their importance one way or the other. Third, most factors for increasing, or decreasing, sales are provided only by one or two participants rather than by everyone or even a strong majority. The discussion, therefore, can concentrate on the one or few factors that everyone, or a good majority, believes to be influential, and focus on agreeing on the extent to which these factors will influence next year's sales—for it is rare to have a consensus about the extent of changes.

Once the budget meeting has concluded, participants agree upon a final forecast. It has exploited the objectivity advantage of statistical methods, which can best identify and extrapolate established patterns, and it has drawn upon inside information and the experience of top management about forthcoming changes and their implications. The approach also directs discussion to where it is most useful and makes the meeting more efficient and effective.

Finally, by having agreed on the factors that will affect sales growth for next year *and* by having estimated the extent of such change, it is possible to evaluate, at the end of next year, the accuracy of top management's predictions versus that of the statistical method(s). As

By extrapolating the historical quantitative information available the best estimate for the growth rate in our sales for 1999 is 3.5%. Such statistical estimate assumes that 1999 will be similar to the previous years. This is the equivalent of saying that no major changes will occur or that these changes will cancel themselves out. If you believe that major changes will indeed occur in 1999, specify them below under the appropriate heading and estimate their positive or negative influence using the 3.5% growth rate as the base.

Factors involved (please specify factor)	Estimated effect of the various factors in changing the estimated growth rate of 3.5%	
	% Positive influence of the factor listed in increasing the sales	% Negative influence of the factor listed in decreasing the sales
Economic		
Industrywide		
Competitive		
Technological		
Others (specify)		
Overall Influence	**% Positive =**	**% Negative =**
Your own estimate of the growth rate	3.5% + % Positive influence − % Negative influence 3.5% +	− =

Table 10-6: *Form used to justify the factors that will influence the quantitative forecast*

such, not only the accuracy of the statistical versus judgmental forecasts can be compared, but the relative accuracy of each participant
can likewise be assessed, along with his or her ability to correctly
predict each of the factors considered important in affecting sales.
Thus, participants can get feedback in the following year about how
well they have predicted, individually and as a group; this should help
them improve the judgmental accuracy of their future predictions. In
addition, the various factors that have affected sales can be evaluated,
providing quantitative information to assess their impact in the future
when similar changes are considered again.

10/4 Conclusion

Judgmental forecasts are indeed indispensable, for they present the
only alternative to predicting systematic changes from established
patterns and/or existing relationships. At the same time, we must be
careful to avoid the biases and other limitations that characterize our
judgment while reducing their negative consequences on forecasting.
The challenge for firms is to exploit both the advantages of statistical
predictions (including their low cost) and the unique ability of human
judgment to deal with systematic changes in patterns/relationships
which statistical methods cannot predict as they can only extrapolate
the continuation of such patterns/relationships.

In this chapter we described judgmental biases and limitations and
suggested an approach using statistical predictions as an objective
anchor; it can be modified judgmentally, based on participants'
experience, inside information, and knowledge about how the future
will be different from the past and present. Given the use of computer
networks (e.g., intranets) and increasingly sophisticated software,
such an approach will be employed to a much greater extent in
the future (see Chapter 12) to improve forecasting accuracy and
effectiveness.

References and selected bibliography

BERNSTEIN, P.L. (1996) *Against the gods: the remarkable story of risk*, New York: John Wiley & Sons.

BOWMAN, E.H. (1963) Consistency and optimality in managerial decision making, *Management Science*, **10** (1), 310–321.

BUNN, D. and G. WRIGHT (1991) Interaction of judgmental and statistical forecasting methods: issues and analysis, *Management Science*, **37**, 501–518.

CLEMEN, R. (1989) Combining forecasts: a review and annotated bibliography, *International Journal of Forecasting*, **5**, 559–584.

CONROY, R. and R. HARRIS (1987) Consensus forecasts of corporate earnings: analysts' forecasts and time series methods, *Management Science*, **33** 725–738.

DAWES, R.M., D. FAUST, and P.E. MEEHL (1989) Clinical versus actuarial judgment, *Science*, **243**, 1668–1674.

DAWES, R.M. (1988) *Rational choice in an uncertain world*, New York: Harcourt Brace Jovanovich.

GARLAND, L.H. (1960) The problem of observer error, *Bulletin of the New York Academy Medicine*, 569–584.

GLASSMAN, J. (1997) In a random universe, the case against funds, *Washington Post Service*, January 4.

GOLDBERG, L.R. (1970) Man vs model of man: a rationale, plus some evidence, for a method of improving on clinical inferences, *Psychological Bulletin*, 422–432.

GOODWIN, P. and G. WRIGHT (1993) Improving judgmental time series: a review of the guidance provided by research, *International Journal of Forecasting*, **9**, 147–161.

GRAHAM, J.R. and C.R. HARVEY (1995) "Market timing and volatility implied in investment newsletters' asset allocation recommendations", Working paper, Duke University Graduate School of Business.

HARVEY, N. (1995) Why are judgments less consistent in less predictable task situations? *Organizational Behaviour and Human Decision Processes*, **63** (3), 247–263.

HENRY, R.A. and J.A. SNIEZEK (1993) Situational factors affecting judgments of future performance, *Organizational Behaviour and Human Decision Processes*, **54**, 104–132.

HOGARTH, R. and S. MAKRIDAKIS (1981) Forecasting and planning: an evaluation, *Management Science*, **27**, 115–138.

JANIS, I.L. (1972) *Victims of groupthink*, Boston: Houghton Mifflin.

KAHNEMAN, D. and A. TVERSKY (1979) Intuitive prediction: biases and corrective procedures, *TIMS studies in management sciences*, **12**, 313–327.

KAHNEMAN, D., P. SLOVIC, and A. TVERSKY (1982) *Judgment under uncertainty: heuristic and biases*, Cambridge, England: Cambridge University Press.

LAWRENCE, M.J. and S. MAKRIDAKIS (1989) Factors affecting judgmental forecasts and confidence intervals, *Organizational Behaviour and Human Decision Processes*, **43**, 172–187.

LAWRENCE, M.J. and M.J. O'CONNOR (1992) Exploring judgmental forecasting, *International Journal of Forecasting*, **8**, 15–26.

——————— (1993) Scale, randomness and the calibration of judgmental confidence intervals, *Organizational Behaviour and Human Decision Processes*, **56**, 441–458.

——————— (1995) The anchoring and adjustment heuristic in time series forecasting, *Journal of Forecasting*, **14**, 443–451.

LAWRENCE, M.J., R.H. EDMUNDSON, and M.J. O'CONNOR (1986) The accuracy of combining judgmental and statistical forecasts, *Management Science*, **32**, 1521–1532.

——————— (1995) A field study of sales forecasting: its accuracy, bias and efficiency, Working paper, School of Information Systems, University of New South Wales, Australia.

MAKRIDAKIS, S. (1990) *Forecasting, planning and strategy for the 21st century*, New York: The Free Press.

——————— (1996) Forecasting: its role and value for planning and strategy, *International Journal of Forecasting*, **12**, 513–539.

MATHEWS, B.P. and A. DIAMANTOPOULOS (1986) Managerial intervention in forecasting: an empirical investigation of forecast manipulation, *International Journal of Research in Marketing*, **3**, 3–10.

MCNEES, S.K. (1990) The role of judgment in macroeconomic forecasting accuracy, *International Journal of Forecasting*, **6**, 287–299.

MEEHL P.E. (1954) *Clinical versus statistical prediction: a theoretical analysis and review of the literature*, Minneapolis: University of Minneapolis Press.

OSKAMP, S. (1965) Overconfidence in case-study judgments, *Journal of Consulting Psychology*, **29**, 261–265.

ROTHCHILD, J. (1988) *A fool and his money: the odyssey of an average investor*, New York: Viking.

SANDERS, N.R (1992) Accuracy of judgmental forecasts: a comparison, *OMEGA International Journal of Management Science*, **20** (3), 353–364.

SILVERMAN, B.G. (1992) Judgment error and expert critics in forecasting tasks, *Decision Sciences*, **23** (5), 1199–1219.

WALKER, K.B. and L.A. MCCLELLAND (1991) Management forecasts and statistical prediction model forecasts in corporate budgeting, *Journal of Accounting Research*, **29** (2) 373–382.

WASON, P.C. and P.N. JOHNSON-LAIRD (1972) *Psychology of reasoning: structure and content*, London: Batsford.

WEBBY, R. and M. O'CONNOR (1996) Judgmental and statistical time series forecasting: a review of the literature, *International Journal of Forecasting*, **12**, 91–118.

WINKLHOFER, H., A. DIAMANTOPOULOS, and S.F. WITT (1996) Forecasting practice: a review of the empirical literature and an agenda for future research, *International Journal of Forecasting*, **12**, 193–221.

Exercises

10.1 In 1996 the giant firm of Philips Electronics lost $350 million on revenues of $41 billion. For the last five years Philips has been having great trouble modernizing itself and turning to profitability. During this time the various chief executive officers that passed through Philips were promising "to fix" Philips' problems but so far they have failed. Could one believe current announcements that Philips' problems will be corrected in the future?

10.2 Glassman (1997) describes the reasons why various investment funds do not outperform the average of the market. Comment on the following quotes from Glassman's article:

> "For the third year in a row, fewer than one-fourth of U.S. stock mutual funds beat the Standard & Poor's 500 index. Once again, the vast majority of professionals who are paid to choose the best stocks could not beat the broad market averages."

> "This year's failure—the ninth in the past thirteen years, according to Lipper Analytical Services Inc.—brings to mind a famous quotation from *A Random Walk Down Wall Street*, by Burton Malkiel: 'A blindfolded monkey throwing darts at a newspaper's financial pages could select a portfolio that would do just as well as one carefully selected by the experts'..."

> "Fund managers are not stupid. Why do they do so poorly? One reason is that, to a great degree, stock-picking is a 'random walk'; stocks are priced so efficiently by the market that finding winners may be a matter of luck. If that is true, then the typical mutual fund will do about what the averages do, minus its fees and expenses. But most do worse. Why?... The biggest problem for managers is that they are frantic rather than patient. The typical fund had a turnover rate of 83 percent for stocks in its portfolio, according to Morningstar..."

> "Managers are manic because they have to show strong short-term returns in order to attract or hold antsy investors. They cannot buy a great underpriced company and wait five years for it to bloom, or they will lose their jobs..."

"...managers have to justify their salaries by appearing to do something..."

"Finally, managers of large funds have to worry about owning too large a chunk of the companies in which they are investing. If you own millions of shares, you will not be able to sell without pushing the price down sharply..."

"Most fund managers do not care about your taxes; their bonuses are determined strictly on pretax returns, and, after all, many investors own funds in tax-deferred retirement accounts..."

"If the market crashes and investors run for the exits, most mutual fund managers will have to sell stocks in order to raise cash to meet the redemption demands of their shareholders. In such a debacle, smart investors will be buying stocks at bargain prices; mutual funds will not have that luxury..."

10.3 The U.S. economy has been growing without interruption since May 1991. The longest previous expansion in the U.S. economy lasted for 105 months while the average post World War II expansion has been lasting a little more than 50 months. What can one say about the current expansion? Can we say how long it will be before it is interrupted by a recession?

10.4 If you were to count, only once, from 0 to 100, how many times will you encounter the number eight?

11

THE USE OF FORECASTING METHODS IN PRACTICE

This chapter describes the usage of the statistical forecasting methods presented in Chapters 3 through 8, based on surveys among forecasting users.

surveys

It also presents empirical evidence concerning the post-sample forecasting accuracy of all major methods—information that is necessary in order to narrow the gap between what forecasting can really achieve and what various users expect. This information is also necessary for providing guidelines so that forecasts (both statistical and judgmental) can be made as accurate as possible while the uncertainty associated with them can be correctly assessed and clearly communicated to potential users. In addition, if more tasks are needed than simply extrapolating established patterns and relationships, then users must be provided with the type of information they need so an appropriate method for their *specific* forecasting situation can be proposed. Such a choice depends upon four factors:

empirical evidence

(a) whether users want simply to forecast, or they also want to understand and influence the course of future events;
(b) the characteristics of the time series;
(c) the time horizon of forecasting;
(d) the number of predictions required.

Finally, this chapter discusses the combination, or averaging, of forecasts and presents evidence from both within and outside the field; it shows that, in the majority of cases, such combining results in more accurate post-sample predictions than the individual methods being averaged. This empirical evidence also demonstrates that the uncertainty of the combined forecasts is smaller than that of the individual methods averaged together.

combination forecasts

11/1 Surveys among forecasting users

There have been more than 35 surveys among forecasting users (Winklhofer et al., 1996) since 1970. These studies have elicited users' responses concerning their familiarity with and usage of various forecasting methods, their satisfaction with such methods, at which area and forecasting horizons these methods have been applied, the magnitude of errors, as well as many other questions. This section summarizes the studies' conclusions and presents some key tables taken mainly from the work of Mentzer and Cox (1984) and of Dalrymple (1987), which is, in our view, the most complete. The interested reader can consult the bibliography at the end of this chapter for additional references or read the survey paper by Winklhofer et al. (1996) concerning the usage of forecasting in practice.

In summarizing their survey of surveys, Winklhofer et al. (1996) conclude that although a great deal of work has been done, some issues (e.g., the role and level of forecasting) have been neglected, and some linkages (e.g., data sources utilized) have been left unexplored. Moreover, Winklhofer and his colleagues observe that while company size and industry membership have been widely utilized to explain differences, other potentially relevant variables, such as environmental turbulence and the degree of formalization or centralization of the forecasting function within the firm, have been ignored. Similarly, they conclude that although certain interrelationships have been examined, others, like those between the resources committed to forecasting and forecast performance, have not. For this reason they propose that more research is needed to cover these neglected issues and aspects in order to make forecasting more useful and relevant for practitioners.

11/1/1 Familiarity and satisfaction with major forecasting methods

level of familiarity

Table 11-1, which is based on the Mentzer and Cox (1984) study, indicates the level of familiarity of more than 150 U.S. managers with a number of subjective and quantitative (objective) methods of forecasting. On the basis of this table and the results of similar questions from other studies (Wilson, 1996; Sanders and Manrodt, 1994; Wheelwright and Clarke, 1976; and Dalrymple, 1975), a number of observations can be made:

judgmental forecasts

1. Forecasting users are very familiar with the subjective (judgmental) methods of jury of executive opinion, sales force composite, and customer expectations.

simple methods

2. Users are also very familiar with the simpler quantitative methods of moving averages, straight-line projection, exponential smoothing, and the more statistically sophisticated method of regression.

3. Moving average is the most familiar of the objective methods, although, from empirical studies, it is not as accurate as the method of exponential smoothing.

4. The Box-Jenkins methodology to ARIMA models is the least familiar of the methods included in Table 11-1. The same is true with other sophisticated methods of which practitioners are not much aware.

ARIMA models

5. Classical decomposition is the second least familiar method. Only about one half of the respondents indicated any familiarity with this method, although it is one of the most useful, since it can distinguish the various subpatterns (seasonality, trend cycle, and randomness) of a data series and can be used to seasonally adjust a data series. Only the Wilson study showed a higher percentage of usage of this method. (Wilson does not report users' familiarity with the various methods.)

time series decomposition

Respondents' overall satisfaction with various methods is shown in Table 11-2. It is interesting that forecasting users are less satisfied with subjective methods than with objective methods, and they are not simply neutral with regard to subjective methods. Dissatisfaction with subjective methods is higher than it is with objective methods. This observation is consistent with the findings discussed in Chapter 10. A number of additional observations can also be made on the basis of Table 11-2:

1. Regression is the method users have the highest level of satisfaction with, despite empirical findings that time series methods are more accurate than explanatory (regression and econometric) methods. However, since regression can be used for purposes other than simply obtaining forecasts, this finding is not, therefore, surprising and proves the point made earlier: higher accuracy is not the only criterion for selecting a certain forecasting method.

regression

2. The method with which users were next most satisfied is exponential smoothing. This finding is consistent with empirical studies reporting that exponential smoothing is capable of considerable accuracy, is easy to understand, and can be used routinely and with little effort to forecast for many, often thousands, of items.

exponential smoothing

Method	Very Familiar	Vaguely Familiar	Completely Unfamiliar
Subjective			
Jury of executive opinion	81	6	13
Sales force composite	79	5	16
Customer expectations	73	7	20
Objective (quantitative)			
Moving average	85	7	8
Straight-line projection	82	11	7
Exponential smoothing	73	12	15
Regression	72	8	20
Trend-line analysis	67	16	17
Simulation	55	22	23
Life cycle analysis	48	11	41
Classical decomposition	42	9	49
Box-Jenkins	26	9	65

Table 11-1: *Familiarity with forecasting methods (as a percentage of those responding). Source: Mentzer and Cox (1984).*

moving average
trend-line analysis

3. The methods of moving average and trend-line analysis also produced a high level of satisfaction. Furthermore, trend-line analysis had one of the smallest percentages of dissatisfied users. This finding is somewhat surprising in light of empirical evidence suggesting that neither method does very well on the criterion of accuracy, and that exponential smoothing tends to outperform both of these methods on many commonly used accuracy criteria. However, both of these methods have intuitive appeal for practitioners. In specific cases the trend-line is utilized for benchmarking (if the future will be a linear extrapolation of the past) purposes, while moving average is used to remove randomness from the data.

Box-Jenkins method

4. Users were the least familiar and the most dissatisfied with the Box-Jenkins method. This result is consistent with empirical findings indicating that the method is difficult to understand

Method	Satisfied	Neutral	Dissatisfied
Subjective			
Jury of executive opinion	54	24	22
Customer expectations	45	23	32
Sales force composite	43	25	32
Objective (quantitative)			
Regression	67	19	14
Exponential smoothing	60	19	21
Moving average	58	21	21
Trend-line analysis	58	28	15
Classical decomposition	55	14	31
Simulation	54	18	28
Life cycle analysis	40	20	40
Straight-line projection	32	31	37
Box-Jenkins	30	13	57

Table 11-2: *Satisfaction with forecasting methods (as a percentage of those responding). Source: Mentzer and Cox (1984).*

and apply while its post-sample accuracy (see below) is often not better than that of much simpler methods, such as exponential smoothing. Wilson (1996) reports a higher satisfaction rate than that indicated in Table 11-2, but the reason is probably because many of his respondents were academics.

5. It is somewhat surprising that classical decomposition does not fare better in Table 11-2. One reason might be that it is as much a tool for analysis as a forecasting method. However, its perceived value is certainly below what the empirical evidence on performance would suggest. Moreover, its ability to decompose a series into seasonality, trend-cycle, and randomness is of high importance and of great intuitive appeal to managers. classical decomposition

6. Finally the satisfaction of users concerning expert systems and neural networks is not high: 21.7% and 30% respectively (Wilson, 1996). expert systems neural networks

Method	Forecast Period					
	D 1–3 months	M-C 0–3 months	D 4–12 months	M-C 3–24 months	D over 1 year	M-C over 2 years
Subjective						
Sales force composite	23.1	37	34.3	36	5.2	8
Jury of executive opinion	18.7	37	29.1	42	6.7	38
Intention to buy survey	10.4 ⎫		11.2 ⎫	24	4.5 ⎫	12
Industry survey	8.2 ⎭		15.7 ⎭		11.4 ⎭	
Extrapolation						
Naive Forecast	34.3	–	17.9	–	0.7	–
Moving average	17.9	24	12.7	22	2.2	5
Percentage rate of change	10.4 ⎫	21	13.4 ⎫	28	8.2 ⎫	21
Unit rate of change	9.7 ⎭		9.7 ⎭		4.5 ⎭	
Exponential smoothing	9.7	24	9.0	17	6.7	6
Line extension	6.0	13	8.2	16	3.7	10
Leading indicators	3.7	–	20.1	–	7.6	–
Quantitative						
Box-Jenkins	6.0	5	3.7	6	2.2	2
Multiple regression analysis	5.2 ⎫		11.9 ⎫	36	4.5 ⎫	28
Simple regression analysis	5.3 ⎭		7.5 ⎭		3.0 ⎭	
Econometric models	2.2	4	10.4	9	7.5	10

M-C: adapted from Mentzer and Cox (1984)

D: adapted from Dalrymple (1987)

Table 11-3: *Percentage of respondents using techniques for different forecast horizons.*

11/1/2 The use of different forecasting methods

Mentzer and Cox (1984), like others before and after them, surveyed the use of different forecasting methods for different forecasting horizons. Their results, summarized in Table 11-3, suggest several points:

1. The jury of executive opinion is the most widely used fore- judgmental forecasts
   casting method; furthermore, its usage is uniform across all
   forecasting time horizons. Although this method has some
   advantages, it also has some serious disadvantages, as discussed
   in Chapter 10.

2. Sales force composites and customer expectations are used less
   for the long-term and more for the medium- and short-terms.
   Overreliance on these two methods, and on the jury of executive
   opinion, introduces considerable bias into forecasting. Empirical findings have shown that salespeople are overly influenced
   by recent events.

3. Exponential smoothing and moving average methods are used exponential
   more for short-term, less for medium-term, and even less for smoothing
   long-term horizons; this is consistent with empirical evidence,
   which indicates that these methods perform best for shorter
   time horizons.

4. It is surprising that the straight-line projection method is used trend-line projection
   for short-term horizons. Given seasonality and cyclical factors,
   ups and downs in the short-term make straight-line extrapolations highly inaccurate. Even for the medium-term, trend-line
   extrapolation is not very accurate, according to empirical studies.

5. The Box-Jenkins method is not used very much for any fore- Box-Jenkins method
   casting horizons, which is consistent with empirical findings.

6. Finally, regression is used most often for medium-term, followed regression
   by long-term, forecasting horizons. This is consistent with
   theoretical reasoning that postulates that in the medium- and
   long-terms, more emphasis should be placed on understanding
   the variables to be forecast and the factors that influence them.
   Such understanding can be substantially aided with regression
   analysis.

The level at which different forecasting methods are used is shown
in Table 11-4. The jury of executive opinion method is used more
than any other method for all forecasting levels except product
forecasting, while customer expectations and sales force composite

Method	Organizational level				
	Industry Forecast	Corporate Forecast	Product Group Forecast	Product Line Forecast	Product Forecast
Subjective					
Jury of executive opinion	26	41	32	32	22
Customer expectations	8	12	18	18	23
Sales force composite	5	20	25	27	24
Objective (quantitative)					
Regression	18	22	21	29	12
Trend-line analysis	13	20	20	21	22
Simulation	7	9	7	4	4
Straight-line projection	6	10	11	10	11
Life cycle analysis	4	4	4	4	6
Moving average	4	9	18	19	20
Exponential smoothing	4	6	14	14	23
Box-Jenkins	2	3	3	2	6
Classical decomposition	2	4	8	7	9

Table 11-4: *Percentage of respondents using different techniques for different organizational level forecasts. Source: Mentzer and Cox (1984).*

methods are used at least as much at the level of the product. As the extent of disaggregation increases, moving average and exponential smoothing methods are used more frequently, while regression is used most frequently at the level of product line forecasts. (This is consistent with both theoretical reasoning and empirical findings.) Finally, straight-line analysis is used about the same amount across all organizational levels, although from a theoretical point of view it is more appropriate at higher levels of aggregation.

The application areas where the various methods are being used are shown in Table 11-5. Production planning is the heaviest user of forecasting, followed by budgeting and strategic planning. Surprisingly, material requirements planning was one of the areas making the least use of forecasting, although it is one that could greatly benefit from accurate forecasts. Perhaps respondents did not distinguish

	Total	Primary Decision	Secondary Decision
Production planning	73	36	20
Budgeting	54	11	25
Stratgetic planning	45	6	18
Sales analysis	29	14	5
Inventory control	26	13	9
Marketing planning	22	8	13
Logistics planning	17	8	3
Purchasing	10	3	7
Material requirements planning	10	3	7
Production planning	4	0	0
		100	100

Table 11-5: *Percentage of respondents for different application areas where forecasts are used. Source: Mentzer and Cox (1984).*

between production planning and material requirements planning, even though material requirements planning precedes production planning.

Finally, Table 11-6 shows the percentage of regular use of forecasting methods by industrial and consumer firms as reported by Dalrymple (1987). Overall, it seems that industrial firms are heavier users than consumer firms. This is surprising; forecasting is usually more accurate for consumer products, because the number of customers is much larger and because cycles influence consumer goods less than industrial products. At the same time, certain statistical methods (moving average and exponential smoothing) are used more by consumer firms than by industrial firms.

The conclusions of surveys among forecasting users leave little doubt that much more can be done to increase the usage of formal forecasting methods in business and other organizations, which are still heavily reliant on subjective forecasting methods. Sanders and Manrodt (1994) make this point in their paper (p. 100):

Method	Percent of Industrial Firms	Percent of Consumer Firms
Subjective		
Sales force composite	33.9	13.0
Jury of executive opinion	25.4	19.6
Industry survey	6.8	8.7
Intentions to buy	6.8	4.3
Extrapolation		
Naive Forecast	18.6	17.4
Leading indicators	16.9	2.2
Moving average	8.5	10.9
Unit rate of change	6.8	6.5
Percentage rate of change	5.1	15.2
Exponential smoothing	3.4	10.9
Line extension	1.7	6.5
Quantitative		
Econometric models	10.2	4.3
Multiple regression	10.2	4.3
Simple regression	5.1	2.2
Box-Jenkins		
Number of firms	59	46

Table 11-6: *Regular usage of sales forecasting techniques by industrial and consumer firms. Source: Dalrymple (1987).*

"Like past investigations (surveys) we found that judgmental methods are the dominant forecasting procedure used in practice. However, two trends may indicate a greater readiness on the part of managers to embrace formal forecasting procedures. First managers indicated greater familiarity with quantitative methods than in past surveys. ... Second, the number of respondents who are dissatisfied with quantitative methods is much lower in this survey than in past surveys."

11/2 Post-sample accuracy: empirical findings

Over the last 30 years numerous empirical studies have compared the post-sample forecasting accuracy of all major forecasting methods using real-life business, economic, financial, demographic, and other data. The major conclusions of these studies can be summarized as follows:

1. **Econometric methods:** Armstrong (1978) surveyed all studies comparing the accuracy of econometric versus alternative methods. He concluded that econometric forecasts were not shown to be significantly better than time series methods in any of the 14 ex post and 16 ex ante empirical tests published in the literature. Moreover, he confirmed that more complex econometric models did not do better than simpler ones.

   econometric methods

2. **Multivariate models (ARIMA, Vector autoregressive, state space, etc.):** Although not many empirical studies published compare the performance of such methods, those that exist do not show any superior accuracy performance for these methods (McNees, 1986; Riise and Tjostheim, 1984; also see 4. below).

   multivariate methods

3. **Non-linear models:** In a survey of the latest developments of non-linear time series modeling, De Gooijer and Kumar (1992, pp. 151–152) conclude,

   non-linear models

   > "No uniformity seems to exist in the evidence presented on the forecasting ability of non-linear models ... Some authors claim that even when a non-linear model gives a better fit to the data, the gain in forecasting will generally not be great; ... Thus, in our opinion the question posed in the heading of this subsection [What is the gain from non-linear models?] is still unanswered."

4. **Macroeconomic forecasts:** Ashley (1988) in a survey of macroeconomic forecasts concludes (p. 363),

   macroeconomic forecasts

   > "Most of these forecasts are so inaccurate that simple extrapolation of historical trends is superior for forecasts more than a couple of quarters ahead."

In a special issue on Macroeconomic Forecasting published by the *International Journal of Forecasting* (October 1990), several models (including econometric and multivariate ones) were examined and the macroeconomic forecasts of the OECD and IMF analyzed. Although some studies report macroeconomic forecasts that are more accurate than simple extrapolations, for short-term horizons, others (e.g., Arora and Smyth, 1990) report macroeconomic forecasts that are inferior to those generated by random walk models. Worse, it does not seem that the accuracy of macroeconomic forecasts improves over time. There is evidence that such accuracy may even deteriorate over time (Ash et al., p. 390).

adaptive methods

5. **Fixed parameter versus adaptive methods:** Although it has been claimed in the past that adaptive models can learn and can therefore forecast more accurately, this claim is not supported by empirical evidence (Gardner and Dannenbring, 1980; Makridakis et al., 1982).

expert systems
neural networks

6. **Expert systems and neural networks:** There is no evidence that such methods do better than simple methods such as exponential smoothing. Thus, until additional empirical studies have been conducted, we cannot say much (see Chatfield, 1993) about the value of expert systems and neural networks.

Although not all the empirical findings are in complete agreement, the following four broad conclusions have been reached and accepted by the great majority of researchers in the field of forecasting (see Fildes and Makridakis, 1995):

simple methods

1. **Simple versus complex methods:** This conclusion indicates that the post-sample accuracy of simple methods is, on average, at least as good as that of complex or statistically sophisticated ones. This seems surprising, as higher statistical sophistication and more complexity should improve a method's ability to more correctly identify and better predict time series patterns. That has not been the case, however. Even extremely simple methods such as single exponential smoothing, which have, in addition, been shown to be special cases of ARMA models, outperform, on average, the ARMA models themselves as well as other sophisticated methods such as econometric and multivariate

ARMA models. The reason is simple: established time series patterns can and do change in the future. Thus, having a model that better fits historical data (the only thing sophisticated or complex methods can achieve) is not a guarantee of more accurate post-sample predictions. It can, for instance, be shown that a perfect fit may be assured by using an polynomial of order $n - 1$, but such a fit can result in disastrous post-sample forecasts. Simple methods, on the other hand, are robust, extrapolating more appropriately the time series pattern. This type of extrapolation provides more accurate results when, for example, the series involved is a random walk whose turning point cannot be predicted.

over-fitting

Table 11-7 shows the Mean Absolute Percentage Error (MAPE) of many time series methods from the Makridakis and Hibon (1979) study. Table 11-8 shows the MAPE of all major time series methods from the M-Competition (Makridakis et al., 1982), where 111 series were used by an expert in each method to predict for up to 18 periods ahead. Even a deseasonalized random walk model (called Naïve 2 in Tables 11-7 and 11-8) outperformed, on average, the Box-Jenkins methodology to ARMA models and that of Bayesian Forecasting. Figure 11-1 shows graphs of the performance of Naïve 2 single and damped exponential smoothing (two very simple methods) versus that of the Box-Jenkins methodology to ARMA models (a statistically sophisticated method) in two different studies (Makridakis and Hibon, 1979; and Makridakis et al., 1982). In Figure 11-1(a) both Naïve 2 and single smoothing outperform the Box-Jenkins methodology. In Figure 11-1(b) the accuracy of the three methods is similar, with Box-Jenkins being more accurate for some horizons and less accurate for others. Overall, however, for all 18 forecasting horizons both Naïve 2 and single smoothing are more accurate than the Box-Jenkins methodology to ARMA models (see Table 11-1).

M-Competition

Other empirical studies (Fildes et al., 1997; Makridakis et al., 1993) have reached the same conclusion: simple methods do at least as well as complex or statistically sophisticated ones for post-sample predictions even when a few series are involved and judgmental adjustments can be made by experts in forecasting.

	Forecasting method	Model	Forecasting horizons							
		Fitting	1	2	3	4	5	6	9	12
	1. Naïve 1	21.9	15.5	18.4	20.4	27.9	28.8	28.6	32.2	34.1
	2. Single moving average	19.5	13.8	16.4	18.7	27.2	28.2	27.8	30.7	32.3
Original	3. Single exponential smoothing	19.5	14.4	16.6	19.0	27.3	28.1	27.9	31.3	33.3
data:	4. Adaptive response rate exponential smoothing	21.2	13.5	15.4	18.0	25.8	26.4	26.0	28.6	30.5
nonseasonal	5. Linear moving average	22.2	17.1	20.3	23.6	34.2	36.5	37.1	44.1	49.6
methods	6. Brown's linear exponential smoothing	20.2	13.2	15.8	18.4	26.5	27.7	27.3	31.2	34.7
	7. Holt's (2 parameters) linear exp. smoothing	20.5	13.3	15.6	18.1	26.2	27.7	27.5	30.5	32.5
	8. Brown's quadratic exponential smoothing	20.8	13.6	15.9	18.1	26.2	28.4	29.0	36.4	43.3
	9. Linear trend (regression fit)	22.5	19.0	19.8	22.3	30.8	31.3	30.6	34.8	38.0
Seasonal and	10. Harrison's harmonic smoothing	11.0	26.4	26.3	27.6	27.4	28.0	29.3	32.2	34.2
nonseasonal	11. Winters' linear and seasonal exp. smoothing	10.9	13.8	14.8	15.4	16.2	17.1	18.4	21.3	23.6
methods	12. Adaptive filtering	11.7	15.6	16.7	16.8	18.9	18.7	19.5	22.9	24.5
	13. Autoregressive moving average (Box-Jenkins)	10.6	14.7	15.0	15.7	16.6	17.1	18.1	21.6	24.3
	14. Naïve 2	10.0	14.5	15.0	15.1	15.3	15.6	16.6	19.0	21.0
Seasonally	15. Single moving average	8.4	12.9	13.6	13.7	13.8	14.3	15.3	17.7	19.8
adjusted	16. Single exponential smoothing	8.5	12.8	13.4	13.8	14.0	14.3	15.6	18.1	20.2
data:	17. Adaptive response rate exponential smoothing	9.2	13.0	14.0	14.5	14.7	15.2	16.2	18.5	20.4
nonseasonal	18. Linear moving average	9.1	15.0	15.6	16.3	16.6	17.4	18.6	22.6	26.4
methods	19. Brown's linear exponential smoothing	8.5	12.9	14.3	14.6	14.9	15.9	17.1	20.3	23.5
	20. Holt's (2 parameters) linear exp. smoothing	9.0	12.0	12.8	13.2	13.7	14.8	16.0	19.7	23.0
	21. Brown's quadratic exponential smoothing	8.7	12.5	14.0	14.7	15.6	17.0	18.6	23.6	28.9
	22. Linear trend (regression fit)	11.4	19.6	20.4	21.1	21.1	21.9	22.8	25.3	27.4

Table 11-7: *Average of the Mean Absolute Percentage Errors (MAPE) of many time series methods applied to all 111 series from the Makridakis and Hibon (1979) study.*

Methods	Model Fitting	Forecasting horizons										Average of forecasting horizons						n (max)
		1	2	3	4	5	6	8	12	15	18	1–4	1–6	1–8	1–12	1–15	1–18	
Naïve 1	14.4	13.2	17.3	20.1	18.6	22.4	23.5	27.0	14.5	31.9	34.9	17.3	19.2	20.7	19.9	20.9	22.3	111
Mov. Average	12.8	14.1	16.9	19.1	18.9	21.8	23.6	23.9	16.3	28.7	31.9	17.3	19.1	20.1	18.9	19.7	20.8	111
Single Exp	13.2	12.2	14.8	17.4	17.6	20.3	22.5	22.7	16.1	28.8	32.5	15.5	17.5	18.5	17.8	18.8	20.1	111
ARR Exp	15.1	13.0	17.1	18.4	18.3	20.7	22.8	22.4	16.1	29.6	32.2	16.7	18.4	19.2	18.3	19.3	20.5	111
Holt Exp	13.6	12.2	13.9	17.6	19.2	23.1	24.9	31.2	22.6	40.4	40.3	15.7	18.5	21.1	21.3	23.4	25.1	111
Brown Exp	13.6	13.0	15.1	19.6	19.5	25.2	27.1	35.0	28.0	54.0	59.6	16.5	19.7	22.8	23.6	26.8	30.3	111
Quad. Exp	13.9	13.2	16.1	21.9	23.2	30.3	34.1	51.5	49.0	103.1	106.0	18.6	23.1	28.4	31.7	40.4	47.7	111
Regression	16.6	17.9	19.9	21.1	21.2	23.2	25.0	26.2	26.1	49.5	60.2	20.0	21.4	22.5	22.9	25.4	29.5	110
Naïve 2	9.1	8.5	11.4	13.9	15.4	16.6	17.4	17.8	14.5	31.2	30.8	12.3	13.8	14.9	14.9	16.4	17.8	111
D Mov. Average	8.1	10.7	13.6	17.8	19.4	22.0	23.1	22.7	15.7	28.3	34.0	15.4	17.8	19.0	18.4	19.1	20.6	111
D Single Exp	8.6	7.8	10.8	13.1	14.5	15.7	17.2	16.5	13.6	29.3	30.1	11.6	13.2	14.1	14.0	15.3	16.8	111
D ARR Exp	9.8	8.8	12.1	14.0	16.1	16.7	18.1	16.5	13.7	28.6	29.3	12.9	14.4	15.1	14.7	15.8	17.1	111
D Holt Exp	8.6	7.9	10.5	13.2	15.1	17.3	19.0	23.1	16.5	35.6	35.2	11.7	13.8	16.1	16.4	18.0	19.7	111
D Brown Exp	8.3	8.5	10.8	13.3	14.5	17.3	19.3	23.8	19.0	43.1	45.4	11.7	13.9	16.2	17.0	19.5	22.3	111
D Quad. Exp	8.4	8.8	11.8	15.0	16.9	21.9	24.1	35.7	29.7	56.1	63.6	13.1	16.4	20.3	22.2	25.9	30.2	111
D Regress	12.0	12.5	14.9	17.2	18.4	19.7	21.0	21.0	23.4	46.5	57.3	15.7	17.3	18.2	18.8	21.3	25.6	110
Winters	9.3	9.2	10.5	13.4	15.5	17.5	18.7	23.3	15.9	33.4	34.5	12.1	14.1	16.3	16.4	17.8	19.5	111
Autom. AEP	10.8	9.8	11.3	13.7	15.1	16.9	18.8	23.3	16.2	30.2	33.9	12.5	14.3	16.3	16.2	17.4	19.0	111
Bayesian F	13.3	10.3	12.8	13.6	14.4	16.2	17.1	19.2	16.1	27.5	30.6	12.8	14.1	15.2	15.0	16.1	17.6	111
Combining A	8.1	7.9	9.8	11.9	13.5	15.4	16.8	19.5	14.2	32.4	33.3	10.8	12.6	14.3	14.4	15.9	17.7	111
Combining B	8.2	8.2	10.1	11.8	14.7	15.4	16.4	20.1	15.5	31.3	31.4	11.2	12.8	14.4	14.7	16.2	17.7	111
Box-Jenkins	N.A.	10.3	10.7	11.4	14.5	16.4	17.1	18.9	16.4	26.2	34.2	11.7	13.4	14.8	15.1	16.3	18.0	111
Lewandowski	12.3	11.6	12.8	14.5	15.3	16.6	17.6	18.9	17.0	33.0	28.6	13.5	14.7	15.5	15.6	17.2	18.6	111
Parzen	8.9	10.6	10.7	10.7	13.5	14.3	14.7	16.0	13.7	22.5	26.5	11.4	12.4	13.3	13.4	14.3	15.4	111
Average	10.7	10.8	13.7	15.5	16.8	19.3	20.8	24.0	19.2	37.5	40.7	14.1	16.1	17.8	18.0	19.9	22.1	

ARR = Adaptive Response Rate
Quad. = Quadratic
Winters = Holt-Winters Exponential Smoothing
Mov. = Moving
Exp. = Exponential Smoothing
D = Deseasonalized

Table 11-8: *MAPE of all major time series methods from the M-Competition (Makridakis et al., 1982), where 111 series were used by an expert in each method to predict for up to 18 periods ahead.*

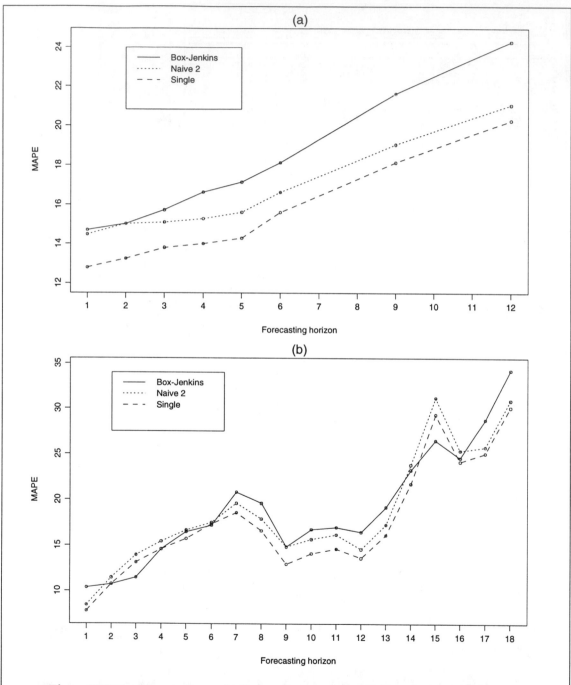

Figure 11-1: *The post-sample forecasting accuracy of Box-Jenkins, Naïve 2 and Single Exponential Smoothing. (a) Makridakis and Hibon study; (b) M-Competition.*

Methods	Forecasting horizons									Average 1988	Overall average
	1	2	3	4	5	6	8	12	15		
Naïve 1	7.3	16.6	20.0	23.9	41.2	34.9	37.9	17.5	24.2	23.8	22.0
Naïve 2	1.1	6.4	15.1	19.9	18.2	12.3	18.0	20.0	15.0	14.3	12.9
Method O/S	2.7	9.1	10.1	16.6	22.1	15.4	14.8	13.8	8.8	13.0	11.9
Single O/S	2.3	8.0	12.1	16.6	19.6	9.9	13.8	21.0	13.6	12.9	11.8
Holt O/S	2.4	9.6	12.1	16.6	24.9	12.3	12.3	18.1	12.4	14.0	12.8
Dampen O/S	2.7	9.5	13.6	16.4	22.8	12.4	12.6	17.8	13.6	14.2	13.1
Single	1.9	6.1	12.1	16.8	20.6	13.0	13.9	18.4	11.9	12.4	11.3
Holt	2.5	9.3	9.9	16.8	23.2	15.1	13.3	18.3	10.7	13.3	12.1
Dampen	2.7	7.9	11.4	16.6	21.0	12.7	13.2	18.9	10.6	11.9	11.0
Long	5.0	16.5	14.7	22.1	52.0	41.4	27.4	12.2	12.6	22.4	20.3
Box-Jenkins	5.2	14.4	13.7	21.0	25.8	19.0	20.1	18.1	16.1	16.5	15.4
Forecaster A	2.3	8.4	10.9	18.4	29.5	16.1	13.4	17.7	10.7	13.9	12.5
Forecaster B	2.6	12.5	6.3	15.8	24.9	23.2	15.8	20.1	21.8	22.5	19.4
Forecaster C	1.4	13.5	14.7	21.9	27.8	19.6	21.4	21.3	14.6	16.5	15.1
Forecaster D	3.4	15.1	15.2	22.6	35.7	21.0	26.0	21.8	22.9	21.9	19.8
Forecaster E	5.3	10.2	11.5	19.0	21.9	16.1	15.8	16.8	11.5	14.6	13.5
Comb exp sm	2.6	8.0	10.6	16.9	24.5	15.1	13.7	17.1	9.0	12.5	11.4
Comb forec	2.0	10.3	9.4	17.5	30.3	19.3	15.8	14.7	7.8	14.5	13.1
Average	3.0	10.8	12.3	18.7	28.3	18.7	17.6	17.7	13.8	16.1	14.6

Table 11-9: *MAPE all series (period Oct 1987–Dec 1988)*

Table 11-9 shows the MAPEs of various methods as well as those of five forecasters, most of them using sophisticated methods. None of the forecasters performed on average, accuracy-wise, better than the three exponential smoothing methods (single, Holt, and damped), while only forecaster A was more accurate than Naïve 2. Moreover, the Box-Jenkins methodology was one of the least accurate methods (see Table 11-9).

2. **Time horizon of forecasting:** This conclusion states that forecast horizon some methods perform more accurately for short horizons while others are more appropriate for longer or long ones. That can

be seen in Table 11-1 and is confirmed by a recent empirical study (Fildes et al., 1997) involving 263 time series.

accuracy measures

3. **Different methods versus various accuracy measures:** Chapter 2 discussed various accuracy measures used in the forecasting literature. If different methods are evaluated using these various accuracy measures (mean square error, rankings, percentage, Theil's U-statistic, etc.), their performance differs depending upon the specific measure used. Table 11-10 shows the performance of different methods, in the Makridakis et al. (1993) study, using ranking as the accuracy measure. The methods that do best in Table 11-10 are not the same as those of Table 11-8.

combination forecasts

4. **The combination of forecasts:** Empirical findings within the field of forecasting and outside (for a survey and annotated bibliography see Clemen, 1989) conclude that the averaging of the forecasts of more than one method results in more accurate predictions than the individual methods themselves. In addition, and equally important, the uncertainty (size of forecasting errors) in the combined forecasts is considerably smaller than that of each of the single methods being averaged (Makridakis and Winkler, 1983). Tables 11-8 and 11-9 show the post-sample forecasting errors for various combination schemes which outperform, on average, the individual methods being combined.

11/3 Factors influencing method selection

Selecting an appropriate method for forecasting should not, under any circumstances, be solely based on the method's accuracy or its statistical sophistication or complexity. Instead, the selection must be made considering the following four factors that are related to the objective (forecasting versus explaining): the data, the characteristics of the data, the type (length between successive values) of data, and the number and frequency of forecasts required for scheduling, planning, or strategy.

Methods	Model Fitting	— Forecasting horizons																		Average of all forecasts	n (max)
		1	2	3	4	5	6	7	8	9	10	11	12	13	14	15	16	17	18		
NAIVE1	15.8	11.9	12.4	12.3	11.7	12.2	12.0	11.9	11.6	11.6	11.2	11.1	10.0	11.1	11.5	11.1	11.5	11.8	11.2	11.62	1001
Mov. Average	13.3	11.8	12.3	11.9	11.9	11.8	11.5	11.0	11.0	10.8	10.8	10.9	10.9	10.7	11.1	10.4	11.0	10.6	10.6	11.28	1001
Single EXP	12.9	11.9	12.2	11.9	11.9	11.9	11.6	10.8	10.8	10.4	10.5	10.7	10.6	10.4	10.9	10.5	10.8	10.6	10.6	11.18	1001
ARR EXP	18.3	12.8	14.0	12.4	13.0	12.1	12.4	10.8	11.2	10.7	11.0	11.3	11.5	11.2	11.6	11.1	11.2	10.8	10.8	11.82	1001
Holt EXP	10.5	10.9	10.9	11.0	10.7	10.9	11.0	11.9	11.4	11.7	12.0	12.0	11.3	11.9	12.4	12.0	11.7	11.6	11.8	11.41	1001
Brown EXP	12.4	10.8	10.9	10.9	10.8	11.2	11.4	12.1	11.8	12.0	11.9	12.0	11.9	12.6	13.0	12.3	12.1	12.3	12.6	11.68	1001
Quad.EXP	13.8	11.8	12.0	12.5	12.1	12.6	13.1	14.1	14.2	13.8	13.8	14.2	14.5	15.5	15.5	15.1	15.0	15.3	15.7	13.68	1001
Regression	15.6	14.2	13.4	12.8	12.2	11.6	11.4	11.6	11.5	11.9	12.3	12.4	11.8	12.0	12.3	11.3	11.2	11.0	11.1	12.08	1001
NAIVE2	11.1	10.4	10.5	10.6	10.8	11.0	10.6	10.4	10.6	10.5	10.2	10.3	10.0	9.8	9.5	10.2	10.0	10.1	9.9	10.36	1001
D Mov.Avrg	8.1	11.4	11.9	12.3	12.3	12.1	11.6	11.5	11.1	11.2	10.8	11.1	10.9	10.1	10.3	10.8	11.0	10.9	10.8	11.34	1001
D Sing EXP	7.6	10.3	10.4	10.6	10.7	10.8	10.5	9.8	9.7	9.6	9.6	9.7	9.8	9.3	9.0	9.7	9.5	9.5	9.4	10.00	1001
D ARR EXP	13.6	11.4	12.4	11.6	12.0	11.5	11.5	10.3	10.5	10.4	10.5	10.2	10.5	10.0	9.7	10.3	10.1	10.0	10.0	10.87	1001
D Holt EXP	4.8	9.4	8.9	9.3	9.7	9.7	9.9	10.4	10.5	10.7	10.5	10.4	10.7	10.8	10.3	10.7	10.4	10.6	10.7	10.09	1001
D brown EXP	6.6	9.4	9.0	9.5	9.7	9.9	10.0	10.6	10.6	10.6	10.8	10.6	10.9	11.0	10.7	11.0	11.0	11.3	11.3	10.29	1001
D Quad. EXP	8.3	10.2	10.2	11.0	11.2	11.6	11.9	12.8	13.1	12.9	13.0	13.0	13.7	13.7	13.5	14.1	14.2	14.4	14.6	12.44	1001
D Regress	12.3	13.3	12.0	12.1	11.4	10.8	10.9	11.0	11.0	11.4	11.4	11.0	11.2	10.7	10.4	10.7	10.2	10.5	10.0	11.21	1001
WINTERS	7.2	9.4	9.0	9.3	9.6	9.7	9.8	10.1	10.4	10.8	10.5	10.5	10.4	10.3	9.9	10.2	10.3	10.3	10.3	9.96	1001
Autom. AEP	9.1	9.8	9.8	10.2	9.7	10.0	10.0	10.5	10.4	10.7	10.8	10.6	10.6	10.9	11.0	10.5	10.7	10.6	10.7	10.32	1001
Bayesian F	15.6	11.0	10.0	10.1	10.3	10.1	10.4	10.4	10.7	10.3	10.3	10.2	10.7	10.5	10.3	10.4	10.7	10.4	10.2	10.38	1001
Combining A	6.7	9.0	8.8	8.9	9.2	9.2	9.4	9.3	9.3	9.4	9.4	9.2	9.4	9.1	8.8	9.3	9.1	9.2	9.4	9.17	1001
Combining B	7.5	9.8	10.0	10.0	10.1	10.3	10.1	9.8	9.8	9.7	9.6	9.7	9.8	9.5	9.1	9.6	9.4	9.6	9.6	9.80	1001
Average	11.0	11.0	11.0	11.0	11.0	11.0	11.0	11.0	11.0	11.0	11.0	11.0	11.0	11.0	11.0	11.0	11.0	11.0	11.0	11.00	

Table 11-10: *Average ranking of all major time series methods from the Makridakis et al. (1982) study where 1001 series were used by an expert in each method to predict for up to 18 periods ahead.*

explanatory models

1. **Forecasting versus explaining:** Often, we may want to better understand the factors that influence the variable we want to forecast (e.g., our sales) than simply to obtain a prediction about the future value of such variable. The reason is that by knowing the various factors that affect, say, our sales we can take steps to influence the sales in desired directions. This obviously can be achieved by increasing the advertising budget, decreasing price, or undertaking other actions that we know will have an impact. To identify such factors and measure their specific influence, however, we must develop an explanatory model (regression or econometric) that can provide such information. Indeed, if such a model provides us with accurate information and if appropriate steps are taken and are successful, we can influence the future direction, and by so doing invalidate (make less accurate) our forecasts.

   For instance, this can happen if a time series model predicts a 10% decline in sales while a regression model tells us that if we increase advertising by 1%, sales will in increase by 2.5%. If we increase advertising by 5%, sales will increase by 12.5% (again, if we are successful), thus not only avoiding a decline but even achieving a 2.5% increase. For these reasons, the choice between explanatory and time series methods, which simply provide us with "black box" type forecasts, is entirely subjective, depending on our objective. If such an objective, however, is to merely obtain forecasts, then time series models are much simpler and cheaper to use while also being, on average, more accurate.

time series
decomposition

2. **Characteristics of time series:** In Chapter 3 a time series was decomposed into seasonality, trend, cycle (or trend-cycle), and randomness. We also saw that seasonality, because of its regularity, presents no special problems and that all methods can predict it about equally well. If we have to make a choice we should, therefore, prefer the simplest approach for estimating seasonality: the classical decomposition method. Even in the case of ARMA models, it is more accurate to first remove seasonality before selecting an ARMA model (see Makridakis and Hibon, 1997); doing so simplifies the selection process and results in a small but consistent improvement in post-sample

forecasting accuracy over the alternative of selecting a seasonal ARMA model. The same is true of the Holt method, which when applied to seasonally adjusted data produces more accurate forecasts than the method of Winters, which is equivalent to Holt but which also identifies and extrapolates seasonality directly (see Makridakis et al., 1982 and 1984).

As seasonality presents no special problems or challenges, the magnitude of randomness and the behavior of the trend-cycle become, therefore, the key to method selection. In general, the larger the randomness the more appropriate the selection of simpler methods. When the randomness dominates the trend-cycles, as is often the case with short-term data, single exponential smoothing is often the most accurate approach as far as post-sample performance is concerned. It should be noted that such a method extrapolates the most recent actual value, once the randomness has been separated (smoothed) from the data pattern, horizontally. That is, it assumes that the direction in the trend in the time series cannot be predicted correctly because of the excessive level of randomness and our inability to predict the next turning points accurately.

randomness

The more the trend-cycle dominates the randomness in our time series, the less appropriate becomes the method of single smoothing to forecast the continuation of the pattern, as cyclical continuity and trend persistence can be extrapolated with reasonable confidence. This is why methods that can more correctly identify and more appropriately extrapolate such a pattern are needed. In the case of little randomness, as with macroeconomics data, ARMA models have been shown to do relatively better than smoothing methods (Makridakis et al., 1982). Similarly, methods such as Kalman and other filters, as well as Parzen's approach, can be used and must be considered.

When there is not much randomness and the trend dominates cyclical fluctuations, Holt's method is to be preferred, as it assumes that the latest smoothed (i.e., without randomness) trend can be extrapolated linearly. However, if the cyclical component dominates the trend, this type of extrapolation often overshoots actual growth, as cyclical turns can be missed, resulting in large errors. Under such a condition damped exponential smoothing is more appropriate since it slows down the extrapolation of trend, as a function of its randomness, and by so doing outperforms Holt's smoothing.

type of data

3. **Type of data:** The type of data (yearly, quarterly, monthly, weekly, daily, etc.) relates to the characteristics of the time series since, in general, randomness diminishes as the level of aggregation increases.

   Thus, yearly data include less randomness than monthly, since averaging 12 months eliminates most of the randomness which by definition fluctuates around zero. For long forecasting horizons, therefore, a method that can correctly identify and extrapolate the trend in the data pattern should be preferred. This is why trend fitting is recommended: it ignores random, and cyclical, fluctuations and concentrates on the long-term increase or decline instead. The dangers, however, of trend fitting were demonstrated in Chapter 9: the choice of the starting date is of extreme importance given the often huge cyclical fluctuations characterizing many series.

   At the other extreme, in daily data randomness dominates while trend is insignificant or not present at all. In such a case, single smoothing is to be preferred as it is the best method for isolating whatever pattern exists in such series by averaging—smoothing—the time series.

   Quarterly data are in between yearly and daily or weekly in terms of trend and randomness. In addition, quarterly data can also exhibit strong cyclical fluctuations as well as seasonality. Since randomness in such data is limited, and the trend-cycle dominates, providing a fair amount of momentum and persistence, it is less likely that the pattern of the series will change considerably. For these reasons, sophisticated methods, which can correctly identify and extrapolate complex patterns, seem to be doing the best with quarterly data and should, therefore, be preferred to simpler methods.

4. **Number and frequency of forecasts:** The number of required forecasts, and their frequency—which relates to their number—is another factor that helps us determine the most appropriate method to select. A greater number of predictions is needed when forecasting on a daily rather than on a monthly basis, or on a monthly rather than a quarterly basis. The number of required forecasts further diminishes when going from quarterly to yearly predictions. This means that when predicting, say, the yearly sales of a company, significant effort can be expended for the predictions involved.

forecast horizon

Thus, the methods considered can include statistically sophisticated ones, which can require a lot of human data to build and human inputs to operate. This cannot be the case, however, when forecasts for the inventory demand of many thousands of items are needed on a monthly, weekly, or even daily basis. In such a situation, automatic methods that require no human input must be used. Thus, from a practical point of view, the greater the number of forecasts and the more frequently they are needed, the simpler and more automatic the methods utilized.

11/4 The combination of forecasts

There is little doubt that combining improves forecasting accuracy. This empirical finding holds true in statistical forecasting, judgmental estimates, and when averaging statistical and subjective predictions (Clemen, 1989). In addition, combining reduces the variance of post-sample forecasting errors considerably (Makridakis and Winkler, 1983). The empirical findings are at odds with statistical theory and point to a rethinking of what is appropriate to forecasting methods and how a method should be selected. As Clemen (1989) concludes,

combination forecasts

> "Using a combination of forecasts amounts to an admission that the forecaster is unable to build a properly specified model. Trying ever more elaborate combining models seems to add insult to injury as the more complicated combinations do not generally perform all that well."

11/4/1 Factors that contribute to making combining work

Several factors, described below, make the accuracy of individual forecasting methods deteriorate and increase the size of errors; combining works because it averages such errors.

1. *Measuring the wrong thing:* In forecasting we often need to estimate demand, but demand data are rarely, if ever, available. Thus, instead of measuring demand we measure such things as orders, production, shipments, or billings. It, of course, is obvious that such proxies of apparent demand introduce systematic biases in measuring the "real" demand and therefore decrease forecasting accuracy.

2. *Measurement of errors:* No matter what we try to measure there are always errors of measurement (including clerical and data processing errors), the size of which can be substantial and systematic. This is particularly true for disaggregate items but can be also observed on aggregate ones whose magnitude range from plus or minus 10 to 15%. Measurement errors also include accounting changes, the way the data are kept, changes in definitions, and what is to be included in the different factors being used. Even if the size of measurement errors is in the neighborhood of 10–15% (which is a minimum that applies to highly aggregate macroeconomic variables), it makes little sense to worry about better methods that would improve forecasting accuracy by 5 or 10%.

3. *Unstable or changing patterns or relationships:* Statistical models assume that patterns and relationships are constant. This is rarely the case in the real world, however, where special events and actions, fashions, cycles, and so forth bring systematic changes and therefore introduce non-random errors in forecasting.

4. *Models that minimize past errors:* Available forecasting methods select the best model by a process that depends upon how well a model minimizes one-step-ahead forecasting errors. However, we often need forecasts for several/many periods ahead, which may not be the most appropriate ones if they are based on models that minimize the one-period-ahead errors. The

remainder of this chapter presents an example of how forecasts can be combined. This illustration also shows how combining can result in more accurate predictions than the individual methods being combined.

11/4/2 An example of combining

Table 11-11 displays the forecasts of single exponential, Holt's, and damped smoothing together with two kinds of combining. One is called optimal and the other simple. In optimal combining, the weights of each of the three methods utilized are determined in an inverse function to the MSE of the model fit of each of the methods (there are also other approaches for specifying optimal weights; see the selected bibliography at the end of this chapter). In simple combining the weights are equal. In other words, the combining is the simple arithmetic average (i.e., the sum of the three predictions divided by three) of the forecasts of the three methods used.

Table 11-11 illustrates that although the MSE of the model fit is at its lowest with Holt's smoothing, followed by damped and single, and even though the MSE of the optimal combining is smaller than that of the simple averaging, in the post-sample predictions the MSE of the simple combining outperforms all alternatives in the great majority of forecasting horizons and in the overall average. The same is true with single exponential smoothing, whose post-sample MSE (as well as Mean Error and MAPE) is the smallest of the three methods although it was the largest of the model fit (see Table 11-11).

The reason is simple and can be seen in Figure 11-2. The historical pattern of the time series has not remained constant during the forecasting phase (the historical growth pattern has slowed down considerably), making Holt's smoothing overshoot the actual, post-sample values. However, when the forecasts of the three methods are combined (averaged) their errors are cancelled out to a great extent (see Figure 11-3).

Moreover, the simple combination of Holt, damped, and single is more accurate than the optimal combining, which gives more weight to Holt than single smoothing. Although such an occurrence does not happen all the time, empirical research has shown that, on average, the simple combining outperforms the individual methods being

Period	Time Series	Single	Holt	Damped	Optimal Combination	Simple Combination
				Model fit forecasts		
1	376	492	367	365	403	408
2	324	457	375	369	397	401
3	341	417	364	367	380	383
4	444	394	361	362	371	373
5	450	409	394	368	390	391
⋮	⋮	⋮	⋮	⋮	⋮	⋮
44	603	563	578	592	578	578
45	694	575	592	590	586	585
46	542	611	631	599	599	599
48	735	581	596	595	591	591
				Model fit errors		
Mean Error or Bias		9.37	1.57	17.77	9.48	9.57
MSE		4278.75	3501.39	3625.17	3540.61	3564.40
MAPE		11.39	10.23	10.40	10.49	10.54
				Post-sample forecasts		
49	628	627	648	607	628	627
50	676	627	653	615	632	632
51	629	627	659	620	636	635
52	600	627	664	623	639	638
53	654	627	670	625	642	641
54	661	627	675	627	644	643
55	606	627	580	628	647	645
56	660	627	686	629	649	647
57	665	627	691	629	651	649
58	595	627	696	629	653	651
59	621	627	702	630	655	653
60	723	627	707	630	657	655
61	608	627	713	640	659	657
62	728	627	718	630	661	658
63	650	627	723	630	663	660
				Post-sample errors		
Mean Error or Bias		19.64	− 38.79	21.58	− 0.67	0.81
MSE		1945.98	3116.47	2003.52	1468.48	1468.76
MAPE		5.21	6.87	5.59	4.85	4.84

Table 11-11: *Forecasts (both model fit and post-sample) of three methods and their simple and optimal combining*

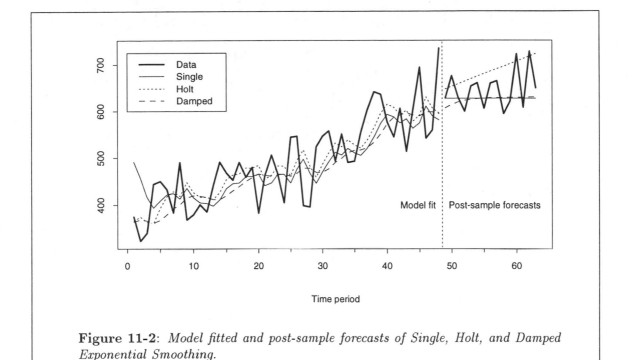

Figure 11-2: *Model fitted and post-sample forecasts of Single, Holt, and Damped Exponential Smoothing.*

combined as well as the optimal combination of forecasts (Makridakis and Winkler, 1983). Moreover, the MSE, relating to the variance or the magnitude of uncertainty in our forecasts, is smaller with the simple combining than with the individual methods themselves or the optimal combining (see Table 11-11). The reason is that averaging cancels out large forecasting errors and diminishes the MSE. The fact that simple combining reduces the MSE of post-sample forecasts is an additional reason for using it in practice, where smaller errors mean less uncertainty, which translates into smaller inventories and, therefore, costs.

The superior performance of combining cannot be easily explained by statistical theory, which postulates selecting models based on how well they fit available data (model fit). This optimal model selection is obviously not done when combining forecasts, as some of the method(s) being combined will be suboptimal (this is clearly the case of single smoothing in Table 11-11, whose MSE is much bigger than the other two methods). However, if the historical pattern changes during the forecasting phase, then combining can

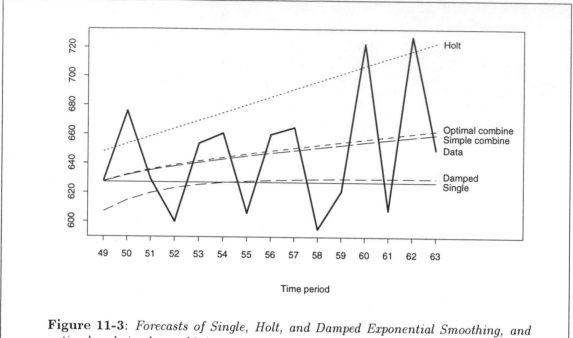

Figure 11-3: *Forecasts of Single, Holt, and Damped Exponential Smoothing, and optimal and simple combining.*

be more accurate than the method that minimizes the MSE of the model fit, which in Table 11-11 corresponds to the method of Holt. Combining, therefore, allows us to more accurately predict and reduce our uncertainty about the future when we are not sure whether or not the historical pattern (or relationship) in our data will continue or be different from that of the past. As can be seen in Figure 11-3, combining averages out the errors of the individual methods being combined and results, therefore, in smaller errors and more accurate and more reliable predictions.

References and selected bibliography

ARMSTRONG, J.S. (1978) Forecasting with econometric methods: folklore versus facts, *Journal of Business*, **51** (4), 549–564.

———————— (1984) Forecasting by extrapolation: conclusions from 25 years of research, *Interfaces*, **14**, 52–66.

ARORA, H.A. and D.J. SMYTH (1990) Forecasting the developing world: an accuracy analysis of the IMF's forecasts, *International Journal of Forecasting*, **6**, 393–400.

ASH, J.C.K., D.J. SMYTH, and S.M. HERAVI (1990) The accuracy of OECD forecasts of the international economy, *International Journal of Forecasting*, **6**, 379–392.

ASHLEY, R. (1988) On the relative worth of recent macroeconomic forecasts, *International Journal of Forecasting*, 4, 363–376.

BUNN, D. and G. WRIGHT (1991) Interaction of judgmental and statistical forecasting methods: issues and analysis, *Management Science*, **37**, 501–518.

CHATFIELD, C. (1993) Neural networks: forecasting breakthrough or passing fad? *International Journal of Forecasting*, **9**, 1–3.

CLEMEN, R. (1989) Combining forecasts: a review and annotated bibliography, *International Journal of Forecasting*, **5**, 559–584.

DALRYMPLE, D.J. (1975) Sales forecasting methods and accuracy, *Business Horizons*, December, pp. 69–73.

———————— (1987) Sales forecasting practices, *International Journal of Forecasting*, **3**, 379–391.

DAVIDSON, T.A. (1987) Forecasters—who are they? Survey findings, *Journal of Business Forecasting*, **6**, 17–19.

DE GOOIJER, J.G. and K. KUMAR (1992) Some recent developments in non-linear time series modelling, testing and forecasting, *International Journal of Forecasting*, **8**, 135–157.

FILDES, R. and S. MAKRIDAKIS (1995) The impact of empirical accuracy studies on time series analysis and forecasting, *International Statistical Review*, **63**, 289–308.

FILDES, R., M. HIBON, S. MAKRIDAKIS, and N. MEADE (1997) The accuracy of extrapolative forecasting methods: additional empirical evidence, *International Journal of Forecasting*, **13**, forthcoming.

GARDNER, E.S. JR. and D.G. DANNENBRING (1980) Forecasting with exponential smoothing: some guidelines for model selection, *Decision Science*, **11**, 370–383.

HANKE, J.E. (1989) Forecasting in business schools: a follow-up survey, *International Journal of Forecasting*, **5**, 259–262.

HANKE, J.E. and K. WEIGAND (1994) What are business schools doing to educate forecasters? *Journal of Business Forecasting*, **13** (3), 10–12.

KOEHLER, A.B. and E.S. MURPHREE (1988) A comparison of results from state space forecasting with forecasts from the Makridakis Competition, *International Journal of Forecasting*, **4**, 45–55.

LO, T. (1994) An expert system for choosing demand forecasting techniques, *International Journal of Production Economics*, **33**, 5–15.

MAINES, L.A. (1996) An experimental examination of subjective forecast combination, *International Journal of Forecasting*, **12**, 223–233.

MAKRIDAKIS, S. and M. HIBON (1979) Accuracy of forecasting: an empirical investigation, *Journal of the Royal Statistical Society Series A*, **142**, 97–145.

——————— (1997) ARMA models and the Box-Jenkins methodology, *Journal of Forecasting*, **16**, 147–163.

MAKRIDAKIS, S. and S.C. WHEELWRIGHT (1989) *Forecasting methods for management*, 5th ed., Chichester: John Wiley & Sons.

MAKRIDAKIS, S. and R. WINKLER (1983) Average of forecasts: some empirical results, *Management Science*, **29**, 987–996.

——————— (1989) Sampling distributions of post-sample forecasting errors, *Applied Statistics*, **38**, 331–342.

MAKRIDAKIS, S., A. ANDERSEN, R. CARBONE, R. FILDES, M. HIBON, R. LEWANDOWSKI, J. NEWTON, E. PARZEN, and R. WINKLER (1982) The accuracy of extrapolation (time series) methods: results of a forecasting competition, *Journal of Forecasting*, **1**, 111–153.

_____ (1984) *The forecasting accuracy of major time series methods*, Chichester: John Wiley & Sons.

MAKRIDAKIS, S., C. CHATFIELD, M. HIBON, M.J. LAWRENCE, T. MILLS, K. ORD, and L.F. SIMMONS (1993) The M2-Competition: a real time judgmentally based forecasting study (with comments), *International Journal of Forecasting*, **9**, 5–30.

McNEES, S.K. (1986) Forecasting accuracy of alternative techniques: a comparison of U.S. macroeconomic forecasts, *Journal of Business and Economic Statistics*, **4**, 5–15.

MEESE, R. and J. GEWEKE (1984) A comparison of autoregressive univariate forecasting procedures for macroeconomic time series, *Journal of Business and Economic Statistics*, **2**, 191–200.

MENTZER, J.T. and J.E. COX JR. (1984a) Familiarity, application and performance of sales forecasting techniques, *Journal of Forecasting*, **3**, 27–36.

MILLER, D.M. (1985) The anatomy of a successful forecasting implementation, *International Journal of Forecasting*, **1**, 69–78.

RIISE, T. and D. TJOSTHEIM (1984) Theory and practice of multivariate ARIMA forecasting, *Journal of Forecasting*, **3**, 309–317.

SANDERS, N.R. (1992) Corporate forecasting practices in the manufacturing industry, *Production and Inventory Management*, **33**, 54–57.

SANDERS, N.R. and MANRODT K.B. (1994) Forecasting practices in US corporations: survey results, *Interfaces*, **24**(2), 92–100.

SCHNAARS, S.P. (1986) A comparison of extrapolation models on yearly sales forecasts, *International Journal of Forecasting*, **2**, 71–85.

SMYTH, D.J. (1983) Short-run macroeconomic forecasting: the OECD performance, *Journal of Forecasting*, **2**, 37–49.

WHEELWRIGHT S.C. and CLARKE D.G. (1976) Corporate forecasting: promise and reality, *Harvard Business Review*, **54**, November–December, pp. 40ff.

WILSON, H. (1996) "IABF members' opinions regarding forecasting methods," Paper presented in the IABF, San Antonio, Texas, May.

WINKLER, R.L. and R.T. CLEMEN (1992) Sensitivity of weights in combined forecasts, *Operations Research*, **40**, 609–614.

WINKLHOFER, H., A. DIAMANTOPOULOS, and S.F. WITT (1996) Forecasting practice: a review of the empirical literature and an agenda for future research, *International Journal of Forecasting*, **12**, 193–221.

Exercises

11.1 Table 11-12 shows the symmetric Mean Absolute Percentage Error of 16 methods of the newest forecasting competi-   M3-IJF Competition
tion (M3-IJF) which compared 3003 time series. (The first
method, Naïve Forecast 2, shows the accuracy of the 1001
series of the M-Competition.)   Relate the results of this
competition with those of the previous ones.

11.2 In the above mentioned competition we still have not combined the various methods to compare their performance with
those of the individual methods being combined. What is your
opinion about how well combining will do?

11.3 The above mentioned competition includes methods that use
neural networks, machine learning, and expert systems to
make their predictions. Contrary to claims that such methods
would outperform the more traditional methods of forecasting,
this has not been the case. Comment on this result.

Methods	Forecasting horizons										Average of forecasting horizons						n (max)
	1	2	3	4	5	6	8	12	15	18	1–4	1–6	1–8	1–12	1–15	1–18	
Naïve 2-MC	9.3	11.5	13.4	15.4	17.8	19.5	17.8	16.0	18.8	20.3	12.4	14.5	15.1	15.4	15.8	16.3	1001
Naïve 2	11.0	11.5	13.9	15.1	15.0	16.2	15.2	16.0	20.1	20.9	12.9	13.8	14.1	14.7	15.3	15.9	3003
Single	9.8	10.5	12.9	14.1	14.0	15.1	13.9	14.7	18.8	19.5	11.8	12.7	13.0	13.4	13.9	14.5	3003
Holt	9.1	10.4	12.8	14.3	15.0	16.2	14.4	15.3	19.6	21.1	11.6	13.0	13.3	13.7	14.3	15.0	3003
Dampen	9.0	9.9	12.0	13.3	13.5	14.4	12.9	14.0	17.7	18.7	11.1	12.0	12.2	12.6	13.1	13.7	3003
Winter	9.6	10.6	13.1	14.5	14.8	16.0	14.4	15.9	20.3	20.8	11.9	13.1	13.4	13.9	14.5	15.2	3003
B-J automatic	9.2	10.4	12.2	13.9	14.0	14.8	13.0	14.1	17.8	19.3	11.4	12.4	12.5	12.8	13.3	14.0	3003
Autobox[1]	9.8	11.1	13.1	15.1	16.0	16.8	14.2	15.4	19.1	20.4	12.3	13.7	13.8	14.0	14.6	15.2	3003
Robust-trend[2]	10.5	11.2	13.2	14.7	15.0	15.9	15.1	17.5	22.2	24.3	12.4	13.4	13.7	14.6	15.4	16.3	3003
ARARMA	9.7	10.9	12.6	14.2	14.6	15.6	13.9	15.2	18.5	20.3	11.8	12.9	13.1	13.5	14.1	14.7	3003
AutomatANN[3]	10.4	12.3	14.2	15.9	16.2	17.8	16.0	16.7	19.8	21.2	13.2	14.5	14.7	15.0	15.6	16.2	3003
FLORES-P-1[4]	9.2	10.5	12.6	14.5	14.8	15.3	13.8	14.4	19.1	20.8	11.7	12.8	13.0	13.3	13.9	14.7	3003
FLORES-P-2[5]	10.0	11.0	12.8	14.1	14.1	14.7	12.9	14.4	18.2	19.9	12.0	12.8	12.8	13.0	13.6	14.3	3003
PP-Autocast[6]	9.1	10.0	12.1	13.5	13.8	14.7	13.1	14.3	17.7	19.6	11.2	12.2	12.4	12.8	13.3	14.0	3003
ForecastPro3[7]	8.6	9.6	11.4	12.9	13.3	14.3	12.6	13.2	16.4	18.3	10.6	11.7	11.9	12.1	12.6	13.2	3003
THETA-Model[8]	10.3	11.1	12.7	13.7	14.4	15.4	13.4	14.2	17.6	19.1	12.0	13.0	13.1	13.4	13.8	14.4	3003
RBF[9]	9.9	10.5	12.4	13.4	13.2	14.2	12.8	14.1	17.3	17.8	11.6	12.3	12.4	12.8	13.2	13.8	3003

[1] Automatic Box-Jenkins ARIMA modeling
[2] Like Holt's method but using the median to extrapolate the trend in the data
[3] Automatic Artificial Neural Network
[4] An expert system that chooses among four exponential smoothing methods
[5] An expert system (as in 4 above) which also includes judgmental modifications
[6] Peer Planner using a family of exponential smoothing methods based on Gardner's damped trend smoothing
[7] A system that selects the best among several methods based on the characteristics of the data
[8] A hybrid forecasting method based on a successive filtering algorithm and a set of heuristic rules for both extrapolation and parameters calibration
[9] A rule based (expert system) forecasting method

Table 11-12: *The average symmetric MAPE (all 3003 data) of the M3-IJF Competition.*

12

IMPLEMENTING FORECASTING: IT'S USES, ADVANTAGES, AND LIMITATIONS

People have always wanted to predict the future to reduce their fear and anxiety about the unknown and an uncertain tomorrow. This desire has been satisfied by priests, astrologers, prophets, fortune tellers, and the like since the dawn of civilization. Today, the need to predict the future is fulfilled in a wide range of ways, from horoscopes to econometric services; such forecasts, however, provide psychological, rather than systematic, value. In this book we have introduced the entire range of available forecasting methods (from the statistically simplest to some of the most sophisticated; from quantitative to judgmental). We have also discussed their use in business and other organizations as well as their predictive, post-sample accuracy beyond available historical data. Finally, we have talked about forecasting's practical value but also its limitations.

prophecy

extrapolation

Regardless of the mathematical complexity of the model, the statistical sophistication of the method, the large number of data, and the power of the computer being utilized, forecasting can never become a substitute for prophecy. Any and all types of statistical predictions are simply extrapolations (or interpolations) of established past patterns and/or existing relationships. Even the majority of judgmental forecasts are based on extrapolating patterns/relationships. For these forecasts to be accurate, therefore, one of two things must happen: either no major changes must occur from the conditions that have prevailed during the past, or such changes must cancel themselves out. Otherwise, forecasting errors, sometimes large ones, are possible (their size will, usually, be proportional to the magnitude of changes involved), unless we can develop appropriate foresight about the direction and extent of the forthcoming changes based on means other than extrapolation.

No matter what is being claimed by those wanting to profit from people's desire to foretell the future, *no* statistical method, or for that matter any other approach, allows us to accurately forecast and/or correctly estimate the extent of future uncertainty when "history does not repeat itself." People, therefore, rightly ask, "Is there a need for a forecasting discipline or indeed a book on forecasting?" The best way to answer this question is with another one: "What is the alternative, since forecasts are required for scheduling, planning, and other future-oriented decisions, including strategic ones, that need predictions as inputs?" It is precisely because forecasts are needed that we must come up with the most rational and economical way of obtaining them. Moreover, such forecasts must be as accurate as possible while the magnitude of forecasting errors, or the extent of uncertainty involved when predicting the future, must be as small as possible but also estimated as realistically as possible.

We have shown (see Chapters 10 and 11) that all empirical evidence available points in the same direction: ad hoc, judgmental forecasts are not necessarily more accurate than statistical ones, particularly when many forecasts are required on a frequent basis. In addition, judgmental predictions underestimate future uncertainty considerably and consistently. Finally, they are much more expensive than statistical ones as they require human time and are often made during meetings that involve several/many people who must use their precious, and expensive, time to come up with the required forecasts. We have, therefore, advocated in this book (in Chapter 10) that judgmental predictions must supplement the statistical ones when and where they can contribute the most: in identifying forthcoming changes and predicting the direction and extent that they will influence the future so that statistical predictions, which can more objectively and correctly identify and extrapolate established patterns and/or existing relationships, can be appropriately modified.

judgmental vs statistical forecasts

This chapter first discusses the uses and limitations of forecasting in terms of the forecasting horizons they intend to satisfy. It then addresses some major organizational concerns involving forecasting, including the perceptions of the preparers and users of forecasts, and ways of improving the forecasting function within firms. Next covered are additional aspects of forecasting requiring creative insights and foresight. Finally, we present some issues related to the future of forecasting and their implications. We predict some major changes, bringing considerable improvements in forecasting effectiveness, when intranets and extranets will be widely used by business firms and non-profit organizations.

12/1 What can and cannot be predicted

Over the last 35 years a considerable amount of empirical evidence and experience with forecasting applications has been accumulated. From such studies (see Chapter 11) several general observations as well as some specific conclusions, based on the time horizon of forecasting, can be drawn.

optimism

Empirical evidence (both from within the field of forecasting and from judgmental psychology) concludes that the vast majority of people are overoptimistic in their forecasts while they also underestimate future uncertainty significantly. Few people who start new businesses, for instance, seriously consider the high probability that they will be bankrupt two or three years later. The same is true of product managers or executives, who are not willing to accept that the sales of their product or their budget estimates may fall by a much bigger amount, or percentage, than they are willing to accept. Otherwise, they will have many sleepless nights, which are readily avoided through overoptimism. Because we often confuse forecasting with wishful thinking or the achievement of some desired objective, we need to have objective forecasts, based on statistical predictions, before utilizing our judgment to forecast.

recency bias

Another general observation based on empirical evidence is what psychologists call the recency bias. We humans remember and are greatly influenced by recent events and their consequences. Stock market crashes, for instance, are probably 90% psychological and 10% real, as people panic and are willing to sell at a highly reduced price because they are afraid that prices will keep declining forever. The same is true during periods of recession, when investments drop significantly because businesspeople are influenced by current bad economic conditions and do not realize that recessions are temporary events lasting for more than one year (the longest postwar recession lasted 18 months). Similarly, research findings have shown that the largest amount of flood insurance is taken out just after a flood and the smallest when the next flood takes place. In other words, people are influenced by the fact that there has been a flood and insure themselves, but as time passes and there is no flood, they believe that they are wasting their money so they cancel their insurance policies. By the time the next serious flood arrives (often many years, or even decades later) few people have remained insured.

Setting uncertainty at realistic levels, separating objective predictions from wishful thinking or the attainment of desired objectives, and realizing that unusual, threatening events have occurred and will continue to do so in the future are critical aspects that must be dealt with while forecasting. The future must be considered realistically and objectively even though doing so may reveal threatening events that will increase uncertainty and raise our anxiety. Most important, the latest event(s) or development(s) must be contemplated with a long-term, historical view in mind so that we will not be unduly influenced by the recency bias that characterizes us. Thus, we must realize, and accept, that a storm (even if it will last some time) will be followed by calm, and that after a prolonged calm a storm will undoubtedly occur, even if we cannot predict its exact timing or its precise force.

12/1/1 Short-term predictions

In the short-term, forecasting can benefit by extrapolating the inertia (momentum) that exists in economic and business phenomena. As changes in established patterns are not likely over a short time span, extrapolating them provides us, most often, with accurate and reliable forecasts. Seasonality can also be predicted fairly well. Empirical evidence has shown that seasonality does not change much or frequently. But even when it changes, it usually does so slowly, in a predictable manner. Thus, once computed it can be projected, together with the momentum of the series being forecast, accurately and reliably in the great majority of cases.

extrapolating

seasonality

Momentum and seasonality constitute the two greatest advantages of using statistical forecasting methods. Such advantages can benefit production planning and scheduling; equipment, personnel, and financial planning; the ordering of raw and other materials; and setting up appropriate levels of inventory, or slack in personnel, to deal with higher levels of demand than the most likely value predicted by our statistical models. As seasonal fluctuations can be substantial and as momentum does exist, their accurate prediction can be used to improve, sometimes substantially, short-term scheduling and planning decisions. Moreover, the uncertainty of our predictions can be reliably estimated in terms of prediction intervals around the most likely prediction(s).

scheduling planning

The larger the number of customers or items involved, the smaller the effects of random forces and the higher the accuracy and reliability of forecasting. Thus, firms selling to consumers not only

estimating
uncertainty

can forecast more accurately but also can estimate the uncertainty of their forecasts more reliably than firms selling to industrial customers. Estimating uncertainty can be used to determine safety stocks (for finished products and materials), slack in personnel and equipment, and financial reserves, so that possible errors in forecasting can be confronted with a minimum of surprise and unpleasant consequences. If organizations do not already use a statistical, computerized system to make short-term forecasts and estimates of uncertainty, our advice would be to do so as soon as possible. Overwhelming empirical evidence (see Chapter 11) shows concrete benefits from using statistical methods (often simple ones) instead of using judgment to make these forecasts and to estimate the uncertainty involved. Equally important, the cost of statistical predictions is considerably less than the corresponding judgmental ones.

cost of prediction

altered patterns

Although few things can happen in the short-term to alter established patterns or existing relationships, some changes are occasionally possible, introducing an additional element of uncertainty. For instance, unexpected events (a fire, a major machine breakdown, a big snowstorm) can take place, or competitors can initiate special actions (advertising campaigns, price decreases, new product introductions). Such unexpected events or actions can change established patterns, thus invalidating forecasts and introducing additional uncertainty (for more details and ways of dealing with special events/actions, see Makridakis and Wheelwright, 1989).

12/1/2 Medium-term predictions

recessions and booms

In the medium-term, forecasting is relatively easy when patterns and relationships do not change. However, as the time horizon of forecasting increases, so does the chance of a change in these patterns/relationships. Economic cycles, for one thing, can and do change established patterns and affect relationships. Unfortunately, however, we have not yet been able to accurately predict the timing and depth of recessions, or the start and strength of booms, using statistical methods. Moreover, economists and other experts have not been more successful than statistical methods in predicting the start or the depth of recessions (Urresta, 1995; Fox, 1997; Makridakis, 1982). This makes medium-term forecasting hazardous, as

recessions and booms can start anytime during a planning horizon
of up to 18 months (the usual length of the medium-term which
includes budget forecasts). In addition, the uncertainty in forecasting increases while becoming less easy to measure or deal with in
practical, concrete terms. This is so because differences between
forecasts and actual results can be substantial, especially in cyclical
industries, where business cycles occur. Moreover, forecasting errors
cease to be independent since recessions affect practically all firms
and products/services, at least those in cyclical sectors.

Medium-term forecasts are needed mostly for budgeting purposes.   budgeting
They require estimates of sales, prices, and costs for the entire
company as well as for divisions, geographical areas, product lines,
and so forth. Moreover, they demand predictions of economic and
industry variables that affect company sales, prices, and costs. When
a recession takes place, all variables being predicted will be influenced
in the same direction and by similar magnitude; thus large errors
can result, which might necessitate the closing down of factories, the
firing of workers, and other unpleasant belt-tightening measures. The
March 1997 announcement of the permanent closing of a Renault
factory in Belgium and the firing of nearly 4,000 additional personnel
were partly caused, according to top management, by the 1996 slump
in the European car market, which was not predicted (indeed, there
were forecasts for growth).

The deeper a recession, the worse the forecasting errors and the
greater the unpleasant surprises and negative consequences. During
a boom the opposite type of error normally occurs, giving rise to
underestimations of demand, personnel needs, and the like. The
inability to predict booms, or the underestimation of their extent,
can result in opportunity losses, with serious negative consequences
for a firm's competitiveness.

Although forecasting services and newsletters claim to be able to   newsletters
predict recessions or booms, empirical evidence has shown beyond
any reasonable doubt that they have not so far been successful. This
means that our inability to forecast recessions and booms as well as
measure the uncertainty involved must be accepted and taken into
account not only during budget deliberations but also in formulating
a strategy that accepts such uncertainty and its consequences. On
the other hand, the end of a recession (once it has started) is easier

to predict. Recessions last about a year, and their length does not fluctuate widely around this average.

cycles

Not all companies are equally affected by cycles. In general, manufacturing firms are more affected than service firms; firms producing or servicing luxury (elastic) goods are more affected than those producing or servicing necessities (inelastic products and services); industrial firms are more affected than consumer firms; and companies in industries where strong competition exists are affected more than those in less competitive ones. These general rules can help executives decide upon the extent of cyclical fluctuations so they can determine what needs to be done to be prepared for the eventuality of a recession or boom. A great deal of information about the length of business cycles, the depth of recessions, and the strength of boom can be gained for specific industries and firms through historical data, which can be decomposed (see Chapter 9) to isolate and study the trend-cycles involved.

recession

In forecasting and planning one thing is sure: after a long boom a recession is inevitable. The only thing not known is when it will start and how deep it will be. Thus, contingency plans, including the buildup of reserves to face the coming recession, become necessary. The same is true during periods of recession. A recovery is certain. The only question is when exactly it will start and how strong it will be. Obviously, there is always the possibility that a recession might last a very long time, or that it may turn into a depression. It will have to end sometime, however.

depression

Although the possibility of a depression exists, it is highly unlikely and cannot be seriously considered; moreover, a firm trying to plan for an extremely long or continuous recession will likely be too conservative in its outlook and actions and overtaken by more aggressive competitors. Although we know that a car can hit us when we are crossing a street, no one can seriously consider never walking because of that possibility. Equally important, only one postwar recession has lasted for more than one year (18 months precisely). Thus, chances are that future recessions will not be much longer than one year.

monitoring

Because recessions and booms cannot be predicted, it becomes necessary to monitor critical variables to know, as soon as possible, when they will arrive. This is the second best alternative to forecasting. It is like having a radar tracking system looking for a possible enemy attack. It cannot tell us when the attack will be launched, but it can warn us once it is on the way. Although monitoring is not forecasting, it prevents executives from being taken completely by surprise when a recession, or boom, arrives. Moreover, it can provide them with a competitive advantage if they can predict the start of the recession (or boom) earlier than their competitors—at least they will not be at a disadvantage.

Another way of anticipating recessions is by looking for imbalances in one's own industry, the economy, or the international financial system. The bigger and the more widespread such imbalances, the greater the chance of a correction, which usually takes the form of a recession. Similarly, the longer the boom, the higher the chance of a recession or vice versa. Thus, all the talk about the end of recessions is premature (the same beliefs were held in the end of the 1960s, just before the 1969/70 recession). Recessions are part of the economic system; the only question is how long and how deep they will be.

In practical terms, it makes little sense to attempt to forecast recessions or booms well in advance. In the past, recessions or booms that had not been forecast occurred, and others that had been predicted did not materialize. Therefore, spending money or resources to predict recessions or booms adds little or no value to future decision making. It is best to accept that such a task cannot provide us with reliable predictions, and to plan budgets by extrapolating established trends and relationships or by making contingency plans having the average recession, or boom, in mind. Subsequently, an organization should be capable of adjusting its plans as soon as monitoring has confirmed a recession or boom. This is where contingency planning *contingency planning* can be of great help. As recessions or booms are certain to arrive, managers can be prepared to face them by having drawn up detailed contingency plans of what to do once the occurrence of a recession or boom of a certain magnitude has been confirmed.

12/1/3 Long-term predictions

Long-term forecasts are primarily needed for capital expansion plans, selecting R&D projects, launching new products, formulating long-term goals and strategies, and deciding the best way of adapting orga-

mega trends
analogies
scenarios

nizations to environmental changes. Long-term predictions are based on the extrapolation of mega trends and on analogies (see Chapter 9). The challenge is to determine, preferably through scenarios, how such trends will affect us and how new technologies (e.g., computers and telecommunications) will influence the future environment and our industry and firm.

The farther away the time horizon of our predictions, the lesser the accuracy of our forecasts, since many things can happen to change established patterns and relationships. The purpose of forecasting in such cases is to build scenarios that provide general directions to where the world economy, or a particular industry, is heading, and to identify the major opportunities as well as dangers ahead.

technology

A big challenge is to predict technological innovations and how they will change the industry, mold competition, and affect the specific organization. New technologies can drastically change established demand, societal attitudes, costs, distribution channels, and the competitive structure of industries and firms. The major purpose of such long-term forecasting is to help the organization develop foresight, form a consensus about the future, and start considering ways of adapting to the forthcoming change—or even actively contributing to changing the industry in desired ways so that the firm can become the leader and profit from such changes.

organizational
consensus

Because long-term forecasting cannot be specific and will always be uncertain, its value lies in helping generate organizational consensuses and in establishing the right sense of direction. At present firms must, for instance, be concerned about the forthcoming Information Revolution and its impact (see Chapter 9), and more specifically how the Internet and similar worldwide networks may affect them in the future.

12/2   Organizational aspects of forecasting

users and preparers

Wheelwright and Clarke (1976), in a survey about the usage of forecasting in business firms, identified some major differences between the perceptions of forecast users (managers and decision makers) and those of forecast preparers. These differences can be seen in Table 12-1, which identifies preparers' and users' abilities as seen

Preparer's Ability	Rating (%)
Understand sophisticated mathematical forecasting tendencies	+1
Understand management problems	-25^a
Provide forecasts in new situations	−42
Provide forecasts in ongoing situations	−13
Identify important issues in a forecasting situation	−30
Identify the best technique for a given situation	−56
Provide cost-effective forecasts	−33
Provide results in the time frame required	−38
User's Technical Ability	
Understand the essentials of forecasting techniques	+27
Understand sophisticated mathematical forecasting techniques	+12
Identify new applications for forecasting	+5
Effectively use formal forecasts	−6
Evaluate the appropriateness of a forecasting technique	+24
User/Preparer Interaction Skills	
Understand management problems (preparers)	−25
Work within the organization (preparers)	−10
Understand management problems (users)	−5
Communicate with preparers of forecasts (users)	−1
Work within the organization in getting forecasts (users)	+2
User's Management Abilities	
Make the decisions required in their jobs	−3
Effectively use formal forecasts	−6
Describe important issues in forecasting situations	−8
Work within the organization in getting forecasts	+2

[a]25% more preparers rated themselves good or excellent than did users.

$$\text{Rating} = 100 \times \frac{\% \text{ users rating good or excellent} - \% \text{ preparers rating good or excellent}}{\% \text{ preparers rating good or excellent}}$$

Table 12-1: *Differences in perceptions of users and preparers of forecasts. Source: Steven C. Wheelwright and Darral G. Clarke (1976), "Corporate Forecasting: Promise and Reality," Harvard Business Review (November–December 1976), copyright © 1976 by the President and Fellows of Harvard College, all rights reserved. Reprinted by permission.*

separately by each group, the users'/preparers' interaction skills, as well as the users' management abilities. Examining the differences in Table 12-1 it is obvious that preparers perceive that they are doing a much better job than users think, while they also perceive that users cannot adequately understand fundamental aspects of forecasting including the selection of the most appropriate method(s). At the same time, preparers think that they understand management and work problems much better than is perceived by users. Such major differences between preparers and users were further supported in a series of questions about those activities whose improvement would be most beneficial to the firm's forecasting efforts. A majority of responses highlighted communication between preparers and users. In addition, management support and data-processing support were also cited as important areas that could significantly enhance the

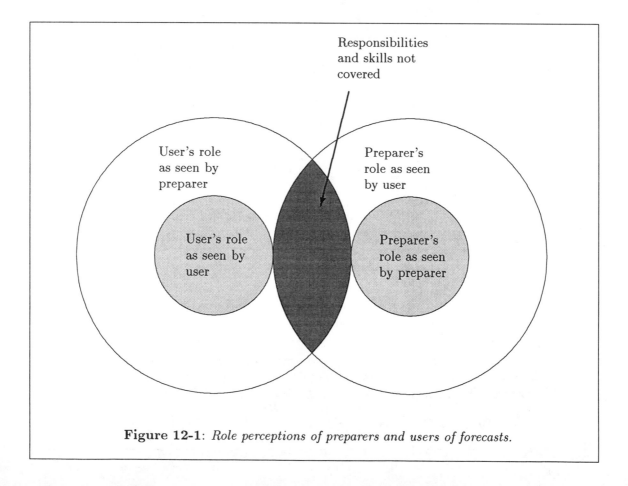

Figure 12-1: *Role perceptions of preparers and users of forecasts.*

value of the firm's forecasting efforts.

Wheelwright and Clarke concluded from their survey that while the communication problem was indeed real, it was merely a symptom of a deeper problem. The problem inherent in a number of the responding firms centered around the definition of the responsibilities and skills of users and preparers. It appeared that both groups had abdicated certain essential tasks and skills to their counterparts, with the result that some of the basics were not being covered. This conclusion is shown graphically in Figure 12-1. Each group appeared to view its own role more narrowly than the role of its counterpart, with the consequence that some responsibilities and skills were not being picked up by either group.

responsibilities

Wheelwright and Clarke identified a range of critical tasks where a significant number of the surveyed firms rated themselves as only adequate or less than adequate in their skills and abilities. For example, in only 15% of the firms did both the user and preparer rate themselves as adequate or more than adequate in understanding management's forecasting problems. In only 29% did both users and preparers rate themselves as adequate or better at identifying the important issues in a forecasting situation.

While these results suggest some basic areas requiring attention, those charged with managing the forecasting function need a mechanism for identifying what is wrong with their own situation and the types of actions to be taken. These issues are discussed next.

12/2/1 Correcting an organization's forecasting problems

Much of the authors' work in forecasting has suggested that a good starting point for improving the forecasting function within organizations is to audit existing problems and opportunities. Although there is some literature on performing such reviews, the bulk of it concentrates on accuracy as the key problem and identifies as causes of the problem the use of poor data, the wrong methods, and the lack of trained forecasters. Without much empirical basis, this literature suggests that an obvious solution to problems of accuracy is the use of improved—by which is generally meant more sophisticated—methods. Not surprisingly, such solutions tend

review existing
problems

to require more sophisticated forecasters or additional training for those already at work. Thus, the typical solution is to replace existing methods with more mathematical ones and to replace and upgrade existing forecasters so that they can handle such methods. Unfortunately, empirical evidence does not support the assumption that sophisticated methods outperform simpler ones (see Chapter 11).

The results of such actions range from slight improvements to frustration and higher turnover among forecasters. Even organizations with trained statisticians and sophisticated methods are frequently disappointed with the performance and impact of their forecasting. This interaction of problem–causes–remedies–results often leads to the undesired scenario summarized in Figure 12-2.

One reason for results being less desirable than expected is that in many organizations forecasting is not a career. Rather, it is part of the assignment of a market planner or a group controller, or it is a temporary job on the way to more important positions. Recommending that these forecasters become experts in sophisticated statistical techniques has been inconsistent with organizational and personal philosophies and objectives, as well as bad advice if the goal is improved accuracy.

In addition, applying a specific method and obtaining a numerical output represent only one step, albeit an important one, in the process of forecasting. Concentrating on accuracy is like trying to melt an iceberg by heating the tip: when forecasting accuracy is slightly improved, other managerial problems of implementation rise to the surface to prevent the full realization of forecasting's promise.

12/2/2 Types of forecasting problems and their solutions

characterize problems

To improve forecasting, one framework that the authors have found useful has as its first step the characterization of problems as one of several types, which are discussed below: credibility and impact, lack of recent improvement, and lack of a firm base on which to build, while solutions center around the opportunities and in adequate training.

Credibility and impact:

Forecasting often has little impact on decision making. This may be caused by a forecast's lack of relevance—in terms of what, when, how, and in which form such forecasts are provided. The problem may be interpersonal, for example, when those who prepare the forecasts and those who use them fail to communicate effectively; or the problem may be one of organizational structure, where forecasting is performed at such a level that it is highly unlikely that it will ever have much impact on decision making. In addition, forecasters tend to concentrate on well-behaved situations that can be forecast with standard methods, and ignore the more dynamic (and often more interesting) change situations that decision makers most want to forecast.

Lack of recent improvements in forecasting:

Forecasting problems arise when forecasting is no longer improving. Sometimes the reason is simply that the resources committed to forecasting have become so stretched in maintaining ongoing procedures that no new development is possible. At other times there may not be enough commitment to attain the next level of substantial progress. This also occurs when organizational change and managerial interface problems are not recognized. The remedies prescribed in Figure 12-2 run into barriers that they cannot overcome. Furthermore, these remedies probably are not helpful, even if accepted by the organization.

Lack of a firm base on which to build:

This is generally a getting-started problem. Resources or emphasis committed to forecasting may be insufficient for substantial impact. Even when resources have been committed, knowledge of good forecasting practice and available methods may be lacking during startup. The problem may also result from an absence of any systematic strategy or plan for improving forecasting.

Major opportunities for improvement:

Organizations frequently describe their forecasting problems in terms of opportunities for substantial improvements. They may

credibility and impact

lack of improvements

lack of firm base

opportunities for improvement

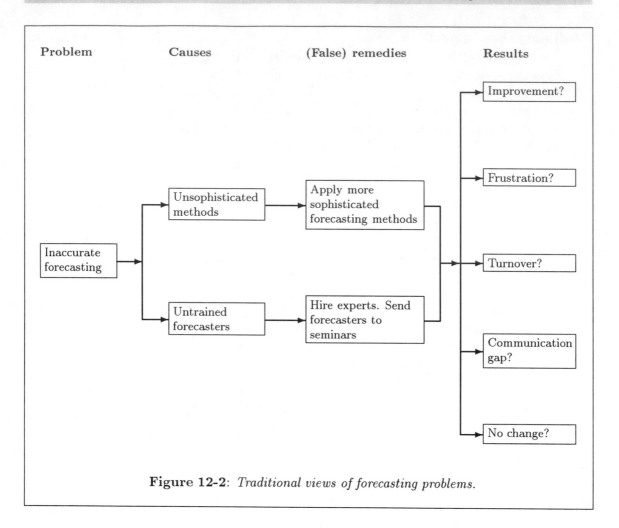

Figure 12-2: *Traditional views of forecasting problems.*

be quite satisfied with what is being done but feel more could be done—particularly if certain areas are not being handled systematically as part of the forecasting system or if performance is not yet at the expected level. Organizations may also feel this way when they think their forecasting approach is extremely vulnerable to changes in the environment, or when changes in their strategy may require (be contingent on) significant improvements in forecasting performance. In any of these situations, major opportunities for improvement must be identified both internally and by benchmarking a firm's performance in various criteria with that of others, preferably those best in forecasting applications.

Training:

Training is the most common remedy when organizations attack forecasting problems. It may also be the most overrated. The emphasis should not be on increasing the forecaster's knowledge of sophisticated methods, since doing so does not necessarily lead to improved performance. Rather, training should consider issues such as how to select a time horizon; how to choose the length of a time period; how to find appropriate data and adjust it for outliers and other, possible, errors; how judgment can be incorporated into a statistical forecast; how large changes in the environment can be monitored; and the level of aggregation to be forecast. Users of forecasts, on the other hand, need training in the pros and cons of alternative methods and in the identification of situations where systematic forecasting can play a major role in improving organizational decision making. Finally, training may help in refining one's approach to implementation and avoiding or minimizing communication problems between the preparers and the users of forecasts.

Underlying such an audit is the notion that both forecasters and the decision makers who use their forecasts tend to do a number of things "wrong," which detracts from realizing the full potential for their organization. As suggested in Table 12-2, Armstrong has identified 16 pitfalls often seen in practice that are characteristic of   mistakes in using forecasting. Table 12-2 also suggests (in the form of a question) the solution for each of those mistakes. As indicated in this checklist, a firm that can answer "yes" to each solution question is doing an outstanding job of avoiding mistakes and getting the most out of its forecasting applications. The larger the percentage of "no" responses for a given situation, the more things are being done incorrectly and the greater the opportunity to improve significantly the way the forecasting situation is being handled.

This section has dealt with possible organizational pitfalls and improvements so that forecasting can become more useful and relevant for those most needing its predictions: the users of forecasts. The changes being suggested will, however, in their great majority, produce marginal improvements, which if taken together can better the forecasting function. At the same time, organizations should look for "big" improvements that may produce revolutionary changes in their approach to forecasts and their usefulness.

1. *Assess the methods without the forecasts.* Most of the discussion should focus on the methods. Which forecasting methods were considered, and which ones were used? The auditor is in a good position, as an outside observer, to say whether the methods are reasonable. (See checklist items 1 through 8.)

2. Given that the methods are judged reasonable, *what assumptions and data were used in the forecast?* (This step may be difficult to separate from the previous step.) One role of the auditor is to judge whether all relevant factors have been examined. In particular, the auditors might help to ensure that key environmental factors have been assessed. (See items 9 through 11.)

3. *An assessment should be made of uncertainty.* This should include upper and lower bounds for each forecast, contingency forecasts, previous accuracy, and the arguments against each forecast. Interestingly, in a study on long-range metals forecasts, Rush and Page found that while 22% of the 27 forecasts published from 1910 to 1940 made explicit references to uncertainties, only 8% of the 63 studies from 1940 to 1964 did so. In other words, the concern over uncertainty decreased over time. (See items 12 through 15.)

4. Finally, *an assessment should be made of costs.* (See item 16.)

Forecasting Methods	No	?	Yes
1. Forecast independent of top management?	___	___	___
2. Forecast used objective methods?	___	___	___
3. Structured techniques used to obtain judgments?	___	___	___
4. Least expensive experts used?	___	___	___
5. More than one method used to obtain forecasts?	___	___	___
6. Users understand the forecasting methods?	___	___	___
7. Forecasts free of judgmental revisions?	___	___	___
8. Separate documents prepared for plans and forecasts?	___	___	___
Assumptions and Data			
9. Ample budget for analysis and presentation of data?	___	___	___
10. Central data bank exists?	___	___	___
11. Least expensive macroeconomic forecasts used?	___	___	___
Uncertainty			
12. Upper and lower bounds provided?	___	___	___
13. Quantitative analysis of previous accuracy?	___	___	___
14. Forecasts prepared for alternative futures?	___	___	___
15. Arguments listed against each forecast?	___	___	___
Costs			
16. Amount spent on forecasting reasonable?	___	___	___

Table 12-2: *Armstrong's forecasting audit checklist. Source: Armstrong, J.S., 1982. "The Forecasting Audit," Chapter 32, The handbook of forecasting, S. Makridakis and S.C. Wheelwright (eds.). New York: John Wiley & Sons, Inc. Reprinted by permission.*

12/3 Extrapolative predictions versus creative insights

Nowadays, when benchmarking is widely used, whatever improvements a firm can achieve in its forecasting function will be easily imitated by others. The widespread use of personal computers, large data banks, and easy-to-use forecasting programs have allowed a large percentage of firms to employ statistical methods to obtain accurate and timely objective predictions. Accurate statistical forecasting has become a competitive requirement, therefore, that provides few unique advantages to today's firms. The same is true of extrapolative, long-term predictions (in particular, general ones), which are readily available for practically everyone interested in obtaining them; they are published in books and are available in a variety of sources. Thus, these provide no strategic advantages even if they are highly accurate.

The substantial growth in the demand for personal computers has, for example, been correctly predicted since the middle 1980s; however, the great majority of firms producing and/or selling such computers went out of business as high growth rates and the prospects of huge profits contributed to creating serious overcapacity, by both existing players as well as new entrants, which fueled competition and reduced profit margins. In final analysis fewer than a dozen firms worldwide have managed to prosper in such a highly competitive environment. On the other hand, Bill Gates became one of the richest men on earth by moving into a direction few considered of major importance at that time: software. IBM was not interested in buying outright the operating system Microsoft offered to run its first personal computers, though it could have easily done so as its bargaining power at that time was huge while that of Gates and Microsoft was nil.

IBM did not want to buy the rights to the operating system because the company did not believe that the software for running the personal computers was important. The premise: they extrapolated the past in a linear fashion. By doing so, they judged the value of personal computers and programs from the perspective of mainframe computers and programs where the obvious winner was the hardware ("big iron"), which provided huge profit margins while the role of software, mostly proprietary, was simply to support the hardware.

extrapolating the past

As well, the price of software was then prohibitively high; only the government, military, or business firms could contemplate buying it.

Gates' insight was to see a whole new market made up of hundreds of millions of personal computers each using its own software that would be cheap enough so that anyone with a computer could afford it. Whether or not Bill Gates was simply lucky or indeed had a creative insight is probably unanswerable. However, he and Microsoft were ready to exploit the opportunities opening up through exploding demand for personal computers, while others were not. In consequence, Microsoft's market value increased above that of IBM's, which found itself in serious trouble precisely because personal computers and cheap software greatly diminished the demand for its mainframe computers as the cost per million instructions of personal computing became less than $1/100$ that of mainframes.

The story of Bill Gates and Microsoft is not unique. The ability to see the future in a new light, not constrained through the linear extrapolation of the past, has always been central to every breakthrough: from Henry Ford's Model T to the latest developments in the Internet. Unless someone is capable of conceiving brand-new ways of utilizing the capabilities available through new technologies, there cannot be a breakthrough. Linear thinking, on the other hand, provides only small, marginal improvements and a lot of competition. Thus, forecasting involves much more than mere extrapolations, which are most relevant for the short-term but of little use for the long run.

creative insights

Forecasting for operational scheduling and planning is based upon the correct identification of established patterns/relationships and their appropriate extrapolation. This extrapolation, although it provides great advantages for operational purposes, can also become the biggest hindrance to succeeding in the long-term because successful forecasting requires creative insights not constrained through the linear extrapolation of the past. Long-term forecasting requires visionaries who are, at the same time, practical realists. They must be capable of breaking from the conventional wisdom of the past and present, and conceive the future in new ways which, by definition, must be based not on tired thinking but on creative insights about forthcoming changes and their implications.

Are all those with creative insights concerning the future success-ful? The answer is a definite no. For every success story there are probably hundreds of failures (Kaplan, 1995); being a pioneer requires taking huge risks that do not pay off in the great majority of cases (Schnaars, 1989). Yet for those pioneers who make it, the payoffs are enormous, justifying the great risks taken to succeed.

12/3/1 Hindsight versus foresight

People are rarely surprised by what has happened (Hogarth and Makridakis, 1981). The Monday morning quarterback syndrome is strong in all of us. After the fact we believe we know what has happened and we can explain with absolute certainty the reasons why those involved were successful visionaries—or outright failures blinded by shortsightedness and unable to recognize and act upon the major changes that affect their firm and industry/market. Hindsight is easy. The big challenge is developing correct foresight about future events whose timing and consequences are not yet known.

At the beginning of 1997, for instance, there was a big debate. On one side were Intel and Microsoft, whose dominance forced consumers into a spiral of buying ever more sophisticated computer programs, such as Windows 95, whose operation required faster computers (i.e., those using Intel's Pentium chip). This spiral of bigger pro-grams/faster computers seemed endless; if buyers wanted to keep up with the newest developments they had to continuously spend large sums on upgrading their computers and on buying bigger, more sophisticated programs. In doing so they improved the profitability of Intel and Microsoft, but they spent a lot of money.

On the other side of the debate were firms like Sun Microsystems, Oracle, and Netscape that argued that there was no need for high-powered personal computers and huge, complex programs capable of meeting the needs of even the most sophisticated users. Instead they proposed a cheap, basic computer box that could run on the Internet (Schlender, 1996). Users could download any program they wished from the Internet to do a specific task: word processing, spelling, etc. Users would not have to pay for a single program containing myriad features they would never use; rather, they would pay only for what was wanted, renting the programs for a single occasion, or on a monthly or yearly basis. The advantage of renting is that in addition to being extremely cheap, as there would be millions of users, the version rented would contain the latest improvements. Since even the largest, specific-purpose program could be run on a cheap basic computer box, users would not have to buy a bigger and faster computer every few years, thereby breaking the spiral and diminishing or destroying the monopolistic power that "Wintel" held over the personal computer market. The result would open up brand-new possibilities.

At present it is not clear whether Intel/Microsoft or Sun/Oracle/Netscape will be the winners of the race to dominate the personal computer market. Maybe there will be one, or the other, or probably a combination of the two. This is where correct foresight is critical, as the consequences of who will win are enormous. At the same time, in a few years when the winner is known it will be easy to say, in hindsight, whether Bill Gates of Microsoft and Andy Grove of Intel were visionary or shortsighted. In other words, saying after the fact that Ken Olsen of Digital and John Akers of IBM were shortsighted has little value. What provides great value is correct foresight about the future. Successful foresight will have to involve new developments that go beyond Internet and computer languages such as Sun's Java. These are not even known at present but will, undoubtedly, become huge commercial successes in the future precisely because of the creative insights of some people who can conceive their commercial value and take specific steps to exploit them to their advantage.

As creative insights will always be in short supply, so will the foresight needed to correctly anticipate major future changes, which when exploited can provide huge commercial benefits. The bottleneck to future success will, therefore, become the creative potential of entrepreneurs and executives who can come up with the foresight required to anticipate those changes that will be in the biggest demand tomorrow.

12/4 Forecasting in the future

In the future we foresee several major changes that will affect forecasting and its use and usefulness. They will be mostly related to the
so-called Information Revolution and are described in the remainder   Information
of this chapter.   Revolution

12/4/1 Data, information, and forecasts

As the cost of computers, communications, and information storage
falls, their usage will increase—to the point that they become util-   '
ities like electricity and telephone. Nearly everyone will be able to
access any databank or source of information desired, and/or store
practically unlimited data on some computer device; this access will   data access
be possible from anywhere. As the dissemination of information
becomes faster and global, market efficiency will improve and local   efficiency
inefficiencies be eliminated. The quality of information will become   information quality
better as more resources are devoted to data collecting and process-
ing. Furthermore, computer programs will analyze and evaluate information and provide expert advice on its meaning and implications.   expert advice
Such advice will also include the identification and extrapolation of
established patterns/relationships, assuming no major changes, or
even providing alternative scenarios under various assumptions of
possible changes so as to aid judgmental forecasting. As a result,
accurate extrapolative predictions will be commonplace and provide
no competitive advantages. Instead, they will be a competitive
requirement every firm will need so as to improve its internal efficiency
and effectiveness and survive in the long run. Externally, as more
organizations and people are capable of accurate extrapolations,
whatever benefits they generate will be quickly discounted, making
all markets more efficient.

A major consequence of super-efficient markets will undoubtedly
be that they behave increasingly like random walks, making it im-   random walks
possible to predict, at least statistically, their turning points. Insignificant, unpredictable events could trigger major turning points
in a fashion similar to the "butterfly effect" in chaos theory, where   chaos theory
some trivial initial condition (such as the air displaced by the flying
of a butterfly in a tropical forest) can instigate a major hurricane

a week or two later. Since business and economic events are, in addition, influenced by psychological factors, the effect of some trivial initial happening could bring considerable changes as its effects are amplified through people's perceptions of the implications. In such an environment competitive advantage will stem from correct, unique, and insightful anticipations of forthcoming changes that are exploited before others realize the opportunities.

12/4/2 Collective knowledge, experience, and forecasting

Successful forecasting requires studying the past and knowing the present. In statistical forecasting historical data are collected and used to identify established patterns and existing relationships, which are subsequently extrapolated to predict their continuation. Such data provide the memory that links the past/present with the future and serves as the basis of forecasting. But in the long run we must break the linearity and through creative insights build the future of our dreams. Many will fail and in a sense pay the price for the few who will manage to achieve success.

groupware

Where much can and needs to be done is in soliciting the collective wisdom of all knowledgeable people in the organization in ways that can improve overall forecasting accuracy and usage while keeping costs as low as possible. This is where groupware run through intranets (and extranets) is bound to play a highly valuable role, improving organizational learning and the accuracy of forecasting, particularly in special, or even unique, cases and when patterns and/or relationships have changed or are about to change.

The three biggest advantages we see in groupware for forecasting purposes are:

ease of interaction

1. Allowing the interaction of several/many people without the need to be physically present in a meeting. This means that their collective wisdom and knowledge can be tapped without the high cost of co-location. Groupware also reduces the influence of dominant individuals (including the boss, who can unduly impose opinions about the future) while speeding up the process of arriving at a consensus forecast(s) because several people can offer opinions simultaneously. Moreover, as useful

background information can be put onto electronic bulletin boards, participants can be better informed before or during a "virtual" meeting. Furthermore, suppliers, customers, and company people working in different departments will have access to the data banks and bulletin boards where information is kept and changes, and their implications, are noted so that their influence on the future can be better estimated;

2. Keeping extensive and detailed records of the factors and options considered as well as the forecasts of the various participants. These records can be used in the future to form the basis of feedback and facilitate learning. Equally important, groupware can record such learning for the future, when other people will be involved in the forecasting process. A new product manager, for example, will not have to start from scratch but can instead learn from records kept in ways that allow for organizational learning beyond specific individuals.

keeping records

3. Facilitating the "unbiasing" of judgmental forecasts (by both providing objective information and illustrating past cases of judgmental biases) and the building of a consensus concerning the future. Such a consensus is particularly valuable for long-term predictions when important technological and other changes can occur and whose consequences can be critical for the firm.

unbiased judgmental forecasts

In our view, groupware will probably affect the field of forecasting more than any other development (in ways that are difficult to envision at present), providing the impetus for more accurate and effective predictions and allowing statistical predictions to be more efficiently and effectively blended (combined) with judgmental ones. To achieve such an objective the advantages of both statistical methods and judgment will have to be exploited while their disadvantages avoided by designing appropriate groupware procedures for doing so. More specifically, the field of forecasting must go beyond its present quantitative bounds and expand to include the following 10 considerations necessary to better understand the factors that influence the future and how they could change past patterns and/or relationships:

1. Economic/market forces (e.g., the law of demand and supply) and biological laws (e.g., the S-shaped increases in growth) that generate and maintain various types of long-term equilibria.

2. People's preferences, tastes, and budget constraints.

3. People's aspirations to change the future in some desired manner or direction.

4. Some people's ability to change the future in some favored way (e.g., through new technologies).

5. Some people's wish to maintain the status quo.

6. Some people's capabilities to control or slow down change (e.g., through monopolies or cartels).

7. Natural events (e.g., a good or bad harvest) and their influence on the economic and business environment.

8. Momentum, or inertia, that sustains established patterns and upholds existing relationships, at least in the short-term.

9. Psychological factors, market inefficiencies, and plain accidents or mere coincidences.

10. Ability to monitor effectively current events and take corrective action if necessary and possible.

This is, we believe, the direction the field of forecasting must take to provide an "all-inclusive" service to those who need predictions about the future upon which to base their plans and strategies. This is, therefore, the big challenge for those in the field: they must go beyond their narrow speciality and provide a service to encompass the above 10 aspects necessary for making accurate and realistic forecasts.

References and selected bibliography

CUSUMANO, M.A. and SELBY, R.W. (1995) *Microsoft Secrets: powerful software company creates technology, shapes markets and manages people*, New York: The Free Press.

DURANT, W. and A. (1968) *The lessons of history*, New York: Simon and Schuster.

FILDES, R. and BEARD, C. (1992) Forecasting systems for production and inventory control, *International Journal of Operations and Production Management*, **12**, 4–27.

FOX, J. (1997) The economic outlook: reasons to worry, *Fortune*, Feb. 3, pp. 16–18.

HOGARTH, R. and MAKRIDAKIS, S. (1981) Forecasting and planning: an evaluation, *Management Science*, **27**, 115–138.

HOWARD, M. (1991) *The lessons of history*, Oxford: Clarendon Press.

KAPLAN, J. (1995) *Startup: a Silicon Valley adventure*, New York: Houghton Mifflin.

MAKRIDAKIS, S. (1982) The chronology of the last six recessions, *Omega*, **10**, 43–50.

————————— (1986) The art and science of forecasting: an assessment and future directions, *International Journal of Forecasting*, **2**, 15–39.

MAKRIDAKIS, S. and WHEELWRIGHT, S.C. (1989) *Forecasting methods for management*, 5th ed., New York: John Wiley & Sons.

ORD, J.K. (1988) Future developments in forecasting: the time series connection, *International Journal of Forecasting*, **4**, 389–401.

SCHLENDER, B. (1996) Sun's Java: the threat to Microsoft is real, *Fortune*, Nov. 11, pp. 87–92.

SCHNAARS, S. (1989) *Megamistakes: forecasting and the myth of rapid technological change*, New York: The Free Press.

URRESTA, L. (1995) Recession? What recession? *Fortune*, June 12, p. 25.

WHEELWRIGHT, S.C. and CLARKE, D.G. (1976) Corporate forecasting: promise and reality, *Harvard Business Review*, **54**, November–December, pp. 40ff.

Exercises

12.1 Describe what can and cannot be predicted while attempting to forecast the future.

12.2 Discuss the value of creating meaningful insights about the future when operating in a competitive environment where information is readily and instantly disseminated.

12.3 Where do you see the field of forecasting going in the future and what can you do to benefit from forthcoming changes in the environment?

12.4 Table 12-2 in this chapter shows Armstrong's Forecasting Audit Checklist. Comment on the value of such checklist and discuss its usefulness in avoiding forecasting biases.

APPENDIX I

FORECASTING RESOURCES

1 Forecasting Software

Every forecaster will need access to at least one forecasting package. The selection of a suitable package can be difficult with thousands of computer packages available which allow some forecasting. There are large packages providing a bewildering array of facilities and able to handle millions of data from thousands of variables. There are small specialized packages which will handle only a few models, often providing facilities which are not available in larger packages. There are statistical programming languages enabling the user to develop their own forecasting methods. There are add-on forecasting functions for spreadsheet packages. The choice of software depends on the forecasting methods available, the ease of data entry and data management, the quality of the output, and a host of other factors associated with the needs of the user.

In this appendix, we summarize a range of forecasting software and give some indication of their usefulness in different contexts.

1/1 Spreadsheets

spreadsheet packages Spreadsheet packages such as Excel, Lotus 1-2-3, and Quattro Pro are used extensively in business. They usually provide some forecasting functions. For example, Microsoft Excel (version 5.0) provides facilities for single exponential smoothing, simple and multiple regression. Add-on functions are available for the most popular packages which provide some additional facilities.

It should be noted that a spreadsheet is not designed for statistical analysis and the facilities which are provided are insufficient for exploratory data analysis, checking model assumptions and comparing several competing forecasting methods. Instead, a spreadsheet functions more as a statistical calculator. Many other packages allow input from Lotus and Excel files, so they provide a useful adjunct to other more powerful forecasting software.

1/2 Statistics packages

General statistics packages usually provide some forecasting facilities. Minitab, SAS, and SPSS are among the most popular statistics packages which are used for forecasting. Each of these packages is available for both mainframes and microcomputers, and can be used via a menu structure or via a command language. Table I-1 summarizes their capabilities. We have also included S-Plus which is not intended to be a general statistics package, but an environment for data analysis and developing statistical applications. However, it comes with a number of useful forecasting facilities. In producing this summary, we have used the Minitab version 11, SAS version 6.12 with the ETS component, SPSS version 7.5 with the Trends module and S-Plus version 4.0. All packages were used on the Windows platform.

Note that although a package may offer a particular method, the ease-of-use and available options can vary greatly between packages. Only where a package has a built-in function to perform a particular method is it marked as available. Each of these packages also has some facilities for programming, enabling the user to implement forecasting methods not provided as a standard option.

General statistics packages are useful for those who require statistical, graphical, and data analysis facilities more generally than just for forecasting. Reviews of statistical software appear regularly in **software reviews** a number of journals including the "Statistical Software Newsletter" which is published with *Computational Statistics and Data Analysis* by Elsevier.

1/3 Specialty forecasting packages

Smaller computer packages are available which specialize in forecasting. These contain a much more limited range of facilities than a general statistics package, but they often contain forecasting tools which are not available in the larger packages. These specialty packages are useful for those whose only statistical needs are related to forecasting. They are also useful in conjunction with a more general statistics package, particularly where they provide facilities which are otherwise unavailable. Most of the specialty forecasting packages are only available on the Windows platform. Among the most popular Windows forecasting packages are Forecast Pro, EViews (a successor of MicroTSP), SIBYL/Runner, Autobox, and SCA. These are summarized in Table I-2. In producing this summary, we have used Forecast Pro 2.0, EViews 3.0, SIBYL/Runner 1.12, Autobox 4.0, and SCA 5.1a (with PC-EXPERT and PC-GSA). Some

Chapter	Method	Minitab	SAS	SPSS	S-Plus
2	Time plots	✓	✓	✓	✓
	Seasonal plots				
	Scatterplots	✓	✓	✓	✓
	Autocorrelation	✓	✓	✓	✓
3	Classical decomposition	✓	✓	✓	
	Census II decomposition (X11)		✓	✓	
	STL decomposition				✓
	Decomposition plot				✓
	Sub-series plot				✓
4	Moving average forecasts	✓			
	Single exponential smoothing		✓	✓	
	ARRSES				
	Holt's method	✓	✓	✓	
	Holt-Winters' additive method	✓	✓	✓	
	Holt-Winters' multiplicative method	✓	✓	✓	
	Other exponential methods		✓	✓	
5	Correlations	✓	✓	✓	✓
	Simple linear regression	✓	✓	✓	✓
	Loess smoothing	✓	✓	✓	✓
6	Multiple linear regression	✓	✓	✓	✓
	Best subsets regression	✓			
	Step-wise regression	✓	✓	✓	✓
	Durbin-Watson test	✓	✓	✓	
	Residual plots	✓	✓	✓	
7	ACF and PACF plots	✓	✓	✓	✓
	Box-Pierce or Ljung-Box tests	✓	✓	✓	
	ARIMA models	✓	✓	✓	✓
	AIC for ARIMA models		✓	✓	✓
	Automatic model selection		✓		
	Simulation of ARIMA models		✓		✓
8	Regression with AR errors		✓	✓	✓
	Regression with ARIMA errors		✓	✓	✓
	Dynamic regression models		✓		
	Intervention analysis		✓	*	
	Multivariate AR models		✓		
	State space models		✓		
	Non-linear models				
	Neural network forecasting				
Other	Comparison of forecasting methods		✓		
	Allows holdout sets		✓		

* only where $\delta(B) = 1$

Table I-1: *Forecasting facilities in Minitab 11, SAS 6.12 (with ETS), SPSS 7.5 (with Trends) and S-Plus 4.0.*

Chapter	Method	Forecast Pro	EViews	SIBYL/ Runner	Autobox	SCA
2	Time plots	✓	✓	✓	✓	✓
	Seasonal plots					
	Scatterplots		✓			✓
	Autocorrelation	✓	✓	✓	✓	✓
3	Classical decomposition			✓		
	Census II decomposition (X11)		✓	✓		
	STL decomposition					
	Decomposition plots					
	Sub-series plots					
4	Moving average forecasts	✓	✓	✓	✓	✓
	Single exponential smoothing	✓	✓	✓	✓	✓
	ARRSES			✓		
	Holt's method	✓	✓	✓	✓	✓
	Holt-Winters' additive method	✓	✓	✓	✓	✓
	Holt-Winters' multiplicative method	✓	✓	✓	✓	✓
	Other exponential methods	✓	✓	✓	✓	✓
5	Correlations		✓	✓	✓	✓
	Simple linear regression	✓	✓	✓	✓	✓
	Loess smoothing					
6	Multiple linear regression	✓	✓	✓	✓	✓
	Best subsets regression					
	Step-wise regression				✓	✓
	Durbin-Watson test	✓	✓	✓		✓
	Residual plots		✓		✓	✓
7	ACF and PACF plots	✓	✓	✓	✓	✓
	Box-Pierce or Ljung-Box tests	✓	✓		✓	✓
	ARIMA models	✓	✓	✓	✓	✓
	AIC for ARIMA models	✓	✓		✓	✓
	Automatic model selection	✓			✓	✓
	Simulation of ARIMA models		✓		✓	✓
8	Regression with AR errors	✓	✓		✓	✓
	Regression with ARIMA errors		✓		✓	✓
	Dynamic regression models				✓	✓
	Intervention analysis				✓	✓
	Multivariate AR models		✓		✓	
	State space models		✓			
	Non-linear models		✓			
	Neural network forecasting					
Other	Comparison of forecasting methods	✓	✓	✓	✓	✓
	Allows holdout sets	✓	✓	✓	✓	✓

Table I-2: *Forecasting facilities in Forecast Pro 2.0, EViews 3.0, SIBYL/Runner 1.12, Autobox 4.0 and SCA for Windows version 5.1a (with PC-EXPERT and PC-GSA).*

of these packages offer a wide range of forecasting facilities; others offer advanced features for a smaller set of methods.

software reviews   Reviews of forecasting packages appear periodically. Recent reviews include Ord and Lowe (1996) and Rycroft (1993, 1995). Regular reviews appear in the *International Journal of Forecasting* and the *Journal of Forecasting*.

1/4 Selecting a forecasting package

Because there is such a large number of different forecasting packages to choose from, many users have difficulty selecting an appropriate package for their needs. The questions below provide some guide in making a selection.

software facilities

1. **Does the package have the facilities you want?** Check that the forecasting methods you wish to use are available in the package. The checklist of methods in Tables I-1 and I-2 may be helpful. You will also need to check data management, graphics, and reporting facilities.

computer platforms

2. **What platforms is the package available on?** Obviously the package must be available on your preferred platform. But it may also be necessary to have it available on several platforms and to be able to transfer files between platforms.

software ease-of-use

3. **How easy is the package to learn and use?** Ask for a demonstration to ensure that the facilities are easy to use. In particular, make sure that it is easy to input and output data in the format you require.

new methods

4. **Is it possible to implement new methods?** The advanced user will want to be able to modify existing methods or implement new methods. This is normally done via an in-built programming language.

interactive software

5. **Do you require interactive or repetitive forecasting?** Often you will need to carry out very similar forecasting tasks each month, or each quarter. These may involve thousands of individual series. In this case, a forecasting package which provides a "batch" facility is useful. But if your forecasting

is always carried out interactively, then the batch facility is unnecessary.

6. **Do you have very large data sets?** Most packages have a limit on the number of observations and the number of variables which can be handled. Be wary of all claims about the size of data sets which can be handled. Such claims are sometimes only true for very powerful computers. If possible, it is best to try the software on your data first.

large data sets

7. **Is there any local support?** Having someone nearby to help is invaluable. Such a person may be a fellow user in the same organization, a member of a local users' group, or a contributor to an Internet news group. Technical support provided by the software vendor is also important, and good documentation is essential. There are also short courses available for the most widely used forecasting packages.

software support

8. **Does the package give the right answers?** A common misconception is that all packages give the same answers. Unfortunately, mistakes have been made, even in some very well-known and widely-used packages. It is a good idea to check output from the package against published results or output from an equivalent analysis in a competing package. Some differences will result from different algorithms being used for numerical computation. But some may result from errors in the program. Numerical inaccuracy can be a problem when very large or very small numbers are involved. This has been a particular problem with most spreadsheets (see Sawitzki, 1994).

numerical accuracy

2 Forecasting associations

The **International Institute of Forecasters** (IIF) is an association that includes both academics and practitioners in the field. It hosts an annual conference which is held one year in North America, and the next outside North America. In addition to the annual conference it also publishes the *International Journal of Forecasting*. The purpose of the International Institute of Forecasters is to foster generation, distribution, and knowledge on forecasting to academics and practitioners throughout the world. The IIF was founded in 1981.

Inquiries about membership of the International Institute of Forecasters should be addressed to:

Stuart Bretschneider
Center for Technology and Information Policy
Syracuse University
Syracuse, NY 13244-1090
U.S.A.

The annual membership is $80 which includes a subscription to the *International Journal of Forecasting* and *The Forum* newsletter.

The **International Association of Business Forecasters** (IABF) includes mostly practitioners in the area of forecasting. In addition to its annual conference it also publishes the *Journal of Business Forecasting* and the joint newsletter (*The Forum*) with the International Institute of Forecasters. The International Association of Business Forecasters is dedicated to:

- enhancing the professional status of users and preparers of business forecasts;
- promoting an understanding and appreciation for the work of professional forecasters among business managers;
- encouraging research in the areas of forecasting methods and systems, and planning;
- promoting dialogue among users, preparers, and academicians engaged in research and teaching of forecasting techniques;
- conducting periodic regional and national conferences, symposia, and similar events to disseminate information about business forecasting and planning;
- helping members learn more about forecasting and planning.

Membership information is available through:

Howard Keen
Conrail
2001 Markets Street 5-B
PO Box 41405
Philadelphia, PA 19101-1405
U.S.A.

The cost of the membership varies according to whether it is a company subscription ($150) or an individual subscription ($30 for the United States and Canada, $35 outside the United States and Canada) or a full-time student ($10).

Membership in the International Association of Business Forecasters includes a $10 discount for the *Journal of Business Forecasting*.

3 Forecasting conferences

The two major forecasting conferences are annual and are organized by the two major associations (IIF and IABF). Both conferences include papers on all principal aspects of forecasting and they are attended by several hundred participants. The IIF conferences include more academic papers and more of the participants are academicians. The IABF conferences include mostly practical, "how to do" papers, and are attended by many practitioners. Several of the papers (usually the most important) presented at these conferences are later published in the *International Journal of Forecasting* and the *Journal of Business Forecasting* respectively. The IIF conference is held one year in North America, and the following year in a city outside North America, while the IABF conference is usually held in the United States.

Forecasting conferences

4 Forecasting journals and newsletters

There are three forecasting journals and a newsletter (*The Forum*) which is published jointly by the two major forecasting associations. In addition, journals in statistics, economics, business and management often include articles on forecasting.

Forecasting journals
Forecasting newsletter

The **International Journal of Forecasting** is (in the opinion of the authors) the leading journal in the field. It publishes high quality academic papers and includes sections on software and book reviews as well as surveys on research on forecasting. It covers all areas of forecasting and occasionally includes papers on the practice of forecasting. Subscriptions to the journal are obtained automatically for the members of the International Institute of Forecasters. For others who are not members, they can obtain subscription information from the Customer Service Department, Elsevier Science, at the following addresses:

PO Box 945	PO Box 211	20-12 Yushima 3-chome
New York, NY 10159 0945	1000 AE Amsterdam	Bunkyo-ku, Tokyo 113
U.S.A.	The Netherlands	Japan

The **Journal of Business Forecasting** is published by the International Association of Business Forecasters and includes mainly articles that are concerned with practical and "how to do it" issues. Subscription information about the journal can be obtained from the International Association of Business Forecasters.

The **Journal of Forecasting** includes mostly academic papers on the various areas of forecasting. Information for subscriptions can be obtained from the publisher, John Wiley & Sons, Baffins Lane, Chichester, Sussex PO19 1UD, England.

The Forum is the joint newsletter of the International Association of Business Forecasters and the International Institute of Forecasters. It contains information about the forecasting conferences as well as various topics of interest to forecasters. It includes reviews of forecasting programs, it contains advertisements from all major developers of forecasting softwares, and lists on how these programs can be obtained. Finally, it publishes short articles and includes news about those working in the field of forecasting.

5 Forecasting on the Internet

There is a rapidly growing collection of forecasting resources on the Internet including time series data, forecasting software, e-mail discussion lists, and information about conferences.

A good place to start is the web page for this book at

www.maths.monash.edu.au/~hyndman/forecasting/

Time Series Data Library

M3-IJF Competition

This contains all the data used in this book and over 500 additional time series from the "Time Series Data Library" which can be used for student projects or self-learning. The 3003 series used in the latest M3-IJF Competition can also be downloaded. There are links to other time series collections, forecasting resources, and forecasting software.

The International Institute of Forecasters has a web page which contains links to other resources, time series data, information about how to join their e-mail discussion list, information about the next International Forecasting Symposium, and more. The web address is

weatherhead.cwru.edu/forecasting/

The home page of the International Association of Business Forecasters is at

www.iabf.org

This includes *The Forum* (the joint newsletter of the IIF and IABF), information about upcoming conferences, and how to join the association.

References and selected bibliography

ORD, K. and S. LOWE (1996) Automatic forecasting, *American Statistician*, **50**, 88–94.

RYCROFT, R.S. (1993) Microcomputer software of interest to forecasters in comparative review: an update, *International Journal of Forecasting*, **9**, 531–575.

RYCROFT, R.S. (1995) Student editions of forecasting software: a survey, *International Journal of Forecasting*, **11**, 337–351.

SAWITZKI, G. (1994) Report on the numerical reliability of data analysis systems, *Computational statistics and data analysis*, **5**, 289–301.

APPENDIX II
GLOSSARY OF FORECASTING TERMS

ACF See Autocorrelation function.

Additive model A model in which the various terms are added together. See also **Multiplicative model**.

Adaptive response rate In many time series forecasting methods, a trade-off must be made between smoothing randomness and reacting quickly to changes in the basic pattern. Adaptive-response-rate forecasting uses a decision rule that instructs the forecasting methodology (such as **exponential smoothing**) to adapt more quickly when it appears that a change in pattern has occurred and to do more smoothing of randomness when it appears that no such change has occurred.

AIC (Akaike's Information Criterion) The AIC provides a measure of the **goodness-of-fit** of a model which takes into account the number of terms in the model. It is commonly used with **ARIMA models** to determine the appropriate model order. The AIC is equal to twice the number of parameters in the model minus twice the log of the **likelihood** function. The theory behind the AIC was developed by Akaike and is based on entropy concepts. See **Order selection criteria**.

Algorithm A systematic set of rules for solving a particular problem. The sets of rules used in applying many of the quantitative methods of forecasting are algorithms.

Applicability Recently, applicability has gained recognition as an important criterion in selecting a forecasting method. Applicability refers to the ease with which a method can be applied to a given situation with a specific user of forecasting. Increased complexity of sophisticated forecasting methods often reduces applicability.

ARMA model This type of time series forecasting model can be **autoregressive** (AR) in form, **moving average** (MA) in form, or a combination of the two (ARMA). In an ARMA model, the series to be forecast is expressed as a function of both previous values of the series (autoregressive terms) and previous error values from forecasting (the moving average terms).

ARIMA An abbreviation for **A**uto**R**egressive **I**ntegrated **M**oving **A**verage. A time series which, when **differenced**, follows an ARMA model is known as an ARIMA model. It is a very broad class of time series models. See **Autoregressive (AR) model**, **Differencing**, **Integrated**, and **Moving average**.

Asymptotically unbiased estimator If the bias of an estimator approaches zero as the sample size increases, the estimator is called "asymptotically unbiased." The formula for **mean squared error** is a biased estimator of variance, but it is asymptotically unbiased. See **Biased estimator**.

Autocorrelated errors When the error terms remaining after application of a forecasting method show **autocorrelation**, it indicates that the forecasting method has not removed all of the pattern from the data. There are several **hypothesis tests** for autocorrelated errors. The **Box-Pierce test** and **Ljung-Box test** check whether a sequence of autocorrelations is significantly different from a sequence of zeros; the **Durbin-Watson test** checks only for first-order autocorrelations after fitting a **regression model**. See **Regression with ARIMA errors** and **Dynamic regression models**.

Autocorrelation This term is used to describe the **correlation** between values of the same time series at different time periods. It is similar to correlation but relates the series for different time lags. Thus there may be an autocorrelation for a time lag of 1, another autocorrelation for a time lag of 2, and so on.

Autocorrelation function The pattern of **autocorrelations** for lags 1, 2, ..., is known as the autocorrelation function or ACF. A plot of the ACF against the lag is known as the *correlogram*. It is frequently used to identify whether or not seasonality is present in a given time series (and the length of that seasonality), to identify appropriate time series models for specific situations, and to determine if data are **stationary**.

Autoregressive (AR) model Autoregression is a form of **regression**, but instead of the variable to be forecast being related to other **explanatory variables**, it is related to past values of itself at varying time lags. Thus an autoregressive model would express the forecast as a function of previous values of that time series.

Backcasting In applying quantitative forecasting techniques based on past errors, starting values are required so certain recursive calculations can be made. One way to obtain these is to apply the forecasting method to the series starting from the end and going to the beginning of the data. This procedure is called backcasting and provides a set of starting values for the errors that can then be used for applying that forecasting method to the standard sequence of starting from the data and forecasting through the end.

Backward shift operator The letter B is used to denote a backward shift by one period. Thus B operating on X_t has the effect of shifting attention to X_{t-1}. Similarly BB or B^2 is the same as shifting attention to two periods back. A first difference for a time series can be denoted $(1-B)X_t$. A second-order difference is denoted $(1-B)^2 X_t$ and a second difference would be denoted $(1-B^2)X_t$. See **Differencing**.

Biased estimator If a formula is defined to calculate a statistic (such as the mean) and the expected value of this statistic is not equal to the corresponding population parameter (e.g., the mean of the population), then the formula will be called a biased estimator. The usual formula for the sample mean is an unbiased estimator of the population mean, but the formula for **mean squared error** is a biased estimator of the variance. See **Asymptotically unbiased estimator**.

BIC (Bayesian Information Criterion) Like the AIC, the BIC is an order selection criteria for ARIMA models. It was invented by Schwarz[1] (1978) and sometimes leads to less complex models than the AIC.

Box-Jenkins methodology George E. Box and Gwilym M. Jenkins have popularized the application of autoregressive / moving average models to time series forecasting problems. While this approach was originally developed in the 1930s, it did not become widely known until Box and Jenkins published a detailed description of it in book form in 1970.[2] The general methodology suggested by Box and Jenkins for applying ARIMA models to time series analysis, forecasting, and control has come to be known as the Box-Jenkins methodology for time series forecasting.

Box-Pierce test This is a test for **autocorrelated errors**. The Box-Pierce Q statistic is computed as the weighted sum of squares of a sequence of **autocorrelations**. If the **errors** of the model are **white noise**, then the Box-Pierce statistic is distributed approximately as a **chi-square distribution** with $h - m$ **degrees of freedom** where h is the number of lags used in the statistic and m is the number of fitted parameters. It is sometimes known as a "portmanteau test." Another portmanteau test is the **Ljung-Box test** which is an improved version of the Box-Pierce test.

Business cycle Periods of prosperity generally followed by periods of depression make up what is called the business cycle. Such cycles tend to vary in length and magnitude and are often dealt with as a separate subcomponent of the basic pattern contained in a time series.

Census II The Census II method is a refinement of the **classical decomposition method**. It attempts to decompose a time series into seasonal, trend, cycle, and random components that can be analyzed separately. This method has been developed by using

---

[1] G. Schwarz (1978) Estimating the dimensions of a model, *Annals of Statistics*, **6**, 461–464.

[2] G.E.P. Box and G.M. Jenkins (1970) *Time Series Analysis*, San Francisco: Holden-Day. Later editions were published in 1976 and 1994 (with G.C. Reinsell).

the empirical results obtained from its application at the United States Bureau of Census and elsewhere. The most widely used variant of the Census II method is **X-11 decomposition**. This has now been superseded by the **X-12-ARIMA** method.

Central limit theorem Regardless of the shape of the population distribution, this theorem states that the **sampling distribution** of the mean of n independent sample values will approach the **normal distribution** as the sample size increases. In practice, when the sample size is sufficiently large (say greater than 30) this theorem is invoked.

Chi-square test Given a standard normal population (i.e., **normal distribution** with mean zero and variance one) and n independently sampled values, the sum of the squares of these sampled values is called a chi-square value with n **degrees of freedom**. The complete set of such chi-square values is called a chi-square distribution. Several statistics have approximate chi-square distributions including the **Box-Pierce** statistic and the **Ljung-Box** statistic. Using these statistics, **hypothesis tests** can be conducted to see if the sample **autocorrelations** are significantly different from zero. See **Sampling distribution**

Classical decomposition method This **algorithm** seeks to decompose the underlying pattern of a time series into cyclical, seasonal, trend, and random subpatterns. These subpatterns are then analyzed individually. See also **Census II**.

Coefficient of determination See **R-squared** and **R-bar-squared**.

Coefficient of variation This statistic is the ratio of the **standard deviation** to the **mean**, expressed as a percent. It is a measure of the relative dispersion of a data series.

Confidence interval Based on statistical theory and probability distributions, a confidence interval, or set of confidence limits, can be established for population parameters such as the mean. For example, a 95% confidence interval will contain the true value of the population parameter with probability 95%. The term *confidence interval* is sometimes inappropriately applied to **prediction interval**.

Correlation coefficient A standardized measure of the association or mutual dependence between two variables, say X and Y. Commonly designated as r, its values range from -1 to $+1$, indicating strong negative relationship, through zero, to strong positive association. The correlation coefficient is the covariance between a pair of standardized variables.

Correlation matrix Most computer programs designed to perform multiple regression analysis include the computation of the correlation coefficients between each pair of variables. The set of these correlation coefficients is often presented in the form of a matrix, referred to as the correlation matrix.

Correlogram See Autocorrelation function.

Covariance This is a measure of the joint variation between variables, say X and Y. The range of covariance values is unrestricted (large negative to large positive). However, if the X and Y variables are first standardized, then covariance is the same as correlation and the range of covariance (correlation) values is from -1 to $+1$.

Critical value In hypothesis testing, the critical value is the threshold for significance. A test statistic beyond the critical value gives a significant result. See Hypothesis testing and P-value.

Crosscorrelation A standardized measure of association between one time series and the past, present, and future values of another time series. This statistic has the characteristics of a regular correlation coefficient and is used in the Box-Jenkins approach to fitting dynamic regression models. It is not covered in this book.

Cumulative forecasting Instead of forecasting values for sequential time periods of equal length, users of forecasting often prefer to forecast the cumulative level of a variable over several periods. For example, one might forecast cumulative sales for the next 12 months, rather than forecast an individual value for each of these 12 months.

Curve fitting One approach to forecasting is simply to fit some form of curve, perhaps a polynomial, to the historical time series data. Use of a linear trend is, in fact, a curve fitting method. Higher forms of curve fitting are also possible, and they frequently provide better results.

Cyclical data See Business cycle.

Cyclical index A cyclical index is a number, usually standardized around 100, that indicates the cyclical pattern of a given set of time series data.

Decomposition See Classical decomposition method, Census II, and STL decomposition.

Degrees of freedom (df) Given a sample of data and the computation of some statistic (e.g., the mean), the degrees of freedom are defined as the number of observations included in the formula minus the number of parameters estimated using the data. For example, the mean statistic for n sample data points has n d.f., but the variance formula has $(n-1)$ df because one parameter (the mean of X) has to be estimated before the variance formula can be used.

Delphi method This qualitative or technological approach seeks to use the judgment of experts systematically in arriving at a forecast of what future events will be or when they may occur. The approach uses a series of questionnaires to elicit responses from a panel of experts.

Dependent variable See Forecast variable.

Depression This term is used to describe that portion of the business cycle in which production and prices are at their lowest point, unemployment is highest, and general economic activity is low.

Deseasonalized data See Seasonal adjustment.

Diagnostic checking A step in time series model building where the estimated errors of a model are examined for independence, zero mean, constant variance, and so on.

Differencing When a time series is **non-stationary**, it can often be made **stationary** by taking first differences of the series—that is, creating a new time series of successive differences ($X_t - $

X_{t-1}). If first differences do not convert the series to stationary form, then first differences of first differences can be created. This is called second-order differencing. A distinction is made between a second-order difference (just defined) and a second difference $(X_t - X_{t-2})$. See **Backward shift operator** and **Seasonal differencing**.

Double moving average When a moving average is taken of a series of data that already represents the result of a moving average, it is referred to as a double moving average. It results in additional smoothing or the removal of more randomness than an equal-length single moving average.

Dummy variable Often referred to as a binary variable whose value is either 0 or 1, a dummy variable is frequently used to quantify qualitative events. For example, a strike/non-strike situation could be represented by a dummy variable. These variables are most commonly used in the application of **multiple regression** analysis. They are also known as *indicator variables*.

Durbin-Watson statistic The Durbin-Watson (DW) statistic, named after its creators, tests the **hypothesis** that there is no **auto-correlation** of one time lag present in the **errors** obtained from forecasting. By comparing the computed value of the Durbin-Watson test with the appropriate values from the table of values of the DW statistic (Table F of Appendix III), the significance can be determined. See **Autocorrelated errors**.

Dynamic regression models A dynamic regression model is a regression model which allows lagged values of the explanatory variable(s) to be included. The relationship between the **forecast variable** and the **explanatory variable** is modeled using a **transfer function**. A dynamic regression model is used to predict what will happen to the forecast variable if the explanatory variable changes. The **errors** from this model are usually described with an **ARIMA model**. Hence, a **regression with ARIMA errors** is a special case of a dynamic regression model.

Econometric model An econometric model is a set of equations intended to be used simultaneously to capture the way in which endogenous and exogenous variables are interrelated. Using such a set of equations to forecast future values of key economic variables is known as econometric forecasting. The value of econometric forecasting is intimately connected to the value of the assumptions underlying the model equations.

Economic indicator An economic indicator is a time series that has a reasonably stable relation (it lags, leads, or is coincident) to the average of the whole economy, or to some other time series of particular interest. Leading indicators are frequently used to identify turning points in the level of general economic activity.

Elasticity This term is used to describe the amount of change in supply or demand when there is a 1% change in price. For a highly elastic product there would be a change greater than 1% in quantity with a 1% in price. The opposite is true for an inelastic product.

Endogenous variable An endogenous variable is one whose value is determined within the system. For example, in an **econometric model** the market price of a product may be determined within the model, thus making that an endogenous variable.

Error A forecast error is calculated by subtracting the **forecast value** from the actual value to give an error value for each forecast period. In forecasting, this term is commonly used as a synonym for **residual**. However, in **regression with ARIMA errors** and **dynamic regression models**, we draw a distinction between errors and residuals. An error is the difference between the forecast obtained from the regression part of the model and the actual value whereas the residual is obtained by subtracting the true forecast value from the actual value.

Error cost function An error cost function states the cost of an error as a function of the size of the error. The most frequently used functional form for this is quadratic, which assumes that the effect of an error is proportional to the square of the error.

Estimation Estimation consists of finding appropriate values for the parameters of an equation in such a way that some criterion will be optimized. The most commonly used criterion is that of **mean squared error**. Often, an iterative procedure is needed in order to determine those parameter values that minimize this criterion.

Ex ante forecast A forecast that uses only information available at the time of the actual forecast. See Ex post forecast.

Ex post forecast A forecast that uses some information beyond the time at which the actual forecast is prepared. See Ex ante forecast.

Exogenous variable An exogenous variable is one whose value is determined outside of the model or system. For example, in an econometric model the gross national product might be an exogenous variable. In a multiple regression equation, the explanatory variables would be exogenous variables.

Explanatory model This type of forecasting model assumes that the variable to be forecast is related to one or more other explanatory variables. Regression models, dynamic regression models, and multivariate ARMA models are the most common forecasting approaches of this type.

Explanatory variable An explanatory variable is one whose values are determined outside of the system being modeled. An explanatory variable is used to predict values of a forecast variable. Explanatory variables are also called *independent variables* and *regressors*.

Exploratory forecasting The general class of technological forecasting methods that seek to predict long-run outcomes are known as exploratory approaches. These contrast with the normative approaches that seek to determine how best to achieve certain long-term results.

Exponential growth If $100 is invested in a bank at 10% compound interest, then the amount grows at an exponential rate. This is exponential growth. Similarly, populations grow exponentially if unchecked. In forecasting, many situations (e.g., sales, GNP) can be modeled as exponential functions.

Exponential smoothing Exponential smoothing methods provide forecasts using weighted averages of past values of the data and forecast errors. They are commonly used in inventory control systems where many items are to be forecast and low cost is a primary concern. The simplest exponential smoothing method is single exponential smoothing (SES), suitable for data with no trend or seasonal patterns. For trended data, **Holt's method** is suitable and for seasonal data, **Holt-Winters' method** may be used. **Pegels' classification** provides a convenient structure in which to study and apply exponential smoothing methods.

Feedback Feedback occurs when there is an interrelationship between two series such that past values of each series affect current values of the other series. If feedback occurs, a **multivariate ARMA model** must be used.

File A file is a collection of data arranged in some order for future reference. When stored on a computer, files may represent actual computer programs for performing certain forecasting methods or simply historical data to be used by those computer programs.

Filter The purpose of a filter, as developed in engineering, is to eliminate random variations (high or low frequencies) so that only the true pattern remains. As applied to time series forecasting, filters generally involve one or more parameters that are used to weight historical values of the series, or of the **residuals** of the series, in some optimal way that eliminates randomness.

First difference See Differencing.

Forecasting Forecasting is the prediction of values of a variable based on known past values of that variable or other related variables. Forecasts also may be based on expert judgments, which in turn are based on historical data and experience.

Forecast horizon The forecast horizon is the length of time into the future for which forecasts are to be prepared. These generally vary from short-term forecasting horizons (less than three months) to long-term horizons (more than two years).

Forecast interval See Prediction interval.

Forecast variable A variable that is predicted by some other variable or variables is referred to as a forecast variable. The forecast variable is also called the *dependent variable* or *response variable*.

Fourier analysis See Spectral analysis.

F-test In statistics the ratio of two mean squares (**variances**) can often be used to test the significance of some item of interest. For example, in **regression** the ratio of "mean square due to the regression" to "mean square due to error" can be used to test the overall significance of the regression model. By looking up an F table, the degree of significance of the computed F value can be determined. See **Hypothesis testing**.

Function A function is a statement of relationship between variables. Virtually all of the quantitative forecasting methods involve a functional relationship between the item to be forecast and either previous values of that item, previous error values, or other **explanatory variables**.

Goodness of fit See AIC, R^2, Mean absolute percentage error (MAPE), and Mean squared error (MSE).

Gross National Product (GNP) The most comprehensive measure of a nation's income is the gross national product. It includes the total output of goods and services for a specific economy over a specific period of time (usually one year).

Heteroscedasticity This condition exists when the errors do not have a constant **variance** across an entire range of values. For example, if the **residuals** from a time series have increasing variance with increasing time, they would be said to exhibit heteroscedasticity. See **Non-stationary** and **Homoscedasticity**.

Heuristic A heuristic is a set of steps or procedures that uses a trial-and-error approach to achieve some desired objective. The word comes from Greek, meaning *to discover or find*.

Holdout set When assessing the performance of one or more models for making forecasts, a group of data is sometimes withheld from the end of the series. This is a holdout set and is not used in the parameter estimation of the models. The forecasts from each of the models can then be compared with this hold-out set to allow genuine forecast assessment. See **Post-sample evaluation**.

Holt's exponential smoothing method Holt's method is an extension of single **exponential smoothing** which allows for trends in the data. It uses two smoothing parameters, one of which is used to add a trend adjustment to the single smoothed value. It is sometimes also called double or linear exponential smoothing.

Holt-Winters' exponential smoothing method Winters extended Holt's exponential smoothing method by including an extra equation that is used to adjust the forecast to reflect seasonality. This form of **exponential smoothing** can thus account for data series that include both trend and seasonal elements. It uses three smoothing parameters controlling the level, trend, and seasonality.

Homoscedasticity This condition exists when the **variance** of a series is constant over the entire range of values of that series. It is the opposite of **heteroscedasticity**. When a series of **residuals** exhibits constant variance over the entire range of time periods, it is said to exhibit homoscedasticity.

Horizontal or stationary data See Stationary.

Hypothesis testing An approach commonly used in classical statistics is to formulate a hypothesis and test the statistical significance of a hypothesis. For example, a hypothesis might be that the **errors** from applying a time series method of forecasting are **uncorrelated**. The statistical test would then be set up to determine whether or not those residuals behave in a pattern that makes then significantly different (statistically) from uncorrelated variables. See *P*-value.

Identification This is the step in time series model building (for ARMA and ARIMA approaches) where patterns in summary statistics such as **autocorrelation functions**, **partial autocorrelation** functions, and so on are related to potential models for the data. The intent is to identify, at least tentatively, an appropriate model so that the next steps in model-building—estimating parameters followed by diagnostic checking—can be pursued.

(It should be noted that this definition and use of the word bears no relationship to the same word as used in the economics literature.)

Impulse response weights If an input time series X exerts its influence on an output variable Y in a dynamic manner over the future time periods, then the set of weights defining this relationship is called the impulse response function. These weights are estimated as part of a **dynamic regression model**.

Independent variable See Explanatory variable.

Index numbers These numbers are frequently used as summary indicators of the level of economic activity and/or corporate performance. For example, the Federal Reserve Board Index of Industrial Production summarizes a number of variables that indicate the overall level of industrial production activity. Similar index numbers can be prepared for economic variables, as well as for corporate variables.

Indicator variable See Dummy variable.

Integrated This is often an element of time series models (the I in ARIMA models), where one or more of the differences of the time series are included in the model. The term comes from the fact that the original series may be recreated from a differenced series by a process of integration (involving a summation in the typical discrete environment).

Interactive forecasting This term has been used to describe forecasting packages that allow the user to interact directly with the data and with the results of alternative forecasting methods.

Intercept In simple regression the constant term is referred to as the intercept of the regression equation with the Y-axis. If the explanatory variable X is 0, then the value of the forecast variable will be the intercept value.

Interdependence If two or more variables are interdependent or mutually dependent, it indicates that their values move together in some specific manner. Thus a change in the value of one of the variables would correlate with a change in the value of the other variable.

Intervention analysis This approach to forecasting is a special case of **dynamic regression models**. It facilitates determining the effects of unusual changes in the **explanatory variables** on the **forecast variable**. The most important characteristic of intervention analysis is that transient effects caused by such changes can be measured and their influence on the forecast variable can be predicted.

Lag A difference in time between an observation and a previous observation. Thus Y_{t-k} lags Y_t by k periods. See also **Lead**.

Lead A difference in time between an observation and a future observation. Thus Y_{t+k} leads Y_t by k periods. See also **Lag**, **Lead time**, and **Leading indicator**.

Leading indicator An economic indicator whose peaks and troughs during the business cycle tend to occur sooner than those of the general economy. Turning points in such an indicator lead subsequent turning points in the general economy or some other economic series, thus signaling the likelihood of such a subsequent turning point.

Lead time This term refers to the time interval between two events, when one must precede the other. In many inventory and order entry systems, the lead time is the interval between the time when an order is placed and the time when it is actually delivered.

Least squares estimation This approach to estimating the parameter values in an equation minimizes the squares of the deviations that result from fitting that particular model. For example, if a trend line is being estimated to fit a data series, the method of least squares estimation could be used to minimize the **mean squared error**. This would give a line whose estimated values would minimize the sum of the squares of the actual deviations from that line for the historical data.

Likelihood The probability that a certain empirical outcome will be observed, conditional on a certain prior outcome. This term is often used in connection with statistics that are maximum likelihood estimators for a population.

Ljung-Box test This is a test for **autocorrelated errors**. It is an improved version of the **Box-Pierce test**.

Local regression Local regression is a form of **smoothing**. A curve is estimated by applying linear **regression** to sections of the data. See **Loess**.

Loess The most popular implementation of **local regression**. It also provides some protection against extreme observations by downweighting outliers.

Logistic curve This curve has the typical S-shape often associated with the product life cycle. It is frequently used in connection with long-term curve fitting as a technological method.

Logarithmic transformation This transformation is applied to remove **exponential growth** in a series. The transformed series consists of logarithms of the original series.

Macrodata These type of data describes the behavior of macroeconomic variables such as GNP, inflation, the index of industrial production, and so on. Macroeconomics deals with the study of economics in terms of whole systems, usually at national or regional levels.

Matrix In mathematical terminology a matrix is a rectangular array of elements arranged in rows and columns. There may be one or more rows and one or more columns in such a matrix.

Maximum likelihood estimation The parameters in an equation can be estimated by maximizing the **likelihood** of the model given the data. For **regression** models with **normally distributed** errors, maximum likelihood estimation is equivalent to **least squares estimation**.

M-Competition The M-Competition (Makridakis et al., 1982, 1984) compared the accuracies of about 20 different forecasting techniques across a sample of 111 time series. A subset of the methods was tested on 1001 series. The last 12 points of each series were held out and the remaining data were available for model fitting. The accuracy was assessed via the **mean absolute percentage error (MAPE)** on the **holdout set**.

M3-IJF Competition The M3-IJF Competition was conducted in 1997 by the *International Journal of Forecasting*. It compared a range of forecasting techniques across a sample 3003 time series. The accuracy was assessed using a range of measures on a holdout set.

Mean The arithmetic average or mean for a group of items is defined as the sum of the values of the items divided by the number of items. It is frequently used as a measure of location for a frequency or probability distribution.

Mean Absolute Percentage Error (MAPE) The mean absolute percentage error is the mean or average of the sum of all of the percentage errors for a given data set taken without regard to sign. (That is, their absolute values are summed and the average computed.) It is one measure of accuracy commonly used in quantitative methods of forecasting.

Mean Percentage Error (MPE) The mean percentage error is the average of all of the percentage errors for a given data set. This average allows positive and negative percentage errors to cancel one another. Because of this, it is sometimes used as a measure of bias in the application of a forecasting method.

Mean Squared Error (MSE) The mean squared error is a measure of accuracy computed by squaring the individual error for each item in a data set and then finding the average or mean value of the sum of those squares. The mean squared error gives greater weight to large errors than to small errors because the errors are squared before being summed.

Medial average The middle number of a data set is the median. It can be found by arranging the items in the data set in ascending order and identifying the middle item. The medial average includes only those items grouped around the median value. For example, the highest and lowest value may be excluded from a medial average.

Median Frequently used as a measure of location for a frequency or probability distribution, the median of a group of items is the value of the middle item when all the items are arranged in either ascending or descending order of magnitude.

Microdata *Micro* comes from the Greek word meaning small. Microdata refers generally to data collected at the level of an individual organization or a company. Microeconomics refers to the study of such data as contrasted with macroeconomics, which deals generally with a regional or national level.

Mixed model In time series analysis a process or model that combines moving average (MA) forms with autoregressive (AR) forms is frequently referred to as a mixed process. See **ARMA models**.

Model A model is the symbolic representation of reality. In quantitative forecasting methods a specific model is used to represent the basic pattern contained in the data. This may be a **regression** model, which is explanatory in nature, or a time series model.

Moving average There are two distinct meanings to this term. First, for a time series we can define the moving average of order K as the average (mean) value of K consecutive observations. This can be used for smoothing (Chapter 3) or forecasting (Chapter 4). Second, in Box-Jenkins modeling the MA in **ARIMA** stands for moving average and means that the value of the time series at time t is influenced by a current error term and (possibly) weighted error terms in the past. See Chapter 7 for examples.

Multicollinearity In **multiple regression**, computational problems arise if two or more **explanatory variables** are highly correlated with one another. The regression coefficients associated with those explanatory variables will be very unstable. In larger sets of explanatory variables, the condition of multicollinearity may not be easy to detect. If any linear combination of one subset of explanatory variables is nearly perfectly related to a linear combination of any other subset of explanatory variables, then a multicollinearity problem is present. See Chapter 6 for details.

Multiple correlation coefficient If a **forecast variable** Y is regressed against several **explanatory variables** $X_1, X_2, \ldots, X_k$, then the estimated Y value is designated $\hat{Y}$. The correlation between $\hat{Y}$ and Y is called the multiple correlation coefficient and is often designated R. It is customary to deal with this coefficient in squared form (i.e., R^2). See Multiple regression, R-squared, and R-bar-squared.

Multiple regression The technique of multiple regression is an extension of simple regression. It allows for more than one explanatory variable to be included in predicting the value of a forecast variable. For forecasting purposes a multiple regression equation is often referred to as a causal or explanatory model.

Multiplicative model A model in which the various terms are multiplied together. See also Additive model.

Multivariate ARMA model Multivariate ARMA models allow several time series which are mutually dependent to be forecast. Each of the series is forecast using a function of its own past, the past of each of the other series, and past errors. This is in contrast to dynamic regression models where there is only one forecast variable and it is assumed that the explanatory variables do not depend on the past of the forecast variable. See ARMA model.

Naïve forecast Forecasts obtained with a minimal amount of effort and data manipulation and based solely on the most recent information available are frequently referred to as naive forecasts. One such naive method would be to use the most recent observation available as the future forecast. A slightly more sophisticated naive method would be to adjust the most recent observation for seasonality.

Neural networks Neural networks are based on simple mathematical models of the way brains are thought to work. They can be thought of as a network of neuron-like units organized in layers. When applied to time series, they provide a non-linear forecasting method.

Noise The randomness often found in data series is frequently referred to as noise. This term comes from the field of engineering where a filter is used to eliminate noise so that the true pattern can be identified.

Non-linear estimation If parameters have to be estimated for non-linear functions, then ordinary least squares estimation may not apply. Under these circumstances certain non-linear techniques exist for solving the problem. Minimizing the sum of squared **residuals** is one common criterion. Another is **maximum likelihood estimation**. Non-linear estimation is an iterative procedure and there is no guarantee that the final solution is the global minimum.

Non-linear forecasting A time series model is non-linear if it cannot be written as a linear function of past observations, errors, and explanatory variables. Non-linear models are capable of reproducing some features in time series, such as chaotic behavior, which are not able to be captured using linear models. See **Neural networks**.

Non-stationary A time series exhibits non-stationarity if the underlying generating process does not have a constant mean and/or a constant variance. In practice, a visual inspection of the plotted time series can help determine if either or both of these conditions exist, and the set of **autocorrelations** for the time series can be used to confirm the presence of non-stationarity or not. See **Stationary**.

Normal distribution This is a probability distribution which is very widely used in statistical modeling. It is the distribution of many naturally occurring variables and the distribution of many **statistics**. It is represented by a bell-shaped curve.

Observation An observation is the value of a specific event as expressed on some measurement scale by a single data value. In most forecasting applications a set of observations is used to provide the data to which the selected model is fit.

Optimal parameter or weight value The optimal, final parameters or weights are those values that give the best performance for a given model applied to a specific set of data. It is those optimal parameters that are then used in forecasting.

Order selection criteria For ARMA **models** of time series, it can be difficult to determine the order of the autoregressive and moving average components of the model. There are several order selection criteria to help make this decision, including the AIC and BIC.

Outlier An outlier is a data value that is unusually large or small. Such outliers are sometimes removed from the data set before fitting a forecasting model so that unusually large deviations from the pattern will not affect the fitting of the model.

Parameter Characteristics of a population such as the **mean** or **standard deviation** are called parameters. These should be distinguished from the characteristics of a sample taken from a population, which are called **statistics**.

Parsimony The concept of parsimony holds that as few parameters as possible should be used in fitting a model to a set of data. This concept is a basic premise of the Box-Jenkins approach to time series analysis.

Partial autocorrelation This measure of **correlation** is used to identify the extent of relationship between current values of a variable with earlier values of that same variable (values for various time lags) while holding the effects of all other time lags constant. Thus, it is completely analogous to **partial correlation** but refers to a single variable.

Partial correlation This statistic provides a measure of the association between a **forecast variable** and one or more **explanatory variables** when the effect of the relationship with other explanatory variables is held constant.

Pattern The basic set of relationships and the underlying process over time is referred to as the pattern in the data.

Pegels' classification Pegels has conveniently classified **exponential smoothing** method into a two-way table with three rows labeled A (no trend), B (linear trend), and C (multiplicative trend), and three columns labeled 1 (no seasonality), 2 (additive seasonality), and 3 (multiplicative seasonality). Cell A-1 represents simple exponential smoothing; cell B-1 represents Holt's two-parameter method; and cell B-3 represents Winters model.

Polynomial In algebra a polynomial is an expression containing one or more terms, each of which consists of a coefficient and a variable(s) raised to some power. Thus $a + bx$ is a linear polynomial $a + bx + cx^2$ is a quadratic polynomial in x. A polynomial of order m includes terms involving powers of x up to x^m. **Regression** models often involve involve linear and higher order polynomials.

Polynomial fitting It is possible to fit a polynomial of any number of terms to a set of data. If the number of terms (the order) equals the number of data observations, the fit can be made perfectly.

Post-sample evaluation The evaluation of a forecasting model using data that were collected after the set of data on which the model was estimated is often referred to as a post-sample evaluation of the forecasting model. Ongoing tracking of the performance of a model is another example of this. See also **Holdout set**.

Prediction interval Based on statistical theory and probability distributions, a forecast interval, or set of forecast limits, can be established for a forecast. For example, a 95% prediction interval will contain the observation with probability 95%. These limits are based on the extent of variation of the data and the **forecast horizon**. Sometimes the term **confidence interval** is inappropriately used instead of *prediction interval*. Prediction intervals are also known as *forecast intervals*.

Probability The probability of an event is expressed as a number from 0 through 1. An impossible event has probability zero. A certain event has probability 1. Classical probability is defined in terms of long-run relative frequency—in a long series of identical trials the relative frequency of occurrence of the event approaches a fixed value called the probability of the event. In Bayesian analysis, probability is defined more subjectively as the encoding of my knowledge about that event. It is the degree of plausibility of the event given all that I know at this time, and is expressed as a number between 0 and 1.

Product life cycle The concept of the product life cycle is particularly useful in forecasting and analyzing historical data. It presumes that demand for a product follows an S-shaped curve growing slowly in the early stages, achieving rapid and sustained growth in the middle stages, and slowing again in the mature stage. See *S-curve*.

P-value Used in **hypothesis testing**. The *P*-value is the probability of obtaining a result as extreme as the one calculated from the data, if the hypothesis to be demonstrated is not true. For example, an **F-test** is used to test whether the slope of a **regression** line is non-zero. In this case, the *P*-value is the probability of obtaining an F value as large as that obtained if, in fact, the line has zero slope. It is customary to conclude that the result is significant if the *P*-value is smaller than 0.05, although this threshold is arbitrary.

Qualitative or technological forecasting Qualitative or technological methods of forecasting are appropriate when the assumption of constancy is invalid (the pattern contained in past data cannot be assumed to continue into the future), when information about the past cannot be obtained, or when the forecast is about unlikely or unexpected events in the future.

Quantitative forecasting Quantitative forecasting methods can be applied when information about the past is available, if that information can be quantified and if the pattern included in past information can be assumed to continue into the future.

R-squared (R^2) In **regression** the square of the correlation between Y (the forecast variable) and $\hat{Y}$ (the estimated Y value based on the set of **explanatory variables**) is denoted R^2. This statistic is often called the coefficient of determination. See **R-bar-squared**.

R-bar-squared $(\bar{R}^2)$ Since the computation of R^2 does not involve the **degrees of freedom** for either SS (sum of squares of deviations due to the **regression** or the SS of deviations in the original Y data, a corrected R^2 is defined and designated $\bar{R}^2$ (*R*-bar squared). See **R-squared**. This statistic can be interpreted as the proportion of **variance** in Y that can be explained by the explanatory variables.

Randomness The noise or random fluctuations in a data series are frequently described as the randomness of that data series.

Random sampling This statistical sampling method involves selecting a sample from a population in such a way that every unit within that population has the same probability of being selected as any other unit.

Random walk A random walk is a time series model which states that each observation is equal to the previous observation plus some random error. Therefore, the change between observations is **white noise**.

Regression A term "regression" dates back to Sir Francis Galton and his work with the heights of siblings in different generations. The heights of children of exceptionally tall (or short) parents "regress" to the mean of the population. Regression analysis today means any modeling of a **forecast variable** Y as a function of a set of **explanatory variables** X_1 through X_k. See **Simple regression** and **Multiple regression**.

Regression coefficients In regression, a **forecast variable** Y is modeled as a function of **explanatory variables** X_1 through X_k. The regression coefficients are the multipliers of the explanatory variables. The estimates of these regression coefficients can be used to understand the importance of each explanatory variable (as it relates to Y) and the interrelatedness among the explanatory variables (as they relate to Y). See **Regression**.

Regression with ARIMA errors In standard regression modeling, it is assumed that the errors are uncorrelated. However, it is common with time series to find that this assumption is not true. When there are **autocorrelated errors**, the correlation in the errors may be modeled by an **ARIMA** model. This combination of a regression model and an ARIMA model for the errors is discussed in Section 8/1. See also **Dynamic regression models**.

Regressor See Explanatory variable.

Residual It is calculated by subtracting the **forecast value** from the observed value to give a residual or error value for each forecast period. In forecasting this term is commonly used as a synonym for **error**, although in some cases we distinguish the two.

Sample A sample is a finite or limited number of observations or data values selected from a universe or population of such data values.

Sampling distribution The distribution of a **statistic** from a finite sample. If many such samples were able to be taken, the collection of possible values of the statistic would follow its sampling distribution.

Sampling error The sampling error is an indication of the magnitude of difference between the true values of a population parameter and the estimated value of that parameter based on a sample.

S-curve An *S*-curve is most frequently used to represent the product life cycle. Several different mathematical forms, such as the logistics curve, can be used to fit an *S*-curve to actual observed data.

Seasonal adjustment Seasonal adjustment is the process of removing seasonality from time series data. It is often done after time series **decomposition**. Seasonal adjustment facilitates the comparison of month-to-month changes. It is used in dealing with such data as unemployment statistics, economic indicators, or product sales.

Seasonal data See Type of data.

Seasonal difference In order to achieve a **stationary** series before applying the Box-Jenkins methodology to time series forecasting, the first or second differences of the data must often be taken. A seasonal difference refers to a difference that is taken between seasonal values that are separated by one complete season. Thus, if monthly data are used with an annual seasonal pattern, a seasonal difference would simply compute the difference for values separated by 12 months rather than using the first difference, which is for values adjacent to one another in a series. See Differencing.

Seasonal exponential smoothing
See Holt-Winters' exponential smoothing.

Seasonal index A seasonal index is a number that indicates the seasonality for a given time period. For example, a seasonal index for observed values in July would indicate the way in which that July value is affected by the seasonal pattern in the data. Seasonal indices are used in **seasonal adjustment**.

Seasonal variation The change that seasonal factors cause in a data series is frequently called seasonal variation.

Serial correlation See Autocorrelation.

Significance See Hypothesis testing.

Simple regression Simple regression is a special case of **multiple regression** involving a single **explanatory variable**. As with multiple linear regression it assumes a linear relationship between the explanatory variable and the **forecast variable**. The relationship is estimated using the method of **least squares** and a set of observed values.

Slope The slope of a curve at a given point indicates the amount of change in the **forecast variable** for a one-unit change in the **explanatory variable**. In **simple regression** the coefficient of the explanatory variable indicates the slope of the regression line.

Smoothing Estimating a smooth trend, usually be taking weighted averages of observations. The term *smoothed* is used because such averages tend to reduce randomness by allowing positive and negative random effects to partially offset each other.

Specification error A type of error often caused either by the incorrect choice of a functional form of a forecasting model or the failure to include important variables in that functional form or model.

Spectral analysis The decomposition of a time series into a set of sine-waves (or cosine-waves) with differing amplitudes, frequencies, and phase angles, is variously known as spectral analysis, harmonic analysis, Fourier analysis, and so on. Each method has specific features but in general they all look for periodicities in the data. Spectral analysis is not covered in this book.

Spencer's weighted moving average The Spencer's weighted moving average is an approach to computing a moving average that will compensate for a cubic trend in the data. It consists of two averages, one for 15 periods and the other for 21 periods. Both have been used widely in many decomposition methods.

Standard deviation A summary statistic (parameter) for a sample (population). It is usually denoted s (σ) for a sample (population), and is the square root of variance. The standard deviation is a measure of the spread in the data (population). For many data sets, about 95% of the observations will be within approximately two standard deviations of the mean.

Standard error Given a population distribution (say a **normal distribution**), a sampling plan (say a simple independent random sampling plan), and a specific statistic (say the mean), then the **sampling distribution** of the mean is a probability distribution with an expected value, a standard deviation, and various other properties. The **standard deviation** of the sampling distribution of a statistic is called the standard error of that statistic.

Standardize Given a sample set of values for X, where the **mean** is $\bar{X}$ and the **standard deviation** is S, the ith value in the set, X_i, is standardized by subtracting the mean and dividing by the standard deviation. The standardized values are often designated by the letter Z.

State space modeling State space models are a matrix representation for univariate and multivariate time series. Many time series models can be written in "state space" form. It provides a convenient structure to handle computations for a wide variety of time series models. There are also some forecasting methods which use the state space model directly. Computations for state space models are carried out using the Kalman recursion equations or Kalman filter. Consequently, state space models are sometimes known as a "Kalman filter" model.

Stationary If the underlying generating process for a time series is based on a constant mean and a constant variance, then the time series is stationary. More formally, a series is stationary if its statistical properties are independent of the particular time period during which it is observed. See **Non-stationary**.

Statistic Given a sample consisting of n values, a statistic is any summary number that captures a property of the sample data. For example, the **mean** is a statistic, and so are the **variance**, the skewness, the **median**, the **standard deviation**, etc. For a pair of variables sampled jointly the **correlation coefficient** is a statistic and so is the **covariance**. The values of a statistic vary from sample to sample, and the complete set of values is called the **sampling distribution** of the statistic.

STL decomposition The STL decomposition method was proposed by William Cleveland and others in 1990 as an alternative to the Census II methods of time series decomposition. The name "STL" is an acronym for "A Seasonal-Trend decomposition procedure based on Loess." See also Loess.

Technological forecasting See Qualitative or technological forecasting.

Time series An ordered sequence of values of a variable observed at equally spaced time intervals is referred to as a time series.

Time series model A time series model is a function that relates the value of a time series to previous values of that time series, its errors, or other related time series. See ARIMA.

Tracking signal Since quantitative methods of forecasting assume the continuation of some historical pattern into the future, it is often useful to develop some measure that can be used to determine when the basic pattern has changed. A tracking signal is the most common such measure. One frequently used tracking signal involves computing the cumulative error over time and setting limits so that when the cumulative error goes outside those limits, the forecaster can be notified and a new model can be considered.

Trading day A trading day is an active day. In many business time series the number of business days in a month or some other specified period of time may vary. Frequently trading-day adjustments must be made to reflect the fact that every January (or similar period) may not include the same number of trading days.

Transfer function A transfer function is part of a dynamic regression model and describes how a change in the explanatory variable is transferred to the forecast variable.

Transformation Transformation involves changing the scale of measurement in variable(s). For example, data can be transformed from a linear to a logarithmic scale, or from a linear to a square root scale. Transformations play two roles: (1) in time series they are used to achieve a series which is stationary in variance and (2) in **regression** they are used to make the relationship linear or to improve the fit of the model.

Trend analysis Trend analysis (or trend-line analysis) is a special form of **simple regression** in which time is the **explanatory variable**.

***t*-test** The *t*-test is a statistical **hypothesis test** used extensively in **regression** analysis to test if the individual coefficients are significantly different from 0. It is computed as the ratio of the coefficient to the **standard error** of that coefficient.

Turning point Any time a data pattern changes direction it can be described as having reached a turning point. For seasonal patterns these turning points are usually very predictable and can be handled by many different forecasting methods because the length of a complete season remains constant. In many cyclical data patterns the length of the cycle varies as does its magnitude. Here the identification of turning points is a particularly difficult and important task.

Type of data In many forecasting methods, such as decomposition, data are classified as having one or more subpatterns. These include a seasonal pattern, a trend pattern, and a cyclical pattern. Frequently, when forecasters refer to the type of data they mean the specific forms of subpatterns that are included in that data.

Unbiasedness A statistic is referred to as an unbiased estimator of a population parameter if the **sampling distribution** of the statistic has a mean equal to the parameter being estimated. See **Biased estimator** and **Asymptotically unbiased estimator**.

Updated forecast Revisions of original forecasts in light of data that subsequently become available after the time period in which the original forecasts were made are often referred to as updated forecasts. This concept is analogous to posterior distributions, although the updating is often much more subjective than in Bayesian analysis and the calculation of posterior distributions.

Validation The process of testing the degree to which a model is useful for making forecasts. The sample data are often split into two segments, one being used to estimate the parameters of the model, and the other being used as a **holdout set** to test the forecasts made by the model. There are many variations on this process of validation.

Variance A summary statistic (parameter) for a sample (population). It is usually denoted S^2 (σ^2). It is the average of squared deviations from the mean.

Vector ARMA model See Multivariate ARMA model.

Weight The term *weight* indicates the relative importance given to an individual item included in forecasting. In the method of moving averages all of those past values included in the moving average are given equal weight. In more sophisticated methods of time series analysis, the problem of model identification involves determining the most appropriate values of those weights.

White noise When there is no pattern whatsoever in the data series, it is said to represent white noise.

Winters exponential smoothing
     See Holt-Winters' exponential smoothing method.

X-11 decomposition The X-11 method for time series decomposition is one of the series of methods which is part of the **Census II** family developed at the United States Bureau of the Census. It was developed in 1967 and was improved in the X-11-ARIMA method. It has now been superseded by the **X-12-ARIMA** method.

X-12-ARIMA decomposition The latest method for time series decomposition from the **Census II** family is X-12-ARIMA. It is an enhancement of the **X-11** method.

APPENDIX III

STATISTICAL TABLES

A: Normal probabilities

Table entry is the probability in the
right-hand tail of a standard normal
distribution (mean 0 and standard
deviation 1). For negative values of z,
probabilities are found by symmetry.

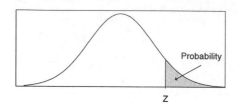

z	\multicolumn{10}{c}{*Second decimal place of z*}
	0.00	0.01	0.02	0.03	0.04	0.05	0.06	0.07	0.08	0.09
0.0	0.5000	0.4960	0.4920	0.4880	0.4840	0.4801	0.4761	0.4721	0.4681	0.4641
0.1	0.4602	0.4562	0.4522	0.4483	0.4443	0.4404	0.4364	0.4325	0.4286	0.4247
0.2	0.4207	0.4168	0.4129	0.4090	0.4052	0.4013	0.3974	0.3936	0.3897	0.3859
0.3	0.3821	0.3783	0.3745	0.3707	0.3669	0.3632	0.3594	0.3557	0.3520	0.3483
0.4	0.3446	0.3409	0.3372	0.3336	0.3300	0.3264	0.3228	0.3192	0.3156	0.3121
0.5	0.3085	0.3050	0.3015	0.2981	0.2946	0.2912	0.2877	0.2843	0.2810	0.2776
0.6	0.2743	0.2709	0.2676	0.2643	0.2611	0.2578	0.2546	0.2514	0.2483	0.2451
0.7	0.2420	0.2389	0.2358	0.2327	0.2296	0.2266	0.2236	0.2206	0.2177	0.2148
0.8	0.2119	0.2090	0.2061	0.2033	0.2005	0.1977	0.1949	0.1922	0.1894	0.1867
0.9	0.1841	0.1814	0.1788	0.1762	0.1736	0.1711	0.1685	0.1660	0.1635	0.1611
1.0	0.1587	0.1562	0.1539	0.1515	0.1492	0.1469	0.1446	0.1423	0.1401	0.1379
1.1	0.1357	0.1335	0.1314	0.1292	0.1271	0.1251	0.1230	0.1210	0.1190	0.1170
1.2	0.1151	0.1131	0.1112	0.1093	0.1075	0.1056	0.1038	0.1020	0.1003	0.0985
1.3	0.0968	0.0951	0.0934	0.0918	0.0901	0.0885	0.0869	0.0853	0.0838	0.0823
1.4	0.0808	0.0793	0.0778	0.0764	0.0749	0.0735	0.0721	0.0708	0.0694	0.0681
1.5	0.0668	0.0655	0.0643	0.0630	0.0618	0.0606	0.0594	0.0582	0.0571	0.0559
1.6	0.0548	0.0537	0.0526	0.0516	0.0505	0.0495	0.0485	0.0475	0.0465	0.0455
1.7	0.0446	0.0436	0.0427	0.0418	0.0409	0.0401	0.0392	0.0384	0.0375	0.0367
1.8	0.0359	0.0351	0.0344	0.0336	0.0329	0.0322	0.0314	0.0307	0.0301	0.0294
1.9	0.0287	0.0281	0.0274	0.0268	0.0262	0.0256	0.0250	0.0244	0.0239	0.0233
2.0	0.0228	0.0222	0.0217	0.0212	0.0207	0.0202	0.0197	0.0192	0.0188	0.0183
2.1	0.0179	0.0174	0.0170	0.0166	0.0162	0.0158	0.0154	0.0150	0.0146	0.0143
2.2	0.0139	0.0136	0.0132	0.0129	0.0125	0.0122	0.0119	0.0116	0.0113	0.0110
2.3	0.0107	0.0104	0.0102	0.0099	0.0096	0.0094	0.0091	0.0089	0.0087	0.0084
2.4	0.0082	0.0080	0.0078	0.0075	0.0073	0.0071	0.0069	0.0068	0.0066	0.0064
2.5	0.0062	0.0060	0.0059	0.0057	0.0055	0.0054	0.0052	0.0051	0.0049	0.0048
2.6	0.0047	0.0045	0.0044	0.0043	0.0041	0.0040	0.0039	0.0038	0.0037	0.0036
2.7	0.0035	0.0034	0.0033	0.0032	0.0031	0.0030	0.0029	0.0028	0.0027	0.0026
2.8	0.0026	0.0025	0.0024	0.0023	0.0023	0.0022	0.0021	0.0021	0.0020	0.0019
2.9	0.0019	0.0018	0.0018	0.0017	0.0016	0.0016	0.0015	0.0015	0.0014	0.0014
3.0	0.0013	0.0013	0.0013	0.0012	0.0012	0.0011	0.0011	0.0011	0.0010	0.0010
3.1	0.0010	0.0009	0.0009	0.0009	0.0008	0.0008	0.0008	0.0008	0.0007	0.0007
3.2	0.0007	0.0007	0.0006	0.0006	0.0006	0.0006	0.0006	0.0005	0.0005	0.0005
3.3	0.0005	0.0005	0.0005	0.0004	0.0004	0.0004	0.0004	0.0004	0.0004	0.0003
3.4	0.0003	0.0003	0.0003	0.0003	0.0003	0.0003	0.0003	0.0003	0.0003	0.0002
3.5	0.0002	0.0002	0.0002	0.0002	0.0002	0.0002	0.0002	0.0002	0.0002	0.0002

B: Critical values for t statistic

Table entry is the point t with the probability p lying above it. The first column gives the degrees of freedom. Use symmetry for negative t values.

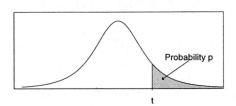

Probability p

t

df	Tail probability p				
	0.1	0.05	0.025	0.01	0.005
1	3.08	6.31	12.71	31.82	63.66
2	1.89	2.92	4.30	6.96	9.92
3	1.64	2.35	3.18	4.54	5.84
4	1.53	2.13	2.78	3.75	4.60
5	1.48	2.02	2.57	3.36	4.03
6	1.44	1.94	2.45	3.14	3.71
7	1.41	1.89	2.36	3.00	3.50
8	1.40	1.86	2.31	2.90	3.36
9	1.38	1.83	2.26	2.82	3.25
10	1.37	1.81	2.23	2.76	3.17
11	1.36	1.80	2.20	2.72	3.11
12	1.36	1.78	2.18	2.68	3.05
13	1.35	1.77	2.16	2.65	3.01
14	1.34	1.76	2.14	2.62	2.98
15	1.34	1.75	2.13	2.60	2.95
16	1.34	1.75	2.12	2.58	2.92
17	1.33	1.74	2.11	2.57	2.90
18	1.33	1.73	2.10	2.55	2.88
19	1.33	1.73	2.09	2.54	2.86
20	1.33	1.72	2.09	2.53	2.85
21	1.32	1.72	2.08	2.52	2.83
22	1.32	1.72	2.07	2.51	2.82
23	1.32	1.71	2.07	2.50	2.81
24	1.32	1.71	2.06	2.49	2.80
25	1.32	1.71	2.06	2.49	2.79
30	1.31	1.70	2.04	2.46	2.75
40	1.30	1.68	2.02	2.42	2.70
50	1.30	1.68	2.01	2.40	2.68
60	1.30	1.67	2.00	2.39	2.66
70	1.29	1.67	1.99	2.38	2.65
80	1.29	1.66	1.99	2.37	2.64
90	1.29	1.66	1.99	2.37	2.63
100	1.29	1.66	1.98	2.36	2.63
∞	1.28	1.64	1.96	2.33	2.58
	80%	90%	95%	98%	99%
			Confidence level		

C: Critical values for F statistic

Table entry is the point F with the probability p lying above it. The first column gives the df in the denominator, the column headings give the df in the numerator. The second column gives the value of p.

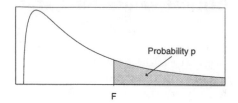

Probability p

F

denom. df₂	p	\multicolumn{10}{c}{numerator df₁}
		1	2	3	4	5	6	7	8	9	10
1	0.10	39.9	49.5	53.6	55.8	57.2	58.2	58.9	59.4	59.9	60.2
	0.05	161.4	199.5	215.7	224.6	230.2	234.0	236.8	238.9	240.5	241.9
	0.01	4052.2	4999.5	5403.4	5624.6	5763.6	5859.0	5928.4	5981.1	6022.5	6055.8
2	0.10	8.53	9.00	9.16	9.24	9.29	9.33	9.35	9.37	9.38	9.39
	0.05	18.51	19.00	19.16	19.25	19.30	19.33	19.35	19.37	19.38	19.40
	0.01	98.50	99.00	99.17	99.25	99.30	99.33	99.36	99.37	99.39	99.40
3	0.10	5.54	5.46	5.39	5.34	5.31	5.28	5.27	5.25	5.24	5.23
	0.05	10.13	9.55	9.28	9.12	9.01	8.94	8.89	8.85	8.81	8.79
	0.01	34.12	30.82	29.46	28.71	28.24	27.91	27.67	27.49	27.35	27.23
4	0.10	4.54	4.32	4.19	4.11	4.05	4.01	3.98	3.95	3.94	3.92
	0.05	7.71	6.94	6.59	6.39	6.26	6.16	6.09	6.04	6.00	5.96
	0.01	21.20	18.00	16.69	15.98	15.52	15.21	14.98	14.80	14.66	14.55
5	0.10	4.06	3.78	3.62	3.52	3.45	3.40	3.37	3.34	3.32	3.30
	0.05	6.61	5.79	5.41	5.19	5.05	4.95	4.88	4.82	4.77	4.74
	0.01	16.26	13.27	12.06	11.39	10.97	10.67	10.46	10.29	10.16	10.05
6	0.10	3.78	3.46	3.29	3.18	3.11	3.05	3.01	2.98	2.96	2.94
	0.05	5.99	5.14	4.76	4.53	4.39	4.28	4.21	4.15	4.10	4.06
	0.01	13.74	10.92	9.78	9.15	8.75	8.47	8.26	8.10	7.98	7.87
7	0.10	3.59	3.26	3.07	2.96	2.88	2.83	2.78	2.75	2.72	2.70
	0.05	5.59	4.74	4.35	4.12	3.97	3.87	3.79	3.73	3.68	3.64
	0.01	12.25	9.55	8.45	7.85	7.46	7.19	6.99	6.84	6.72	6.62
8	0.10	3.46	3.11	2.92	2.81	2.73	2.67	2.62	2.59	2.56	2.54
	0.05	5.32	4.46	4.07	3.84	3.69	3.58	3.50	3.44	3.39	3.35
	0.01	11.26	8.65	7.59	7.01	6.63	6.37	6.18	6.03	5.91	5.81
9	0.10	3.36	3.01	2.81	2.69	2.61	2.55	2.51	2.47	2.44	2.42
	0.05	5.12	4.26	3.86	3.63	3.48	3.37	3.29	3.23	3.18	3.14
	0.01	10.56	8.02	6.99	6.42	6.06	5.80	5.61	5.47	5.35	5.26
10	0.10	3.28	2.92	2.73	2.61	2.52	2.46	2.41	2.38	2.35	2.32
	0.05	4.96	4.10	3.71	3.48	3.33	3.22	3.14	3.07	3.02	2.98
	0.01	10.04	7.56	6.55	5.99	5.64	5.39	5.20	5.06	4.94	4.85

11	12	13	14	15	20	25	30	60	120	∞
60.5	60.7	60.9	61.1	61.2	61.7	62.1	62.3	62.8	63.1	63.3
243.0	243.9	244.7	245.4	245.9	248.0	249.3	250.1	252.2	253.3	254.3
6083.3	6106.3	6125.9	6142.7	6157.3	6208.7	6239.8	6260.6	6313.0	6339.4	6365.8
9.40	9.41	9.41	9.42	9.42	9.44	9.45	9.46	9.47	9.48	9.49
19.40	19.41	19.42	19.42	19.43	19.45	19.46	19.46	19.48	19.49	19.50
99.40	99.42	99.42	99.43	99.43	99.45	99.46	99.47	99.48	99.49	99.50
5.22	5.22	5.21	5.20	5.2	5.18	5.17	5.17	5.15	5.14	5.13
8.76	8.74	8.73	8.71	8.7	8.66	8.63	8.62	8.57	8.55	8.53
27.13	27.05	26.98	26.92	26.9	26.69	26.58	26.50	26.32	26.22	26.13
3.91	3.90	3.89	3.88	3.87	3.84	3.83	3.82	3.79	3.78	3.76
5.94	5.91	5.89	5.87	5.86	5.80	5.77	5.75	5.69	5.66	5.63
14.45	14.37	14.31	14.25	14.20	14.02	13.91	13.84	13.65	13.56	13.46
3.28	3.27	3.26	3.25	3.24	3.21	3.19	3.17	3.14	3.12	3.10
4.70	4.68	4.66	4.64	4.62	4.56	4.52	4.50	4.43	4.40	4.36
9.96	9.89	9.82	9.77	9.72	9.55	9.45	9.38	9.20	9.11	9.02
2.92	2.90	2.89	2.88	2.87	2.84	2.81	2.80	2.76	2.74	2.72
4.03	4.00	3.98	3.96	3.94	3.87	3.83	3.81	3.74	3.70	3.67
7.79	7.72	7.66	7.60	7.56	7.40	7.30	7.23	7.06	6.97	6.88
2.68	2.67	2.65	2.64	2.63	2.59	2.57	2.56	2.51	2.49	2.47
3.60	3.57	3.55	3.53	3.51	3.44	3.40	3.38	3.30	3.27	3.23
6.54	6.47	6.41	6.36	6.31	6.16	6.06	5.99	5.82	5.74	5.65
2.52	2.50	2.49	2.48	2.46	2.42	2.40	2.38	2.34	2.32	2.29
3.31	3.28	3.26	3.24	3.22	3.15	3.11	3.08	3.01	2.97	2.93
5.73	5.67	5.61	5.56	5.52	5.36	5.26	5.20	5.03	4.95	4.86
2.40	2.38	2.36	2.35	2.34	2.30	2.27	2.25	2.21	2.18	2.16
3.10	3.07	3.05	3.03	3.01	2.94	2.89	2.86	2.79	2.75	2.71
5.18	5.11	5.05	5.01	4.96	4.81	4.71	4.65	4.48	4.40	4.31
2.30	2.28	2.27	2.26	2.24	2.20	2.17	2.16	2.11	2.08	2.06
2.94	2.91	2.89	2.86	2.84	2.77	2.73	2.70	2.62	2.58	2.54
4.77	4.71	4.65	4.60	4.56	4.41	4.31	4.25	4.08	4.00	3.91

	p	1	2	3	4	5	6	7	8	9	10
	0.10	3.23	2.86	2.66	2.54	2.45	2.39	2.34	2.30	2.27	2.25
11	0.05	4.84	3.98	3.59	3.36	3.20	3.09	3.01	2.95	2.90	2.85
	0.01	9.65	7.21	6.22	5.67	5.32	5.07	4.89	4.74	4.63	4.54
	0.10	3.18	2.81	2.61	2.48	2.39	2.33	2.28	2.24	2.21	2.19
12	0.05	4.75	3.89	3.49	3.26	3.11	3.00	2.91	2.85	2.80	2.75
	0.01	9.33	6.93	5.95	5.41	5.06	4.82	4.64	4.50	4.39	4.30
	0.10	3.14	2.76	2.56	2.43	2.35	2.28	2.23	2.20	2.16	2.14
13	0.05	4.67	3.81	3.41	3.18	3.03	2.92	2.83	2.77	2.71	2.67
	0.01	9.07	6.70	5.74	5.21	4.86	4.62	4.44	4.30	4.19	4.10
	0.10	3.10	2.73	2.52	2.39	2.31	2.24	2.19	2.15	2.12	2.10
14	0.05	4.60	3.74	3.34	3.11	2.96	2.85	2.76	2.70	2.65	2.60
	0.01	8.86	6.51	5.56	5.04	4.70	4.46	4.28	4.14	4.03	3.94
	0.10	3.07	2.70	2.49	2.36	2.27	2.21	2.16	2.12	2.09	2.06
15	0.05	4.54	3.68	3.29	3.06	2.90	2.79	2.71	2.64	2.59	2.54
	0.01	8.68	6.36	5.42	4.89	4.56	4.32	4.14	4.00	3.89	3.80
	0.10	3.05	2.67	2.46	2.33	2.24	2.18	2.13	2.09	2.06	2.03
16	0.05	4.49	3.63	3.24	3.01	2.85	2.74	2.66	2.59	2.54	2.49
	0.01	8.53	6.23	5.29	4.77	4.44	4.20	4.03	3.89	3.78	3.69
	0.10	3.03	2.64	2.44	2.31	2.22	2.15	2.10	2.06	2.03	2.00
17	0.05	4.45	3.59	3.20	2.96	2.81	2.70	2.61	2.55	2.49	2.45
	0.01	8.40	6.11	5.18	4.67	4.34	4.10	3.93	3.79	3.68	3.59
	0.10	3.01	2.62	2.42	2.29	2.20	2.13	2.08	2.04	2.00	1.98
18	0.05	4.41	3.55	3.16	2.93	2.77	2.66	2.58	2.51	2.46	2.41
	0.01	8.29	6.01	5.09	4.58	4.25	4.01	3.84	3.71	3.60	3.51
	0.10	2.99	2.61	2.40	2.27	2.18	2.11	2.06	2.02	1.98	1.96
19	0.05	4.38	3.52	3.13	2.90	2.74	2.63	2.54	2.48	2.42	2.38
	0.01	8.18	5.93	5.01	4.50	4.17	3.94	3.77	3.63	3.52	3.43
	0.10	2.97	2.59	2.38	2.25	2.16	2.09	2.04	2.00	1.96	1.94
20	0.05	4.35	3.49	3.10	2.87	2.71	2.60	2.51	2.45	2.39	2.35
	0.01	8.10	5.85	4.94	4.43	4.10	3.87	3.70	3.56	3.46	3.37
	0.10	2.96	2.57	2.36	2.23	2.14	2.08	2.02	1.98	1.95	1.92
21	0.05	4.32	3.47	3.07	2.84	2.68	2.57	2.49	2.42	2.37	2.32
	0.01	8.02	5.78	4.87	4.37	4.04	3.81	3.64	3.51	3.40	3.31
	0.10	2.95	2.56	2.35	2.22	2.13	2.06	2.01	1.97	1.93	1.90
22	0.05	4.30	3.44	3.05	2.82	2.66	2.55	2.46	2.40	2.34	2.30
	0.01	7.95	5.72	4.82	4.31	3.99	3.76	3.59	3.45	3.35	3.26

11	12	13	14	15	20	25	30	60	120	∞
2.23	2.21	2.19	2.18	2.17	2.12	2.10	2.08	2.03	2.00	1.97
2.82	2.79	2.76	2.74	2.72	2.65	2.60	2.57	2.49	2.45	2.40
4.46	4.40	4.34	4.29	4.25	4.10	4.01	3.94	3.78	3.69	3.60
2.17	2.15	2.13	2.12	2.10	2.06	2.03	2.01	1.96	1.93	1.90
2.72	2.69	2.66	2.64	2.62	2.54	2.50	2.47	2.38	2.34	2.30
4.22	4.16	4.10	4.05	4.01	3.86	3.76	3.70	3.54	3.45	3.36
2.12	2.10	2.08	2.07	2.05	2.01	1.98	1.96	1.90	1.88	1.85
2.63	2.60	2.58	2.55	2.53	2.46	2.41	2.38	2.30	2.25	2.21
4.02	3.96	3.91	3.86	3.82	3.66	3.57	3.51	3.34	3.25	3.17
2.07	2.05	2.04	2.02	2.01	1.96	1.93	1.91	1.86	1.83	1.80
2.57	2.53	2.51	2.48	2.46	2.39	2.34	2.31	2.22	2.18	2.13
3.86	3.80	3.75	3.70	3.66	3.51	3.41	3.35	3.18	3.09	3.00
2.04	2.02	2.00	1.99	1.97	1.92	1.89	1.87	1.82	1.79	1.76
2.51	2.48	2.45	2.42	2.40	2.33	2.28	2.25	2.16	2.11	2.07
3.73	3.67	3.61	3.56	3.52	3.37	3.28	3.21	3.05	2.96	2.87
2.01	1.99	1.97	1.95	1.94	1.89	1.86	1.84	1.78	1.75	1.72
2.46	2.42	2.40	2.37	2.35	2.28	2.23	2.19	2.11	2.06	2.01
3.62	3.55	3.50	3.45	3.41	3.26	3.16	3.10	2.93	2.84	2.75
1.98	1.96	1.94	1.93	1.91	1.86	1.83	1.81	1.75	1.72	1.69
2.41	2.38	2.35	2.33	2.31	2.23	2.18	2.15	2.06	2.01	1.96
3.52	3.46	3.40	3.35	3.31	3.16	3.07	3.00	2.83	2.75	2.65
1.95	1.93	1.92	1.90	1.89	1.84	1.80	1.78	1.72	1.69	1.66
2.37	2.34	2.31	2.29	2.27	2.19	2.14	2.11	2.02	1.97	1.92
3.43	3.37	3.32	3.27	3.23	3.08	2.98	2.92	2.75	2.66	2.57
1.93	1.91	1.89	1.88	1.86	1.81	1.78	1.76	1.70	1.67	1.63
2.34	2.31	2.28	2.26	2.23	2.16	2.11	2.07	1.98	1.93	1.88
3.36	3.30	3.24	3.19	3.15	3.00	2.91	2.84	2.67	2.58	2.49
1.91	1.89	1.87	1.86	1.84	1.79	1.76	1.74	1.68	1.64	1.61
2.31	2.28	2.25	2.22	2.20	2.12	2.07	2.04	1.95	1.90	1.84
3.29	3.23	3.18	3.13	3.09	2.94	2.84	2.78	2.61	2.52	2.42
1.90	1.88	1.86	1.84	1.83	1.78	1.74	1.72	1.66	1.62	1.59
2.28	2.25	2.22	2.20	2.18	2.10	2.05	2.01	1.92	1.87	1.81
3.24	3.17	3.12	3.07	3.03	2.88	2.78	2.72	2.55	2.46	2.36
1.88	1.86	1.84	1.83	1.81	1.76	1.73	1.70	1.64	1.60	1.57
2.26	2.23	2.20	2.17	2.15	2.07	2.02	1.98	1.89	1.84	1.78
3.18	3.12	3.07	3.02	2.98	2.83	2.73	2.67	2.50	2.40	2.31

	p	1	2	3	4	5	6	7	8	9	10
	0.10	2.94	2.55	2.34	2.21	2.11	2.05	1.99	1.95	1.92	1.89
23	*0.05*	4.28	3.42	3.03	2.80	2.64	2.53	2.44	2.37	2.32	2.27
	0.01	7.88	5.66	4.76	4.26	3.94	3.71	3.54	3.41	3.30	3.21
	0.10	2.93	2.54	2.33	2.19	2.10	2.04	1.98	1.94	1.91	1.88
24	*0.05*	4.26	3.40	3.01	2.78	2.62	2.51	2.42	2.36	2.30	2.25
	0.01	7.82	5.61	4.72	4.22	3.90	3.67	3.50	3.36	3.26	3.17
	0.10	2.92	2.53	2.32	2.18	2.09	2.02	1.97	1.93	1.89	1.87
25	*0.05*	4.24	3.39	2.99	2.76	2.60	2.49	2.40	2.34	2.28	2.24
	0.01	7.77	5.57	4.68	4.18	3.86	3.63	3.46	3.32	3.22	3.13
	0.1	2.91	2.52	2.31	2.17	2.08	2.01	1.96	1.92	1.88	1.86
26	*0.05*	4.23	3.37	2.98	2.74	2.59	2.47	2.39	2.32	2.27	2.22
	0.01	7.72	5.53	4.64	4.14	3.82	3.59	3.42	3.29	3.18	3.09
	0.10	2.90	2.51	2.30	2.17	2.07	2.00	1.95	1.91	1.87	1.85
27	*0.05*	4.21	3.35	2.96	2.73	2.57	2.46	2.37	2.31	2.25	2.20
	0.01	7.68	5.49	4.60	4.11	3.78	3.56	3.39	3.26	3.15	3.06
	0.1	2.89	2.50	2.29	2.16	2.06	2.00	1.94	1.90	1.87	1.84
28	*0.05*	4.20	3.34	2.95	2.71	2.56	2.45	2.36	2.29	2.24	2.19
	0.01	7.64	5.45	4.57	4.07	3.75	3.53	3.36	3.23	3.12	3.03
	0.10	2.89	2.50	2.28	2.15	2.06	1.99	1.93	1.89	1.86	1.83
29	*0.05*	4.18	3.33	2.93	2.70	2.55	2.43	2.35	2.28	2.22	2.18
	0.01	7.60	5.42	4.54	4.04	3.73	3.50	3.33	3.20	3.09	3.00
	0.10	2.88	2.49	2.28	2.14	2.05	1.98	1.93	1.88	1.85	1.82
30	*0.05*	4.17	3.32	2.92	2.69	2.53	2.42	2.33	2.27	2.21	2.16
	0.01	7.56	5.39	4.51	4.02	3.70	3.47	3.30	3.17	3.07	2.98
	0.10	2.84	2.44	2.23	2.09	2.00	1.93	1.87	1.83	1.79	1.76
40	*0.05*	4.08	3.23	2.84	2.61	2.45	2.34	2.25	2.18	2.12	2.08
	0.01	7.31	5.18	4.31	3.83	3.51	3.29	3.12	2.99	2.89	2.80
	0.10	2.81	2.41	2.20	2.06	1.97	1.90	1.84	1.80	1.76	1.73
50	*0.05*	4.03	3.18	2.79	2.56	2.40	2.29	2.20	2.13	2.07	2.03
	0.01	7.17	5.06	4.20	3.72	3.41	3.19	3.02	2.89	2.78	2.70
	0.10	2.79	2.39	2.18	2.04	1.95	1.87	1.82	1.77	1.74	1.71
60	*0.05*	4.00	3.15	2.76	2.53	2.37	2.25	2.17	2.10	2.04	1.99
	0.01	7.08	4.98	4.13	3.65	3.34	3.12	2.95	2.82	2.72	2.63
	0.1	2.76	2.36	2.14	2.00	1.91	1.83	1.78	1.73	1.69	1.66
100	*0.05*	3.94	3.09	2.70	2.46	2.31	2.19	2.10	2.03	1.97	1.93
	0.01	6.90	4.82	3.98	3.51	3.21	2.99	2.82	2.69	2.59	2.50
	0.10	2.73	2.33	2.11	1.97	1.88	1.80	1.75	1.70	1.66	1.63
200	*0.05*	3.89	3.04	2.65	2.42	2.26	2.14	2.06	1.98	1.93	1.88
	0.01	6.76	4.71	3.88	3.41	3.11	2.89	2.73	2.60	2.50	2.41
	0.10	2.71	2.31	2.09	1.95	1.85	1.78	1.72	1.68	1.64	1.61
1,000	*0.05*	3.85	3.00	2.61	2.38	2.22	2.11	2.02	1.95	1.89	1.84
	0.01	6.66	4.63	3.80	3.34	3.04	2.82	2.66	2.53	2.42	2.34

11	12	13	14	15	20	25	30	60	120	∞
1.87	1.84	1.83	1.81	1.80	1.74	1.71	1.69	1.62	1.59	1.55
2.24	2.20	2.18	2.15	2.13	2.05	2.00	1.96	1.86	1.81	1.76
3.14	3.07	3.02	2.97	2.93	2.78	2.69	2.62	2.45	2.35	2.26
1.85	1.83	1.81	1.80	1.78	1.73	1.70	1.67	1.61	1.57	1.53
2.22	2.18	2.15	2.13	2.11	2.03	1.98	1.94	1.84	1.79	1.73
3.09	3.03	2.98	2.93	2.89	2.74	2.64	2.58	2.40	2.31	2.21
1.84	1.82	1.80	1.79	1.77	1.72	1.68	1.66	1.59	1.56	1.52
2.20	2.16	2.14	2.11	2.09	2.01	1.96	1.92	1.82	1.77	1.71
3.06	2.99	2.94	2.89	2.85	2.70	2.60	2.54	2.36	2.27	2.17
1.83	1.81	1.79	1.77	1.76	1.71	1.67	1.65	1.58	1.54	1.50
2.18	2.15	2.12	2.09	2.07	1.99	1.94	1.90	1.80	1.75	1.69
3.02	2.96	2.90	2.86	2.82	2.66	2.57	2.50	2.33	2.23	2.13
1.82	1.80	1.78	1.76	1.75	1.70	1.66	1.64	1.57	1.53	1.49
2.17	2.13	2.10	2.08	2.06	1.97	1.92	1.88	1.79	1.73	1.67
2.99	2.93	2.87	2.82	2.78	2.63	2.54	2.47	2.29	2.20	2.10
1.81	1.79	1.77	1.75	1.74	1.69	1.65	1.63	1.56	1.52	1.48
2.15	2.12	2.09	2.06	2.04	1.96	1.91	1.87	1.77	1.71	1.65
2.96	2.90	2.84	2.79	2.75	2.60	2.51	2.44	2.26	2.17	2.06
1.80	1.78	1.76	1.75	1.73	1.68	1.64	1.62	1.55	1.51	1.47
2.14	2.10	2.08	2.05	2.03	1.94	1.89	1.85	1.75	1.70	1.64
2.93	2.87	2.81	2.77	2.73	2.57	2.48	2.41	2.23	2.14	2.03
1.79	1.77	1.75	1.74	1.72	1.67	1.63	1.61	1.54	1.50	1.46
2.13	2.09	2.06	2.04	2.01	1.93	1.88	1.84	1.74	1.68	1.62
2.91	2.84	2.79	2.74	2.70	2.55	2.45	2.39	2.21	2.11	2.01
1.74	1.71	1.70	1.68	1.66	1.61	1.57	1.54	1.47	1.42	1.38
2.04	2.00	1.97	1.95	1.92	1.84	1.78	1.74	1.64	1.58	1.51
2.73	2.66	2.61	2.56	2.52	2.37	2.27	2.20	2.02	1.92	1.80
1.70	1.68	1.66	1.64	1.63	1.57	1.53	1.50	1.42	1.38	1.33
1.99	1.95	1.92	1.89	1.87	1.78	1.73	1.69	1.58	1.51	1.44
2.62	2.56	2.51	2.46	2.42	2.27	2.17	2.10	1.91	1.80	1.68
1.68	1.66	1.64	1.62	1.60	1.54	1.50	1.48	1.40	1.35	1.29
1.95	1.92	1.89	1.86	1.84	1.75	1.69	1.65	1.53	1.47	1.39
2.56	2.50	2.44	2.39	2.35	2.20	2.10	2.03	1.84	1.73	1.60
1.64	1.61	1.59	1.57	1.56	1.49	1.45	1.42	1.34	1.28	1.21
1.89	1.85	1.82	1.79	1.77	1.68	1.62	1.57	1.45	1.38	1.28
2.43	2.37	2.31	2.27	2.22	2.07	1.97	1.89	1.69	1.57	1.43
1.60	1.58	1.56	1.54	1.52	1.46	1.41	1.38	1.29	1.23	1.14
1.84	1.80	1.77	1.74	1.72	1.62	1.56	1.52	1.39	1.30	1.19
2.34	2.27	2.22	2.17	2.13	1.97	1.87	1.79	1.58	1.45	1.28
1.58	1.55	1.53	1.51	1.49	1.43	1.38	1.35	1.25	1.18	1.06
1.80	1.76	1.73	1.70	1.68	1.58	1.52	1.47	1.33	1.24	1.08
2.27	2.20	2.15	2.10	2.06	1.90	1.79	1.72	1.50	1.35	1.11

D: Inverse normal table

Critical values for the standard normal distribution. Table entry for p and C is the point z with probability p lying above it and probability C lying between $-z$ and z.

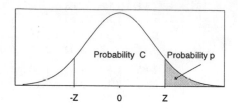

C	p	z	C	p	z
50%	0.25	0.674	96%	0.02	2.054
60%	0.2	0.842	98%	0.01	2.326
70%	0.15	1.036	99%	0.005	2.576
80%	0.1	1.282	99.5%	0.0025	2.807
90%	0.05	1.645	99.8%	0.001	3.090
95%	0.025	1.960	99.9%	0.0005	3.290

E: Critical values for χ^2 statistic

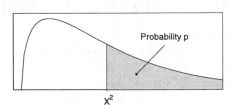

Probability p

x^2

Table entry is the point X^2 with the probability p lying above it. The first column gives the degrees of freedom.

df	Probability p					
	0.1	0.05	0.025	0.01	0.005	0.001
1	2.70	3.84	5.02	6.63	7.87	10.83
2	4.60	5.99	7.37	9.21	10.59	13.82
3	6.25	7.81	9.34	11.34	12.83	16.27
4	7.77	9.48	11.14	13.27	14.86	18.47
5	9.23	11.07	12.83	15.08	16.75	20.52
6	10.64	12.59	14.44	16.81	18.54	22.46
7	12.01	14.06	16.01	18.47	20.27	24.32
8	13.36	15.50	17.53	20.09	21.95	26.12
9	14.68	16.91	19.02	21.66	23.58	27.88
10	15.98	18.30	20.48	23.20	25.18	29.59
11	17.27	19.67	21.92	24.72	26.75	31.26
12	18.54	21.02	23.33	26.21	28.30	32.91
13	19.81	22.36	24.73	27.68	29.82	34.53
14	21.06	23.68	26.11	29.14	31.31	36.12
15	22.30	24.99	27.48	30.57	32.80	37.70
16	23.54	26.29	28.84	32.00	34.26	39.25
17	24.76	27.58	30.19	33.40	35.71	40.79
18	25.98	28.86	31.52	34.80	37.15	42.31
19	27.20	30.14	32.85	36.19	38.58	43.82
20	28.41	31.41	34.17	37.56	39.99	45.31
21	29.61	32.67	35.47	38.93	41.40	46.80
22	30.81	33.92	36.78	40.28	42.79	48.27
23	32.00	35.17	38.07	41.63	44.18	49.73
24	33.19	36.41	39.36	42.98	45.55	51.18
25	34.38	37.65	40.64	44.31	46.92	52.62
26	35.56	38.88	41.92	45.64	48.29	54.05
27	36.74	40.11	43.19	46.96	49.64	55.48
28	37.91	41.33	44.46	48.27	50.99	56.89
29	39.08	42.55	45.72	49.58	52.33	58.30
30	40.26	43.77	46.98	50.89	53.67	59.70
40	51.81	55.76	59.34	63.69	66.77	73.40
50	63.17	67.50	71.42	76.15	79.49	86.66
60	74.40	79.08	83.30	88.38	91.95	99.61
70	85.53	90.53	95.02	100.43	104.21	112.32
80	96.58	101.88	106.63	112.33	116.32	124.84
90	107.56	113.15	118.14	124.12	128.30	137.21
100	118.50	124.34	129.56	135.81	140.17	149.45

F: Values of the Durbin-Watson statistic

Table entry gives DW_L and DW_U for a 5% one-sided test of the Durbin-Watson statistic. n = number of observations; k = number of parameters (so number of explanatory variables is $k - 1$).

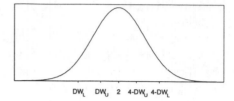

	$k=2$		$k=3$		$k=4$		$k=5$		$k=6$	
n	DW_L	DW_U	DW_L	DW_U	DW_L	DW_U	DW_L	DW_U	DW_L	DW_U
15	1.08	1.36	0.95	1.54	0.82	1.75	0.69	1.97	0.56	2.21
16	1.10	1.37	0.98	1.54	0.86	1.73	0.74	1.93	0.62	2.15
17	1.13	1.38	1.02	1.54	0.90	1.71	0.78	1.90	0.67	2.10
18	1.16	1.39	1.05	1.53	0.93	1.69	0.82	1.87	0.71	2.06
19	1.18	1.40	1.08	1.53	0.97	1.68	0.86	1.85	0.75	2.02
20	1.20	1.41	1.10	1.54	1.00	1.68	0.90	1.83	0.79	1.99
21	1.22	1.42	1.13	1.54	1.03	1.67	0.93	1.81	0.83	1.96
22	1.24	1.43	1.15	1.54	1.05	1.66	0.96	1.80	0.86	1.94
23	1.26	1.44	1.17	1.54	1.08	1.66	0.99	1.79	0.90	1.92
24	1.27	1.45	1.19	1.55	1.10	1.66	1.01	1.78	0.93	1.90
25	1.29	1.45	1.21	1.55	1.12	1.66	1.04	1.77	0.95	1.89
26	1.30	1.46	1.22	1.55	1.14	1.65	1.06	1.76	0.98	1.88
26	1.32	1.47	1.24	1.56	1.16	1.65	1.08	1.76	1.01	1.86
28	1.33	1.48	1.26	1.56	1.18	1.65	1.10	1.75	1.03	1.85
29	1.34	1.48	1.27	1.56	1.20	1.65	1.12	1.74	1.05	1.84
30	1.35	1.49	1.28	1.57	1.21	1.65	1.14	1.74	1.07	1.83
31	1.36	1.50	1.30	1.57	1.23	1.65	1.16	1.74	1.09	1.83
32	1.37	1.50	1.31	1.57	1.24	1.65	1.18	1.73	1.11	1.82
33	1.38	1.51	1.32	1.58	1.26	1.65	1.19	1.73	1.13	1.81
34	1.39	1.51	1.33	1.58	1.27	1.65	1.21	1.73	1.15	1.81
35	1.40	1.52	1.34	1.58	1.28	1.65	1.22	1.73	1.16	1.80
36	1.41	1.52	1.35	1.59	1.29	1.65	1.24	1.73	1.18	1.80
37	1.42	1.53	1.36	1.59	1.31	1.66	1.25	1.72	1.19	1.80
38	1.43	1.54	1.37	1.59	1.32	1.66	1.26	1.72	1.21	1.79
39	1.43	1.54	1.38	1.60	1.33	1.66	1.27	1.72	1.22	1.79
40	1.44	1.54	1.39	1.60	1.34	1.66	1.29	1.72	1.23	1.79
45	1.48	1.57	1.43	1.62	1.38	1.67	1.34	1.72	1.29	1.78
50	1.50	1.59	1.46	1.63	1.42	1.67	1.38	1.72	1.34	1.77
55	1.53	1.60	1.49	1.64	1.45	1.68	1.41	1.72	1.38	1.77
60	1.55	1.62	1.51	1.65	1.48	1.69	1.44	1.73	1.41	1.77
65	1.57	1.63	1.54	1.66	1.50	1.70	1.47	1.73	1.44	1.77
70	1.58	1.64	1.55	1.67	1.52	1.70	1.49	1.74	1.46	1.77
75	1.60	1.65	1.57	1.68	1.54	1.71	1.51	1.74	1.49	1.77
80	1.61	1.66	1.59	1.69	1.56	1.72	1.53	1.74	1.51	1.77
85	1.62	1.67	1.60	1.70	1.57	1.72	1.55	1.75	1.52	1.77
90	1.63	1.68	1.61	1.70	1.59	1.73	1.57	1.75	1.54	1.78
95	1.64	1.69	1.62	1.71	1.60	1.73	1.58	1.75	1.56	1.78
100	1.65	1.69	1.63	1.72	1.61	1.74	1.59	1.76	1.57	1.78

Table entry gives DW_L and DW_U for a 1% one-sided test of the Durbin-Watson statistic. n = number of observations; k = number of parameters (so number of explanatory variables is $k - 1$).

n	$k = 2$ DW_L	DW_U	$k = 3$ DW_L	DW_U	$k = 4$ DW_L	DW_U	$k = 5$ DW_L	DW_U	$k = 6$ DW_L	DW_U
15	0.81	1.07	0.70	1.25	0.59	1.46	0.49	1.70	0.39	1.96
16	0.84	1.09	0.74	1.25	0.63	1.44	0.53	1.66	0.44	1.90
17	0.87	1.10	0.77	1.25	0.67	1.43	0.57	1.63	0.48	1.85
18	0.90	1.12	0.80	1.26	0.71	1.42	0.61	1.60	0.52	1.80
19	0.93	1.13	0.83	1.26	0.74	1.41	0.65	1.58	0.56	1.77
20	0.95	1.15	0.86	1.27	0.77	1.41	0.68	1.57	0.60	1.74
21	0.97	1.16	0.89	1.27	0.80	1.41	0.72	1.55	0.63	1.71
22	1.00	1.17	0.91	1.28	0.83	1.40	0.75	1.54	0.66	1.69
23	1.02	1.19	0.94	1.29	0.86	1.40	0.77	1.53	0.70	1.67
24	1.04	1.20	0.96	1.30	0.88	1.41	0.80	1.53	0.72	1.66
25	1.05	1.21	0.98	1.30	0.90	1.41	0.83	1.52	0.75	1.65
26	1.07	1.22	1.00	1.31	0.93	1.41	0.85	1.52	0.78	1.64
27	1.09	1.23	1.02	1.32	0.95	1.41	0.88	1.51	0.81	1.63
28	1.10	1.24	1.04	1.32	0.97	1.41	0.90	1.51	0.83	1.62
29	1.12	1.25	1.05	1.33	0.99	1.42	0.92	1.51	0.85	1.61
30	1.13	1.26	1.07	1.34	1.01	1.42	0.94	1.51	0.88	1.61
31	1.15	1.27	1.08	1.34	1.02	1.42	0.96	1.51	0.90	1.60
32	1.16	1.28	1.10	1.35	1.04	1.43	0.98	1.51	0.92	1.60
33	1.17	1.29	1.11	1.36	1.05	1.43	1.00	1.51	0.94	1.59
34	1.18	1.30	1.13	1.36	1.07	1.43	1.01	1.51	0.95	1.59
35	1.19	1.31	1.14	1.37	1.08	1.44	1.03	1.51	0.97	1.59
36	1.21	1.32	1.15	1.38	1.10	1.44	1.04	1.51	0.99	1.59
37	1.22	1.32	1.16	1.38	1.11	1.45	1.06	1.51	1.00	1.59
38	1.23	1.33	1.18	1.39	1.12	1.45	1.07	1.52	1.02	1.58
39	1.24	1.34	1.19	1.39	1.14	1.45	1.09	1.52	1.03	1.58
40	1.25	1.34	1.20	1.40	1.15	1.46	1.10	1.52	1.05	1.58
45	1.29	1.38	1.24	1.42	1.20	1.48	1.16	1.53	1.11	1.58
50	1.32	1.40	1.28	1.45	1.24	1.49	1.20	1.54	1.16	1.59
55	1.36	1.43	1.32	1.47	1.28	1.51	1.25	1.55	1.21	1.59
60	1.38	1.45	1.35	1.48	1.32	1.52	1.28	1.56	1.25	1.60
65	1.41	1.47	1.38	1.50	1.35	1.53	1.31	1.57	1.28	1.61
70	1.43	1.49	1.40	1.52	1.37	1.55	1.34	1.58	1.31	1.61
75	1.45	1.50	1.42	1.53	1.39	1.56	1.37	1.59	1.34	1.62
80	1.47	1.52	1.44	1.54	1.42	1.57	1.39	1.60	1.36	1.62
85	1.48	1.53	1.46	1.55	1.43	1.58	1.41	1.60	1.39	1.63
90	1.50	1.54	1.47	1.56	1.45	1.59	1.43	1.61	1.41	1.64
95	1.51	1.55	1.49	1.57	1.47	1.60	1.45	1.62	1.42	1.64
100	1.52	1.56	1.50	1.58	1.48	1.60	1.46	1.63	1.44	1.65

Source: The Durbin-Watson tables are taken from J. Durbin and G.S. Watson (1951) "Testing for serial correlation in least squares regression," *Biometrika*, **38**, 159–177. Reprinted with the kind permission of the publisher and the authors.

G: Normally distributed observations

Random independent observations
from a standard normal distribution
(mean 0 and standard deviation 1).

0.807	0.550	-0.076	0.147	-0.768	-0.022	-0.671	0.395	0.497	1.008
-1.746	2.101	0.473	2.058	-1.133	0.129	-0.251	-0.685	-0.290	0.034
-0.528	-0.121	-1.262	-0.780	1.173	-0.826	-0.698	0.196	1.590	0.019
-0.487	-0.227	-1.218	0.102	0.541	-0.281	0.634	1.226	-1.755	-0.432
0.548	-0.331	-0.163	0.229	-0.915	-0.406	0.028	-1.653	-0.509	0.635
0.946	0.015	2.992	-0.649	-1.070	0.921	1.012	-0.765	-0.506	-0.128
-1.143	-2.068	-0.449	0.111	0.189	-1.488	0.655	-0.958	-0.472	-1.116
-0.508	-0.500	1.207	0.661	-0.428	0.465	0.282	2.406	0.250	0.331
-0.055	-0.708	0.206	-0.247	-1.333	-0.713	-1.803	-0.016	2.784	0.698
1.722	-0.046	0.158	0.753	-1.180	-0.284	-0.101	-0.289	0.679	1.019
-0.775	-1.225	1.163	-0.677	-0.158	0.184	-0.152	-0.149	0.395	-1.486
-0.425	-0.450	-1.267	-0.254	2.049	-0.195	-0.137	-0.629	-0.085	-0.623
0.052	0.571	-0.057	-0.018	0.023	0.342	1.105	0.891	0.957	0.090
-1.568	0.714	0.372	-2.171	0.001	1.457	-1.583	1.199	0.533	-0.595
-0.402	-0.528	1.679	0.102	-0.933	0.691	0.131	-1.041	-0.381	0.704
-0.379	-1.091	0.702	-1.718	1.925	0.608	1.580	0.110	0.595	-0.894
-0.219	2.480	0.876	0.333	-0.748	0.209	0.173	-0.822	-0.428	-0.515
1.102	-0.964	-0.597	-1.281	-0.493	-0.828	1.862	0.076	-0.238	-0.109
-0.067	-0.592	0.532	-0.136	0.673	-0.184	0.698	1.035	-0.740	2.658
-0.766	-0.547	-0.750	0.070	-0.105	2.796	0.521	-0.528	-0.087	-1.108
-0.040	0.244	0.926	-0.163	-0.882	0.686	-0.351	-0.928	1.128	-0.910
-0.840	-0.276	0.063	0.751	2.457	-1.881	-2.265	0.486	0.293	1.080
0.472	0.150	-1.024	1.265	1.163	-1.864	-1.052	-1.258	-0.246	0.212
-0.238	0.306	-1.478	-1.045	-0.314	0.393	0.507	-0.616	-0.624	-1.839
-1.838	1.940	0.836	0.379	0.450	-3.152	-0.251	1.744	1.088	-0.453
-1.347	-0.498	0.928	-2.171	0.227	-0.401	-0.896	2.266	-1.087	1.406
-0.597	-0.337	0.643	-1.093	0.012	0.735	1.313	-0.542	-1.709	0.114
-0.758	1.332	0.177	-0.394	1.939	0.656	-1.052	0.107	2.193	0.314
-0.629	-1.170	-1.099	-0.914	-0.605	0.451	1.529	-0.706	0.053	0.566
-0.127	0.310	0.881	0.385	0.507	-0.724	1.166	-1.139	0.417	0.979
-1.060	0.780	-0.769	0.558	-0.925	-1.875	-1.737	0.601	-0.096	2.050
-0.748	1.106	-0.558	-1.638	-1.830	1.303	0.190	0.374	1.127	-0.934
-0.747	-0.951	-1.259	-0.153	0.104	-0.520	-0.285	0.448	0.871	-0.447
-0.516	0.563	1.507	0.655	-1.207	0.437	-1.498	0.613	-0.357	0.560
-0.111	-0.359	-1.762	0.332	0.000	-0.650	1.212	0.390	-0.868	1.736
0.554	1.107	-0.204	-0.040	-0.114	0.813	-1.071	-0.321	0.974	-1.463
-0.388	0.527	1.205	-0.238	-0.003	-0.138	-0.926	-1.503	-0.464	-0.388
-0.846	-1.411	0.963	1.980	-0.399	0.258	1.279	-1.105	2.107	-0.769
-1.617	-1.017	0.722	-1.925	-0.128	-0.637	0.550	0.485	2.008	1.008
-1.787	-0.691	0.557	-0.856	0.216	0.695	-0.917	-0.500	0.540	0.137

Author Index

Subject Index